Freedom in the World

The findings of the *Comparative Survey of Freedom* and the Map of Freedom include events up to 1 January 1992.

Freedom in the World
Political Rights & Civil Liberties
1991-1992

Freedom House Survey Team

R. Bruce McColm
Survey Coordinator

Dale Bricker
James Finn
Jonathan D. Karl
Douglas W. Payne
Joseph E. Ryan
George Zarycky

Freedom House

First published in 1992

Cover design and map by Emerson Wajdowicz Studios, N.Y.C.

The Library of Congress has catalogued this serial title as follows:

Freedom in the world / —1978–
New York : Freedom House, 1978–
v. : map; 25 cm.—(Freedom House Book)
Annual.
ISSN 0732-6610=Freedom in the World.
1. Civil rights—Periodicals. I. R. Bruce McColm, et al. I. Series.
JC571.F66   323.4'05-dc 19   82-642048
AACR 2   MARC-S
Library of Congress   [84101]
ISBN   0-932088-74-0 (pbk. : alk. paper)
             0-932088-75-9 (cloth : alk. paper)

Distributed by National Book Network
4720 Boston Way
Lanham, MD 20706

3 Henrietta Street
London WC2E 8LU England

Contents

Foreword

Freedom House is a non-profit organization based in New York that monitors political rights and civil liberties around the world. Established in 1941, Freedom House believes the effective advocacy of civil rights at home and human rights abroad must be grounded in fundamental democratic values and principles.

The *Comparative Survey of Freedom* is an institutional effort to monitor the political rights and civil liberties in 183 nations and 62 related territories on an annual basis. Freedom House began earlier efforts to record the progress and decline in freedoms during the 1950s in reaction to racial violence in the United States. The first year-end review of freedom was sparked in 1955 by the kidnapping and murder of Emmet Till, a fourteen-year old black in Mississippi. An all-white jury subsequently acquitted the two white men indicted for the crime.

During those early years, the project was called the Balance Sheet of Freedom, and later the Annual Survey of the Progress of Freedom. By the late 1960s, the Freedom House Board of Trustees felt there was a need to create a single standard by which to measure and record the development of freedom around the world.

When Freedom House's *Comparative Survey of Freedom* was finally established in the early 1960s, democracy was in a perilous state both at home and abroad: Spain, Portugal and Greece were under military rule; the world's largest democracy, India, would soon declare martial law; an American president faced the possibility of impeachment; and the prospects for liberalization—not to say democratization—in Eastern Europe, Latin America and Asia were dim. The past decade has seen unprecedented gains in freedom over much of the world.

Today, the *Comparative Survey of Freedom* has become a year-long project produced by our regional experts, foreign consultants and human rights specialists and derives its information from a wide-range of sources. Freedom House regularly conducts fact-finding missions around the world to gain a more immediate impression of the nature and scope of political transitions. During the past year, Freedom House personnel visited Cuba, Czechoslovakia, El Salvador, Guatemala, Haiti, Hong Kong, Hungary, India, Indonesia, Japan, Mexico, Poland, Romania, South Africa, the Soviet Union and Suriname. During these on-site visits, Freedom House makes efforts to meet a cross-section of political parties and associations, human rights monitors, representatives of both the private sector and independent trade unions, academics, foreign and local journalists, security forces and insurgent movements where they existed.

Throughout the year, we consult a vast array of published source materials, ranging from reports of other human rights organizations to regional publications and newspapers. Most valued to us are the many human rights activists, journalists, editors and political figures around the world who keep us informed on a regular basis of their nations' situations, sometimes at great risk to themselves and their families. As always, the Survey is dedicated to them and their struggle for freedom.

The 1990-1991 *Survey* was conducted by a Freedom House project team: R. Bruce McColm, the coordinator who also serves as the executive director of Freedom House; Dr. Joseph Ryan, a comparative political scientist; Jonathan D. Karl and James Finn, general editors; Douglas W. Payne; George Zarycky; Dale Bricker; and Maria Vitagliano. The *Survey* team is especially grateful to the extraordinary talents of the editorial team of Jonathan D. Karl, James Finn, Mark Wolkenfeld and editorial assistant Pei C. Koay without whom this book would never be completed. The *Survey* team also appreciates the dedicated work of this year's research assistants: Perry Bechky, Carla Copeland, Susanna Corwin, Robert Daniels, Charles Graybow, Edward Lipman, Roksolana Luchkan, Michael McNerney, Raluca Oncioiu, Christina Pendzola, Thomas Ragsdale, Yermolay Solzhenitsyn, Elizabeth Szonyi and Craig Webster.

The findings of the *Survey* are accompanied by independent, regional essays written by acknowledged experts in their field: William J. Barnds, Asia; J. Leo Cefkin, Africa; James Finn, United States; Douglas W. Payne, Latin America; Don Peretz, Middle East; Robert L. Pfaltzgraff, Jr., Soviet Union; Wayne C. Thompson, Western Europe.

As always, Freedom House welcomes criticism and comments on our findings. Throughout the year, this exchange of views makes us constantly review and improve our findings.

Freedom House receives funding from private individuals, corporations, labor unions and private foundations for all its activities. We especially want to express our appreciation to the Pew Charitable Trusts, which have provided the main support for the *Comparative Survey of Freedom* over the past twenty years. We also want to thank the Lynde and Harry Bradley Foundation for its continued support and assistance in this endeavor. ■

The United States: The Sole but Uneasy Superpower

James Finn

During the course of 1991 the United States underwent several great shifts in its self understanding, shifts which have yet to reach a full resolution. These shifts reflect both the new role the United States has necessarily assumed in international affairs as the sole superpower in the world, and a renewed concentration on domestic affairs that this new status allows and that an increasingly uneasy and discontented electorate demands.

War in the Persian Gulf

The most notable event in the early months of the year was the war in the Persian Gulf. The immediate cause of the conflict was Iraq's invasion of Kuwait during the previous year. In late November 1990, after months of intense diplomatic negotiations by the Bush administration, the United Nations Security Council authorized a twenty-eight nation alliance dominated by the United States to expel Iraqi forces from Kuwait if President Saddam Hussein did not withdraw them by mid-January. Overcoming substantial domestic and Congressional resistance to his policies, President Bush rallied to win a supporting vote from Congress. In spite of the U.N. authorization and a united America, Saddam defied the ultimatum. On 16 January President Bush ordered massive air strikes on Iraqi forces in both Iraq and Kuwait. On 23 February allied ground forces attacked and within three days

Saddam's forces were crushed, forced to return to a country whose infrastructure had been shattered. Confounding dire predictions, the conflict was much shorter and the number of American casualties substantially lower than even the most optimistic forecasts had estimated.

Most of the country supported the administration's policy during the crisis in the Gulf, followed the war on TV, and joined in an almost euphoric celebration of the victory. Analysts drew early and large implications from the Gulf war and its outcome: It confirmed the leading role of the United States in international affairs; it strengthened the role of the U.N.; it showed that the USSR and the U.S. could cooperate on major issues that would once have divided them; it made a case for the need for considerable U.S. military forces even though the major threat from the USSR had rapidly eroded; it wrote finis to the Vietnam syndrome and allowed the country to embrace Vietnam veterans along with those Americans who served in the Gulf; it brought the American people together. It also revealed a president who was highly skilled in international negotiations and forceful in the execution of policies to which he was committed. The entire episode, it was generally agreed, left George Bush in an almost impregnable position for reelection in 1992—unless the economy went bad.

Beneath the euphoria and celebration, however, there were some lingering doubts and concerns. The Defense Department had imposed tight restrictions on reporting from the war zone during the fighting. Media representatives complained at the time and, in a subsequent report addressed to Defense Secretary Dick Cheney, seventeen top news executives described the restrictions as "real censorship." The public, however, tended to be sympathetic to the military judgment. More worrisome to those who followed the conflict closely was the decision to end the war leaving Saddam in power. Even stripped of most of his military forces and subject to further U.N. restrictions on Iraq's behavior, he could, it was argued, be a major irritant in mid-East affairs for an indefinite future.

The unraveling Soviet Union

The rapidly unfolding events in the Soviet Union confirmed that the United States had become at the beginning of this decade unchallenged as the single superpower. The failed August coup that attempted to overthrow Mikhail Gorbachev marked a climactic point in the fall of the Communist party and the disintegration of the Soviet empire. Even as centralized power was being fragmented, Washington attempted to shore up the center, maintaining close ties with Gorbachev rather than forging new, strong ties with the leaders of the increasingly independent republics, most notably Boris Yeltsin, president of Russia. The result was to heighten the tension between two discordant aspects of U.S. policy. The first, based on the desire for "international stability," favors the continuation of a union that could direct from a center the multifarious political, economic and military forces that were formed within the Soviet Union. The second, employing traditional American values and concepts, favors

self-determination, pluralism and democracy and, thus, the aspirations of political entities with the requisites necessary to be able to function as sovereign states.

In late November, the Bush administration suddenly shifted course, chose the second option, and announced that it would grant recognition to the Ukraine "expeditiously" if the upcoming December referendum on Ukraine's independence passed and the republic met certain specified conditions. This was a clear signal that the administration believed the Gorbachevian center would not hold.

Since the once-feared Soviet Union has devolved into a mendicant, it presents challenges and opportunities to the United States, as well as its allies, that are of a different order than those of former decades. The major problems now involve such issues as economic and technological aid to the republics of the "Soviet Union," and the limitation on and destruction of nuclear weapons.

While the Gulf war and U.S.-Soviet relations have, understandably, dominated public attention in 1991, U.S. interests extended to a vast range of issues of varying degrees of importance. The United States has attended, intermittently and inconclusively, to the dilemmas posed by the possibility of a European community based on new political and monetary agreements, a community foreshadowed by the decisions made by the twelve nations of the European Community when they met in Maastricht, The Netherlands, early in December. High representatives of the U.S. participated in the Moscow human rights conference of the Conference on Security and Cooperation in Europe. In the face of sharp criticism, the Bush administration continued active engagement with China at the cost of lowering its voice on human rights abuses. With seemingly tireless, vigorous diplomacy Secretary of

State James Baker brought Israeli, Arab and Palestinian leaders together in a Madrid conference in October for the first of what was expected to be a series of meetings. The mere fact of their speaking directly to each other in public sessions was regarded as an historic breakthrough in Arab-Israeli relations. The U.S. pushed for a "fast-track" free-trade agreement with Mexico, stressing recent economic advances within that country rather than the electoral fraud that continues. It continues to search for the elusive guide to good and non-fractious economic relations with Japan.

Domestic concerns

Neither the foreign policy successes, however dramatic, nor the continuing foreign policy debates, however charged, did more than temporarily distract Americans from their domestic concerns. The list has become familiar: continuing recession and rising unemployment; falling tax revenues and increasing budget gaps; rising costs of education without commensurate improvement; drugs, crime and a growing prison population; political and corporate chicanery and corruption; growing number of single-parent families living in poverty; discrimination, quotas and affirmative action; rising health costs and inadequate health plans; the "politically correct" and cultural censorship.

The 106th Supreme Court Justice

As frequently happens in American life, particular events served as both dramatic examples and symbols of sharply contested issues. One of the most dramatic was initiated by President Bush when he nominated Judge Clarence Thomas, a young conservative, up-from-poverty black, to succeed retiring Justice Thurgood Marshall on the Supreme Court. After apparently completing a demanding examination by the Senate Judiciary Committee, Judge Thomas seemed headed for certain confirmation by the full Senate when a last-minute, public charge of sexual harassment brought him back before the Judiciary Committee. An entranced nation watched the long televised proceedings as Anita Hill, a black lawyer who had worked under Clarence Thomas, charged that ten years earlier he had verbally harassed her, as he rebutted her charges and sharply criticized the very process he was participating in, and as a number of impressive character witnesses testified for each of them. The confirmation hung in the balance until, on 16 October, by a voice vote of 52-48 the full Senate returned him as the second black and the 106th Supreme Court Justice of the United States.

A number of revelations flowed from these dramatic proceedings: The American public was entranced but not edified by the proceedings. Overwhelmingly, they judged the process to be demeaning to almost everyone involved. The process itself is now under scrutiny and is likely to be revised before the next nomination to the Supreme Court.

The issue of sexual harassment has been elevated to a much higher and wider range of attention than previously. It is now on the national agenda.

The number of highly educated, successful and articulate black people who testified revealed that blacks have advanced in American society to a degree that concern about minority rights had obscured.

The number of black witnesses who were politically conservative shattered the assumption that there is "a black view" on major political issues and that it is voiced by the leaders of the most recognized black organizations. It is now clear that there is a pluralism of political and cultural views in the black community.

The reaction of the American public, who supported Clarence Thomas by a large majority, revealed a gap between them and their political leaders.

The majority of men and women held similar views on the proceedings and the outcome, challenging the existence of the purported gender gap and the claims of several women's organizations that they represented the views of most American women.

Of passing interest but of no domestic political import, the foreign press generally ignored the debate or dismissed it as what they viewed as one of America's irregular moralistic spasms.

The Louisiana run-off

A regional event that, nevertheless, drew intense national interest was the contest for governor of Louisiana. The character of the two opposing candidates ensured that it would mix strong racial and cultural emotions with economic fears of job loss and increased taxes. To the consternation of the national Republican Party, which repudiated him, David Duke, a white supremacist and open anti-Semite for most of his adult life, ran as a mainstream, conservative Republican. He was opposed by Edwin Edwards, a former high-rolling governor who had been previously indicted on corruption charges but never convicted. The tenor of the debate between the two men and the feeling of the voters who were faced with the choice between them was captured in one campaign slogan that read "Vote for the crook, not the bigot."

In the runoff Duke was soundly trounced but not before he had shown that he could exploit public concern over

serious issues-crime, welfare and affirmative action-to heighten racial tensions and turn some whites and blacks against each other. Even as he lost the election, Duke propelled himself and his message into an ongoing national debate.

Other politicians, running at the national, regional or local level were keenly aware of voter anxiety and anger over the impact the stagnant economy was having on their lives. Across the country, taxes rose and budgets were cut; large corporations reduced both staff and top-level executives. Mill workers, farmers and merchants said they were discontented with the present and very uneasy about the future.

This uneasy discontent made American citizens more sensitive to and sour about what they saw as corrupt political and financial practices. The Savings and Loan (S & L) debacle of 1990-which has continuing reverberations in banking and the real-estate business, further weakening an already weak housing market-was followed in 1991 by the revelation of the far greater international scandal of the Bank of Credit and Commerce International. BCCI had $20 billion in deposits when it was seized by Western regulators in early July following years of investigation by three Congressional committees, the Federal Reserve Board, the Justice Department and the Manhattan District Attorney's office on charges of money laundering, extortion, kickbacks, etc. The byzantine intricacies of the BCCI, which was 77 percent owned by the government of Abu Dhabi and which operated in seventy-nine countries, were too complicated for most people to follow, but the towering fact of the scandal was evident, as was the sense that it would add to the tax burden of the average taxpayer.

For many people, one figure served as the symbol of what went wrong. For many years, Clark Clifford was regarded in the nation's capital as the insiders' insider. He knew as well as anyone, it was said, how to tread the corridors of power. When the illegal and corrupt practices of BCCI began to surface, it was revealed that he had made large sums of money as chairman of First American Bankshares, a bank that was secretly and illegally owned by BCCI, and that Mr. Clifford professed himself ignorant of that ownership. That a man of Mr. Clifford's probity must necessarily be charged either with lying or with uncharacteristic naïvete roused feelings of resentment against Washington insiders.

The S & L and the BCCI scandals were too widespread and complex for focused citizen anger, but several much narrower issues were directly targeted: the Keating five, the five senators who received large campaign contributions from even as they extended considerable senatorial aid to Charles Keating, and the Senate Ethics Committee that seemed reluctant to move against their peers; the many House members who, without penalty, regularly overdrew their accounts at the House bank and members who totted up high, unpaid bills at the House restaurant. It was a mark of the citizens' sensitivity that members of Congress felt the heat for what they had long regarded as standard operating procedure.

Minority rights-and wrongs

In less directly political terms, the United States continued its treatment of minorities and their real and alleged rights in ways that were often judged to be erratic or self-contradictory. For example, in the name of diversity, various provisions made on college campuses to draw minorities into the mainstream led in some cases to self-segregated ethnic groups. Efforts to reduce the use of terms and remarks that some people found offensive because they were based on gender, sex, and race imposed a subtle form of censorship that Victorian society would have found restrictive. In the meantime sleaze merchants enlisted the aid of civil rights organizations, and MTV continued to stretch the limits of what the public will allow. The head of a department in one of New York's colleges gave public anti-Semitic speeches but was protected from dismissal because he has academic tenure. During the Gulf war one college prohibited students from displaying the American flag out of deference to the feelings of those who opposed the war. And the examples multiplied.

The year ended with general unease about the economy, a sense of growing racial and ethnic tensions, a noticeable desire to cut military expenditures in favor of domestic programs, a general ambivalence about the role that the United States should assume in international affairs, and uncertainty about the leadership credentials of those who were beginning to present themselves as presidential candidates. ▬

James Finn, editor of Freedom Review, *is editorial director of Freedom House.*

The USSR and Eastern Europe: The Uncertain Road to Reform

Robert L. Pfaltzgraff, Jr.

In the former Soviet Union and in Eastern Europe, once part of the Soviet empire, there was significant progress in the past year in establishing political and legal systems that respect and protect fundamental human rights. But such change has come as a result of a turbulent process of reform, which carries with it a high risk of potential reversals. The rise of nationalism and a yearning for political freedom among the many peoples living in the regions within what was once known as the Soviet Bloc have been instrumental in bringing about political and economic reforms for which Western states had long been pressing. However, some states, including Bulgaria, Romania and Albania, not to speak of the various portions of Yugoslavia and the Soviet Union, still have a long way to go on the path of democratic reform. In many cases former Communist party elites and the beneficiaries of the party-state administrative-command structure, which were at the heart of the totalitarian Communist regimes, remain in or close to power.

The emergence of multiparty systems

Multiparty political systems and legal systems that incorporate a respect for basic human rights and press freedoms have emerged in Poland, Hungary, Czechoslovakia and, to a lesser degree, in Bulgaria. Even the Stalinist regime in Albania bowed in 1991 to the demands

of protestors calling for greater political and economic freedoms. Mostly free elections have taken place in Poland, Czechoslovakia, Hungary and Bulgaria (which held its second post-Communist national election in June 1991). In Albania, student demonstrations in December 1990 helped convince President Alia to hold the country's first free multiparty elections in its history only three months later. However, all of those elections were marred by factionalism and bitter political differences with nationalist, anti-Semitic and authoritarian overtones. In some cases, former and present Communist party elites managed to retain power. The Albanian Workers' Party (Marxist-Leninist) claims that it won a plurality of the vote in an election that was judged by observers from the Conference on Security and Cooperation in Europe (CSCE) to have fallen far short of its standards for free and fair elections.

In Bulgaria, a partially free election saw the party of the old *nomenklatura*, which changed its name from the Bulgarian Communist Party to the Bulgarian Socialist Party, win a plurality of the vote. In Romania, the victory of Ion Iliescu, the pro-Soviet Romanian Communist Party apparatchik turned social democrat, was marred by charges of voter fraud. Iliescu has since demonstrated authoritarian tendencies in his use of miners to battle pro-democratic protestors in the streets of Bucharest and in his support of large police and military organizations. In May 1991, a number of former National Salvation Front (NSF) parliamentary deputies split off into a "dissident" faction committed to "true social democracy." This group is also highly critical of Iliescu's intolerance of other political options and the highly centralized nature of the NSF that, they argue, could "open the way for the establishment of one-man rule and personality cult."

New arrangements in Central Europe

The democratic revolutions of Eastern Europe and the USSR have contributed to the emergence of new cooperative arrangements in Central Europe. Hungarian, Polish and Czechoslovak leaders agreed in Visegrad on 15 February 1991 that they would cooperate in the areas of security, economic relations, transportation and energy in order to achieve four primary goals: (1) the full restoration of each state's independence, democracy and freedom; (2) the dismantling of the structure of Communist rule; (3) the establishment of parliamentary democracies and modern constitutional states united in a common commitment to respect human rights and fundamental freedoms; (4) and the integration of Eastern Europe into the general European political, economic and security arrangements.

In contrast, governments in Romania, Bulgaria and Albania have taken important steps in moving away from totalitarian Communist rule, but still have a long way to go in rejecting authoritarian tendencies and an obsession with maintaining "order" at the expense of human liberties. In Bulgaria, such authoritarian tendencies have been manifested in the government's opposition to the registration of an ethnic Turkish Movement for Rights and Freedoms, which managed to win twenty-three seats

in the Bulgarian parliament in the June 1990 elections. Racism and ethnic discrimination have also emerged in Romania, where anti-Hungarian, anti-Gypsy, and anti-German sentiments have gained strength in recent months. The Romanian authorities have defended the "individual rights" of all ethnic groups, but not their right to collective "privileges" in Romanian society.

Unfortunately, nationalism and efforts by recalcitrant Communist and socialist party elites to hold on to their privileges have in some cases, and in varying degrees, inhibited the emergence of more pluralistic political systems committed to protecting individual freedoms. In the former USSR as well as Yugoslavia, Romania, Albania and Bulgaria, individuals who prospered under totalitarian Communist rule either remain in control or are fighting rear-guard actions to protect their position and status. Such groups, opposed to the fall of totalitarian systems—in Bulgaria, Albania and until recently the USSR—have drafted laws to limit free expression and turned to military force to achieve their ends. The violence in the Baltics in January 1991 and the attempted coup against Gorbachev in August 1991 were the most vivid demonstrations yet of the continuing, though greatly reduced, military and political threat from antidemocratic forces.

Separatist movements & civil war

The civil war in Yugoslavia provides a vivid example of the dangers inherent in a political struggle in which Communist party and military elites are committed to holding the country together by suppressing separatist movements fueled by nationalism and a desire for greater political freedoms. The flowering of democracy in Yugoslavia in 1990 has since been overshadowed by a resumption of the Balkan wars. Ethnic rivalries and tensions, which had long been suppressed by Communist rule, have erupted into violence as ethnically based leaders in Slovenia, Croatia, Montenegro and Macedonia press their demands for complete and total independence from the Serb-dominated Yugoslav federal structure. (Albanian and Bulgarian government officials have raised the specter of a wider war by establishing their vital interest in the fate of Albanians and Macedonians living inside Yugoslavia. Both Albania and Greece could also conceivably become involved in a wider regional conflict over the fate of an independent Macedonia.) The spark that touched off the pow-der keg came on 25 June 1991, when the republics of Croatia and Slovenia voted to leave the Yugoslav federation. Since then, the Serb-dominated Yugoslav High Command has shown little willingness to compromise in its goal to unify a greater Serbia (minus possibly Slovenia). The split of the eight-member presidency on 4 October 1991 into Serb and Croat-dominated factions, with each claiming to be Yugoslavia's official government, has greatly complicated efforts by the European Community to reach a permanent cease-fire and an end to the fighting.

There are numerous hurdles yet to be cleared on the road to reform in Eastern Europe and the former Soviet empire. The economic devastation wrought by state socialism has made it difficult for freely elected governments to achieve rapid economic growth. The optimism of the 1989-1990 period has waned as a pervasive sense of malaise and uncertainty about the future of democracy in Eastern Europe spreads. The potential threat to democratic reforms inherent in the economic crisis has been clearly shown by the recent surge in political violence in Romania.

The violence eventually forced former Prime Minister Petre Roman to resign in September 1991, but not before he warned that miners rioting in Bucharest for the overthrow of Iliescu and Roman were seeking to launch a "Communist putsch from be-low" and "dissolve" all the democratic institutions.

In Czechoslovakia little progress has been made in rooting out the old bureaucracy which still survives in the central bodies and federal ministries. In the Czech and Slovak Republics, former Communist party members now openly advocate anti-reform agendas through the Party of the Democratic Left (formerly the Slovak Communist Party), the Czechoslovak Communist Party, the Communist Party of Bohemia and Moravia, Slovak National Party, the Movement for a Democratic Slovakia, and to a lesser degree the Czechoslovak Social Democracy party (led by Valtr Komarek and criticized by Rudolf Battek as a party dominated by "Communists and crypto-Communists"). The Communist movement in Czechoslovakia still shows some signs of life, even after the failure of the coup attempt in Moscow. The unity shown by opposition forces during the velvet revolution of November 1989 did not last beyond late 1990. In early 1991, the Czech Civic Forum and the Slovak Public Against Violence split up into four separate parties, leaving the Communist party as the largest single party in the Federal parliament and the third largest group in the parliaments of the Czech and Slovak republics. Although many former CP members appear to be genuine converts to democracy, many others are not. One of the most vocal advocates of a more authoritarian approach, as well as a leading advocate for Slovak independence, is Vladimir Meciar, the former Communist prime minister of Slovakia, who was dismissed in April 1991 for using secret police material to blackmail political opponents. Ironically, Meciar has been supported by the former leader of the Communist reform movement, Alexander Dubcek, who has called Meciar a "persistent defender of Slovak interests." President Havel has been Meciar's most vociferous critic, particularly since they oppose one another on the central issue facing Czechoslovakia today: whether Slovakia will remain part of a unified Czech and Slovak Federal Republic.

Nationalism & federalism

The rise of nationalism in the Czech and Slovak republics has hurt the democratic reform movement because some of the strongest advocates of political and economic reforms, including Jan Carnogursky (Slovak prime minister and the leader of the Christian Democrats) and Havel have strongly endorsed the idea of federation. The Slovak indepen-dence movement appeared to be gaining strength in 1991 as officials discussed holding a referendum on the issue. The referendum, which could be held before the end of December 1991, calls for complete independence for both republics within one year if more than 50 percent of the voters in any one republic vote in favor of secession.

Throughout Eastern Europe and the former Soviet empire, the broad-based democratic movements that were at the forefront of the anti-Communist revolu-tions of 1989 and 1991 have regressed into factionalism, and remain more closely identified with individuals, e.g., Russian President Boris Yeltsin, Polish President Lech Walesa and Havel, rather than with ideas. Many liberal and centrist politicians in Poland, Czechoslovakia and Russia look with apprehension at what are seen as the authoritarian tendencies of Yeltsin

and Walesa, as well as Havel's opposition to Slovak independence. They fear that in the event of economic and political chaos Yeltsin and Walesa may opt for a more authoritarian style of rule, while Havel may feel compelled to use force to prevent Slovak nationalists from taking power. Walesa has already sought special powers to rule by decree in order to push through an unpopular economic austerity plan. In late July 1991 Walesa was quoted as saying that, "If I was to face anarchy, or widespread strikes, if the situation turned out dramatic, I would have to rely on force to save the country."

Human rights: opportunities & danger

Nevertheless, the present diffusion of power within the former Soviet empire provides both opportunities and obstacles for improving human rights. On the one hand, the failure of the Soviet experiment in totalitarian communism has virtually destroyed the police state that Bolshevik leaders had erected as a pillar of the "socialist" system. How or even whether it can be reconstituted remains an open question. This has created an unprec-edented opportunity for democracy to blossom and for democratic institutions to establish roots that can survive the tur-moil of political, economic and cultural upheaval, although much uncertainty looms in the months just ahead.

It appears that the destruction of the Stalinist superstructure and the search for a "new Soviet man" was sealed on 5 September 1991, when the meeting in Moscow of the Congress of People's Deputies passed a Declaration of Human Rights and Freedoms, which declared in its preamble that, "No group, party or state interests may be placed above the interests of the individual." Articles 1 and 3 of the Declaration appeared to be based on the U.S. Constitution and accepted norms of international law on human rights. Article 1 declares that:

> Every person possesses natural, inalienable and inviolable rights and freedoms. They are sealed in laws that must correspond to the universal declaration of human rights and other international norms and this declaration.

Article 3 establishes a concept unique in the history of Russian and Soviet jurisprudence: that all citizens are considered "equal before the law and have an equal right to protection by law, irrespective of nationality, social origin, language, sex, political or other convictions, religion, place of residence, property status or other circumstances."

Transforming instruments of repression

The instruments of Soviet repression are also undergoing what appears to be a radical transformation. The KGB is being reorganized under the leadership of Vadim Bakatin, a self-proclaimed "radical centrist" who had broken with the Communist Party of the Soviet Union (CPSU) in late 1989 and was well known among U.S. officials as a man who wanted to reform the organization and its practices to accord with Western standards for the role of police forces in society. Both Bakatin and the new minister of internal affairs, Viktor P. Baranikov, had also been well known before the coup attempt for their efforts to eliminate Communist party cells from the Ministry of Internal Affairs (MVD). Gorbachev and Yeltsin have also advocated a move towards a "rule of law" that would protect the achievements of the democratic reform movement.

However, much of this progress has been made only with the reluctant

support of Gorbachev, who tried, unsuccessfully, to prevent the dissolution of the CPSU and republic-level party organizations in many of the former Soviet republics. Gorbachev has also adopted the seemingly contradictory positions of acting as a staunch defender of the union and a supporter of the "constitutional right" of every republic to "self-determination." In the end, Yeltsin's agenda triumphed. In all of the former Soviet republics the assets of the Communist parties are now either being nationalized or distributed. On 24 August, Gorbachev decreed an end to all activities by "political parties and political movements" in the USSR Armed Forces, USSR KGB, USSR MVD, and other government organizations. "Gorbachev's" decrees were actually modeled on Boris Yeltsin's presidential edict of 20 July, which banned all organized political activity in workplaces and outlawed discrimination and preferences based on an individual's membership in a political party or public organization.

In an effort to loosen the party apparat's grip on power, Yeltsin and Gorbachev have had to impose constraints on political activities that, depending upon how the relevant decree is interpreted, go farther than many Western societies would find acceptable. It may be the price citizens must pay to dismantle a totalitarian system that had stifled political freedoms for over seven decades. However, to ensure that the decrees do not become the basis for a new tyranny, Gorbachev included in them paragraphs defending the "constitutional right" of former CPSU members employed in government bodies to participate in "political activity outside those bodies" and declaring that governmental bodies should "not allow any violations of civil rights" during their restructuring.

The breakup of the USSR

The breakup of the Soviet Union has unleashed nationalist passions that threaten to inhibit and overwhelm further progress in promoting and defending respect for fundamental human rights in many of the former Soviet republics. The deep divisions between Russian and Union leaders and officials, who generally advocate the formation of a loose confederation of states, and nationalist and democratic reformers in the former Soviet republics, who generally seek greater independence from Moscow, have created a condition in which there is a very real threat that the Soviet Union could, like Yugoslavia, erupt into a civil war. In some Soviet republics the threat to progress in promoting democratic reforms comes not so much from Balkanization as from the less pernicious possibility of Lebanonization. Long suppressed ethnic tensions have erupted into protests and violence in Armenia, Azerbaijan, Moldavia, Tadzhikistan and Kyrgyzstan. Ethnic violence continues in Nagorno-Karabakh, South Ossetia, northern Moldavia, and other parts of the former Soviet Union. Georgia is on the brink of a bloody civil war. The potential for open conflict between the "sovereign states" of some sort of voluntary union in place of the Soviet Union has not been entirely removed as a result of Yeltsin's mediation of the Armenian-Azeri dispute over Nagorno-Karabakh. The Russian government has also established a potential *casus belli* in the form of a declaration that it would review existing borders if any neighboring republics with large populations of ethnic Russians, e.g., the Ukraine, Byelorussia, and Kazakhstan, broke away from the Union. In statements before the attempted coup, President Gorbachev pointed to the inherent dangers in such a declaration and responded with sharp criticism and a warning that the union

must be held together, and that Republic borders should be considered immutable. Gorbachev's preferred alternative until August 1991, one that President Bush openly supported in his Kiev address to the Ukrainian Parliament on 1 August 1991, was to conclude a new treaty that would hold the union together and grant the republics a significant degree of autonomy to legislate domestic policy, carry on nominal foreign policies, and declare themselves "sovereign federated states."

However, on 1 December, Ukraine voted overwhelmingly for independence under the leadership of Leonid M. Kravchuk, who won Ukraine's first presidential election. Russia granted immediate diplomatic recognition. The election outcome was the *coup de grace* for Gorbachev's efforts to form a new union from the remains of the old Soviet Union. On 8 December the presidents of the three Slavic republics—Ukraine, the Russian Federation, and Byelorussia—signed a declaration declaring an end to the USSR as a geopoltical reality and the formation of a Commonwealth of Independent States.

The proposed union treaty, which was initialed on 23 April 1991 by nine of the fifteen constituent republics, offered only a limited form of sovereignty that would not allow constituent republics to achieve complete sovereignty in formulating policy with regard to their economy, defense and internal security. Nevertheless, Gorbachev's own proteges in the military High Command and Committee for State Security (KGB) at-tempted to prevent the formal signing of that treaty by launching two abortive attempts to deprive Gorbachev of his powers: the first, a constitutional maneuver that failed in June 1991, and the second, two months later, the attempt on 19-20 August forcibly to overthrow him. Before the abortive coup, Gorbachev's intransigence and reluctance to dismantle completely the union structures appeared to be very similar to the inflexibility evident among the Serbian generals controlling the Yugoslav federal army. In the face of rising nationalism, the growth of non-Soviet armed forces, and a collapsing economy the reconstitution of some form of central authority may not be possible without compromising the struggle for democracy in the former Soviet empire.

Nascent democratic movements

Among the greatest threats to democratic reforms in the USSR are the millions of people who prospered as members of the *nomenklatura*, and the strands in Russian culture that favor an iron hand and collectivism. Gorbachev's former adviser on ideology and foreign policy, Alexander Yakovlev, has warned that a "lumpen conscience" among the millions of Russians who did not take part in the recent democratic revolution "might win and begin to crush everything." Advocates of a new authoritarian regime, including the nationalist leader of the not-so-liberal Liberal Democratic party Vladimir Zhirinovskiy, may find themselves the benefactors of growing popular support both with-in and beyond the cities. Other so-called "loyal Communists," whom Gorbachev has defended for their commitment to social-ism and opposition to the coup, may rally around organizations like the Communists for Democracy faction headed by Alexander Rutskoy.

To date, much of the political opposition to Communist rule has been popularly based, without any organized leadership by a large political party or group. The most popular of the nascent democratic opposition umbrella groups is the Movement for Democratic Reform (MDR), which includes former minister of foreign affairs, Eduard Shevardnadze, and Alexander Yakovlev. The next largest group is Democratic Russia, which is an umbrella organization rather than a well organized political party. The remaining groups, movements, and parties that have been formed since late 1989 represent a broad spectrum of political agendas, ranging from monarchism to libertarianism. Despite the growth of such groups, Russia's vice-president, Aleksandr Rutskoy, was candid and correct when he spoke at the memorial service for three students killed during the coup attempt: "Some people are now thinking that democracy has already triumphed, and that ahead lies an open road for democratic freedoms. But this, esteemed comrades, is far from being so."

While most of the non-Russian independence movements have agendas with nationalist overtones, the overwhelming majority of their leaders and supporters are committed to securing for their own people greater political and economic freedoms. Whether they will succeed in this great endeavor remains to be seen. Much hangs in the balance. For the U.S. and its Western allies, the protracted effort to deny communism the benefit of external expansion has succeeded. What lies ahead is the formidable task of building representative political institutions and market-oriented economies. If the opportunities are great, so are the dangers and obstacles. Just as the U.S. and its allies evolved a cold war strategy based on the containment of communism, we will need a strategic framework within which to forward the process of democratization based on freedom and independence. Despite the obvious gains of recent years and months, we remain far from this objective. ■

Robert L. Pfaltzgraff, Jr., is president of the Institute for Foreign Policy Analysis and Shelby Cullom Davis Professor of International Security Studies at the Fletcher School of Law and Diplomacy, Tufts University.

Asia: Progress, Stalemates, and a Setback

William J. Barnds

The collapse of Soviet communism and the disintegration of the USSR reverberated throughout Asia in 1991, and these events have not yet played themselves out. Other external developments, such as the Gulf war and the growing United Nations' role in dealing with regional conflicts, are affecting the political context within which national affairs are conducted. Together with local developments, these trends served to improve the prospects for peace, human rights and democracy in much of Asia.

The Soviet-American agreement to halt weapons shipments to Afghanistan could in time reduce the level of violence in the decade-old civil war, which is now continuing basically because of internal Afghan conflicts. India lost its superpower patron as Moscow no longer had the will or the ability to provide large-scale economic and military support to New Delhi. Pakistan's declining value to the United States as an arms conduit to Afghanistan, and its continued clandestine nuclear weapons program led to a halt in U.S. aid. The dwindling and possible end of the U.S. military presence in the Philippines and the planned reduction of U.S. armed forces in East Asia, together with America's declining economic position in the region, indicate that American influence on all issues— including human rights and democracy— probably will slowly diminish. The European Community and Japan announced that henceforth one factor governing their foreign aid distribution will be the recipient country's record on human rights and democracy, but they have yet to demonstrate how high a priority such issues will have.

Australia, New Zealand, Japan and India remained functioning democracies— although rising political, ethnic and religious violence posed a growing threat to the Indian polity. Pakistan, Singapore, Malaysia and Sri Lanka maintained systems based upon elections and representative governments, but with significant limits on civil liberties imposed by entrenched institutional forces or ethnic conflicts. A major breakthrough dramatically improved the prospects for peace and even democracy in Cambodia, and Bangladesh and Nepal moved from authoritarianism toward democracy. Only in Thailand, which experienced a military coup, was there a significant setback for political freedom.

Northeast Asian development

The Chinese regime's continued inability to deal with the aftermath of the widespread anti-government demonstrations of 1989 and the related problem of how to modernize a nation economically while maintaining tight political controls dominated events in that country. The regime's dilemmas were intensified by the failure of the August coup in the Soviet Union, the ensuing collapse of communism and the ongoing fragmentation of the USSR itself. While Beijing publicly reacted circumspectly to the coup and its failure, private party documents made clear that Soviet developments left China's rulers even more fearful and defensive than previously. Although China's population is over 90 percent ethnically Han, there was evident fear that independence movements in Soviet Central Asia—and Mongolia's move away from communism—could spill over into China's sensitive border regions. Continued popular alienation in Tibet was kept in check only by repression. More ominously, rising demands for formal independence in Taiwan added to Beijing's woes.

Domestic repression was widespread but uneven. There was cautious movement toward renewed economic reform, and Beijing's unsuccessful 1990 efforts to exert greater economic control over provincial governments in China's more prosperous areas forced Beijing's hardline conservatives to tolerate considerable regional autonomy. Despite efforts at renewed indoctrination of a Marxist ideology that few officials or citizens believed in any longer, China continued to allow large numbers of students to go abroad for study, thus risking "spiritual pollution." Yet many dissidents languished in prison without a trial, pressure on religious groups increased, and the media remained stridently dogmatic.

The regime still benefits from the economic gains made (particularly by the peasantry and the southern coastal provinces) since the late 1970s, but this is a wasting asset. China's aging rulers are divided and on the defensive, having lost their legitimacy in 1989 but not their control of the country's powerful security forces. They also benefit from the lack of organized opposition. Citing Poland,

Deng Xiaoping reportedly said China is fortunate not to have to contend with a Solidarity or a Catholic church. Yet Deng's plans to institutionalize reform and establish a mechanism for an orderly transfer of power have been shattered, and many observers believe that China's lack of a civic culture makes the outlook for political reform questionable. The regime fears that tackling basic structural economic problems could cause new political unrest, necessitating either further repression or a surrender of power that many Chinese desire but also fear could lead to national disintegration or something approaching the chaos of the 1920s and 1930s.

Continued progress toward political reform occurred in a Taiwan moving steadily if cautiously toward a more democratic system. President Lee Teng-hui, the first native Taiwanese to hold that office, ended the "period of Communist rebellion" on 1 May, thus easing legal constraints on dealing with the mainland. This was followed by abolition of the most draconian provisions of the island's sedition laws in May, which permitted more open political life in Taiwan. The opposition moved to exploit the new atmosphere by pressing for the repeal of anti-sedition provisions of the Criminal Code, which have been used to prevent discussions of independence. This move by the increasingly assertive Democratic Progressive Party (DPP) reflects the party's move toward open advocacy of *de jure* independence for Taiwan, a stance which frightens the influential main-landers within the Kuomintang (KMT) and which has caused an alarmed Beijing to warn it would not tolerate a formal declaration of independence. Thus as both the Chinese and Taiwanese governments move toward a more pragmatic stance on issues involving trade, investment and travel, and Beijing accepts Taiwan's membership in some international groupings, the upsurge of pro-independence moves may complicate or even undermine the progress made to date. With political—though perhaps not public—opinion polarizing, the December elections for a new National Assembly to replace the one elected on the mainland in 1947 will be a test of the island's ability to continue on the path of political reform and ultimately create a new and fully democratic constitution appropriate to present-day realities and aspirations.

The Republic of Korea (ROK) maintained the trend toward pluralism of recent years—itself a sign of progress— while successfully conducting the first local council elections in thirty years on 26 March. While voter turnout was low, the elections could be an important step toward decentralization in a country whose political life has long been dominated by Seoul. Yet Korean democracy remains a delicate plant. Its political parties have shallow roots, being largely the instruments of individual political leaders seeking personal power, and compromise and the idea of a "legal opposition" remain alien. The brutal tactics of the police when dealing with radical demonstrators led President Roh Tae Woo to accept his prime minister's resignation, reshuffle his cabinet, and adopt a more flexible approach to dealing with public protests. These helped to keep moderate students—and the urban workers and the middle class—from joining the radicals.

Southeast Asia: one step forward, one step back

Most nations of Southeast Asia continued along the paths of recent years. Indonesia under President Suharto allowed somewhat more open dissent in a few areas,

but continued to use forceful and often brutal methods in dealing with openly dissident groups, some of which have few historic links to the rest of Indonesia and want no part of Indonesian rule. Vietnam remained stalled in its efforts to move beyond its earlier liberalizing reform successes in agriculture, which have alleviated but not eliminated its bleak economic situation.

Hanoi is unwilling to supplement cautious attempts at further economic reform by any significant political liberalization, and faces drastic cuts in— or even the end of—Soviet aid as well as Moscow's demands for repayment of past loans. Hanoi rests its hopes on trade with and aid from the capitalist world after a Cambodian settlement—but fears such links could increase the appeal of democratic values.

The Philippines experienced a less tumultuous year politically, but made little progress on enacting and implementing badly needed economic and social reforms during President Aquino's last full year of her term. Next year's national, regional and local elections will test the country's commitment to fair and peaceful campaigning and polling, and will affect strongly the degree of public confidence in the post-Marcos political system. Slow but continued progress marked the government's struggle against the Communist-led National People's Army insurgency—often by methods strongly criticized by human rights groups—and private militias in parts of the country continued the Filipino tradition of political violence. The eruption of Mt. Pinatubo in June, which rendered the U.S. base at Clark Field useless, was followed by huge mudflows sparked by typhoons. The ensuing dislocations, following those brought about by the impact of the Gulf war, will be further exacerbated by the Philippine Senate's 16 September rejection of new U.S.-Philippines base agreement, which—whatever its psychological benefits for Filipino's sense of independence—will cost the country at least $500 million annually.

Myanmar (Burma) continued its record of xenophobia, ineptitude and brutality. The three-decades old military regime has led one of southeast Asia's richest countries back to subsistence living unknown since pre-modern times—a feat that makes Mikhail Gorbachev look like an economic genius! After responding to nationwide protests in 1988 by agreeing to national elections, the regime has simply ignored the results since hastily assembled opposition forces won an overwhelming victory in 1989. Facing economic sanctions from the U.S. and the EC—but only partially from Japan—the military regime relies on drug exports, deforestation for a world hungry for wood, and arms imports from a China in search of any friends it can find to keep itself in power in Myanmar. Despite its apparent control of the levers of power, reported purges of the civil service and dissent within the military suggest the regime is on the defensive. In October the Nobel Peace Prize was awarded to Daw Aung San Suu Kyi, the daughter of the leader of the country's independence movement, who led the opposition to victory in 1989 and is now under house arrest. The award could embarrass Japan and Myanmar's Southeast Asian neighbors, who argue in favor of "constructive engagement" and are concerned about Western emphasis on human rights, but its impact on their policies—or those of the military regime—is problematical.

One regional issue that demonstrates the complexities and inconsistencies of international life surfaced in October when Hong Kong's British rulers and

Vietnam agreed to the mandatory return of tens of thousands of Vietnamese boat people who have been classified as economic migrants rather than political refugees. If carried out over the next few years, such a policy could lead to Vietnamese agreements with other Southeast Asian countries with sizeable numbers of boat people. International objections and U.S. opposition halted similar efforts in the past, but Hong Kong officials point out that Hong Kong has for years returned illegal entrants from China and that the United States routinely turns back would be refugees from such countries as Haiti. And despite the fact that most of Hong Kong's citizens are themselves earlier escapees from China, they apparently accept and even support the moves to expel the Vietnamese.

Thailand, which had moved steadily toward a democratic system in the 1980s, took a major step backward with the 23 February military coup which ousted the country's first fully elected government since 1976. The military claimed their action was based upon the government's widespread corruption and vote-buying, and on its efforts to establish a "parliamentary dictatorship" that was trying to dominate the long-powerful civilian bureaucracy and the military. While the Thai people, due to four years of double-digit economic growth and disgust with the elected government's corruption, accepted the coup, most observers who remembered the Thai military leadership's history of less than squeaky clean behavior regarded their action as basically designed to protect the military's traditional powerful role. Appointment of a respected group of civilian technocrats and the promise of elections by April 1992 won the military some initial support, but the dominant role given military officers in the body established to write a new constitution soon dismayed many Thais. The military faces no immediate threat to its power, but some Thai political leaders and citizens have begun to challenge it openly, causing divisions within the regime. More basically, it is unable to devise a method of fulfilling its promise to reestablish democracy while protecting its traditional role and power.

A major breakthrough for Cambodia occurred on 23 October when the four contending Cambodian factions and eighteen nations signed an agreement designed to bring peace and representative government to that strife-torn nation. Over two years of negotiations following the Vietnamese troop withdrawal in 1989 led to the complicated plan, which provides for United Nations administration of the country under broad guidance by the Cambodian Supreme National Council representing the four factions— the previous Communist government, the notorious and fanatic Khmer Rouge Communists, and two non-Communist guerrilla groups. The government declared a formal end to communism in mid-October. A cease-fire officially began immediately, the military forces of the four groups are to be reduced by 70 percent, foreign military support is to end, and 350,000 refugees along the Thai border are to return. The U.N. administration will help organize free elections in early 1993 to elect a constituent assembly charged with drafting a democratic constitution, and the signers of the treaty have committed themselves to provide the resources to rebuild the country.

The agreement represents half of a miracle; the other half involves implementing it successfully. The minefields ahead—involving both the huge number of mines planted in the country that need to be located and removed, and the many potential disputes and conflicts that could still occur—are daunting. Probably none is as serious as securing Khmer Rouge compliance with the provisions that greatly reduce its military strength, which would in turn weaken its political base by limiting its ability to intimidate large numbers of Cambodians. Many observers are skeptical on this point because the Khmer Rouge has extensive military stocks and its acceptance of the agreement suggests far less of a change of heart than a tactical move. Yet at worst the agreement should improve conditions in Cambodia, and could even bring an end to its long nightmare.

South Asian progress

Despite South Asia's many monumental problems—extreme poverty, religious and ethnic disputes and violence, and fragile political institutions and authoritarian traditions in several countries—democracy not only held its own but gained ground during 1991. Although Pakistan continued to experience considerable political and ethnic violence, the government—with power divided between President Ghulam Ishaq Khan and Prime Minister Nawaz Sharif, who was elected late in 1990— continued to function and to move the country slowly to a more market-oriented economy. The Tamil-Singhalese civil war in the northern and eastern parts of Sri Lanka continued, but with the democratically elected Sinhalese government slowly extending its power—often through the use of indiscriminate violence and economic blockades that hurt the innocent as well as the insurgents.

The Tamil guerrilla forces, originally motivated by a desire to establish a separate Tamil state because of past Singhalese discrimination, now appear addicted to violence for its own sake. Outside of Tamil-controlled or -contested areas life has returned to some normalcy, with the economy rebounding and the government able to hold and win peaceful local elections everywhere but in the northern and eastern provinces in May. Yet with no conclusion of the regional civil war in sight Sri Lanka's future as one nation is problematical.

The 6 March collapse of India's second minority government formed after the indecisive November 1989 elections forced the country to hold new general elections. Even though no elections were scheduled for Kashmir (torn by the bloody conflict between undisciplined Indian security forces and Muslim militants protesting past discrimination by New Delhi) and were postponed in strife-torn Punjab and Assam, the election campaign began with more killing, intimidation and vote-rigging than any previous election. Fears that India was becoming ungovernable were dramatically increased by the assassination of former Prime Minister Rajiv Gandhi on 21 May, apparently by a South Indian Tamil-terrorist resentful of Gandhi's sending the Indian army to help the Sri Lankan government subdue the Tamil rebellion there. (Ironically, the Tamil rebels had originally been supported and supplied by Indian intelligence acting under the author-ity first of Prime Minister Indira Gandhi and then of her son, Rajiv.)

Some observers thought the trend toward political violence demonstrated that India was headed toward semi-chaos or authoritarian rule even though the general election, although postponed briefly, was soon held and resulted in the Congress Party winning a strong plurality. Other observers argued that any country that could cope with the many shocks to its political system experienced by India in recent years and still operate in a basically democratic manner had reserves of strength and resiliency. At least in the short term, the latter group

has proven correct. India's new Congress-led government has moved vigorously to adapt market-oriented economic reforms, although it had little choice in view of its need for Western aid, given Soviet inability to continue to help prop up its heavily regulated economy. Such reforms could revive the economy, which slowed after expanding by 5 percent annually during the 1980s—the best record since independence. Yet some progress in reducing the growing level of political violence by dealing constructively with the country's seemingly intractable ethnic, religious and caste conflicts is necessary to assure the survival of democracy and adequate protection for the lives and liberties of Indian citizens.

Bangladesh held its first free and honest elections on 27 February, following widespread political agitation which finally led to the resignation of the authoritarian regime of President H.M. Ershad, who came to power as the result of a military coup in 1982. The Bangladesh Nationalist Party (BNP), led by Khaleda Zia, wife of former army commander and later President Ziaur Rahman, won 140 of the 300 contested seats. The Awami League, headed by Hasina Wajed, wife of the country's first prime minister, won 84 seats. (Both husbands were assassinated, one indication of the turmoil the country has experienced since its birth in 1971.) The new government formed by Prime Minister Zia faced massive economic problems growing out of the Gulf crisis and a massive cyclone that struck the country on 30 April, rendering millions homeless and devastating huge areas of farmland. The tasks of running a near subsistence economy that depends overwhelmingly on foreign aid for its development projects is perhaps even less daunting than that of developing a democratic political culture and institutions, which will test the wisdom and skills of the many inexperienced politicians, including the prime minister.

Nepal, in 12 May elections that official foreign observers said were fair, saw the Nepali Congress (NC) win 110 of the 205 seats in the House of Representatives in the country's first free elections since 1959. The non-party village council system (dominated by King Birenda and feudal elements) had been discredited by its poor performance and rising demands for democracy, and was sacrificed by the king to avoid risking even wider and bloodier popular unrest than he faced throughout 1990. He granted a new constitution lodging sovereignty in the people (a move whose implications are unclear since most Nepalis believe the king is an incarnation of the Hindu god Vishnu) and instituted multi-party elections. The second largest number of seats (69) in the May election was won by the Communists, which raises questions about the stability of the system. Since several of the NC's few experienced leaders lost in the elections the task of dealing with the country's formidable problems and delicate domestic political and international issues has fallen to a small group of relatively inexperienced leaders. Thus the progress made so far is modest compared to the challenges ahead. ▄

William J. Barnds has served as president of the Japan Institute of America and as staff director of the Subcommittee on Asian and Pacific Affairs of the House Foreign Affairs Committee.

Africa:
A Truly Historic Year

J. Leo Cefkin

There are solid reasons to judge 1991 as a true watershed in Africa's affairs. One-party regimes are falling. Multi-party democracy is the order of the day.

One-party rule, it had been said, was a peculiarly African form of government which alone met the needs for nation-building in a multi-tribal setting. Oppression and suppression were judged essential for public order. In fact one-party rule was typically corrupt. It fostered leadership intent on entrenching its own power. Often it provided ascendancy for one ethnicity to the detriment of others. Presidents for life or leaders empowered by coups were the rule. Promises for development remained unfulfilled. Incompetents could not be turned out of office.

Multi-party democracy now holds out an opportunity for state and nation building. Periodic free and fair elections promise stability. These changes, at least in part, reflect the demise of Communist rule in the Soviet Union and in the former East bloc countries. The Cold War is over, and Moscow's clients no longer enjoy Kremlin support. Of concern there is now the possibility that the countries of Europe and, especially, the United States will neglect Africa. At a time when Africans are most in need of encouragement to develop their potentially prosperous democracies such a prospect is unfortunate.

The fall of the leaders

African dictatorships came to an end in 1991. Long-serving presidents were turned out of office. Ethiopia's Mengistu Haile Mariam, perhaps the most despised dictator on the continent, was forced to flee his country and take refuge in Zimbabwe. His seventeen years in power were marked by extreme ruthlessness. On coming to power he ordered the execution of sixty officials of Haile Selassie's government. He personally shot to death five rivals during a banquet in the former emperor's palace. A number of diplomats defected. He made no effort to negotiate a settlement with the Eritrian and Tigrean guerrillas and fought a failing war of suppression. By adapting a hardline Marxist stance and imposing collectivization on over 1 million peasants, he reduced farm production and exacerbated the famine of 1984-85.

Mengistu had intensified the fighting after the ouster of Selassie in 1974 aided by Cuban troops, Soviet arms and financial aid. Nevertheless, victory was not in prospect. When the Cubans withdrew, and Moscow cut its assistance and advised negotiations, defeat on the battlefield followed. Mengistu's future became dubious and he fled, leaving the country in shambles and the economy bankrupt.

The Ethiopian Peoples Revolutionary Democratic Front (EPRDF) took power in Addis Ababa promising democracy and ethnic rights in a reconstituted Ethiopia. Meles Venawi, leader of the EPRDF, was chosen president pending general elections within two years. A new openness has spawned an explosion of public expressions and demonstrations for varied causes. Eritrea established its own provisional government and may opt for independence. Meles has been negotiating with the Eritreans to gain access to sea ports and to promote economic ties. Hundreds of senior officers of the previous regime have been detained and threatened with trials.

Two other military rulers with a baleful record for oppres-sion and self-aggrandizement were also ousted; Hissene Habre in Chad and Siyad Barre in Somalia. Habre, having lost French military aid, could not withstand the challenge of a rival guerrilla force. He fled the country in disgrace. Barre, with his troops fighting a losing battle, abandoned Mogadishu to the guerrillas of a rival clan within the Somali nation. Corruption, a failing economy, and brutal suppression narrowed his support to that of his own clan group.

Coups toppled regimes in Lesotho and Mali. Presidents, acceding to demands for multi-party elections, were voted out of office, including the long-standing presidents of Benin, Cape Verde, Sao Tome and Zambia.

Free and fair elections

Most startling was the defeat of Kenneth Kaunda in Zambia, not that it was unexpected, since opinion polls showed Kaunda running behind his opponent. Kaunda is one of the great leaders of African independence. His principle of humanitarian social-ism dictated a benign authoritarian rule. His stalwart stand against white supremacy imposed sacrifices on the Zambian economy and paid "the high price of principle" in the cause of justice. Zambia's economy deteriorated over the years. Corruption by those around Kaunda demoralized the populace.

The Movement for Multi-party Democracy (MMD) gained broad support for an end to one-party elections in favor of a multi-party contest. Frederick Chiluba, their candidate for president, proved an attractive rival. The MMD championed democracy and a market economy, with the promise of turning malaise into prosperity.

Free and fair elections have offered a way out from on-going civil wars. Despite the Angola/Namibian agreement of 1988, which authorized Namibian independence and withdrawal of Cuban troops from Angola, the civil war continued without any prospect for victory. The Popular Movement for the Liberation of Angola (MPLA) refused to surrender power. The Savimbi-led National Union for Total Independence of Angola (UNITA) insisted on full participation in a democratized Angola. Both Moscow and Washington, respec-tive supporters of the rival par-ties, urged a negotiated settlement. Portugal, with the support of the U.S. and the USSR, undertook the mediatory role. The basis for internal settlement improved as the Angolan government gave up its Marxist orientation and embraced the principles of multi-party democracy and a market-driven economy.

Mediation facilitated an MPLA/UNITA agreement that provided for a cease-fire and for transition to a demo-cratic political system. The agreement of 31 May 1991 accepted continuation of the Angolan government through a transitional phase. The cease-fire was to be supervised by a Joint Political and Military Commission with shared MPLA and UNITA membership. As a result, a 600-member international monitoring group observes implementation of the accord. Over 200,000 soldiers were to be demobilized and replaced by a military force of 50,000 containing MPLA and

UNITA military units. Both parties had advocated elections. The MPLA proposed a three-year transition while UNITA demanded one year. A compromise settled the matter with the voting scheduled for September-November 1992.

Already a few dozen parties have beep organized. To qualify for participation in the balloting a party must have a minimum of 3,000 members with at least 140 in fourteen of Angola's eighteen provinces. Alliances are likely. UNITA's strength lies among the Ovimbundu people, the largest ethnic group. It also enjoys support among other ethnicities. MPLA is rooted in the Mbundu communities, but also has a following in the coastal cities. MPLA's chief disadvantage is its single-minded concentration on defeating UNITA. As much as 70 percent of its budget went for military expenditures. It has, nevertheless, a year or more to prove its competence.

Despite the fall and execution of President Samuel Doe, the warring factions in Liberia continued their strife. Wanton bloodletting had induced seven West African countries, members of the Economic Community of West African States (ECOWAS), to dispatch an intervening force to pacify the country. They endorsed Amos Sawyer as a transitional president, a respected personality who had eschewed affiliation with any faction. The National Patriotic Front of Liberia (NPFL), led by Charles Taylor, challenged the decision. Sawyer and the West African peacekeeping force con-trolled the capital, Monrovia. The NPFL held sway in the hinter-land. The stalemate was broken when Taylor accepted the West Africans offer of elections within six months in return for the disarming of all Liberian military personnel. The agreement was hailed by the Nigerian commander as, "total commitment of all Liberians to rid their beloved country of...arms and ammunition."

War and terrorism

Rwanda became a battlefield between the majority Hutu people and the ruling Tutsi minority. Prior to its independence, a Hutu uprising established their rule of the country. Tutsis fled into exile, mainly to Uganda. In 1991 a Tutsi-led group, the Rwanda Patriotic Front (RPF), invaded Rwanda seeking to overthrow the government. The challenge failed, although the RPF continued harassment in the countryside.

The RPF was accused of eco-terrorizing for destroying the scarce (320) gorilla population of northern Rwanda. After the shootings, it is estimated that no more than 110 remain. The situation was troubling enough to energize establishment of a peacekeeping force composed of fifteen soldiers each from Uganda, Burundi, Tanzania and Zaire to monitor the Rwanda-Uganda border. Rwanda President Juvenal Habyarimana proposed constitutional changes that would make Rwanda a multi-party democracy. The RPF could then compete in an election. Opposition parties were legalized, and a number of then have been formed. Elections have been promised for 1992.

Several African states are going through chaotic times. Zaire is a prime example. In September, soldiers protesting unpaid wages ran amok, looting, maiming and killing. The populace joined in the disorder. Stores in Kinshasa were looted and boarded up. Expatriates, who dominated Zaire's formal economy, have packed up and fled. The government doesn't govern. Jobs are gone. President Mobutu Sese Seko, Zaire's dictator for twenty-six years, is the main cause of the turmoil.

He lives on his yacht on the Congo River. He doesn't dare enter Kinshasa for fear of being lynched. He is reputed to have accumulated a great fortune stashed away abroad. Yet, he clings to power by military force. An opposition has as yet been unable to dislodge him. Western countries and international organizations have suspended their aid programs. France and Belgium sent in military forces for the limited purpose of evacuating their nationals. However, in the words of a European diplomat, "Zaire is not an important country for Europe and America anymore." Seemingly, nobody cares and a solution is not in sight.

South Africa

In South Africa the 1991 session of Parliament marked the end of an era, the era of apartheid. What remains of apartheid as law is the disenfranchisement of blacks which will end as the new order is put in place. Negotiations for a new constitution, spelling out the restructured political system, are pending. Al-ready established are the principles of a multi-party democracy, majority rule, and the protection of individual freedom in a bill of rights. An all-party gathering to decide on the constitution-writing process and the content of the document was the next step, but it had to be preceded by a Conference of the African National Congress (ANC). The July meeting in Durban led to the formulation of the ANC position.

In the preceding months, the ANC undertook an impressive grass-roots discussion on leadership and policy and elected dele-gates to the Conference. The elected leadership, with Nelson Mandela as president, represents the moderate wing. A National Executive Committee and a smaller leadership group were also selected. The executive bodies reflect the full spectrum of ANC membership but also reinforce the alliance with the COSATU trade unions and the South African Communist Party (SACP). Leadership was given a broad mandate to implement policy guidelines. Most significant in these guidelines is the emphasis on negotiating the transition to majority rule.

Long and arduous negotiations are assured. President F.W. de Klerk has called for an all-party conference to get the process underway. A seemingly absurd situation emerged in which the government, under the ruling National Party (NP), which benefits from the *status quo,* pressed for constitutional deliberations, while the ANC, the organization that demands majority rule as soon as possible, delayed the process. The ANC, the Pan Africanist Congress (PAC), and other groups met in October to establish a Patriotic Front (PF) in order to present a united stance in confronting the government. They agreed to call for a preliminary meeting in order to press for an interim government and an elected Constituent Assembly to write the constitution. However, the groups comprising the PF retained their separate identities. In fact, in a two-day conference convened to set up rules and an agenda for the constitutional revision gathering, the PAC withdrew, charging that the NP and the ANC were in collusion on the future constitution.

The legitimacy of the government was compromised when it was revealed that state funds were given to the Inkatha Freedom Party to organize rallies. Cabinet members argued that this was an appropriate use of government money, because Inkatha opposed sanctions, a position also held by the government. However, it was readily recognized that the state was funding a party to rival the

ANC. "Inkathagate" undermined the government's claim to the right to oversee the transition to a post-apartheid era.

The PF demands the resignation of the de Klerk government and its replacement by a regime of national unity. The NP refuses to surrender. They are not a defeated force. De Klerk proposes, instead, a broadening of the government to include ANC and other participants in the decision-making process. The ANC calls for an elected Constituent Assembly to write the constitution. De Klerk wants to work out constitutional provisions in advance of any election. The issue of property rights is a major concern. ANC leaders talk of nationalization, redistribution of wealth, and a refusal to honor the state's financial obligations, positions which are exceedingly threatening. If these are pressed by the ANC, an agreed upon settlement may become impossible. At the same time, ANC leadership denies the adoption of the foregoing provisions. Mandela's warm embrace of Castro and Qadhafi, and the ANC's support for Saddam Hussein raise suspicions about their protestations for democracy.

The government of South Africa possesses formidable police power. ANC/PF strength rests on its ability to mobilize mass action.

In November, a strike was called to demand that the recently-enacted Value Added Tax (VAT) be cancelled. VAT replaced the General Service Tax. At issue was not the tax *per se* but the government's failure to consult with the ANC/COSATU/SACP, and PF. The *New Nation,* the ANC newspaper, explained this flexing of muscles as a vital "linkage between mass action and negotiations...." Should the strike fail, "our struggle will be dealt a cruel blow from which the democratic movement may never recover...." The strike was widely supported.

A major impediment to successful negotiations is the large-scale recourse to violence, claiming thousands of lives. Intimidation and violence seem to be an unrelenting aspect of South Africa's political culture. The uses of force have many sources. It was the way the government ruled. It was a tactic for revolutionary change. It was the formula for resolving ethnic differences and ideological conflict. It was the means used by town-ship gangsters. More recently, it was spawned by clashes between people living in squatter locations and those in the all-male hostels set up for workers from other parts of the country.

The government, the ANC and Inkatha have been preoccupied with efforts to bring the killing to an end. While acrimonious exchanges continued, a national peace effort sponsored by church and business groups persevered in deliberations which resulted in a National Peace Accord. Violence continues, but the mechanism set up under the Accord has been useful.

A political culture conducive to resolution of issues cannot be created instantaneously. This is acknowledged by groups, such as the Institute for Multi-Party Democracy, that are devoted to developing tolerance among rival groups and teaching the values essential for democracy.

The lifting of sanctions

On 10 July 1991 President Bush lifted sanctions contained in the Comprehensive Anti-Apartheid Act (CAAA). As a courtesy to the ANC his decision followed their Conference. Bush's action was acclaimed by the daily press as a vital step toward improved economic conditions in South Africa. While the ANC opposed the move, the reaction to it by the leadership was muted. The *New Nation* did not editorialize against it. They merely re-ported a statement from a member of the Congressional Black Caucus, pledging renewed efforts to reverse the president's action. The lifting of sanctions was not even denounced by ANC leaders.

Despite claims that sanctions were essential to force the de Klerk govern-ment to stay on course toward the post-apartheid order, the sanctions had become, in fact, a lever of political influence for the ANC, which wanted to make the determination as to when sanctions could best end.

Sanctions had effectively dried up foreign investment. Trade was, at best, marginally affected. With the termination of sanctions, South Africans hoped that American investment would grow quickly. Nevertheless, there is general recognition of the fact that private investment gravitates toward the profit-able.

The CAAA of 1986 had been passed over Reagan's veto. To win adoption, the law had to include more than just sanctions. Thus it called for the peaceful transfer of power. It castigated terrorism, particularly necklacing. The president was required to report to Congress on the ANC and its ties with the South African Communist Party (SACP). The law also spelled out conditions for lifting sanctions, including the freeing of Mandela and other political prisoners. Banned organizations had to be unbanned. The state of emergency had to be lifted, apartheid laws repealed, and negotiations with legitimate black leadership had to commence. With these conditions met, the president was obligated to terminate sanctions.

The most troubling criterion was the release of political prisoners. Persons guilty of murder and other acts of violence for political goals were on the ANC list of political prisoners. The government considered them criminals in many cases. Bush required that the United States make its own judgment based on its criteria of political prisoners. Given Washington's long-standing hostility to violent acts, Bush agreed with Pretoria's position that all political prisoners had been released.

Preliminary meetings to organize the Convention for a Democratic South Africa were held 29 and 30 November. Twenty groups were represented with only the pro-apartheid right-wing white groups and a black consciousness organization refusing to participate. As noted, the Pan African Congress withdrew. The structure, agenda, and timing of the December sessions were settled, raising the hope that divisive issues can be accommodated. Cyril Ramaphosa, secretary general of the ANC, expressed the general feeling of delegates with his assessment. "The possibility of achieving this goal through negotiation has now become real..." and "more than ever, we are convinced that we are walking the last mile."

Decisions about the process are difficult to make. Issues of federalism, bicameralism, and separation of powers are sure to produce intense debate. Yet, given the spirit of accommodation, at the end of 1991 they did not seem beyond solution. ▬

J. Leo Cefkin, professor emeritus, Colorado State University, was in 1991 a Fulbright Professor at Rhodes University in South Africa.

The Middle East: War & its Aftermath

Don Peretz

The Gulf War and its consequences dominated nearly every aspect of developments in the Middle East during 1991. All nations in the region were involved either as participants or as recipients of the economic impact of the crisis. The crisis and the war that followed from it caused a massive exodus from several Middle East countries creating one of the most severe refugee problems in recent years. Although the United States vehemently denied that there was any linkage between the Gulf crisis and the Arab-Israel conflict, victory over Iraq by an allied consortium led to a peace conference between Israel and its neighbors during October.

The political confrontation that began in August 1990 between Iraq and an American dominated alliance organized through the United Nations continued to escalate until President George Bush decided to take military action against Baghdad. On 16 January 1991, the day after a deadline for Iraq's withdrawal from Kuwait passed without compliance, American, British, Kuwaiti and Saudi Arabian forces launched a massive air campaign against the invading army. The air strikes were reportedly aimed at destroying command and control centers, air defenses, Scud surface-to-surface missile launchers, and airfields in preparation for an allied land invasion.

Although twenty-eight countries contributed forces to the operation and it was conducted under the United Nations flag, it was planned, managed and commanded by the United States. Iraq attempted to involve Israel in the war by firing dozens of Scud missiles into heavily populated areas of Tel-Aviv, Haifa and their environs. However, the U.S. persuaded Israel to refrain from retaliation and to permit the allied forces to take care of the situation; the U.S. feared that Israeli participation in combat against Iraq would jeopardize the alliance, which included several Arab states hostile to Israel. In repayment for its restraint the Israeli government was rewarded by the U.S. with Patriot anti-Scud missiles and additional financial assistance.

Continued efforts through the United Nations by the Soviet Union, France, the PLO, Jordan, China and other governments to persuade Iraqi President Saddam Hussein to withdraw from Kuwait or to effect some other compromise failed despite the heavy air bombardments. Consequently the allies initiated a ground invasion of Iraq and Kuwait with over 700,000 soldiers on 23 February. Within three days the Iraqi forces were defeated, suffering hundreds of thousands of casualties and losing tens of thousands of prisoners. President Bush ordered the allied forces to suspend military operations on 27 February. In the truce and cease-fire agreements that followed, Iraq agreed to comply with the twelve U.N. resolutions on the Gulf crisis, to completely withdraw from Kuwait, and to release all property and spoils of war and prisoners seized since August. New U.N. resolutions also required Iraq to accept responsibility for the war and to pay for war damages. The U.N. also continued the economic and military embargo imposed during the crisis, preventing Iraq from importing goods or from selling oil abroad, its principal source of foreign exchange.

Post-war scene in Iraq...

Within Iraq there was a total breakdown of civil government among the Shi'ite Muslim population in the south and among the Kurds in the northern provinces of the country. However Saddam Hussein managed to retain his office and continued to rule the country for the rest of the year. His attempt to suppress the Shi'ite and Kurdish uprisings with brutal force led to allied intervention in the Kurdish areas where American and other troops were sent to protect civilian populations and to assist the hundreds of thousands of refugees who fled across the border to Turkey. The Iraqi government attempted to end the Kurdish uprising through negotiations based on extending autonomy to the minority. By the end of the year no agreements with the Kurds or other internal dissidents were reached, but Iraqi forces were still prevented from imposing their authority in many northern areas of the country.

In terms of military expenses, casualties, refugees and damage to both Iraq and Kuwait, the war was one of the most costly since World War II. By the end of the year the total cost of military operations was around $50 billion, most of it paid by the U.S. with promises of contributions to cover nearly all this amount from Western European allies

and Japan. Allied casualties were very light, fewer than a 1,000. However, estimates of Iraqi soldiers killed were as high as 100,000. The impact of the war on the Iraqi civilian population was equally disastrous; tens of thousands of civilians became casualties during the combat operations and after the war as a result of widespread hunger and the collapse of transportation, irrigation and other vital components of the nation's infrastructure. Most of the country's electricity supply was knocked out, which meant that irrigation networks for agriculture were disrupted, hospital services were badly damaged, and public transport rendered inoperable.

Following a visit to Iraq during March by the under-secretary-general of the U.N. to survey after-effects of the war, he reported "that nothing that we had seen or read had quite prepared us for the particular form of devastation which has now befallen the country. The recent conflict has wrought near apocalyptic results upon the economic infrastructure of what had been...a rather highly urbanized and mechanized society. Now, most means of modern life support have been destroyed or rendered tenuous. Iraq has, for some time to come, been relegated to a pre-industrial age, but with all the disabilities of post-industrial dependency on an intensive use of energy and technology (UNSC S/ 22366)."

...and in Kuwait

Kuwait also suffered extensive damage, most of it caused by the retreating Iraqi army. Many public buildings and other facilities were either destroyed or left badly damaged. Much of the country's machinery, industrial equipment, vehicles, libraries and other public and private property were looted and carted off to

Baghdad before the war, and by the retreating Iraqis during February. Thousands of Kuwaiti citizens were killed, imprisoned and tortured by the invaders during the occupation. As Iraqi troops withdrew, they attempted to undermine the basis of Kuwait's economy, its petroleum industry, by torching or blowing up more than 700 of the country's approximately 800 oil wells. Before the war Kuwait depended for more than 90 percent of its income on export of about 1.5 million barrels of oil a day. By the end of 1991 after all the oil well fires were extinguished, production was back to 620,000 bpd with expectation that it would reach 800,000 by mid-1992. It was estimated that two more years would be required to reach full pre-war production levels. In the interim Kuwait borrowed abroad and used for reconstruction some of the more than $100 billion its rulers had deposited in foreign accounts.

...and other countries

At least 5 million people from over thirty countries were displaced by the war and the crisis that preceded it according to estimates of American and international relief officials. One State Department officer characterized the upheaval as "a world on the move." An analyst at the U.S. Committee for Refugees observed: "This was surely one of the largest migrations ever; I can't recall an instance in which so many people moved in so short a time." During the first phase of the exodus before the war more than 1.5 million people fled from Iraq, Kuwait and other Gulf countries. They included 700,000 Egyptian workers in both countries, 380,000 Kuwaitis fleeing from the invasion, 250,000 Palestinian workers from several Gulf states, and 350,000

Asians employed in the region. The latter included 150,000 from India and tens of thousands from Pakistan, Sri Lanka Bangladesh, Vietnam, Thailand and the Philippines. About 1 million Yeminis fled to their homeland from Saudi Arabia when they were expelled because of Yemen's refusal to support the U.N. measures against Iraq. Most of the Asian and Middle Eastern refugees became an economic burden in their home countries where unemployment rates were already high. Furthermore, many left behind life savings, homes and other property which they had acquired through years of service in the Middle East. Remittances which they had been sending to families in the home countries amounting to between $1 and $2 billion a year were also lost.

During the War only a little over 100,000 refugees were on the move. However, after the war more than 2 million, mostly Iraqi Kurds and Shi'ites, fled in less than a week. By April most of the Kurds had returned to Iraq from Turkey and Iran although many were unable to reach their homes. Iran reported that several hundred thousand Shi'ites still feared to return. The crisis was particularly acute in Jordan, where more than 250,000 Palestinians, mostly from Kuwait, found refuge. Several thousand Iraqis also arrived in Jordan after the war fleeing from Saddam Hussein's repression and/or the severe economic after-effects of combat. The refugee influx amounted to approximately a 5 percent population increase in a country whose economy was in shambles. Because of King Hussein's temporary alliance with Saddam Hussein during the crisis most of the country's foreign aid had been stopped and the U.N. embargo prevented trade with Iraq, Jordan's principal economic partner until 1990.

Middle Eastern countries that were allied with the U.S. during the war were able to reverse many of the economic setbacks. Egypt, whose economy was disrupted during the crisis because of income cutbacks in tourism, overseas remittances, Suez Canal tolls, and oil exports, more than made up for these losses when the U.S. and its European creditors made arrangements to forgive up to half of the country's $50 billion foreign debt. This more than compensated for overall losses due to the war which President Husni Mubarak estimated at some $20 billion.

Israel was compensated for its restraint during the war with substantial additions to the near $3.2 billion it has received annually in American aid. The additions included $650 million for destruction, "pain and suffering" resulting from Iraqi missile attacks, a special military grant of $700 million, $400 million in housing guarantees voted by Congress last summer and several smaller items. These additions were assured before the squabble between the Bush administration and Prime Minister Yitzhak Shamir over Israel's expectation of a further $10 billion in housing loan guarantees to cover construction of homes for new, mainly Soviet, immigrants during the next five years.

Political consequences of the Gulf War

Political consequences of the war were problematic. True, Saddam Hussein's attempts to disrupt the Middle East status quo were aborted. After the war U.N. investigation teams discovered that Iraq's experiments in and development of nuclear, chemical and biological weapons were far more advanced than had been believed. These discoveries were made despite Iraq's attempts to conceal its

work on nonconventional weapons. The war also demonstrated the extent to which the Cold War had disappeared as a major influence in determining U.S. and other policies in the region. Rather than obstructing allied efforts to restore the status quo, the Soviet Union cooperated in undermining Saddam Hussein's plans, although Moscow did not actively join the military campaign in the Gulf.

The war did little if anything to diminish the Middle East arms race. The region continued to be the world's largest market for the sale of conventional weapons with increased purchases by several nations. These included new sales by the U.S. to Saudi Arabia of $3.3 billion for Patriot missiles, $1.6 billion to Egypt to include 46 F-16 jet fighters, and $350 million to Israel for a Patriot battery. Opponents of the arms race urged the U.S. to use its unprecedented influence in the region to promote arms cuts rather than additional sales. But others argued that a unilateral approach would be unwise, that if arms reduction were to succeed there would have to be general compliance with limitation agreements.

Regional problems of economic and social development remained critical. The Middle East is an area with countries among those with the highest per capita income, such as the United Arab Emirates and Saudi Arabia, and classified by the U.N. as among the world's ten most impoverished, Yemen. One of the most critical problems is the shortage of water and the consequent danger of international disputes over its sources. Turkey's construction of the massive Ataturk Dam is perceived as a danger by both Syria and Iraq. Israel's use of water from the occupied West Bank and Gaza is also seen as a threat by Palestinians. King Hussein recently observed that although he could conceive few reasons for war between Jordan and Israel, he might be compelled to fight for water.

The Madrid peace conference

It was hoped that some of these problems would be confronted in the third stage of the Middle East peace conference which opened in Madrid during October. The conference was convened by the U.S. and the Soviet Union following the Moscow summit between Presidents Bush and Gorbachev last July. Before agreement by all parties to the Arab-Israel conflict to participate in the conference could be obtained, Secretary of State James Baker made eight trips to the Middle East to negotiate the necessary details of conference site, agenda, qualifications of participants, sponsorship, and the like.

Although the U.S. had denied that the Gulf crisis was in any way linked with the Arab-Israel conflict, there is little doubt that one of the principal results of the war was a decision by the U.S. and the Soviet Union to renew attempts to deal with the dispute. One of Israel's conditions for agreeing to Soviet co-sponsorship was reestablishment of full diplomatic relations with Moscow. Thus following the visit to Israel by Soviet Foreign Minister Pankin the two countries exchanged ambassadors for the first time since relations were broken during the 1967 war.

An initial obstacle to the conference was a series of restrictions that Israel placed on the meeting. The Shamir government opposed any representation by Arab inhabitants of Jerusalem, by those with PLO affiliation or membership, or by Palestinians living outside the West Bank and Gaza. The Palestinians would not be permitted to have separate representation, but would have to be part

of a Jordanian delegation. Shamir also insisted that the general opening session, which included all participants and observers, be limited to a day or two; that this session would have to be followed by direct face-to-face meetings between Israel and its antagonists—Syria, Lebanon and a joint Jordanian/Palestinian delegation. During the second phase of face-to-face meetings, bilateral agreements would be worked out dealing with the various issues in dispute between Israel and its neighbors. At the third phase of the conference to occur simultaneously with bilateral negotiations, regional problems such as the arms race, water disputes, and development issues would be dealt with.

Until only days before the conference convened, it was uncertain who would attend. But when the first session opened in Madrid during October all invited parties appeared. The delegations included the two sponsors, the U.S. and the Soviet Union, Israel, Syria, Lebanon and Jordan/Palestine. Additional observers included Egypt, the Gulf Cooperation Council, and the European Economic Community (EEC). The conference opened with speeches by Presidents Bush and Gorbachev, the foreign minister of Egypt, and the chief representatives of the Israeli, Syrian, Lebanese and Jordanian/Palestinian delegations.

Although meetings between Israel and each of the other participants had taken place during previous years in one form or another, the conference was an historic occasion because it was the first public forum dealing with the Arab-Israel conflict in which Israel and all its immediate neighbors had directly addressed each other. After the formal opening sessions it was uncertain when and where the following bilateral meetings would take place. Debate between Israel and Syria was acrimonious, Israel insisting that the conference continue in the Middle East where sessions would alternate between sites in Israel and the surrounding countries. Syria and the other Arab participants demanded that sessions continue at some venue in Europe, preferably Madrid. Furthermore, Syria indicated that it would refuse to join the meetings dealing with regional issues until Israel returned *all* territories it had occupied during the 1967 war.

Relations between Israel and the Jordanian/Palestinian delegation were less confrontational. There were civil, even friendly exchanges between the Israeli and Arab participants, but each party left Madrid still determined to reconvene at a site of its own choice. Following the Madrid meetings, Secretary of State Baker indicated that the U.S. would mediate the continuing debate, as it has continued to do, in Washington D.C., where the next meetings were held.

Indications were that the peace conference would be long drawn out with many months of initial discussion about procedure, protocol and similar matters before dealing with such controversial substantive issues as territory, borders, refugees, compensation and the like.

Other Middle East areas

Elsewhere in the Middle East there was relative stability. Although some militant Iranian leaders threatened Arab partici-pants in the peace conference with assassination, and an international anti-peace-conference rally was organized in Teheran, President Hashemi Rafsanjani and other senior officials associated with him appeared to gain the upper hand in their conflict with conservatives and

religious fundamentalists. Reorientation of their policies away from confrontation with the West was indicated by their approach to world financial markets for development funds and normalization of ties with Arab Gulf states. President François Mitterrand's announcement that he would visit Iran in exchange for a visit by President Rafsanjani to Paris was symbolic of the diminishing tension between Iran and the West. Iran also cooperated in helping to obtain the release of Western hostages held in Lebanon by militant pro-Iranian funda-mentalist factions.

Lebanese government forces backed by the Syrian army continued to extend their authority in most parts of the country and to disarm the various militias. However terrorists affiliated with the militant fundamentalist factions intensified their activity at the end of the year, escalating attacks on the Israeli-held security zone in south Lebanon and bombing the administration building of the American University of Beirut.

In elections for the Turkish parlia-ment during October, the party of President Turgut Ozal was defeated, although he insisted that he would remain in office to complete his seven-year term of office which ends in 1996. Indications were that it would be difficult to form a stable government since none of the three largest parties won more than 28 percent of the vote. Diversity of ideology and party programs made the establishment of a new government with a coherent program very difficult.■

Don Peretz, a specialist on Middle Eastern affairs, is professor of political science at the State University of New York, Binghamton.

Latin American Democracy: In Search of the Rule of Law

Douglas W. Payne

In most of Latin America, people can choose their governments through the ballot box. However, the basis of rule in all but a few countries remains power, not law. In general, politics is still dominated by traditional elites who operate with impunity in a culture of entrenched corruption, while most people continue to struggle for survival amid deepening poverty and unchecked political and criminal violence.

Optimism about the region stems from the apparent consensus among today's Latin leaders in favor of economic modernization. But while it is true that inefficient state-run economies must be overhauled if Latin America is to emerge from its protracted economic crisis, it is also true that the cornerstone of a modern state is the rule of law. No amount of economic growth will ensure the survival of weak democratic systems unless there is an established legal framework in which the powerful are held accountable for their behavior, and the political rights and civil liberties of the majority are guaranteed.

Latin America's social and economic inequities are unmatched in the world. With an average per capita income of $1,950, the region is ahead of the rest of the Third World. Yet, according to the United Nations Development Program, in 1991 62 percent of Latin America's 437.7 million people lived in poverty, 160 million in extreme misery. And despite the return to elected government, the gap between rich and poor continues to widen, while the middle class, the anchor of any established democracy, is being driven back into poverty. Disillusionment is evident in the regionwide increase in voter abstention and the unceasing migration to first world countries.

Nonetheless, many Latin Americans remain undaunted by the lock on political power of unbridled elites and the inordinate influence retained by unrepentant militaries. New civic organizations and advocacy groups are appearing every year—peasant federations, worker movements, *barrio* associations, and small business, professional, legal service, and human rights organizations. These groups are chiseling away at the tradition of centralized authority, as each in its way is demanding a say in how the rules are made after the votes are counted.

This nascent civic society, inspired by the power of the democratic idea propelled through modern media, and emboldened by the ability to connect with counterparts around the world through computer networks, fax, and portable video equipment, represents the first serious challenge to the age-old Latin idea that power is more important than law. In some countries it has begun to spawn a new, younger generation of political figures independent of the personalistic vehicles and patronage machines that still dominate party politics. Even the poorest of the poor, barely subsisting in the burgeoning informal economies that account for more than 50 percent of the work force in some countries, have demonstrated an ability to organize themselves in social and economic units more democratic and efficient than the central governments that shun them.

The question is whether the democratic determination of the majority can overcome the authoritarian structures that block the path to truly representative government. After more than a decade of elections, the culture of corruption, violence and impunity rooted in Spanish and Portuguese colonialism has changed little. Latin American elites speak the language of democracy and compete with each other for votes because the developed world—upon which their economic interests depend—now expects them to, just as it once expected them to be anti-Communist. Underneath the free-market economic policies they have adopted lies an engrained system of bribes, kickbacks, privileges and institutional corruption that will take several generations to root out, and that will not go gently. Meanwhile, as they demand relief from interest payments on a foreign debt of $450 billion, they continue to harbor an estimated $180 billion in capital flight investments abroad.

Venezuela: no exception

Venezuela, after three decades of elected civilian government, is generally considered one of Latin America's more solid democracies. But Venezuela's institutions are showing signs of extreme strain, and current trends there bring into sharper focus the conditions that undermine democratic aspirations throughout the region.

Like most Latin governments, the administration of President Carlos Andres Perez has imposed a harsh austerity program to narrow a gaping budget deficit and secure new loans from the international financial community. At the same time, it has promised the Venezuelan people that market reforms will result in improved economic conditions. But for the strapped majority, the promise seems empty when elite life styles remain uneffected and drug and corruption scandals involving the government, the military and big business are exploding in the media.

Not surprisingly, Venezuela has been the scene of increasing social unrest. Demonstrations and labor actions have been met by force and hundreds of people have been killed. The military and security forces are virtually immune from prosecution for human rights violations, while hundreds of protesters remain imprisoned without ever having been to court. At the same time, no one has ever gone to jail under Venezuela's 1983 anti-corruption law because political and economic power hold sway over the nominally independent judiciary.

In Venezuela there is also evidence of a systematic attempt to stifle journalistic investigations into official corruption and human rights violations. In recent years, the country's energetic media have been subject to intimidation through government wire-taps, physical threats, and arrests under a variety of emergency and media-licensing laws. In 1991, the Inter-American Press Association expressed alarm at the continuing high rate of journalists killed in Latin America due to political and drug-related violence. But it denounced with equal fervor the newer pattern of more sophisticated intimidation by elected governments such as that of Venezuela.

The emergence of independent, probing media has been one of the most positive developments in Latin America over the last decade. In country after country, journalists have exposed the layers of corruption in governmental, judicial and financial institutions, and the continuing violation of human rights. The media have also played a key role in giving voice to nongovernmental and civic groups struggling for recognition.

However, rather than making an effort to be held accountable, governments have sought to find ways to circumscribe the media, which has served only to diminish their already flagging legitimacy. The antagonism toward one of democracy's main pillars and the failure to establish strong, independent judicial systems reflect a narrow belief that with the return to civilian rule, all that is needed to solve Latin America's problems is renewed economic growth.

Why Chile is different

Under the Pinochet dictatorship, market economists were given a free hand to privatize state enterprises and open the country to foreign investment. The Chilean economy has grown by 5 percent or better annually since 1985, compared with negative growth in most other countries in the region. But economic growth came at a severe price—the brutal suppression of political dissent and one of the worst human rights records in Latin America. And still, nearly 40 percent of Chileans continue to live below the poverty line.

But unlike most other Latin countries, Chile has a history of respect for democratic values and civic participation. Prior to the 1973 coup, the country experienced 150 years of nearly uninterrupted democratic rule, and even seventeen years of military dictatorship could not eradicate Chile's democratic political culture rooted in the respect for

law. During the transition to civilian rule that culminated in the 1989 elections, democratically structured political parties and an array of independent civic institutions came quickly back to life. As a result, the government of President Patricio Aylwin is broadly representative and responsive to a wide social base.

It is therefore alarming to see a number of elected leaders in other countries resorting to executive decree to impose economic readjustment programs—for example, President Carlos Menem of Argentina and President Alberto Fujimori of Peru—and relying on force to put down dissent. This trend points to a regression into some hybrid form of authoritarian democracy which retains the formal trappings of democratic rule, but excludes most citizens from meaningful political participation—an inherently unstable situation no matter how much economic growth is achieved. Latin America may have returned to civilian rule, but only in Chile has there been a return to democracy.

Mexico: free trade, unfree politics

Mexico is the envy of many Latin American governments. President Carlos Salinas has carried out a remarkable overhaul of the Mexican economy, putting his country first in line to benefit from the Bush administration's hemispheric free trade initiative. But Salinas has had the advantage of one-party rule through which to carry out his economic program. Independent political activity is allowed, but there is little separation between the state and the long ruling Institutional Revolutionary Party (PRI), and elections are inherently unfair and tainted by fraud. Some modest political reforms have been made in recent years, but Mexico remains the most authoritarian state in Latin America outside of Cuba.

Salinas has argued that economic reform must come first for there to be a smooth transition to a modern Mexico. But an authoritarian system cannot survive long in a market economy. Events around the world in recent years, from China to Eastern Europe, demonstrate that opening economic systems increases the social and political pressure for democracy. In Mexico, and indeed throughout Latin America, breaking down commercial barriers also means the dismantling of psychological barriers of anti-modernity which have sustained authoritarian traditions for centuries. Given today's international climate and modern communications technology, foreign investment dollars now come with democratic values and models of civic society which, as they take hold, exert increasing pressure on the pyramidal structures of Mexican politics.

Salinas will soon have to choose between initiating the transition to a democratic rule of law or trying to put the genie back in the bottle, which would require force, undermine his economic successes, and ultimately fail. That is the lesson other governments in the region should be learning from Mexico. Instead, many appear more impressed by the support for Salinas coming from the U.S. and the international financial community, which unfortunately can be read as a signal that resorting to anti-democratic methods to hasten economic modernization will be tolerated.

A question of political culture

In this century, Latin America has experienced three waves of democratization, each one progressively stronger and involving more countries. The first was wiped out by worldwide depression and the rise of fascism in the 1930s. The second succumbed to the Cold War during which the region was whipsawed by the competing superpowers. Now, however, there is a global trend toward democratic rule and the influence of extreme ideologies has diminished. Only Fidel Castro, who appears bent on making the final chapter of the Cold War an ugly episode, still refuses to see the writing on the wall. This time around, the fate of democracy in Latin America will be determined by the Latin Americans themselves.

At the 1991 general assembly of the Organization of American States (OAS), Latin American representatives led the thirty-three member nations (including the U.S., Canada and the English-speaking Caribbean) in resolving to assist any elected government in the region threatened by or overthrown in a military coup. That was particularly welcome given the OAS's poor record of supporting democracy since its founding in 1948. And the OAS indeed responded swiftly and firmly to the overthrow of Haiti's first freely elected government.

But democracy is more than the difference between military and civilian rule. Increasing social upheaval has prompted speculation about coups in a number of Latin countries, including Venezuela, Peru and Brazil. However, while the possibility cannot be discounted, most Latin militaries appear more interested in preserving their elite status as armed corporations than in jumping back into power. Of greater concern is the impunity with which political and economic powerbrokers continue to operate, and the exclusion of most people from the decision-making process except at election time.

If Latin American leaders are to breath new life into the OAS as a force for democracy, they must revisit its charter, which calls for adherence to the principles of *representative* democracy and the rule of law. Adherence to those principles has been achieved only in Costa Rica and most of the countries of the English-speaking Caribbean. Chile appears to be back on the right track.

Poverty, drugs and the foreign debt are commonly perceived as threats to democratization. The Latin American political class makes such a case in arguing for debt relief and international economic aid, particularly from the U.S. A case also can be made that the first world shares part of the responsibility for the region's ills, having provided support for military rule in the past and providing the main market for illicit drugs now.

But the fact remains, the problems affecting Latin America are primarily the result of anti-democratic traditions that continue to define its political culture today. Nearly all of Latin America's current leaders have said their goal is to bring their countries into the modern world. But the transformation of Latin American nations into modern, democratic states requires that old traditions give way to a new set of democratic values. Political cultures evolve slowly, but it happens. Twenty years ago Spain and Portugal, the original colonizers of

Latin America, were ruled by dictatorships. Now they are solid, representative democracies.

Thus far in Latin America, ordinary people are ahead of their leaders in embracing democratic values. That is evident in the growth of organized civic activity over the last decade. The danger is that business-as-usual at the top will lead to cynicism and disillusionment among aspiring citizens. For example, what can Brazilian public school teachers making less than $100 a month think when local legislators in the state of Rio de Janeiro give themselves salaries greater than that of the president of the United States?

Elected government is but the first step in the long and complex process of democratization. The weight of the past will prevent some Latin American countries from making further progress, and the Central American and Andean nations are actually in danger of regressing. But for nearly all the countries in the region, the transition to a democratic rule of law—a cultural transformation—still lies ahead. ▄

Douglas W. Payne is Freedom House director of hemispheric studies.

Western Europe: More Freedom and its Problems

Wayne C. Thompson

With the collapse of communism 700 million people from Moscow to Dublin live in democracies where free elections provide the only legitimate claim to power and which are basically committed to freedom, individual rights, and some variant of capitalism.

Western Europeans see more than a dozen independent nations emerging out of the rubble of the Soviet empire, in desperate economic circumstances, with borders in dispute, ethnic hatreds, and millions of discontented and frightened citizens tempted to seek better lives in the West. Western European countries led the way in recognizing the newly independent Baltic states of Estonia, Latvia and Lithuania, which are reaching out for Western economic and diplomatic help. Ukrainian independence, chosen by a free election on 1 December, paves the way for the fourth largest state in Europe, with 52 million people and more territory than France. On 8 December Ukraine joined Russia and Byelorussia to form a Commonwealth and to liquidate the Soviet Union. This act raised the question of whether it would complicate implementation of the 1991 Strategic Arms Reduction Talks (START) agreement and the 1990 Conventional Forces in Europe (CFE) breakthrough.

Yugoslavia has come unglued and is the scene of the first full-scale war in Europe since 1945, pitting the Serbian-dominated federal army against an independence-minded Croatia. The EC tried to stop the violence, and failed, prompting EC Commission president, Jacques Delors, to lament that "the EC is a little like a child confronted with an adult crisis." Germany sympathized with independent Croatia and Slovenia. Spain, France and Britain worried about the effect of unrestrained self-determination on Basque, Catalan, Corsican and Scottish independent movements in their own countries. French and German calls for "European buffer units" in Yugoslavia were rejected by other partners who feared that the EC could become trapped in a deadly quagmire of military intervention.

The EC's failure spurred the U.N. into action, which dispatched former American Secretary of State Cyrus Vance to Yugoslavia to seek a peaceful settlement.

NATO and a new European defense identity

Western European impotence in Yugoslavia underscored the need for a new post-Cold War security structure as a precondition for a politically united Europe. Another reminder was the August coup attempt in the Soviet Union, which threatened to eliminate central control over 12,000 tactical nuclear weapons dispersed throughout the USSR. The West's first response came not from Europe but from President George Bush who, in September, proposed sweeping cuts, going far beyond the START agreement reached in July calling for a 30 percent reduction in U.S. and Soviet long-range missiles. European allies unanimously backed Bush, and a badly shaken Mikhail Gorbachev not only matched Bush's unilateral move, but added to it.

Western Germans, who live with the world's heaviest concentration of atomic weapons, were delighted. Chancellor Helmut Kohl stated: "President Bush's decision implies that all American short-range nuclear weapons and nuclear artillery will be removed from German soil. In the name of all Germans I want to thank the president for that." NATO will retain about half of its atomic bombs on dual-capacity aircraft to deter possible future threats. Britain and France will have to decide what to do about their nuclear systems.

There is a consensus that a new European defense identity and strategy is necessary, but none on the roles NATO and the EC will play in it. No European country wants the withdrawal of all American troops, which have already been reduced from 320,000 before the 1991 Gulf War to only 260,000 today and will go to about 150,000 by 1995. The issue has become entangled with the ongoing debate about the scope of European political union, with many Europeans arguing that the EC must develop its own security structure if it is ever to have political clout commensurate with its economic power. In a general way, the Americans also want the Europeans to bear a greater responsibility for their own defense, but not in competition with NATO, which remains the major pillar for American leadership in Europe.

Britain and Italy, supported by the Netherlands, stepped forward in October to argue that the nine-nation Western

European Union (WEU—all EC countries except Greece, Denmark and Ireland) should serve as a strategic bridge between the EC and NATO, but France objected that the plan would subordinate the EC's defense identity to NATO. It found an ally in Germany; in October the two countries proposed the creation of an all-European army, beginning with an expansion of the tiny French-German brigade to corps size of about 40,000 soldiers.

At the November summit meeting of NATO leaders in Rome, President Bush declared bluntly: "If, my friends, your ultimate aim is to provide independently for your own defense, the time to tell us is today." There were no takers, but the relationship between a new European defense identity and NATO was left undefined. EC leaders agreed in December that it would be separate from but "linked to" NATO. The Atlantic Alliance created a North Atlantic Cooperation Council to provide for regular consultation with the USSR and central Europe. NATO's outdated doctrine of containing Soviet power through "forward defense" and "flexible response" was replaced by one more suited to the changed European environment. Smaller, highly mobile, conventional and multinational forces are to be created which can be deployed on short notice anywhere within NATO territory, and which can help manage unpredictable crises and instability in eastern Europe, the Balkans, the Mediterranean area and beyond.

The road to greater European unity

At its summit meeting in December in the Dutch city of Maastricht the EC agreed to create a single European currency and central bank, and to move toward common defense and foreign and economic policies by the end of the century. Britain expressed reluctance to relinquish more sovereignty to the EC. Facing a difficult election against a reinvigorated Labour Party in 1992 and under attack from the "Eurosceptics" within his own Conservative Party, notably Margaret Thatcher, Prime Minister John Major found it hard to compromise with his continental partners.

Despite the difficulty of "deepening" the EC unity, other European countries are eager to join. The relatively poor countries of eastern Europe probably will have to wait a long time. But the EC and the seven European Free Trade Association (EFTA) countries agreed in October to form a European Economic Area (EEA) creating a market of 380 million customers extending from the Mediterranean to the Arctic and accounting for over 40 percent of world trade. EFTA members will enjoy the EC's "four freedoms": of goods, services, capital and people, but EEA does not include agriculture, fish, energy, coal and steel. EFTA members will have to live under EC rules although they will have no voice in their writing; this lack of representation will give them added incentive to join the EC as full members.

"Freedom to travel" vs. "freedom to settle"

The greatest perceived threat to freedom in Western Europe is the influx of newcomers from the crucibles of the Soviet Union, central and southeastern Europe, the southern rim of the Mediterranean and, most recently, Asia. Their presence in comparatively homogeneous, tolerant and stable countries raises the issues of rights and duties for immigrants as well as natives. In Western European countries, anti-immigrant sentiment is rising. Opinion surveys in the fall revealed that about three-fourths of

western Germans and French and about two-thirds of the British object to new immigrants. Right-wing parties vow to protect the livelihood of the native-born, at a time of high unemployment and slow economic growth.

In France the Socialist minority government of President François Mitterrand has been beset by 10 percent unemployment and protest demonstrations from civil servants, nurses and farmers. His acerbic prime minister, Edith Cresson, has the lowest popularity ratings of any French premier in more than a decade. One of every three newborns has a foreign parent. The 5 million Arabs in France constitute one-tenth of the population. French historian Jean-Marie Domenach remarked: "Even as we are integrating all Europe, we can see a Muslim community that cuts across European lines, a sort of thirteenth nation of the European Community. This is a fear that is growing all across Europe." According to a 1991 government survey, 71 percent of the French think their country has too many Arabs, 42 percent admit to hostility toward them, and 94 percent believe that racism has become "rampant" in France.

No party reaps as much benefit from this deplorable situation as the National Front, whose slogan is, "France for the French." Its leader, Jean-Marie Le Pen, hammers away at "invading Muslim hordes," and leaders of the country's respectable parties have begun to borrow from his xenophobic vocabulary. Cresson recommended that illegal immigrants should be deported by the planeload. Gaullist leader Jacques Chirac criticized their "odor" and "noise," and former President Valery Giscard d'Estaing warned of an "invasion" of immigrants. He called for nationality laws based on blood to replace the current statutes which grant French citizenship automatically to anyone born on French soil. In

October, 32 percent of respondents to a poll said they generally agreed with Le Pen's ideas, even though 76 percent rejected the notion of his receiving a ministerial post, and 65 percent believed that he and his party are "a danger for democracy."

In neighboring Belgium the coalition government of Wilfried Martens crashed in September on the familiar rocks of Flemish-Walloon French linguistic rivalry, necessitating early parliamentary elections in November. The results were startling: the anti-immigrant Flemish Vlaams Blok, which campaigned under the banner, "Our People First," jumped from two to twelve seats in the lower house and emerged as the largest party in the country's second-largest city, Antwerp. It also did well in the capital, Brussels, where half the newborns are now from Arab parents. Martens called the results "an extreme shift to the right" for which the traditional politicians bore a "heavy responsibility."

One year of German unity

On 3 October Germany's low-keyed celebration of its first year of unification was overshadowed by fears of unemployment in the east, resentment in the west toward the cost of unification, moving the nation's capital to Berlin, and the shock of a frightening upsurge of violent racist attacks in both parts of the country. Polls show little support for right-wing violence. Nevertheless, anti-foreigner sentiment is high, even though immigrants comprise only about 6 percent of western Germany's population, and 2 percent of eastern Germany's. Bundestag President Rita Süssmuth reminded her countrymen that "attacks against asylum-seekers and foreigners in Germany reawaken fears outside our country which are fostered by our past. With our

experience under the Nazi reign of violence, we Germans know the fundamental importance of asylum as a human right." On 9 November, the first anniversary of the Berlin wall's collapse and the fifty-third anniversary of the Nazi Kristallnacht rampage against Jews, the street brawls of several hundred young neo-Nazis (uneducated itinerant thugs) in eastern Germany stole some of the spotlight from 100,000 demonstrators across the country who marched against racism. The court system in the East is still mostly non-functional, as former Communist judges are screened or replaced, and therefore cannot prosecute attackers. Human-rights campaigners form human chains and all-night vigils to protect asylum-seekers from harm. A group of leading intellectuals issued a declaration saying that "a vast majority of citizens are ashamed that people once again fear pogroms in Germany." President Richard von Weizsäcker made three visits to the homes of victims to show his concern.

In 1990, 193,000 asylum-seekers arrived in Germany, and in 1991 the number grew to 230,000. This is roughly half the total of refugees in all of Europe and does not count arrivals of ethnic Germans from eastern Europe (400,000 in 1990), who receive immediate citizenship and full rights. Many Germans, including Chancellor Kohl and his ruling Christian Democratic Party (CDU), which is losing political ground in both East and West to the opposition Social Democratic Party (SPD), partly blame the untenable situation on Article 16 of the Basic Law, which grants political asylum to all who claim it. Interior Minister Wolfgang Schnäuble maintains that "freedom to travel can-not mean freedom to settle" in a richer country. Article 16 had been inspired by the fact that many German anti-Nazis, such as Willy Brandt, had been saved during the Hitler era because they found asylum in democratic countries and by the fact that thousands of Jews perished because other countries had turned them away. Opinion polls show that 70 percent of Germans still favor granting asylum to political refugees, but many believe that this right has been abused: although more than 90 percent of refugees were refused permanent asylum, as many as 40 percent still managed to stay for "humanitarian reasons." Because the Liberals, who are part of the ruling coalition, and the opposition Social Democrats reject any alteration of Article 16, the government resorted to new procedures: all asylum-seekers are sequestered in "collective housing" on abandoned military bases, and their applications are processed in six weeks. Those who are rejected are to be deported quickly. It remains to be seen if these new measures will work and whether Germany can avoid adopting a quota system for legal immigration.

Germany must also continue to face its Communist past. In the 6 million Stasi files is information surreptitiously gathered over forty years, threatening to destroy lives and reputations, but also promising to exonerate innocent citizens who face defamatory charges, hearsay, slander and lies. To protect the rights of citizens, Bonn has allowed individuals access to their own files, while threatening journalists with three-year jail terms if they publish information from them without permission. This restriction prompted charges of press muzzling from journalists and civil liberty advocates, who called the decision the most serious effort at limiting freedom of the press since the Hitler era. It threatens to create a situation similar to that in West Germany earlier when many prominent Nazis were permitted to resume their

careers after 1945 without a review of their histories in well-kept Nazi records.

In the German literary world, noted East German authors, such as Christa Wolf and Sacha Anderson, are being accused by fellow writers of having been Communist stooges and Stasi collaborators. In September, four young ex-East German border guards, who maintained that they were merely following orders, were put on trial for killing a man trying to flee to the West. Since former party chief Erich Honecker remained in Moscow and other top leaders have escaped prosecution, accusations have been made that only the menial operatives of the East German state were being called to justice. These charges were fueled when the legendary former head of East Germany's foreign intelligence service, Markus Wolf, returned to Germany from exile in the Soviet Union and was released on $30,000 bail, a paltry sum for a man who now is paid at least that much for interviews with the sensation-hungry Western press.

Before 1989 Austrians were surrounded on three sides by the Communist bloc; now their country is a bustling thorough-fare to the East. Austria's businessmen are enthusiastic, but its general public is apprehensive. The civil war in Yugoslavia has sent thousands of refugees over the border, adding to the half million foreigners (out of a total population of 7.8 million) already living in Austria. In Vienna's provincial elections in November Jîrg Haider's anti-immigration, right-wing Freedom Party captured 22.6 percent of the votes and became the country's second-largest party. This represented a remarkable comeback for Haider, who in June had been forced to resign as Carinthia's governor because he had praised Hitler's "employment policy," a remark which seemed to endorse concentration camps and slave labor.

Anti-foreigner sentiment was given a more sinister dimension when an October Gallup poll conducted for the American Jewish Committee revealed that 39 percent of Austrian respondents held the view that "Jews have caused much harm in the course of history"; 31 percent preferred not to have Jews for neighbors, but even higher percentages were averse to living near Poles, Slovenes, Croats, Serbs and Turks. Unlike the Germans, the Austrians have never engaged in a cathartic debate about their Nazi past, hiding behind the comfortable official interpretation that they were Hitler's first victims. In a long-overdue gesture Chancellor Franz Vranitzky acknowledged in July that many Austrians had supported Hitler and had taken a hand in his crimes; he apologized for the atrocities Austrians had committed.

In the fall Switzerland experienced several fire-bombings of dwellings harboring immigrants. After the October parliamentary elections the Swiss woke up to find that thirteen right-wing representatives demanding curbs on newcomers had won seats in the lower house; this is the strongest xenophobic contingent in two decades. Its presence does not endanger the comfortable 75 percent majority of the four parties which have ruled the country for four decades. The government declared its intention to apply for EC membership, which for the first time is supported by a majority of Swiss.

Changing attitudes in Scandinavia

In September Sweden's Social Democrats had their worst election since the 1920s. In his inaugural address to parliament, the winner, Prime Minister Carl Bildt, chairman of the Moderate Party which presented itself to voters as "the Party of freedom," called the elections "a question of a revolution in freedom of choice," and declared that "the age of collectivism in Sweden is over."

Faced with a stalled economy and declining international competitiveness, voters turned against the power of the large institutions and centralized decision-making process which are the hallmarks of the "Swedish model." Young voters especially opted for the nonsocialist parties. Described as the "Interrail generation," they returned from wide travel with the impression that other Western Europeans enjoyed more freedom of choice in their lives. The young Bildt had never been a student revolutionary and had actively opposed his country's support of North Vietnam in the 1960s and 1970s. In 1980-81 he spent much time in Poland and returned convinced that "freedom and democracy are conditions for peace and cooperation." As the first twentieth-century Swedish prime minister who is a passionate European, he will press hard for his country's admission to the EC, to which it formally applied in July; Swedes now favor membership 3 to 1.

The nonsocialist victory does not mean, though, that Bildt has a Thatcheresque mandate to reverse the welfare state. He aims to stop its growth and trim it around the edges. This is especially true since his four-party coalition has a minority of seats in the Riksdag. It will be dependent for crucial votes on the neophyte populist, anti-politician New Democracy Party, led by the flamboyant and eccentric Count Ian Wachmaeister, an industrialist and amusement park owner who is a fervent believer in individual freedom and free markets. His party railed against taboos in Sweden such as expensive alcohol and advocated expulsion of immigrants with criminal records.

Perhaps the greatest encouragement for Bildt can be found in neighboring Denmark, where Poul Schlüter's shaky right-of-center minority governments have ruled for nine years. Not only has he clung to power, but he has presided over dramatic improvements in Denmark's economy: in 1991 it had a current account in surplus and the lowest inflation rate in the OECD. The debilitating conflicts over EC and NATO policy are over, but the shadow of unwanted immigrants remains: a 1991 poll revealed that half of all Danes blame foreigners for housing shortages and unemployment (10.8 percent). Norway's prime minister, Mrs. Gro Brundtland, has less to be thankful for. She viewed her Labor Party's 30.5 percent of the votes in September's local elections as a defeat. The daily *Aftenposten* concluded that "first and foremost the elections were a victory for EC opponents." Norway, which had a new monarch in January— Harald V—again faces the wrenching emotionally charged decision of whether to join the EC. Membership may prove essential if its larger neighbor, Sweden, is admitted. An exasperated Brundtland declared that "the only reason why I will not throw in my cards now is because no one else can take over."

Conditions in Finland are worse. Its first nonsocialist government in twenty-five years, formed in April by Prime Minister Esko Aho, inherited an economy devastated by the collapse of the country's best customer—the USSR—pulling Finland's GNP down by 5 percent and its industrial production by 15 percent in 1991. The government is committed to privatizing much of the economy, and, despite strong opposition from farmers, will probably apply for EC membership in 1992, a move which polls say is supported by two of three Finns. Aho is the first Finnish leader to

question the 1948 friendship treaty with the USSR. He asked that it be renegotiated so that the neutrality which it requires would not be an obstacle to joining the EC.

Southern Europe

If the Swedish elections signaled a move away from a state-fettered economy, the October voting in Portugal demonstrated the steadiness of Prime Minister Anibal Cavaco Silva's free market policies, economic privatization, and encouragement of private initiative and foreign investment. They have given the country five years of steady economic growth, averaging 4.6 percent annually since entering the EC in 1986. For the first time since the founding of the Portuguese Republic eighty-one years ago, a democratically elected party (PDS— Social Democrats) has won two consecutive absolute majorities. This is a stunning change for a country whose only previous periods of political stability were under fascist dictatorship. The main losers were on the left, especially the Communists (PCP) who were handed their worst result since the 1974 "carnation revolution": under 9 percent. Although Western European Communist parties are declining everywhere, the PCP was especially punished for its ideological rigidity and the fact that it supported the unsuccessful coup attempt against Gorbachev in August. The disillusioned, more educated party members are defecting in droves.

Under Prime Minister Felipe Gonzalez, Spain's government made a crucial decision during the 1991 Gulf war to support its allies actively. At first, this was unpopular in a country whose last war outside its borders was in 1898, when Cuba was lost to the U.S. However, as in many other Western

European countries, public opinion swung around when reports of Iraqi atrocities in Kuwait began arriving. Gonzalez asserted that "for the first time in modern history, Spain has stood where it should be." This marked a defining moment in the country's efforts to end its long isolation and shoulder more international responsibility. It buoyed Spanish confidence and helped sweep away memories of fascist sympathies in the Second World War. A reward was that Madrid became the venue of the first Middle East peace conference that brought Israelis and Arabs together at the negotiating table. Spain will remain in the international spotlight throughout 1992 because it will host a world exposition in Seville and the Olympic Games in Barcelona. Of course, this world attention provides temptations for Catalan and Basque terrorists to publicize their causes, which are rejected in voting booths. The EC's recognition of the Baltic republics and the crisis in Yugoslavia have inflamed nationalist sentiment in decentralized Spain. Catalonia's leader, Jordi Pujol, has developed close links with the Slovene government and declared his region to have the same rights as Lithuania.

Italy's fiftieth government in forty-five years, led by Giulio Andreotti, faces both internal and external challenges. The Mafia is not in retreat and is spreading its tentacles into the industrialized North. This prompted the government to create a special post, dubbed the Italian "FBI," within the attorney general's office to coordinate the fight against organized crime. As a rich country, despite a frightening budget deficit, Italy attracts refugees seeking a better life. Waves of Albanians, travelling across the Adriatic Sea in overcrowded boats, washed ashore, only to be penned into coal docks and a local soccer stadium, which they proceeded to wreck out of anger at this

reception. One Caritas relief worker complained that "the police threw food at them like in a zoo." Stung by criticism against such rough treatment, the Italian government adopted a new policy to prevent an exodus of impoverished Albanians. It reached a security agreement with Albania under which Italian naval vessels help it patrol its shores. It also established a large emergency aid program within Albania itself. Italian soldiers distribute food and advice on improving the infrastructure, as a forerunner to a longer-term program to help stabilize the Balkan country's ailing economy.

Greece faces a similar problem, as thousands of ethnic Greeks from North Epirus flee Albania. In 1991 Constantine Mitsotakis became the first Greek prime minister to visit Tirana to seek constructive ways to deal with the influx of refugees, who are also arriving from Bulgaria, Poland and Turkish Kurdistan, as well as from the USSR, where about a half million Greek-speaking Pontians live. These newcomers seek not only better economic living conditions, but a freer political environment. Greeks demonstrated again in September their sensitivity to infringements on their freedom. The editors of seven newspapers went to jail rather than comply with a new law which, precipitated by the 1989 assassination of Mitsotakis' son-in-law by the terrorist November 17 group, prohibited them from publishing statements from terrorists. This measure reminded too many Greeks of the censorship practices during the military dictatorship from 1967 to 1974. Behind bars, the editors vowed that "the battle we started will not end here. We will continue—in or out of prison." ▬

Wayne C. Thompson is professor of political science at the Virginia Military Institute.

The Comparative Survey of Freedom 1991-1992: Between Two Worlds

R. Bruce McColm

The twentieth century is dramatically closing on one grand historical epoch that began with the Russian Revolution and the signing of the Treaty of Versailles, and ended with the breach in the Berlin Wall and eventual implosion of the Soviet Union. The last three-quarters of a century have been defined by a bitter clash of ideologies, two World Wars, the Holocaust, the Gulag, the Chinese Cultural Revolution, and their reproduction in many smaller conflicts throughout the developing world. This old epoch remains the bloodiest era in human history and may well be viewed in the future as an aberrant period. Yet remarkably, the liberal democratic idea, which faced three waves of reverses in the 1920s, 1940s and 1970s, triumphed over the challenge posed by fascism in the first part of this era and over communism and its derivatives in the second.

The past three years have seen the greatest expansion of freedom in history. Over one-third of the nations on earth, encompassing nearly 30 percent of the earth's population, have consciously decided to radically alter their political systems for more open and democratic forms of government. The twenty-first century will again challenge liberal democracy with questions concerning its ability to produce prosperity and a just social system.

Free societies—an all-time high

Last year's *Survey*, reflecting the triumphal revolutions in Central Europe and the dramatic transformation of the former Soviet Union, recorded the freest year in its 21-year history. It was the first year in which both the number of Free countries and their populations outnumbered the Not Free countries and their populations. This year India, the world's most populous democracy, fell to Partly Free for the first time since martial law was declared in 1975, thereby significantly altering the population figures. Even with such a significant loss, the number of Free societies continued to rise to an all-time high of 76. More remarkably still, the *Survey* found that there were 91 democracies and another 35 countries in some form of democratic transition—a staggering 126 out of the 183 nations evaluated—compared to forty-four democracies in 1972 and 56 in 1980.

The sweep and depth of this global transformation are stunning when compared to the different periods of democratic development. Harvard professor Sam Huntington has identi-fied three "long waves" of democracy. The first began in the early nineteenth century with the extension of the right to vote in the United States and continued until the 1920s. During this period, some 29 democracies came into being. With the accession to power of Benito Mussolini in Italy in 1922, the first reversal began, lasting until 1942, when the number of the world's democracies had been reduced to twelve.

The triumph of the Allied Forces in World War II triggered a second

Freedom in the World—1992

The population of the world this year is estimated at 5.374 billion residing in 183 sovereign states and 62 related territories, a total of 245 places. The level of political rights and civil liberties as shown comparatively by the Freedom House Survey is:

Free: 1,359.3 billion (25.29) percent of the world's population) live in 76 of the states and in 48 of the related territories.

Partly Free: 2,306.6 billion (42.92 percent of the world's population) live in 65 of the states and 4 of the related territories.

Not Free: 1,708.2 billion (31.79) percent of the world's population live in 42 of the states and 10 of the related territories.

Ten-Year Record of the Survey

SURVEY DATE	FREE		PARTLY FREE		NOT FREE		WORLD POPULATION
	(population in millions)						
January '81	1,613.0	(35.90%)	970.9	(21.60%)	1,911.9	(42.50%)	4,495.8
January '82	1,631.9	(35.86%)	916.5	(20.14%)	2,002.7	(44.00%)	4,551.1
January '83	1,665.1	(36.32%)	918.8	(20.04%)	2,000.2	(43.64%)	4,584.1
January '84	1,670.7	(36.00%)	1,074.8	(23.00%)	1,917.5	(41.00%)	4,663.0
January '85	1,671.4	(34.85%)	1,117.4	(23.30%)	2,007.0	(41.85%)	4,795.8
January '86	1,747.2	(36.27%)	1,121.9	(23.29%)	1,947.6	(40.43%)	4,816.7
January '87	1,842.5	(37.10%)	1,171.5	(23.60%)	1,949.9	(39.30%)	4,963.9
January '88	1,924.6	(38.30%)	1,205.4	(24.00%)	1,896.0	(37.70%)	5,026.0
January '89	1,992.8	(38.86%)	1,027.9	(20.05%)	2,107.3	(41.09%)	5,128.0
January '90	2,034.4	(38.87%)	1,143.7	(21.85%)	2,055.9	(39.28%)	5,234.0
January '91	2,088.2	(39.23%)	1,485.7	(27.91%)	1,748.7	(32.86%)	5,322.6
January '92	1,359.3	(25.29%)	2,306.6	(42.92%)	1,708.2	(31.79%)	5,374.2

wave of democratic development that crested in the early 1960s with 36. The second period of reversal occurred during the period of decolonization in the developing world and the rise in regional conflicts, bringing the number down to 30 by 1974. One can debate whether Professor Huntington's 1974 date is the appropriate start of the third wave of democracy, but the explosion in democracies over the past few decades to 91, with another nearly three dozen countries waiting in the wings, demonstrates the lengthening and deepening of democratic development as a global phenomenon. Before the "fourth wave" that Huntington predicts for the twenty-first century, we can anticipate a period of reversal, the extent of which will depend in some measure on whether the West can help the new and fragile democracies

transform their short-term gains into a permanent reality.

The end of this historical epoch with its intense ideological rivalries doesn't mean the end of the social conflicts and conditions which shaped the contours of debate and war over the past 75 years. The collapse of communism and authoritarian states around the world has the potential, not yet fully realized, of releasing long-repressed ethnic and national antagonisms rooted in a longer historical memory. The virtual end of the Cold War has led to significant progress in negotiating a political end to conflicts from Southern Africa to Southeast Asia but it also removes superpower constraints on intense national, ethnic and religious enmities throughout the Third World and possibly even in the post-Communist societies themselves. Three major events affecting this year's

Survey—the disintegration of the Soviet Union, the deterioration of freedom in India and the tragedy of Yugoslavia, the most intense conflict in European history since World War II—are warnings that the world might enter a period of global decomposition marked by explosive incidents of ethnic and racial warfare before this era of democratic development can be completed.

The democratic changes of the past decade have been attributed to a wide-range of impersonal historical factors such as the integration of the global economy, the cross-boundary appeal of new information technologies and the growing desire of nation-states to become re-integrated into larger regional economic and political communities. To a large extent the past decade has represented a global revolution against a wide array of political elites, revolutionary vanguards and bureaucratic restraints. This democratic revolution for the most part has been healthy, liberating societies from the oppressive political control of both authoritarian and totalitarian regimes and empowering millions and millions more people.

A common denominator of the political struggles around the world is their ideological focus, the desire to replace oppressive regimes with more pluralist and open societies. It is within this context that the threat posed by existing national movements should be evaluated. As Timothy Garton Ash reminds us in *The Magic Lantern*, his account of the 1989 revolutions in Central Europe, the crowds we saw in Poland, Hungary, Czechoslovakia and Romania, in a sea of national flags and singing long-repressed national hymns, are patriotic, not nationalist. Rediscovered pride in one's own nation does not necessarily imply hostility to other national or ethnic groups. What is

surprising about events in the former Soviet Union during the last year is not the upsurge in ethnic violence, such as occurred in Georgia, Moldavia and Azerbaijan, but the relative ease with which the attempted August coup was thwarted and a new commonwealth was called into existence by the Brest declaration. What appears extraordinary to date is how the independence and national movements within the former Soviet republics have so far embraced democratic principles and expressed concern for ethnic minorities. Yet the full reaction to the demands for greater autonomy by hundreds of subnationalities has not yet been seen. The civil war in Yugoslavia, with the Serbian repression of other nationalities, may be a dark portent of future ethnic strife.

A springtime of nations

During the peaceful revolutions within Central Europe, many commentators likened the period to 1848, the springtime of nations. For a century after this watershed year until the Communist deep freeze, Central Europe was a battlefield of both nations and classes. Central European democratic leaders such as Hungary's Janos Kis argue that the nation-states as constituted by the Treaty of Versailles after World War I are obsolete and must be transformed into new federations that can accomodate the desires of sub-nationalities for political autonomy. Even so, and despite the difficult situation of ethnic minorities in a number of countries, the list of potential conflicts is much shorter than it was before the Iron Curtain. Likewise, twenty-two African countries this year adopted multi-party systems, abandoning the one-party state and its rationale: that it unites culturally distinct entities in countries with artificial borders.

National and ethnic conflicts in these regions may grow again either between or within states, especially if the global economic situation deteriorates. After World War II potential conflicts in Western Europe were alleviated by an improvement in the region's economic reconstruction and the larger process of integration into a common market and community. Indeed, what has been striking about new agitations of political nationalism in industrialized Western countries is the instability and impermanence of these movements when compared with the strength and stability of national identities they claim to express.

The modern national movements that have dominated the political transformation of post-Communist societies have been essentially coalitions of democratic organizations and associations united against what they considered an historically obsolete mode of political organizations, namely the Leninist state. In this sense, the movements in the post-Communist world might be regarded as successors to those nationality movements directed against the moribund political structures of the Hapsburg, Tsarist and Ottoman empires. However, it is clear from recent state policies adopted by representatives of these movements that one of their first steps will be to petition for membership in the European Community, or in the case of independent former Soviet republics to join a new commonwealth, also with an idea toward European integration.

Racialist or ethnic movements or groups such as Austria's proto-Nazi Freedom Party and the Czechoslovakian Republican Party represent a different and worrisome nationalist strain. Most of these groups are essentially negative and divisive. Their existence depends, in large part, on a rejection of modern modes of political organization, both national and supranational. New global migration patterns and efforts at regional integration—such as the recent Maastricht agreement by the twelve-member European Community or the North American Free Trade Zone—may temporarily increase racial animosity as citizens's national identity seems threatened.

Resurgent democratic values

Democratic values are clearly resurgent today. Viewed over the long course of human history, however, most democracies have been short-lived. During the three periods of reversals, democracies have collapsed from political failure, succumbed to internal division, and been destroyed by revolution, civil war and foreign invasion. The rise of a populist, nationalist challenge to the new democracies may come as an ironic result of democracy's sucess, not failure, over the past decade, especially during the last three years. Over the last decade, there have been 28 successful democratic transitions around the world, the largest wave of liberalization in the history of mankind. The Freedom House 1992 Comparative *Survey* reflects the state of freedom in the world during the most significant period of political change in history. During 1989, the year of the Central European revolutions, 27 countries changed their ratings. Last year another 56 nation-states, or over one-third of the world, registered changes in their numerical ratings because of real political events rather than methodological considerations. This year again saw 56 changes in ratings, maintaining the unprecedented rate of change established the previous year. The *Survey* found that 39 countries improved their human rights situation this year, continuing last year's upward trend of 36. Declines were registered by another 17. Twenty-four nations improved their category ranking and only six reversed their ranking. More impressive is the fact that nearly 1.5 billion people or roughly 28 percent of the world's population came to live in societies where there has been a conscious attempt to replace their political systems with a more democratic alternative over the last three years.

Of the 183 nations evaluated by the *Survey*, 91 have democratic systems, 15 of which are considered in the Partly Free category; another 35 governments are in varying degrees of a transition to a more open and pluralistic system. Once major political competitors to liberal democracy, Communist states have been reduced to six, and traditional monarchies to twelve; military regimes number eighteen. Of all the nations Freedom House tracks, 38 remain one- or dominant-party political systems. The liberal democratic idea has triumphed as the preferred model for political develop-ment. It is sobering to note that in 57 of the 126 countries that are either democratic or in transition to democracy, military, para-military and security forces play a significant political role. Any shift in the military's allegiance to the democratic process could jeopardize this global trend.

The desire for freedom may be an inherent human characteristic but the habits and behavior of democracy must be learned over time. The Freedom House Comparative *Survey*, which monitors political rights and civil liberties in 183 nations and 62 related territories, this year classified 76 nations and 48 territories as Free, 65 nations and 4 terri-tories as Partly Free and 42 nations and 10 territories as Not Free. The findings represent a gain of 11 countries in the

Free category and a decline of 8 in the Not Free category since January 1991.

A significant three-year trend

This year's findings continue a three-year trend of a significant reduction in the number and percentage of the world living in Not Free societies. Since our January 1990 findings, 15 additional countries have gained a Free status, 18 additional are in Partly Free, and there has been a reduction of 17 societies in the Not Free category. For the sake of comparison, fifteen years ago, 43.9 percent of the world lived in Not Free societies, which is 12.1 percent more than in 1992. The world population has increased by 1.36 billion people since 1977, while people living in Not Free societies have actually declined in real terms by 56.4 million. On the other hand the population of Free societies has increased by 570 million from fifteen years ago, and Partly Free societies have increased by 847.9 million over this same period, a net combined gain of 1.418 billion people.

According to the *Survey*, out of a world population of 5.37 billion people, 1.36 billion, (25 percent) live in countries categorized as Free, 2.31 billion, (43 percent) in Partly Free, and 1.71 billion, (32 percent) in Not Free societies. However, a world without India and China, which account for a combined 2 billion people, would show 1.36 billion, or 40 percent of the earth's population, living in Free societies, 1.51 billion, or 44 percent, in Partly Free societies and 560 million people, or 16 percent, in Not Free societies.

This significant reduction in Not Free societies over the last several years should encourage increased efforts to bring pressure on those societies that remain closed. Peace negotiations marginally improved the human rights situation in Angola, Cambodia, Ethiopia, Lebanon, Mozambique and Liberia. But the aftermath of the Gulf War and the beginning of new Middle East peace talks have not apparently encouraged a liberalization process throughout the region from Afghanistan, Iran, Iraq and Syria to Saudi Arabia, Somalia and the Sudan. Cuba, Laos, North Korea and Vietnam remain defiant in the face of massive changes within the former Communist world. Burma and the People's Republic of China deny their citizens even the most elementary human rights. Indeed, within the ruling circles of Beijing there has been a debate over whether to reverse their program of economic reform.

Over two-thirds of the world lives in Free or Partly Free societies. Yet, these societies are often characterized by institutions that have become dysfunctional or corrupt. The new democracies frequently lack a vibrant civil society, where citizens may freely participate in national life and form the variety of voluntary associations that are indispensable for democratic development. In many countries undergoing a democratic transition, such as El Salvador, Guatemala, the Philippines and Pakistan, cultures that encourage intolerance and exclusivity—attitudes encouraged by conditions of war—may provide the greatest obstacle to national development. The question for these societies is whether authoritarian and paramilitary structures and organizations within the new democracy can be overcome and dismantled. Throughout the newly emerging democracies, citizens are pressing for reforms to make government more accountable, legislatives more effective, legal systems more accessible and citizen groups more active. Accountability, responsiveness and tolerance will be necessary to curb the endemic violence in many of these societies and to foster the greater stability which comes with democracy.

Within the American society itself citizens express their fear that the world's oldest democracy is in jeopardy of becoming dysfunctional by tax revolts, withdrawal from electoral politics and open cynicism. While the world is experiencing a democratic revival of unprecedented magnitude, the U.S. and the industrialized democracies should engage in a period of reform, restoring and strengthening their public institutions so that they deserve respect and support. During this year of a presidential campaign, the debate might start with what America's role in the new world should be and what kind of society the U.S. wants to become.

Fifty years ago, Freedom House was created to counter the growing forces of isolationists, protectionists and nationalists who believed the United States should avoid entanglements in the darkness enveloping Europe. During a period of global economic and political change, where the line between domestic and foreign issues is increasingly blurred, we are again hearing the refrains of those who would retreat into a new nationalism. These are siren voices to which we should turn a deaf ear. Freedom House urges our society to turn inward, not to isolationism, but for reflection on a democratic renewal both at home and abroad. ■

The Survey 1992
The Year in Review

The difficulties in evaluating the state of freedom around the world have been inherent in the *Survey* project since its inception 21 years ago. This has been especially true over the past three years as the rate of political change around the world has accelerated in an unprecedented manner.

For example, in 1989, an unusually volatile period compared to past *Surveys*, 27 countries changed their ratings. The following year 56 nations, or over one-third of the world, changed because of real political events rather than from any methodological reconsiderations. Again in 1991, the world experienced radical political movement as 58 countries changed in their ratings. 41 countries improved their human rights situations, comparable to 36 the year before, while declines were registered by 17, compared to 20 the year before. 1991 saw 31 countries change their category ratings, compared to 17 the year before, moving between the categories "Free," "Partly Free" and "Not Free." Of these 24 nations improved categories, while 7 lost ground.

The *Survey* itself has expanded this year. The dissolution of the Soviet Union and the creation of the Commonwealth of Independent States have generated fifteen new national entities—the three Baltic countries of Estonia, Latvia and Lithuania and the twelve former republics of the Soviet Union. For the first time, *Freedom in the World* provides an account and the rating of political rights

31 Countries that changed categories

Country	1991	1992
Albania	Not Free	Partly Free
Angola	Not Free	Partly Free
Antigua and Barbuda	Free	Partly Free
Bangladesh	Partly Free	Free
Benin	Partly Free	Free
Bulgaria	Partly Free	Free
Cape Verde	Partly Free	Free
Central African Republic	Not Free	Partly Free
Congo	Not Free	Partly Free
Estonia*	--	Free
Ethiopia	Not Free	Partly Free
Georgia	--	Not Free
Guinea-Bissau	Not Free	Partly Free
Haiti	Partly free	Not Free
India	Free	Partly Free
Latvia*	--	Free
Lebanon	Not Free	Partly Free
Lesotho	Not Free	Partly Free
Lithuania*	--	Free
Mali	Not Free	Partly Free
Mongolia	Partly Free	Free
Mozambique	Not Free	Partly Free
Nepal	Partly Free	Free
Niger	Not Free	Partly Free
Romania	Not Free	Partly Free
Sao Tome and Principe	Partly Free	Free
Slovenia	--	Free
Thailand	Free	Partly Free
Uganda	Partly Free	Not Free
Yugoslavia	Partly Free	Not Free
Zambia	Partly Free	Free

* Formerly under control of the Soviet Union; new to the *Survey*.

and civil liberties in each former Soviet Republic. The Marshall Islands and Micronesia have moved from being considered as related territories to nation-states. By the close of 1991. the Survey recognized Slovenia and Croatia as separate national entities with the anticipation that more former states of Yugoslavia will gain their independence this year. Northern Ireland and Eritrea have been added to the category of related territories.

By a rather generous estimate, the *Survey* team estimates nearly 35 countries are at varying stages of a democratic transition. The number of democracies in the world has more than doubled in a twenty year period from 44 in 1972 to 91 in 1992. The rapid political transformation of the world raises questions about the longevity of these new democracies and the future success of those undergoing the transition process. These changes are threatened by the lack of institutional infrastructure, the absence of the rule of law, cultures of endemic violence and a persistence of civil strife between ethnic and sub-nationalities. This year's *Survey* freezes the world at an important transitional phase, which may be a democratic interlude before another cycle of political reversals begin.

Category changes

Fourteen nations joined the Free community this year. Two former United States Trust territories—the **Marshall Islands** and **Micronesia**—made the switch from related territories to independent countries. Six former Communist countries—**Bulgaria**, **Estonia**, **Latvia**, **Lithuania**, **Mongolia** and **Slovenia**—improved from Partly Free to a Free rating. The African nations of **Benin**, **Cape Verde**, **Sao Tome and Principe** and **Zambia** held competitive, multiparty

---

The 13 Worst Violators of Human Rights

Afghanistan
Burma (Myanmar)
China
Cuba
Equatorial Guinea
Haiti
Iraq
Korea, North
Libya
Somalia
Sudan
Syria
Vietnam

---

elections. The Asian countries of **Bangladesh** and **Nepal** completed their democratic transitions this year.

Bulgaria elected its first non-Communist government in forty-six years when the opposition Union of Democratic Forces (UDF) edged out the Bulgarian Socialist Party (formerly the Bulgarian Communist Party) in the October vote for the new 240-member parliament. Growing ethnic tensions and a deteriorating economy marked by a severe cut in Soviet imports marred the political transition.

Fifty-one years after being forcibly incorporated into the **Soviet Union**, **Estonia** held a plebiscite on independence with 78 percent of eligible voters supporting the proposition. The attempted 19 August coup against Gorbachev prompted the country to declare independence, which was recognized by the European community. Under a a new constitution, a national Congress is to be elected in 1992, replacing the current Supreme Council.

Nineteen-ninety-one opened with a violent crackdown by MVD Black Berets in **Latvia** but ended with independence as a March referendum yielded nearly three-quarters of the population supporting "a democratic state." Left unresolved

17 Gains in Freedom without changing category	10 Declines in Freedom without changing category
Belize	Ecuador
Cambodia	Egypt
Chad	Ghana
Colombia	Guatemala
Comoros	Japan
Gabon	Morocco
Grenada	Pakistan
Jordan	Peru
Kuwait	Suriname[*]
Liberia	Tunisia
Mauritius	
Nigeria	[*] Moved from 4,3 to 6,4 to 4,4
Paraguay	within the year
Portugal	
Togo	
Zaire	
Zimbabwe	

is the question of citizenship for the 40 percent of the population who are non-Latvian.

Eighty-four percent of voters in **Lithuania** cast 90 percent of their ballots for the creation of an independent and democratic state. For the months leading up to the August coup attempt in Moscow, Vilnius was under siege by Soviet troops but soon after that the country's independence was recognized.

Mongolia continued its fast but rocky transition to a democratic, market-oriented society. Fears of a Communist resurgence prompted the passing of a law barring government officials from party membership. Freedom of religion has been introduced in this largely Buddhist country, and monasteries are being refurbished and reopened.

Bangladesh's road to democracy began late in 1990 when President Lt. General Hossain Mohamed Ershad resigned after weeks of civil disorder by those protesting his authoritarian rule. February's elections were held with a minimum of violence and a large turnout from the country's 62 million voters. In

mid-June, the government announced that the country would adopt a Westminster-style political system. A national referendum on this matter passed by a margin of 84 percent to 15 percent.

The Himalayan kingdom of **Nepal** held its first multiparty elections in more than thirty years as 11 million citizens registered to vote. The liberal Nepali Congress led by Girija Prasad Koirala won a slight majority over a strong Communist alliance.

The central western African country of **Benin** made important strides toward consolidating its democratic transition be-gun in 1990. In March, the country held the first competitive presidential race in its post-independence history. After two rounds of balloting, Nicephore Soglo defeated the long-ruling general, Ahmed Kerekou.

Eleven years after its constitution ratified one-party rule, **Cape Verde** held its first multi-party elections since it won its independence from Portugal in 1975. Former PAICV (African Party for the Independence of Cape Verde) activist Carlos Veiga led his young opposition party, the Movement for Democracy, to a landslide victory in the January elections.

Following last year's approval of a new constitution calling for a multiparty system, a mixed economy, freedom of expression and the right to strike, **Sao Tome and Principe** held both legislative and presidential elections.

After eighteen years of government by independence figure Kenneth Kuanda, **Zambia** returned to a multiparty system with the stunning victory of trade union leader Frederick Chiluba and his multi-ethnic Movement for Multiparty Democracy (MMD). Observers believe the Zambian elections will cause **Kenya**, **Zimbabwe** and **Tanzania** to reconsider their opposition to multipartyism.

Three Free countries—**Antigua and Barbuda**, **India**, and **Thailand**—dropped to Partly Free this year. In the Caribbean nation of Antigua and Barbuda aging Prime Minister Vere Bird continued to resist calls for political reform amid the over-whelming domination of that country's politics by the Antigua Labor Party.

For the first time since the declaration of martial law in 1975, Freedom House rated **India** Partly Free after three consecutive years of deterioration in the human rights record of the world's most populous democracy. Nineteen-ninety-one was an extraordinary year for India as Tamil separatists assassinated former Prime Minister Rajiv Gandhi during the most violent election campaign in the country's history, which resulted in thousands of deaths. Open revolt continued in **Jammu and Kashmir**, and Indian security forces continued to use harsh measures to quell the uprising.

The military returned to power in **Thailand** by toppling the elected government of Prime Minister Chatichai Choonhavan last February. A new constitution released in November appears to guarantee the military's continued domination of the political system.

Within the category of Free, the Central American country of **Belize** continued to improve as the Security Intelligence Service (SIS) was dissolved, the Belize Human Rights Commission created and an independent board was formed to oversee state-owned media. After last year's constitutional crisis, **Grenada** held new elections that led to installation of a new government this year. **Portugal** privatized its media and **Mauritius** held its cleanest elections ever.

Twelve countries moved from Not Free to Partly Free this year.

For the first time in sixty years, **Albania** held contested elections and formed a coalition government after the victorious Communists were forced to acquiesce to opposition demands, paralyzing strikes and the flight of thousands of people to **Italy**, **Greece** and **Yugoslavia**.

Two years after the execution of Nicolae Ceausescu, **Romania** has made slight progress in its political transition. The year saw the parliamentary opposition call for a transitional government to replace the National Salvation Front. Throughout the year, the Civic Alliance, the popular umbrella organization for the democratic opposition, managed to organize strikes, demonstrations and rallies throughout Bucharest, Timisoara and other major cities.

Nine African nations moved into Partly Free following the adoption of multipartyism throughout the continent. After sixteen years of civil war in **Angola**, representatives of the MPLA government and the UNITA guerrilla movement signed a peace accord that provides for a cease-fire, the creation of a joint political and military commission to guide the transition, and the promise of elections in 1992.

The year also saw the overthrow of the Communist regime of the Dergue in **Ethiopia** and the forced exile of Hailie Miriam Mengistu to **Zimbabwe**. A transitional government led by the Ethiopian Revolutionary Democratic Front (EPRDF) was established to guide the country's transition.

Mozambique made slow progress toward the adoption of a multiparty system, postponing elections until 1992 and continued the negotiations between the ruling Mozambique Liberation Front (Frelimo) and Mozambique National Resistance (Renamo). An aborted coup attempt in June demonstrated the degree to which the military was demoralized.

The **Central African Republic**, the **Congo**, **Mali**, and **Niger** proceeded toward adopting multipartyism and allowed increased participation by opposition political parties. In May, **Guinea-Bissau's** ruling PAIGC paved the way for the transformation of this one-party state by allowing other parties to function legally. **Lesotho's** military government began a transition. It was overthrown by another military government, but the transition continued.

After sixteen years of civil war, peace began to take hold in **Lebanon** under the terms of the 1989 Arab league-sponsored Taif Accord. The government of President Elias Hrawi announced elections for the spring of 1992.

Four nations fell from Partly Free to Not Free this year—the former Soviet republic of **Georgia**, **Haiti**, **Uganda** and **Yugoslavia**.

President Jean-Betrand Aristide, the first freely elected leader in **Haiti's** history, fled Port-au-Prince following a military coup on 30 September 1991. By November, the Organization of American States (OAS) and the military government began to hold negotiations for the restoration of constitutional rule and the return of the deposed president but there was no progress by the end of the year.

Uganda continued its decline of last year as the administration of President Museveni became more repressive. Counter-insurgency efforts begun last year in the eastern and western parts of the country continued with renewed voracity.

Fighting in **Yugoslavia** between Croatians and the Serbian militias backed and armed by the federal army has killed at least 5,000 and left some 350,000 homeless. All the various cease-fires brokered by the European Community have collapsed, leading Germany to recognize Slovenia and Croatia. Violence could easily spread to newly "independent" Bosnia-Herzegovina and Kosovo.

Throughout the Partly Free category, there was noticeable movement in a number of countries. **Algeria** faced demonstrations and violence between police and Islamic fundamentalists who threatened to destabilize the Benjedid government and derail that country's democratic experiment. As the year came to a close, Algeria was attempting to break the political pattern in the region by holding the first round of genuinely free elections in December. Observers felt the military would prohibit the winning Islamic Salvation Front (FIS) from forming a government.

The de Klerk government in **South Africa** began all-party talks to discuss the drafting of a new constitution and the transition to full participation in government before 1994. Political violence continues to mar the black townships with blame assigned to all political forces.

In **Nigeria**, Africa's most populous country, presidential primaries and final elections for a civilian head of government are still scheduled to take place in 1992.

In Latin America, the **Guyana** government of President Desmond Hoyte delayed the 1991 elections because of serious irregularities with voter registration. Neighboring Suriname's democratically elected government of Ronald Venetiaan still must confront the power of the 3,000-member military led by Commander Desi Bouterse, who overthrew the last elected government in December 1990. The Fujimori government in **Peru** engaged in the violation of human rights, while being confronted with the savage activities of the Shining Path guerrilla organization. Negotiations in **Guatemala** between the military and the guerrilla movements have become deadlocked, while violence from street crime and military-linked death squads increased this past year. The Chamorro government in **Nicaragua** continued to be plagued by the Sandinista control of the security apparatus.

El Salvador's on-again, off-again negotiations between the Cristiani government and the FMLN guerrilla movement appears on-again as the year closes with prospects for peace in 1992 slightly better than before. **Paraguay** continued to progress with the May election of Carlos Filizzola, a labor leader, as mayor of Asuncion and the December elections for a constituent assembly to draft a new constitution. **Colombia** oversaw the drafting of a new constitution and coaxed the leaders of the Medellin drug cartel into surrendering.

The **Soviet Union** for all intents and purposes ceased to exist on 8 December with the Brest declaration that proclaimed a new commonwealth of the **Russian Republic**, **Belarus (Byelorussia)** and **Ukraine**. Within the ensuing two weeks, the nine remaining republics followed

suit and declared their independence. The key milestone of the past year was the leadership of President Boris Yeltsin of the **Russian Republic** in thwarting the 19 August coup attempt against Mikhail Gorbachev by military and Party hardliners. About 2.2 million voters went to the polls in **Armenia** and elected Levon-Petrosyan president from six candidates. Russian President Boris Yeltsin and **Kazakhstan** President Nazarbayev brokered meetings between both sides in the Nagorno-Karabakh conflict. Since 1988 hundreds have been killed and hundreds of thousands made homeless in the Armenian-Azeri battle. Mr. Nursultan Nazarbayev won election as Kazakhstan president unopposed with virtually no opposition in parliament. The May election in **Georgia** of former political prisoner Zviad Gamsakhurdia quickly led to a dictatorial government, engaged in jailing its opposition and repressing the ethnic Ossetians. Old-time Communist leaders won competitive but unfair elections in **Tajikistan** and **Uzbekistan**. The death-blow to the Soviet Union was dealt by the overwhelming vote on 2 December in the elections in **Ukraine**, where about 83 percent voted to approve the parliament's independence declaration.

Some of the more interesting developments came in Not Free countries, where **Burkina Faso**, **Cameroon**, and **Guinea** engaged in official repression against dissidents while they haltingly moved to multipartyism. The Arap Moi government in **Kenya** continued to crack down on dissent and rejected all proposals for a national referendum on multi-partyism until the Zambian elections and international pressure caused the president to signal his approval of greater liberalization in the year ahead. **Liberia's** civil war threatened to re-ignite as the conflict left hundreds of thousands of refugees in neighboring countries and approximately 10,000 dead. **Djibouti** was flooded with an influx of 30,000 refugees from **Somalia** and another 35,000 from **Ethiopia**. The Obiang regime in **Equatorial Guinea** was remarkable in its attempts to forestall internal pressures for multiparty elections. Nine political parties in opposition to the current regime are presently in exile in neighboring **Gabon** and **Cameroon**.

Somalia's Siad Barre and **Chad's** Hissein Habre suffered the same fate as Ethiopia's Mengistu. The current Somalian government of Ali Mahdi Mohammed can boast of control over half the capital on any given day. After twenty-six years, **Zaire's** President Mobutu Sese Seko ruled the central African country in seclusion from a yacht on the Zaire River. Demonstrations, clashes between opposition supporters and the security forces, labor strikes and frequent calls for the President's resignation continued throughout the year. The rise of opposition to the regime generated the creation of some 250 political parties.

Besides **Haiti**, the Western Hemisphere's only other Not Free country is Castro's **Cuba**. In complete defiance of the changes in the former Communist world, Castro reaffirmed single-party Marxist-Leninist rule during the Fourth Cuban Communist Party (PCC). The government attacked the small dissident political and human rights organizations that called for political reform.

Decades of civil war and violence in **Cambodia** came to an apparent end on 23 October when four rival factions signed a peace treaty in Paris. The agreement calls for a substantial U.N. peace-keeping presence in the country, while granting a major role to the internationally condemned Khmer Rouge.

Burma's ruling military junta tightened its control over the country, jailing dissidents, banning several political parties, and battling ethnic rebel groups in the countryside. Aung San Suu Kyi, the daughter of independence hero Aung San, received both the Nobel Peace Prize and the European Parliament's Sakharov Human Rights Award in absentia for her leadership of the democratic movement. Despite international pressure on the regime, she remains under house arrest, virtually incommunicado.

Both **Laos** and **Vietnam** strengthened their commitments to a one-party state while continuing a modest program of economic reform. The Stalinist regime of Marshall Kim Il-Sung in **North Korea**, strapped for economic support, began talks with the **Republic of South Korea**.

The collapse of Soviet communism ignited a major debate among leaders in the ruling Communist party of the **People's Republic of China** over whether to revert to classical Maoism or push ahead with market-oriented reforms. Since the crack-down at Tiananmen Square two years ago, China's security forces have beefed up surveillance of foreigners and possible dissidents. Democracy activists were officially charged as "counter-revolutionaries" in late 1990 and received sentences ranging from two to thirteen years of imprisonment. The government says that 715 in all were tried, but Western observers claim another 250 were still waiting court action. Western estimates of China's prison population place it in the neighborhood of 20 million, with approximately 10 percent regarded as political prisoners.

The Middle East remains singly impervious to the political changes sweeping the rest of the world. **Jordan** continues with its liberalization. **Saudi**

Arabia and **Kuwait** have made public noises about greater liberty. But the Gulf War left the **Iraqi** government of Saddam Hussein in power, seeking revenge on his Shiite population in the South and the Kurds in Northern Iraq. The United Nations accused the Baghdad regime of driving another 200,000 Kurds from their homes since October. **Iran** emerged from its international isolation as an important post-Gulf war power. Iran opened its doors to over 1 million Kurdish refugees and supplied weapons and support to the Shiite uprisings in Iraq. However, Iran remains one of the world's major violators of human rights, embarking on a chilling series of extrajudicial killings and assaults on opponents of the regime both at home and abroad. Throughout the summer, radicals cracked down on violations of Islamic law.

The *Survey* underscores Freedom House's concern that the enhancement and support of democratic movements and human rights organizations abroad be seen as consistent with American national interests. The current trend toward democratization can only be consolidated through a concerted effort to provide technical expertise and moral support to those risking their lives for a freer, more peaceful future. ▬

The Map of Freedom—1992

(Numbers refer to the map, pages 62-63)

FREE STATES

9	Argentina
10	Australia
11	Austria
13	Bahamas
15	Bangladesh
16	Barbados
18	Belgium
19	Belize
20	Benin
23	Bolivia
25	Botswana
26	Brazil
29	Bulgaria
33	Canada
35	Cape Verde Isls.
40	Chile
49	Costa Rica
51	Cyprus (G)
52	Cyprus (T)
223	Czechoslovakia
53	Denmark
55	Dominica
56	Dominican Republic
58	Ecuador
230	Estonia
66	Finland
67	France
71	The Gambia
72	Germany
76	Greece
78	Grenada
86	Honduras
88	Hungary
89	Iceland
94	Ireland
96	Israel
97	Italy
99	Jamaica
100	Japan
104	Kiribati
106	Korea (S)
228	Latvia
229	Lithuania
114	Luxembourg
122	Malta
123	Marshall Islands
126	Mauritius
129	Micronesia
131	Mongolia
180	Namibia
135	Nauru
136	Nepal
137	Netherlands
141	New Zealand
148	Norway
153	Papua New Guinea
224	Poland
159	Portugal
166	St. Christopher-Nevis
167	St. Lucia
169	St. Vincent and the Grenadines
171	Sao Tome & Principe
243	Slovenia
177	Solomon Isls.
181	Spain
186	Sweden
187	Switzerland
195	Trinidad & Tobago
199	Tuvalu
203	United Kingdom
204	United States
206	Uruguay
140	Vanuatu
208	Venezuela
212	Western Samoa
217	Zambia

RELATED TERRITORIES

4	Amer. Samoa (US)
5	Andorra (Fr-Sp)
7	Anguilla (UK)
138	Aruba (Ne)
12	Azores (Port)
21	Bermuda (UK)
27	Br. Vir. Is. (UK)
34	Canary Isls. (Sp)
36	Cayman Isls. (UK)
157	Ceuta (Sp)
39	Channel Isls. (UK)
43	Christmas Is. (Austral.)
44	Cocos (Keeling Isls.) (Austral.)
48	Cook Isls. (NZ)
57	Rapanui/Easter Is. (Chile)
63	Falkland Is. (UK)
64	Faeroe Isls. (Den)
68	French Guiana (Fr)
69	French Polynesia (Fr)
222	French Southern & Antarctic Terr. (Fr.)
75	Gibraltar (UK)
77	Greenland (Den)
79	Guadeloupe (Fr)
80	Guam (US)
95	Isle of Man (UK)
113	Liechtenstein (Swz)
117	Madeira (Port)
127	Mahore (Fr)
124	Martinique (Fr)
158	Melilla (Sp)
130	Monaco (Fr.)
132	Montserrat (UK)
139	Ne. Antilles (Ne)
225	New Caledonia (Fr)
145	Niue (NZ)
146	Norfolk Is. (Austral.)
147	No. Marianas (US)
17	Belau (Palau) (US)
220	Pitcairn Islands (UK)
160	Puerto Rico (US)
162	Reunion (Fr)
165	St. Helena and Dependencies (UK)
165a	Ascencion
165b	Tristan da Cunha
168	St. Pierre-Mq. (Fr)
170	San Marino (It)
192	Tokelau (NZ)
198	Turks & Caicos. (UK)
210	Virgin Isls. (US)
211	Wallis & Futuna Isls. (Fr)

PARTLY FREE STATES

2	Albania
3	Algeria
6	Angola
8	Antigua & Barbuda
237	Armenia
238	Azerbaijan
14	Bahrain
233	Belarus
22	Bhutan
37	Central African Republic
45	Colombia
46	Comoros
47	Congo
244	Croatia
59	Egypt
60	El Salvador
62	Ethiopia
65	Fiji
70	Gabon
81	Guatemala
83	Guinea-Bissau
84	Guyana
90	India
91	Indonesia
98	Ivory Coast
101	Jordan
240	Kazakhstan
235	Kyrgystan
109	Lebanon
110	Lesotho
116	Madagascar
119	Malaysia
121	Mali
128	Mexico
234	Moldova
133	Morocco
134	Mozambique
142	Nicaragua
143	Niger
144	Nigeria
151	Pakistan
152	Panama
154	Paraguay
155	Peru
156	Philippines
163	Romania
201	Russia
173	Senegal
175	Sierra Leone
176	Singapore
179	South Africa
182	Sri Lanka
184	Suriname
185	Swaziland
42	Taiwan (China)
236	Tajikistan
190	Thailand
193	Tonga
196	Tunisia
197	Turkey
241	Turkmenistan
231	Ukraine
242	Uzbekistan
73	Yemen
218	Zimbabwe

RELATED TERRITORIES

87	Hong Kong (UK)
245	Northern Ireland
115	Macao (Port)
221	Western Sahara (Mor)

NOT FREE STATES

1	Afghanistan
28	Brunei
205	Burkina Faso
30	Burma (Myanmar)
31	Burundi
102	Cambodia
32	Cameroon
38	Chad
41	China (PRC)
50	Cuba
54	Djibouti
61	Equatorial Guinea
239	Georgia
74	Ghana
82	Guinea
85	Haiti
92	Iran
93	Iraq
103	Kenya
105	Korea (N)
107	Kuwait
108	Laos
111	Liberia
112	Libya
118	Malawi
120	Maldives
125	Mauritania
150	Oman
161	Qatar
164	Rwanda
172	Saudi Arabia
174	Seychelles
178	Somalia
183	Sudan
188	Syria
189	Tanzania
191	Togo
200	Uganda
202	United Arab Emirates
209	Vietnam
215	Yugoslavia
216	Zaire

RELATED TERRITORIES

24	Bophuthatswana (SA)
219	Ciskei (SA)
214	East Timor (Indo.)
232	Eritrea
226	Irian Jaya (Indo.)
227	Kashmir (India)
149	Occupied Territories (Isr.)
213	Tibet (China)
194	Transkei (SA)
207	Venda

This map is based on data developed by Freedom House's *Comparative Survey of Freedom*. The *Survey* analyzes factors such as the degree to which fair and competitive elections occur, individual and group freedoms are guaranteed in practice, and press freedom exists. In some countries, the category reflects active citizen opposition rather than politcal rights granted by a government. More detailed and up-to-date *Survey* information may be obtained from Freedom House.

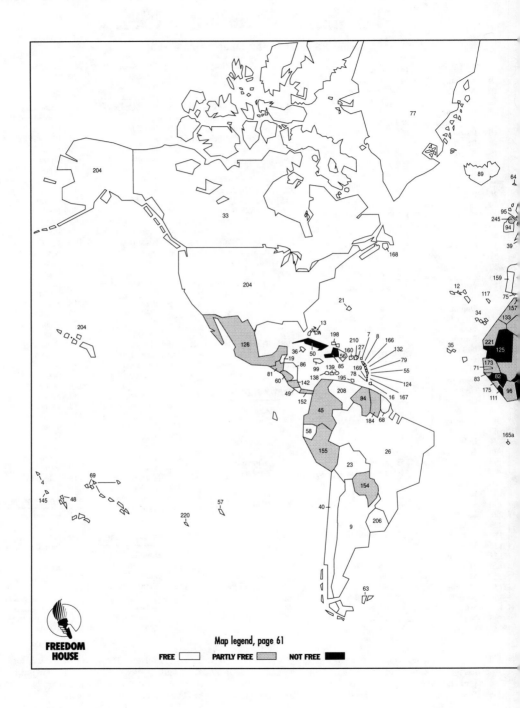

Map legend, page 61

FREEDOM
HOUSE

FREE ☐   PARTLY FREE ▨   NOT FREE ■

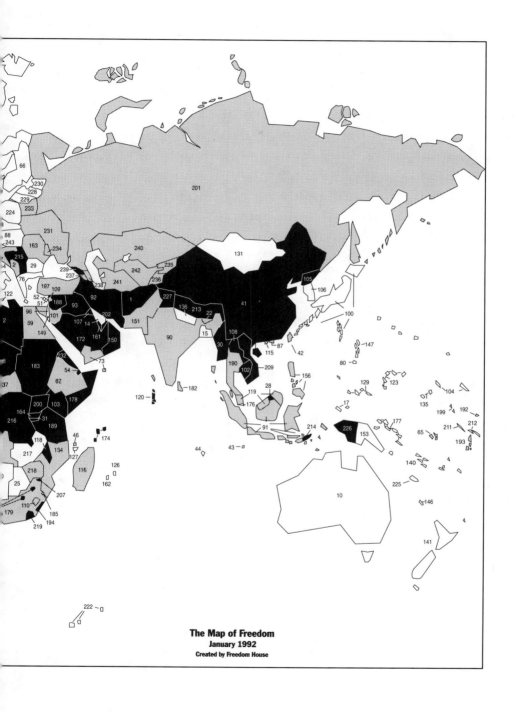

The Map of Freedom
January 1992
Created by Freedom House

The Comparative Survey of Freedom 1991-1992 Survey Methodology

Joseph E. Ryan

The purpose of the *Comparative Survey of Freedom* since its inception in the 1970s has been to provide an annual evaluation of political rights and civil liberties everywhere in the world.

The *Survey* attempts to judge all places by a single standard and to point out the importance of democracy and freedom. At a minimum, a democracy is a political system in which the people choose their authoritative leaders freely from among competing groups and individuals who were not chosen by the government. Putting it broadly, freedom is the chance to act spontaneously in a variety of fields outside the control of government and other centers of potential domination. Normally, Westerners associate the adherence to political rights and civil liberties with the liberal democracies, such as those in North America and the European Community. However, there are also such Third World democracies as Costa Rica and Botswana. In another case, Western Samoa combines political parties and competitive elections with power for the *matai*, the heads of extended families.

Freedom House does not view democracy as a static concept, and the *Survey* recognizes that a democratic country does not necessarily belong in our category of "free" states. A democracy can lose freedom and become merely "partly free." Peru and Colombia are examples of such "partly free" democracies. In other cases, countries that replaced military regimes with elected governments can have less than complete transitions to liberal democracy. El Salvador and Guatemala fit the description of this kind of "partly free" democracy. (For an explanation of the designations "free," "partly free," and "not free," see the section on The Map of Freedom below.)

Just as democracy is not a static concept, the *Survey* itself adapts to changing conditions. Readers of the previous editions of the *Survey* will note that the ratings of many countries and related territories have changed since 1989. Events have changed some ratings, but other changes reflect methodological refinements developed by this year's *Survey* team.

Definitions and categories of the *Survey*

The *Survey*'s understanding of freedom is broad and encompasses two sets of characteristics grouped under political rights and civil liberties. **Political rights** enable people to participate freely in the political process. By the political process, we mean the system by which the polity chooses the authoritative policy makers and attempts to make binding decisions affecting the national, regional or local community. In a free society this means the right of all adults to vote and compete for public office, and for elected representatives to have a decisive vote on public policies. A system is genuinely free or democratic to the extent that the people have a choice in determining the nature of the system and its leaders.

The *Survey* employs checklists for these rights and liberties to help determine the degree of freedom present in each country and related territory, and to help assign each entity to a comparative category.

The checklist for political rights asks whether (a) the head of state and/or head of government or other chief authority, and (b) the legislative representatives, are elected through free and fair elections. Freedom House considers the extent to which the system offers the voter the chance to make a free choice among competing candidates, and to what extent the candidates are chosen independently of the state. The checklist asks specifically whether there are fair electoral laws, equal campaigning opportunities, fair polling and honest tabulation of ballots.

The mechanics of the election are not the only concern. We also examine whether the voters are able to endow their elected representatives with real power, or whether unelected elements reduce or supersede this power. In many Latin American countries, for example, the military retains a significant political role, and in Morocco the king maintains significant power over the elected politicians.

A fully free political system must allow the people to organize in different political parties or other competitive political groupings of their choice, and the system must be open to the rise and fall of these competing parties or groupings. The *Survey* looks for the occurrence of a significant opposition vote, *de facto* opposition power, and a possibility for the opposition to increase its support or gain power through elections. The definition of political rights also includes a country's right of self-determination and its citizens' freedom from domination by the military, foreign powers, totalitarian parties, religious hierarchies, economic oligarchies or any other powerful group. The more people suffer under such domination, the less chance the country has of getting credit for self-determination.

Finally, the *Survey* examines minority rights and subnational political power: Do cultural, ethnic, religious and other minority groups have reasonable self-determination, self-government, autonomy or participation through informal consensus in the decision-making process? Is political power decentralized, allowing for local, regional and/or provincial or state administrations led by their freely elected officials? (For entities such as tiny island nations, the absence of a decentralized system does not necessarily count as a negative in the *Survey*.)

For traditional monarchies that have no parties or electoral process, the *Survey* gives discretionary credit for systems that provide for consultation with the people, encourage discussion of policy, and allow the right to petition the ruler.

Freedom House does not have a culture-bound view of democracy. The *Survey* team rejects the notion that only Europeans and those of European descent qualify as democratic. The *Survey* demonstrates that, in addition to those in Europe and the Americas, there are free countries with varying kinds of democracy functioning among people of all races and religions in Africa, the Pacific and Asia. In some Pacific islands, free countries can have competitive political systems based on competing family groups and personalities rather than on European or American-style parties.

Civil liberties are the freedoms to develop views, institutions and personal autonomy apart from the state. The checklist for civil liberties begins with a requirement for free and independent media, literature and other cultural expressions. In cases where the media are state-controlled but offer pluralistic points of view, the *Survey* gives the system credit. The checklist also includes the rights to have open public discussion and free private discussion, and freedom of assembly and demonstration. Freedom House looks for evidence that a country or territory allows freedom of political or quasi-political organization. This includes political parties, civic associations, ad hoc issue groups and so forth.

The *Survey* considers whether citizens are equal under the law, have access to an independent, nondiscriminatory judiciary, and are respected by the security forces. Freedom House does not mistake constitutional guarantees for the respect for human rights in practice. The checklist also includes protection from unjustified political terror, imprisonment, exile or torture, whether by groups that support or oppose the system, and freedom from war or insurgency situations. Freedom from war and insurgency situations enhances the liberties in a free society, but the absence of wars and insurgencies does not in itself make an unfree society free.

The standards for civil liberties also include free trade unions and peasant organizations or equivalents, free professional and other private organizations, free businesses or cooperatives, and free private and public religious expression and free religious institutions. For tiny island countries and territories and other small entities with low populations, the absence of unions and other types of association does not necessarily count as a negative unless the government or other centers of domination are deliberately blocking association.

The checklist for civil liberties has an item on personal social freedoms, which include such aspects as gender

equality, property rights, freedom of movement, choice of residence, and choice of marriage and size of family. The *Survey* also rates equality of opportunity, which includes freedom from exploitation by or dependency on landlords, employers, union leaders, bureaucrats or any other type of denigrating obstacle to a share of legitimate economic gains. Equality of opportunity also implies a free choice of employment and education. Extreme inequality of opportunity prevents disadvantaged individuals from enjoying a full exercise of civil liberties. Typically, desperately poor countries and territories lack both opportunities for economic advancement and the other liberties on this checklist.

The final point on the civil liberties checklist is freedom from extreme government indifference or corruption. When governments do not care about the social and economic welfare of large sectors of the population, the human rights of those people suffer. Gross government corruption can pervert the political process and hamper the development of a free economy.

The *Survey* rates political rights and civil liberties separately on a seven-category scale, 1 representing the most free and 7 the least free. A country is assigned to a particular category based on responses to the checklist and the judgments of the *Survey* team at Freedom House. The numbers are not purely mechanical; they also reflect judgment. The team assigns initial ratings to countries by awarding from 0 to 2 points per checklist item, depending on the degree of compliance with the standard. The highest possible score for political rights is 18 points, based on up to 2 points for each of nine questions. The highest possible score for civil liberties is 26 points, based on up to 2 points for each of thirteen questions.

After placing countries in initial categories based on checklist points, the *Survey* team makes minor adjustments to account for factors such as extreme violence, whose intensity may not be reflected in answering the checklist questions. These exceptions aside, in the overwhelming number of cases, the checklist system reflects the real world situation and is adequate for placing countries and territories into the proper comparative categories.

The map on pages 62-63 divides the world into three large categories: "free," "partly free," and "not free." The *Survey* places countries and territories into this tripartite division by averaging the category numbers they received for political rights and civil liberties. Those whose category numbers average 1-2.5 are considered "free," 3-5.5 "partly free," and 5.5-7 "not free." The dividing line between "partly free" and "not free" falls within the group whose category numbers average 5.5. For example, countries that receive a rating of 6 for political rights and 5 for civil liberties, or a 5 for political rights and a 6 for civil liberties, could be either "partly free" or "not free." The total number of raw points is the factor which makes the difference between the two. Countries and territories with combined raw scores of 0-14 points are "not free," and those with combined raw scores of 15-29 points are "partly free." "Free" countries and territories have combined raw scores of 30-44 points.

The differences in raw points between countries in the three broad categories represent distinctions in the real world. There are obstacles which "partly free" countries must overcome before they can be called "free," just as there are impediments which prevent "not free" countries from being called "partly free." Countries at the lowest rung of the "free" category (category 2 in political rights, category 3 in civil liberties) differ from those at the upper end of the "partly free" group (category 3 in both). Typically, there is more violence and/or military influence on politics at 3,3 than at 2,3 and the differences become more striking as one compares 2,3 with worse categories of the "partly free" countries.

The distinction between the least bad "not free" countries and the least free "partly free" may be less obvious than the gap between "partly free" and "free," but at "partly free," there is at least one extra factor that keeps a country from being assigned to the "not free" category. For example, Bahrain (6,5) has a system of consultation between ruler and subjects, and rights of petition. These are examples of aspects that separate this country from its "not free" neighbor, Iraq (7,7). The gap between "partly free" and "not free" is easier to see if one compares Lesotho (6,4) with Burma (7,7). Lesotho began moving from dictatorship towards democratic transition in 1991, and it expanded civil liberties. By way of contrast, Burma (Myanmar) halted and reversed democratic trends after the opposition won the legislative election in 1990. The Burmese military crushed dissent and reinforced its harsh rule.

Freedom House wishes to point out that the designation "free" does not mean that a country has perfect freedom or lacks serious problems. As an institution which advocates human rights, Freedom House remains concerned about a variety of social problems and civil liberties questions in the U.S. and other countries that the *Survey* places in the "free" category. Similarly, in no way does an improvement in a country's rating mean that human rights campaigns should cease. On the contrary, we wish to use the *Survey* as a prod to improve the condition of all countries.

The approach of the *Survey*

The *Survey* attempts to measure conditions as they really are around the world. This approach is distinct from relying on intense coverage by the American media as a guide to which countries are the least free. The publicity given problems in some countries does not necessarily mean that unpublicized problems of other countries are not more severe. For example, while U.S. television networks are allowed into Israel and El Salvador to cover abuses of human rights, they are not allowed to report freely in North Korea, which has far less freedom than the other two countries. To reach such comparative conclusions, Freedom House evaluates the development of democratic governmental institutions, or lack thereof, and also examines the quality of civil society, life outside the state structure.

Without a well-developed civil society, it is difficult, if not impossible, to have an atmosphere supportive of democracy. A society that does not have free individual and group expressions in nonpolitical matters is not likely to make an exception for political ones. As though to prove this, there is no country in the *Survey* that places in category 6 or 7 for civil liberties and, at the same time, in category 1 or 2 for political rights. In the overwhelming majority of cases in the *Survey*, countries and territories have ratings in political rights and civil liberties that are within two categories of each other.

Readers should not necessarily interpret the ratings as a commentary on the intentions of particular governments. Rather, the ratings represent Freedom House's evaluation of the countries and territories' situations, which are formed

by both governmental and nongovernmental factors.

The *Survey* rates both countries and related territories. For our purposes, countries are internationally recognized independent states whose governments are resident within their officially claimed territories. In the unusual case of Cyprus, we give two ratings, since there are two governments on that divided island. In no way does this imply that Freedom House endorses Cypriot division. We note only that neither the predominantly Greek Republic of Cyprus nor the predominantly Turkish Republic of Northern Cyprus is the *de facto* government for the entire island. A few internationally recognized states, such as Monaco and San Marino, count as related territories here, due to their officially dependent relationships with other states. With those exceptions, related territories consist mostly of colonies, protectorates, occupied territories and island dependencies. Although many countries recognize the PLO as the government of Palestine, we do not count Palestine as an independent country, because the PLO does not govern a Palestinian state. This edition of the yearbook carries experimental ratings of the republics of the former Soviet Union and ratings for Slovenia and Croatia, the newly recognized former republics of Yugoslavia. Due to their increasing international recognition, Marshall Islands and Micronesia change status from related territories to independent countries in this *Survey*.

The *Survey* excludes uninhabited related territories and such entities as the U.S.-owned Johnston Atoll, which has only a transient military population and no native inhabitants. Since most related territories have a broad range of civil liberties and some form of self-government, a higher proportion of them have the "free" designation than do independent countries.

The 1992 *Survey* has made additions in its coverage of related territories. We list Eritrea as a related territory of Ethiopia, and Northern Ireland as a related territory of the U.K. In these cases and others, such as Tibet and Kashmir, the separate listing allows Freedom House to call attention to the human rights situation in areas in which there are serious questions about self-determination. ▬

The Tabulated Ratings

The accompanying Table of Independent Countries (pages 572-573) and Table of Related Territories (page 574) rate each country or territory on seven-category scales for political rights and civil liberties. Each entity is then placed in a broad category of "free," "partly free" or "not free." On each scale, 1 represents the most free and 7 the least free.

Political rights

In political rights, generally speaking, states rated 1 come closest to the ideals suggested by the checklist questions, beginning with free and fair elections. Those elected rule. There are competitive parties or other competitive political groupings, and the opposition has an important role and power. These entities have self-determination or an extremely high degree of autonomy (in the case of related territories). Usually, those rated 1 have self-determination for minority groups or their participation in government through informal consensus. With the exception of such entities as tiny island countries, these countries and territories have decentralized political power and free subnational elections.

Countries and territories rated 2 in political rights are free, but are less free than those rated 1. Such factors as violence, political discrimination against minorities, and foreign or military influence on politics are present and weaken the quality of democracy.

The same factors that weaken freedom in category 2 may also undermine political rights in categories 3, 4 and 5. Other damaging conditions are at work as well, including civil war, very strong military involvement in politics, lingering royal power, unfair elections and one-party dominance. However, states and territories in these categories still have some elements of political rights, such as the freedom to organize nongovernmental parties and quasi-political groups, reasonably free referenda, or other significant means of popular influence on government.

Typically, states and territories with political rights rated 6 have systems ruled by military juntas, one-party dictatorships, religious hierarchies and autocrats. These regimes allow only some minimal manifestation of political rights such as competitive local elections or some degree of representation or autonomy for minorities. A few states in category 6 are traditional monarchies that mitigate their relative lack of political rights through the use of consultation with their subjects, toleration of political discussion, and acceptance of petitions from the ruled.

Category 7 includes places where political rights are absent or virtually nonexistent, due to the extremely oppressive nature of the regime or extreme oppression in combination with civil war.

Civil liberties

States and territories rated 1 in civil liberties come closest to the ideals of freedoms of expression, assembly and demonstration, religion and association. They also do the comparatively best job of protecting the individual from political violence and from harms inflicted by courts and security forces. Entities in this category have free economic activity and tend to strive for equality of opportunity. There is no such thing as complete equality of opportunity, but free places tend to come comparatively closer to the ideal than less free ones. In general, these countries and territories are comparatively free of extreme government indifference or corruption.

The political entities in category 2 in civil liberties are not as free as those rated 1, but they are still relatively free. In general, these countries and territories have deficiencies in three or four aspects of civil liberties. In each case, the country is otherwise generally free.

Independent countries and related territories with ratings of 3, 4 or 5 have progressively fewer civil liberties than those in category 2. States in these categories range from ones that are in at least partial compliance with virtually all checklist standards to those which have partial compliance with only eight standards. Some countries have a mixture of good civil liberties scores in some areas and zero or partial credit in others. As one moves down the scale below category 2, the level of oppression increases, especially in the areas of censorship, political terror and the prevention of free association. There are also many cases in which groups opposed to the state carry out political terror that undermines other freedoms. That means that a poor rating for a country is not necessarily a comment on the intentions of the government. The rating may simply reflect the real restrictions on liberty which can be caused by nongovernmental terror.

Typically, at category 6 in civil liberties, countries and territories have a few partial rights. For example, a country might have some religious freedom, some personal social freedoms, some highly restricted private business activity, and relatively free private discussion. In general, these states and territories severely restrict expression and association. There are almost always political prisoners and other manifestations of political terror.

At category 7, countries and territories have virtually no freedom. An overwhelming and justified fear of the state's repressive nature characterizes the society.

The accompanying Tables of Combined Average Ratings average the two seven-category scales of political rights and civil liberties into an overall freedom rating for each country and territory. ▬

Introduction to Country and Related Territory Reports

The Survey team at Freedom House wrote reports on 183 countries and 62 related territories. As we prepared to go to press, former Soviet and Yugoslav republics began receiving international recognition. There was enough time in our production process to write a separate report on Ukraine, as we had already done for Estonia, Latvia, and Lithuania. Reports on eleven other former Soviet republics appear under USSR (former). All former Soviet republics have separate listings on the comparative charts in the book. While Slovenia and Croatia have separate listings in our comparative charts, the information on them appears under Yugoslavia.

The Marshall Islands and Micronesia change from related territories to independent countries in this edition. However, with the addition of Eritrea and Northern Ireland, the number of related territories remains unchanged from the last yearbook's total of 62.

Each report begins with brief political, economic, and social data. This information is arranged under the following headings: **polity, economy, political rights, civil liberties, status, population, purchasing power parities (PPP), population, life expectancy,** and **ethnic groups**. More detailed information follows in an **overview** and in an essay on the political rights and civil liberties of each country.

Under **polity**, there is an encapsulated description of the dominant centers of freely chosen or unelected political power in each country. Most of the descriptions are self-explanatory, such as Communist one-party for China or

parliamentary democracy for Ireland. Such non-parliamentary democracies as the United States of America are designated presidential-legislative democracies. European democratic countries with constitutional monarchs are designated parliamentary democracies, because the elected body is the locus of most real political power. Only countries with powerful monarchs (e.g. the Sultan of Brunei) warrant a reference to the monarchy in the brief description of the polity. Dominant party polities are systems in which the ruling party (or front) dominates government, but allows other parties to organize or compete short of taking control of government. There are other types of polities listed as well. Among them are various military and military-influenced or -dominated regimes, transitional systems, and several unique polities, such as Iran's clergy-dominated parliamentary system. Countries with genuine federalism have the word "federal" in the polity description.

The reports label the **economy** of each country. Non-industrial economies are called traditional or pre-industrial. Developed market economies and Third World economies with a modern market sector have the designation capitalist. Mixed capitalist countries combine private enterprise with substantial government involvement in the economy for social welfare purposes. Capitalist-statist economies have both large market sectors and government-owned productive enterprises, due either to elitist economic policies or state dependence on key natural resource industries. Mixed capitalist-statist economies have the characteristics of capitalist-statist economies plus major social welfare programs. Statist systems have the goal of placing the entire economy under direct or indirect government control. Mixed statist economies are primarily government-controlled, but also have significant private enterprise. Developing Third World economies with a government-directed modern sector belong in the statist category. Economies in transition between statist and capitalist forms may have the word "transitional" in the economy description.

Each country report mentions the category of **political rights** and **civil liberties** in which Freedom House classified the country. Category 1 is the most free and category 7 is the least free in each case. **Status** refers to the designations "free," "partly free," and "not free," which Freedom House uses as an overall summary of the general state of freedom in the country.

Each entry includes a **population** figure which is sometimes the best approximation that is available. For all cases in which the information is available, the Survey provides **life expectancy** statistics.

Freedom House obtained the **Purchasing Power Parities (PPP)** from the U.N. Development Program. These figures show per capita gross domestic product (GDP) in terms of international dollars. The PPP statistic adjusts GDP to account for real buying power. For some countries, especially for newly independent countries, tiny island states, and those with statist economies, these statistics were unavailable.

The Survey provides a listing of countries' **ethnic groups**, because this information may help the reader understand such questions as minority rights which the Survey takes into account.

Each country summary has an **overview** which describes such matters as the most important events of 1991 and current political issues. Finally, the country reports contain a section on **political rights** and **civil liberties.** This section summarizes each country's degree of respect for the rights and liberties that Freedom House uses to evaluate freedom in the world. These summaries include instances of human rights violations by both governmental and non-governmental entities.

Reports on related territories follow the country summaries. In most cases, these reports are comparatively brief and contain fewer categories of information than one finds in the country summaries. ■

Afghanistan

Polity: Communist one-party
Economy: Statist
Population: 16,600,000
PPP: $710
Life Expectancy: 42.5
Ethnic Groups: Pashtun, Tajik, Uzbek, Hazara

Political Rights: 7
Civil Liberties: 7
Status: Not Free

Overview:

In 1991 the quest for a negotiated political settlement in Afghanistan continued to be elusive. Since the withdrawal of Soviet forces from Afghanistan in February 1989 several different formulas aimed at reconciling the Afghan resistance with the Kabul regime have failed. Afghan President Mohammad Najibullah has tenaciously remained in power, continuing an inconclusive battle with the factionalized Muslim resistance. Although the United States and the Soviet Union have been the primary patrons of the two opposing sides for a dozen years, during the past two years the two countries have also endeavored to play the role of chief peacemakers.

The Afghan civil war began after the Soviet Union's invasion in December 1979. The Soviets deposed president Hafizullah Amin, the leader of the Khalq faction of the Communist People's Democratic Party of Afghanistan (PDPA), and replaced him with his longtime rival, Babrak Karmal. Amin's ruthless Marxist tactics and programs had generated mounting resistance in the country, leading the Soviets to decide that without an intervention they would lose control over the country. The invasion culminated in Amin's death, and put the Parcham faction of the PDPA in power. In May 1986, with the Soviets unable to crush the resistance despite having in excess of 100,000 troops in the country, Mohammed Najibullah replaced Karmal as PDPA general secretary after the latter's visit to Moscow for "health" reasons.

For more than a decade the Soviet Union's invasion was repeatedly condemned by the U.N. and the world community. More than 1 million Afghans—80 percent of them civilians—were killed by Soviet bombs, napalm, chemical gases, artillery, mines and bayonets. The war also displaced 5 million Afghans, creating the largest refugee population in the world.

Throughout the war the *mujahideen* resistance have relied primarily on guerrilla hit-and-run tactics, but have also shelled major cities, including Kabul, which resulted in the indiscriminate killing of many civilians. The core of the Pakistan-based mujahideen—officially represented by a government-in-exile formed in February 1989—comprises a loose and fractious coalition of seven moderate and fundamentalist Sunni Muslim groups. Several of the moderate parties have advocated the return of exiled King Zahir Shah, who was stabbed and wounded in November 1991 at his villa in Rome by an assailant disguised as a journalist.

There are also nine relatively small Afghan Shiite mujahideen groups based in Iran. The Pakistan supported mujahideen have argued that the Iranian-based groups have done little fighting in the twelve-year war against the Soviet-backed government in Kabul, but now want to have a large share of power. Since the war began the United States has supplied the resistance with an average of $200 million per year in military aid, as well as sizeable outlays for humanitarian assistance.

In an effort to gain control of the divided country, Najibullah has attempted to move away from the Communist past and the Soviet Union's many years of political, economic and cultural domination. Over the years he had changed his name from "Najib" back to "Najibullah," in an effort to sound more Muslim. He became president of the Republic of Afghanistan, deleted the word "Democratic" from the country's name, and offered the Muslim guerrillas a plan for both "national reconciliation" and the formation of a coalition government. The Parcham faction of the PDPA also underwent a change in name, becoming the Watan (Homeland) Party in June 1990 with Najibullah as its chairman. The president's speeches, which were usually peppered with references to socialism and revolutionary victory, now focus on the role of the private sector in national economic life. A similar metamorphosis has occurred in the country's cultural life and educational system. The teaching of Russian has been replaced with French, and atheistic indoctrination gave way to the teaching of Islam.

The quick disintegration of the Soviet center has posed a grave problem to the Soviet-allied government in Kabul which, in 1990, had received from the USSR $3.4 billion in military aid, in addition to another $700 million in economic assistance, mostly food, clothing and fuel. The Soviets continued this level of aid in 1991. The emergence of Boris Yeltsin as the most powerful de facto leader in the fragmenting Soviet Union posed a threat to Najibullah's regime. Even before his election as president of the Russian republic on 12 June 1991 Yeltsin repeatedly stated that Russia would cease its support of all client states in the third world, including Afghanistan. In September 1991 Najibullah made a personal appeal to Yeltsin to not to block Soviet aid in arms, fuel and food, fearing that further discontent in his impoverished country could spark a coup against him.

An official agreement to this effect was reached in Moscow on 13 September 1991 between Soviet Foreign Minister Boris D. Pankin and Secretary of State James A. Baker III. They announced that both countries would cease all weapons deliveries to their respective combatants in Afghanistan by 1 January 1992, and urged other countries to follow suit. The latter statement was directed primarily at Saudi Arabia, which has been bank-rolling the mujahideen for more than a decade. It was understood, however, that this important U.S.-Soviet agreement could not insure an end to the fighting, because both Najibullah and the mujahideen were reported to have stockpiled enough weapons and supplies to last for two years.

The U.S.-Soviet joint communiqué also called for "an independent and non-aligned Afghanistan" to be attained by a "democratic and free electoral process." A major rift between the Afghan resistance and Najibullah has been his refusal to step down from the presidency before an interim government holds elections. A second recurring problem has been the mujahideen's unwillingness to conduct negotiations for a political settlement directly with Najibullah.

A flurry of diplomatic activity aimed at finding a peaceful solution to the war began in the spring of 1991. On 21 May U.N. Secretary-General Javier Perez de Cuellar issued a peace plan calling for an intra-Afghan dialogue which would evolve into an internationally assisted interim government, free and fair elections, cessation of hostilities, and an end to military assistance by all foreign parties. The U.N. proposal was promptly endorsed by the U.S. and the USSR, but the role of Najibullah in the interim government remained problematic. Moscow insisted that a cease-fire precede the formation of the interim government, which should include Najibullah. While some moderate mujahideen factions approved the plan, most of the resistance groups did not.

In July U.N. Secretary-General Perez de Cuellar announced his readiness to convene a peace conference representing all sides in the Afghan conflict, but later that month talks broke down between rival resistance factions who were trying to draft their own peace plan. A newly formed twenty-eight-member commission set up to represent the resistance parties dissolved after feuding mujahideen groups argued over their allotted number of seats on the commission. However, at a conference on 28-29 August held in Teheran, Iran, Pakistan and their Afghan mujahideen allies were able to form a joint delegation to seek clarifications on the U.N. proposal.

The failed August coup in Moscow and the ascendancy of Boris Yeltsin at the end of the summer signaled new hope for an end to the Afghan conflict. On 10 November an eleven-member mujahideen delegation led by Burhanuddin Rabbani, the president of the Pakistan-based interim government, arrived in Moscow. The delegation included all nine Shiite groups based in Iran and four of the seven parties based in Pakistan, although the three fundamentalist mujahideen groups boycotted the trip. It was the first large-scale reception of Afghan resistance leaders in Moscow, and in the words of Rabbani the talks had "surpassed all expectations."

On 12 November the delegation was received by Soviet and Russian foreign ministers Boris Pankin and Andrey Kozyrev, and later met with Pankin's successor, Eduard Shevardnadze, as well as Russia's vice-president, Alexander Rutskoy. The two most important items on the agenda were a final political settlement of the Afghan conflict and the return of the remaining 75-80 Soviet prisoners of war. After meeting with a group of the POWs' parents, Rabbani stated that he would "do everything possible" to win their freedom.

On 15 November a landmark joint communiqué, signed by Rabbani and Pankin, was issued in Moscow stating that power in Kabul should be handed over to an Islamic transitional government, which should then hold a general election within two years. The statement also contained a denunciation of the Red Army's invasion of Afghanistan in 1979. Unlike previous Soviet statements, there was no demand that Najibullah and his Homeland Party should play the senior role in the interim government. However, the Najibullah government drew comfort from the fact that at least the Moscow communiqué did not exclude it from the peace process, and expressed confidence that as long as it enjoys the support of the army, it cannot be left out of future negotiations.

Despite the peace initiatives in 1991, the bitter legacy of the civil war continued to ravage the country. There were ongoing battles for control of towns, garrisons and provinces. Moscow has supplied the Kabul regime with a large number of SCUD missiles, which have continued to be launched into mujahideen-controlled areas of the country. Thirty-five Moscow-supplied SCUD missiles were fired on Khost during the mujahideen's assault on the city from 17-31 March. The heavily fortified city in south-eastern Afghanistan finally fell to the resistance, however, causing a major setback to the Kabul government; the battle consolidated mujahideen control over 80 percent of the countryside. Najibullah's forces continued to maintain control of the major cities. In October and December the mujahideen launched offensives on the city of Gardez, the capital of Paktia province and the hometown of Najibullah and other key government officials. The ten-day battle in mid-October left at least 400 mujahideen fighters dead, largely due to intensive bombing by government warplanes.

**Political Rights
and Civil Liberties:**
Citizens of Afghanistan cannot change their government democratically. President Najibullah is both head of state and head of the ruling Watan (Homeland) party.

The twelve-year civil war has taken a great toll on the Afghan people. In addition to the more than 1 million Afghans killed since the 1979 Soviet invasion, 5 million Afghan refugees continue to live in camps in Pakistan and Iran, unable to return because their homes are destroyed, the agricultural infrastructure is in ruins, and the rural areas littered with deadly land mines left from the war.

Both mujahideen and regime forces have been accused of committing widespread human rights violations, including torture, disappearances, executions of political enemies and POW's, forced conscription, and attacks on civilian areas.

Arbitrary arrest and detention of people suspected of anti-government activities is routine in Kabul. In March, Amnesty International called on the government to end torture and long-term detention without trial of some 3,000 political prisoners, some of whom have been held in isolation for almost a decade. Although the government claims it has abolished special tribunals set up to try political crimes, the judiciary is controlled by the party-state apparatus.

The government maintains monopoly control over the media and even private criticism of the regime can result in detention.

Although a 1990 law on assembly allows demonstrations and strikes that do not violate "public security," and a law on association allows the formation of any group that does not desire the overthrow of the regime, new parties are practically non-existent. The Central Council of Trade Unions is a party-dominated umbrella organization for labor, and the ruling Watan party officially supervises all religious organizations.

Albania

Polity: Dominant Party (transitional)
Economy: Statist (transitional)
Population: 3,300,000
PPP: na
Life Expectancy: 72.2
Ethnic Groups: Albanians (two main ethnic linguistic groups: Ghegs, Tosks, 96 percent), Greeks (2.5 percent)

Political Rights: 4
Civil Liberties: 4
Status: Partly Free

Overview:
In 1991 Albania saw its first free election in sixty years and the subsequent formation of a coalition government when the victorious Communists were forced to acquiesce to opposition demands after paralyzing strikes, severe food shortages and the flight of thousands of Albanians to Italy, Greece and Yugoslavia. But by year's end, the government of Premier Ylli Bufi resigned after the opposition Democratic Party withdrew from the government. President Ramiz Alia asked nonparty intellectual Vilson Ahmeti to form an interim government and elections were scheduled for 1992.

President Ramiz Alia, head of the Communist Albanian Party of Labor, has led the country since the death of Stalinist strongman Enver Hoxha in 1985. The Socialist

People's Republic of Albania was established as a one-party Communist regime in 1946 led by Hoxha. Fluctuating from Stalinism to a home-grown Maoism, Hoxha eventually severed relations with the USSR and China, completing the international isolation of Albania. Under Hoxha, all religion was forbidden, and the notorious, 30,000-member secret service, the Sigurimi, became an intrusive force of state control.

On 11 December 1990, responding to student protests and growing public dissatisfaction, President Alia ended the Communist monopoly on power, opening the tiny Balkan country to political pluralism. With the legalization of organized political opposition, the Democratic Party of Albania became the first independent political party. Four more parties—the Republican Party, the Ecology Party, the Agrarian Party and an ethnic Greek party—and a human rights organization were registered during the first two months of 1991 and several more soon followed.

The opposition scored its first victory on 16 January 1991 when President Alia met demands of striking coal miners and postponed the country's first multi-party elections from 10 February to 31 March, thus allowing the new parties time to campaign. The government banned demonstrations unrelated to the elections on 1 March, but the ban was largely ignored and thousands of Albanians held daily demonstrations against the government. A hunger strike by 700 students and professors forced the government to drop Hoxha's name from Tirana University. Most protests were aimed against insufficient privatization measures and economic deterioration, police brutality and the Sigurimi.

More than 59 percent of Albania's voting population voted in the spring elections. The ruling Party of Labor won 169 of 250 seats while the Democratic Party led opposition parties with 75 seats. While the ruling party maintained control of the government and the power to choose the president, the Democratic Party gained enough seats to form a meaningful opposition. Although President Alia lost his seat in the legislative body to an unknown opposition candidate, the new Party of Labor-dominated parliament re-elected him president on 30 April.

The elections were not entirely free and fair. The ruling party benefited from a well-established infrastructure, control over police and security forces, and a monopoly on media access. The opposition also charged that on several occasions its members and candidates were harassed and intimidated by authorities. The Democratic Party protested that it had not been allowed to campaign in the rural areas, where over 60 percent of Albania's citizens live. The Communists also dominated the Central Election Commission and zonal polling commissions. Foreign observers were not permitted to monitor the election.

The election results caused outbreaks of violence in Albania's northern cities (Democratic Party strongholds) and in Tirana, the nation's capital. Applications for foreign visas rose immediately, as did illegal border crossings. On 2 April army units in Shkoder killed four protesters, including Democratic Party leader Arben Broxi, shot in the back while trying to calm anti-government demonstrators. As protests and violence escalated, the Democratic Party decided to boycott Parliament until those responsible for the Shkoder crimes were brought to trial. On 26 April the government issued a report on the role of the security forces in the killings, and seven officials were arrested.

In May a chrome miners' strike grew into a general strike, paralyzing public transportation and all major industries in the country. The strikers, organized by the newly formed Union of Free and Independent Trade Unions, demanded higher wages, an investigation of the Shkoder killings, the right to religious holidays, better conditions for working women, and an end to falling living standards.

The crippling fifteen-day general strike brought down the newly elected Communist cabinet on 4 June. The next day, President Alia named Ylli Bufi, an alternate member of the Party of Labor's Central Committee, to replace Fatos Nano as head of government and to form a new, non-partisan parliament. The twenty-four members of the new cabinet renounced their Party affiliations. Twelve had belonged to the Party of Labor (renamed the Socialist Party of Albania on 12 June), seven to the Democratic Party, and the rest to the Republican, Agrarian and Social Democratic parties. The new coalition parliament, the first non-Communist dominated government since 1944, was charged with running the country until new elections in 1992. The Democratic Party took control over economic issues; during the year the party's popularity eroded because of their failure to improve the food supply and halt a surge of unemployment that exceeded 30 percent. Inflation also hovered at 30 percent by the fall.

Economic instability, the removal of travel restrictions and a lack of trust in the government prompted thousands of Albanians to seek asylum in neighboring countries. Exodus to Greece began in late December 1990. Although most refugees came from the ethnic Greek enclave in southwest Albania, the Greek government, faced with its own economic problems, tried to prevent their entry. In early February 1991 would-be emigrants without travel documents rioted in Durres and other ports after police prevented them from boarding vessels bound for Italy. The Albanian government described the refugees flooding coastal cities and virtually paralyzing the ports as "economic migrants," ineligible for international legal protection given those fleeing political persecution. Clashes between police forces and refugees resulted in a number of casualties, and military rule was established in some ports to maintain order.

In August a ship carrying some 10,000 Albanians was blocked from docking by the Italian navy. Hundreds jumped overboard and swam to shore. Italy's refusal to admit more Albanians led to violent clashes between the police and refugees in the port of Bari. On 17 August Italian authorities began deporting Albanians airlifting emergency food supplies to Albania.

Unrest flared up in September, with thousands of demonstrators in Tirana calling for the resignation of Alia. In November 4,000 oil workers went on strike in the southern town of Ballsh. Industrial strikes involving tens of thousands of workers and a walkout of hundreds of independent radio and TV personnel continued through the month.

Throughout the year, the country's economy remained in shambles. Four decades of state-planned economy and debilitating isolation made Albania the poorest country in Europe. Unable to feed its people, the government sought international humanitarian aid. American military cargo planes began airlifting some 280,000 pounds of food supplies, much of it left over from the Gulf War.

In 1991 Albania took some steps towards privatization: the government lifted a twenty-year-old ban on foreign credits, loans and investments, reintroduced private farming, and abolished the State Planning Commission. The European Bank for Reconstruction and Development recommended that Albania become its forty-second member.

Albania has re-established diplomatic relations with the U.S. and other countries, and has sought to join the Commission on Security and Cooperation in Europe (CSCE) and the European Economic Community.

Political Rights and Civil Liberties:

In 1991 Albania held direct, multi-party elections based on the majority system for the 250-seat, unicameral People's Assembly. Irregularities and allegations of fraud marred the process. Albanians did not have a direct say in the presidential elections, as the Communist-dominated People's Assembly elected Ramiz Alia (he had lost his parliamentary seat).

Political parties, civic organizations, independent trade unions and student groups are able to organize freely. In 1991 the Democratic and Republican parties published Albania's first two independent newspapers, *Rilindja Demokratike* and *Republika.* On 30 April a transitional constitutional law placed radio, television and other official news media under parliamentary control. The state-media had previously reflected a pro-Communist bias, especially during the electoral campaign.

The state extended official recognition to political parties, a miners' union, and a human rights organization. However, it denied students the right to organize a union, and the minister of education closed Tirana University on 1 March in an effort to stifle the student movement. On 7 March Alia, responding to the coastal refugee crisis, banned all "abnormal gatherings of people" in Tirana, and in the ports of Durres, Vlora and Shengjin. In April the Internal Affairs Ministry began issuing passports to Albanians who had fled illegally.

On 5 January the government began freeing political prisoners. Agitation, attempting to defect, propaganda against the state and religious propaganda are no longer political crimes, and those convicted on such counts have been pardoned. But the government announced it would not free prisoners who were found guilty of terrorism, espionage, sabotage or subversion.

The opposition accused the government of using political unrest as an excuse to arrest opposition leaders. On 17 June the leading Albanian human rights activist, Arben Puto, asserted that Albanian prisons still held 100 political prisoners. The Forum for the Defense of Human Rights asked for a general amnesty for all Albanian prisoners, because they had no legal assistance during trials.

The issue of internal exiles remained a serious human rights concern. For decades, Albania subscribed to the principle of "objective responsibility," according to which an entire family could be punished for a crime committed by one of its members. Thousands were expelled from their houses and workplaces and resettled in remote villages. In 1991 these "internees" were freed to return to their place of origin, but lack of funds often made returning impossible.

The judicial system remains weak, not fully independent and reflects a lack of legal expertise (Hoxha banned legal practice in 1967). May 1990 laws lifted the twenty-three-year-old ban on religion, and the transitional constitutional law declared that the Albanian secular state observes "freedom of religious beliefs and creates conditions in which to exercise it." Churches and mosques—Albania is 70 percent Muslim, 20 percent Orthodox and 10 percent Catholic—are now open and can hold legal services. On 11 February workers formed the country's first independent trade union federation, the Confederation of Independent Trade Unions of Albania (BSPSh).

Algeria

Polity: Dominant party
Economy: Statist
Population: 26,000,000
PPP: $2,470
Life Expectancy: 65.1
Ethnic Groups: Arabs (75 percent), Berbers (25 percent)

Political Rights: 4
Civil Liberties: 4
Status: Partly Free

Overview:

In 1991, pro-Iraq demonstrations and violence between police and Islamic fundamentalists threatened to destabilize the government of President Chadli Benjedid and derail Algeria's trail-blazing democratic experiment. But as the year came to a close, Algeria held the first part of a scheduled two-round elections.

As 1991 began, domestic events, such as sectarian violence between Christians and Muslims, were quickly overshadowed by the start of the Gulf War in mid-January, when tens of thousands of people and parties of virtually all political affiliations took to the streets to express support for Iraq. As the Paris International Broadcast Service reported: "From the Islamic fundamentalists of the Islamic Salvation Front to the democrats of the Socialist Forces Front and the Rally for Culture and Democracy...there has not been a single discordant note in Algerian political state-ments. They are unanimous in supporting Iraq and Saddam." Many of Algeria's forty political parties formed the National Committee for Support of the Iraqi People, an anti-American umbrella group which expressed support for Iraq and the Palestinians.

In anticipation of violence surrounding pro-Iraqi demonstrations, security around the country was tightened, and forces surrounded the U.S. embassy. In February, demonstrators in Algiers stoned the U.N. office and burned the U.N. flag as police dispersed them with tear gas. Protestors also targeted Algeria's former colonial power: the French news agency was bombed, a French teacher beaten, the French consulate sacked and the Air France Office torched.

After initially condemning Iraq's invasion of Kuwait, President Benjedid's National Liberation Front (FLN) government publicly assailed the American-led offensive against Iraq and "U.S. domination of the U.N." in response to pro-Iraq fervor. In addition, Algeria sent two medical teams and six tons of medical supplies to Iraq. Algerian officials privately told Western diplomats they had to support Iraq or the pro-Iraq movement would destabilize the government and result in an Islamic fundamentalist victory in upcoming national elections.

The Islamic Salvation Front (FIS), the nation's leading fundamentalist party and the most popular opposition group, rejected the government's moderate stance and called for direct military support for Iraq. FIS leaders also demanded President Benjedid's resignation and the immediate conversion of Algeria into an Islamic state. The FIS announced that if it won in the national elections, it would commit itself to the implementation of Islamic law and prosecute former government officials.

During the Gulf War, President Benjedid postponed elections for June, hoping that the pro-Iraq and Islamic fervor would subside. The government and democratic forces seemed to agree on putting off the elections, since neither of them would have benefited from having them in the midst of such strong Islamic sentiment.

After the Gulf War, Algeria began preparation for national elections, announced for 27 June. But Algeria's eight major opposition parties protested the election rules and called for a general strike. There was intense jostling in April and alliance-building among Algeria's political groupings and continued protest of the election rules. On 26 May 20,000 people marching on the president's office were met by road blocks and riot police. The next day, 100,000 people marched down the city center.

As the campaign season opened on 1 June the FIS expanded its demands to include the resignation of President Chadli and the establishment of an Islamic state. On 4 June a demonstration involving tens of thousands of people exploded into violence between police and fundamentalists, leaving at least seven people dead, including a police officer.

President Benjedid immediately declared a state of emergency, sent tanks and troops into the capital, postponed the elections again, and dismissed Prime Minister Mouloud Hamrouche's government. The violence continued until early July and resulted in a reported 60 deaths and over 2,000 arrests.

On 1 July the two leaders of the FIS, philosophy teacher Abassi Madani and his deputy, clergyman Ali Belhadj, were arrested and charged with seven crimes, including inciting the citizens to take up arms against the state, setting up unauthorized armed forces, and kidnapping and torturing security force members. The army insisted that the men be tried in military court, while Algerian human rights groups maintained the jurisdiction belonged to civilian courts.

President Benjedid quickly consulted with the leaders of major non-fundamentalist opposition parties on the formation of a new government. He appointed as prime minister former Foreign Minister Sid Ahmed Ghozali, a known reformer without strong ties to the ruling FLN. The prime minister subsequently named a reformist cabinet which included two women.

The government then invited all opposition parties, including the FIS, to participate in a forum held 30 July on what to do next, namely how to reform the electoral law, the opposition's main grievance. The FIS did not attend, however, as the conditions it put forth—the lifting of the state-of-siege and the release of its eight leaders—were not met before the forum. The jailed FIS leaders began a hunger strike, demanding the formation of an independent commission to investigate the events surrounding their arrests.

Throughout the summer President Benjedid, the National Assembly and opposition groups haggled inconclusively over election rules while the FIS boycotted negotiations demanding the release of their leaders from prison. By the end of September the government lifted a four-month state of emergency which had severely curtailed political activity, but the standoff over election rules continued.

At issue were the number of seats in parliament and the practice of proxy voting. Approved by the parliament, proxy voting would allow husbands to vote for their wives. Opposed by President Benjedid and Prime Minister Ghozali, the issue of proxy voting was referred to the Constitutional Council, a body set up in 1989 to review laws passed by parliament, which—to the dismay not only of FLN old-guard but also the FIS—vetoed Parliament's decision.

In late October President Benjedid announced an election date of 26 December. During the pre-election period political parties demonstrated and campaigned openly, but economic hardship plagued Algeria as the election date neared. Out of a work force of 5 million, 1.5 million Algerians are unemployed, and an estimated 200,000 are added to their ranks each year. The government's price-freeing economic reform program provoked strikes protesting deteriorating buying power. Fearing political fallout reminiscent of 1988 food riots, the government struggled to make up a $2.5 billion shortfall, restore public faith in the economic reform program, and boost living standards.

On 26 December, Algeria held a parliamentary election, with 49 parties and 5,712 candidates. The FIS won a landslide victory, taking 189 out of the 430 seats in only the first round of voting, in which 58 percent of Algerians cast ballots. The FLN won 15 seats, while the Socialist Forces Front (FFS) took 25 places. In anticipation of winning the additional 27 seats needed for a majority in the second round of voting scheduled for 15 January 1992, the FIS called for implementing *shar'ia,* or Islamic law, while proposing to respect democratic rights. FIS leaders proposed to ban the consumption of alcohol, impose segregation of males and females in schools, and force women to wear the veil. The FLN and other secular parties implored Algerians not to vote for the FIS in the second round and accused the fundamentalists of manipulating the vote. Some groups suggested calling off the second round of elections. Algerians, traditionally western, and with close ties to Europe, reportedly voted for the FIS simply to bring down the ruling FLN, which they view as corrupt and incompetent.

Political Rights and Civil Liberties:

In 1991 the right of the Algerian people to choose their government by democratic means was tested on the national level. Algeria's fragile democratic experiment began in 1988 after food riots and a government crackdown killed over 500 students. Mounting domestic political opposition forced the ruling FLN to put forth a sweeping liberalization plan. In June 1990 free and fair local elections produced resounding victories for the leading Islamic fundamentalist opposition party, the FIS.

With a few notable exceptions, Algerians are free to exercise rights of speech, press, association and assembly. But during a state of emergency which lasted from June to the end of September, these rights, in addition to guarantees for a fair trial, were suspended. During the emergency, military tribunals were set up, and security forces given special powers of search and detention. Over 2,000 people were arrested in demonstrations and the leaders of the leading Islamic fundamentalist party remain in prison.

Algerian law limits pre-arraignment detention for questioning a suspect to forty-eight hours, after which the suspect must be charged or released. Accused persons held in detention have access to their lawyers at any time. Free legal counsel to defendants who cannot afford lawyers is provided by the Algerian Bar Association.

All political parties can freely publish their own periodicals and set up media stations, and millions of Algerians receive CNN and European television via satellite. While a new press code outlaws spreading false information, threatening state security or public unity, and insulting Islam, criticism of the government has been met with relatively little interference (except during the state of emergency). However, the FIS newspapers have been banned since August 1991 and the press code requires that all publications be written in Arabic, unless special permission is granted to use other languages. Some foreign publications, such as the Paris-based *Jeune Afrique* are also banned.

The FLN has loosened its grip over most associations and professionals, including the FLN-related General Union of Algerian Workers (UGTA), which can now represent union members with greater independence. Although the UGTA is still the only legal labor organization, at least two new professionals' unions have formed with tacit government acceptance. The right to strike is guaranteed by the new constitution, yet reportedly strikers have occasionally been arrested on charges of "disturbing the right to work" of other workers.

Islam is the official religion, as established under the constitution, but there are no Islamic courts, and the tiny Christian and Jewish communities are allowed to freely practice their faith. With the rise of Islamic activism, harassment and discrimination against women has reportedly increased. Women cannot obtain a divorce and are considered to be under the guardianship of their husbands, fathers or brothers; physical abuse of women is for the most part culturally acceptable. Following its victory in the first round of elections, the FIS proposed to fully Islamicize Algerian society.

Algerians are free to travel within the country, although traveling abroad is made difficult by strict currency controls.

Angola

Polity: Transitional
Economy: Statist
Population: 8,500,000
PPP: $840
Life Expectancy: 45.5
Ethnic Groups: Ovimbundu (37 percent), Kimbundu (25 percent), Kongo (13 percent), mulatto (2 percent), European (1 percent)

Political Rights: 6
Civil Liberties: 4
Status: Partly Free

Overview:

On 31 May 1991 the ruling Popular Movement for the Liberation of Angola (MPLA) government and the opposition National Union for the Total Independence of Angola (UNITA) signed an accord intended to finally end Angola's sixteen year civil war. Initialed in Lisbon, Portugal, the peace accord calls for multi-party elections by the last quarter of 1992. As 1991 neared its end the MPLA and UNITA were generally adher-ing to the peace accord's provisions and the cease-fire between the two groups was still holding with only sporadic exception. Meanwhile, in another important development, the ruling MPLA officially abandoned Marxism-Leninism as its official ideology in April, positioning itself as a social democratic party for the upcoming elections.

A former Portuguese colony located on the Atlantic coast of southwest Africa, Angola gained independence in 1975 after fourteen years of guerrilla war led by the three principal independence movements: Holden Roberto's National Front for the Liberation of Angola (FNLA), operating primarily in the north among the Bakongo people and militarily moribund since the late seventies; the Marxist-Leninist, Soviet-backed MPLA, headed by the poet Agostinho Neto, and dominant in and around the capital of Luanda in a region largely populated by the Kimbundu; and UNITA, led by Dr. Jonas Savimbi and most active in the central highlands among the Ovimbundu.

Since the departure of the Portuguese, the MPLA regime, headquartered in Luanda, has obtained widespread international recognition as the *de jure* government of Angola. The current president of the republic is Jose Eduardo dos Santos; in mid-1991, Fernando Franca Van-Dunem was appointed by the president to serve as prime minister during the transition leading up to multi-party elections. Though UNITA now concedes legitimacy to the MPLA's People's Republic of Angola, until 1991 the rebel movement sustained a guerrilla war against the Luanda regime and operated as the sole *de facto* authority within the southeastern one-third of the country.

The independent history of Angola began after the Portuguese commissioner left the country on 10 November 1975. The MPLA, which controlled the environs of Luanda, immediately declared its People's Republic. Two weeks later, the associated FNLA-UNITA forces, which then controlled much of the rest of the country, announced the creation of a republic based in the city of Huambo and began an ultimately unsuccessful military drive on the capital. Before the year was up, pursuant to its "internationalist duty" and courtesy of a Soviet airlift, Cuba had dispatched 20,000 troops to Angola to buttress the MPLA regime. Over the next several years, the Cuban presence grew to over 50,000. With the virtual elimination of the FNLA by 1979, Savimbi's UNITA forces, sustained in part by millions of dollars in U.S. aid and the occasional help of South African forces, waged guerrilla war against the MPLA government in Luanda.

The MPLA party congress in December of 1990 approved constitutional reforms legalizing opposition political parties, allowing free expression, and permitting direct election of the president. The party also endorsed the turn towards a market economy. However, peace talks at the end of 1990 reached an impasse when the MPLA demanded that UNITA lay down its arms before being recognized as a legal political party.

The May peace accord provided for a permanent cease-fire supervised by MPLA and UNITA representatives with international observers. The landmark agreement also called for multi-party elections to be held in September 1992, the creation of a neutral police force monitored by United Nations observers, and the cessation of military assistance by Soviet and American governments to their respective clients. In addition, the accord calls for the concentration of MPLA and UNITA troops in specified areas outside of population centers and their merger into a single national armed force.

Because the newly integrated armed forces are to be made up of 40,000 troops, the vast majority of the MPLA/UNITA combined forces of 125,000 are to be demobilized. With the large number of guns circulating in the country, there is widespread concern over the possibility that demobilized soldiers and guerrillas may take up banditry if unable to succeed as civilians.

Although the MPLA formally legalized the creation of other political parties, Angola will remain a one-party state until the multi-party elections because of President dos Santos's exclusion of other political parties in the transitional government. The impact of this arrangement on the outcome of the 1992 elections will be compounded by the MPLA's control over foreign assistance—and, thus, substantial patronage—to Angola during the critical period leading up to the election. Meanwhile, the MPLA-controlled People's Assembly has forbidden political parties from accepting foreign financial aid, required that party headquarters be in Luanda, and ruled that party leaders must be physically present within Angola during the six month period leading up to the election in 1992. Such unilateral directives seem to be designed to constrain the organizing activity of the opposition; the MPLA is clearly using its monopoly on power for partisan advantage.

The political opening created by the peace accord has permitted exiled and unarmed internal political forces, the so-called "third force" parties, to enter Angolan public life and prepare for elections. To date, apart from the MPLA and UNITA, parties expected to compete in the September 1992 polling include the reviving FNLA and the strongly emerging Democratic Renovation Party. Most joined together to form the National Opposition Council alliance in late October 1991. All announced parties have demanded a voice in the transition process, and many have called for a sovereign national conference to create a broad-based interim government. In November 1991, the Angolan government proposed a non-sovereign conference to set up electoral mechanisms for 1992.

UNITA has dismissed the third force parties as MPLA fronts, denounced any sovereign national conference as a "civilian coup d'état," refused to participate in the non-sovereign conference, and said it prefers to rely on its bilateral transition agreement with the MPLA. UNITA, whose lengthy armed struggle prevented the MPLA from completely monopolizing power in Angola, remains expressly confident of victory in the up-coming election.

As 1991 wore on the primary difficulty in satisfying the terms of the accord was gathering the soldiers of both sides to the conflict in pre-determined assembly points as quickly as required. Adequate food for all the troops expected to assemble was reportedly in question. The delay was in turn said to be delaying the formation of the integrated national armed forces. Both the MPLA and UNITA charged each other with stalling the release of political prisoners, and the government showed signs of wavering on the September 1992 date for elections. UNITA ended its long absence in Luanda by establishing a headquarters there.

The political transition will be complicated by an Angolan economy in ruins. The civil war resulted in over 500,000 deaths, and over 1 million people were internally displaced. The country has a foreign debt of some $650 million. Managers and technicians are desperately lacking and economic output low due to the effects of war and the creation of poorly managed state-owned farms and industries, but the closing of inefficient state enterprises will result in unemployment for an estimated 20 percent of the adult population. The government has made some recent moves in the direction of privatization and deregulation. The International Monetary Fund and the World Bank have been assisting attempts at restructuring. Less than 10 percent of the rail system is currently operational, in part a consequence of UNITA sabotage during the war. Because of Angola's dependence on oil for 95 percent of its foreign exchange earnings, rising oil prices due to the Gulf Crisis make short-term economic prospects for Angola somewhat brighter. The country also has rich but largely unexploited deposits of iron ore and diamonds.

A drought continues to afflict wide portions of the country with famine, exacerbating the dislocation and deprivation already suffered by the population as a consequence of the civil war. International relief efforts began in 1991 in an atmosphere of uncertainty as UNITA and the government each expected that the other would use the humanitarian assistance to resupply its own combatants and supporters.

Political Rights and Civil Liberties:

Angolans have not yet been given the opportunity to democratically change their government, but the 1991 peace accord provides for multi-party elections by the end of 1992. Following the end to an MPLA ban on other political parties, several parties registered and began organizing for the upcoming elections.

Angola's sixteen year civil war led to persistent reports of political killings, torture, and disappearances perpetrated by government forces and by UNITA. The MPLA security police still reportedly operate with advisors formerly associated with the disbanded East German Stasi. In the past, suspects in political cases have been held by the government without charge for up to three months. The judiciary has not been independent of MPLA control since independence, and it is still too early to determine whether or not new legislation will guarantee that the courts meet internationally recognized standards of fairness and impartiality in the future. However, during the course of 1991 the National Assembly abolished capital punishment, formally established judicial independence and the right of *habeas corpus,* guaranteed trade union independence, and gave legal assurance of the right to assembly. The government also granted an amnesty for all political crimes committed against the regime before the 31 May signing of the peace accord.

In the past citizens and dissidents in a given part of Angola could not express contrary views freely without risking persecution by the armed movement in power in that region. With rare exceptions the government-controlled press reflects official MPLA policy, while UNITA media reflects that movement's own official policy. The president has stated that the government has no intention of privatizing the broadcast media, despite movement toward a mixed economy. The government has announced that it intends to return former church properties that were expropriated. Until 1991 workers could not form independent trade unions and had to be members of the MPLA-controlled National Union of Angolan Workers.

Antigua and Barbuda

Polity: Dominant party
Economy: Capitalist-statist
Population: 100,000
PPP: na
Life Expectancy: 72.0
Ethnic Groups: Black (89 percent), other (11 percent)

Political Rights: 3
Civil Liberties: 3
Status: Partly Free

Overview:

The government of eighty-two-year-old Prime Minister Vere Bird struggled to recover from the 1990 scandal involving the transshipment of Israeli arms through Antigua to Colombian drug lords. Opposition parties and civic groups stepped up demands for the government to comply with the recommendations for political reform made by a distinguished British jurist whose report implicated high government officials in the arms deals.

Antigua and Barbuda is a member of the British Commonwealth. The British monarchy is represented by a governor-general who acts as ceremonial head of state, but the islands became self-governing in 1969 and gained independence in 1981. Formally a parliamentary democracy, Antigua and Barbuda has been dominated by Prime Minister Bird's Antiguan Labour Party (ALP) for nearly two decades.

In a 1989 general election free of violence but marred by irregularities and fraud, the ALP maintained almost complete dominance of the parliament, capturing fifteen of the sixteen seats it held in the House. The opposition United National Democratic Party (UNDP) won one seat and the Barbuda People's Movement (BPM) won the Barbuda seat. Also competing were the leftist Antigua Caribbean Liberation Movement (ACLM), the Barbuda National Party (BNP) and the Barbuda Independent Movement (BIM). In separate elections two weeks later, the BPM took all five Barbuda Council seats.

As in previous elections, the opposition charged that the ALP exerts undue influence over the nominally independent electoral supervisor and uses bribery and intimidation at polling time. In response to a petition filed by UNDP, a high court annulled the results in one constituency. Before it could rule on six other contested constituencies, ALP parliament members holding the contested seats resigned, the government announced by-elections, and the ALP named a new election supervisor. The UNDP boycotted the by-elections, stating that they would not participate until reforms were made in the electoral system.

In the aftermath of the 1989 elections, the ruling ALP confronted a looming succession crisis as Vere Bird Jr. and Lester Bird competed for the party mantle held for decades by their now ailing father, with Papa Bird favoring Bird Jr. The rivalry became a full-scale clash with the outbreak of the Israeli arms scandal in 1990.

The brouhaha began in April 1990 when the government of Colombia publicly protested that Israeli arms had been sold to the Antiguan government and shipped to the Medellin drug cartel in Colombia with the knowledge of Bird Jr., the minister of Public Works and Communication and national security advisor. Bird Jr. denied the allegation, but his brother Lester, the deputy prime minister and foreign minister, convinced his father to allow an independent judicial inquiry.

A commission of inquiry headed by prominent British jurist, Louis Blom-Cooper, began its investigation in June and issued a report in November 1990 which implicated Bird Jr. and Lt. Col. Clyde Walker, the chief of the ninety-member Antiguan Defense Force. The report concluded that the country faced being "engulfed in corruption" and had fallen victim to "persons who use political power as a passport to private profit."

The prime minister tried unsuccessfully to defuse opposition calls for his resignation by agreeing to dismiss Walker and ban Bird Jr. from politics for life. His stalling on the reform recommendations by Blom-Cooper—including administrative reforms, anti-corruption legislation, and the establishment of a government ombudsman office— led to the resignation of Lester Bird and other key cabinet officials in March 1991. Lester then joined in a series of large demonstrations organized by opposition parties, churches and civic groups to demand compliance with the Blom-Cooper report.

The government responded by passing a limited anti-corruption bill in parliament, but the legislation failed to quell mounting protests. With the added pressure caused by a three-year economic downturn, Prime Minister Bird finally asked his son Lester to return to the cabinet. Lester accepted, saying he had been given a mandate to "devise and lead a political and economic recovery program." Opposition parties seemed temporarily placated by the move, but warned of renewed protests unless serious governmental reform was undertaken. The next national elections are constitutionally due by 1994.

Political Rights and Civil Liberties:

Technically, citizens are able to change their government by democratic means, but elections are tainted by serious irregularities and undue influence exerted by the ruling party on the electoral authorities.

The political system is parliamentary, consisting of a seventeen-member House of Representatives elected for five years and an appointed Senate. In the House of Representatives, there are sixteen seats for Antigua and one for Barbuda. Eleven senators are appointed by the prime minister, four by the parliamentary opposition leader, one by the Barbuda Council and one by the governor general. Barbuda has achieved limited self-government through the separately elected Barbuda Council. Political parties, labor unions and civic organizations are free to organize and express themselves and an independent Industrial Court mediates labor disputes between unions and the government. The free exercise of religion is respected.

The judiciary is relatively independent, with further recourse available through an inter-island court of appeals for Antigua and five other small former British colonies in the Lesser Antilles. There are no political prisoners.

Newspapers are associated with political parties and include the outspoken leftist weekly, *Outlook*. Some have been subject to systematic legal harassment by members of the ruling ALP. Radio and television are either owned by the state or members of the Bird family; the opposition charges both with favoritism. Such charges were lent weight in 1990 as the Antigua Broadcasting Service declined to provide live coverage of the arms scandal inquiry, despite the approval of the jurist heading the investigation. Upon returning to the cabinet in September 1991, Lester Bird said that government-run media would be revamped and opened to all points of view.

Argentina

Polity: Presidential-legislative democracy
Economy: Capitalist
Population: 32,700,000
PPP: $4,360
Life Expectancy: 71.0
Ethnic Groups: Europeans (mostly Spanish and Italian), Mestizos, Indians, Arabs

Political Rights: 1
Civil Liberties: 3
Status: Free

Overview:

President Carlos Menem overcame a series of government corruption scandals as the Peronist party made advances in the 1991 midterm elections, primarily on the strength of the government's success in cutting inflation. However, Menem's tendency to rule by decree to bypass congressional opposition, including factions within his own party, resulted in widespread criticism that he was governing undemocratically.

The Argentine Republic was proclaimed upon achieving independence from Spain in 1816. A federal constitution was drafted in 1853. In this century, democratic governance was frequently interrupted by military takeovers. The end of the dictatorship of Juan Peron (1946-55) led to a period of instability marked by left-wing violence and repressive military rule. After the military's defeat by the British in the 1982 Falkland/Malvinas war, Argentina returned to civilian and democratic government in December 1983.

In 1983 most of the constitutional structure of 1853 was restored. The president and vice-president are designated for six-year terms by a 600-member electoral college. The electoral college is chosen on the basis of proportional representation, with each of the twenty-three provinces as well as the federal district of Buenos Aires having twice as many electors as the combined number of senators and deputies. The legislature consists of a 254-member Chamber of Deputies directly elected for six years, with half the seats renewable every three years, and a forty-six-member Senate nominated by the legislatures of each of the twenty-three provinces for nine-year terms, with one-third of the seats renewable every three years. Provincial and municipal governments are elected.

In the 1983 election, the moderate-left Radical Civic Union (UCR) won a decisive victory over the Peronist Justicialist Nationalist Movement (MNJ) and President Raul Alfonsin was inaugurated in December 1983. Following the prosecution of former military leaders for human rights abuses during the "dirty war" against leftist guerrillas, the Alfonsin administration was buffeted by three military rebellions led by the hard-line *carapintada* (painted face) faction of the army.

In primary elections held in 1988 the UCR nominated Eduardo Angeloz for president, and the Peronists selected Menem. On 14 May 1989, amid Argentina's worst economic crisis ever, Menem won the presidency with 49 percent of the vote and the Peronists secured a working majority in the legislature. President Menem was inaugurated in July 1989, the first time in 61 years that one democratically elected civilian had succeeded another.

Menem campaigned as a populist in the traditional Peronist manner, but upon taking office he stunned followers by initiating a market-based economic reform program. By February 1991, however, the program had collapsed, inflation had soared to 28 percent a month, and Menem was swamped by corruption scandals involving government officials and members of his family. Menem turned the tide with a new stabilization plan that cut inflation to less than two percent a month by the start of mid-term elections in August. In the elections, held over the course of four months, voters proved to be more concerned with economic security than political scandals, and the Peronists retained a working majority in the Congress.

However, with the Peronists divided over his program to dismantle Argentina's statist economy, Menem increasingly resorted to implementing policy by decree. In October 1991 he swept away dozens of rules and restrictions in a massive economic deregulation. The decree, praised by economists, did not require prior congressional approval. But it was harshly criticized by the media and legislators, including Peronists, who charged Menem with ruling undemocratically. Menem's response: "I prefer to be authoritarian with public support rather than democratic with the support of 20 percent."

Menem also has relied on presidential powers to pardon 280 officers and civilians accused of corruption and human rights violations—including eighteen generals, admirals, and former junta members convicted in 1984—a clear attempt to placate the restive military. After the armed forces high command put down a fourth *carapintada* mutiny in December 1990, the chances of a military coup appeared greatly reduced. Since 1983 there has been little civilian support for military rule, as there had been during previous economic crises, although Menem's decree returning responsibility for internal security to the military in the wake of food riots in 1990 met with only mild disapproval. Also, government efforts to reduce the military budget generally have been applauded.

Emboldened by his political revival in the second half of 1991, Menem started talking about constitutional reform to allow for presidential reelection. However, if his economic reform falters or fails to deliver the promised rewards, Argentina's notoriously volatile public opinion could quickly turn against him once again.

Political Rights and Civil Liberties:

Citizens are able to change their government through free and fair elections. Constitutional guarantees regarding right to organize political parties, civic organizations and labor unions are generally respected. However, the constitutional separation of powers has been undermined by President Menem's growing tendency to rule by decree. The political landscape is dominated by two parties, but there are dozens of other parties, from Communist and Trotskyist on the left to fascist on the right.

The nation's Catholic majority enjoys freedom of religious expression. However, the Jewish community, numbering around 350,000, was targeted in 1991 by a wave of anti-Semitic vandalism. The community also was alarmed by the emergence of the National Workers Party (PNT), an avowed Nazi organization founded in 1990 by a former Peronist. However, the Menem administration curtailed PNT activities, using the 1988 law which prescribes prison sentences for racial or religious discrimination, and won praise from Jewish leaders for its efforts against anti-Semitism.

Newspapers are privately owned, vocal and uncensored. There are numerous independent dailies reflecting various points of view. Television and radio broadcasting are both private and public. In 1991, there were an increasing number of incidents of media intimidation by security forces and shadowy groups apparently linked to orthodox Peronist factions. Those most frequently targeted were journalists and publications investigating government corruption. Buenos Aires-based international media covering corruption stories received threats in July from the previously unheard-of Peronist Moralization Commando.

Labor is well organized and politically strong. The nation's 3 million organized workers are dominated by the Peronist General Confederation of Labor (CGT). But union influence has diminished in recent years because of corruption scandals, internal divisions, and restrictions on public sector strikes decreed by Menem.

During the urban food riots in 1989-90, over a dozen deaths and over 1,000 arrests were reported during the government crackdown. In 1991, amid labor strife and a mounting crime wave, human rights groups reported an increase in incidents of illegal arrests and searches, and violent intimidation by police and security forces.

The human rights community is well organized and consists of numerous organizations dating back to the 1970s. These groups played an influential role in the prosecution of military officers during the Alfonsin administration. However, after condemning Menem's pardoning of officers convicted for human rights violations, rights groups have received anonymous threats, and on at least four occasions in 1991 activists' offices were sacked by unidentified raiders and documentation stolen. In a further act of intimidation, the chairwoman of the Mothers of the Plaza del Mayo, the country's most prominent rights organization, was charged in federal court with breaking a law that forbids insulting the president.

The judiciary is an independent body headed by a nine-member Supreme Court. There are also federal appeals courts and provincial courts. The judicial system proved effective in handling the numerous human rights and criminal cases brought against military officers and former leftist guerrilla leaders during the Alfonsin administration. In general, however, it remains weak, inefficient, overpoliticized (Menem overrrode the legislature to pack the Supreme Court in 1990), and undermined by the corruption which is endemic to all branches of the government.

Australia

Polity: Federal parliamentary democracy
Economy: Capitalist
Population: 17,500,000
PPP: $14,530
Life Expectancy: 76.5
Ethnic Groups: European (95 percent), Asian (4 percent), aborigines (1 percent)

Political Rights: 1
Civil Liberties: 1
Status: Free

Overview:
 Taking advantage of a slumping economy, Paul Keating became prime minister of Australia in December 1991 after ousting Robert Hawke through a no-confidence vote. The ruling Australian Labor Party (ALP) also faced criticism for its natural resource and environmental policies.

Claimed by British Captain James Cook for the Crown in 1770, Australia became self governing in 1901. The country's economic and foreign policy began a shift towards its Asian neighbors in the 1970s, and the government officially abandoned a "White Australia" immigration policy in 1973. The Labor Party has won four consecutive national election victories since 1983.

Treasurer Paul Keating launched his first challenge to Hawke's leadership on 30 May 1991 when he announced that in November 1988 the prime minister had secretly agreed to retire some time after the 1990 election. The controversy prompted a no-confidence vote in Parliament in June, which Hawke won by a vote of 66-44. Emboldened by the victory, Hawke announced that he would run again in the next election, due by March 1993. In addition to the divisive vote, however, Hawke's party faced an ongoing Royal Commission investigation into alleged corruption in three of the five state governments under its control. With unemployment at 10.5 percent, Labor's MPs voted 56-51 on 19 December to replace Hawke with Keating.

The government dealt a major blow to the mining industry on 18 June when it placed a ban on prospecting at a sacred Jawoyn Aboriginal site in the Northern Territory. Hawke reasoned that "the Jawoyn have said 'no' and mean 'no.'" However, the Jawoyn themselves were divided over the mining, which would bring them jobs and revenue. The industry anticipated the mining project would add $50 million per year to the economy, and saw the refusal as a precedent which could lead to a loss of investor confidence in the country.

The government further angered the mining industry (responsible for almost half the country's exports) by vetoing an attempt to permit more than three uranium mines to operate in Australia. Despite the controversy, the ALP barely discussed uranium mining at its party conference in June, and Hawke angered the party's conservative wing and business supporters by breaking a promise to speak out against mining restrictions. Hawke also angered environmentalists by promising to set aside certain old growth forest areas for industrial logging in order to cut a trade deficit in paper products.

The mining and environmental controversies came in the wake of a major economic reform program announced in March 1991 designed to help the manufacturing sector, promote investments in certain natural resources projects, and lower consumer prices. The government plans to reduce protective tariffs from the current 10-15 percent down to 5 percent between 1993 and 1996. These measures are in response to Australia's deepest recession in over fifty years.

A Royal Commission report released on 9 May highlighted the unequal treatment of Australia's Aboriginal minority in the nation's criminal justice system. The four-year study indicated that although government spending on Aboriginal matters had increased significantly since the early 1970s, the Aborigines still remain the country's most disadvantaged group. In a sample year Aborigines were incarcerated at a rate of over fourteen times that of the general population, often for minor offenses, and once in jail were more likely to commit suicide or be killed by guards then their non-

Aboriginal counterparts. In 1989 the government established the Aboriginal and Torres Straits Islander Commission, designed to give Aborigines greater discretion in managing their affairs on a regional and national basis.

Australia's biggest concerns abroad were with two of its larger trading partners, the United States and Malaysia. Relations with the latter have been strained since 1986, when Prime Minister Hawke called the hanging of two Australians in Malaysia on drug charges a "barbaric act." On 23 July 1991 Foreign Minister Gareth Evans met with Malaysian Prime Minister Mahathir Mohamad out of concern that Australia's trade with Malaysia and its political allies would suffer because of souring relations. United States wheat sales to traditional Australian markets such as Yemen angered Australian exporters and led to harsh press criticism of American and European agricultural export subsidies.

Australia's federal parliament consists of a 76-member Senate and a 148-member House of Representatives, with the prime minister and the cabinet responsible to the House. In the House, the ALP holds 78 seats, the Liberal-National coalition holds 69, and an independent holds one. In July 1990, the government proposed a streamlining of the federal system because of charges that the present arrangement results in an unnecessary duplication of functions between the federal government, the six state governments, and the governments of the Northern Territory and the Australian Capital Territory of Canberra. In 1991 the government called for a debate on leaving the British Commonwealth by 2001 in light of the country's independent foreign policy and growing trade ties with Asia. The proposed move, which would end Queen Elizabeth's role as the ceremonial head of state, has aroused heated passions, and in July an entertainer and a radio broadcaster broke out into a brawl while discussing it on live national television.

Political Rights and Civil Liberties:

Australians can change their government democratically, suffrage is universal and there is a fine for not voting. Although the Australian constitution does not contain a formal bill of rights, fundamental freedoms are respected in theory and practice and there is an independent judiciary. Freedoms of speech and of press are respected and protected, although there is growing concern over the limited concentration of media ownership. A leading newspaper group and two television networks have been forced into bankruptcy and two competing businessmen, Kerry Packer and Rupert Murdoch, own a large share of the private media.

Complete freedom of religion exists, and during the Persian Gulf crisis Prime Minister Hawke issued a strong statement asking Australians not to harass the country's Arab and Muslim populations. Workers' rights are advocated by over 300 active trade unions. Legislation passed in the 1980s prohibits gender discrimination and calls for equal employment opportunities for women.

Austria

Polity: Federal parliamentary democracy
Economy: Mixed capitalist
Population: 7,700,000
PPP: $12,350
Life Expectancy: 74.8
Ethnic Groups: Austro-German (97 percent), Slovenian and Eastern European immigrant and refugee groups

Political Rights: 1
Civil Liberties: 1
Status: Free

Overview:

Major news stories in Austria in 1991 concerned the forthcoming retirement of President Kurt Waldheim, controversy over pro-Nazi statements by a provincial governor, Chancellor Franz Vranitzky's statement on Austrian responsibility for Nazi crimes, and the country's new role in Europe.

1991 was the first full year of the latest coalition government run by the Social Democratic Party (SPO), which was called the Socialist Party until 1991, and the Christian Democratic Austrian People's Party (OVP). In the general election in October 1990, the senior partner in the ruling coalition, the SPO, won 43 percent of the vote. Its junior partner, the more conservative OVP, garnered only 32 percent, losing 17 seats in the lower house. Picking up conservative votes, the right-wing populist Freedom Party took 17 percent of the vote and 33 seats, a gain of 15 seats. The environmentalist Greens attracted 4.5 percent and won 9 seats, a gain of one.

The Republic of Austria was founded in 1918 after the defeat of its predecessor, the Austro-Hungarian Empire, in World War I. Austrian independence ended in 1938 when Nazi Germany annexed its territory. After Germany's defeat in World War II, the Republic of Austria was reborn in 1945, but the Western Allies and the Soviet Union occupied the country until 1955 when they signed the Austrian State Treaty, guaranteeing Austrian neutrality and restoring its national sovereignty.

The Austrian head of state is President Kurt Waldheim, who was elected directly for a six-year term in 1986. The president belongs to the People's Party, but his position is primarily ceremonial. He appoints the chancellor, the government's chief executive, whose party or coalition commands majority support in the National Council, the 183-member lower house of parliament. Its members are elected directly for four-year terms. The upper house is the 63-member Federal Council, which the provincial assemblies choose by proportional representation. Federal Council members have four- to six-year terms, depending on the term of their respective provincial assemblies. The chancellor is Social Democrat Franz Vranitzky, who took office in 1986. Following inconclusive National Council elections in 1986, the SPO began a grand coalition government with the OVP. Following the People's Party's disappointing performance in the 1990 election, the Socialists announced their willingness to renew the coalition in order to keep the Freedom Party out of government.

In 1990 Joerg Haider, the Freedom Party leader, gave controversial campaign speeches against Austrian neutrality and the growing number of immigrants. Haider tried to appeal to the growing sentiment against foreigners in Austria, and to revive nationalism. He had shocked the SPO in 1989 by winning the provincial election in Carinthia and forming a coalition with the local People's Party.

Haider's views forced him from office in 1991 when he gave a speech endorsing the Nazis' labor policies. National leaders of both major parties condemned his comments, and the local OVP withdrew from its coalition with Haider's Freedom Party, causing Haider to lose a confidence vote in the provincial legislature.

The Freedom Party made significant gains in local and regional elections in 1991. It tripled its share of the vote in the provinces of Styria and Upper Austria. In the Viennese municipal election, the party more than doubled its portion of the vote and surpassed the OVP to become the second largest party in the city. Voters responded favorably to the party's anti-immigrant stance.

Austria's international reputation has been damaged by allegations concerning President Waldheim's activities during the Nazi period. Consequently, most political leaders were pleased when Waldheim announced in June 1991 that he would not be a presidential candidate in the 1992 election.

Realizing that the Waldheim case and the Haider controversy had undermined Austria's liberal democratic image, Chancellor Vranitzky declared in July 1991 that Austria must accept a share of moral responsibility for the sins of the Third Reich. This statement represented a break from the more popular Austrian view that Austrians had been Hitler's first victims and were therefore absolved of guilt.

Since the collapse of communism in Eastern Europe in 1989, Austria has sought to redefine its international role. It used to present itself as a bridge between the two camps in Europe, but is now seeking to join the European Community by 1995. The EC is positive towards Austrian membership on political and economic grounds, but is concerned that Austrian neutrality could cause problems if the Community gets involved in defense policy.

Because of growing concern over the civil war that broke out in neighboring Yugoslavia, the Austrian government dispatched troops to patrol its border with the country. Austria called for peace in Yugoslavia, but the Yugoslav federal government claimed that Austria supported secessionist movements politically and militarily. The Austrian government denied these charges and Chancellor Vranitzky blocked a proposal to grant diplomatic recognition to Slovenia, but the chancellor did admit that Austrian companies had exported hunting rifles across the border.

Political Rights and Civil Liberties:

Austrians have the right to change their government democratically. Four parties won seats in the 1990 National Council elections. Nazi organizations are illegal, and the 1955 State Treaty prohibits Nazis from enjoying freedoms of assembly and association. However, for many years old Nazis found a home in the Freedom Party, which expresses thinly veiled Nazi sympathies.

The country's provinces have significant local power and can check federal power by choosing the members of the upper house of parliament. There is a Slovenian minority which has had some disputes with the Austro-Germans over bilingual education.

The media are generally very free, but rarely used restrictions on press freedom allow the removal of publications from circulation if they violate laws on public morality or security. Broadcast media belong to an autonomous public corporation. There is freedom of religion for faiths judged consistent with public order and morality. Recognized denominations must register with the government.

The judiciary is independent. Refugees have long used Austria as the first point of asylum when they leave Eastern Europe and the Soviet Union. Until mid-March 1990, Austria had an open door policy for people fleeing Eastern Europe. Since 15 March 1990 Austria has required that all prospective newcomers apply for a visa first. The country concluded that it needed to draw a distinction between economic refugees and politically persecuted arrivals.

Business and labor groups are strong and play a major role in formulating national economic policy. Most Austrian workers must belong to Chambers of Labor, which represent workers' interests to the government. Trade unions, on the other hand, negotiate for workers with management.

Bahamas

Polity: Parliamentary democracy
Economy: Capitalist-statist
Population: 300,000
PPP: $10,590
Life Expectancy: 71.5
Ethnic Groups: Black (85 percent), white (15 percent)

Political Rights: 2
Civil Liberties: 3
Status: Free

Overview:

The Commonwealth of the Bahamas, a member of the British Commonwealth, became internally self-governing in 1967 under the leadership of Lynden O. Pindling and the Progressive Liberal Party (PLP). Independence, which was not supported by the opposition Free National Movement (FNM), was granted in 1973. The British monarchy is represented by a governor-general.

Under the 1973 constitution there is a bicameral parliament consisting of a forty-nine-member House of Assembly directly elected for five years, and a sixteen-member Senate with nine members appointed by the prime minister, four by the leader of the parliamentary opposition, and three by the governor-general. The prime minister is the leader of the party commanding a majority in the House. Islands other than New Providence and Grand Bahama are administered by centrally appointed commissioners.

The PLP under Prime Minister Pindling has remained in power since independence. At the two most recent parliamentary elections of 1982 and 1987, the PLP retained control of the House of Assembly but fell short of the three-quarters majority it had previously enjoyed. In the 1987 elections, the PLP won thirty-one seats, the FNM sixteen and independents two. The results were expected to be closer as evidence revealed in U.S. courts pointed to high official corruption in connection with narcotics trafficking. The PLP countercharged that it was the FNM that was involved in the drug trade. The FNM alleged that electoral fraud had taken place, charging that throughout its tenure, the PLP government had enhanced its electoral advantage by dispensing favors to supporters.

In April 1990 the PLP increased its majority in the assembly to thirty-two seats when independent parliamentarian Perry G. Christie re-entered the PLP fold by accepting a cabinet position offered by Prime Minister Pindling. In a by-election in June marred by charges of fraud by both parties, the FNM narrowly retained its Marco City, Grand Bahama, parliamentary seat vacated by the death of FNM leader Cecil Wallace-Whitfield. Hubert A. Ingraham was selected by the FNM as the new official opposition leader.

The next national election is constitutionally due by September 1992. In the fall of 1991, however, Prime Minister Pindling appeared to place the PLP on a campaign footing, suggesting that elections might be called sooner. His government also introduced in parliament a series of electoral reforms to limit fraud opportunities such as double voting. The opposition FNM supported the measures but called also for a provision requiring photographs on voter IDs.

Political Rights and Civil Liberties:

Citizens are able to change their government by democratic means, although recent elections have been marked by irregularities and allegations of fraud by all sides. Constitutional guarantees regarding the right to organize political parties, civic organizations and labor unions are generally respected, as is the free exercise of religion. Labor, business and professional organizations are generally free. There is a right to strike, but demonstrations are often broken up by police, with demonstrators subject to temporary detention, as was the case during a state employees strike at the end of 1988. Nearly 30 percent of the work force is organized and collective bargaining is extensive.

There is an independent Grand Bahama Human Rights Association, as well as at least two other independent rights groups, which frequently criticize the government on police, constitutional and other issues. In recent years, there have been continuing reports of police brutality during the course of arrests and interrogations. Human rights groups have also criticized harsh conditions and overcrowding in the nation's prisons.

A major concern is the condition of the illegal Haitian immigrant population, which in 1991 was estimated at 50,000, nearly 20 percent of the Bahamian population. The influx has created tension because of the strain on government services during a period of creeping economic recession. The government has tried to develop programs to better integrate the Haitian population, but human rights groups charge that Haitians are treated inhumanely by the authorities and the public, and in many cases are deported illegally. The problem was expected to worsen with an increase in Haitian refugees following the overthrow of Haitian President Jean-Bertrand Aristide in September 1991.

Full freedom of expression is constrained by strict libel laws which the government uses against the independent press. On occasion, newspapers have been ordered by the government not to print certain materials. Radio and television are controlled by the government-owned Broadcasting Corporation of the Bahamas and often fail to air differing points of view.

The judicial system is headed by a Supreme Court and a Court of Appeal, with the right of appeal under certain circumstances to the Privy Council in London. There are local courts, and on the outer islands the local commissioners have magisterial powers.

Despite recent anti-drug legislation and a formal agreement with the United States in 1987 to suppress the drug trade, there is lingering evidence that drug-related corruption continues to compromise the Bahamian Defense Force, the judicial system and government at the highest levels.

Bahrain

Polity: Traditional monarchy
Economy: Capitalist-statist
Population: 500,000
PPP: $9,490
Life Expectancy: 71.0
Ethnic Groups: Bahraini (63 percent), other Arab (10 percent), Asian (13 percent), immigrant groups, Iranian

Political Rights: 6
Civil Liberties: 5
Status: Partly Free

Overview:

In 1991, the Persian Gulf War shook the tiny island country of Bahrain, polluting its crops and driving foreign bankers away from this hub of Gulf finance. Bahrain played an important role in the war effort by providing military bases for United States and other allied forces in their campaign against Iraq.

The Al Khalifa family has ruled this Persian Gulf nation as a traditional monarchy since 1782. The country is currently ruled by Emir Sheikh 'Isa ibn Salman Al Khalifa, his eldest brother (the prime minister) and his son (the Crown Prince). Once a British protectorate, the country became independent in 1971 and established a constitutional monarchy. Approved in June 1973, the constitution made the emir the hereditary ruler and established a National Assembly with thirty popularly elected members. In 1975, however, the emir began to rule by decree, as he was entitled to do under the constitution. One of his decrees was to suspend the constitutional provision for an elected assembly and dissolve the National Assembly, which he found to be dominated by "alien ideas."

The ruling family is Sunni Muslim while roughly 60 percent of the population is Shiite. The regime is increasingly wary of the possibility of a fundamentalist upheaval, especially since the Iranian revolution of 1979. The most threatening underground opposition groups have been the Iran-backed Shiite Islamic Front for the Liberation of Bahrain, which launched a coup attempt in 1981 and the Islamic Call Party which seeks to establish an Islamic state. There are two secular radical groups with apparently limited appeal.

As 1991 began war tensions were deeply felt, prompting the government to close schools and issue gas masks and emergency instructions. Bahrain, which has an accord with the U.S. for navy services dating to the end of World War II, provided bases for American and other allied military presence in the Gulf, stationing over 200 U.S. warplanes and 15,000 military personnel.

Following the war's end in late February, Bahrain began strengthening ties with neighboring states. In August the Bahraini Foreign Ministry called a meeting to resolve a traditional border dispute with Qatar. In September an evolving trade alliance with Iran culminated in the signing of a letter of understanding on trade and development, outlining cooperation in industrial projects and the exchange of industry experts. In October Bahrain took part in the region's attempt to form a more peaceful post-war order by attending the Middle East peace conference in Madrid.

Political Rights and Civil Liberties:

In a limited way, citizens participate politically by attending the emir's open-air audiences, but political rights are otherwise sharply curtailed. Criticism of the regime's legitimacy is not tolerated, political parties are proscribed, and meetings with any political undertones are banned.

Although newspapers are privately owned, traditionally they adhere to government positions: past censorship and suspensions by the Information Ministry has produced self-censorship. Foreign journalists have had their credentials revoked for unfavorable coverage. Radio and television are state-owned.

Some private professional associations are allowed to function, and public religious events are tolerated, but they too are monitored closely for possible political discussions. "Workers' committees," composing over 10 percent of the work force, are sponsored by the government. Workers do not have the right to strike, and expatriate workers, half of the work force, are not allowed to form unions.

Jews, Baha'is and expatriate Christians are allowed to practice their faith in their own place of worship. Sunni Muslims are generally better off than Shiites. They hold better jobs—including key government jobs—and have easier access to social services. Citizens are free to move within the country, while passports for foreign travel have been denied in the past for political reasons.

Unconfirmed reports of torture against suspected leftists by the Security and Intelligence Service continue to be received. Arbitrary, prolonged and incommunicado detention is practiced, and security laws allows for broad arrest powers against suspected political activists.

Women face far fewer cultural and legal restrictions than do women in other Islamic societies, but there have been reports of physical abuses of expatriate female domestics.

Bangladesh

Polity: Parliamentary democracy **Political Rights:** 2
Economy: Capitalist-statist **Civil Liberties:** 3
Population: 116,600,000 **Status:** Free
PPP: $720
Life Expectancy: 51.8
Ethnic Groups: Bengali (98 percent), Bihari (1 percent),
various tribal groups (1 percent)

Overview:

Following free elections in February 1991 featuring nearly 2,800 candidates from over 100 parties, Khaleda Zia was named Bangladesh's first female prime minister. Within months, the country adopted a parliamentary system, ending sixteen years of presidential rule. Critical developments facing the new government included a deadly cyclone and the sixteen-year insurgency of 600,000 mostly Buddhist and Hindu Chakma tribesmen concentrated near the India-Burma border.

The country's road to democracy began late in 1990 when President Lt. Gen. Hossain Mohammad Ershad, chairman of the National Party (*Jatiya Dal*) that seized power in a bloodless 1982 coup, abruptly resigned on 6 December after weeks of escalating civilian protest against authoritarian rule. In January police charged Ershad with possession of illegal arms and sent him for trial to a special court, while the government accused him of receiving kickbacks in an aircraft purchase from Britain.

The transitional government set up after Ershad's downfall quickly made preparations for a transition to democratic rule. Former Supreme Court Justice Shahabuddin Ahmed, who took over as caretaker president, scheduled elections on 27 February for 300 directly elected seats to the 330-member unicameral National Assembly (thirty appointed seats are reserved for women). The two leading opposition parties to Ershad's *Jatiya Dal* were the Awami League, headed by Sheikh Hasina, daughter of the late president Sheikh Mujibur Rahman, and the Bangladesh National Party (BNP), led by Khaleda Zia, widow of the late president Ziaur Rahman. Although Ershad and other members were under arrest, the *Jatiya Dal* was allowed to field candidates after appealing an earlier ban to the Election Commission.

By the end of January the three mainstream political groupings had failed to reach an electoral alliance. In addition to the eight-party Awami League and the seven-party grouping led by the BNP, a new front called the Democratic Unity Group (GOJ), which brought together leftists, Communists and socialists of various shades, entered 120 races. The fundamentalist Muslim *Jamaat-e-Islami* also fielded a strong slate of candidates.

In contrast to other votes, the 27 February election was held with minimal violence and a large turnout of the country's 62 million eligible voters. The BNP won 139 seats, with 88 going to the Awami League, and 18 to the *Jamaat-e-Islami* party. The BNP chose 28 of 30 seats reserved for women, with two going to the Islamic party. The jailed Ershad won a seat in parliament, but was later removed following his conviction on several charges. On 5 March Acting President Ahmed named Khaleda Zia prime minister, and appointed 11 cabinet ministers and 20 ministers of state from the BNP.

In an attempt to ensure political stability after sixteen years of executive presidency and military rule, the government announced in mid-June that the country would adopt a Westminster-style parliamentary form of government. The opposition Awami League welcomed the constitutional change, which was approved by the required two-thirds margin in parliament. The change called for parliament to elect a president, who would be the ceremonial head of state. In a 15 September national referendum Bangladeshis approved the proposed change by a margin of 84 percent to 15. Four days later Prime Minister Zia was sworn in as head of government, completing the change to parliamentary government. On 25 September the parliament approved the BNP-nominated Abdur Rahman Biswas, speaker of the Parliament, to the presidency.

The country's political rehabilitation was hampered by a deadly cyclone and tidal wave on 29 April which killed at least 140,000 people and left 10 million homeless. The government complained about insufficient foreign aid, with $120 million pledged to relieve the $1.5 billion in estimated damages. On 16 May an American task force of almost 8,000 troops, diverted en route home from the Persian Gulf, began full-fledged operations to transport food and medicine to remote parts of the stricken region. The presence of U.S. troops, however, touched off protests in the capital, Dhaka.

Other issues included the trial of former President Ershad, the ongoing guerrilla war in the Chittagong Hill Tracts (CHT), and the country's sluggish economy. In mid-June Ershad was found guilty of possessing illegal weapons and sentenced to ten years in jail. The conviction touched off violent protests in Dhaka by 2,000 Ershad-backers. In September Ershad was indicted again, this time for smuggling gold from Singapore. The trial began on 15 October. The insurgency in the CHT is led by the outlawed Shanti Bahini (Peace Force) guerrillas, who have been fighting for CHT autonomy since the early 1970s. On 21 October the government offered amnesty, free food and money for weapons surrendered by the estimated 5,000 guerrillas. However, on 6 November Buddhist rebels fired into a boat with 30 Muslim settlers, killing at least five people. The fighting had claimed some 5,000 lives since 1974, and 30,000 had fled to India to escape the insurgency.

Political Rights and Civil Liberties:

In 1991, Bangladeshis exercised their right to democratically elect their government. International observers rated the 27 February parliamentary election generally "free and fair." A national referendum endorsed the government's decision to scrap the presidential system in favor of a parliamentary form. Civil courts are considered fair and the judiciary is independent. In January more than 150 prisoners, many of them jailed for political offenses, were granted amnesty. The new government also agreed to release 3,683 prisoners convicted by Ershad's martial law courts. The government's action ended two weeks of violent prison protests at Khulna, Jessore, Comilla, Dhaka and Chittagong jails. Prisoners had demanded the release of all those jailed since 1982, better food and living conditions. Amnesty International reported that 35 prisoners were killed in Dhaka Central Jail on 9 and 10 April by paramilitary units, ostensibly for trying to escape.

After nine years of government censorship the press in Bangladesh enjoyed new-found freedoms in 1991. Publications were permitted to write freely and critically without fear of reprisals. Since Ershad's ouster, over a dozen new newspapers—both in English and vernacular languages—were launched in Dhaka. The new government did crack down on one newspaper, however. The editor and publisher of the Bengali *Ajer Kagoj* were arrested in June for a "highly defamatory and objectionable" report which accused the finance minister of fraud. The arrest sparked a wave of protests, and the two were released on bail. During the campaign both leading parties promised to make radio and television into autonomous corporations.

The rights of assembly and association are generally respected. In 1988, Islam was declared the state religion, but the government generally respects the rights of Buddhist, Hindu and Christian minorities. Yet, Hindu-Muslim antagonisms have led to violence in the CHT and elsewhere. Freedom to move within the country is, with some exceptions, unrestricted, and citizens can freely emigrate or travel abroad. Only 3 percent of the labor force belongs to unions. In 1991, there were several strikes, including those by government workers, ferry operators and state-run jute and textile mill workers.

The fate of some 250,000 Bihari, Urdu-speaking Muslim refugees who opted for East Pakistan after the partition of the subcontinent in 1947, but favored (West) Pakistan in the 1971 civil war, continued to be a major human rights issue. Scattered in squalid refugee camps, the Bihari await emigration to Pakistan, but the issue remains in a diplomatic tangle involving the U.N., India, Pakistan and Bangladesh. Another humanitarian concern is the monthly influx of Burmese Muslims escaping religious persecution. Official figures put the number of Burmese Muslims who fled to Bangladesh since the 1970s at 500,000.

Barbados

Polity: Parliamentary democracy
Economy: Capitalist
Population: 300,000
PPP: $6,020
Life Expectancy: 75.1
Ethnic Groups: Black (80 percent), white (4 percent), mixed (16 percent)

Political Rights: 1
Civil Liberties: 1
Status: Free

Overview:

The governing Democratic Labour Party (DLP) was returned to office in the general election held in January 1991. But Prime Minister Erskine Sandiford soon came under severe pressure from political opponents, business and labor because of his austerity program aimed at bringing the country out of a two-year economic slump.

Barbados, a member of the British Commonwealth, became internally self-governing in 1961 and achieved independence in 1966. The British monarchy is represented by a governor-general.

The system of government is a parliamentary democracy. The bicameral parliament consists of a twenty-eight-member House of Assembly (the twenty-eighth seat was added in 1991) elected for five years by direct popular vote, and a twenty-one-member Senate, with twelve senators appointed by the prime minister, two by the leader of the parliamentary opposition, and seven by various civic interests. Executive authority is invested in the prime minister, who is the leader of the political party commanding a majority in the House.

Since independence, power has alternated between two centrist parties, the DLP under Errol Barrow until 1976, and the Barbados Labour Party (BLP) under Tom Adams from 1976 until Adams' death in 1985. Adams was succeeded by his deputy, Bernard St. John, but the BLP was soundly defeated in the 1986 elections. The DLP took twenty-four seats to the BLP's three and Barrow returned as prime minister. Barrow died suddenly in June 1987 and was succeeded by Erskine Sandiford.

The DLP's majority was reduced in February 1989 when four House members, led by former finance minister Richie Haynes, broke away from the DLP to form the National Democratic Party (NDP). As per the constitution, Haynes became the leader of the opposition on the strength of the NDP's four-to-three seat advantage over the BLP. The ruling DLP retained twenty seats.

Economic issues dominated the campaign for the 1991 election. The gross domestic product declined in 1990 for the first time in seven years, primarily because of decreased revenues from tourism, manufacturing and the sugar industry. Higher oil prices, a result of the Persian Gulf crisis, cut into already dwindling hard currency reserves. The opposition parties pressed their cases on unemployment, which the government put at 17-18 percent, and increasing drug abuse and crime, particularly among youth.

Nonetheless, the DLP was able to win an eighteen-seat majority in the January 1991 election. The BLP, led by former foreign minister Henry Forde, bounced back from its dismal 1986 showing to take ten seats. The NDP failed to break the two-party system, winning no seats. Voter participation dipped to 62 percent, down from 76 percent in 1986.

Amid the continuing economic slide, the Sandiford government began pushing austerity legislation, including a public sector pay cut which passed in the House by only one vote. Further legislation tied to the government's unpopular economic stabilization program appeared to be in trouble as the BLP mobilized against it. In early November, the country was crippled by a two-day general labor strike and mass demonstrations, a level of turbulence not seen in Barbados in over twenty years. The unions were backed by the BLP, the churches and most of the media. The business community demanded that Sandiford resign. Sandiford rejected the demand, but his government appeared ill-prepared to weather what looked to be a continuing storm.

Political Rights and Civil Liberties: Citizens are able to change their government through free and fair elections. Constitutional guarantees regarding freedom of religion and the right to organize political parties, labor unions and civic organization are respected. Apart from the parties holding parliamentary seats and the NDP, there are other political organizations including the small left-wing Workers' Party of Barbados. Human rights organizations operate freely. There are two major labor unions and various smaller ones, which are politically active and free to strike.

Freedom of expression is fully respected. Public opinion expressed through the news media, which is free of censorship and government control, has a powerful influence on policy. Newspapers are privately owned, and there are two major dailies. There are both private and government radio stations. The single television station, operated by the government-owned Caribbean Broadcasting Corporation (CBC), presents a wide range of political viewpoints.

The judicial system is independent and includes a Supreme Court that encompasses a High Court and a Court of Appeal. Lower court officials are appointed on the advice of the Judicial and Legal Service Commission. The government provides free legal aid to the indigent.

In 1991 human rights concerns centered around the rising crime rate and the justice ministry's decision to return to the practice of flogging as punishment for armed robbery. Judicial whipping had not been used for several decades, but its use was never abolished by law. Human rights groups protested that flogging violated a constitutional ban on torture or inhuman and degrading punishment.

Belgium

Polity: Parliamentary democracy
Economy: Capitalist
Population: 9,900,000
PPP: $13,010
Life Expectancy: 75.2
Ethnic Groups: Fleming (55 percent), Walloon (33 percent), mixed and others (12 percent), including Moroccan, Turkish, and other immigrant groups

Political Rights: 1
Civil Liberties: 1
Status: Free

Overview: The top news stories in Belgium in 1991 concerned the collapse of the governing coalition, the general election and immigrant riots.

Modern Belgium dates from 1830 when the territory broke away from the

Netherlands. A constitutional monarchy, Belgium has a largely ceremonial king who symbolizes the unity of this ethnically divided state. The Dutch-speaking Flemings comprise about 55 percent of the population, while the Francophone Walloons make up about 33 percent. The remainder includes a small German minority near the German border. The country is divided into separate linguistic zones for the Flemings, Walloons, Germans, and multi-cultural Brussels. For much of Belgian history, the Walloons dominated culture and the economy, while Flemings had no legal status.

Due to ethnic divisions, Belgians have political parties split along linguistic lines. Both groups have their own parties ranging across the political spectrum. The bicameral parliament has a Senate made up of directly and indirectly elected members, and a directly elected Chamber of Representatives. Members of both houses of parliament serve terms of up to four years. The heir to the throne (King Baudouin's nephew) has the right to a Senate seat. The current Senate has 181 members and the Chamber of Representatives has 212.

A center-left government under Christian Democratic Prime Minister Wilfried Martens was in office from 1987 to late 1991. The governing coalition consisted of both Socialist parties, both Christian Democratic parties, and Volksunie, the moderate Flemish nationalist party. Parties outside the coalition included Vlaams Blok, the militant Flemish party; two Green parties; two right-wing Liberal parties; Walloon Federalists; Flemish libertarians; and the French-speaking Front. Completing the first two-thirds of a reform program, Martens's coalition government instituted protections for minority language rights in linguistically mixed areas, established an elected regional assembly for Brussels and increased devolution of powers to the regions. In October, however, the coalition government broke up before it could restructure the Senate and institute elected assemblies for Flemish and Walloon areas. Disputes between the Flemish and Walloon parties over government contracts caused the breakup of the ruling coalition.

Voters elected a new Chamber of Representatives on 24 November. The Christian Democrats, Socialists, Francophone Liberals, and Volksunie lost seats. Vlams Blok, the Greens, Flemish right-wing liberals, Flemish Libertarians, and the Francophone National Front made gains. The small Francophone Federalists held their ground. As a result of the election, it became tougher to form a government. The government parties lost a combined fourteen seats. The king asked Guy Verhofstadt, a right-wing Flemish Liberal, to form a government. When Verhofstadt failed, the king turned to Melchior Wathelet, a bi-lingual, Francophone Christian Democrat. Since the voters increased the standing of environmentalist and anti-immigrant parties, the new government will be under pressure to address their concerns.

In recent years, the large influx of immigrants from Third-World countries has been a source of tension. Young Moroccan immigrants rioted for several nights in May 1991 in Brussels, driving through the streets throwing firebombs at buildings and vehicles. The riots sprang from the Moroccans' feelings of discontent with their social and economic conditions. Moroccans and Turks do much of Belgium's manual labor.

Martens's government faced criticism on international issues in 1991. During the Persian Gulf War, Belgium allegedly refused to provide ammunition to Britain, which fought in the anti-Iraq coalition. However, the Belgian government claimed that it had merely stalled military assistance which it provided later. The government suffered further embarrassment after the foreign ministry granted an entry visa to Walid Khaled, a spokesman for the terrorist Fatah Revolutionary Council. Prime Minister Martens ordered Khaled's expulsion after someone reported recognizing the foreign visitor on the street. Three foreign ministry officials resigned over the incident.

In 1991 Belgium dispatched troops to Zaire (the former Belgian Congo) to maintain some degree of order and evacuate Belgian nationals. The Belgians were reacting to the violence and looting which grew as the Mobutu dictatorship collapsed.

Political Rights and Civil Liberties:

Belgians have the right to change their government democratically. Voting is compulsory, and nonvoters are subject to fines. Numerous political parties organize freely, usually along ethnic lines. Each language group has the right to autonomy within its own region. However, tensions and constitutional disputes arise when members of one group get elected to office in the other's territory and refuse to take competency tests in the regionally dominant language. The voters elect regional councils, but the national government appoints the provincial governors.

In general, there is freedom of speech and of the press. However, libel laws may have some minor restraining effects on the press, and there are restrictions on civil servants' criticism of the government. Autonomous public boards govern the state television and radio networks, and ensure that public broadcasting is linguistically pluralistic. The state has permitted and licensed private radio stations since 1985. The overwhelming number of workers belong to trade union federations.

Religious freedom is respected in Belgium. The state recognizes and subsidizes Christian, Jewish and Muslim institutions. Other faiths have complete freedom. The monarch and his consort have a religious role. According to Belgian tradition, the seventh child born to any Belgian family has the king or queen as his or her godparent.

The judiciary is independent. The government appoints judges for life tenure. Belgium has a generally good record on prisoners' rights questions, but there have been some problems with extended pretrial detentions. Since 1985 the municipalities around Brussels have had the right to refuse to register new residents from countries outside the European Community.

Belize

Polity: Parliamentary democracy
Economy: Capitalist
Population: 200,000
PPP: na
Life Expectancy: 69.5
Ethnic Groups: Majority of mixed ancestry, including black, Carib, Creole and mestizo

Political Rights: 1
Civil Liberties: 1
Status: Free

Overview:

Belize is a member of the British Commonwealth. The British monarchy is represented by a governor-general. Formerly British Honduras, the name was officially changed to Belize in 1973. Internal self-government was granted in 1964 and independence in 1981. Because neighboring Guatemala refused to recognize the new state, Britain agreed to provide for Belize's defense. In 1991 Guatemala agreed to recognize Belize but refrained from dropping its historic claim to an undefined part of Belizean land. A 1,500-member British military force remains in Belize pending resolution of the dispute.

Belize is a parliamentary democracy with a bicameral National Assembly. The assembly consists of a twenty-eight-seat House of Representatives with members elected to five-year terms. Members of the Senate are appointed, five by the governor-general on the advice of the prime minister, two by the leader of the parliamentary opposition, and one by the Belize Advisory Council.

In the country's first post-independence election in December 1984, the center-right United Democratic Party (UDP) won twenty-one seats in the House, overturning thirty years of rule by George Price's center-left People's United Party (PUP) which took the remaining seven. The UDP's Manuel A. Esquivel replaced Price as prime minister.

In the most recent national elections, held in September 1989, Price returned as prime minister as the PUP won fifteen seats in the House to the UPD's thirteen. A third party, the Belize Popular Party (BPP), was unable to win any seats.

In early December 1989, the PUP followed its return to national office with a victory in Belize City Council elections. The PUP won all nine of the council seats, ending twelve years of UDP control of local government in the nation's capital, where nearly 30 percent of the population resides. In subsequent municipal elections held in March 1991, the PUP won majorities in five out of country's seven Town Boards. The next national elections are due in 1994.

Political Rights and Civil Liberties:

Citizens are able to change their government through free and fair elections. While the UDP and the PUP dominate the political scene, there are no restrictions on the right to organize political parties. Civic society is well established, with a large number of nongovernmental organizations working in the social, economic and environmental areas. Labor unions are independent and free to strike. There are nearly a dozen active trade unions, and close to a third of the work force is unionized. Disputes are adjudicated by official boards of inquiry, and businesses are penalized for failing to abide by the labor code. There is freedom of religion.

The judiciary is independent and nondiscriminatory and the rule of law is guaranteed. The formation of a Security Intelligence Service (SIS) by the UPD government in 1988 to combat drug traffickers was criticized by the PUP, and led to the creation of the Belize Human Rights Commission to address charges of physical and verbal abuse and wrongful arrests by security forces. The SIS was a major issue of the 1989 electoral campaign and the PUP dissolved it after returning to office at the end 1989.

In recent years, human rights concerns have focused on the plight of migrant workers and refugees from neighboring Central American countries and charges of labor abuses by Belizean employers. Among an estimated 30,000 aliens in Belize, 6,000 have registered under an amnesty program implemented in cooperation with the United Nations High Commissioner for Refugees. There also has been concern about the increase in violent crime. Most of the 700-member police force goes unarmed, but the human rights commission has warned of the potential for abuses with the use of a few dozen soldiers of the 600-member Belize Defense Force to augment street patrols.

There are five independent newspapers representing various political viewpoints. Belize has a literacy rate of over 90 percent. Radio and television, however, have played an increasingly prominent role in recent years. There are fourteen privately owned television stations including four cable systems. At the end of 1990 the PUP made good on its 1989 campaign promise to reduce government involvement in the broadcast media by creating an independent board to oversee operations of government-owned outlets.

Benin

Polity: Presidential-legislative democracy
Economy: Statist-transitional
Population: 4,800,000
PPP: $1,050
Life Expectancy: 47.0
Ethnic Groups: Aja, Bargu, Egba, Fon, Somba, Tem, Yoruba

Political Rights: 2
Civil Liberties: 3
Status: Free

Overview:

In 1991, this narrow, central-west African country became a trend-setter in Francophone Africa by conclusively rejecting strongman president General Ahmed Kérékou the first time he faced a competitor in multi-party elections. Benin's democratization began in 1990, when a national conference assumed control of the country and appointed a transitional government to prepare for democracy. After both local and national elections in early 1991, the transition culminated in March when two rounds of balloting for president resulted in victory for Kérékou's opponent, Nicephore Soglo, the prime minister of the transitional government.

The Republic of Dahomey achieved its independence from France on 1 August 1960. General Kérékou seized power in a 1972 coup, renamed the country "Benin" in 1975 and established a Marxist-Leninist state under the banner of his Benin People's Revolutionary Party (PRPB). Political orthodoxy was advanced and safeguarded by the militant Youth League, and both real and suspected political enemies suffered arbitrary arrest, imprisonment, torture and extrajudicial execution. By 1988 the state was effectively bankrupt, bled by official corruption and incompetence, and besieged by widespread work stoppages and student-led strikes. In June 1989 legislative "elections" under the one-party system were held for the 206-member National Assembly. The official results were a foregone conclusion: a "popular" ratification of the *status quo*. On 2 August 1989 the National Assembly elected Kérékou to another five-year term. Its authority reconfirmed, the regime met with exiled opposition figures in Paris in December 1989 to negotiate a consensus on how the country might pull itself out of its economic morass.

The resulting Paris agreement laid the foundation for Benin's transition to multiparty democracy. Within months a special joint session of the Assembly and the Cabinet was held, producing dramatic results: the abandonment of Marxism-Leninism as the official state ideology; the separation of state and party; the creation of the post of prime minister; and the announcement of a national conference representing the various sectors of Benin's society in order to draft a new constitution. By accepting a measure of political liberalization, Kérékou expected that the conference would grant him society-wide support for harsh new austerity measures that his government intended to implement. What he got was not what he had in mind. Instead, the conference stripped him of power.

Deciding that its mandate was nothing less than a complete transformation of the political system, the conference set up a committee to draft a new democratic constitution, asserted sovereignty over the country, and selected an interim prime minister, Nicephore Soglo, to lead the country through a year-long transition to competitive elections. After a brief period of national speculation about the president's possible response to the Convention's far-reaching actions, Kérékou formally approved the selection of Soglo, a former World Bank official, and endorsed the conference's decisions. The president retained his functions as head of state and chief of the Armed Forces, but legislative power during the transition period and ultimate control over Kérékou was entrusted to a thirty-member High Council of the Republic (HCR). Installed on 12 March 1990, the new government was the result of a "civilian coup d'etat" that alarmed other one-party regimes on the continent faced with mounting domestic political opposition. Indeed, political reform in Benin during the last two years has explicitly served as a model for other countries in Africa moving towards greater democratization.

The first multi-party elections were held throughout the country in November 1990 for local offices and the new constitution was approved in a referendum three weeks later. In February 1991, 1,800 candidates competed in elections for the new 64-seat National Assembly. A requirement that political parties run in all six provinces prevented political parties too closely identified with a particular ethnic group or region from participating. After the election legislative responsibility was handed over to the Assembly by the HCR. In contrast to the one-party legislature of the prior regime, 16 political parties are represented in the new National Assembly.

On 10 March 1991, after competing against thirteen other announced candidates for the presidency, Soglo won 37 percent to Kérékou's 26 percent. Two weeks later Soglo won the runoff election with over 67 percent of the vote. Soglo's electoral support was overwhelmingly concentrated in the center and south of the country, while Kérékou scored his highest vote totals in the north, his region of origin. Ethnic clashes broke out during the runoff in northern Benin; local Kérékou partisans attacked southerners, primarily Fons, suspected of voting for Soglo. Two people were killed and at least twenty wounded, while thousands fled south to avoid further attacks. Ill-founded allegations by Kérékou that his supporters were being subjected to wide-spread threats and physical coercion in the south, and his warning that he would not step down if he determined that the elections had been rigged, caused concern in light of his control over the military. Although there were scattered reports of vote-buying, voter intimidation, ballot-box stuffing, and the use of state resources to improperly aid the campaigns of those in the transition government, impartial observers described the elections as generally free and fair.

Ill with a variety of ailments during the last stage of the campaign, Soglo spent time in France for medical treatment before returning for his inauguration as president on 5 April.

While the transitional administration managed to decrease the budget deficit somewhat during 1989 and early 1990, Soglo now faces the formidable task of tackling the country's economic problems with a potentially unpopular austerity program. The country remains very poor and has already been hit by budget cuts made under IMF restructuring guidelines. Schools and hospitals lack needed supplies, and their staffs have gone for extended periods without receiving their salaries. Despite campaign promises to increase the number of schools and hospitals, and create new employment opportunities, one of the economic measures to be taken by the new government will be to prune an oversized public sector. Up to 6,000 civil servants could lose their jobs over the next four years as the extensive nationalization of the prior regime is reversed. The new government has said that it intends to take legal action to retrieve public funds embezzled by officials of the former regimes.

Political Rights and Civil Liberties: A constitution approved by referendum in 1990 provides Benin's citizens the means to change their government democratically. In an indication of growing pluralism, Soglo's choice for speaker of the new Assembly lost in July 1991, when legislators chose Adrien Houngbedúi who had been an unsuccessful minor candidate for president. Reforms in the judicial and legal system have begun, but some Beninois are already complaining that the president's democratic mandate has given him the idea that he is not restrained by the rule of law. Angered by criticism of foreign leaders, President Soglo threatened in August to restrict the media's freedom of expression. The national media, including those outlets owned by the state, vigorously covered the political transition and reflected a wide range of political views.

There are no major restrictions on religion, and both domestic and international travel are unrestricted. The right to strike is now constitutionally protected, and civil servants have gone on strike demanding retraining programs and wage hikes. The independent Benin Commission on Human Rights exists to guard against recurrence of the widespread human rights violations of the previous regime. The new government does not want to court trouble by appearing to "settle old scores" with officials of the prior regime, so initiative is being left with private citizens to seek redress for human rights abuses and political persecution suffered before the new government took office.

Bhutan

Polity: Traditional monarchy
Economy: Pre-industrial
Population: 700,000
PPP: na
Life Expectancy: 48.9
Ethnic Groups: Bhotia (60 percent), Nepalese (25 percent), indigenous (15 percent), Tibetan refugees

Political Rights: 6
Civil Liberties: 5
Status: Partly Free

Overview: In 1991 this last remaining Himalayan Buddhist kingdom nestled on the Sino-Indian border continued to slowly modernize an almost medieval culture under thirty-five-year-old King Singye Wangchuk. Many of these efforts were targeted for the south, where a year earlier violent clashes occured between government troops and Nepalese.

A 150-member National Assembly, two-thirds of which is elected every three years by universal suffrage (with the remaining third designated to several religious bodies and secular interests supported by the monarch), enacts legislation. It meets twice a year, for less than two weeks at a time. The king does not have the power of veto, but can send bills back to the Assembly for reconsideration. On all crucial issues, the king's decisions are implemented. The monarch appoints a Council of Ministers and a nine-seat Royal Advisory Council, all of whom also hold seats in the National Assembly.

The major political problem facing the king continued to be the demands of the Hindu Nepalese minority. In 1988, in a move to safeguard Bhutanese identity, the king, who is a member of the indigenous Drukpa tribe, ordered a census aimed at disenfranchising illegal immigrants. He chose 1958 as the cut-off date for legal migration, outraging Nepalese who had entered later. Bhutan also began curbing the influx of Indians, most of whom are Hindus, which led Indians across the border to encourage Hindu Nepalese in the Bhutanese south to raise protests.

In 1989 the king further fueled Nepalese resentment by banning the teaching of Nepali in schools and saying everyone should wear the national dress and do their hair in the Drukpa style. The government argued that it was merely seeking to enforce a "Bhutanese way of life," including national dress, architectural styles and languages.

Although Bhutan forbids political parties, the Nepalese Bhutan People's Party (BPP) and other outlawed organizations based in India were formed in 1990, ostensibly to press for greater democracy. However, regional experts—including many in India—saw the BPP as representing essentially economic refugees and thought its emphasis on democracy merely a ploy to gain international sympathy.

In September 1990 there were bloody clashes throughout southern Bhutan. The BPP claimed that soldiers killed over 300 people during peaceful protests. This report was denied by eyewitnesses who said that several thousand armed Nepalese militants crossed the border from India and tried to foment an uprising among Bhutanese of Nepali descent. No large scale violence was reported in 1991. Recently the government distributed land to landless peasants in the area, and targeted the south for greater economic development. The BPP has charged that government officials favor investors linked to the royal family, thus practicing economic discrimination. Since 1986, 10,000 people (mostly Nepalese) have been expelled for working in the country without permits.

While the country's fifth Five-Year Plan (1981-86) targeted transport, telecommunications, geological exploration and hydroelectric power for development, the sixth (1987-92) concentrated on increasing popular participation in government development programs and on the improvement of public services. "I don't think Bhutan's political future and the well being of our people, our security and our sovereignty can be determined by one individual," the king said in March. Thirty years ago Bhutan did not have a currency, and although its economy still largely operates on a barter basis, and is predominantly of an agricultural subsistence nature, exports of fruit, coal, stone, dolomite and cement are on the rise. English is taught in schools, an increasing number of people are sent abroad for education, and high priority has been given to the creation of skilled labor.

India has guided Bhutan's foreign policy since 1949, but the country has been gradually increasing its ties with the outside world. It has joined the World Bank, the International Monetary Fund, the Asian Development Bank, and has been conducting annual negotiations with China on Sino-Indian border disputes. During the 1980s

Bhutan established independent diplomatic ties with the Maldives, Norway, Sweden, Switzerland, Austria, Finland, Japan, Sri Lanka and the European Community. No more than 3,000 tourists can enter Bhutan each year. There are no television stations in Bhutan, and satellite dishes and antennas were banned to prevent the reception of foreign broadcasts. However, a new television network is in the works with Japanese technical guidance and assistance.

Political Rights and Civil Liberties: The people of Bhutan cannot change their government democratically. Freedoms of assembly, association, speech and press are not protected by law. Political parties are discouraged, and there are no independent associations of any sort. The existence of a right to a fair public trial is questionable. Judges, appointed by the king, are accountable to him, and are in charge of investigation, filing charges, prosecution, and judging defendants. There is no jury or court-appointed defense attorney. Citizens can make final appeals to the king.

There is one government newspaper, but foreign publications are freely available (12 percent of the country's adults can read). The king can be criticized in the National Assembly, but not in the media. Government radio broadcasts in four languages for three hours a day.

Tibetan Tantric Buddhism is the state religion, and the government subsidizes shrines and monasteries. The 6,000 Buddhist monks hold significant political clout, and Buddhist interests are reserved a number of seats in the National Assembly as well as in the Royal Advisory Council. Hindus do have the right to practice their religion, but proselytizing is not permitted. Conversions are illegal. Recently, major Hindu festivals have been declared national holidays, and the king has urged many of the country's 12,000 Buddhist monks (one-half of whom receive government aid) to increase their input into social works. Although land is divided equally between sons and daughters, opportunities for women are limited. New laws do favor women in alimony issues, but only 10 percent of government employees are women. The industrial work-force makes up less than 1 percent of Bhutan's population, and there is no labor-related legislation.

Bolivia

Polity: Presidential-legislative democracy
Economy: Capitalist-statist
Population: 7,500,000
PPP: $1,480
Life Expectancy: 54.5
Ethnic Groups: Mixed (25-30 percent), Quechua Indian (30 percent), Aymara Indian (25 percent), European (10-15 percent)

Political Rights: 2
Civil Liberties: 3
Status: Free

Overview: In 1991, the coalition government of President Jaime Paz Zamora overcame a serious constitutional crisis stemming from a conflict of powers between the executive and the judiciary. But it was widely criticized for ordering the participation of the military in a U.S.-assisted program against cocaine trafficking.

Since achieving independence from Spain in 1825, the Republic of Bolivia has endured recurrent instability and extended periods of military rule. The armed forces, responsible for over 180 coups in 157 years, returned to the barracks in 1982, and the 1967 constitution, suspended in 1969, was restored with the election of President Hernan Siles Suazo. The July 1985 election of President Victor Paz Estenssoro of the Nationalist Revolutionary Movement (MNR) marked the first peaceful transfer of power between two democratically elected presidents in twenty-five years.

The constitution provides for a president elected for a four-year term by universal adult suffrage and a Congress consisting of a 130-member House of Representatives and a 27-member Senate similarly elected for four years. If no presidential candidate receives an absolute majority of the votes, Congress makes the selection from among the three leading contenders. Although the constitution calls for biennial municipal elections, local balloting was conducted in 1987 for the first time in thirty-nine years.

The MNR candidate in the 7 May 1989 election was Gonzalo Sanchez de Lozada, President Paz's planning minister and architect of a market-oriented austerity program that had ended hyperinflation and rationalized the economy. The two main challengers were Hugo Banzer, whose conservative Nationalist Democratic Action (ADN) had formed an alliance with the government in support of the MNR's economic program, and Jaime Paz Zamora of the social democratic Movement of the Revolutionary Left (MIR).

The balloting resulted in a virtual three-way tie as Lozada obtained a slim plurality over Banzer in second and Paz Zamora in third. Although international observers praised the electoral process, the tight finish led to mutual accusations of fraud, and fierce horse-trading in the new Congress where the MNR took forty-nine seats, the ADN forty-six and the MIR forty-one. Banzer finally decided to back Paz Zamora for president in exchange for the ADN receiving over half the cabinet positions. Paz Zamora was elected president by Congress in August 1989.

Municipal elections were held on 3 December 1989. The MIR-ADN coalition, known as the Patriotic Accord, lost in a number of cities, but won in the capital, La Paz. The elections were marked by voter apathy, with abstention running close to 40 percent, and the increasing strength of non-traditional political forces, particularly the Conscience of the Fatherland party headed by the television talk-show host and ardent nationalist, Carlos Palenque.

Since taking office President Paz's efforts to privatize money-losing state industries and open Bolivia, the poorest country in South America, to foreign investment have been hindered by a series of labor strikes led by the Bolivian Workers Central (COB). In late 1990, however, economic issues took a back seat after a dispute between the government and the MNR, over control of the Supreme Court and the electoral courts, mushroomed into a constitutional crisis. When the Supreme Court sided with the MNR, the government used its parliamentary majority to impeach eight of the twelve Supreme Court justices. The court then threatened to annul election results from 1989 in three key regions, which would have left the government without legal standing.

The crisis finally was resolved in May 1991. The eight justices were reinstated and both sides agreed in a behind-the-scenes deal to depoliticize the judicial and electoral systems. Elements of the agreement emerged during the summer, when plans for a new voter registration for the 1993 national elections were announced, and a new electoral court consisting of five politically independent magistrates was created. Magistrates previously were appointed by the three main political parties, and the court's impartiality remained in question. The government also named a 15-member judicial reform commission.

In the meantime, municipal elections scheduled for 1 December 1991 were expected to reveal how much support the government had lost by agreeing to cooperate with the U.S. in an anti-drug program involving the Bolivian military. In recent years, Bolivia has become the world's second largest producer of cocaine. But the government's U.S.-assisted program drew political fire from peasant unions representing Bolivia's 50,000 coca farmers; the COB, the nation's largest labor confederation; and every opposition political party.

Political Rights and Civil Liberties: Citizens are able to change their government through democratic means. Constitutional guarantees regarding free expression, freedom of religion, and the right to organize political parties, civic groups and labor unions are generally respected. However, political expression is restricted by recurring violence associated with labor strife and the billion-dollar-per-year cocaine trade. Also, the emergence of a handful of small left-wing guerrilla groups has caused an overreaction by security forces against legitimate government opponents. And, even though the languages of the indigenous population are officially recognized, the 40 percent Spanish-speaking minority still dominates the political process.

The political landscape features two dozen legal political parties ranging from the fascist right to the radical left. There are also a number of Indian-based peasant movements, which in 1991 began talking about demanding full autonomy within Bolivia for the various Indian "nations."

There continues to be strong evidence that drug money has penetrated the political process through the corruption of government officials and the military, and through electoral campaign financing. The drug trade also has spawned private security forces that operate with relative impunity in the coca-growing regions.

Unions are permitted to strike and have done so repeatedly against the government's economic liberalization program, which has left more than 20 percent of the work force idle. In response, the government has often resorted to force. Workers still have a generous social welfare program and are usually compensated when dismissed from state-owned enterprises.

The judicial system, headed by a Supreme Court, has been more effective since the return to civilian rule, but it remains over-politicized and subject to the compromising power of drug traffickers. The resolution of the constitutional crisis described above resulted in the naming of a reform commission mandated to make the judiciary more independent. There are nine District Courts; local courts try minor offensives.

There are human rights organizations, both government-sponsored and independent. Allegations of police brutality and harsh prison conditions including torture have increased in the last year and there have been reports of intimidation against independent activists.

The press, radio and television are privately owned and free of censorship since the end of military rule. There are a number of daily newspapers including one sponsored by the influential Catholic church. Public opinion polling is a growth industry. Five years ago there was no television; in 1989 there were forty-seven television stations. The impact was most evident in 1989 in the media-based campaigns of the prominent political parties. In 1991, however, the media protested a new law passed by the Congress which limits paid political messages. Also, journalists covering corruption stories have been subject to threats and occasional violent attacks.

Botswana

Polity: Parliamentary democracy and traditional chiefs
Economy: Capitalist
Population: 1,300,000
PPP: $2,510
Life Expectancy: 59.8
Ethnic Groups: Tswana (95 percent), Baswara, Kalanga and Kgalagadi (4 percent), European (1 percent)

Political Rights: 1
Civil Liberties: 2
Status: Free

Overview:

This land-locked, thinly populated, southern African country, is one of the few working democracies on the continent. Major news stories in 1991 concerned the economy, a major development project, the formation of an opposition coalition and a major land dispute.

Formerly the British colony of Bechuanaland, Botswana gained its independence in 1966. Although it was one of the poorest countries in the world at the time of independence, large-scale mining of its principal resource, diamonds, has led to 13 percent economic growth and a foreign exchange reserve among the highest in the Third World. However, the increasing dependence on diamonds—which now account for 63 percent of exports and 50 percent of gross domestic product—is a source of concern because diamond mines are already working at full capacity.

Despite Botswana's increasing wealth, most citizens engage in subsistence farming and 60 percent of the population earns less than $100 a year. In 1991 the government set aside approximately $100 million for urban development, and spent another $14.1 million modernizing the rural infrastructure, including the establishment of new primary schools. Unfortunately, Botswana's harsh climate (much of the country's land is either marsh or desert) makes growth difficult for the agricultural sector. The government increased the minimum wage by 12 percent in May 1991, but the impact will be minimal because most of the population is self-employed. Botswana also suffers from an unemployment rate of over 25 percent. Currently, only 5,000 people work in Botswana's three diamond mines, although a recent agreement between the Botswana government and De Beers of South Africa, which holds the government-sanctioned monopoly, to open a diamond cutting factory will provide an extra five hundred jobs. The government's inability to solve the unemployment problem has led to significant growth of jobs in unlicensed businesses, employing more than 6,000 each year.

The Botswana government had planned to make the water of the Okavango Delta, a vast area of swampland, into a constant, usable water source for the surrounding villages. This would have involved dredging forty kilometers of the Boro River. The government, acknowledging the project's environmental costs, argued that it was crucial for local villages already experiencing chronic water shortages. Villagers, however, began to protest the arrival of the construction crews. Before long, the protest became national and international—even Greenpeace got involved. Finally, at the January *kglota,* the traditional tribal debating forum in Botswana society, strong dissent convinced the government of the need to suspend the project.

The chief of state and head of government is Dr. Quett K.J. Masire, leader of the Botswana Democratic Party (BDP), which has held power since independence. The Parliament consists of a National Assembly and a consultative House of Chiefs. Locally, Botswana is divided into nine districts and five towns, all governed by councils. In 1990 the two main opposition parties, the Botswana National Front (BNF) and the Botswana People's Party, along with the Botswana Independence Party (BIP) and the Botswana Progressive Union (BPU), tried to form a united opposition front. However, the BIP pulled out after the BNF threatened violence if the BDP kept winning elections. In October 1991 opposition parties again formed a coalition called the Botswana Peoples Progressive Front, this time excluding the BIP. One intention of the new coalition's platform is to make Botswana less dependent on South Africa.

Political Rights and Civil Liberties:

The people of Botswana have the power to democratically change their government, but the same party has controlled the country since it gained independence in 1966. The judiciary is considered fair and independent. The press is free and presents opposition viewpoints. Although the Botswana Press Agency is part of the Department of Information and Broadcasting, it operates with a large measure of autonomy and is often critical of the government. There are no restrictions on either religion or freedom of movement.

In May 1991 Botswana received some attention in the press for its treatment of the Basawra, commonly known as the Bushman. Although the Basawra have been traditionally nomadic, drought and government wildlife protection policies have forced these people to make more permanent settlements. The government has encouraged settlements by designating reservations on which the Basawra can live. Conditions on these settlements are harsh; the Basawra survive mostly on government food rations, while local farmers and government officials often exploit Basawra women. As the Baswars's land becomes increasingly valuable, other parties have become interested for commercial purposes. When, in 1991, the Botswana government tried to take away some of the land from the Basawra, protests from both local development organizations and the Norwegian government temporarily stopped confiscation. However, the central government is still putting pressure on the local council to allocate at least some of the land for commercial purposes.

Unions are well organized and have the right to strike, but first they must submit to a mandatory arbitration procedure. There is only one major labor confederation, the Botswana Federation of Trade Unions. In November 1991, 50,000 manual workers staged a two-day strike, demanding a six-fold increase in salary. Not only did they fail to get their demands, but 12,000 strikers were fined.

Brazil

Polity: Presidential-legislative democracy
Economy: Capitalist-statist
Population: 153,300,000
PPP: $4,620
Life Expectancy: 65.6
Ethnic Groups: Caucasian (54 percent), mixed (39 percent), black (6 percent), pure Indian (less than 1 percent)

Political Rights: 2
Civil Liberties: 3
Status: Free

Overview:

President Fernando Collor de Mello's second year in office was marked by economic deterioration, the threat of renewed hyperinflation, and political isolation. With special interest blocs in the Congress plotting to limit his executive powers and the military growing restless, many in Brazil questioned whether Collor's presidency would survive until the end of his five-year term.

Brazil retained a monarchical system after gaining independence from Portugal in 1822, but became a republic in 1889. Democratic rule has been interrupted by long periods of authoritarian rule, most recently under military governments from 1964 to 1985.

The return to civilian rule in 1985, the result of a controlled transition transacted by the military with opposition political parties, culminated in the 1985 electoral college balloting won by Tancredo Neves. Neves died soon after and Jose Sarney, his vice-presidential running mate, became the first civilian president in twenty-one years. Direct elections for a bicameral Congress were held in 1986. The Senate and the Chamber of Deputies formed a constituent assembly that produced a new constitution.

The 1988 constitution provided for a president to be directly elected on 15 November 1989 for a five-year term. The Congress was retained, with a 72-member Senate directly elected for eight years and a 503-member Chamber of Deputies directly elected for four years. Brazil is divided into 26 states and the Federal District of Brasilia. State governors and legislatures are elected, as are municipal governments. The constitution provides for a national plebiscite in 1993 to decide whether to keep the presidential system, change to a parliamentary system, or reestablish a monarchy.

The top contenders among the 22 candidates in 1989 were Collor, a political newcomer and candidate of the center-right National Reconstruction Party (PRN), Luis da Silva of the Marxist-oriented Workers' Party (PT), and Leonel Brizola of the social democratic Democratic Labor Party (PDT). The main issues were Brazil's massive foreign debt, uncontrolled inflation, corruption, crime, and the deteriorating living conditions of the nation's poor, who make up nearly two-thirds of the population.

In the first round, Collor obtained 28 percent of the vote. Silva edged out Brizola for second. Collor won the runoff a month later, taking 53 percent of the vote. He was inaugurated on 15 March 1990, the first directly elected president in nearly three decades.

With a strong popular mandate, the forty-two-year-old Collor vowed to "kill" inflation, clean out government corruption, and privatize one government-owned company every month. However, after eighteen months and two economic shock programs, inflation was again pushing 20 percent a month, the country remained in a deep two-year recession, and Collor's popular support was evaporating amid corruption scandals involving his wife and close advisors.

Moreover, his plan to overhaul the statist economy and attract foreign investment remained blocked by a hostile Congress wielding the 1988 constitution, a populist document that mandates spending on behalf of a vast array of special interests and makes structural reform virtually impossible. When Congress—a diverse and generally feckless group of nineteen parties tied to labor, big business and regional interests—rejected Collor's package of constitutional amendments in September 1991, the political system reached political deadlock.

In October a number of political parties led by the Social Democratic Party of Brazil (PSDB) attempted to stage a "constitutional coup." With polls showing popular support for a parliamentary system, the idea was to advance the 1993 plebiscite to 1992. A vote in favor of a parliamentary system would not necessarily mean Collor could not complete his five-year term. But it would reinforce his lame-duck status, and Congress could at any time set the date for the changeover which would greatly reduce the power of the presidency. In November the PSDB initiative lost in the Senate by only three votes, but renewed efforts to limit Collor's authority were expected.

As the political and economic crises deepened, the military, already hurt by defense budget cuts and Collor's exposure and cancelation of a secret atomic-bomb project, grew restive. A number of ranking officers spoke out about the armed forces as guarantors of internal order. Despite such ominous rhetoric, the military did not appear inclined to take power again. At the same time it also showed little interest in backing Collor.

Political Rights and Civil Liberties: Citizens are able to change their government through free and fair elections. Constitutional guarantees regarding free expression, freedom of religion and the right to organize political parties and civic organizations are generally respected. Over two dozen political parties span the political spectrum. However, alarming levels of criminal violence and police corruption, fueled by economic recession and the burgeoning drug trade, have created a climate of generalized insecurity.

Numerous independent human rights organizations are active. Despite the constitutional guarantees against torture and inhuman treatment during confinement, rights groups report extensive and systematic abuses in police detention centers and in the over flowing, violence-plagued prisons. Vigilante "death squads," linked to the police and financed by local merchants, are responsible for thousands of extra-judicial killings a year. Violence, including murder, against the 35 million children living in poverty, at least a quarter of them living in the streets of burgeoning urban centers, is systematic, with hundreds, possibly thousands, of "street kids" murdered annually. Various government initiatives thus far have failed to curtail these practices.

The judicial system is headed by a Supreme Court whose members must be approved by the Senate. The Court was granted substantial administrative and financial autonomy by the 1988 constitution, but remains bureaucratic, overloaded and chronically corrupt. There are federal courts in the state capitals and states have their own judicial systems. There are also special labor and electoral courts. In March 1991 the Supreme Court ruled that a man can no longer kill his wife and win acquittal on the ground of "legitimate defense of honor," but in subsequent cases juries ignored the high ruling, as they are entitled to do.

At the local level, courts are under-financed, poorly staffed, intimidated by monied interests, and overwhelmed by the national crime wave. As a result, there is little public confidence in the judicial system and poorer citizens, beset by inflation and unemployment, have resorted to lynchings, with hundreds of mob executions reported in 1991. The middle class, already shrinking and unable to afford costly private security measures, has been targeted by kidnappers who often operate in league with underpaid, corrupt police.

There has also been an increase in violence associated with land disputes. Two percent of Brazil's landowners control nearly 60 percent of arable land, and the poorest 30 percent share less than two percent of the land. In recent years, hundreds of activists, Catholic church workers and rural unionists have been killed by paramilitary groups hired by large landowners, with only a handful of cases brought to court. Rubber tappers, environmentalists, and Indian tribes continue to be targets of violence, including assassination, associated with the huge Amazon basin development projects initiated under military rule, and the gold rush in the far north. The constitution gives Brazil's quarter million Indians legal sanction. However, not until 1991 did the government create Indian reserves, and it is uncertain whether the government can guarantee the security of these lands.

Industrial labor unions are well organized and politically influential. The right to strike is permitted by the 1988 constitution. Although unions have protested that subsequent legislation is vague and restrictive, the populist constitution guarantees job security to public workers with more than five years service, and hundreds of strikes have been carried out during Collor's time in office.

Virtually all forms of media constraints were removed by the 1988 constitution. The press is privately owned, vigorous and uncensored. There are daily newspapers in most major cities and many other publications throughout the country. Radio is mostly commercial. Although overseen by a government agency, television is an independent and powerful political instrument; roughly two-thirds of the population is illiterate. The huge TV Globo dominates, but there are three other networks, plus educational channels.

Brunei

Polity: Traditional monarchy
Economy: Capitalist-statist
Population: 300,000
PPP: na
Life Expectancy: 73.5
Ethnic Groups: Malay (65 percent), Chinese (20 percent), other (15 percent)

Political Rights: 6
Civil Liberties: 5
Status: Not Free

Overview:

Proclaimed an independent sultanate in January 1984, this tiny oil-rich Islamic monarchy on the northern tip of Borneo is ruled by Sultan Muda Hassanal Bolkiah. The constitution permits the sultan, whose family has ruled the area for over 500 years, to override decisions of the legislative and executive bodies.

In 1962 a party opposed to the sultan won a large majority in legislative elections, and in December an armed uprising was put down with the aid of British troops. The sultan then assumed emergency powers for two years, which have been renewed ever since.

In 1990 the government released six political prisoners held since a failed coup attempt against the late Sultan Omar Ali Saifuddin. Five of the six were former members of the Brunei People's Party (PRB), which was outlawed after the 1962 uprising. Also in 1990, the government released two members of the Brunei National Democratic Party (BNDP), arrested under the Internal Security Act in 1988. By the end of year, the government claimed to have released all political prisoners.

In 1991 Brunei continued to prosper from oil and liquefied natural gas revenues. Brunei boasts the highest per capita gross national product in the world, no debts and an estimated $30-40 billion in financial reserve.

Since 1962 there has been no notable social unrest and unparalleled economic prosperity. Oil revenues and interest on invested reserves enable the government to provide free medical care in modern facilities, and university training. Per capita income is over $20,000, government workers receive generous salaries and low- or no-interest loans to purchase homes, cars, and appliances. There is no income tax.

Political Rights and Civil Liberties:

The citizens of Brunei do not have the means to change their government democratically. The judiciary is based on a British model and is generally independent. But suspects may be detained without trial for renewable two-year terms under the Internal Securities Act (ISA). There is no formal political opposition, and in the past political parties were banned. Although freedoms of speech and the press are not restricted by law, government-owned television, radio and major newspaper steer clear of controversial issues. Islam is the state religion, but the constitution provides safeguards for Christian and Buddhist minorities. The Chinese minority are not citizens, but few have emigrated from this prosperous country. There are no travel restrictions for citizens, permanent residents or expatriates, although the latter face some restrictions on overseas travel. Trade unions are legal, but must be registered with the government. Total membership is less than 5 percent of the workforce, and there have been no strikes in recent history.

Bulgaria

Polity: Parliamentary democracy
Economy: Statist-transitional
Population: 9,000,000
PPP: na
Life Expectancy: 72.6
Ethnic Groups: Bulgarian (Slavic) (85 percent), Turkish (9 percent), Gypsy (3 percent), Macedonian (3 percent)

Political Rights: 2
Civil Liberties: 3
Status: Free

Overview:

In 1991 Bulgaria elected its first non-Communist government in forty-six years when the opposition Union of Democratic Forces (UDF) edged out the Bulgarian Socialist Party (formerly the Bulgarian Communist Party) in 13 October voting for the 240-member unicameral parliament. Other critical developments included growing ethnic tensions, a deteriorating economy marked by a severe cut in Soviet imports, Iraq's failure to pay a $2 billion debt, spiraling inflation and unemployment, and the former coalition government's foot-dragging in implementing reforms.

In June 1990 Bulgaria held its first multi-party elections since the fall of the thirty-five-year-old Communist regime of Todor Zhivkov. The BSP won 211 parliamentary seats in the then-400-member National Assembly, making it the only Communist party in Eastern Europe to return to power after free elections. The UDF opposition won 144 seats and the Movement for Rights and Freedom (MRF), an ethnic Turkish group not registered as a party, won 23 seats. By the end of 1990 political turmoil and a wave of high-level political resignations beset Bulgaria. On 1 August parliament named UDF leader Zheliu Zhelev president of Bulgaria after the abrupt resignation of President Petar Mladenov. Petar Beron, Zhelev's replacement as head of the 16-member UDF, was forced to resign after disclosures that he once worked for the secret police. On 29 November, three months after being elected, BSP Prime Minister Andrei Lukanov stepped down after weeks of demonstrations and strikes. His ability to govern was weakened by his refusal to form an all-BSP government and the UDF's persistent refusal to join a coalition. On 20 December parliament approved a transitional coalition government headed by Prime Minister Dimitur Popov, a Sofia municipal judge without party affiliation nominated by President Zhelev.

In the first half of 1991 recriminations and rancor seemed to paralyze the government. The UDF had split into two factions. The so-called center bloc, dominated by the revived Social Democratic Party under Petur Dertliev, included 60 members of parliament who insisted elections should not be held until a new constitution had been drawn up. They also criticized the tough anti-inflationary policies advocated by the International Monetary Fund (IMF). The UDF's other faction, dominated by the right wing, including the Monarchist Party, was led by UDF Chairman Filip Dimitrov, who took over after the resignation of Beron. This faction maintained that the BSP was placing a brake on reforms and wanted elections as soon as possible, regardless of whether a constitution had been drawn up.

On 28 May parliament voted to hold a nationwide referendum on whether Bulgaria should become a monarchy or remain a republic, but reversed itself eight days later under intense public criticism.

On 12 July Bulgaria became the first former Communist country to adopt a new constitution that enshrined its commitment to build a free and democratic society. In a four-hour ceremony, 309 of the (then) 400 deputies signed the new constitution which called for political pluralism and proclaimed the inviolability of private property. The constitution debate had touched off a twenty-three-day hunger strike by lawmakers from the national and royalist wing of the UDF, who argued that it was passed by a parliament dominated by the former Communist party. The constitution was also opposed by the Turkish minority because the document stated that no political party should be based on ethnic background. The Turkish MRF had walked out of parliament in May, protesting that the constitution was discriminatory against Turks; the thirty-nine MRF parliamentarians returned on 24 July after new national elections were announced for the fall.

In August former Prime Minister Lukanov resigned as deputy chairman of the BSP to protest its refusal to condemn the coup attempt against Soviet leader Mikhail Gorbachev. Although politically weakened by the June 1990 vote, the BSP remained the dominant force, both in the cabinet and the parliament. It did its best to leave a socialist imprint on new legislation, and consistently opposed radical market reforms and measures that might deprive the *nomenklatura* of positions and benefits they once enjoyed.

In the October legislative elections, the UDF narrowly defeated the BSP by a margin of 34.3 percent (110 seats) to 33.1 percent (106 seats). MRF won 7.5 percent of the vote—passing the 4 percent hurdle necessary to place deputies in parliament—and won 24 seats in parliament. International observers concluded the election was fair.

The BSP's strong showing came at a time when other East European former Communist parties—with the exception of those in Romania, Serbia and Albania—had vanished from the political scene. The BSP also won overwhelmingly in the countryside, leaving intact a power base on the local level. The main losers in the elections were the 34 smaller parties and coalitions that failed to win the necessary 4 percent needed to get seats.

Few Bulgarian politicians were happy that the Turkish MRF held the balance of power. The Supreme Court had ruled that an ethnic Turkish party could not contest the elections, but the decision was reversed after international diplomatic pressure. Anti-Turkish sentiments persisted, even as all parties condemned the forced assimilation under Zhivkov of ethnic Turks in the early 1980s and the expulsion of 350,000 in 1989.

On 29 October President Zhelev expressed concern that growing ethnic tensions and a polarized parliament could destabilize the new government. UDF leader Dimitrov said he planned to form a one-party government without the BSP.

On 4 November Stefan Savov, a senior UDF official, was elected chairman of the National Assembly, the first non-Communist to head parliament since 1944. The following day, President Zhelev asked Dimitrov to form a new government after Premier Popov and his coalition resigned. On 11 November 30,000 BSP supporters marched in Sofia to protest a draft law on the confiscation of the party's property.

Parliament announced on 13 November that direct elections for president and vice president would be held on 12 January 1992.

As in all post-Communist East European countries, economic reform was a central issue. Early in the year the Popov coalition government announced plans to scrap subsidies on many basic goods and utilities beginning 1 February. The decisions meant sharp price rises for consumers already facing a severe winter and chronic shortages of food and fuel. The plan included a comprehensive macroeconomic stabilization and price liberalization program to bring down inflation. The program was launched in the face of a moratorium on fresh credit by Western banks because of a 1990 BSP government suspension of all principal and interest payments on the country's $11 billion debt. Bulgaria was also affected more than other East European countries by the switch to hard-currency trading with the Soviet Union and the collapse of COMECON, the socialist trading organization. More than 80 percent of Bulgaria's trade had been with the USSR and other East European countries, particularly East Germany. A shortfall in Soviet energy supplies, cancelled contracts and general upheaval in the trading patterns in Eastern Europe added to Bulgaria's ills. At the end of 1990 industrial output had fallen by 25 percent and exports by 27 percent.

The government's decision to liberalize and increase prices by 250 percent, raise interest rates and cut consumer spending received backing from the IMF. Bulgarian officials forecast that unemployment could rise to between 300,000 to 400,000 over the next few years. The agricultural sector in the countryside, a BSP bastion, was hampered by old-style Communist thinking and the lack of a comprehensive agricultural program. While a land law aimed at returning Bulgarian agriculture to private hands was passed, there was a three-year moratorium on land sales. Farmers also complained about government bans on agricultural exports and export taxes of more than 30 percent on meat products, cereal and cheese.

In October the economy suffered a further jolt when the Soviet Union suddenly cut off electricity supplies to Bulgaria. Earlier in the month the Soviets stopped supplying coal until the end of the year. Moreover, Bulgaria agreed to cut back capacity at the Kozlodui nuclear power plant after international inspectors concluded that four of the six Chernobyl-type reactors had to be closed for safety reasons.

As in other East European countries, Bulgaria faced the challenge of prosecuting former officials of the old regime. On 6 June Stoyan Ovcharov, a former economics minister, was convicted of abuse of office and sentenced to two years' imprisonment. Former Party boss and leader Zhivkov, seventy-nine, was put on trial on 25 February for misappropriating $4 million worth of state property. He was also accused of allowing top Communist officials to buy apartments, cars and weekend houses at giveaway prices. The trial was suspended on 15 April pending completion of a medical report on Zhivkov's health. In August the Bulgarians asked the Soviets to extradite General Vladimir Todorov, a former intelligence chief in the Bulgarian interior ministry, wanted for questioning in the 1978 "umbrella murder" in London of exiled dissident Georgi Markov.

Political Rights and Civil Liberties:

In October 1991 Bulgaria held the second national legislative election since the overthrow of the Communist regime in 1989. A multi-party system was enshrined in a new constitution adopted in July 1991, and October's parliamentary elections were deemed fair by international observers. Judicial reforms were begun in 1990 and Bulgarian law and general practice provide for public trials in criminal cases. A handful of political prisoners, among them Muslim activists, are believed to be in custody.

Citizens freely express their views and freedoms of association and assembly are generally accepted. However, in rural areas these rights have been circumscribed through intimidation and inhibition resulting from over four decades of Communist rule. The law on association provides for legal registration of independent groups. Hundreds of political, social, cultural, human rights and union organizations are registered. A Macedonian rights group was denied registration after a court deemed it was an ethnically-based, separatist group.

Over 700 newspapers continue to be published (135 are owned by private businessmen and 120 are associated with political parties), although shortages of newsprint and facilities and February's price hikes affected circulation. In March, the Union of Bulgarian Journalists threatened to strike over the sharp rise in the cost of paper and several publications ceased publication for financial reasons. The broadcast media are also facing competition, mainly from foreign stations.

The predominant Orthodox church—in addition to Roman Catholic, Uniate and Protestant churches—function under some government regulation, and the issue of church property has yet to be finally decided. Although the government has pledged to remove all restrictions on Muslims (ethnic Turks and Bulgarian Pomaks), restrictions exist on Turkish-language instruction and on the availability of religious materials.

There are few restrictions on international and domestic travel, and special residence permits are no longer needed for major urban areas. An independent trade union, Podkrepa, has over 500,000 members.

Burkina Faso

Polity: Dominant party (military-dominated)
Economy: Mixed statist
Population: 9,400,000
PPP: $650
Life Expectancy: 48.2
Ethnic Groups: Bobo, Busansi, Dafi, Dagari, Dogon, Fulani, Guin, Gurma, Lobi, Malinke, Minianka, Mossi, Nunuma, Samo, Sehufo, Sia, other

Political Rights: 6
Civil Liberties: 5
Status: Not Free

Overview:

Burkina Faso's transition to multi-party democracy stalled during the December 1991 presidential election when all five candidates challenging the incumbent withdrew from the race in a gesture of protest. They did so after the regime refused to meet an opposition deadline to set the date for a national conference. President Blaise Compaore was re-elected by default. Two withdrawn candidates were fired on by unknown gunmen. Legislative elections scheduled for mid-January of 1992 were suspended.

This landlocked, arid, and extremely poor central-west African country (known as Upper Volta until 1984) has been ruled since October 1987 by President Compaore through the broad-based Popular Front (FP). In the thirty-one years since it gained independence from France, Burkina Faso has never changed its head of state through direct multi-party elections. Compaore himself came to power by overthrowing Captain Thomas Sankara in 1987. Sankara had come to power during a military coup in 1983 when he overthrew the junta of Surgeon General Jean-Baptiste Ouédraogo. Compaore was an important participant in the 1983 coup, which his regime refers to as a "revolution."

Officially founded in April 1989, the FP is a collection of political parties and trade unions, in which the military-dominated and leftist Organization for Popular Democracy-Labor Movement (ODP-MT) is the first among equals. Critics charge that other organizations within the Front were created either by the national leadership or allowed to join the Front in order to convey an image of political pluralism. President Compaore has asserted a commitment to multi-partyism and legalized several parties of diverse political orientation in 1991. In addition, the ODP-PT stated in March 1991 that it was no longer a Marxist-Leninist party, redefining itself as a "revolutionary mass political party" committed to development of a Burkinabé market economy.

The Compaore government's "democratic opening" was launched at the First Congress of the Popular Front, held in March 1990, which resolved to write a new constitution. President Compaore stated his opposition at the time of the Congress to the development of a multi-party system, seeing it as something that foreigners would manipulate in order to whittle away at Burkinabé sovereignty. It was political unity, he said at the time, that "protected the country against capitalist exploitation." Nevertheless, before the end of 1990 an appointed constitutional commission had presented a draft constitution to the president which outlined a multi-party system in which there would be separation of powers among the three branches of government and a directly elected head of state. The national legislature adopted the constitution in December 1990, and by the beginning of 1991 there were fifteen new political parties. The president publicly declared a change of heart, acknowledging in interviews that a pluralistic democracy "pursued well" could result in a higher degree of national satisfaction. In a June 1991 referendum, 93 percent of voters supported the new constitution, although reportedly over half of the registered voters neglected to vote. After the referendum, Compaore dissolved the government and appointed a transitional government to oversee the change to multi-partyism. Opposition leaders complained that the transitional administration was composed entirely of members of the ODP-PT and parties artificially constructed by the regime.

Throughout 1991 the political opposition resisted the government's program for political change. In February two of the political parties not within the FP called for a dissolution of the Front and its replacement by an all-party interim government which would organize elections. On 23 March, a growing alliance of opposition parties outside the FP formed the Coordination of Democratic Forces (CDF). The CDF took issue with certain constitutional provisions and the government's unilateral decisions on the transition to democracy. These included setting the term of office for president at seven years, holding the upcoming presidential elections before legislative elections, and refusing to agree to the convening of a national conference. The CDR charged that though the government has solicited comments about proposed official actions, it has never seriously bothered to secure the opposition's consent before acting, and afterward presented all actions taken as settled fact. On several occasions representatives of the CDF either refused to participate or staged walkouts at meetings with the government in protest. After Compaore formed the transitional government in June, the CDF demanded that a sovereign national conference be called in order to give them access to decision-making power.

The regime and its supporters in the pro-government Alliance for the Respect and Defense of the Constitution (ARDC) rejected the call for a national conference as anti-constitutional. Calling the opposition "reactionary conference advocates," they accused the CDF of attempting to mount a "civilian coup d'état." ODP-MT partisans at the highest level warned that they would employ unspecified "old tactics" to put an end to what they alleged were attacks on the revolution of August 1983 and everything it embodied. Some opposition leaders responded by claiming that the government was planning a campaign of assassination and kidnapping; the government denied the charges. A consultative meeting convened on 31 July without CDF representatives issued a report which asserted that a sovereign national conference would unconstitutionally call into question the legitimacy of the head of state and his government.

The CDF charged that the December 1991 presidential elections were a sham intended to give a veneer of legitimacy to an undemocratic, military-dominated regime. The CDF and government supporters each continued to release communiqués demanding and rejecting the national conference option, each declaring that its own terms for the transition to democracy were the only basis for national reconciliation. The opposition gave the government a deadline of 30 September to convene a conference. When the deadline was ignored, a protest demonstration culminated in a clash that left 40 people injured. Other demonstrations followed, and the level of violence rose. Partisans on both sides attacked one another with rocks and clubs in the street, while residences and political headquarters were the targets of fire-bombs and gun-fire. Events culminated in the assasination of one of the withdrawn presidential candidates and the shooting of another by parties unknown in mid-December, after Compaóre won an election in which only a quarter of those registered to vote bothered to do so.

Political Rights and Civil Liberties: The people of Burkina Faso cannot change their government democratically. There are now several opposition political parties, but they all must accept the "historical necessity" of the 1983 coup as a tacit precondition for their legalization. Revolutionary courts try corruption cases, while criminal and civil cases are adjudicated fairly by the regular court system. In July 1991 amnesty was granted for all political offenses committed since independence which resulted in sentences. The remaining detainees that had participated in a coup attempt in December 1989 were released, and Captain Boukary Kabore, a Sankara loyalist living in Ghana who was reported by the government to have been the mastermind of the plot, returned from exile. Vigilante brigades, the "Revolutionary Committees," were disbanded.

The government Written Press Board oversees the press, and the government maintains a monopoly in the domestic media. The government has pledged its acceptance of the principle of a free press, but in 1991 the regime continued to restrict press freedoms. There are no significant restrictions on freedom of religion; foreign travel is usually unencumbered. Nonpolitical business, social, cultural and religious organizations are generally free to function. Members of those organizations which were deemed by the government to be engaged in impermissible political activity have been subjected to dismissal, premature retirement, or administrative transfer to remote areas of the country. Though unions have the right to strike and enjoy relative independence, explicitly anti-government activities have not been permitted in the past.

Burma (Myanmar)

Polity: Military
Economy: Mixed statist
Population: 42,100,000
PPP: $660
Life Expectancy: 61.3
Ethnic Groups: Burman (68 percent), Karen (7 percent), Shan (6 percent), Rakhine (4 percent), Chin, Kachin, Mon and Arkanese totalling 1 million

Political Rights: 7
Civil Liberties: 7
Status: Not Free

Overview: Burma's ruling military junta tightened its control over the country in 1991, jailing dissidents, banning several political parties, and battling ethnic rebel groups in the countryside. However, leading opposition figure Aung San Suu Kyi brought attention to the plight of the Burmese people by receiving two major international awards.

Massive, peaceful demonstrations in 1988 brought an end to twenty-six years of military rule by General Ne Win's Burmese Socialist Program Party (BSPP). Through its "Burmese Way to Socialism," the BSPP impoverished what was once one of the region's richest countries. The army eventually smashed the uprising and killed over 3,000 demonstrators, and in September 1988 created the State Law and Order Restoration Council (SLORC), led by General Saw Maung and Brigadier General Khin Nyunt, to rule the country. Ne Win is said to be the ultimate authority behind the junta. At the time, the SLORC's three main goals were to restore order, improve internal transportation and basic services, and hold multi-party elections.

Multi-party elections were eventually held on 27 May 1990. The National League for Democracy (NLD) surprised the junta by winning 392 of the 485 seats contested, while the SLORC-sponsored National Unity Party, the successor to the BSPP, won only 10 seats. Although some analysts feel the SLORC underestimated popular support for the NLD, others think the junta called elections to flush out and arrest the middle members of the NLD leadership. Since the election hundreds of NLD members, including many elected to parliament, have been jailed. In December 1990 some elected NLD leaders formed a shadow government in rebel-controlled territory near the Thai border, but so far it has not received international recognition.

In the months after the election, the junta claimed it would transfer its power to the NLD-led government as soon as a new constitution was drafted. But in April, deputy armed forces commander General Than Shwe said "at present we cannot find any organization that can govern the country in a peaceful and stable manner," adding that the country's political parties were "unfit to rule." By 8 September the government formally nullified the results of the May 1990 elections. SLORC member Lieut. General Aung Ye Kyaw announced that the junta intended to rule for another five to ten years.

The SLORC spent much of 1991 consolidating its power. In February it banned the Anti-Fascist People's Freedom League, which had led Burma's struggle for independence in the 1940s, and arrested general secretary Cho Cho Kyaw Nyein for allegedly meeting with dissident students. Three other political parties were soon banned; a fifth, the Party for National Democracy, had been banned in December 1990 after its head, Dr. Sein Win, became the prime minister of the shadow government.

Fearing it would be next on the list, the NLD dropped chairman Tin Oo and dynamic secretary general Aung San Suu Kyi from its leadership on 23 April. Both had been sentenced to house arrest on 20 July 1989 and had become symbols of the opposition movement. Suu Kyi, the daughter of independence hero Aung San, has not accepted the government's offer of exile from Burma. She remains under house arrest, virtually incommunicado, saying she will not leave the country until all political prisoners are freed and the SLORC puts a civilian government in place. In 1991 she received both the Nobel Peace Prize and the European Parliament's Sakharov human rights award in absentia. Following a Nobel ceremony in London honoring Suu Kyi in December, students held a rally at Rangoon University, the first significant protest in two years. Opposition groups said 900 students were arrested, and the government closed all universities in the country.

Suu Kyi's awards added to growing international pressure on the regime. The forty-three-nation United Nations Human Rights Commission voted unanimously in a 26 February closed-door session in Geneva to condemn the Burmese government for human rights abuses. Sadako Ogata of Japan, who observed conditions in Burma in November 1990, had not been allowed to meet with political prisoners or dissidents during her investigation. Her report to the Commission described a closed society living in fear of a repressive regime that showed no signs of relinquishing power. It noted that the SLORC continued to detain "a large number of persons, including prominent political leaders of political parties" and had refused to answer to "serious and persistent allegations of torture and mistreatment" of these political prisoners. In June the government refused entry to another U.N. inspector from Japan, Yozo Yokota. However, on 18 October, just four days after the Nobel Committee made its announcement, the government agreed to allow Yokota to visit Burma, but without seeing Suu Kyi. On 29 November the U.N. unanimously adopted a resolution condemning the regime for its human rights violations and continuing military rule.

Several countries have backed the U.N.'s position. The United States imposed trade sanctions against Burma in July, citing its poor human rights record and lack of active measures to eradicate its opium crop. Since the SLORC assumed power, the country has become the world's leading opium producer, with much of it being shipped out of the "Golden Triangle" region via the old Burma Road. The State Department also made access to U.S. textile markets more difficult by allowing a bilateral agreement to expire. However, the U.S., Canada and the European Community have been unable to persuade the ASEAN nations—Brunei, Indonesia, Malaysia, the Philippines, Singapore and Thailand—to put pressure on the Burmese government. Meeting in July with their leading Western trading partners, several ASEAN delegates said that aid and trade should not be linked to human rights issues, and they would not interfere with Burma's internal problems. Many nations have imposed arms embargoes against the regime, but in 1991 China agreed to provide $900 million worth of military equipment, including jet fighters, about half of which will be paid for in rice and wood. Diplomats said closer Sino-Burmese relations have been a critical factor in the SLORC's decision to stay in power.

Sporadic fighting continued in 1991 between the government and various ethnic rebel groups, such as the Karens, Mons, and Shans, who have been seeking independence or autonomy for the past several decades. Government forces overran a key Mon base in the southeast on 21 January during a dry season offensive. Troops also came within ten miles of the Karen National Union stronghold, near the Thai border, which is also where the shadow government was located. In October the government admitted that opposition troops had entered the Bogale district in the Irrawaddy delta, which had not seen fighting in nearly two decades.

Many government attacks have been launched from inside Thai territory, financed by concessions granted to Thai companies to log the teak forest near the Thai-Burmese border. In the past several years, the government has accommodated some rebel groups by granting them business concessions, often in the lucrative opium trade, in return for a cease-fire. However, the Karen and Karenni have refused to cooperate with the government, seeking instead greater autonomy, if not indpendence.

Since the 1988 popular uprising, the SLORC has forcibly relocated up to a half-million of Burma's urban poor to squalid satellite towns under the pretext of providing better living conditions. Many experts feel the junta is attempting to clear major cities of possible sources of unrest. In the countryside, villagers are routinely forced to work as porters for the military, often either dying of exhaustion or killed after having outlived their usefulness. Many are forced to walk ahead of army units as human minesweepers. Thousands have fled to refugee camps in Thailand.

The government has also been systematically destroying Muslim towns in Burma's Arakan state near the Bangladesh border since late 1989, possibly to stir up popular support among ethnic Burmese in the area. The government launched a similar campaign in 1978, causing in excess of 200,000 Muslims to pour into Bangladesh. Thousands of Burmese troops have been moved into the region, and another exodus of Muslims has begun.

Political Rights and Civil Liberties: Burmese citizens lack the democratic means to change their government. The State Law and Order Restoration Council (SLORC) has nullified the results of the May 1990 election and taken complete control of the country. Shadowy strongman Ne Win, who has been the force behind the military's internal intervention in Burma since 1958, is apparently still exerting control from behind the scenes. Many of those elected in 1990 have been placed either under house arrest or in jail, and several political parties have been banned. Political parties must be registered with and approved by the government. Dissident students and other activists have been tortured, and several political prisoners have died at Rangoon's Insein jail. The SLORC controls the mass media, and has banned activities which oppose its policies or existence. Public criticism of the regime is punishable by the death penalty, imprisonment, or hard labor. Martial law orders announced in 1989 permit military commanders to conduct summary trials and executions in military tribunals.

The SLORC has imposed an 11 PM to 4 A.M. curfew, banned outdoor meetings of more than four people, and imposed a permit requirement for indoor gatherings. The government forces students, parents and lecturers to sign pledges promising not to engage in behavior which would threaten the junta. The SLORC requires civil servants to answer in writing a list of thirty-three questions, which include, "Are you in favor of a CIA intervention?" and "Is Burma the United States of America?" Another question, "Should a person who is married to a foreigner become the leader of Burma?", clearly refers to opposition leader Aung San Suu Kyi, who is married to a Briton.

Relations between the SLORC and religious groups were badly damaged in 1990 after security forces killed several monks involved in anti-government demonstrations and raided monasteries. To convince the population, which is 85 percent Buddhist, that all is forgiven, high-ranking military leaders are often shown on television giving color televisions and other gifts to monks. Internal security forces monitor Christian, Muslim and animist religious groups, and have outlawed some groups of monks opposed to the government. Workers are forbidden to unionize or strike.

Burundi

Polity: One-party (military)
Economy: Mixed capitalist
Population: 15,800,000
PPP: $550
Life Expectancy: 48.5
Ethnic Groups: Hutu (85 percent), Tutsi (14 percent), Twa pygmy (1 percent)

Political Rights: 7
Civil Liberties: 6
Status: Not Free

Overview: In 1991 the Republic of Burundi, a densely populated and poor former Belgian colony bordering on Rwanda, Zaire, Tanzania, and Lake Tanganyika, remained a one-party state. National political life is dominated by the thirty-one member Military Committee for National Salvation (CMSN) and the Unity for National Progress (Uprona), the country's only legal political party. Burundi has periodically been wracked by tribal violence between the majority Hutu tribe and the minority Tutsis, who control the government and the army. An insurgent group attacked government installations and forces in November, but it was reportedly repulsed.

The Tutsis historically have asserted for themselves a role as overlords over the Hutu. The country's most traumatic episode of inter-tribal violence occurred in 1972, when as many as 100,000 persons died in what was in effect a pogrom against the Hutu. The last major outbreak of violence in Burundi was in August 1988 when thousands of people, mostly Hutus, were killed in the country's two northern provinces. Despite the potential for violent Hutu rebellion and Tutsi reaction, President Pierre Buyoya has progressively widened a political opening, allowing Tutsis and some Hutu to serve in his government. The prime minister, Adrien Sibomana, is a Hutu. Major Buyoya, who seized control of the state from another Tutsi military regime in a September 1987 coup, explicitly rejected a multi-party system before 1991, arguing instead that "democracy within a single party" would foster national unity.

In December 1990, Uprona approved a draft National Unity Charter at an extraordinary party congress. The Charter, which had been proposed by the president earlier that year, is intended to formally abolish ethnic-based discrimination and to approve the creation of a new constitution to further democratization. In a referendum held 5 February 1991, some 90 percent of the voters endorsed the charter. A month later, the president established a constitutional commission charged with drafting the new constitution. In April, without giving specifics, the prime minister cautioned that there are single party countries where people have more liberties, where the press is freer, and where human rights are more respected than in the multi-party countries. Nevertheless, the president has stated that the constitutional commission will recommend some form of multi-partyism when it releases its report in March 1992. The commission has decided that political parties are not to be regionally, ethnically, or religiously affiliated.

Despite the presence of Hutus in the Buyoya government, an active opposition to continuing Tutsi hegemony is manifest in the existence of certain Hutu political movements of varying militancy and clandestine activity. These include the Party for the Liberation of the Hutu People (Palipehutu), the Burundi Democratic Front, and *Ubumwe*. Palipehutu denies that it is either violent, subversive or anti-Tutsi. *Ubumwe* has launched guerrilla attacks against the regime, as it did on an army base in southern Burundi in August 1990. In 1991 the government reassured Rwanda that Burundi would not be used as a staging ground for guerrilla attacks against Rwandan territory. At the same time, Burundi sought its own reassurance that the Rwandan government in Kigali would stifle inflammatory articles in its nation's press written by Palipehutu, and also assist in controlling the border between the two countries to keep subversive elements from entering Burundi. Although Palipehutu has asserted in interviews that it is committed to non-violent political change, it was accused of launching attacks in November and December 1991 on the capital of Bujumbura and countryside to the northwest. Government troops were able to re-establish order after two days of fighting during which 270 persons were reported to have been killed.

Burundian refugees are found in Tanzania, Rwanda, Zaire and other countries. Virtually all are Hutus who fled the massacres of former years. The president established a commission in January 1991 to deal with the reintegration of refugees seeking repatriation into Burundian national life.

Political Rights and Civil Liberties: **B**urundi remains a militarily dominated one-party state in which the people cannot change their government democratically. The regime has promised a new constitution which will allow for the formation of multiple political parties. Any new constitution is likely to have strong guarantees of minority rights, as those who rule the country today are of the minority Tutsi ethnic group. The judiciary is not independent of the government or the ruling CMSN. Separate courts deal with military and criminal (civil) cases. A State Security Court created to deal with political offenders was abolished in October 1991. The police and state security agents still make arrests without warrants. Despite announcements of amnesties in 1989 and 1990, Hutu activists and political leaders continue to be arrested and held in indefinite detention as political prisoners. Dozens of Hutus were arrested and detained in mid- and late 1991 on the political grounds of "stirring up ethnic hatred" by being Palipehutu sympathizers and organizers. At the same time, security forces killed other Hutus when attempted arrests of alleged organizers of Palipehutu infiltrators were resisted. The government announced in February 1991 that it had approved the formation of two nongovernmental human rights organizations, though members accuse the government of creating obstacles to their activities. The government controls all media, and open political debate is generally limited to Uprona meetings. Nonpolitical associations are permitted, but must be registered with the government; political parties other than Uprona are banned and freedom of assembly restricted. The Buyoya regime has abandoned the repressive anti-religious policies of its predecessor, but all religious associations must register with the government and cannot engage in activities deemed "political." There are regulations on domestic travel, but emigration and foreign travel are generally unencumbered. The majority Hutu tribe still faces *de facto* discrimination on many levels of society, despite the National Unity Charter and the presence of several Hutus in the Buyoya administration. The national Trade Union Confederation is controlled by Uprona, and worker rights are effectively curtailed.

Cambodia

Polity: Transitional
Economy: Statist
Population: 7,100,000
PPP: na
Life Expectancy: 49.7
Ethnic Groups: Khmer (93 percent), Vietnamese (4 percent), Chinese (3 percent)

Political Rights: 6
Civil Liberties: 6
Status: Not Free

Overview: **D**ecades of civil war and violence in Cambodia came to an apparent end on 23 October 1991 when four rival factions signed a peace treaty in Paris. The agreement calls for a substantial United Nations presence in the country, and grants a major role to the internationally condemned Khmer Rouge.

The five permanent members of the United Nations Security Council—China, Great Britain, France, the Soviet Union and the U.S.—provided the framework for the treaty, which allows the U.N. to essentially run the country in the interim period before elections are held. Under the terms of the agreement, former Cambodian leader Prince Norodom Sihanouk heads a twelve member Supreme National Council (SNC), composed of six representatives of the former government and two representatives from each of three rebel groups. The SNC will delegate power to the United Nations Transitional Authority in Cambodia (UNTAC) and hold the country's U.N. seat. UNTAC will supervise five key government ministries—Defense, Finance, Foreign Affairs, Information and Public Security. A series of talks in 1991 resolved the highly sensitive issues of disarmament, the nature of elections, and the post-settlement role of the Khmer Rouge.

Cambodia entered a period of neutrality under Prince Sihanouk after achieving its independence from France in 1953. A violent suppression of a peasants' revolt in 1967, combined with a stagnant economy and anger over the use of Cambodian territory by rival Vietnamese forces, led to a bloodless coup by Prime Minister and army General Lon Nol in March 1970. The rightwing Lon Nol regime fell in April 1975 after years of losing battles to the Communist Khmer Rouge. Once in power, the Khmer Rouge undertook a ruthless program of radical agrarian reform. During its reign, an estimated 1 to 3 million Cambodians died of torture or starvation. Vietnam invaded Cambodia in December 1978, ousted the Khmer Rouge, and installed the Communist government of the Kampuchean People's Revolutionary Party, under the leadership of Khmer Rouge defector Heng Samrin.

In 1982 three anti-Vietnamese groups formed the Coalition Government of Democratic Kampuchea to overthrow the government. Led by Prince Sihanouk, the three groups were: the Chinese-backed Khmer Rouge, with an estimated 30,000 to 40,000 troops; the Sihanouk National Army, led by the prince, with up to 20,000 troops; and the Khmer People's National Liberation Army, led by former prime minister Son Sann, with roughly 10,000 soldiers. In mid-1988, Vietnam removed 50,000 of the estimated 120,000-140,000 troops it had stationed in Cambodia, and announced a complete withdrawal in September 1989. The U.S. withdrew diplomatic recognition from the guerrilla coalition in July 1990, and offered to negotiate directly with Vietnam in an effort to solve the conflict and prevent the Khmer Rouge from returning to power. Talks on the U.N. proposal broke down in December 1990.

Sporadic fighting continued in the first few months of 1991 as all sides tried to increase their military leverage heading into the next round of negotiations. Talks were complicated by the government's demands that any disarmament be postponed until after the election and for assurance that the Khmer Rouge would never return to power. The government claimed the Khmer Rouge, notorious for its ability to hide weapons and blend into the civilian population, could never be effectively demobilized and would retain an advantage if all sides were required to give up their arms.

The new round of talks got off to a slow start. Prime Minister Hun Sen agreed in Jakarta on 2 June to allow Prince Sihanouk to serve as chairman of the SNC in return for being named vice-chairman. The prime minister also called for a tribunal to try former Khmer Rouge leaders on charges of genocide. On 6 June, Chinese Foreign Minister Qian Qichen announced his country's approval of Hun Sen's position as SNC vice-chairman, and added that China continued to favor the U.N. plan as a basis for further negotiations and had not sent arms to the Khmer Rouge for several months. The same day, however, the Khmer Rouge leadership said it could not accept Hun Sen's proposed position as vice-chairman of the SNC, and urged its troops to resume fighting, temporarily ending a fragile cease-fire implemented on 1 May. But on 24 June the four factions agreed to stop receiving foreign arms and renewed the cease-fire. In addition, plans were laid to establish the SNC's headquarters in Phnom Penh by November.

China agreed to host a follow-up meeting in Beijing in July, which marked the first visit by Prime Minister Hun Sen to the country that had backed the Khmer Rouge's efforts to overthrow his government. At the Beijing conference, the four factions formally named Prince Sihanouk as the head of the SNC. They also agreed that the delegation holding the SNC's U.N. seat will be led by the Prince and will include Hun Sen and Khmer Rouge leader Khieu Samphan. The Prince quit his position as nominal head of the resistance forces, and declared himself to be "completely neutral." Significantly, Vietnam retired its notoriously anti-China foreign minister, Nguyen Co Thach, in July. Many diplomats said a settlement would be possible only if China and Vietnam decided to end what amounted to a proxy war in Cambodia.

The talks gained momentum when the government agreed to a demobilization plan during another meeting in Thailand in late August. Under the plan, troops and ammunition are to be placed in temporary quarters under U.N. supervision, with 70 percent of the forces being demobilized by the time elections are held. The factions agreed that Prince Sihanouk will have the final vote if the SNC becomes deadlocked over an issue, although a U.N. representative in Cambodia will ultimately determine whether the SNC's decisions abide by the peace plan. With the negotiations moving faster, Hun Sen dropped his insistence on a specific reference to the Khmer Rouge's "genocide." The talks then suddenly broke down over a final barrier: the specifics of the election process.

While the Prince remained optimistic, Khmer Rouge leader Khieu Samphan insisted "the war is still going on." Samphan's admission that former Khmer Rouge leader Pol Pot—who presided over the starvation and bloodshed of 1975-1978—is still active in the rebel group provoked minimal international response. Thai government officials had told reporters in early August that the former leader had been in Thailand in June directing his rebel group's participation in the talks. However, Samphan claimed Pol Pot is only in charge of the Khmer Rouge's National Institute of Research and Defense and would be a "simple Cambodian citizen" after the settlement.

The final major breakthrough occurred at the United Nations on 20 September when the groups agreed on an electoral formula. Previously, the Cambodian government had insisted on a single-seat constituency, first-past-the-post system, which would allow it to take full advantage of its administrative network throughout the country. The opposition, particularly Son Sann, who potentially has the least base of support, favored a nationwide proportional representation system which would assure it of winning some seats. The parties accepted a compromise featuring a proportional system using Cambodia's twenty provinces as constituencies. Each faction would be expected to do well in its stronghold. Premier Hun Sen reasoned that the Khmer Rouge would win fewer seats this way than under a national proportional vote.

One last obstacle arose just weeks before the leaders met in Paris. Sometime in September, Khmer Rouge operatives kidnapped the elected leaders of a refugee camp, known as Site Eight, on the Thai border. Khmer Rouge officials then went into the camp in an effort to force the refugees to register with them for repatriation in

Cambodia. The peace plan expressly prohibits any of the factions from resettling refugees, which would presumably be done to build up an electoral base in areas under that faction's control. The Khmer Rouge ended its latest forced relocation attempt after a harsh warning from the U.N. Security Council.

With the signing of the treaty imminent, Cambodia's Kampuchean People's Revolutionary Party—at that point, still the only legal political party in the country — called a special party congress on 17-18 October. The party officially dropped its Marxist-Leninist ideology, announced its approval of a multi-party political system and a market economy, and changed its name to the Cambodian People's Party. The party also named Chea Sim as its new leader, and dropped longtime party chief Heng Samrin to the meaningless position of honorary president.

On 23 October the leaders of the four factions—Prince Sihanouk, Sonn San, Prime Minister Hun Sen, and Khieu Samphan—signed the treaty along with represen- tatives of eighteen other countries. The agreement calls for a new constitution to be drafted by a 120-member national assembly to be freely elected, possibly within twenty-one months. It also calls for the release of all political prisoners. In October, Hun Sen's government, which had previously denied having any political prisoners, released an initial group of 442. In what will be its largest project ever, the U.N. will commit up to 30,000 soldiers and administrators to run the country and monitor the cease-fire until the elections are held, at a cost in excess of $1 billion.

Thousands of Cambodians turned out for the Prince's dramatic return to Phnom Penh on 14 November and watched him ride to the Royal Palace in a 1963 sedan. Foreign governments have been invited back to the capital, and the United States sent a special representative in early November. Even with the treaty, many have warned that the Khmer Rouge could be gearing up for a violent return to power. Several weeks after the Paris ceremonies, relief workers and others in the countryside said the radical rebel group had begun hiding soldiers and weapons in remote areas.

Events late in the year threatened the peace process. On 20 November, Hun Sen unexpectedly named Sihanouk president of the country after the prince and his followers entered into a coalition with the government to alienate the Khmer Rouge. On 27 November, a raging mob bloodied and nearly lynched Khieu Samphan upon his return to the capital, with many Cambodians vowing revenge on all Khmer Rouge leaders for the deaths of their relatives. Sensing the peace plan could unravel, on 6 December Sihanouk temporarily dropped plans for the coalition. On 21 December, crowds gathered in Phnom Penh protesting both the return of Khmer Rouge leaders and the government's economic policies and corruption, the first major demonstration in the capital in 16 years. The following day, at least three were killed and 25 injured in further unrest, and the government imposed a nighttime curfew on the capital. The Supreme National Council finally met in Phnom Penh on 30 December and called for a rapid deployment of the U.N. troops.

Political Rights and Civil Liberties:

The October 1991 peace treaty installed an interim govern- ment composed of the four rival factions which had been fighting for control of Cambodia. Until then the Communist Kampuchean People's Revolutionary Party (KPRP) had been the only legal political party, although rebel groups controlled substantial parts of the country. Elections for a national assembly are scheduled to be held by mid-1993.

Under the KPRP regime, political prisoners were routinely tortured and sent to "re-education" camps. Defendants had few procedural rights, and many trials were conducted in secret. The government controlled all media. Citizens did not have the right of free assembly, and all organizations had to be approved by the government. Only state-approved labor associations were permitted. While Buddhism is the official religion, recently some Protestant, Roman Catholic and Muslim communities were allowed to practice their religions. Brutal conditions were reported in areas under Khmer Rouge control, especially in camps for displaced persons. In the months leading up to the peace agreement, the Khmer Rouge repeatedly attempted to relocate refugees into areas it controlled in order to increase its voting base in anticipation of eventual elections.

Cameroon

Polity: One-party
Economy: Capitalist
Population: 11,400,000
PPP: $1,670
Life Expectancy: 53.7
Ethnic Groups: Adamawa, Bamiléké, Beti, Dzem, Fulani, Mandari, Shouwa, other—over 100 tribes and 24 languages

Political Rights: 6
Civil Liberties: 6
Status: Not Free

Overview:

When President Paul Biya officially legalized opposition parties on 19 December 1990, multi-party democracy seemed close at hand. But by the end of 1991, violent confrontation and stalemate resulted in military rule instead of democracy.

In 1991 the newly legalized political opposition demanded a sovereign national conference to organize a change of regime, but the president refused to concede supreme authority to the opposition by allowing such a conference to take place. While the government and opposition argued over the organization of political change, violent anti-government strikes and demonstrations broke out repeatedly in many areas of the country.

The current territory of the Republic of Cameroon, located on the Gulf of Guinea in west-central Africa, was formed in 1961 with the merger of former British and French colonial possessions. This dual Anglo-French colonial heritage is still felt in the often sharp divisions between the 20 percent Anglophone minority and the 80 percent Francophone majority. Additional racial, tribal, religious and political divisions initially led to a loose federal structure emphasizing separate regional governments. By 1965, however, a shift to a centralized unitary regime had begun, culminating in the political dominance of President Ahmadou Babatoura Ahidjo in 1972. In 1982 however, Ahidjo resigned and elevated his friend Prime Minister Paul Biya to the presidency. Running as the sole candidate, Biya was officially elected president in 1984. Soon thereafter, the unicameral 150-member National Assembly eliminated the office of prime minister, thereby vesting all executive power in Biya. The present unitary system calls for a strong presidency directly elected by universal suffrage, with the power to appoint and dismiss government ministers, governors, other provincial officials, and members of the legislature at will.

On 22 April 1991 at Biya's bidding, however, the 150-member National Assembly passed legislation recreating the post of prime minister and mandating the release of all political prisoners. On 25 April Biya appointed as prime minister Sadou Hayatou, a northerner trusted in the international financial community, to head an interim government leading to legislative elections before the end of the year. But the oppositon dismisses the legislature as a rubber stamp and its election as insignificant.

Competitive elections of a sort were held for the first time in 1988, but all of the candidates were approved by the leadership of the ruling single-party CPDR (Cameroon People's Democratic Rally). In the face of strong public pressure by those disillusioned with Biya's one-party state, President Biya announced his commitment in principal to multi-partyism in June 1990. Although fourteen parties were active by early April of 1991, the promise of a smooth evolution toward multi-party democracy was short-lived. The CPDM itself seemed to be fragmenting into pro- and anti-reform wings, with many in the ruling coterie around Biya opposed to the type of political liberalization that would end their further dominance. Many of those in the highest levels of the government and the military come from Biya's own Beti ethnic group, and there seems to be an attempt to rally intra-ethnic support by framing the opposition to the regime in terms of an anti-Beti movement by the allegedly self-serving Bamiléké of the former British part of Cameroon.

Among the stronger opposition parties are: the Social Democratic Front (SDF), whose region of greatest strength lies where anglophones predominate in the northwest; the leftist Union of Cameroonian Peoples (UPC), which is strongest in the area of Douala and the Littoral Province; the largely Muslim and northern-oriented National Union for Democracy and Progress (UNDP) which descends from the party ex-President Ahidjo founded during his rule; the Union of Democratic Forces of Cameroon (UFDC), which has some strength around the capital of Yaounde; and the National Movement for Democracy (MND) of Yondo Black.

A united front of most of the opposition parties and political associations (the NCCOP) was created to demand a national conference, the dissolution of the CPDM-monopolized legislature, a new constitution establishing a decentralized confederation of elected regional governors, full amnesty for political prisoners and exiles, and an end to all censorship and the government's monopoly on access to broadcasting. They also demanded an independent electoral commission, revision of the electoral code, and an end to the regime's clandestine revision of the electoral register. Despite calls for his resignation, President Biya has repeatedly declared that he will not step down before his term expires in 1993. The government has continued to insist that a national referendum to validate proposed reforms undertaken in the existing constitutional framework is more democratic than a national convention. It also dismissed demands for an independent electoral commission and refused to recognize the NCCOP as a legal organization. The opposition responded by threatening to boycott any elections, arguing that they would certainly be rigged.

Despite bans on public gatherings, anti-government demonstrations began in earnest by early April. Violent crackdowns by government security forces took over 70 lives by November. Not all the deaths were due to police misconduct. One student, for example, was severely burned at the university when anti-government agitators set him on fire; his elder brother was believed to have been a police informer. Nevertheless, the vast majority of deaths were caused by security police firing into crowds.

In late May, despite having earlier dismissed the protests as symptomatic of an "infantile malady," Biya put seven of the country's ten provinces under military rule. In response, opposition groups gathered on 15 June and adopted a *Ville deserte* policy (often referred to as "operation dead cities and deserted country"). This campaign of civil disobedience involved work stoppages, transport strikes, rallies, marches and boycotts. In an attempt to force all of the citizenry to participate in strikes and shut-downs some opposition militants stoned vehicles on the road and looted the premises of shopkeepers who kept their businesses open. There were street clashes between government supporters and opponents, leading to more deaths. Some shopowners were arrested for observing the strike, and the locks on their shops were broken on order of authorities. Attempting to stop further demonstrations and public disruptions, the government banned opposition groups from working together within the NCCOP on 26 June, accusing them of using terrorist methods. In July, Biya specifically outlawed six organizations involved in the campaign, including independent human rights groups, on grounds that their activities jeopardized public order and state security. Leaders of opposition groups have been repeatedly arrested in an attempt to stop the campaign against the government.

The opposition and the government finally decided to meet in talks to try to break the deadlock. Convening at the end of October, the parties heard the prime minister, asserting the right to chair the proceedings and set the agenda, refuse to address any matters other than opposition access to state-run media and revision of the electoral code. The regime would not discuss a national conference. When the opposition rejected his framework for discussion, talks were stalemated.

Political Rights and Civil Liberties:

Despite the legalization of multiple political parties, the people of Cameroon do not have the right to change their government by democratic means. Legislative elections have been scheduled for 16 February 1992, although opposition participation is uncertain. Opposition leaders are against holding any elections before a national conference, fearing electoral fraud by the government.

Courts are generally not subject to government interference when dealing with nonpolitical matters. However, there have been public charges of pervasive judicial corruption. Security laws limit freedom of expression and the ability of citizens to openly criticize their government. Military tribunals have tried civilians for political offenses, but now the new state security courts handle such cases under subversion statutes. The details of charges may be withheld in such trials, defendants may be denied effective counsel, and there is no automatic right of appeal upon conviction. There are no limitations on preventive detention for defendants formally indicted, and governmental officials at many levels have the power to administratively detain individuals without charge or trial. The security forces regularly employ such extrale-gal means of discouraging political dissent, as harassment, beatings and torture.

Despite the government's pledge in mid-1990 to end censorship, in 1991 the regime continued to actively stifle the independent media. Journalists have been arrested, opposition newspapers censored, and the amount of newsprint available to nongovernmental publications has been intentionally restricted in order to limit their circulation. Nonetheless, banned periodicals are often printed in Nigeria and smuggled across the border into Cameroon, and a burgeoning independent press of over sixty publications continues to vigorously criticize the regime for corruption and repression. The government publishes two newspapers and controls television and radio, all of which reflect official government positions and deny access to dissenting voices.

The 27 December 1990 issue of the independent *Le Messager* contained an open letter sharply criticizing President Biya and the sincerity of his pledge to move toward democracy. The response was immediate: the issue was confiscated from the stands, and both the author of the letter and the director of the paper were arrested for defaming political institutions and insulting the head of state. After a trial in which the defense was not allowed to present its case, the defendants were given suspended sentences and fined.

Unions are controlled by the government under the umbrella Organization of United Cameroonian workers (OCWU). Strikes are illegal. Freedom of association is restricted and opposition organizations have been banned. There are also restrictions on freedom to travel outside the country. Freedom of religion is not respected with regard to certain evangelical Protestant sects.

Canada

Polity: Federal parliamentary democracy
Economy: Capitalist
Population: 26,800,000
PPP: $17,680
Life Expectancy: 77.0
Ethnic Groups: British, French, other European, Asian, Caribbean black, aboriginal (Indian and Inuit), others

Political Rights: 1
Civil Liberties: 1
Status: Free

Overview:

In 1991, Canadian news was dominated by controversy and debate over Quebec sovereignty, the Canadian constitution, political scandals and economic stress.

The French and British colonized Canada in the seventeenth and eighteenth centuries. Following the Treaty of Paris in 1763, Britain governed both the Francophone and Anglophone areas until it granted home rule with the British North America Act (now called the Constitution Act) in 1867. The British monarch remains the titular head of state, acting through the largely ceremonial Canadian governor-general. Britain retained a theoretical right to rule over the Canadian Parliament until 1982, when Canadians established complete control over their own constitution.

The Canadian Parliament is bicameral. The House of Commons has 295 members elected from single-member districts (ridings). The Senate has more than 100 members whom the government appoints to represent the country's provinces and territories. The provinces have some significant local powers.

Canada adopted an overhauled constitution in 1982 and added a charter of rights and freedoms, which common law had covered previously. Limiting the binding nature of the rights and freedoms, one constitutional clause, known as the "notwithstanding clause," permits provincial governments to exempt themselves from applying the charter within their jurisdictions. After holding out against the new constitution, Quebec agreed to accept it in 1987 in return for a recognition by the federal government and the other provinces that Quebec constitutes a "distinct society" within Canada. This was the heart of the Meech Lake accord, named after the location of the constitutional negotiations. Quebec invoked the "notwithstanding clause" to keep its provincial language law which restricts the use of English in signs. Many English-speaking municipalities reacted by declaring themselves official English zones. There was a widespread feeling among Anglophone Canadians that recognizing Quebec as a distinct society in the constitution could give it extraordinary powers to limit the rights of non-French Canadians. Generally, Anglophone Canadians did not dispute Quebec's distinctive nature, but questioned whether its distinct status justified curtailing the Charter of Rights and Freedoms and whether Quebec deserved to have constitutionally implied powers unavailable to other provinces.

Under the terms of the deal, all provinces had to ratify the Meech Lake accord by 23 June 1990. But after months of national debate, Newfoundland and Manitoba doomed the accord by failing to ratify it.

The defeat of Meech Lake was a sharp political setback for Canadian Prime Minister Brian Mulroney. His Progressive Conservative Party had won the 1988 federal parliamentary election with strong support in Quebec. A bilingual Quebecker, Mulroney had sought to keep his province within Canada through the adoption of the Meech Lake agreement. The pact's failure angered Quebec's Francophone majority and increased support for Quebec sovereignty.

With the death of the Meech Lake accord, the Quebec government appointed a panel, the Belanger-Campeau Commission, to investigate provincial constitutional options. In March 1991 the commission recommended a referendum on sovereignty for Quebec by 26 October 1992. The Belanger-Campeau commissioners were split on the question of holding a referendum before negotiations with the national government. Quebec's Liberal Premier Robert Bourassa demanded that Canada approve radically decentralized government or face such a referendum. His plan called for exclusive provincial control over twenty-two fields of government. Bourassa would leave the central government with exclusive jurisdiction over defense, customs, currency and wealth equalization among the provinces. Mulroney attacked the Bourassa plan, saying, "I will never acquiesce in reducing our national government to the status of a conference center, a financial clearing house, or an inter-provincial welfare agency." The prime minister dismissed Quebec sovereigntists as "dream merchants," and rejected the idea of a "part-time" Canada. Mulroney shuffled his cabinet in April 1991, and appointed former Prime Minister Joe Clark to the new post of Minister for Constitutional Affairs. Mulroney and Clark hope to keep Canada intact with constitutional reforms acceptable to both Quebec and the other provinces.

Quebec's opposition party, Parti Quebecois (PQ), has announced that after winning a provincial election it would establish an independent Quebec and negotiate a division of assets with Canada.

Attempting to prevent secession and buy time, Mulroney appointed a panel chaired by Keith Spicer to solicit the views of the Canadian public on the constitution and the political system. The Spicer Commission held a series of public hearings, the Citizens' Forum on Canada's Future, which allowed 350,000 people to vent their frustration with the political system and offer solutions to the Quebec question and other major issues. The Spicer Commission reported in 1991 that the country was out of sync with itself, disgusted with its leadership, opposed to provincial privilege (except in Quebec), and desirous of radical change. The commissioners backed proposals protecting the country's national symbols, ending local ignorance of other regions, reforming the structure of the Canadian Senate, granting self-government to the Indians, reviewing the policy of bilingualism, and making some concessions to Quebec to keep it within Canada. The Spicer Commission supported educating Canadians on the consequences of an independent Quebec.

In September 1991 the Mulroney government introduced a package of constitutional reforms. The major elements included: recognition of Quebec as a distinct society; an elected Senate with guaranteed aboriginal representation; Indian and Inuit self-government; decentralization of many governmental responsibilities to the provinces; entrenchment of property rights in the constitution; freer movement of people, goods, and services within Canada; a requirement of majority votes from both major language groups to pass linguistic and cultural bills in the Senate; restrictions on use of the "notwithstanding clause"; and a "Canada clause," which would enshrine national values and purposes in the constitution. Initial political action was mixed. Opposition politicians tended to view the package as a bargaining tool. Critics questioned the meaning of the proposed property rights clause, and wondered about the implications for divorce settlements, Indian land claims, and zoning laws. The provincial government of Ontario countered with a proposal for adding social rights to the constitution.

The possible break-up of Canada has many serious implications. For example, no one is sure whether a sovereign Quebec would be automatically entitled to participate in Canada's existing trading arrangements with other countries, most notably with the U.S. Other possible costs of independence include severe economic stress and loss of territory for Quebec. The Canadian government granted Quebec resource-rich territories in 1898 and 1912. In 1991 some Canadians suggested removing these areas from Quebec before independence. The Canadian Institute of Strategic Studies raised the possibility of civil war, especially if the Cree Indians attempted to withdraw their lands from Quebec. The province's departure from Canada would leave Francophones in other Canadian provinces without Quebec's political and cultural protection.

Aside from the debates over Quebec and the constitution, scandals strained the political system in 1991. In July a justice of the peace approved corruption charges against sixteen Progressive Conservative politicians, former officials, aides and law enforcers. Former Quebec businessman Glen Kealy, an alleged victim of the corruption, had led a three-year campaign to prosecute the group for fraud, bribery, kickbacks and obstruction of justice. Holding a protest sign and a toy pig, Kealy had stood daily in front of Parliament and had heckled Mulroney and other Conservatives. In 1991 Kealy attracted national support for the charges. However, in September prosecutors dropped most of the Kealy-initiated charges except for those against former Public Works Minister Roch La Salle. At the provincial level, William Vander Zalm, the premier of British Columbia, resigned in April over a conflict of interest scandal involving his family's theme park.

Canada suffered from a severe recession in 1991. The unemployment rate climbed over 10.6 percent, and was especially high in manufacturing areas. As of 1 January the country also began enduring a national goods and services tax (GST). Coupled with provincial sales taxes, the GST drove record numbers of Canadian consumers to shop in the United States. Other signs of economic strain were strikes by postal workers and civil servants.

Many Canadian companies moved their locations across the border in 1991, taking advantage of the Canadian-American free trade agreement, which Mulroney had championed in the 1988 election. The major opposition parties, the Liberals and the social democratic New Democrats, had opposed the deal as detrimental to Canada's economic and cultural interests. Under the pact, major trade barriers between the two countries will disappear during the 1990s. In 1991 the U.S. and Canada decided to speed up tariff reductions. With mixed feelings, Canada joined the U.S. and Mexico in negotiations over a North American free trade area. By having started bilateral free trade talks with Mexico, the U.S. left Canada with little choice about joining the negotiations. Quebeckers wondered about their place in an expanded free trade zone, especially since the province has a strongly interventionist economic policy.

Beyond North America, Canada's most significant international activity in 1991 was its role in the Persian Gulf War. On 22 January the House of Commons voted to back the U.N. effort to force Iraq out of Kuwait. Canada sent ground troops, ships and air power to the region, and took part in attacks on military targets in Iraq and Kuwait.

Traditionally, Canadians have held that theirs is basically a major-party-dominated system but, at the federal and provincial levels, there is an increasingly fractious multi-party system. The leading opposition party to Mulroney's Conservatives (Tories) is the Liberal Party, headed by Jean Chretien, who became leader at a party convention in 1990. Chretien faced political difficulties in 1991 after charges that he flip-flopped over whether or not Canada could amend the constitution without Quebec's approval. The second opposition party is the social democratic New Democratic Party (NDP), led by Audrey McLaughlin. The NDP received a major boost when it captured control of the province of Ontario in 1990, and the provinces of British Columbia and Saskatchewan in 1991. Formed by dissident Conservatives and Liberals in the House of Commons and headed by ex-Conservative Lucien Bouchard, the Bloc Quebecois advocates sovereignty for Quebec. The fast-growing, anti-bilingual Reform Party surpassed the Conservatives in many opinion polls in 1991, and threatened to undercut the Tories in the West at the next general election. Some other purely regional parties exist at the provincial level. The most notable of them is Parti Quebecois (PQ), which also advocates sovereignty for Quebec. In April 1991 the PQ endorsed Bloc Quebecois at the federal level. Some trade union supporters of PQ are considering forming their own social democratic labor party in the event of an independent Quebec.

Political Rights and Civil Liberties:

Canadians have the right to change their government by democratic means at the federal, provincial and local levels. Due to canvassing every five years by government census-takers, Canada has nearly 100 percent effective voter registration. The provinces, especially Quebec, have significant powers. Canada is moving to give more autonomy to its aboriginal inhabitants. In 1991 Ontario granted Indians self-government and resource development within the province. Following Indian demands, federal leaders have discussed including specific Indian rights in new constitutional amendments. Canada negotiated with the Inuits (Eskimos) to carve an Inuit-governed territory, Nunavut, out of the Northwest territories.

In general, civil liberties are very strong and protected by the Charter of Rights and Freedoms. However, the "notwithstanding clause" allows liberties to be curtailed by provincial governments. Unevenly enforced laws prohibit some forms of pornography and hate literature. In 1991, Canadanian Customs seized over 700 books destined for a gay bookstore in Toronto, but the volumes remained available at other locations. At the same time, the government prepared to end its policy against recruiting and promoting homosexuals in the military.

The media are generally free, but there are some restrictions. There is an autonomous government broadcasting system, the CBC, which has both English and French channels. There are also private broadcasters, magazines and newspapers. In 1991 the Canadian Radio Television and Telecommunications Commission relaxed rules that dictated the precise mixtures of music radio stations could play. Mulroney caused an uproar in 1991 by appointing John Crispo to the CBC's governing board. A right-wing academic, Crispo is hostile to the CBC, and applauded budget cuts which wiped out eleven stations. Asserting that the network's news coverage is unfair, Crispo called the CBC a "lousy, left-wing, liberal, NDP, pinko network." The NDP government of Ontario announced plans in March 1991 to eliminate "sexist" advertising.

A generous welfare system supplements a largely open, competitive economy. The government privatized Petrocanada, the national oil corporation, in 1991. Property rights for current occupants are generally strong, but increasing Indian land claims have led to several rounds of litigation and negotiation.

Trade unions and business associations are free and well-organized. The Canadian Supreme Court ruled in February 1990 that Quebec's ban on public sector strikes was unconstitutional, because the collective bargaining agreements were not translated into English. In 1991 the Supreme Court upheld Ontario's labor relations system which puts teachers into unions based on sex and religion.

Religious expression is free and diverse. However, there are some special rules about religious education. Since the founding of the Canadian government in 1867, there have been state-supported religious (or "separate") school systems in various provinces, but not all denominations have government-backed systems. Complying with an appeals court ruling in 1990, the province of Ontario ordered its public schools to avoid education in a particular religion, but it also specified that the schools may provide an education about religions in general. In 1991, Jewish and Protestant groups in Ontario challenged the provincial policy of giving financial aid to Catholic schools. They charged that the subsidies violated the freedom of religion and equality sections in the Charter of Rights and Freedoms.

The judiciary is independent, and the courts often overturn government policy. Judges have constitutional protection from political interference.

The Supreme Court strengthened the rights of the accused in June 1990 when it ruled that confessions are inadmissible as evidence if police obtain them undercover from those who have refused to be questioned. In October 1990 the Supreme Court ruled in favor of the constitutional right to be tried within a reasonable time, which Justice Peter Cory described as six to eight months. As a result, courts threw out tens of thousands of cases in 1991. Cory responded that the lower courts were taking the ruling too rigidly. A Quebec judge ruled in 1991 that prosecutors have the right to conduct a trial of Indians in French, and that the section of the criminal code which guarantees a right to be tried in French or English did not apply to Quebec. The court drew a distinction between the right to understand and the right to be understood.

Quebec's language laws limit the cultural and educational rights of non-French Canadians. For example, immigrants may not send their children to Anglophone schools in Quebec, although Anglo-Canadians may do so under some circumstances. Anglophone children may attend English schools in Quebec if at least one parent is an Anglophone Canadian and if that parent had an English-language education for the last three years of secondary school. In 1991 the U.N. Human Rights Commission accepted a case dealing with Quebec Bill 178 which bans English on outdoor commercial signs in the province. A funeral home operator is arguing that the sign law violates international human rights standards.

1991 brought significant developments in freedom of movement. Canada gave resident status to Mohammed Al-Mashat, the former Iraqi ambassador to the U.S. Meanwhile, there was a growing backlog of other refugee claimants including people from Anglophone Caribbean countries. An immigration adjudicator declared unconstitutional a section of the Immigration Act permitting the government to certify a person a danger and ineligible for refugee status. Since the Charter of Rights and Freedoms applies to all on Canadian soil, refugee claimants tend to stay for at least two years while awaiting a guaranteed hearing.

Cape Verde

Polity: Presidential-parliamentary democracy
Economy: Mixed statist
Population: 400,000
PPP: $1,410
Life Expectancy: 67.0
Ethnic Groups: Overall ethnic unity among all racial groups, Mestiço/Mulatto, Black African, European

Political Rights: 2
Civil Liberties: 3
Status: Free

Overview:

Cape Verde began 1991 with a heavy turnout in its first multi-party elections since it won independence from Portugal in 1975.

Carlos Veiga, a former activist in the long ruling African Party for the Independence of Cape Verde (PAICV), led the eight-month-old opposition party Movement for Democracy (MPD) to a convincing victory in a parliamentary poll on 14 January with some 65 percent of the vote. The MPD won 56 of 79 seats at stake in the new national legislature. In presidential elections held on 17 February MPD-supported independent candidate and former Supreme Court Justice Antonio Mascarenhas Monteiro beat the ruling president, Aristides Pereira. For fifteen years, Pereira ruled as leader of the PAICV while it was the sole legal party in the country. The new administration plans to draft a new constitution to replace the quasi-Marxist one inherited from the previous regime.

A cluster of ten islands and smaller islets off the coast of west-central Africa, Cape Verde began its post-colonial existence politically linked to Guinea-Bissau, another former Portuguese dependency located on the west African mainland. The leadership of Cape Verde severed this connection in 1979 after the government in Guinea-Bissau was overthrown in a coup. The 1980 Capeverdian constitution established a single-party state under the tutelage of the leftist PAICV, with legislative authority vested in a unicameral National People's Assembly.

The move toward multi-partyism began officially at a PAICV party congress held in February of 1990. The leadership advocated constitutional amendments to pave the way for competitive elections and eliminate reference to the guiding role of the PAICV in society. The national legislature later voted to permit alternative party slates in parliamentary polling and universal suffrage in direct elections for president. President Pereira subsequently resigned his PAICV leadership post in preparation for running for president as an independent—new electoral regulations stated that presidential elections could not be party based. Pedro Pires was then appointed prime minister and official standard bearer for the PAICV, only to resign from office months later after conceding electoral defeat to Carlos Viega and the MPD.

Upon taking office, the new government demanded that ex-officials of the PAICV regime return furnishings allegedly stolen when they vacated government residences. Abandoning their offices almost immediately after their defeat at the polls, the PAICV also demonstrated little interest in helping to facilitate a smooth transition to the new government. The Veiga government later accused the PAICV of organizing a campaign of destabilization and disinformation against the new government in order to scare off foreign investors and drum up support for itself among foreign leftists.

In May 1991 partisans of the Independent and Democratic Capeverdian Union (UCID) marched in protest when the Supreme Tribunal of Justice rejected the party's bid for legalization on the basis that its application was not in order. A similar ruling before the January elections had kept the UCID off of the ballot. The Veiga government endorsed the speedy legalization of the UCID, and promised to revise legislation dealing with political parties.

The MPD won ten of fourteen local councils in elections marked by a low turnout on 15 December 1991.

Cape Verde has among the highest per capita incomes in West Africa. Many citizens survive on remittances sent by expatriates to family members still living on the islands or from Social Security checks sent to retirees who have spent their working lives in the U.S. These are the primary sources of foreign exchange earnings for the nation because agricultural opportunities are limited on the arid islands and the fishing industry is still underdeveloped. The new government hopes to boost the economy by encouraging foreign investment and developing the tourism industry.

Political Rights and Civil Liberties: In 1991 Cape Verde held competitive elections for the first time since independence. Criminal and civil cases are generally adjudicated fairly and expeditiously; the new government intends to abolish the local "popular tribunals" staffed by individuals chosen by the PAICV. There are no known political prisoners. Public criticism of the government is now tolerated. Freedoms of religion, association and assembly are all respected. The new government has abolished the FSOP security force and the ideologically inspired peoples' militias. Unions no longer need belong to the formerly PAICV-affiliated labor federation, the *Central Sindical*.

Central African Republic

Polity: One-party (military)
Economy: Capitalist-statist
Population: 3,000,000
PPP: $780
Life Expectancy: 49.5
Ethnic Groups: Baya (34 percent), Banda (27 percent), Mandja (21 percent), Sara (10 percent)

Political Rights: 6
Civil Liberties: 5
Status: Partly Free

Overview:

Following pro-democracy protests in 1991, the Central African Republic's government announced its commitment to establish multi-party democracy. By the end of the year, however, no elections had been held or announced.

This former French colony has been under the leadership of General André Kolingba since 1981, when he overthrew the regime of Colonel Jean-Bedel Bokassa. General Kolingba immediately established the Central African Democratic Assembly (RDC) as the sole legal political party. Kolingba rule has been marked by superficial calls for democracy, but with no tangible results.

In 1990, during an extraordinary congress, the RDC declared that it would try to eradicate corruption in the government, and meet the demands of striking teachers by raising their salaries. The congress also declared itself in favor of greater freedom of expression and of the press. However, the RDC categorically rejected the institution of a multi-party system, saying the "multi-party system does not constitute an absolute basis of democracy."

In October 1990 violent demonstrations broke out after police prevented the meeting of the Coordinating Committee for the Convening of a National Conference (CCCN), an opposition group calling for a national conference to revise the system of government. Police also arrested several members of the group.

As a response to continuing protests by students and their supporters, General Kolingba declared in his New Year address that he would call another congress of the RDC to revise the constitution, create an elected office of prime minister and "strengthen democratic institutions." By March there was a new prime minister—Edouard Franck—but he was appointed by Kolingba, not elected. Franck is a former government clerk and protégé of General Kolingba. The Congress also increased the power available to the Parliament, still completely controlled by Kolingba's party. In April, when these "reforms" did not pacify increasingly restive opposition groups, General Kolingba announced that the RDC would reconsider its decision and accept multi-party democracy.

This stated policy reversal did not calm the population. On 29 April 1991 the civil servants' unions called for a general strike to protest the frequent delays in the payment of their salaries. Teachers, students, civil servants, press, health personnel, rural development workers, and finance sector workers all participated in the strike. Strikers also demanded multi-partyism and a national conference on the future of the Central African Republic. Violence increased as the strikers engaged in pillaging and the government retaliated with tear gas. In June workers initiated a series of weekly "Operation Ghost Towns," during which virtually all work ceased for twenty-four hours. Finally, on 2 July 1991 the RDC approved a bill to introduce multi-party democracy. However, since this legislation did not appease the strikers, Kolingba arrested at least twenty-five union leaders and banned all union activities. At first, workers began to return to their jobs. However, strikes, sometimes violent, resumed in August. Kolingba finally relented in September with a declaration of clemency that freed the union leaders and reduced the sentence of former Emperor Jean-Bedel Bokassa from life to twenty years hard labor. However, the head of the CCCN was arrested on 29 August, allegedly for a common law offense. Attempts at new demonstrations in October by the opposition and student movement were stopped by the security forces. A mediator appointed by the government offered 19 February 1992 as a date for the national conference. However, this was rejected by the opposition, who insisted that a conference be convened on 19 November. Preliminary consultations between the opposition and the regime on fixing a date for the conference began on 9 November, but were suspended due to the poor health of the government mediator. In an attempt to appease the opposition, the government lifted the ban on union activity on 1 November. At the end of the year, multi-party democracy remained elusive to the people of the Central African Republic.

Political Rights and Civil Liberties: The Central African Republic remains a one-party state dominated by RDC; citizens do not have the power to change their government democratically. In 1991, however, opposition parties were legalized for the first time; eleven parties had been registered as of December. Although criticism of the government is not uncommon in the RDC-controlled parliament, it remains subservient to the president. Although the constitution guarantees equal rights for all citizens, one group, the Bamingua (Pygmies) are frequently discriminated against. Despite the RDC's calls for greater freedom of expression, the government-controlled media reflect official policy and citizens still cannot openly criticize the government. In 1991 government troops violently dispersed several peaceful demonstrations. Except for select political cases, the government does not interfere in the judicial process, which appears relatively fair. However, inadequate, incompetent staffs and loose interpretation of evidence (sometimes involving witchcraft and sorcery) often compromise judicial proceedings.

There is little interference in religion, and freedom of movement is generally unrestricted. On 11 September all roadblocks, except those set up for customs, were removed. After a seven-year ban, labor unions were allowed to form and have generally been free from government interference.

Chad

Polity: Military-transitional
Economy: Capitalist
Population: 5,100,000
PPP: $510
Life Expectancy: 46.5
Ethnic Groups: Arab, Bideyat, Daza, Hadjarai, Kanembu, Maba, Sara,Teda, Zaghawa, 20 distinct other groups

Political Rights: 6
Civil Liberties: 6
Status: Not Free

Overview: The most significant event in Chad during 1991 was the consolidation of the new regime of Idris Deby. In November

1990 Chadian rebels under the command of Deby rolled out of their bases in Sudan's neighboring Darfur region and attacked army garrisons in eastern Chad. Routing government forces, the insurgents captured the capital by 2 December. President Hissein Habre fled to Cameroon and Deby assumed the presidency.

Deby, a former army commander, had fled Chad in April 1989 after a coup attempt he reportedly led against Habre failed. After fleeing, Deby formed the Patriotic Salvation Movement (MPS) and from his sanctuary in Sudan, began to plan Habre's ouster from his sanctuary in Sudan. Although Deby was backed by Libya as well as the Sudan, he has been deeply anti-Libyan in the past.

Located in north-central Africa, Chad gained independence from France in 1960. Upon the withdrawal of French troops in 1965, domestic factions began to struggle for control, presaging an on-again, off-again civil war. After years of conflict, two main factions emerged: Hissein Habre's Armed Forces of the North (FAN) and the People's Armed Forces (FAP), led by Goukouni Oueddei. Both groups cooperated in the formation of a government in 1979 with Oueddei serving as president and Habre as defense minister. A rift, however, led to renewed fighting. By the end of 1980, the FAP, with Libyan assistance, succeeded in forcing Habre to withdraw from the capital of N'Djamena. Fighting continued until 1983, when Habre, with French assistance, overthrew Oueddei's regime and became president.

Shortly after taking power, Habre began challenging Libyan occupation of parts of northern Chad, including the mineral-rich Aouzou Strip. In March 1987, after sporadic fighting to recover the region, Habre's forces overran Libyan positions and pursued Mu'ammar al-Qadhafi's soldiers into southern Libya. By November of 1988, Qadhafi formally terminated the war. In August 1989 Chad and Libya agreed to give themselves one year to bilaterally negotiate a solution to their dispute over the Aouzou strip, and, failing this, to have the issue taken up by the International Court of Justice. However, discussions between Libya and Chad over the disputed Aouzou strip did not progress, and Habre and Qadhafi agreed to refer the border dispute to the Court. The process was suspended on 2 December 1990 as Idris Deby, with Libyan assistance, overthrew Habre. Since rising to power, however, Deby has not cooperated with the Libyans; he has pledged to fight to regain complete Chadian sovereignty over the Aouzou Strip. Clashes were reported between Libyan and Chadian forces in the contested region during May 1991.

Declaring that the MPS will institute a multi-party democracy and guarantee freedom of expression, religion and association, Deby dissolved the National Assembly and suspended the constitution within days of taking power. He later assumed the presidency as head of a provisional administration, which was replaced in March by a more conventionally organized government with a prime minister. In February 1991 a "committee of experts" drew up a national charter and a new constitution, which is to remain in effect for thirty months. At the end of this interim period, there is to be a national referendum to vote on whether or not to accept a new constitution. There is no firm date yet for national elections, and though the new regime initially promised municipal and then regional elections before 1991 ended, they were not held. But the government has emphasized that democratization presupposes order and security, which is a particularly tall order in Chad. Among notable Chadians who may eventually be allowed to contest political power in multi-party elections is ex-President Goukouni Oueddei.

The regime finally came out with a draft law providing for the legalization of political parties in October 1991, and announced that a sovereign national conference will be convened in May or June of 1992. The president named a commission in December 1991 to prepare for the national conference. The ruling MPS has exempted itself from registration requirements and has already begun to organize for elections. However, political movements, such as the National Conference Forum, are being launched, and will likely transform themselves into legal opposition parties when allowed to do so. Several political opposition movements merged with the MPS during 1991.

In the fall of 1991 armed opposition groups stepped up attacks on government officials and garrisons. In September former army troops of the Goran ethnic group, supporters of the deposed Hissein Habre, attacked government positions in Tibesti. In October active troops of the Hadjarai ethnic group, allegedly on behalf of Interior Minister and Vice Chairman of the MPS Maldoum Bada Abbas, attacked an arms depot and other positions in the capital city N'djamena. During the October clashes, an estimated 150 died and Abbas was arrested. The year ended with another outbreak of fighting, this time in the Lake Chad area. The last week of December saw clashes between Deby's army and forces of the pro-Habre Movement for Democracy and Development. Most conflict in Chad has an inter-ethnic basis.

Political Rights and Civil Liberties:

Chadians do not have the right to change their government democratically. Upon taking power in December 1990, President Deby suspended Hissein Habre's recently adopted 1989 constitution, claiming at the time that the rights therein guaranteed had never been respected. The suspended document included provisions which formally guaranteed freedom of association and expression, the right to a fair trial and freedom from arbitrary arrest and humiliating or degrading treatment while detained. According to the President, a proposed replacement is to have many of the same rights among its provisions.

President Deby abolished the Habre political police force, but he has maintained the National Security Force. The president claimed at the beginning of his government that there are no longer any political prisoners in Chad. Some of the Hadjarai involved in the October uprising were reportedly tortured and executed after their capture. The government claims that others arrested on suspicion of involvement were later released.

The regime warned journalists of using "freedom of the press to discredit the institutions of the Republic." On 8 August a Chadian journalist was arrested for publishing an investigative report which displeased the government. Nevertheless, a national union of journalists was legalized in October.

Workers have formed a new labor federation, the Union of Chadian Trade Unions. Doctors and nurses as well as communications workers went on strike during 1991 over unpaid salaries. The Chadian Human Rights League was set up 1991, and publicly issued protests at reported abuses by the Deby government.

Chile

Polity: Presidential-legislative democracy
Economy: Capitalist
Population: 13,400,000
PPP: $4,720
Life Expectancy: 71.8
Ethnic Groups: Mestizo, Spanish, other European, Indian

Political Rights: 2
Civil Liberties: 2
Status: Free

Overview:

The September 1991 decision by Chile's Supreme Court to try two former military security chiefs accused of murder in civil courts was a milestone in the effort by the government of President Patricio Aylwin to strengthen civilian authority over the military. The decision, coupled with new constitutional reforms and the scheduling of the first municipal elections in two decades, indicated that Chile remained on the road to regaining its status as a model democracy in Latin America.

The Republic of Chile was founded after achieving independence from Spain in 1818. Democratic governance predominated in this century until the overthrow of the socialist government of Salvador Allende in 1973. General Augusto Pinochet, who became head of state in 1974, dissolved the Congress and outlawed independent political activity. Until August 1988 the government operated under either a state of siege or other states of exception.

The 1980 constitution, approved in a state-controlled plebiscite, established a permanent tutelary role for the military in a transition to a "protected" democracy. However, it also provided for a second plebiscite in which voters could reject another eight-year presidential term for a government candidate. In October 1988, 55 percent of Chilean voters said "no" to a second term for General Pinochet, which meant the government was constitutionally bound to hold competitive presidential and legislative elections in 1989.

The 1988 campaign of the 16-party "Command for the No" was based on reforming the constitution. After the plebiscite, right-wing supporters urged Pinochet to negotiate with the Command, leading to an agreement on 54 constitutional changes that were passed in a July 1989 plebiscite. Changes included increasing the number of elected senators in the Congress from twenty-six to thirty-eight (nine would still be appointees of the Pinochet government); the end of the ban on Marxist parties; and the reduction of the presidential term from eight years to four.

The center-left Coalition for Democracy (formerly the Command for the No) nominated Christian Democratic leader Patricio Aylwin for president. Right-wing parties backed either Hernan Buchi, Pinochet's former finance minister, or business-man Francisco Errazuriz. Because Aylwin vowed not to make major changes in the free-market, free-trade thrust of the economy, civil-military relations were the main issue. The 1980 constitution allows Pinochet to remain commander of the army, the strongest branch of the 57,000-man armed forces, until 1997.

On 14 December 1989 Aylwin won the presidency with 55.2 percent of the vote, with Buchi taking 28.9 percent, and Errazuriz taking 14.4 percent. The Coalition for Democracy secured a 72-48 majority in the 120-member Chamber of Deputies, and won 22 of the 38 elected Senate seats. But with nine senators appointed by the outgoing government, it fell short of a majority in the 47-seat Senate. Ammending the constitution requires a two-thirds majority in both houses.

In its first two years, the Aylwin government has made significant progress in diminishing the military's autonomy. In 1990 it created a Truth and Reconciliation Commission to investigate human rights violations committed under military rule. Pinochet protested, but the heads of the air force, navy and national police agreed to cooperate, indicating a willingness to respect the constitutional prohibition against military interference in political affairs. Pinochet indulged in some saber rattling, but it appeared that a significant number of his own officers supported an apolitical role for the army.

On 4 March 1991 the government's human rights report was released, implicating the military and the secret police at the highest levels in the death or disappearance of 2,279 people between September 1973 and March 1990. But it appeared doubtful that those responsible would be prosecuted. In 1978 the Pinochet regime issued an amnesty for all political crimes, and the Supreme Court, packed by Pinochet before leaving office, opposed the Aylwin government's efforts to lift it.

However, after persistent coaxing by Aylwin, the Supreme Court made a dramatic turnaround on a related issue—the 1976 murder in Washington of former Chilean ambassador to the U.S., Orlando Letelier, and his assistant, Ronni Moffit. In September, just before the statute of limitations ran out, the court ordered the arrest of the alleged perpetrators of the crime—General Juan Manuel Contreras and Colonel Pedro Espinosa—after ruling that they be tried in civilian courts. The expected backlash from the army never materialized, underscoring Pinochet's growing isolation and the enhanced authority of the civilian government.

Although a successful prosecution of the Letelier case would not establish accountability for the crimes investigated by the Truth and Reconciliation Commission, it would breach the wall of impunity around the military and renew the possibility of lifting the 1978 amnesty. In the meantime, Aylwin, whose opinion poll ratings have been consistently 70 percent or better, was expected to move on curtailing the military's autonomy in other areas, including budget and troop reductions. The next national elections are scheduled for December 1993.

Political Rights and Civil Liberties:

Citizens are able to change their government through free and fair elections. Following the passage of a constitutional amendment by the Congress in mid-1991, municipal elections, the first since the return to civilian rule, were scheduled for June 1992. Religious expression is unrestricted, and most of the laws limiting political expression were eliminated by the 1989 constitutional reforms. Any political party can achieve legal status, and the political spectrum runs from Marxist to fascist.

Since the constitutional reforms of 1989, any person or group is free to start, edit, operate and distribute newspapers or magazines without government permission. The Aylwin government has committed itself to complete media freedom, but a number of restrictive laws remain on the books, including one that grants power to military courts to convict journalists for libeling members of the armed forces. In September 1991, Manuel Cabiese, editor of *Punto Final*, was arrested on charges of defaming Pinochet, the first time the military had utilized this law under the new government. On occasion the media also has been targeted by left-wing terrorists. In September the general manager of *El Mercurio*, the nation's major newspaper, was abducted, but two months later his kidnappers still had neither identified themselves nor stated their demands.

Radio is both private and public. Independent radio played a key role in the 1988 plebiscite and the 1989 election with extensive coverage of independent, parallel vote counts. The national television network is operated by the state, but open to all political voices. There are three noncommercial television stations run by universities. During the 1988 and 1989 campaigns, all parties were allotted time on the state-run network. The 1989 campaign featured a nationally televised debate between the presidential candidates.

In 1990 negotiations between the government, labor unions and the private sector led to partial reform of the draconian labor code inherited from the Pinochet regime. However, a law banning public sector strikes remains on the books and was employed in 1991 by the government against strikes by miners, teachers and health workers. The government eventually dropped charges against strike leaders, but appeared reluctant to fulfill its promise of complete labor reform amid ongoing budget disputes with public sector workers.

Under Pinochet the power of military courts was greatly expanded at the expense of the civil court system. The Aylwin government has made significant headway in reversing the process, but the Supreme Court continues to refuse to hear cases regarding rights abuses by the military under Pinochet.

There were over 400 political prisoners when the Aylwin government took office. By October 1991 all but 83 had been pardoned. The remaining prisoners, convicted of violent actions by military courts, were to have their cases retried in civil courts, pending the passage of new legislation in the Congress.

In the first half of 1991 there was a wave of terrorist actions by remnants of the Manuel Rodriguez Patriotic Front (FPMR), the former armed wing of the Communist Party, and the bizarre anarcho-hedonist Lautero Front. Human rights groups expressed concern about new anti-terrorist legislation which permits police entry without a warrant in certain circumstances. Terrorist activity continued sporadically through the remainder of the year, but the police appeared to be responding in a generally responsible manner.

In August 1990, Chile ratified the Inter-American Convention on Human Rights and formally recognized the jurisdiction of the Inter-American Human Rights Court for the interpretation and enforcement of the provisions contained in the convention.

China

Polity: Communist one-party
Economy: Statist
Population: 1,148,300,000
PPP: $2,470
Life Expectancy: 70.1
Ethnic Groups: Han Chinese (93 percent), Azhuang, Hui, Uygur, Yi, Miao, Manchu, Tibetan, Mongolian, others

Political Rights: 7
Civil Liberties: 7
Status: Not Free

Overview:

The collapse of Soviet communism in 1991 ignited major debate among leaders in the ruling Communist party over whether to revert to classical Maoism or push ahead with market-oriented reforms launched a decade ago. Two years after the bloody crackdown against the pro-democracy movement in Tiananmen Square, the governing gerontocracy sought ways to safeguard its rule in the face of pressures from local and provincial leaders for faster economic reforms, as well as from the international community on the country's human rights record. Other major issues in 1991 included the prosecution of pro-democracy activists, a faltering economy and serious flooding in the summer that left thousands dead in 15 provinces. By year's end, it remained unclear who would succeed the octogenarians in power. What was clear was the government's public commitment to socialism. During September celebrations marking the forty-second anniversary of the People's Republic of China, Prime Minister Li Peng said that "no tempest will shake the people's determination to move along the path of building socialism under the leadership of the Communist Party of China." But the year was marked by an ongoing schism in the CCP and government over reforms.

The People's Republic of China (PRC) was established as a one-party Communist state in 1949 after Mao Zedong's victory over the Nationalists, led by Chiang Kai-Shek. The dominant political force in the country is the Chinese Communist Party (CCP), although eight smaller parties are allowed to exist under a CCP umbrella, the Chinese People's Political Consultative Conference. The unicameral National People's Congress (NPC) serves as the legislative body, though it is subservient to the CCP. The NPC confirms the president, vice-president and premier of State Council. In 1982 a new constitution reinstated the post of president; it is currently held by Yang Shankun, but is considered a largely ceremonial position. The chairman of the Party (replacing the liberal-minded Zhao Ziyang who has been under house arrest since June 1989) is Jiang Zemin, and the premier is Li Peng. Although eighty-seven–year–old Deng Xiaoping no longer holds an official position, he remains the highest political arbiter in China.

In 1991 Beijing tried to keep its grip on the reins of power, but in order to achieve this aim, the government sought to combine Western economic mechanisms with ideological intolerance and state-enforced uniformity. The CCP vowed not to relax its vigilance against "foreign forces trying to subvert socialism." Party Chairman Jiang said that the seventy-year experience of Chinese communism "boils down to one point: we must integrate the fundamental principles of Marxism with the concrete realities of the Chinese revolution and national development and keep to our own road."

But the strife between the Party's hardline and pro-reform factions spilled onto the front pages of China's state-run press when the USSR abandoned communism in August. By fall, Chinese newspapers began carrying more statements about "class struggle," there were calls for intensifying Marxist education, and leaders of many work units warned employees not to meet with foreigners. While Party elders (or "old comrades" as they are known in China) were united in their disgust at the collapse of Soviet communism, they held differing views on the pace of economic reform and the selection of younger leaders. Aging Party leaders seemed intimidated by the erosion of state control over the economy, but they conceded that economic reform had produced material gains that had lessened the chances of the type of overthrow that toppled East European regimes in 1989.

On 22 October, Party Chief Jiang warned that "without economic development and prosperity there will be no political stability." But hardline Communists argued that in order for the Party to survive, it had to revert to "class struggle," by indoctrinating citizens to rid China of capitalism, liberalism and other forces inimical to the working class. Reformers appeared to prevail at a Party working conference on the economy in Beijing in late September. "All work must be subordinate to and serve the core of economic construction," President Yang Shangkun said in a nationally televised speech days after the conference ended.

As expected, hardliners attacked reform plans. Two weeks after Yang's 9 October address, hardliners published a front-page commentary in the *Guangming Daily* titled "In Concentrating Forces on Economic Construction We Cannot Ignore Politics." The piece railed against "incorrect thinking and behavior." As part of the apparently broadbased drive to reassert Maoist orthodoxy, propaganda chief Wang Renzhi in the fall drafted a plan for promoting class struggle as a way to battle subversion. Justice Minister Cai Cheng asserted in early November that Chinese law could "not be divorced from politics," but must serve as a class tool in fighting enemies of the proletariat.

Other hardliners, such as Vice President Wang Zhen and ideologue Deng Liqun, called "Mao Zedong thought" "the most valuable asset of the Chinese nation," and advocated a "resolute struggle" against "capitalistic reform." Wang, a believer in Party control, had been one of the strongest supporters of economic reform and the establishment of special economic zones.

Deng's opponents did manage to slow market-oriented reforms with a government austerity drive in the fall of 1988 and shelved them after Tiananmen Square in June 1989. Yet, by November 1991, there were several underlying factors that may have tilted the future balance in favor of reformers. China's intractable economic problems demanded market solutions. More than two-thirds of China's state-run enterprises were running at a loss, contributing to a state budget deficit that Chinese officials estimated grew 60 percent in 1991.

Moreover, political support for economic reform remained strong among China's provincial leaders, especially in prosperous coastal areas that benefited from private enterprise, such as Guandong and Fujian provinces. The provinces vigorously opposed attempts by Party hardliners to re-centralize economic decision-making in Beijing and retract powers delegated to localities during the 1980s.

The hopes of the reformists were raised with the elevation of former Shanghai mayor Zhu Rongji to the post of vice-premier. Zhu was widely known for his bold experiments with reform in the Shanghai of the 1980s, and is considered a protégé of Zhao Ziyang. However, he was given the difficult task of overhauling state industry, which forced him to raise the specter of bankruptcies, something that hardliners could use against him in the future.

In 1991 the power of the central government was challenged by headstrong provincial leaders and by the efficiency of small-scale economic activity. In February, Jiang Zemin and Li Peng toured several key provinces to diffuse tension surrounding the demands of regional authorities for more latitude from Beijing in local policy-making. In May provincial leaders made strong calls to move ahead with market reforms. The central government could not afford to disregard them because local authorities gained power over collecting taxes, and the coffers in Beijing have been consistently short of the needed revenues.

By the summer, economic reforms seemed to be moving forward again. In June the *People's Daily* advocated strengthening the ten-year-old contract managerial system. Plans for a new labor planning system were also outlined: the state would continue to regulate the number of workers and the total sum of wages of a state-owned enterprise, but the enterprise itself would be independent in employing workers and assigning jobs. There were also plans for transferring responsibility for pensions, health services, and social security payments to insurance companies, making it easier for enterprises to fire workers. Having fulfilled the target dictated by the plan, enterprises would be allowed to retain excess profits and output. The official news agency reported that the government had signed agreements with 90 percent of the state enterprises, making them responsible for their profits and losses. Stock markets reopened in Shenzhen and Shanghai. Li Peng has mingled ideological pronouncements with calls for price reform and the creation of a service industry. Prices of basic industrial inputs (coal, steel, electricity) have been raised closer to the real market value. "It is necessary to develop marketable products... to make great efforts to open up markets" said the premier in June.

Nowhere has economic decentralization been more pronounced than in the PRC's foreign trade. From 1978 to 1990 China's trade turnover went from $21 billion to $115 billion, the largest increase in the world over that period. The state-established Foreign Trade Corporations of the past had been replaced by several thousand new foreign trade companies. Taiwanese companies increased their investments in the mainland, and 58 percent of Hong Kong's exports in 1990 were actually re-exports of goods manufactured in China. An estimated 20 percent of Hong Kong's currency circulates in China's southern Guangdong Province.

Although China's official unemployment rate was 4 percent, an estimated 100 million jobless peasants have flooded urban centers. Per capita income in China is about $300, but 110 million people earn less than $62 a year. Despite the record 1990 harvest, rural incomes only rose by 1.8 percent (low demand caused grain prices to fall), while urban wages were increased in 1990 by 10 percent (after accounting for inflation). The standard of living is higher in cities than in the countryside, in part due to the government's concerted efforts to reduce the volatility of the urban atmosphere. In the spring of 1991 the price of grain was increased by 25 percent (the first increase since the 1960s), but the workers were compensated with a 16 percent wage increase in advance of the price changes.

Political Rights and Civil Liberties:

The Chinese do not have the right to change their government democratically. The regime does not allow independent parties or political groupings, and the CCP dominates all aspects of daily life.

The government has complete control over the media, and still jams BBC and Voice of America broadcasts. Freedom of expression is severely curtailed. But in a highly unusual case, one of China's leading writers, Wang Meng, filed a libel suit against a cultural newspaper controlled by hardliners for publishing a "letter" that charged the writer with criticizing Deng Xiaoping. While no newspaper in Beijing dared write about the lawsuit, a literary journal and several newspapers in various parts of China ran the story, suggesting that an anti-hardline faction in Beijing supported the coverage to embarrass and confront hardliners.

The constitution guarantees rights "of assembly, of association, of procession, and of demonstration....as long as they don't infringe upon the interests of the state," but they exist largely on paper. Individual contacts with foreigners are discouraged. Video cameras and telephone bugs follow foreigners who come to Beijing and establish local acquaintances. The secret police often open and censor mail.

China's security network consists of the Ministry of State Security, the Ministry of Public Security, the People's Armed Police, and the People's Liberation Army. Security forces reportedly use torture and arbitrary arrests in maintaining public order. In an effort to eliminate corruption within the Party and the People's Armed Police, in October 1990 the government passed a new law enabling citizens to sue officials who abuse authority. In May 1991 the government announced a campaign against police corruption. After 1989 the government stopped debate about making the judiciary "more autonomous and less arbitrary," and the judiciary remains, in effect, simply an arm of the security apparatus. Trials are, in effect, sentencing hearings, with a conviction rate of 99 percent. An Australian human rights group reported that out of 16,000 criminal cases in Shanghai in 1990, there were only 30 acquittals.

At the end of 1990 the government officially charged democracy activists that had already been imprisoned for eighteen months with "counterrevolutionary offenses." After a series of trials from January to March, thirty-six people were convicted and received sentences ranging from two to thirteen years of imprisonment. The government says that all 715 cases related to the 1989 Tiananmen Square demonstrations have now come to trial, but Western estimates conclude 250 people were still awaiting trial as of April 1991. Security forces urged student leaders and intellectuals to confess their errors and "to correct their attitude" in exchange for lighter sentences. According to Western estimates, there are roughly 20 million people in China's prisons. Approximately 10 percent are regarded as political prisoners.

Since 1990, according to Chinese authorities, close to 1,000 pro-democracy activists were released from detention without charge. But many of those released continued to face harassment by public security authorities, the loss of employment, housing, and travel restrictions.

In the fall of 1991 China held several mass public trials and executions of alleged drug traffickers. Chinese authorities said they uncovered 5,400 drug cases in the first half of the year, a 50 percent increase from the comparable period in 1990. In November, 10 political prisoners in northeastern China announced plans for a hunger strike to protest dismal prison conditions, beatings and forced labor. The strike was to coincide with the 15 November visit of U.S. Secretary of State James Baker, the highest-level U.S. official to visit the country since the Tiananmen square massacres. Prior to the visit, a secret fifteen-page document criticized U.S. concerns for human rights as "garbage," and said that President Bush's policies were designed to encourage the development of "internal forces of opposition" to overthrow the Communist regime. During his visit Baker asked the Chinese to free pro-democracy political prisoners, but several dissidents were detained to prevent them from meeting with Baker's aides. The three-day talks ended with little progress toward easing China's suppression of human rights.

There was also evidence that China has been exporting products manufactured by forced labor. On 24 October, in an apparent move to counter U.S. criticism, the government announced that it had dismissed a factory official and warned another about the export of goods made by prison labor.

Chinese citizens must carry an identification card at all times and register with the Public Security Bureau to spend a night away from home. Each citizen is assigned to a work unit, and must obtain the unit's permission to travel, to marry, to divorce and to have a child. Street committees monitor the activities in each neighborhood, providing the state with an established apparatus for surveillance. The authorities require college students to submit a written statement regarding their position on the events of June 1989, in order to graduate.

Over the course of the past year, there has been a significant increase in the persecution of Catholics and Protestants. In December 1990 at least 23 Roman Catholic priests were arrested in Hebei, to prevent them from serving Christmas mass in unofficial churches (the official Catholic Patriotic Association is controlled by the state, and does not recognize the Vatican's authority). In February 1991 more cases of detention of bishops, priests and laymen were reported. In July the Pope named Ignatius Gong Pin Mei to the position of Cardinal. He had spent 30 years in Communist jails, and his replacement in Shanghai was arrested when the July announcement was made. There are also persistent reports of torture against Buddhist monks and nuns.

China's draconian birth-control policy has continued in 1991, as in the past decade, yet population continues to grow. Beijing's "one-child policy" is enforced by birth-control officials with the help of neighborhood committees. There are 13 million volunteers in the monitoring system for pregnancies. If a woman who has already exceeded her limit becomes pregnant, she is harassed and threatened until she agrees to an abortion. In urban areas it is virtually impossible to obtain permission to have a second child, whereas in rural areas, and especially among ethnic minorities, the government does not enforce the policy as strictly. There have been many cases of physical compulsion to abort or sterilize, and in Gansu Province people with severe mental defects have been prohibited from having children. Since 1987 ultrasonic testing to determine the sex of the fetus has been prohibited in China. Traditionally, the rural Chinese have considered girls less valuable than boys, because men work in the fields and continue to live at home after marriage, thereby being in a position to take care of the aged parents, while girls simply go off to their husband's household. Five percent of all infant girls (one-half million) are unaccounted for by the time they should be five years old. Western analysts believe that many are either drowned, adopted or raised secretly.

There are no free trade unions or other private organizations, although free businesses and cooperatives continue to receive encouraging signs from the Party leadership.

Colombia

Polity: Presidential-legislative democracy
Economy: Capitalist-statist
Population: 33,600,000
PPP: $3,810
Life Expectancy: 68.8
Ethnic Groups: Mestizo (58 percent), Caucasian (20 percent), Mulatto (14 percent), Black, (4 percent), Indian (1 percent)

Political Rights: 2
Civil Liberties: 4
Status: Partly Free

Overview:

During his first eighteen months in office, President Cesar Gaviria Trujillo oversaw the writing of a new constitution designed to broaden political participation and coaxed leaders of the Medellin drug cartel into surrendering in exchange for leniency. Nonetheless, criminal and political violence continued at alarming levels, and the prospects for Gaviria's ambitious plan to strengthen democracy remained uncertain.

Colombia achieved independence from Spain in 1819. The Republic of Colombia was established under the 1886 constitution, and the Liberal and Conservative parties traditionally have dominated the political system. In 1957 the two parties established a National Front under which they participated equally in government. After 1974 the two parties competed in direct presidential and congressional elections. Municipal elections were held for the first time in 1988.

Gaviria, the Liberal party candidate, was elected president in May 1990, and after taking office initiated the process for writing a new constitution. On 9 December 1990 voters selected a 74-member constituent assembly that included politicians from left to right, former left-wing guerrillas, human rights lawyers, labor leaders, Protestant pastors, and native Indian leaders. The assembly was granted unrestricted power and its decisions were not subject to ratification.

The new constitution went into effect on 5 July 1991 and provided for the immediate dissolution of the Congress elected in 1990. It called for new elections in October for an expanded bicameral Congress and 27 departmental governors. Until the new Congress was sworn in, President Gaviria would govern with the advice and consent of a multi-party 36-member "legislative commission."

The new constitution was designed to break the traditional oligarchical grip on government and curtail institutionalized corruption. It abolishes the system of discretionary funds that allowed members of Congress to pay for patronage and re-election campaigns at public expense. It penalizes absenteeism, restricts government-funded travel abroad, prohibits legislators from holding second jobs, and bars relatives from running for office.

The 1991 constitution also limits the powers of the president. It not only takes away the power to appoint departmental governors, but also creates the elective office of vice-president, limits presidents to single four-year terms, gives Congress veto powers over the Cabinet, gives monetary policy to a largely independent central bank, and restricts state-of-siege powers to ninety days.

The new constitution is also among the world's wordiest; it contains 397 articles reflecting the various special interests of its writers. One local observer described it as "constitutional populism." The document will regulate so many areas of the nation's political, social and economic life that many legal experts warned of the potential for juridical gridlock.

Despite the constitutional overhaul, the outcome of the 27 October 1991 elections indicated that Colombian society would be slow to absorb the package of political reforms. Despite a new voter system that gives all parties equal billing on the ballots and the participation of more than a dozen highly diverse political parties, only three out of every ten eligible voters turned out. The 70 percent abstention rate was high even by Colombian standards. One reason was voter exhaustion—this was the fourth election in two years.

But voters also stayed away because the level of political violence, high to begin with, escalates during electoral campaigns. During the 1990 campaign, hundreds of people—including three presidential candidates—were killed by drug traffickers, left-wing guerrillas, and the military. While somewhat less bloody, the 1991 campaign saw party offices bombed and hundreds of people killed, including at least half a dozen candidates.

The results of the election also showed that for the time being Liberals and Conservatives would continue to dominate the political system. The Liberals won 56 of 102 seats in the Senate and 86 of the 161 seats in the Chamber of Representatives. The Conservatives, running divided under three banners, took 24 seats in the Senate and 44 in the Chamber. The two traditional parties therefore ended up controlling 78 percent of the Senate and 81 percent of the Chamber. The Democratic Alliance M-19, a former guerrilla group that made strong showings in the 1990 elections, trailed, winning only 10 percent of the vote.

The Gaviria government had hoped that the new 1991 constitution and a more inclusive Congress would help entice Colombia's two remaining active guerrilla groups to lay down their arms and join the political system. Negotiations with the Revolutionary Armed Forces of Colombia (FARC) and the National Liberation Army (ELN), the country's two oldest and most battle-hardened guerrilla groups, began in Caracas in June. But the government broke off talks when the guerrillas launched major offensives to disrupt the electoral process in the fall. A second round of talks appeared to break down in November.

President Gaviria also sought to reduce drug-related violence and corruption—both have reached astounding levels in the last five years and seriously weakened the authority of the state. He stunned the country by issuing a series of decrees which allowed Medellin cartel leaders to plead guilty to only one crime if they turned themselves in. Cartel leaders, including Medellin kingpin Pablo Escobar, held out until it was clear the new constitution would ban extradition, the only thing they have ever feared. Gaviria favored the ban, the linchpin of his "pacification process," but according to *Semana*, a Colombian weekly, the cartel assured its passage by bribing over half the members of the constituent assembly.

During his election campaign in 1990, Gaviria argued that giving in to the cocaine traffickers would mean forfeiting the nation's sovereignty. When Escobar and his entourage surrendered in June 1991, they took up residence in a secured compound in Escobar's home state, complete with amenities and high-tech communications gear. Critics charged that Escobar would be able to conduct business as usual and that it had been the state, not the traffickers, that had surrendered.

By the end of 1991 it appeared that Escobar's house arrest had limited his influence in the drug world. But with the basic infrastructure of the drug trade still intact, including assassination teams and paramilitary units, a new generation of leaders had emerged in a somewhat decentralized Medellin cartel. Also, the equally powerful Cali cartel simply ignored Gaviria's enticements and successfully branched out into the heroin trade. Colombia's drug traffickers have proved masters of adaptation, and in all likelihood drug-related violence and corruption will remain threats to the country's democratic institutions for the foreseeable future.

Political Rights and Civil Liberties:

Citizens are able to change their government through democratic elections, and the 1991 constitution provides for much broader participation in the political system, including two reserved seats in the Congress for the country's Indian minority. It also expands religious freedom by ending the privileges of the Catholic church which has long enjoyed the advantages of an official religion. However, constitutional rights regarding free expression and the freedom to organize political parties, civic groups and labor unions are severely restricted by political and drug-related violence and the government's inability to guarantee the security of citizens, institutions and the media. Violence during electoral campaigns is a primary cause of high voter abstention rates.

Political violence continues to take more lives in Colombia than in any other country in the hemisphere, with an average of nearly ten killings, disappearances or kidnappings per day in the first eight months of 1991. Those responsible include the military and security forces, drug traffickers, left-wing guerrilla groups, right-wing paramilitary groups, and hundreds, possibly thousands, of assassins-for-hire. Another category of killings in recent years is the "social clean-up"—the elimination of drug addicts, street children and other marginal citizens by police-sponsored "popular militias." All of these elements continue to operate with a high degree of impunity.

There are a number of independent human rights organizations, but rights activists themselves, as well as labor, peasant and student organizations, are consistently the targets of violence and intimidation. In the fifteen-month period between January 1990 and March 1991, 138 trade union members were killed, according to the International Confederation of Free Trade Unions, making Colombia the most dangerous country in the world for labor organizations.

In the last ten years, the entire judicial system was severely weakened by the onslaught of the drug cartels and generalized political violence. Much of the system has been compromised through corruption and extortion. In the last six years, nearly 300 judges and court personnel as well as a justice minister and an attorney general have been killed.

Under the new constitution, the judiciary, still headed by a Supreme Court, was revamped. An adversarial system similar to that in the U.S. was adopted and government prosecutors will be able to use government security services to investigate crimes. Previously, judges investigated crimes without the help of major law enforcement agencies.

The new measures may help to reduce the level of common crime, but the judiciary remained ill-equipped and vulnerable as it faced its biggest test: trying the Medellin cartel leaders who surrendered in 1991. To protect the judiciary from drug-traffickers, President Gaviria instituted a system of 84 "faceless judges," and "witnesses with no names." But the judges are under protection only while on duty, and many witnesses remain too fearful to testify. Also, nearly half the nation's other 4,500 judges are still unprotected. Less than 5 percent of all criminal proceedings result in sentences. In the fall of 1991 most of the nation's judges held a series of strikes in demand of better security, greater resources and higher pay.

Upon enactment of the 1991 constitution, the government lifted the state of siege imposed in 1984 in response to drug-related violence. It was hoped that removing the measures would diminish the sense of impunity within the army and security forces. However, the military was untouched by constitutional reform; no demands were made on spending accountability and mandatory military service was left intact. Moreover, the new constitution guarantees that cases involving police and military personnel accused of human rights violations will be tried in military rather than civilian courts.

The media are both public and private. Radio includes government and independent stations. Television is a government monopoly. The press, including several major daily newspapers, is privately owned and uncensored. Although no sector of Colombian society has been left untouched, the predominantly anti-drug press and broadcast media have been hit especially hard by the drug traffickers. Since 1980 dozens of journalists have been murdered, twelve alone in the first ten months of 1991. Numerous others have been kidnapped and nearly every newspaper, radio station and television news program is repeatedly threatened. A number of newspapers have been forced to close their regional offices and a few radio stations have gone off the air.

Comoros

Polity: Transitional
Economy: Capitalist
Population: 500,000
PPP: na
Life Expectancy: 55.0
Ethnic Groups: Africans, Arabs, East Indians

Political Rights: 4
Civil Liberties: 3
Status: Partly Free

Overview:

In August 1991 the Comoros experienced an attempted "civilian coup d'état" when the country's Supreme Court unsuccessfully tried to remove the president from power on grounds of alleged unfitness to govern further. In November, President Saïd Mohamed Djohar agreed to form a new coalition government with opposition figure Mohamed Taki.

The Comoros, a tiny state consisting of three islands in the Indian Ocean off Madagascar, declared its independence from France in 1975. The first head of state in the independent country, Ahmed Abdallah Abderrahman, served only briefly before being ousted in a coup, but resumed leadership of the country in 1978 after seizing power with the assistance of a group of mercenaries under the command of Colonel Bob Denard. Abdallah stood for election unopposed in 1978 and 1984, successfully consolidating the power of his one-party regime. Though successful in staving off a succession of coup attempts over the next five years, in late 1989 Abdallah was assassinated, reportedly on orders of Colonel Denard. Supreme Court Justice Djohar was installed as interim president while Denard and twenty-one other mercenaries had to leave the country under pressure from the French government.

In March 1990 the Comoros held its first multi-party presidential elections since independence. In the second round, Djohar of the Comoran Union for Progress defeated former Federal Assembly President Mohamed Taki of the National Union for Democracy in the Comoros by 55 to 45 percent. The election, however, was marred by irregularities and allegations of fraud. Despite a challenge by Taki, winner of the first round, the Supreme Court validated the results.

Following the elections, Taki partisans staged anti-Djohar demonstrations and, in August 1990, the government asserted it had foiled a coup attempt. Taki was charged in February 1991 with criminal complicity in the attempted coup, and an international warrant was issued for his arrest. Efforts at extraditing Taki, who had fled to France, were dropped when he reached agreement in Paris to form the coalition "national union government" with President Djohar in November.

The opposition seemed unreconciled to Djohar's election victory. Six anti-government parties, allied in an Opposition Union, boycotted a roundtable conference to develop constitutional revisions in May 1991 after the regime rejected demands that the conference be given sovereignty and that the government be considered only one party among many in attendance. The government also refused to submit the results of the conference to a national referendum. A major complaint aired at the round-table was the lack of government posts held by residents of Moheli, the smallest of the three islands making up the country.

On 3 August the Supreme Court suddenly decided by unanimous vote to remove Djohar from office, a move loudly welcomed by some in the opposition. The Court asserted that Djohar was mentally impaired, that his administration of the country had been "negligent," and that he was imperiling national unity by allegedly refusing to deal with Moheli's grievance. Under the Comoran constitution, the chief justice of the Court takes over as head of state if the executive president is incapacitated. The Supreme Court chief justice who attempted to assume the presidency, Ibrahim Halidi, is the father of one of Djohar's unsuccessful competitors for the executive presidency in the 1990 election campaign, Hassane Mohamed Halidi of the Movement for Democracy and Progress (MDP).

President Djohar stated in a radio address that the members of the Court had badly misunderstood the constitution, and that Comoran democracy needed to be protected by those "nostalgic for the old days of the rule of force." He threatened to arrest the leadership of the MDP and ban the party. The head of security for the Chief of State, a member of the French military, publicly announced that the move to remove Djohar was illegal. Chief Justice Halidi was placed under house arrest. There were demonstrations for and against the attempted take over. On 15 August a state of emergency was declared, but it was lifted in less than a month. The opposition charged that France was interfering with Comoran internal affairs by actively support-ing Djohar in his defiance of the impeachment process. It further called for a sovereign national conference in order to change the status quo.

November's international conference of Francophone nations, which Djohar attended in Paris, provided an opportunity for the president and the exiled Taki to confer. Taki announced that his meeting with the president produced an understanding to convene a national conference in the Comoros which labor, political and religious leaders would attend. Taki said that he and other opposition figures would immedi-ately return to Moroni, the Comoran capital, to participate in the new administration.

The agreement followed other efforts by the president since the attempted coup to bring members of various opposition parties into his government. But Djohar's own Unity (UDZIMA) party publicly complained of the president's accommodation with opposition party leaders, and on 18 November said that it would go into opposition to the regime in the Federal Assembly.

President Djohar indicated that one of his greatest economic challenges had to do with the necessity of pruning back the large number of civil servants on the public payroll. This was also an issue of concern to France, which reportedly still pays approximately 60 percent of the Comoran budget. At the same time, the government hopes to develop the tourism industry and to increase the foreign sales of vanilla and the perfume essence of ylang-ylang.

Political Rights and Civil Liberties:

In 1990 the Comoros held its first multi-party elections since gaining independence from France in 1970. Despite allegations that the elections were fraudulent, and the unwillingness of some in the opposition to accept defeat, consolidation of democracy in the Comoros continued in 1991. The judicial system is based on both Islamic law and the French legal code. In civil and criminal cases, the judiciary is independent, but security provisions allow for indefinite detention. Public criticism of the government is tolerated and there are many discussion groups and political groupings. The government-controlled media tend to follow the government line, and the independent press resists sporadic government attempts at censorship and control. Foreign publications generally enter the country unimpeded. Private cultural and community organizations exist. Although Islam is the state religion, adherents of other faiths are allowed to worship freely. There are no serious restrictions on freedom to travel. Trade unions and strikes are permitted.

Congo

Polity: Transitional
Economy: Mixed statist
Population: 2,300,000
PPP: $2,120
Life Expectancy: 53.7
Ethnic Groups: Bakongo, Bangi, Bomitaba, Bonojol, Ikasa, Kota, Kunyi, M'Bochi, Pande, Sanga, Sundi, Teke, Vili, Yombe, pygmies, other

Political Rights: 6
Civil Liberties: 4
Status: Partly Free

Overview:

In 1991 the Republic of the Congo, a former French colony located in central-west Africa, vaulted ahead of many of the other African countries transforming themselves to multi-party states. The process of political change, which the long-ruling Congolese Labor Party (PCT) intended to develop at its own pace and define strictly on its own terms, came to have its own momentum. A sovereign national conference, ruled out by the president in mid-1990, took place from 25 February to 10 June and largely assumed governance of the Congo from the PCT regime.

Ten years after winning independence in 1960 the Congo became, as the "African

People's Republic of the Congo," a one-party, Marxist-Leninist state run by the PCT. Seizing control in a coup in 1979, General Denis Sassou-Nguesso ruled until early 1991 as chairman of the PCT and president of the country. However, the national conference in early 1991 decided that the functions of a president would thereafter be limited to signing international treaties and representing the country at formal ceremonies. The office of the president is no longer as powerful as that of the prime minister nor is it partisan; Sassou-Nguesso has resigned his chairmanship of the PCT.

The liberalization of national political life began in earnest in mid-1990 when the PCT Central Committee issued a communiqué stating that the Party would drop Marxism-Leninism as its official ideology. The communiqué also said that the PCT was committed in principle to institutionalization of such rights as those of assembly, expression and association, and that the country would likely move toward multi-partyism in 1991. The Central Committee recommended that a national convention with an essentially consultative role be held to debate the specifics of a transformation, and set a timetable for multi-party elections. A few months later the Committee legalized the formation of new political parties. On 10 December 1990, the PCT officially abandoned Marxism-Leninism and adopted a social democratic platform.

As of 1 January 1991 duly registered political parties in the Congo acquired the right to be recognized legally and to operate freely. Although some seventy parties have announced their intent to join the political arena, some in the opposition charged that a number of parties were secretly launched and financed by the PCT as a ruse to control the national conference and confuse the electorate. With the freer atmosphere now prevailing within the country, Congolese political exiles have returned to the country to form new political parties.

In attempting to lay down its own terms for the transition to multi-partyism, the PCT government took steps which were frequently ignored or even abrogated by the opposition, such as passing legislation requiring registering political parties to pay a fee of nearly $4,000. The opposition decided not to recognize this law as binding. In early January, President Sassou-Nguesso announced his intention of appointing a government of "national union and dialogue" rather than a transitional government, and stated that the national conference to establish an electoral timetable would be held in late February. He soon appointed as prime minister a retired army general who had earlier resigned from the PCT in accordance with the move toward military depoliticization.

The opposition, however, rejected the idea of a government of "national union and dialogue" as unacceptable, appointed another prime minister in early June at the end of the three-and-a-half month long national conference, and affirmed, over government protest, that the conference and its decisions were "sovereign." Though officials of the PCT regime repeatedly warned that actions by the national conference verged on being insurrectionary, in the end the Sassou-Nguesso administration accepted the measures adopted by the conference as binding.

During the conference, the regime was repeatedly excoriated for its corruption, incompetence and waste. Its history of preferences for certain ethnic groups and regions was denounced. Attendees cited systematic violations of human rights, the political manipulation of the judiciary, and frequent arbitrary arrests and the use of torture. They called for the disbanding of revolutionary tribunals and political police, the constitutionally guaranteed separation of powers, the repatriation of the embezzled public funds now in private accounts overseas, and even the immediate resignation of the president and his government. The conference went on to direct that legislative institutions be disbanded and that a new constitution be drafted. In the end, a new legislative High Council of the Republic (CSR) of 153 members was created to implement the national convention's decisions during a one-year period of transition. Municipal elections are slated for January 1992, legislative elections for the following March, and presidential elections for May or June 1992. Andre Milongo, a former official of the World Bank, was elected transitional prime minister by the conference. Sassou-Nguesso stayed on as president with substantially reduced authority.

Since the end of the national conference, President Sassou-Nguesso has reacted resentfully to the new administration's attempt to ignore him. The National Alliance for Democracy, a coalition of some forty political parties and associations, has rallied to the side of the president and the PCT, accusing the transitional government of instituting politically motivated prosecutions against those of ethnic groups heavily represented in the former regime. Meanwhile, an anti-PCT alliance entitled the Coordinated Forces of Change accused Monsignor Ernest Kombo, chairman of the CSR and the national conference, of treason for being too conciliatory towards Sassou-Nguesso and the other former leaders of the PCT regime.

Within two months of the close of the national conference, the High Council of the Republic directed the transitional government headed by Prime Minister Milongo to institute legal action against former government officials suspected of misappropriating public funds and other improprieties. In late October 1991, an ex-finance minister and leader of the PCT was sentenced to 15 years in prison for having embezzled 45 million dollars of government funds for non-governmental purposes. In addition, the president's brother was arrested for diverting state money for his own purposes.

In November the transitional government adopted legislation excluding anyone who had been accused of participating in financial irregularities from standing for office in up-coming elections. This would effectively exclude Sassou-Nguesso. In December a new constitution was adopted, with plans to hold a referendum on it in January 1992. Also in December, a French magazine alleged that France had intervened diplomatically to prevent a coup against the new administration on behalf of the president. The aborted take-over was reportedly planned by the Army chief of staff and the former director of intelligence.

The Congo has the highest per capita debt in the world. Apart from foreign assistance, the economy is heavily dependent on revenues from oil. Some from the political opposition have charged that the regime's program of "privatization" is nothing more than a virtual give away of state properties to ranking PCT officials. One of the most important tasks of the transition government is to regularize public finances.

Political Rights and Civil Liberties:

The Congolese people have not yet had the opportunity to change their government democratically, but multiparty elections are scheduled for the first half of 1992. Freedom of expression, association and religion are guaranteed in a new constitution approved in a November 1991 referendum. The judiciary has created a professional group to defend its members against manipulation by other branches of government. The Presidential Guard is in the process of being disbanded.

Despite resistance from the regime, many of the journalists working for the state-controlled broadcast media have successfully managed to depoliticize their news coverage over the past year. On 4 January, in a test of strength between the government and independent-minded broadcast journalists, the interior minister banned the state radio from covering opposition parties and their activities and then suspended journalists who refused to limit their news coverage. The director general of Congolese Radio and Television accused the suspended journalists of inciting popular revolt and of broadcasting false information. After a brief strike, the suspended journalists were reinstated without apparent restriction. There has been a recent proliferation of newspapers and magazines independent of government control which freely criticize the PCT regime. But, in September, eleven radio journalists were fired for criticizing the transitional government.

The umbrella Congolese Trade Union Confederation (CSC) was controlled by the PCT until September of 1990, when a labor congress demanded that members of the Party's Central Committee be removed from positions of leadership within its constituent unions. Unions are now allowed to form without affiliating with the CSC. Labor strikes by air traffic controllers, teachers, judicial personnel and other civil servants were common in 1991.

Costa Rica

Polity: Presidential-legislative democracy
Economy: Capitalist-statist
Population: 3,100,000
PPP: $4,320
Life Expectancy: 74.9
Ethnic Groups: Spanish with Mestizo minority

Political Rights: 1
Civil Liberties: 1
Status: Free

Overview:

The popularity of President Rafael A. Calderon Jr. plunged in 1991 due to the harsh effects of his government's economic austerity program. In April 1991 the country's economic difficulties were exacerbated by a powerful earthquake which devastated Puerto Limon, a nerve center of the national economy. By mid-year, potential candidates from the opposition National Liberal Party (PLN) were already scrambling for the presidential nomination for the February 1994 election.

The Republic of Costa Rica achieved independence from Spain in 1821 and declared itself a republic in 1848. Democratic constitutional government was instituted in 1899 and briefly interrupted in 1917 and 1948. The 1949 constitution, which proscribes the formation of a national army, has been the framework for democratic governance ever since.

The constitution provides for three independent branches of government. The president and the fifty-seven-member Legislative Assembly are directly elected for four years, and are prohibited from succeeding themselves. The Assembly has co-equal power, including the ability to override presidential vetoes. Members of the judicial branch are elected by the Assembly.

The most recent election, held in February 1990, was preceded by fierce primary campaigns in both major parties. In the primaries, the social democratic PLN elected Carlos Manuel Castillo as its presidential nominee and the conservative Social Christian Unity Party (PUSC) elected Calderon. By September 1989, seventeen political parties from across a wide political spectrum were registered by the independent, five-member electoral tribunal. For the tenth time in forty years, the executive branch turned control of the nation's police over to the electoral authorities during the election period.

Calderon led in the polls as the PLN tried to overcome widespread publicity surrounding charges of drug trade connections among high party officials. A number of PLN leaders were forced to resign party positions in the wake of damaging reports of involvement issued by a special Assembly commission.

The campaign was marked by mutual accusations of corruption and illegal campaign funding by both major parties. Opinion polls, however, showed the electorate to be more interested in economic issues. In an effort to diminish the impact of the "poll wars" characteristic of Costa Rican campaigns, the electoral tribunal prohibited the publication of opinion polls during the month prior to the vote.

Nearly 80 percent of the electorate went to the polls on 4 February 1990. Calderon defeated Castillo by 51.4 percent to 47.3 percent. Exit polls showed many voters had turned away from the PLN because they feared an excessive concentration of power in one party; the PLN had held the presidency for two straight terms, and sixteen out of the previous twenty years. The other candidates netted a combined total of less than 2 percent, reinforcing the two-party system.

In the Assembly races, the PUSC and the PLN swapped positions; the PUSC rose to a majority position with 29 members (up from 25), while the PLN dropped to 25 (down from 29). The three remaining seats were won by the left-wing Pueblo Unido party, the Cartagines Agricultural Union, and the Generalena Union. The PUSC also won a majority of the local races that took place in the country's 81 municipal districts.

After taking office in May 1990, the Calderon administration began implementing an austerity and privatization program in an effort to reduce a widening public sector deficit and a mounting foreign debt. The program received high marks from international creditors and private economists, but provoked a widespread backlash, including a series of public-sector labor strikes, from a population used to some of the best social services in Latin America. As Calderon's rating in the polls plummeted in 1991, no less than six presidential aspirants began contending for the PLN nomination. The early battle within the PLN reflected, in part, the struggle to fill the vacuum left by Nobel Laureate and former President Oscar Arias.

Other key issues in 1991 included drug-related corruption—Costa Rica has become a major transshipment point for South American cocaine traffickers—and violent land disputes between peasant organizations and large-scale farmers. Both issues underscored Costa Rica's tenuous status as the only demilitarized state in the region.

Costa Rica has been an easy target for drug traffickers because it has no army, navy or air force. But calls for upgrading the national police force have been countered by alarm over the proliferation of paramilitary groups in the hire of rural landowners.

These private "auxiliary police" were legalized in 1981 as a way to reinforce the scant anti-crime resources of the regular police. By 1991, however, their numbers had reached an estimated 15,000—30 percent larger than the regular police. They were increasingly being used against peasants in the battle for land in rural areas.

Coupled with the difficult economic situation, the security and drug-related corruption problems will test the institutions of Latin America's strongest democracy in the decade ahead.

Political Rights and Civil Liberties:

Citizens are able to change their government through free and fair elections. Constitutional guarantees regarding freedom of expression, freedom of religion and the right to organize political parties, civic organizations and labor unions are respected.

Labor unions are active and permitted to strike. There were a series of stoppages in 1991 by various federations over the increased cost of living and the government's privatization program. There also was continued confrontation between independent labor unions and the so-called Solidarismo movement. The unions, with support from the International Confederation of Free Trade Unions (ICFTU), charge that Solidarismo is a private sector instrument for coopting workers and denying collective bargaining rights guaranteed by the constitution. The unions received further backing in May 1991 from the International Labor Organization (ILO) which called on the Calderon government to reform the country's labor code to prevent Solidarismo groups from impeding union activities. The government responded by proposing legislation to prevent anti-union discrimination.

Press, radio and television are free of censorship. There are a number of independent dailies and weeklies serving a society that is 90 percent literate. Television and radio stations are commercial, with six private television stations providing an increasingly influential forum for public debate. Freedom of expression, however, is marred by a twenty-year-old licensing requirement for journalists. A 1985 Inter-American Human Rights Court ruling determined that licensing of journalists is incompatible with the American Convention on Human Rights.

The judicial branch is fully independent, its members elected for eight-year terms by the Legislative Assembly. There is a Supreme Court with power to rule on the constitutionality of legislation, as well as four courts of appeal and a network of district courts. The members of the Supreme Electoral Tribunal are elected by the Supreme Court.

In recent years, the judiciary has been called upon to investigate unprecedented charges of human rights violations made by the four-year-old, independent Costa Rican Human Rights Commission and other rights activists. A number of cases, including allegations of arbitrary arrests and accusations of brutality and torture committed in secret jails, have been made against special police units since 1989, leading to the formation of a special legislative commission to investigate rights violations.

The judicial system also has been marked by mounting delays in the hearing of cases, which have created a volatile situation in overcrowded prisons and increased inmate violence. The root of the problem appears to be the nation's economic slump, which has led to a rise in crime at a time of budgetary cutbacks affecting the judicial branch.

Cuba

Polity: Communist one-party
Economy: Statist
Population: 10,700,000
PPP: na
Life Expectancy: 75.4
Ethnic Groups: Relatively homogeneous admixture of
Caucasian and black

Political Rights: 7
Civil Liberties: 7
Status: Not Free

Overview:

Following the failed coup by hardliners in the Soviet Union, Moscow moved closer to cutting Cuba's economic life line. Fidel Castro, however, remained defiant. The fourth Cuban Communist Party (PCC) congress held two months later reaffirmed single-party Marxist-Leninist rule. With Castro calling for the "Zero Option," in effect the devolution into a pre-industrial society cut off from the rest of the world, the question was how much longer the Cuban people could tolerate him.

Cuba achieved independence from Spain in 1898 as a result of the Spanish-American War. The Republic of Cuba was established in 1902, remaining subject to U.S. tutelage under the Platt Amendment until 1934. On 1 January 1959 left-wing guerrilla forces under Fidel Castro overthrew the right-wing dictatorship of Fulgencio Batista, who had ruled for eighteen of the preceding twenty-five years.

Since 1959 Castro has dominated the Cuban political system. Under his direction Cuba was transformed into a one-party, Marxist-Leninist state. Communist structures were formally institutionalized by the 1976 constitution approved at the first congress of the PCC.

The constitution provides for a National Assembly whose members emerge from an indirect electoral process controlled by the PCC leadership. Theoretically, the Assembly designates a Council of State which appoints a Council of Ministers in consultation with its president who serves as head of state and chief of government. In reality, Castro is responsible for every appointment. As president of the Council of Ministers, chairman of the Council of State, commander-in-chief of the Revolutionary Armed Forces (FAR) and the first secretary of the PCC, Fidel Castro controls every lever of power in Cuba. The PCC is the only political party authorized by the constitution, and it controls all governmental entities from the national to the municipal level. All political activity outside the PCC is outlawed.

Castro has defied the radical changes that have swept through the Communist world, reaffirming Cuba's adherence to Marxism-Leninism and making "Socialism or death" the official battle cry. Since 1986 the PCC has been conducting a "rectification" program designed to eradicate any semblance of capitalist behavior in society, and any political behavior, either inside or outside the PCC, that appears to take its cue from events in the Soviet Union and Eastern Europe.

After a February 1990 plenum the PCC announced that its 4th Congress would be held in 1991 and would be aimed at reinforcing the rectification process and "perfecting a single, Leninist party based on the principles of democratic socialism." The plenum also was marked by a shuffle of the party leadership that strengthened Castro's direct control over the Party, the military and the government. The assignment of Brigadier General Sixto Batista to head the Committees for the Defense of the Revolution (CDRs), the Party's neighborhood watchdog network, signaled the increased importance assigned to the CDRs in suppressing dissent.

In the fall of 1990, already facing a diminishing flow of Soviet aid, Castro announced that Cuba was entering a "special period in peacetime," a euphemism for a drastic austerity program involving severe cutbacks in energy consumption, and more stringent rationing of food and consumer items. In 1991 the economic situation grew even worse. Moscow granted only a reduced, one-year trade pact that it ultimately was unable to fulfill; by October the Soviet Union had shipped only a third of the goods promised.

The failed coup in the Soviet Union in August 1991 ended Castro's last hope that he would not be cast adrift. In September, Mikhail Gorbachev announced an end to military aid, and Moscow indicated that in 1992 all trade with Cuba would shift to a world market commercial basis, ending the sugar-for-oil swap that has long favored Cuba. With Cuba nearly out of hard currency reserves to purchase oil, Castro called on Cubans to prepare for the "Zero Option," a preindustrial, subsistance economy.

The fourth congress of the PCC held in October appeared to douse any expectations that Castro might change his hard-line position. Before the congress every human rights organization on the island made public statements urging "profound democratic changes," including free elections, a general amnesty of political prisoners, the lifting of travel restrictions, and respect for basic human rights. The government responded with mob attacks orchestrated by state security forces and the jailing of eight rights activists.

At the October congress, Castro tried to convey an aura of increased openness. But in the end he scornfully rejected pluralist democracy as "complete rubbish," and one-party rule was reconfirmed, with a few cosmetic changes thrown in for international consumption. The PCC Politburo was expanded to include younger members, but the result was a further concentration of people loyal to Castro. The congress also reconfirmed the "unchanging revolutionary, anti-imperialist and internationalist basis" of Cuban foreign policy and pledged "fraternal unity" with China, Vietnam and North Korea.

The economic strategy document approved by the congress gave priority to wooing foreign investment, especially from Latin America, and rapid development of the island's tourist trade. But, Latin countries, struggling to make the economic adjustments for participation in the global economy, showed little interest in investing in Cuba's collapsing economy. And while Cuba's tourism effort has been relatively successful, the proceeds are insignificant compared with the loss of Soviet subsidies.

At the end of 1991 the question was how long the Cuban people could survive on a diet of sunshine and deprivation. Although the power of Cuba's formidable security forces seemed to rule out a Romania-style social explosion, it was difficult to believe the Castro regime could hold out indefinitely.

Political Rights and Civil Liberties:

Cubans are unable to change their government through democratic means. All political and civic organization outside the confines of the PCC is illegal. Political dissent, spoken or written, is a punishable offense. With the possible exception of South Africa, Indonesia and China, Cuba under Castro has had more political prisoners per capita for longer periods than any other country. The educational system, the judicial system, labor unions, professional organizations, cultural groups and all media are tightly controlled by the state; outside of the Catholic church, whose scope remains severely limited by the government, there is no semblance of independent civil society.

Since 1989 Cuba's small community of human rights activists and political dissenters has been subject to regular and severe crackdowns. In the months before Cuba hosted the August 1991 Pan American games, the government waged a stepped-up campaign of repression against the slightest expressions of discontent. Nearly three dozen activists or dissenters were jailed or placed under house arrest. Others were assaulted in the streets and in their homes by plainclothes police and the newly formed "rapid action brigades," mobs organized by state security through the neighborhood Committees for the Defense of the Revolution (CDRs). A similar crackdown took place prior to the PCC congress in October 1991.

There are continued allegations of torture in the prisons and in psychiatric institutions, where a number of the dissidents arrested in recent years have been incarcerated. Since 1990 the International Committee of the Red Cross has been denied access to prisoners. According to Cuban rights activists, more than 100 prisons and prison camps hold between 60,000 to 100,000 prisoners of all categories. According to international human rights organizations, there are between 200 and 300 political prisoners. In 1991 the United Nations voted to assign a Special Representative on human rights in Cuba, but the Cuban government categorically refused to cooperate.

Freedom of movement and freedom to choose one's residence, education or job are greatly restricted. Attempting to leave the island secretly is a punishable offense and also applies to those who help Cubans escape. In 1991, however, enforcement was relaxed as Castro turned to a traditional safety valve for ridding the island of dissenters. Similarly, Castro also lowered the age to twenty for people wanting to travel abroad, provided that the host nation gave them a visa.

People who practice religion are formally discriminated against, unless they pledge loyalty to the government and its stated goals. At the fourth PCC congress held in 1991, Castro announced that religious believers would be allowed to join the Communist party. The Church hierarchy issued a statement responding to this announcement, saying that religious discrimination would end when the government allows Communist party members to join the Church and when Catholics are given access to leading positions in Cuban society.

As was evident during the 1989 show trials of officers charged with drug trafficking, and during the trials of human rights activists in 1990 and 1991, due process is alien to the Cuban judicial system; the job of defense attorneys accepted by the courts is to guide defendants in their confessions.

The government also has continued restricting the ability of foreign media to operate in Cuba. In 1990 a Czech reporter and a Mexican television crew were expelled. In 1991, four foreign journalists—from the U.S., Poland, and two from Spain—were expelled for attempting to cover the PCC congress, from which the international media was barred.

Cyprus (Greek)

Polity: Presidential-legislative democracy
Economy: Capitalist
Population: 538,000
PPP: $8,380, sector not specified
Life Expectancy: 76.2
Ethnic Groups: Greek, Turk

Political Rights: 1
Civil Liberties: 1
Status: Free

Cyprus (Turkish)

Polity: Presidential-parliamentary democracy
Economy: Capitalist
Population: 172,000
PPP: $8,380, sector not specified
Life Expectancy: 76.2
Ethnic Groups: Turk, Greek

Political Rights: 2
Civil Liberties: 2
Status: Free

Overview:

In 1991 the Turkish and Greek sectors of Cyprus remained divided—politically, culturally and physically—despite renewed efforts to integrate the two communities into one sovereign state.

Since Cyprus achieved independence from Greece in 1960, communal tensions and violence have plagued it. A 2,000-strong U.N. peacekeeping force was introduced in 1964. In 1974 Greek rightists staged a coup in Nicosia, and Turkish paratroopers secured the northern third of the island, allegedly to defend the Turkish-speaking community. Since then, the country has been split into a Greek south and a Turkish North. After the invasion, about 200,000 Greek Cypriots moved to the south and 40,000 Turkish Cypriots moved to the north. In 1983 the Turkish Cypriots proclaimed an independent Turkish Republic of North Cyprus (TRNC), recognized as a state by Turkey, but branded illegal by the U.N. Security Council.

Today, Greek and Turkish Cypriot forces face each other over an island-dividing buffer zone patrolled by U.N. peacekeeping forces. The U.N. Security Council resolutions, which Turkish leader Rauf Denktash rejects, require that Turkey withdraw its estimated 35,000 Turkish troops and 50,000 Turkish settlers from northern Cyprus.

As 1991 began both Turkish Cypriot leader Rauf Denktash and Greek Cypriot leader George Vassiliou supported the allied forces in the Gulf War against Iraq. Throughout the crisis, Cyprus hosted a number of foreign embassies, thousands of refugees and foreign nationals fleeing Iraq and Kuwait, and over 800 U.N. dependents, mainly from Jordan and Israel.

The end of the Gulf War in late February brought renewed urgency to the Cyprus problem. Yet, the Turkish and Greek Cypriot leaders remained intractably polarized on the issue. Greek Cypriot leader George Vassiliou proposed that the island be governed as a federation under a strong central government, and that Turkish Cyprus be reduced from 38 percent to no more than 28 percent of the country, in order to more accurately represent the 18 percent of the population that is Turkish. Turkish Cypriot leader Rauf Denktash, however, refused any territorial concessions and proposed a confederation of two equal states, a weak confederal government and recognition of the Turkish Cypriots as a separate people.

In March 1991 the European Community Parliament, of which Greece, unlike Turkey, is an associated member, unanimously endorsed the implementation of U.N. Security Council resolutions which maintain the illegality of the TRNC. Greece appealed to the international community to enforce the U.N. resolutions and compared the Turkish invasion of Cyprus to the Iraqi invasion of Kuwait.

The summer brought new hope for rapprochement. President Bush visited Greece in July and renewed pressure, especially on the Turkish Cypriot administration, for progress in negotiations. The U.S. State Department proposed a five-party conference to be attended by representatives of the Greek and Turkish Cypriot sides, the Greek and Turkish governments and the Cyprus Government. The Greek government was encouraged by Turgot Ozal's rejection of Turkish Cypriot representatives' criticism of the proposal as not acknowledging the statehood of the TRNC. However, Greek Cypriots were disappointed when President Bush did not call for the withdrawal of the Turkish forces.

U.N. Secretary General Javier Perez de Cuellar also stepped up diplomatic attempts to get the two sides to agree to the implementation of U.N. Security Resolutions, advocating one state comprising two politically equal communities. The resolutions include drastic reduction of Turkish and Greek troops on the island, and joint security structures at a federal and community level. Denktash said the TRNC was prepared to concede to a land realignment of 29 percent of the island, including the long disputed enclave of Varosha.

However, unable to come to terms on key issues, the Cypriot leaders could not accept President Bush's invitation—contingent upon a narrowing of differences—to meet with him in September. Turkish demand for the recognition of Turkish Cyprus remained the main point of disagreement. U.N. Secretary General Perez de Cuellar backed the Greek Cypriot refusal to recognize the TRNC and continued to advocate the implementation of the U.N. resolutions.

On 1 October Greek Cypriots paraded their military might in a celebration marking the thirty-first anniversary of independence. But President Vassiliou stated he was ready for full demilitarization if Turkey withdrew its troops from north Cyprus.

Similarly, upon the eight anniversary of the TRNC in late November President Denktash reiterated demands for "equality and sovereignty," and adopted the slogan of "no land for peace."

In 1991 the Turkish Cypriot community suffered from internal divisions: since the May 1990 general elections, opposition parties, who claim to represent at least half the electorate, have boycotted the legislative assembly to protest an electoral law which gave Denktash's ruling party 34 of the Assembly's 50 seats, despite winning only 34 percent of the vote. The opposition, which won 46 percent of the vote, got only 16 seats. An October poll revealed that in contrast to Denktash's hardline position, 82 percent of Turkish Cypriots favor a unified Cypriot federation.

Both the Turkish and Greek Cypriot economies suffered from a decline in tourism brought on by the Gulf War and a fall in agricultural production due to drought and recession.

Political Rights and Civil Liberties:

Both the Turkish Republic of Northern Cyprus (TRNC) and the Republic of Cyprus (Greek) are multiparty systems marked by vigorous debate. Elections in both are considered free and fair. The approximately 1,000 Greek Cypriots and Maronites living in the north may vote in elections in Greek Cyprus.

The TRNC is a presidential-parliamentary system dominated by President Denktash's ruling National Unity Party (NUP). The popularly elected president serves a five year term and appoints a prime minster. A unicameral, fifty-member Assembly is also elected for five-year terms.

The Republic of Cyprus is governed by a presidential-legislative system. A popularly elected Greek president serves for five years and appoints his own cabinet. A House of Representatives is vested with legislative authority.

All Cypriot workers have the right to strike. Most of the labor force is unionized and trade unions in both Greek and Turkish Cyprus are independent and function freely. The Cyprus Turkish Trade Unions Federation (TURK-SEN) and the largely Greek Cyprus Workers' Confederation (SEK), both affiliated with the International Confederation of Free Trade Unions (ICFTU) carry on a mutually supportive exchange which includes reciprocal visits, joint educational activities and cooperation on union issues. Child labor laws and health and safety provisions are effectively enforced in both areas.

All Cypriots and foreign residents are free to practice their own religion. Turkish authorities have reportedly eased travel restrictions to and from the south.

Although both governments control radio and television broadcasting, the private printed press is uncensored and critical. Rights of privacy are respected. Trials are public and generally considered fair.

Czechoslovakia

Polity: Federal-presidential parliamentary democracy
Economy: Statist transitional
Population: 15,700,000
PPP: na
Life Expectancy: 71.8
Ethnic Groups: Czech (65 percent), Slovak (30 percent), Magyar, other

Political Rights: 2
Civil Liberties: 2
Status: Free

Overview:

Two years after the 1989 "velvet revolution" ended forty-one years of hard-line Communist rule, Czechoslovakia faced the prospect of Slovakia's secession, the fragmentation of the Civic Forum, and controversies over the pace of economic reform and the fate of former Communists.

President Václav Havel, playwright and former political prisoner, finished his second year in office trying to forge a federal constitutional framework that would maintain national unity and satisfy demands for greater autonomy by Slovakia, the largely Catholic, industrialized republic of 5 million that comprises one-third of the country. In April he called for a national referendum on the fate of the federation. However, this attempt to bypass the legislature and go directly to the electorate was hampered by federal parliamentarians unable to decide on the referendum's wording. By law, a referendum can only be held before the beginning of the electoral campaign, which was scheduled to start in January 1992 for elections in June.

From the start of 1991, Czech and Slovak politicians met regularly without coming to any agreement on the future of the 73-year-old Czechoslovak federation.

Slovak politicians demanded assurance that Prague, the federal capital, would not dictate all aspects of the the republic's economic and political life. Toward the end of the year, Slovak politicians said they would push through a separate Slovak constitution, including provisions for an independent president and army, which would supposedly come into effect only if they failed to win enough concessions from the Czechs on a new constitution.

On 11 November Prime Minister Marian Calfa's federal government met in emergency session and announced it would take a more active role in talks about future Czech-Slovak relations. The same day President Havel arrived in Bratislava, Slovakia's capital, temporarily shifting his office from Prague for a week to confront and appease Slovaks whose complaints of second-class citizenship in the federation had grown more vocal toward year's end. Several days earlier, on 28 October, President Havel was pelted with eggs by angry Slovaks in Bratislava when he arrived straight from a U.S. visit to commemorate the founding of the country in 1918.

On 2-3 November, Czech, Slovak and federal representatives agreed at a meeting at President Havel's country house that three new constitutions—Czech, Slovak and federal—should be adopted before May 1992. A new treaty between the republics would serve as a basis for the constitution. Politicians on both sides, however, disagreed on whether the treaty should be immediately binding, or merely serve as an instrument to enable new constitutions to be adopted.

On 12 November parliamentary leaders from the Czech and Slovak republics failed to agree on how to share power, increasing the possibility of the country's breakup. In an 88-point treaty that would have served as a basis for a federal constitution, there was disagreement on 22 points. The problems centered on Slovakia's economic hardship resulting from the country's push toward a market economy.

Although polls consistently showed that most Slovaks did not want to secede, and only the Slovak National Party (which had 14 percent in parliament) openly called for independence, political, historic and economic factors led to widespread anxiety in the eastern republic. Unemployment in Slovakia in September reached 9.5 percent, while it remained around 5 percent in the Czech republic. Burdened with large, inefficient factories geared for Soviet markets, entire sections of the Slovakian economy spiraled downwards. In particular, the defense industry, of which 80 percent is located in Slovakia, stopped production following a unilateral decision by Prague in the wake of the November 1989 revolution. Slovakian leaders also complained that out of some 3,000 joint ventures with Western companies, only 600 landed in Slovakia, a reflection of the federal government's promotion of the larger Czech lands.

Growing support for a new federal-Slovak relationship led to a rise in new parties and caused a split in the umbrella Public Against Violence (PAV), Civic Forum's counterpart in Slovakia. The split occurred in March when then-Slovakian Prime Minister Vladimir Meciar was ousted through a parliamentary decision after he left the coalition government to form his own party, the Movement for a Democratic Slovakia. He charged the leadership of the PAV, which won the majority of votes in Slovakia in 1990, with being too close to Prague. By year's end, he was the most popular politician in Slovakia, supported by workers, trade unionists and inhabitants of the poor rural regions of central Slovakia.

Current Slovak Prime Minister Jan Carnogursky, leader of the Christian Democratic Movement (CDM), was forced to become more vocal in supporting Slovakian sovereignty. The split led to weakening of the government coalition (CDM-PAV), when the PAV lost half its deputies to Meciar's party. Despite internal discord, the PAV continued to support a unified country.

The pace of economic reforms and emerging political differences also caused a split early in 1991 in the broad-based Civic Forum, which spearheaded the 1989 "velvet revolution" and won 51 percent of the vote in the 1990 elections. Václav Klaus, the powerful, pro-market federal finance minister, led a group of young supporters to create the Civic Democratic Party (ODS) in January. Right-wing and avidly free market, the ODS identified itself with the British Conservative Party and the French Republican Party. With an economic platform supporting a fast-track privatization program and integration with Western Europe, the ODS was the most popular party in Czech lands.

Dissidents in the former Civic Forum regrouped under the Civic Democratic Movement (OH). Among them are prominent dissidents who became ministers when Civic Forum won the elections, including Jiri Dienstbier, the foreign affairs minister and chairman of the party, and Petr Pithart, the prime minister of the Czech government. OH, while supporting economic reforms, positioned itself more toward the center of the political spectrum. While both ODS and OH had an equal number of deputies in the Czech parliament (each holding about 20 percent), OH had more difficulty gaining public support than the ODS.

Another new group was the Civic Democratic Alliance (ODA), whose supporters included important ministers such as Vladimir Dlouhy, the federal economics minister widely considered the most important man in the federal government after Klaus, and Tomsz Jezek, the Czech minister of privatization.

In addition to Slovakian separation and the new political groupings, another major issue facing the country in 1991 was what to do about former Communists. In February, Czechoslovakia began screening more than 1,000 top officials—parliament members, government ministers and their aides—to discover which ones were informers for the secret police under the Communist regime. Officials said at the time that about 100,000 Czechoslovakians were persuaded, coerced or paid to spy on fellow citizens. But dismissals of some officials prompted charges that the screenings would take on the character of witch hunts. On 1 March the government announced that eight senior Communists, among them former chief ideologue Vasil Bilak, were being indicted for embezzling millions of dollars. On 22 March, in a special session of parliament broadcast live on television, an investigatory commission read the names of 10 members of parliament found to have collaborated at one time or another with the secret police. Among those listed was Jan Kavan, founder of Palach Press in London, widely known as having played a leading role in first publishing and distributing the works of such dissidents as Václav Havel.

On 5 September federal lawmakers asked that the Communist party be outlawed. Four days later, the government proposed that all former Communist government officials, secret agents and paramilitary troops be banned from holding state jobs. The proposed ban concerned all elected or appointed positions in the state political and economic administration, as well as courts, the army, police and state media. Candidates for positions of ministers, their deputies and advisers, as well as ministerial department heads, would need to be certified and produce written proof that investigations had revealed no links to human rights violations under Communist rule. On

17 September Václav Vales, a vice premier and chief coordinator of Czechoslovakia's economic reform, resigned amid speculation linking him to the former Communist secret police. "I am disgusted by the unjust attack against his person," President Havel told reporters in a bitter statement. "I am disgusted because I have verified that such accusations are totally unfounded."

On 5 October authorities began screening all civil servants and members of state-owned organizations as part of a new law directed at former Communist party officials and collaborators. The law, called *lustrace*, propelled particularly by Klaus's deputies, barred all Communists and collaborators from holding public office for the next five years. It targeted all those listed in the files of the once-feared secret police, regardless of the causes which led their names being inscribed there. The law came under heavy criticism from all sides on the grounds that it presumed guilt.

Another central issue during 1991 was the pace and scope of economic restructuring. In January the government introduced a program of price liberalization and stabilization that has dramatically reduced inflation—from 26 percent in January to nothing between June and September. Also in January, the currency was made partially convertible and the International Monetary Fund announced a $1.8 billion loan to Czechoslovakia, its biggest loan to date to any of the new democracies in Eastern Europe. At the end of January the government began auctioning off several hundred thousand state-owned stores to private buyers. On the first round of bids only Czechoslovakians were allowed to take part, including anyone who was a citizen as far back as 1948.

Under a new law announced in February, the government said it planned to return hundreds of thousands of businesses and other properties confiscated by the former Communist government to the original owners or their heirs, who had until the end of September to claim old property. Only 10 percent of formerly private property was covered by the law. The future of legally nationalized properties and former church land was covered by a broader privatization law.

Czechoslovakian farming also underwent changes as parliament passed a bill returning almost all farmland confiscated by the Communists. Some 3.5 million original landowners were eligible to reclaim property. The new law meant that cooperatives would have to start paying rent for the land they farm. In mid-June, foreign investors were offered the chance to buy total or partial control of 50 leading Czech enterprises singled out as prime candidates for privatization.

On 11 November, Czechoslovakia postponed for two months the start of a privatization plan to auction shares of about 3,000 companies. Finance Minister Klaus opposed the delay, saying it would cost the country millions of crowns (Czechoslovakian currency). Several hundred thousand people were said to have paid 1,000 crowns, or about $30, to register coupon "checkbooks" for the program. Officials at the privatization ministry of the Czech republic said more time was needed to evaluate the worth of assets of state companies.

Overall, the Czechoslovak economy is projected to do well after all reform measures are put in place over the next five years. But in 1991 measured industrial output declined 30 percent. Gross national product was expected to decline by some 20 percent. The decline in exports to former socialist countries depressed total export volume by 15 percent. In the first eight months of 1991 the dollar value of exports to the Soviet Union was down by 38 percent in comparison with the same period of

1990, while those to the rest of Eastern Europe fell by 11 percent. In 1991 the volume of exports to market economies was also expected to contract.

Finally, in June the last 917 Soviet soldiers and their 83 family members left Czechoslovakia, the last of 73,000 soldiers and 18,500 officers stationed there since 1968. In July parliament voted unanimously to end the country's membership in the Warsaw Pact.

Political Rights and Civil Liberties: Citizens of Czechoslovakia have the democratic means to change their government under a multiparty system. The independent judiciary is no longer subject to control by any political force. Criminal offenses are adjudicated in fair and open public trials. Overtly "political offenses" were scrapped from the judicial code in 1990. Citizens are free to criticize the government. However, the passage of a bill, known as *lustrace*, banned from public offices and jobs anyone suspected of having collaborated with the Communist government. Many intellectuals and politicians oppose the law on legal and moral grounds. The rights of freedom of assembly and association are respected. A lively independent press is free from government interference and newspapers and books represent diverse viewpoints.

Czechoslovakians enjoy religious freedom. On 19 July the federal parliament approved legislation that would return nearly 200 religious buildings confiscated by Communist authorities to their original owners. It also formally restored the standing of churches after four decades of repression. There are no restrictions on domestic or foreign travel. Over 90 percent of workers belong to independent labor organizations.

Denmark

Polity: Parliamentary democracy
Economy: Mixed capitalist
Population: 5,100,000
PPP: $13,610
Life Expectancy: 75.8
Ethnic Groups: Overwhelmingly Danish, a small German minority, various small immigrant groups

Political Rights: 1
Civil Liberties: 1
Status: Free

Overview: In 1991 the leading issues in Danish politics included the country's involvement in the European Community, proposed links with Sweden, and the passage of the government's budget.

The country's role in the European Community (EC) has been a divisive issue. Denmark joined the EC in 1973, but it was only recently that most political parties have agreed to work within a united Europe. The largest opposition group, the Social Democratic Party, remains critical of the Community's machinery but has taken a more pro-Europe stance since 1990.

On 5 December 1991, the Parliament voted against committing Denmark yet to a joint European defense structure and a common European currency. Six parties with an overwhelming majority in Parliament took these positions. Danes will settle European issues through referenda.

In March 1991 the parliament approved negotiations with Sweden on building a bridge and tunnel connection between the countries. If completed, the project would link the two Nordic economies more closely, and would affect shipping companies and other business sectors which have depended on Denmark's separation from the rest of Scandinavia.

Denmark is the oldest monarchy in Europe and the only Scandinavian country presently a member of the European Community. Today the role of royalty in state functions is largely ceremonial. Since 1972 the ceremonial head of state has been Queen Margrethe II. Real political power rests with the parliament, the *Folketing*, a unicameral chamber consisting of 179 members. Of the 179 in the Folketing, 135 are elected in seventeen districts. As autonomous regions, Greenland and the Faroe Islands each send two representatives to the Folketing. The remaining 40 Danish seats are allocated on a proportional basis to representatives chosen from parties which receive more than two percent of the popular vote.

Because of the large number of parties and the 2 percent hurdle requirement, parliamentary politics are marked by shifting and collapsing coalitions. The most recent shift occurred in the December 1990 parliamentary elections, when the Radical Liberal Party left the ruling coalition with the Conservatives. However, Poul Schlüter and his Conservative Party were able to maintain a minority government in coalition with the Liberal Party. Serving as prime minister since 1982, Schlüter has maintained various coalitions. After the 1990 vote, the Conservative-Liberal coalition held 59 seats and the Social Democrats 69. The government maintains its margin over the opposition with the support of small centrist and conservative parties. On 1 February 1991 the Social Democrats, not wanting another general election two months after the last one, kept the government in power by abstaining from the vote on the budget.

Political Rights and Civil Liberties:

Danes have the right to change their government democratically. There is a wide range of political parties—including a Communist party, a radical right-wing party, a green party and a party advocating the philosophy of nineteenth century economist Henry George. Freedoms of assembly and association are respected in practice.

There is a free press and a large selection of publications reflecting a variety of opinions, including forty-five daily newspapers. The state finances radio and television broadcasting, but the editorial boards operate independently. Independent radio stations are permitted, but are regulated tightly by the government.

Over 90 percent of the populace is affiliated with the Lutheran Church, which is the established church of Denmark and receives its finances from the state. However, there is freedom of worship for all. Although discrimination based on race, gender and language is illegal, there have been reports of attacks by civilians on recent non-Nordic immigrants.

Workers have the right to organize and strike. However, in 1991 the Queen's staff filed a complaint in the European Court of Human Rights about their lack of a labor contract, which they have been trying to obtain since 1973. Approximately 90 percent of the wage earners in Denmark are affiliated with free trade unions. The umbrella organization in the labor movement is the Danish Federation of Trade Unions (DFTU), which is linked with the Social Democratic Party. Labor organizations not affiliated with the DFTU have met with fierce resistance from the more established unions and their federation.

Djibouti

Polity: One-party
Economy: Capitalist
Population: 400,000
PPP: na
Life Expectancy: 48.0
Ethnic Groups: Isas, Afars, Arabs

Political Rights: 6
Civil Liberties: 5
Status: Not Free

Overview:

In 1991 Djibouti was rocked by an alleged attempt to overthrow the government in January, an ethnic uprising in the northern part of the country in November and December, and the entry into the country of thousands of Ethiopian and Somalian refugees fleeing the collapse of regimes in neighboring countries.

President Hassan Gouled Aptidon and his Popular Rally for Progress (RPP) have ruled this northeastern African republic since independence was granted by France in 1977. A member of the Somali-speaking Isa, the single largest ethnic group in the country, the president was indirectly elected by the Chamber of Deputies at independence and has since been directly re-elected twice in one-party elections. Although Gouled has consistently named a member of the rival Afar tribe as prime minister, Isas effectively controls the ruling party, the army and the bureaucracy.

In 1981, Afars, disturbed that Gouled ran unopposed, formed the Djibouti Peoples' Party (PPD). Shortly after, PPD leaders were arrested and a National Mobilization law established a one-party system. Since then all candidates have been RPP members. Reassessing one-party rule in light of the continent-wide move toward multi-partyism, the RPP decided in March 1991 that a move toward political pluralism outside of the single-party framework was unnecessary in Djibouti. Perhaps as a result of the civil war that broke out in November in northern Djibouti, Aptidon said that a referendum on multi-partyism would be held within six months of the ouster of the "foreign armed bands" from the country. In 1987 a former Gouled associate and RPP member, Robleh Awaleh, created the National Djibouti Movement for the Installation of Democracy (MNDID). In 1990 it joined with other dissidents and underground groups in exile to form the Union of Democratic Movements.

During the pre-dawn hours of 9 January the Tadjoura military barracks were attacked by an unknown group. One soldier was killed and four others reportedly injured. The government claimed the attack was launched by subversives in a bid to capture quantities of arms and ammunition. The government's sense that it was under siege—Gouled saw the attack as part of an attempted coup d'état—precipitated a series of measures against political dissidents. At virtually the same time, sixty-eight people were arrested in a cemetery in the capital for holding what authorities deemed to be a "suspicious" meeting. All but two were later released. Within days, Ali Aref Bourhane, an Afar and leader of colonial Djibouti from 1967 to 1977 was arrested. The Gouled regime charged that Aref was behind the attack on the garrison as well as a larger conspiracy by Afar elements to assassinate the current leadership and seize power. Other Djiboutians were arrested and temporarily detained in 1991 after requesting permission from the authorities to hold rallies in favor of multi-partyism.

In January the arrest of Aref and a number of other prominent Afars suspected of plotting a coup d'état sparked a public demonstration in the city of Djibouti that was broken up by security forces. The government immediately banned further demonstrations and rounded up hundreds of individuals for questioning in connection with the alleged coup attempt. Armed clashes between the military and armed individuals were reported throughout the year, both in the Afar-populated north of the country and in the south where disaffected Somali clans live. A number of individuals were arrested in connection with these incidents; detainees were variously charged with endangering state security, membership in a criminal organization, attempted murder, and murder. Further attacks against government personnel and structures occurred in October 1991 in southern Djibouti, but it was unclear whether the attackers were foreign troops, as the Djiboutian government claimed, or Djiboutian commandos, as political exiles asserted.

By far the greatest threat to the regime began in November, when Afar guerrillas of the three-month-old Revolutionary Front for Unity and Democracy (FRUD) attacked several Djiboutian army bases in the northern part of the country. The government claimed that a substantial number of the attackers were in fact Ethiopian nationals attempting to realize their dream of creating a unified Afar state out of adjacent pieces of Djibouti, Eritrea and Ethiopia. Preferring to present the conflict as the result of external aggression, the Gouled regime called for French assistance and denied that its repression of the indigenous Afar population in Djibouti may have provoked the insurgency. The Union of Democratic Movements charged that Djiboutian soldiers in the besieged towns of Obock and Tadjoura were firing on defenceless Afar civilians. In mid-December, police opened fire during a raid on an Afar district of the capital, killing as many as 36 and wounding 50.

In addition to fighting between government and opposition groups, Djibouti faced an influx of approximately 30,000 refugees in early 1991. The refugees crossed into Djibouti from neighboring Somalia in early 1991 when forces of the Siad Barre regime and their dependents fled the victory of the rebel Somali National Movement. In May they were joined in Djibouti by some 35,000 Ethiopians fleeing from the Eritrean port of Asab as Ethiopia fell to the Eritrean People's Liberation Front. Young unemployed Djiboutians have demonstrated against the continued presence of job-seeking foreigners in Djibouti. A clash between Isas and those of the Oromo ethnic group in a neighboring area of Ethiopia touched off rioting in Djibouti when Isas attacked Oromo refugees. Between forty and sixty were reported dead.

The government of Djibouti hosted two reconciliation conferences in 1991 for the various armed factions in neighboring Somalia which had gained control over portions of their country in the wake of the fall of the dictator Siad Barre. Conspicuously absent was the Somali National Movement, a guerrilla movement in northern Somalia which had unilaterally declared an independent "Republic of Somaliland," and which rejected calls for a return to national Somalian unity.

Political Rights and Civil Liberties: Citizens do not have the means to change their government democratically. There is no secret ballot and citizens must cast votes in "for" and "against" boxes in public.

In political cases the State Security Court is not independent of the government, defendants are not entitled to the legal counsel of their choice, and the tribunal's decision may not be appealed. Political dissidents are usually detained without charge for extended periods of time. As many as 300 detainees were allegedly tortured in 1991, some prisoners have been extrajudicially executed after their arrest by officials, and people have been attacked in their homes by security police. The prime minister, Barkat Bard, has claimed that there are no political prisoners in Djibouti. Although he has also said that the Djiboutian constitution does not permit execution, a court sentenced a man to death for the 1987 bombing of a restaurant in which 12 people were killed and many more injured.

All media are government controlled, and criticism of the regime, the RPP, or government policies is not allowed. Journalists are considered civil servants. Freedom of speech and association is severely constrained. Public demonstrations require prior authorization; violators face imprisonment if they fail to obtain previous permission. Cultural and commercial associations are permitted.

Tribalism and clan division are exacerbated by the government's favoritism toward the president's own Mamassan clan within the Somali-speaking Isa tribe. Djibouti is predominantly Sunni Muslim, but Islam is not the official religion. There is no official pressure to abide by Muslim diet and dress regulations. Expatriates worship freely. Freedom of travel inside and outside the country is respected, except for trips to South Africa or Israel. The country has a large refugee population, but the authorities have usually not recognized the refugee status of those fleeing civil war in neighboring countries. With the reported exception of Isas who have fled Somalia, refugees have at times been forcibly repatriated. All unions must belong to a government-controlled labor federation.

Dominica

Polity: Parliamentary democracy
Economy: Capitalist
Population: 100,000
PPP: na
Life Expectancy: 76.0
Ethnic Groups: Black and mulatto

Political Rights: 2
Civil Liberties: 1
Status: Free

Overview: The Commonwealth of Dominica has been an independent republic within the British Commonwealth since 1978.

Internally self-governing in 1967, Dominica is a parliamentary democracy headed by a prime minister and a House of Assembly with twenty-one members elected to five-year terms. Nine senators are usually appointed, five by the prime minister and four by the opposition leader in the House.

Prime Minister Eugenia Charles, the first woman to head a government in the English-speaking Caribbean, narrowly won a third term in general elections held on 28 May 1990. Although opinion polls had pointed to an easy victory, the ruling

Dominica Freedom Party (DFP) won in just eleven of the twenty-one constituencies. The two-year-old centrist United Workers Party (UWP), led by Eddison James, former head of the Banana Growers Association, took second with six seats and replaced the leftist Dominica Labor Party (DLP), which came third with four seats, as the official opposition.

The main issues of the 1990 campaign—the sluggish economy, development strategy, and the government budget—carried over into 1991. The debate peaked in April when the opposition parties united behind a motion of no-confidence against the government. But the motion was defeated when all eleven DFP members in parliament voted against it.

In recent years there has been controversy over municipal elections. In 1988 Prime Minister Charles postponed elections for the city council of Roseau, the capital of the country. She argued that the polling would interfere with sanitation and environmental projects. Opposition parties denounced the move as political and accused Charles of authoritarian behavior. The DFP has also been charged with gerrymandering in Portmouth, the other town governed locally by a city council.

Political Rights and Civil Liberties:

Citizens have the right to change their government democratically. There are no restrictions on the right to organize political, labor or civic organizations. The small population of Carib Indians (approximately 2,500), many of whom live on a 3,700-acre reserve northeast of the capital, have been represented by the DLP, but recently have been demanding more direct representation in the affairs of the country.

Freedom of religion is generally recognized. However, the small Rastafarian community charges that their religious rights are violated by a policy of cutting off the "dread locks" of those who are imprisoned. The Rastafarians also charge that non-Dominican Rastafarians are illegally banned from entering the country.

The press is generally free, varied and critical. Television and radio, both public and private, are open to views from across the political spectrum. Opposition parties have charged that the board appointed to oversee state-run media is manipulated by the government. Nonetheless, in 1990, television was used for the first time as an effective campaign tool by all parties, particularly the UWP.

There is an independent judiciary and the effectiveness of the rule of law is enhanced by the court system's embrace of the inter-island Eastern Caribbean Supreme Court. There are no political prisoners. The government has criticized the attendance of citizens at conferences in Cuba and Libya, but does not restrict travel to the countries.

The Dominica Defense Force (DDF) was disbanded in 1981 following attempts to overthrow the government by supporters of former Prime Minister Patrick John with the assistance of the DDF. John was convicted in 1986 for his involvement in the coup attempt and given a twelve-year prison sentence. He was released by executive order in May 1990.

Dominican Republic

Polity: Presidential-legislative democracy
Economy: Capitalist-statist
Population: 7,300,000
PPP: $2,420
Life Expectancy: 66.7
Ethnic Groups: Complex, mestizo and mulatto (70 percent), Caucasian (15 percent), and black (15 percent)

Political Rights: 2
Civil Liberties: 3
Status: Free

Overview:

The government of President Joaquin Balaguer, unrecognized by a significant sector of the opposition and besieged by labor strikes and a worsening economic crisis, held on for a second year. The aging Balaguer tried to defuse opposition protests by hinting that elections, constitutionally scheduled for May 1994, might be moved up to 1992.

Since achieving independence from Spain in 1821 and Haiti in 1844, the Dominican Republic has endured recurrent domestic conflict. The assassination of General Rafael Trujillo in 1961 ended thirty years of dictatorial rule but led to renewed turmoil. The military overthrow of the elected government of Marxist Juan Bosch in 1963 led to civil war and U.S.-Organization of American States military intervention in 1965. A truce was imposed and in 1966, under a new constitution, civilian rule was restored with the election of Joaquin Balaguer of the right-of-center Social Christian Reformist Party (PRSC).

The 1966 constitution provides for a president directly elected for four years, a Congress consisting of a 120-member Chamber of Deputies, and a thirty-member Senate, also directly elected for four years. The Senate elects the judges of the Supreme Court. The governors of the twenty-six provinces are appointed by the president. Municipalities are governed by elected mayors and municipal councils.

Balaguer was reelected in 1970 and 1974 but defeated in 1978 by Silvestre Antonio Guzman of the social democratic Dominican Revolutionary Party (PRD). Guzman's inauguration marked the first time in the country's history that a democratically elected president had transferred power to an elected successor. The PRD repeated in 1982 with the election of President Salvador Jorge Blanco, but Balaguer was elected again in 1986, as the PRD was stricken with factional strife.

The main candidates in the 16 May 1990 general election were the eighty-three-year-old Balaguer and the eighty-year-old Juan Bosch, who had moved his left-wing Dominican Liberation Party (PLD) in a more moderate direction. The other candidates were the PRD's Jose Pena Gomez, and Jacobo Majluta, who had split from the PRD to form the Institutional Revolutionary Party (PRI). Four minority-party candidates also competed.

The main campaign issues were the country's strapped economy, poverty and unemployment, and government corruption. Although marred by sporadic violence resulting in a number of deaths and injuries, the campaign was one of the most wide-open and democratic in the nation's history. In addition to daily rallies, voters were inundated by political advertisements, radio and television talk show discussions, and relentless campaign coverage by nearly a dozen daily newspapers.

Under the observation of former U.S. President Jimmy Carter and other international observers, voters turned out on 16 May 1990 to cast ballots for president and legislative and municipal candidates. The abstention rate of 40 percent was the highest since the establishment of democratic rule. The initial count gave Balaguer a razor-thin edge over Bosch, with Pena Gomez coming in a strong third. A potentially explosive situation developed when the two leading candidates claimed victory, with Bosch crying fraud and threatening to send his followers into the streets. With Carter mediating, however, both front-runners agreed to await a recount by the Central Electoral Council in the presence of international observers.

The recount was not completed until June, and Balaguer, with 35.1 percent of the vote against 33.8 percent for Bosch, was not officially declared the winner until 13 July. Balaguer's PRSC, however, lost its legislative majority. In the Chamber of Deputies, Bosch's PLD took 44 seats, the PRSC took 42, the PRD 32, the PRI two. In the Senate, the PRSC obtained 16 seats, the PLD took 12, and the PRD 12.

President Balaguer, now in his sixth term, is in the weakest political position of his career. Bosch refuses to recognize his government, declaring it "illegitimate." PLD-backed labor strikes in demand of Balaguer's resignation continued throughout 1991 and have undermined the government's economic restructuring program. Balaguer has been able to hold on by negotiating with other parties of the divided opposition, and hinting that the next elections will take place in May 1992. Pena Gomez, who has feuded on and off with Bosch for decades, announced in late 1991 that the PRD would not join Bosch in pressing for Balaguer's resignation, but would seek to defeat him through elections. Pena Gomez appears to be the frontrunner if and when the two doyens of Dominican politics pass from the scene.

Political Rights and Civil Liberties: Citizens are able to change their government through regularly scheduled elections, but a significant increase in electoral fraud in recent years threatens the integrity of the system. Constitutional guarantees regarding free expression, freedom of religion and the right to organize political parties and civic groups are generally respected. But political expression is often restricted by the climate of violence associated with political campaigns and government-labor clashes, and by the repressive measures taken by security forces and the military.

There are over a dozen political parties that occupy a wide spectrum and regularly run candidates in elections. However, the activities of small leftist parties, including the Dominican Communist Party (PCD) which was legalized in 1977, are occasionally curbed. Eight small left-wing parties urged their supporters to abstain from voting in the 1990 elections.

Labor and peasant unions are well organized. While legally permitted to strike, they are often subject to government restraints and repression. Labor has become more militant with the deterioration of the economy, and the government has responded with force to break up labor actions. General strikes have been repressed by the military, resulting in dozens of deaths and hundreds of injuries. Moreover, the right to organize unions and bargain collectively is not recognized in the country's twenty-three free trade zones. In 1991 the government promised to reform the labor code to establish worker rights in those areas.

The government has also come under harsh criticism from international bodies and human rights organizations for the slave-like conditions of Haitians, including children, forcibly and illegally recruited to work on state-run sugar plantations. In response to the pressure, in June 1991 the government began repatriating tens of thousands of the estimated 750,000 Haitians living illegally in the Dominican Republic. Rights groups charged that the government systematically mistreated, robbed, and abused the people it expelled, including an undetermined number of people with Dominican citizenship. The 30 September 1991 military coup in Haiti ended hopes for talks between Haiti and the Dominican Republic to consider protection of migrant worker rights.

Human rights groups are independent and active. In 1991 these groups reported a number of disappearances, as well as poor prison conditions and continuing allegations of police brutality and arbitrary arrests by the security forces.

The press, radio and television are mostly privately owned. Newspapers are independent and diverse but occasionally subject to government pressure through denial of advertising revenues. There are dozens of radio stations and at least six commercial television stations, but broadcasts are subject to government review. In September 1989 the Supreme Court ruled that the licensing of journalists was unconstitutional.

The Supreme Court, whose members are elected by the Senate, operates in a generally independent manner. The court appoints lower court judges and is also empowered to participate in the legislative process by introducing bills in the Congress.

Ecuador

Polity: Presidential-legislative democracy
Economy: Capitalist-statist
Population: 10,800,000
PPP: $2,810
Life Expectancy: 66.0
Ethnic Groups: Complex, Indian (approximately 30 percent), mestizo (50 percent), Caucasian (10 percent), and black (10 percent)

Political Rights: 2
Civil Liberties: 3
Status: Free

Overview:

The social democratic government of President Rodrigo Borja, besieged by a hostile legislature and losing popularity because of its economic austerity policies, was reduced to lame-duck status as the nation geared up for the May 1992 presidential election. The unprecedented political assertiveness of Ecuador's indigenous movements, representing an estimated third of the voting-age population, loomed as the main wild card in a free-wheeling campaign.

The Republic of Ecuador was established in 1830 after achieving independence from Spain in 1822. The nation's history has been marked by interrupted presidencies and periods of military rule. The most recent military government paved the way for a return to civilian rule with a new democratic constitution approved by referendum in 1978.

The 1978 constitution provides for a president elected for a four-year term by universal adult suffrage. If no candidate wins a majority in the first round of voting, the two top finishers compete in a second round. There is a seventy-two-member unicameral National Chamber of Deputies with fifty-nine members elected on a provincial basis every two years, and twelve elected on a national basis every four years.

In the January 1988 general election, Sixto Duran of the ruling, right-wing Social Christian Party (PSC) ran a poor third to Rodrigo Borja of the social democratic Democratic Left (ID), and Abdala Bucaram of the populist Ecuadorian Roldosist Party (PRE). Borja defeated the fiery Bucaram in the May 1988 runoff and was inaugurated in August 1988, succeeding President Leon Febres Cordero of the PSC. Borja became the third democratically elected president since the return to civilian rule in 1979.

Borja took office with majority support in the Chamber thanks to a governing alliance with the Christian democratic Popular Democracy (DP); Borja's ID had won 31 seats in January and the DP 8. The other seats were divided among nine other parties, a number of which supported Borja's candidacy but later joined the opposition.

In late 1989 and through the first half of 1990, strains in the ID-DP coalition threatened Borja's parliamentary majority. However, the ID and DP seemed compelled to maintain the alliance in response to increased cooperation between right-wing and populist parties, particularly in coastal Guayaquil, the country's largest city and traditional base of right-wing political forces.

In the 17 June 1990 legislative elections, Borja's ID lost all but fourteen of its seats. A resurgent PSC ended up with sixteen seats, the PRE finished with thirteen, and the DP retained its eight. In a surprisingly strong show, the Marxist Socialist Party (PS) doubled its previous representation to eight seats.

Since mid-1990, the PSC, PRE, PS and a number of smaller parties have joined together to block government policy initiatives by using a narrow parliamentary majority to impeach six cabinet ministers. The government maintains that impeachment proceedings, allowed by the constitution, are part of a campaign to undermine the ID's electoral prospects in the May 1992 national elections. Nevertheless, given the fragmented nature of Ecuadoran politics, it is likely that institutional confrontations will remain a staple of government activity for the foreseeable future.

Borja's presidency has also been marked by mounting labor pressure against the government's economic measures. In 1990 and 1991, the major unions, led by the United Workers Front (FUT) which backed Borja's candidacy in 1988, carried out a series of strikes against his government's economic austerity measures.

By the fall of 1991 there were seventeen political parties registered for the May 1992 elections and at least ten offered presidential candidates. The leader in the opinion polls was Sixto Duran, who split from the PSC to form the Republican Union party (UR), followed by Abdala Bucaram, the controversial populist who has expressed admiration for Adolf Hitler and wears a mustache to match. Raul Baca, who was expected to be the ID candidate, was trailing badly.

However, the unprecedented political assertiveness of the nation's indigenous groups, which account for an estimated third of the population, loomed as a potentially key factor in the 1992 election. In June 1990 the National Confederation of Indigenous Nationalities of Ecuador (Conaie) stunned Ecuador's establishment by mobilizing more than a million people across the country in what is referred to as "the uprising." Conaie's demands include land grants and special sovereignty for the indigenous population, including oil and mineral rights, and the disbanding of paramilitary units established in the countryside by large landowners.

Negotiations between the government and Conaie broke down in May 1991, primarily over the land and sovereignty questions, and a tense showdown ensued when Conaie militants staged a two-day occupation of the national legislature. In September Conaie announced that it would mount a massive boycott of the 1992 elections, including actions to prevent voting on indigenous territory. Its slogans—e.g. "Five hundred years of oppression, five hundred years of resistance"—are rooted in the indigenous protest against honoring the 500th anniversary of Spain's discovery of the Americas.

Conaie also moved to set up an "Indian Parliament." This gave ammunition to landowners, who claim Conaie is determined to undermine national sovereignty by setting up "a state within a state," and provoked a strident statement by the Ecuador's nationalist military calling for President Borja "to neutralize the work of extremist movements seeking the legalization of an Indian state." By year's end, the government was struggling to find the middle ground upon which to renew negotiations with Conaie.

Political Rights and Civil Liberties:

Citizens are able to change their government democratically. Constitutional guarantees regarding freedom of expression, religion, and the right to organize political parties, labor unions and civic organizations are generally respected. There are nearly two dozen highly competitive political parties, ranging from radical right to radical left.

Labor unions are well organized and permitted to strike. A number of national and local work stoppages have taken place during the Borja administration. In 1991 labor strife escalated as the government initiated legislation to liberalize the labor code.

Newspapers, including at least six dailies, are privately owned or sponsored by political parties. They are free of censorship and generally outspoken. Radio and television are privately owned and supervised by two independent associations. There are nearly a dozen television stations, most of which are commercial. On 9 October 1991 the nation's radio stations went silent for an hour to protest the Borja government's denial of a radio frequency to a station owned by an opposition political leader. In Ecuador stations are privately owned, but the government controls the frequencies.

Under the 1978 constitution, an independent judiciary is headed by a Supreme Court appointed by the legislature. During both the Febres and Borja administrations, however, the Court has been caught in a tug of war between the executive and legislative branches. Under Borja, questions of judicial impartiality remain, particularly on issues involving party nominations and allegations of government corruption. The Supreme Court supervises the superior courts which, in turn, supervise the lower court system.

Independent human rights organizations operate freely and there are frequent allegations of police brutality and torture by security forces. In 1991 the government dissolved a police investigative unit implicated in many abuses and announced a human rights training program for police, but rights activists charge that abuses are still committed with impunity because police personnel are tried in police courts rather than civil courts.

Egypt

Polity: Dominant party
(military-dominated)
Economy: Mixed statist
Population: 54,500,000
PPP: $1,930
Life Expectancy: 60.3
Ethnic Groups: Eastern Hamitic (90 percent), Greek, Syro-
Lebanese, other

Political Rights: 5
Civil Liberties: 5
Status: Partly Free

Overview:

In 1991 the major news in Egypt surrounded the country's
central role in the Persian Gulf War—sending 45,000 troops
(the second largest army contingent) to Saudi Arabia to join
the U.S.-led international coalition. In the wake of the allied victory over Iraq, Egypt
emerged a decisive diplomatic force in the post war Middle East.

Although most Egyptians supported the president's position in the war against
Iraqi dictator Saddam Hussein, a vocal segment of the population expressed support
for Iraq; Islamic fundamentalist, leftist secular opposition and student groups held
several pro-Iraq rallies during the crisis. Pro-Iraqi feelings, however, were tempered by
repeated reports of the mistreatment and killing of Egyptians formerly working in Iraq.
The government stepped up efforts to censor critics and responded harshly to the pro-
Saddam demonstrations. Police forces used tear gas and clubs to disperse demonstrators in the streets and on university campuses. Human rights observers expressed
concern over the wave of arrests, administrative detentions and military court proceedings against citizens who criticized the government's position on the war.

Ostensibly a multi-party parliamentary democracy, Egypt remains dominated by
President Hosni Mubarak and his ruling National Democratic Party (NDP), which
controls both houses of parliament. Since the 1952 overthrow of the monarchy, real
power has been exercised by the ruling elite with strong ties to the military. The
traditional role of the People's Assembly, Egypt's national legislative assembly, has
been to approve the policies of the president. President since the 1981 assassination of
Anwar Sadat, Mubarak is both head of state and chairman of the NDP. Elected
indirectly by a two-thirds majority vote of the People's Assembly, the president is also
commander-in-chief and is empowered to appoint and dismiss the prime minister and
cabinet ministers. Mubarak, however, has been slowly cultivating a multi-party system
and has, in fact, made Egypt one of the more open societies in the Arab world. But
political liberalization has been thwarted by a set of emergency laws in effect since
the assassination of Sadat. The emergency laws ban public assembly and allow wide
powers, such as arbitrary arrest and detention of suspects, to the police. At the end of
April 1991 Parliament ratified the unpopular laws for another three years. The motion
was reportedly passed with no debate.

Emerging victorious from the Gulf War, President Mubarak sought concrete
economic and political gains for his country. In exchange for Egypt's war effort and
to offset the losses in revenues caused by the war, in the spring several Gulf states
and the U.S. slashed Egypt's $50 billion foreign debt by half. Egypt's plans for
dominance in the new Arab order were complicated in May, when Gulf states
expressed their desire to have the U.S. supply the core of the security force in Saudi

Arabia. Egypt responded with plans to send its troops home, belying its resentment at what many saw as betrayal by the Gulf Cooperation Council (GCC) countries, particularly Kuwait. Egyptians believed that Kuwait had not given Cairo its due credit for garnering Arab support for the presence of allied forces and helping militarily in the effort against Iraq.

On 15 May, signalling Egypt's importance as a regional power, Egypt's deputy premier and foreign minister, Esmet Abd al-Meguid, was elected secretary-general of the Arab League. Riding a wave of confidence bolstered by the Gulf War, toward the end of May, President Mubarak announced plans for a courageous, IMF-dictated, economic reform. The tough austerity measures, which include severe cuts in subsidies caused concern about potential social unrest, as Egypt is one of the poorest countries in the Arab world.

In June diplomatic tensions with Israel heightened. Egypt expressed frustration at Israeli President Yitzhak Shamir's alleged lack of cooperation in plans for an American sponsored Arab-Israeli peace conference and Israel's unwavering position on the Israeli-occupied territories. At month's end, Egyptian and Israeli positions became even more polarized when Egypt backed the PLO's demands for a major role for the U.N. and the presence of PLO delegates at the proposed conference. But by the fall, Egypt played a major role in the attempt to resolve differences between Israel and its Arab neighbors at the Middle East peace conference in Madrid.

At home, thousands of people, many of them students and Islamic fundamentalists, demonstrated against the Madrid conference. Under Egypt's emergency law, Egyptian security forces arrested and detained around 200 people; 37 demonstrators were referred to the public prosecution on charges of distributing leaflets rejecting the peace conference. Egypt's Muslim Brotherhood publicly rejected the talks, which it declared were aimed for the "sell out of Palestine."

In 1991 Cairo was again hit by sectarian violence. In September, tensions between Coptic Christians and Muslims exploded when Muslim fundamentalists shouting "The Christians are the enemies of Allah!" entered a neighboring Copt village to destroy and loot Coptic churches, stores and houses.

On 21 November the United Nations Security Council unanimously recommended Boutros Ghali, Egypt's sixty-nine-year-old deputy prime minister, to replace Javier Perez de Cuellar as the next U.N. secretary general. Mr. Ghali would be the first person from either the Arab world or Africa to head the U.N.

Domestically, the legitimacy of the National Assembly remained in question. At year's end, 25 deputies faced accusations of electoral fraud and 9 others faced allegations of drug dealing.

Political Rights and Civil Liberties:

Restrictions on political activities limit the ability of Egyptian citizens to change their government democratically. Freedom of press, political association and assembly were increasingly circumscribed in 1991.

Although theoretically a multi-party democracy, Egypt is dominated by the president and his party. The ruling NDP is virtually unopposed in the People's Assembly; the assembly essentially serves as a rubber stamp of executive decisions. The illegal but tolerated Muslim Brotherhood, along with the Labor Party, comprise the largest opposition bloc. Electoral fraud orchestrated by ruling party officials remains a common practice in Egypt.

Egypt's emergency laws, in effect since the 1981 assassination of Anwar Sadat, limit the constitutionally guaranteed right of political assembly and grant wide powers to the police. In 1991 human rights activists expressed concerned about the arrest and administrative detention of journalists, students and political activists opposed to Egypt's role in the Gulf War. Human rights organizations also noted a sharp increase in reports of torture and disappearance of political dissidents.

Egypt has eight legal political opposition groups which are allowed to organize, hold rallies, publish their views, and enter candidates in elections. However, all prospective political parties are required by law to apply for legal status to a committee dominated by the ruling NDP. The Muslim Brotherhood, the Communists and the Nasirites continue to be denied legal status as political parties. In 1991 the government-ordered dissolution of the Arab Women's Solidarity Association signalled even further restrictions on political association.

Despite crackdowns on association and assembly, President Mubarak hasn't completely abandoned the cautious path of political liberalization begun by his predecessor, the late Anwar Sadat. This is evident in the increasing degree of free criticism of the administration in opposition newspapers. Both legal and illegal opposition groups publish views critical of the regime in their own periodicals with little government interference. However, many journalists who criticized Egypt's role in the Gulf War were arrested. Egyptian radio and television, owned and controlled by the state, are lively compared to mass media in other Arab countries, but fail to present fully the diverse political views that exist in Egypt, and, during political campaigns, provide disproportionately wide coverage of ruling party candidates.

Egyptian workers have the right to organize and join local labor committees linked with national trade unions, which are required to affiliate with Egypt's single labor federation, the NDP-dominated Egyptian Trade Union Federation (ETUF). The labor law provides for a system of arbitration to resolve disputes about wages and working conditions. The Criminal Code provides penalties of up to two years imprisonment for those who strike, and more severe punishments for those who incite others to strike. Collective bargaining is allowed in the private sector, but not in the public sector, which employs the most union members.

Islam, Christianity and Judaism are Egypt's recognized religions. The majority of Egyptians are Sunni Muslims and Coptic Christians. Egypt generally protects freedom of religious expression, but conversion from Islam is discouraged by the government, and Christian missionaries who proselytize Muslim Egyptians may be prosecuted. Persons suspected of involvement in militant Islamic activities are routinely and arbitrarily detained by security forces.

The Egyptian judiciary, which has four types of regular courts, and two types of special courts (the Court of Ethics and State Security Courts), is relatively independent of the executive branch of government. Though State Security Courts are less independent because their decisions may be challenged by the executive, there are procedural safeguards (such as the right to legal counsel) that protect the rights of the accused. The Court of Ethics and its investigating agency, the Office of the Socialist

Prosecutor, has been criticized as potentially dangerous to the judicial system. In 1991 human rights activists criticized the investigation and prosecution of civilians in the military court system.

Although they are denied official recognition by the government, human rights groups in Egypt, such as the Egyptian chapter of the Arab Organization for Human Rights, continue to promote respect for human rights in Egypt with relatively little government interference.

El Salvador

Polity: Presidential-legislative democracy (military influenced)
Economy: Capitalist-statist
Population: 5,400,000
PPP: $1,950
Life Expectancy: 64.4
Ethnic Groups: Mestizo (89 percent), with small Indian and Caucasian minorities

Political Rights: 3
Civil Liberties: 4
Status: Partly Free

Overview:

The announced suspension of offensive actions by left-wing guerrillas in November 1991, and the government's response that it would take corresponding measures, appeared to pave the way for a formal ceasefire agreement in El Salvador's civil war by the end of the year. However, fears remained that the hatred and mistrust built up during a dozen years of civil war could still derail the delicate negotiating process.

El Salvador declared independence from the Captaincy General of Guatemala in 1841. The Republic of El Salvador was established in 1859. More than a century of civil strife and military rule followed. The 1970s were marked by mounting conflict between the army and left-wing groups. The 1979 coup by reformist officers was the first breach in the historical alliance between the military and the landed oligarchy. But the the new junta's attempt to institute a democratic opening was undermined by the outbreak of civil war as the Marxist Farabundo Marti National Liberation Front (FMLN) squared off against the military and right-wing forces.

Despite the conflict, Salvadorans elected a constituent assembly in 1982. A democratic constitution was drafted in 1983, and Jose Napoleon Duarte was elected president in 1984. The 1983 constitution provides for a president and vice-president elected by direct popular vote for five-year terms, and a unicameral National Assembly elected for a three-year term. Municipal elections are held every three years.

Duarte's Christian Democratic party (PDC) defeated the right-wing National Republican Alliance (ARENA) in the 1985 legislative and municipal elections. ARENA was founded in 1981 by Roberto d'Aubuisson, a cashiered army officer linked to right-wing death squads, who lost to Duarte in the 1984 election.

After being marginalized by three democratic elections in four years, the FMLN turned to bombings, civilian assassinations and attacks on the country's economic infrastructure. In 1987, however, exiled political leaders allied with the FMLN accepted Duarte's invitation to return to El Salvador and formed the Democratic Convergence (CD). At the same time, ARENA took a moderate turn as businessman

Alfredo Cristiani replaced d'Aubuisson as ARENA's president and led the party to victories in the 1988 legislative and municipal elections.

The 19 March 1989 presidential election offered the widest array of choices in the country's history as eight parties, ranging from left to right, nominated candidates. The main contenders were ARENA's Cristiani, the PDC's Fidel Chavez Mena, and the CD's Guillermo Ungo. Cristiani won a first-round victory with 54 percent of the vote.

President Cristiani offered to negotiate a ceasefire and the FMLN's integration into the political system. But, in November 1989, the FMLN mounted its largest offensive in nine years, during which six Jesuit priests were murdered by the army. The offensive showed that the FMLN remained a potent military force, but lacked the popular support to overthrow the government. It also proved the government could not end the war—a requirement for reactivating the economy—through military means. Confronting a deteriorating stalemate, both sides agreed in April 1990 to U.N.-mediated negotiations to end the war.

During the next fifteen months, as fighting continued, FMLN and government negotiators in Mexico City reached a series of partial accords on human rights verification, and electoral and judicial reform. When the talks deadlocked over the question of military reform and how to guarantee the guerrillas' security after they lay down their arms, the discussions were moved to New York. Those talks produced a general agreement that the guerrillas would be incorporated into a new national police in exchange for giving up their demand to integrate members into the army. The accord also called for reducing the size of the army and "purifying" it of human rights violators, and the creation of an oversight commission made up of representatives from the government, the military, the FMLN, and the six political parties represented in the National Assembly.

The process bogged down again in October when negotiators returned to Mexico to work out the details of implementing the New York accord. As fighting continued to rage in El Salvador, how to arrange a ceasefire remained the stickiest point. The FMLN appeared to break the ice in mid-November when it announced a unilateral suspension of "offensive actions and economic sabotage." President Cristiani called that a "signal of good will" and stated that the government and the army would take "corresponding measures." A number of key issues remained unresolved, including the organization of the new police force and the reduction and reform of the military. But both sides, as well as U.N. mediators, predicted the signing of a formal ceasefire before the end of 1991.

For a peace agreement to last, Salvadorans will have to overcome decades of hatred and distrust. While the government and the FMLN leadership now believe that continuing the war is a futile enterprise, there are recalcitrants on both sides that maintain an all-or-nothing view of El Salvador's future and are capable of disrupting a delicate accord. The negotiating process was marked by an increase in right-wing death squad activity, complaints from the military, and terrorist actions by guerrilla units that believe FMLN negotiators have sold out. The potential remained for the violent settling of scores, anarchy, and yet another escalation of the conflict.

El Salvador's fragile democratic institutions have survived over a decade of civil war and have been strengthened, at least on paper, by agreements reached during the negotiating process. But they will continue to be tested, as will the U.N. mediators, during what could be a bloody peace.

Political Rights and Civil Liberties:

Citizens are able to change their government democratically. The constitution guarantees free expression, freedom of religion and the right to organize political parties, civic groups and labor unions. However, political expression and civil liberties continue to be restricted by the actions of FMLN guerrillas and right-wing death squads, and by repressive measures of the military against left-wing political parties, and labor, peasant, university, and human rights organizations.

Political rights have widened significantly since the lifting of the state of emergency and the administration of an amnesty in 1987. The return of left-wing political exiles has presented voters with the widest choice and most open campaigns in the country's history. There are now a dozen or more active political parties ranging from right to left, six of which won seats in the 84-member National Assembly in the March 1991 election. Electoral reforms made in 1991 appeared to strengthen the independence of the multipartisan electoral commission.

Political rights, however, remain limited by murder at both ends of the political spectrum. Political killings committed by the military and right-wing death squads reached 800 per month in 1980-82. According to Tutela Legal, the Catholic Church's human rights office, the rate had dropped to 8 per month in 1987. But the frequency has risen again in recent years to possibly as high as two dozen per month. There also has been an increase in reports of torture of detainees in the custody of the police and the military.

In mid-1990, the FMLN formally ended its stated policy of summary executions of elected officials and right-wing figures, but assassinations—including the murder of two unarmed U.S. soldiers—have continued during FMLN offensives designed to strengthen its position during the peace negotiations.

Underlying all rights abuses is the absence of an effective system of justice. The judicial system is understaffed, riddled with corruption, and intimidated by the military and security forces. The September 1991 conviction of two officers in the 1989 murder of six Jesuit priests marked the first time military officers had been held accountable for human rights violations, despite overwhelming evidence of military involvement in the deaths of thousands of civilians. But a not-guilty verdict on seven other soldiers involved in the case, in addition to evidence of a military cover-up to protect higher-ranking officers and not-guilty verdicts after obvious jury intimidation in other cases, strongly suggested the convicted officers had been used as scapegoats to deflect pressure from international rights organizations and the U.S. Congress.

Promising developments in 1991 included agreements between the government and the FMLN on judicial reform, and the establishment of a U.N. mission in El Salvador to monitor human rights violations by both sides and compliance with an eventual peace agreement. A 100-member U.N. mission set up shop in August. In November, the National Assembly approved constitutional amendments allowing for an independent judicial council that will make nominations for the Supreme Court and other judicial posts, with nominees requiring confirmation by the Assembly. The government and the FMLN also agreed on creating a new national police, separate from the defense ministry and under civilian command. But ultimately, impunity for rights violators, in particular the military, will be broken only when perpetrators know they will be prosecuted for abusing civilians—and not just in cases that draw international attention.

The wider political space continues to be reflected in the press, radio and television. Most media are in private hands, but the limited, right-wing perspective has opened considerably. Election campaigns feature televised interviews with all candidates and debates between left- and right-wing politicians. Opinion polls are a thriving industry and given wide coverage in publications that span the political spectrum from right to left. The media, however, remain targeted by political violence. Several journalists have been killed and a number of outlets bombed in the last two years, and others are subject to intimidation by the military and security forces.

During the Duarte years, labor, peasant and university organizations reestablished themselves after being decimated in 1980-82. Strikes, as well as marches and other forms of assembly, are permitted and occur frequently. However, labor unions remain subject to violent intimidation and crackdowns by right-wing death squads and the military. In 1990 and 1991, thousands of trade unionists were detained, hundreds abused, with eighteen unionists killed between January 1990 and April 1991 according to the International Confederation of Free Trade Unions.

Equatorial Guinea

Polity: Military
Economy: Capitalist-statist
Population: 400,000
PPP: na
Life Expectancy: 47.0
Ethnic Groups: Bubi, Fang, Puku, Seke

Political Rights: 7
Civil Liberties: 7
Status: Not Free

Overview:
In 1991 Equatorial Guinea's one-party regime continued to resist any movement towards the return of multi-party elections. The government has offered only vague plans for a liberalization of the political process.

This former Spanish colony in west-central Africa—consisting of mainland Rio Muni and the islands of Bioko, Elobey Chico, Elobey Grande, Annobon, and Corisco—became an independent republic in 1968. Macias (later Macie) Nguema Biyogo of the Popular Ideal of Equatorial Guinea was elected president, defeating Bonifacio Ondo Edu of the Movement for the National Unity of Equatorial Guinea. In 1969, amid inter-ethnic and political turmoil, President Macie seized emergency powers and unleashed a decade-long reign of terror. Declaring himself president for life in 1972, he crushed virtually every segment of society: suppressing the Roman Catholic Church; shutting down the school system; expelling Nigerian contract workers who harvested cacao, the mainstay of the economy; sinking the fishing fleet to prevent people from escaping; forcing the exodus of most remaining Spaniards and skilled and educated citizens; and murdering and publicly crucifying opponents.

On 3 August 1979 President Macie was overthrown by his nephew Teodoro Obiang Nguema Mbasogo in a military coup. Macie was hunted down and eventually executed for crimes that included treason and genocide. On assuming power, Colonel

Obiang formally banned political parties and oversaw the drafting of a new constitution, adopted in 1982, which provides for a president elected for seven years and a Council of State. A unicameral Chamber of People's Representatives consists of members handpicked by the president. In 1987, President Obiang launched the Democratic Party of Equatorial Guinea (PDGE), the only legal party. On 25 June 1989, running unopposed, Obiang was elected in the first presidential election since the coup. Obiang and a Fang ethnic group clique from Rio Muni wield disproportionate political power over national affairs. President Obiang's birthday is a national holiday.

The Central Committee of the PDGE stated in a resolution in late November 1990 that the country could adapt itself to "political pluralism." However, some 30 Equatoguineans were arrested and imprisoned when they publicly demanded multiparty democracy. The group included prominent government officials such as the vice-president of the national legislature, the president of the Supreme Court, and the minister of defense. The legislative vice-president, Antonio Ebang Mbele, who was reported to have later gone into exile, had proposed that there be a debate on the possibility of introducing multi-partyism.

Meanwhile, the leadership of the PDGE set up a Political Information and Awareness Commission to make sure that the country understood that political pluralism as conceived of by the Party did not include any "ideologies imported from the outside." State radio broadcasts in early 1991 claimed that in all areas where the Commission had visited, people had strongly rejected multi-partyism, favoring instead an "authentic system adapted to the Equatorial Guinian people's natural development."

Despite this alleged popular support for one-party rule, in May the PDGE Central Committee recommended to the government that a multi-party system be adopted. During a PDGE national congress held in early August 1991 participants formally directed President Obiang Nguema Mbasogo to conduct a successful transition to multi-partyism. However, the government has not yet acted to provide a process allowing for the legalization of political parties, and the president has warned against "premature and disorderly democratic changes." Without specifying a timetable, he has stated that the constitution will be revised and then put to a referendum, after which legislation will be adopted allowing for political parties, independent trade unions, freedom of association and the press, and amnesty for political offenders.

Nine political parties in opposition to the current regime are presently in exile in neighboring Gabon and Cameroon, as well as in Spain. In 1991 they set up a coordinating body to focus on collectively applying pressure on the regime to allow for their legal operation within the country. They have called for a national conference of all Equatoguinean social and political movements in order to redesign the political system. In June 1991 three of these movements formed an alliance to heighten the pressure on the regime in Malabo for a sovereign national conference.

With the assistance of the World Bank and the International Monetary Fund, the Obiang regime is still trying to rebuild an economic structure almost completely eradicated during the Macie years. Recent measures include the introduction of a convertible currency and the encouragement of foreign investment. Equatorial Guinea has abundant timber and fishing resources, as well as practically moribund cacao and coffee sectors that have potential for revival.

Political Rights and Civil Liberties: Citizens of Equatorial Guinea do not have the power to change their government democratically. Although citizens have not been free to criticize the government or to propose alternatives to the existing one-party regime, a resolution of the August 1991 congress of the ruling PDGE called for a new law that would regulate freedom of the press and expression. All media are government-owned. Members of the rubber-stamp Chamber of People's Representatives who have attempted to demonstrate some independence of the president have been arrested and imprisoned.

Independent political association and assembly are banned, and nonpolitical groups must register with the government. Freedom of religion in this largely Roman Catholic country is restricted, and Protestant sects have been harassed or persecuted. Internal travel is generally free. The August 1990 the PDGE congress called for free trade unions, but none exist yet and the right to strike is still prohibited. Unemployed citizens can be subject to periods of forced labor.

Despite a provision in the 1982 constitution that prohibits the use of torture or inhumane forms of punishment, there have been repeated reports of human rights abuses under the current regime, although at a level substantially reduced from the nearly genocidal level which occurred during the Macie period. The security police are vigilant and active. Despite constitution prohibitions, arbitrary arrests and detentions are common. Laws are enacted by decree. The judicial system is weak and cannot effectively review executive policies, since it is subject to the power of the president to appoint and dismiss judges at his pleasure.

In March 1991 the government set up a human rights commission headed by the speaker of the Chamber of People's Representatives. Its role is not yet clear.

Estonia

Polity: Presidential-parliamentary democracy
Economy: Statist transitional
Population: 1,566,000
PPP: na
Life Expectancy: na
Ethnic Groups: Estonian (61 percent), Russian, Ukrainian, other (36 percent)

Political Rights: 2
Civil Liberties: 3
Status: Free

Overview: In 1991, two years after proclaiming "sovereignty" and 51 years after being forcibly incorporated into the Soviet Union under the Hitler-Stalin Pact, Estonia won diplomatic recognition from the international community. Other key issues included the economy and the question of citizenship, which would effect the nation's non-Estonian minority.

Estonia was an independent state between the two World Wars. The U.S. never recognized Estonia's annexation by the Soviet Union. With the advent of Soviet leader Mikhail Gorbachev's liberalization policies in 1985, Estonians began to press demands for greater autonomy. An Estonian Popular Front (EPF) and other political organizations were created, which included reform Communists and non-party intellectuals. Initially, a number of pro-independence advocates were expelled to the

West. In November 1988 the Estonian Supreme Soviet (later Council) adopted a declaration of sovereignty proclaiming that its laws superseded those of the Soviet Union. A year later it declared the 1939 Hitler-Stalin Pact "null and void."

The rise of the EPF led to the proliferation of other groups, including the pro-Moscow Interfront and the United Council of Labor Collectives (UCLC), whose largely Russian constituents opposed the rise of Estonian nationalism. A pro-Moscow umbrella group called the Committee for the Defense of Soviet Power and Civil Rights was subsequently formed.

By the time of the 1990 Estonian Supreme Council elections, the EPF had split, with four parties running under its banner: the Peasant Party, the Democratic Labor Party the Liberal Democratic Party and the Social Democrat Independence Party. Other pro-independence parties included the Union of Labor Collectives of Estonia and the Green Party. Another key organization was the Congress of Estonia, a product of the Estonian Citizens Committee, an opposition movement set up in February 1989 by the Estonian National Independence Party and made up of former dissidents and long-time nationalists. The Citizens Committee rejected Soviet institutions, including the Supreme Soviet, as illegitimate and began a campaign to register individual citizens, as well as those who sought citizenship in a future independent Estonia, with the aim of forming a congress to discuss Estonia's new political order. Over 700,000 people who had registered as citizens took part in elections to the Congress from 24 February to 1 March 1990. On 11-12 March, the elected delegates convened the Congress of Estonia as a 499-member alternative parliament. Some in the Congress called for a boycott of elections for the republic's Supreme Council.

On 18 March 1990, Estonians went to the polls in the first free elections since 1940. The EPF and its allies won 49 seats, 29 went to the Free Estonia and Communist Party, and the Committee for the Defense of Soviet Power (including four seats reserved for the military), won 27. The pre-election factionalism in the Communist party finally caused a split after the vote, as most delegates came out in favor of full independence. The openly pro-independence forces did not win two-thirds of the seats, and could not make constitutional changes. The anti-independence forces did not gain enough votes to constitute a one-third minority.

In March 1991, Estonia—joined by Lithuania, Latvia, Georgia, Armenia and Moldavia—boycotted Soviet President Mikhail Gorbachev's referendum on maintaining the USSR as a "renewed federation." On 3 March, two weeks before Gorbachev's all-union referendum, Estonia held a plebiscite on independence; about 78 percent of eligible voters answered "yes" to the question, "Do you want the restoration of the state sovereignty and independence of the Republic of Estonia?" Even though Estonia called for a formal boycott of the all-union referendum, central bureaucracies organized voting. The Estonian Supreme Council announced that it would not participate in talks on the union treaty or accept the union treaty in any form. On 30 March the Supreme Council declared that Estonia had entered a transition period leading to full independence.

Early in 1991 the government of Prime Minister Edgar Savisaar and President Arnold Ruutel, chairman of the Supreme Council, was asked to resign by pro-Moscow demonstrators, raising fears that the Soviet government was ready to crack down on Estonia as it did in Lithuania in January, when notorious OMON "Black Berets" attacked installations.

The attempted 19 August coup against President Gorbachev prompted Estonia to declare full independence the following day. On 27 August the European Community recognized the independence of Estonia and the other two Baltic nations—Lithuania and Latvia. The U.S. formally recognized the three new states on 2 September and the USSR Congress of People's Deputies followed on 4 September. On 17 September the United Nations General Assembly voted by acclamation to accept the applications of Estonia, Latvia and Lithuania. On 24 October, Estonia and the other Baltic states were admitted as associate members of the North Atlantic Treaty Organization (NATO).

The sensitive issue of citizenship raised tensions between the Popular Front and the Congress of Estonia. In 1939, shortly before the Baltics were seized by the Soviets, Estonians made up 88 percent of the population; by 1989, however, that figure had dropped to 61.5 percent since the Soviets had brought thousands of foreign workers to Estonia as industrial labor.

In August, shortly after independence, a 60-member Constituent Assembly was formed representing both the EPF-led Supreme Council and the alternative Congress of Estonia. Its task was to draft a new constitution in accordance with which a new parliament would be elected in 1992. On 9 September the parliamentary citizenship commission introduced to the Supreme Council a draft citizenship law that had been in the works for over a year. The law eliminated automatic citizenship for spouses and amended the text to allow mothers, as well as fathers, to pass on citizenship. It also increased the minimum residence qualification for citizenship to 10 years and required a loyalty oath. The law set up a complicated pattern of requirements that placed citizens and potential citizens in three categories: first, those who had been citizens of the interwar republic and their descendents; second, those who had permanent resident status in Estonia on 30 March, the day the Supreme Council declared the beginning of a transition period, were granted the option of applying for citizenship or retaining their current citizenship (if they chose naturalization, the state would waive the requirement for competence in the Estonian language and ten years' residence); third, those who settled in Estonia after 30 March might retain their current citizenship or apply to become naturalized after they had lived in Estonia for 10 years by taking a loyalty oath and demonstrating knowledge of Estonian.

The draft law set off heated debate centered on language and residency waivers. The Congress of Estonia issued a protest accusing the Supreme Council of "national treason." The main argument centered on whether the massive postwar migration of non-Estonians threatened to undermine Estonian culture. A few days after the law was announced, hundreds of Estonians rallied in Tallinn to protest a law that granted automatic citizenship to non-ethnic Estonians.

A revised draft specified only two groups—citizens of the interwar period and applicants for citizenship. It also eliminated the residence and language waivers for applicants. Acceptance of the revised draft signaled the emerging power of the Congress of Estonia. On 7 November the Supreme Council voted 64 to 14 to adopt the citizenship law.

On 11 September Prime Minister Savisaar told Estonian radio that the dreaded Soviet "black berets" would be withdrawn by the end of the year, as well as a 700-strong police regiment. A 750-member prison guard division would leave by July 1992. In October the KGB deputy chairman told a press conference in Moscow that the KGB would be dissolved in the Baltic states.

Like other post-Communist states in Europe, Estonia faced the daunting challenge of establishing a viable market economy. At the end of 1991 inflation was running at 120-130 percent, as price reforms went into effect. Privatization was launched in 1990, when Estonia permitted the sale of state-owned service trade and catering companies. In early April 1991 Estonia passed legislation which attempted to set a framework for returning land confiscated after 1940 to its rightful owners. But privatization in the country was hindered by collective and state farms. On 18 October the Supreme Council passed a land law that returned nationalized land to its former owners, but did not specify compensation. In May 1991 the government announced plans to sell 17 large enterprises and its intention to put up for sale a 10 percent stake of all medium and large companies. In September the U.S. promised $14 million in aid to be split among the three Baltic states. On 29 October the government approved a proposal to liberalize import-export regulations. It eliminated quotas and licensing requirements and would not levy taxes on imported and exported goods purchased with hard currency. Certain categories of goods in short supply—food products, lumber, cement, liquor, tobacco and bearskins—would still be subject to quotas, regardless of the method of payment.

Political Rights and Civil Liberties:

Estonians have the means to change their government democratically and elections are scheduled for 1992. A draft of a new constitution has yet to be finalized. Steps had been undertaken at year's end to make the judiciary independent and codify safeguards and guarantees. Freedom of speech is respected, and there is a lively independent press. In October a color weekly, *Den' za dnme,* catering to Russian-speakers, appeared on the newsstands. Freedom of association and assembly are respected and there are generally no constraints on domestic or international travel. Freedom of religion is guaranteed. There has been some concern about the rights of non-Estonians, particularly Russians. Independent labor associations and unions exist.

Ethiopia

Polity: Transitional
Economy: Statist
Population: 50,000,000
PPP: $350
Life Expectancy: 45.5
Ethnic Groups: Afar, Amhara, Anuak, Harari, Oromo, Somali, Tigrinya, others

Political Rights: 6
Civil Liberties: 5
Status: Partly Free

Overview:

1991 marked the end of the military dictatorship which had ruled Ethiopia for fourteen years. Known as the Dergue and headed by Lieutenant Colonel Mengistu Haile Mariam, the regime was one of most ruthless and deadly on the African continent. The country is currently run by a self-proclaimed "transitional" government led by the Ethiopian People's Revolutionary Democratic Front (EPRDF).

The dominant movement within the broader EPDRF coalition is the Tigrean People's Liberation Front (TPLF) of the northern Ethiopian province of Tigre. Formed in 1975 as a Marxist-Leninist movement opposed to the military-dominated communism of the Dergue, the TPLF's leadership is said to have evolved in recent years away from an admiration for Stalinist Albania toward a belief in a mixed economy and political pluralism. It now characterizes itself as "revolutionary democratic." The TPLF was tutored in guerrilla tactics by the Eritrean People's Liberation Front (EPLF), which has fought to detach Eritrea from Ethiopia. [*See related territories report on Ethiopia.*] Over the years the TPLF extended its control from Tigre province in the northern highlands of Ethiopia south in the direction of Addis Ababa. It allied itself within the EPDRF to a few other ethnically-based rebel movements opposed to the Dergue, including the Oromo People's Democratic Organization (OPDO) and the Ethiopian People's Democratic Movement (EPDM), the latter group largely made up of Amharic speakers. As its sphere of armed control grew, the EPDRF maintained a position of unwillingness to negotiate with the Mengistu government.

In 1990 Mengistu had made some vague promises to open up the political system to non-violent opposition movements and the economic system to free market forces. But 1990 ended with Ethiopia still under the oppressive rule of the "Red Negus," or emperor. In its final months the Mengistu regime had suffered from the loss of military and economic aid from the Soviet Union and East Bloc. However, 1991 began with some positive signs for the Dergue. Since it had consistently voted as a member of the U.N. Security Council to support measures against Iraq, the government anticipated that its cooperation would lead to an end to further Arab aid for the allegedly pro-Iraqi Eritrean People's Liberation Front (EPLF), fighting to detach Eritrea from Ethiopia. Further, the Dergue's quiet grant of permission for the Israeli government to transport Falasha Jews out of Ethiopia to Israel reportedly won some surreptitious military assistance.

Negotiations held in late February 1991 in London between the Mengistu government and the EPLF were soon adjourned due to irreconcilable differences. The talks were succeeded almost immediately by armed offensives launched by both the EPLF and EPRDF against government troops. The EPRDF's objective was quickly achieved and the momentum of victory carried the insurgents south against crumbling government defenses. Month after month, government troops were defeated each time they took a stand, and there are estimates that a quarter of them died during the insurgent offensive.

In late April, under pressure from a deteriorating military situation, though still in control in the capital Addis Ababa and environs, the regime called for a ceasefire and offered to form a coalition government of transition to multi-party elections with all political forces committed to the unity of Ethiopia. Sensing the government's weakening position, the rebels showed little interest. By mid-May EPRDF guerrillas and allies were only 150 kilometers from the nation's capital. Finally seeing the handwriting on the wall, Mengistu fled to family-owned property in Zimbabwe on 21 May after the government of President Robert Mugabe assured his sanctuary. Less than a week later, Israel was allowed to fly out approximately 14,500 Falasha Jews.

As the rebels closed in on Addis Ababa, their representatives and the regime finally agreed to meet in London in late May for talks organized by the United States. By this time, what was left of the central government did not even have effective control over its own troops clustered in the capital. Within a day of convening negotiations in London on 27 May forces of the EPRDF, with American approval, entered Addis

Ababa to prevent a complete breakdown of order within the panicked city. Troops of the anti-Dergue coalition moved south and east to consolidate their control throughout the country and a transitional coalition government was formed.

A conference was opened in the beginning of July in order to gather together twenty-six Ethiopian political groups who had opposed the dictatorial Mengistu regime. The leader of the TPLF/EPDRF and "acting head of state," Meles Zenawi, was formally elected chief of state for the period of the transitional government. A charter was adopted which set up an 87-member Council of Representatives charged with drafting a constitution and aiding in the governance of the country until internationally supervised multi-party elections could be held two years later. The conference also called for the creation of an independent judiciary, establishment of justiciable civil liberties and political rights, and particular respect for the right of ethnic groups to self-determination.

Before free and fair elections are held, the present transitional government will need to cope with a variety of opposition forces which will test its new-found commitment to the principles of political pluralism. There is significant support for maintaining the territorial integrity of Ethiopia. This pro-unity Ethiopian nationalism is adamantly opposed to the possibility of independence for Eritrea, despite the EPRDF's firm control over that province.

Ethiopia is considered to be one of the world's poorest countries. Drought, exacerbated by agricultural collectivization with its disastrous effects on crop production, has led to repeated famines. Although the January 1991 party program of the EPRDF called for state ownership of land and key sectors of the economy, since deposing the Mengistu regime the party's leadership has asserted that it supports a mixed economy. As evidence, it points to its encouragement of free trade and non-collectivized farming in the regions of Ethiopia that it had liberated prior to total victory. However, real property will not be returned to private ownership. Hundreds of thousands of peasant soldiers conscripted by the prior regime will have to be demobilized and reintegrated into the economy.

Political Rights and Civil Liberties:

Ethiopians are not yet able to chose their government democratically. However, the new regime has preferred when possible to govern by achieving consensus among representatives of the country's ethnic populations. Though democratic institutions are still in the preliminary stages of formation, the government has publicly and repeatedly asserted its commitment to an independent judiciary, free press, and respect for fundamental human rights.

The last months of the prior regime saw mass forced military conscription, requisitioning of famine supplies for its army, and the effort of its internal security force to violently root out any suspected support for the insurgency among civilian populations still under government control. The new regime acted quickly to abolish the security force, stop forced conscriptions, and pledge to work cooperatively with international famine relief agencies. But forced conscription and human rights abuses were reportedly also common in areas "liberated" by the TPLF.

The transitional government has promised fair trials to officials of the prior regime after a special independent tribunal is set up and criminal investigations are made. Reportedly, high-level and mid-level officials, both military and civilian, are to be subjected to political re-education.

Fiji

Polity: Military-civilian transitional
Economy: Capitalist
Population: 700,000
PPP: $3,610
Life Expectancy: 64.8
Ethnic Groups: Indians (49 percent), Fijian (46 percent), other Pacific islanders, Chinese (6 percent)

Political Rights: 6
Civil Liberties: 4
Status: Partly Free

Overview:

Fiji's first national elections since a 1987 military coup were postponed in 1991 due to organizational problems. The vote, now scheduled for mid-1992, will be held under a military-installed constitution designed assure ethnic Fijians a parliamentary majority.

For several decades after the British claimed Fiji as a dependency in 1874, large numbers of Indian agricultural workers migrated to the islands. The 1986 census recorded 329,000 ethnic Fijians, 348,000 Indians and 37,000 people of other races. These demographics allowed an Indian-dominated government, led by Prime Minister Timoci Bavadra, to be elected in April 1987 behind a coalition of the Indian-backed National Federation Party (NFP) and the trade union-supported Fiji Labor Party (FLP). Later in 1987, the predominantly ethnic Fijian army, led by Lieutenant Colonel Sitiveni Rabuka, shocked the South Pacific region by staging a pair of bloodless coups which overthrew the elected government. The army installed Ratu Sir Kamisese Mara, whose now-defunct Alliance Party had ruled Fiji from its independence in 1970 until the 1987 elections, as prime minister of an interim government.

In January 1990 the coup leaders returned the country to civilian rule, and promised elections within twenty-four months. In July the interim government changed the constitution to grant ethnic Fijians a perpetual parliamentary majority. The constitution reserves for them 37 of the 70 seats in the House of Representatives and 24 of the 34 Senate seats. The unelected Great Council of Chiefs, a group of traditional rulers, will appoint the ethnic Fijian Senate seats and select the president. The prime minister, who will hold most of the executive authority, will be chosen by the president from among members of the House.

In March 1991 the Great Council of Chiefs approved the formation of the Fijian Political Party (FPP) to unite ethnic Fijians. However, it is uncertain how many ethnic Fijians will actually vote for the FPP. Many do not want a society based on traditional rule and resent the Chiefs' involvement in politics. In addition, Melanesian western Fijians feel they are underrepresented by the FPP and the Chiefs, who are mainly Polynesian eastern Fijians. Rabuka's election in October 1991 as FPP president came as a blow to the Chiefs, who fear the ambitious coup leader might wrest control of the party from them.

The main opposition coalition may unravel before the election. In July the NFP decided to contest the vote, but in September the FLP announced that it would boycott the election as a protest against the constitution. The FPP also has to contend with the multi-ethnic All National Congress (ANC). This fast growing party, formed in April 1991 by popular cabinet minister Apisai Tora, is expected to get strong support from the dissident ethnic Fijians. On 25 July Prime Minister Mara removed Tora from the cabinet after the latter spent several months criticizing the government and refused to quit his post as ANC president.

Political Rights and Civil Liberties: Fijians cannot change their military-installed government democratically. Elections planned for 1991 have been postponed until mid-1992. The 1990 constitution ensures that a majority of the seats in both houses of parliament and at least half of the civil service positions will be held by ethnic Fijians. The constitution includes a bill of rights, but allows the parliament to suspend fundamental rights in the event of an alleged threat to national security. Freedom of speech has been largely restored after being suppressed in the wake of the 1987 coups, and political dissidents frequently speak out against the government. The government has arrested several people for publishing "malicious material" under the Public Order Act, and privately owned media therefore practice some self-censorship. Newspaper editorials generally do not criticize the government but opposition viewpoints are printed. Assembly for political purposes must be approved by the government.

The judiciary is independent of the government, and there are no reported political prisoners. The Fiji Intelligence Service has broad authority to conduct personal searches, intercept mail and tap telephones, although it is unclear to what extent such surveillance is actually used. Freedom of religion is guaranteed by the constitution and respected in practice, but the political situation and Sunday commercial restrictions have strained relations between Hindu Indians and ethnic Fijians. In July 1991, 3,000 Methodists staged an anti-Muslim rally and called for a Christian state. Freedom of travel is unrestricted. Strikes are legal and free trade unions are permitted. In April 1991 the government introduced the Sugar Industry Special Protection Decree and the Protection of the National Economy Decree, which would have allowed it to impose fines and jail sentences for disrupting the "orderly planting or growing or harvesting of sugar cane" or other industries. In July the government withdrew the decrees just days before Indian-led unions planned to hold nationwide strikes. Sugarcane workers had successfully organized a six-week walkout to protest the measures.

Finland

Polity: Presidential-parliamentary democracy
Economy: Mixed capitalist
Population: 5,000,000
PPP: $13,980
Life Expectancy: 75.0
Ethnic Groups: Finns (94 percent), Swedes, Lapps

Political Rights: 1
Civil Liberties: 1
Status: Free

Overview: Hit by a recession in 1991, Finland developed closer economic ties with the European Community and voted the governing coalition out of office in March parliamentary elections.

Located in Northern Europe, Finland lived under Swedish and Danish domination for centuries until it became a Russian territory in 1809. Finland achieved independence in 1917, but lost territory to the Soviet Union during World War II. Following the war, two presidents dominated Finnish politics: J.K. Paaskivi (1946-56) and Uhro Kekkonen (1956-81). Social Democrat Mauno Koivisto has been president since 1981. Adopted on 17 July 1919, the present constitution provides for a 200-seat parliament elected by universal suffrage and based upon proportional representation. The president, elected to a six-year term, appoints the prime minister from the party or coalition which commands the majority of the parliament. The president can initiate and veto legislation and is directly responsible for foreign affairs. In addition, the president may dissolve the parliament at any time and call for elections.

Since World War II, Finland's foreign policy has been defined by its neutrality in the Cold War. Until recently, the Soviet Union heavily influenced Finnish politics and occasionally interfered with presidential elections and cabinet selections. The first governing coalition to rule without the Communists took office in 1972. In 1989, Soviet President Mikhail Gorbachev visited Finland and assured the Finns that they were free to make their own policies.

In March 1991 parliamentary elections, the ruling coalition of Social Democrats and Conservatives was voted out of office. The Center Party increased its representation in the parliament and formed a new coalition government with the Conservatives, the Swedish People's Party, and the Finnish Christian Union. The Social Democrats joined the Left Alliance, the Greens, the Rural Party, and the Liberals in the opposition. Women hold about 40 percent of the parliamentary seats, and a new intake of young M.P.s has reduced the body's average age to below 40. At 36, Esko Aho of the Center Party is the youngest prime minister in Finland's history. The youngest parliamentarian, 23-year-old Minna Karhunen, said about the new parliament, "I think we are going to have fun."

The new government faces worsening economic conditions and an unemployment rate (7.5 percent) at a record post-war level. The Central Organization of Employers demanded a 10 percent wage cut, but the government responded to the recession with a proposed ban on vacation pay and other cuts equal to a 5 percent wage reduction. On 3 October 1991 workers responded by protesting against the proposed cuts with Finland's largest political demonstration in almost four decades. Industrial workers sought to protect their excellent benefits and seven weeks' paid vacation.

Largely because of its close ties to the Soviet Union, Finland remained outside of the European Community (EC), but the Finnish government is now taking steps towards joining the EC. In June 1991 the government pegged the Finnish Mark to the European Currency Unit (ECU), thereby facilitating a smooth transition into the united Europe. Finland has also joined the new European Economic Area (EEA).

Political Rights and Civil Liberties:

Finns have the right to change their government democratically. Freedom of assembly, association and press are guaranteed by law. The Finnish Broadcasting Company controls most of the radio and television programming in Finland. There are both Finnish and Swedish programs. With the demise of the Soviet Union, Finns have greater freedom to write and speak about their neighbors' policies. In late 1991, three major daily newspapers closed for financial reasons. The state finances two established churches in Finland: Lutheran and Orthodox. Both churches may teach their beliefs in the public schools. Approximately 88 percent of the Finnish population is Lutheran, but religious freedom is respected for all faiths. Workers have the right to organize. The Swedish-speaking minority (7 percent of the population) has autonomy, cultural rights, and a political party.

France

Polity: Presidential-
parliamentary democracy
Economy: Mixed capitalist
Population: 56,700,000
PPP: $13,590
Life Expectancy: 76.4
Ethnic Groups: French, regional minorities (Corsican, Alsatian, Basque, Breton), and various Arab and African immigrant groups

Political Rights: 1
Civil Liberties: 2
Status: Free

Overview:

The major issues in France during 1991 surrounded immigration policy, separatist militants in Corsica, a flamboyant new prime minister, economic distress, French involvement in the Persian Gulf War, and a wave of protest marches and strikes.

Since the French Revolution in 1789, France has had various republican, imperial and monarchical forms of government. The current system of government, the Fifth Republic, dates from 1958. As designed by Charles De Gaulle, the presidency is the dominant institution in this mixed presidential-parliamentary system. The people elect the president directly through a two-round system. In the first round, candidates of all parties appear on the ballot. If no candidate reaches a majority, a runoff takes place between the two top finishers. The parliamentary bodies are the 577-member National Assembly, which the people elect directly, and the 318-member Senate, which is chosen by an electoral college of local elected officials. However, the foregoing constitutional arrangements could change in 1992. President François Mitterrand is proposing changing the length of presidential terms, adding proportional representation to legislative elections, and strengthening parliamentary power and judicial authority.

A Socialist, Mitterrand has been in power since 1981. During his first term, Mitterrand's polices included the nationalization of several major industrial groups and banks. As the economy weakened in the mid-1980s, the Socialists abandoned many of their statist polices. After the Socialists lost the 1986 National Assembly election to the center-right, Mitterrand appointed Gaullist leader Jacques Chirac prime minister. During this period of so-called ideological cohabitation in government, France denationalized many previously nationalized enterprises. After the National Assembly elections of 1988, the Socialists and their Left Radical allies regained power. Mitterrand appointed moderate Socialist Michel Rocard prime minister.

Rocard received credit for a stable currency and lower inflation. His polices included a partial privatization of nationalized firms. Under his plan, private shareholders could buy up to a 49 percent stake in state-owned banks and industries. During the recession, subsidies were in short supply, so companies needed to turn to private sources for capital. Due to the Socialists' shaky working majority in the National Assembly, Rocard reached out to the political center to pass legislation. Looking to shore up the party, Mitterrand replaced Rocard with Edith Cresson in May 1991. Cresson, a more radical Socialist than Rocard, began to capture international attention with critical comments about the rigid Japanese lifestyle. She also alleged that Englishmen and other non-Latin European males were disproportionately homosexual and uninterested in women.

Cresson astounded Socialist supporters and opponents alike with a new immigration policy. She announced a crackdown on illegal immigrants, stricter standards for issuing visas, especially in political asylum cases, and the possibility of mass expulsions of immigrants. The Right hailed these policies; many Socialists attacked them. The new prime minister appeared to be responding to rising anti-immigrant sentiment among the French public. At the same time, government statisticians projected that the country would continue to need more immigrants to maintain the size of its labor force.

During 1991 there were several incidents of violence by and against immigrants. In March, after a security guard shot an Arab youth to death, there were riots in the Paris suburbs. In May a riot suspect who suffered from asthma died in police custody after officers refused him medicine. In June there were several clashes between police and Arab immigrant youths. The children of the Harkis, pro-French families forced out of Algeria, took to the streets in several locations, using force to vent their frustration with their economic plight. In July a court convicted a paratroop squad of terrorizing an immigrant neighborhood; in late 1990, the soldiers used clubs, iron bars, and brass knuckles in indiscriminate attacks on immigrants, injuring five civilians. As punishment, the troops received fines and suspended jail sentences of six to twelve months, and lost their rights to vote and bear arms. In addition, the military expelled them.

Led by Jean-Marie Le Pen the anti-immigrant National Front has become the focal point for voters with racial and other frustrations. Le Pen has equated racism with patriotism in his speeches, but has had to pay a price for his remarks. Back in 1987 Le Pen dismissed the Nazi Holocaust as a mere "detail" of history. Eleven religious and human rights groups sued him. In 1990 a judge ruled that Le Pen would have to pay the legal costs for his opponents in the case and would also have to give them one franc each in symbolic damages. In March 1991 an appeals court raised Le Pen's fine to the equivalent of $167,000. In a separate case, an appeals court overturned a 1988 fine on Le Pen for comparing a cabinet member to Nazi crematory ovens. The court held that Le Pen's comment was tasteless but legally tolerable.

In November 1991 Bruno Megret, deputy leader of the National Front, proposed an extreme program to deal with immigrants. The proposals called for chartering boats to deport foreigners; building guarded camps to hold those awaiting deportation; voiding naturalizations dating back to 1974; basing naturalization on blood not residency; limiting the building of mosques; setting a quota limiting the number of immigrant children allowed in each classroom; stopping welfare payments to immigrant families; laying off foreign workers before French workers; establishing a separate social security system for foreigners; and giving scholarships to foreigners only if they leave France after completing their education. Le Pen said the party would decide later whether to make this program official party policy.

France suffered from economic difficulties in 1991. Unemployment climbed to over 9.5 percent. Cresson's government responded with higher required social security contributions and cuts in some spending programs. Several types of employees (transport workers, air traffic controllers, printers, auto workers, and broadcast employees) expressed dissatisfaction with the economy through strikes. Steel workers in Normandy held two executives in captivity to protest feared layoffs. Thousands of farmers marched on Paris to oppose falling prices for their products and to stop trade liberalization and reforms of European Community agricultural policies. When health care professionals demonstrated in Paris, riot police fired tear gas at nurses and injured marchers.

The French government also had to deal with a wave of Corsican separatist violence in 1991. Corsica, a Mediterranean island, is more Italian than French in culture. A splinter group of the National Liberation Front of Corsica took 12 hostages and destroyed 40 vacation homes in January 1991. Few Corsicans want independence, but most want recognition of local linguistic and cultural rights. The Socialist government introduced legislation for greater Corsican autonomy. Separatist militants continued their campaign with attacks on foreign tourists in June 1991.

In foreign policy France began 1991 attempting to prevent a war in the Persian Gulf. The French peace plan linked the Palestinian question to an Iraqi withdrawal from Kuwait. Once the war started, the French took part in the multi-national force to evict Iraq from Kuwait. Both houses of parliament approved military action over-whelmingly. Only the Communists, the National Front, and some dissident Socialists voted against French involvement in the war. Later in the year, France dispatched troops to Zaire to protect foreigners and minimal stability during the collapse of order in that African country. Within Europe, France and Germany proposed a new continental army. The proposal raised questions about the future role of NATO and the United States in European defense.

Political Rights and Civil Liberties:

The French have the right to change their government democratically. The electoral system allows the French to elect a new president every seven years and a new National Assembly at least once every five years. Under the Fifth Republic constitution, the president has significant emergency powers and the right to rule by decree under certain circumstances. Reacting against the weak executives of earlier forms of government, De Gaulle insisted on a strong presidency when he supervised the creation of the Fifth Republic in 1958.

France's anti-terrorist policy includes the expulsion of suspected Basque terrorists, a procedure that is also applied to foreigners believed to be assisting Middle Eastern terrorist organizations. The laws contain "urgency" procedures which allow the government to expel foreigners without any possibility to appeal the decision. In 1991 the government deported Abdelmoumen Diouri, a Moroccan dissident author, after he refused to halt publication of a book critical of Moroccan King Hassan II. The government charged Diouri, a twenty-year resident, with having close ties to Libya and Iraq. In response to protests by human rights groups, France rescinded the deportation.

Religious freedom is respected. Religious schools receive financial assistance from the national government. The press is largely free, but there are some restrictions on expression, and the government subsidizes journalism and registers journalists. The state is secretive, and limits criticism of the president. For example, the government charged two journalists with "breach of confidence" following their use of a classified police document in researching a book on terrorism. They were acquitted. The broadcast media became increasingly free and competitive in the 1980s. There is no government monopoly; private radio stations are growing. During the Persian Gulf

War, the government banned and seized videocassettes which praised Saddam Hussein and insulted the West. The government also prohibited female journalists from covering the front line forces.

In 1991 the government legalized the widespread security agency practice of compiling dossiers on thousands of French citizens. Previously, intelligence agents had no legal authorization to do this. The Interior Ministry announced that individuals would be able to review the files concerning them.

The judiciary can rule against actions of the government. In 1991 after the government ordered a magistrate off a case involving illicit campaign contributions to the Socialists, a court ordered the continuation of the investigation. Also in 1991 a court convicted the country's former anti-terrorism chief for helping to fabricate a case against three suspected Irish guerrillas.

Business, agricultural and labor groups have freedom of association. The labor movement has competing Communist and non-Communist federations.

Gabon

Polity: Dominant party transitional
Economy: Capitalist
Population: 1,200,000
PPP: $3,960
Life Expectancy: 52.5
Ethnic Groups: Binga, Duma, Fang, Lumbo, Mpongwe, Seke, Shogo, other

Political Rights: 4
Civil Liberties: 3
Status: Partly Free

Overview:

In 1991 the power of Gabon's longtime strongman Omar Bongo continued to be challenged by an increasingly confident opposition. Important events included the ratification of a new constitution and a parliamentary walkout by opposition members. For the first time since the country's independence in 1960, membership in the National Assembly is no longer limited to members of the ruling party. President Omar Bongo, head of state in a one-party regime for twenty-four years, now portrays himself as non-partisan in the new multi-party regime.

Situated on the west coast of Central Africa, Gabon gained independence from France in 1960. Its leader at the time, President Leon M'Ba, successfully created a one-party state under his Gabon Democratic Bloc (BDG). M'Ba died in 1967 and was replaced by his Vice President, Albert-Bernard—later known as Omar after his conversion to Islam—Bongo. Bongo outlawed all opposition groups and maintained the one-party rule of a newly renamed BDG, now the Democratic Party of Gabon (PDG). President Bongo was last elected in 1986 to a seven-year term,running unopposed as the sole PDG candidate. Presidential elections are scheduled for 1993.

Widespread political unrest prompted Bongo to take steps toward multi-partyism in 1990, culminating in legislative elections in October. Though not free from controversy and allegations of rigging, they were judged relatively fair by impartial observers. Due to the charges of irregularity at the polls, three seats were re-contested in November, and five more in March 1991. Ultimately, Bongo's PDG maintained a slim majority, which stands at sixty-three seats to fifty-seven for the opposition. The total of sixty-three seats includes three seats held by independents, who are allied with the PDG. The largest opposition parties, whose memberships by and large come from the same region or are of the same ethnic group, are the Gabonese Progress Party (PGP), with seventeen seats, the National Rally of Lumberjacks (RNB), also with seventeen, and the Movement for National Recovery (Morena) with seven seats.

In November 1990, when the election results were in, President Bongo directed Prime Minister Casimir Oye Mba, the head of the transitional government and a respected figure in the international financial community, to form a new government. A new cabinet contained representatives of five of the largest opposition parties. Although the PDG held only one-third of the ministerial portfolios, it held the most important ones, including Foreign Affairs, Territorial Administration, Defence and Finance.

The country's democratic transition continued in 1991. In January, the National Assembly rejected the government's proposed budget in an unusual display of independence, apparently because the plan called for too much spending on the military and presidency and for too little on social services. On 15 March the legislature adopted a new constitution, providing for a semi-presidential system and guarantees on political and individual liberties, in addition to the establishment of a constitutional court.

On 24 March violence occurred at Kango, sixty miles east of the capital of Libreville, during re-contested elections for five National Assembly seats. At a rally, RNB leader Father Paul Mba-Abessole stirred up his supporters with calls for the immediate resignation of the prime minister, dissolution of the national assembly, and new nationwide elections held on the basis of a new system of electoral districts and monitored by international observers. His followers then reportedly pillaged polling places and blockaded the main highway and clashed with security forces.

In May a bloc of opposition parties calling itself the Democratic Opposition Coalition (COD) began a boycott of the Assembly. The COD—which included the RNB—demanded the dissolution of the PDG-dominated government, as well as abolition of institutions not in line with the new constitution, such as the High Court of Justice and the Grand Chancellery of National Orders. The parties also pressed for the end of the governing party's lock on coverage in the broadcast media, and for the rapid establishment of institutions called for in the constitution but not yet set up. Prime Minister Oye-Mba presented his government's resignation to Bongo on 7 June, but on 18 June Bongo directed him to form a new government, which he did. Apparently sensing that Bongo was serious about implementing the new constitution, the boycotters returned to their seats on 20 June. In September, the COD demanded that a new electoral code be drawn up, one which ensures that certain regions not receive over-representation in the Assembly. The opposition alliance also called for a general amnesty to be granted political prisoners and exiles.

In foreign affairs, Bongo has continued Gabon's historically close relations with France, including a well-publicized March visit to Paris by President Bongo during which he spoke enthusiastically about democratic reform in Gabon. Bongo has also indicated his willingness to visit South Africa in order to encourage further reform there. The Gabonese political opposition has denounced the inordinate influence which foreigners are alleged to wield over the Bongo government.

Though Gabon has one of the highest per-capita incomes in Africa, a substantial portion of the government's budget is earmarked for foreign debt servicing, and the national wealth is sapped by high inflation and deeply-rooted corruption in the public sector. Given the government's limited social spending, periodic attempts to enact austerity measures meet with stiff popular and political resistance. The government has promised greater accountability and transparency in the management of national resources and public finances.

Political Rights and Civil Liberties:

Under a new constitution, citizens of Gabon can change their government democratically. The first multi-party legislative elections were held in 1990 and presidential elections are scheduled for 1993.

Proceedings in criminal cases are generally fair, but prisoners in security cases can still be held without charge. Prison conditions are harsh, and beating is standard during interrogations. Most of the few political prisoners are charged with involvement in an abortive 1989 coup attempt. In April, President Bongo reduced the prison terms of eight involved in the coup and he later pardoned political detainees with two or less years to serve of their sentences.

Restrictions on freedom of the press continued to be lifted in 1991, although the opposition still charges the state-controlled media, including the daily *L'Union*, with pro-government bias. An increasing number of independent publications print investigative reports and take views vigorously at variance with those of the government. The government announced plans in late October to provide regular access to the state-owned broadcast media for opposition spokesmen and leaders.

Freedom of religion is respected in this 60 percent Christian nation, and there are no significant restraints on domestic or foreign travel. Restrictions on association and assembly have been loosened in the past year; political rallies and meetings are generally not interfered with unless either there is potential or actual violence, or organizers do not give the government the requisite three-day notice prior to a public gathering. Organization in unions is hindered by the mandate that all unions must be associated with the government Labor Confederation of Gabon (COSGYA), long dominated by the ruling party. Although the right to strike is restricted and government employees cannot join unions, work stoppages and protests continued common in 1991.

The Gambia

Polity: Presidential-legislative democracy
Economy: Capitalist
Population: 900,000
PPP: $650
Life Expectancy: 44.0
Ethnic Groups: Mandingo (40 percent), Fulani (19 percent), Wolof (15 percent), Jola (10 percent), Serahuli (8 percent)

Political Rights: 2
Civil Liberties: 2
Status: Free

Overview:

The main issues in the Gambia during 1991 were a briefly contemplated alliance between the government and the main opposition party, the president's temporary decision not to seek re-election, spillover from unrest in neighboring Senegal, and the country's participation in a regional peacekeeping unit in Liberia.

Located in West Africa, The Republic of The Gambia is a narrow country split along its length by the Gambia River of West Africa and bordered on three sides by Senegal. President Sir Dawda Jawara and his People's Progressive Party (PPP) have led the country since its independence in 1965. Jawara has been directly elected under a multi-party system since 1982. Although the PPP has maintained political dominance for almost three decades, opposition parties operate freely and have contested every election.

The unicameral, directly elected House of Representatives has 51 members who serve for five-year terms. In the 1987 election, the PPP won thirty-one seats, while the opposition National Convention Party (NCP) won five. The other seats are filled by nominated members, traditional chiefs, and those holding certain specified legislative positions. Legal political parties not holding seats include the Gambian People's Party, the United Party, the leftist People's Democratic Organization for Independence and Socialism, and the right-of-center People's Democratic Party, formed in September 1991. Presidential and legislative elections are scheduled for 1992.

In July 1991 the PPP rejected an NCP proposal to form a governing coalition or an alliance. The NCP had sought to abandon its role as the official legislative opposition. Apparently secure in its leadership role, the PPP prefers that there continue to be an official opposition in the parliament. At the local level the Parliamentary Act of 1990 came into effect in April, allowing for the first direct municipal council elections in the Gambia's history. Although the majority of races were won by the PPP, opposition candidates had strong showings in many constituencies.

Gambia's top foreign affairs issues in 1991 involved Senegal and the upheaval in Liberia. Some Senegalese military officers attempting to put down an insurgency in Senegal's southern Casamance district have accused Gambia of ignoring the use of Gambian territory as a temporary refuge for rebels of the Casamance Democratic Forces Movement (MFDC). The Gambia has responded by directing the Senegalese government to apply to Gambian courts for the extradition of any expatriate rebels accused of violent acts in the Casamance. In addition, the parliament adopted legislation in April making subversion against a friendly foreign power from within Gambian territory a crime punishable by life imprisonment. However, the government denies that its territory has been used to systematically ferry arms to insurgents operating inside of Senegal.

In early December, President Jawara suddenly announced that he would not be standing again for president in 1992. As a result of the outcry that followed the news, mainly from those in the president's ruling party, within two weeks Sir Dawda agreed to see re-election after all.

The Gambian population enjoys a relatively high standard of living in comparison with others in the region. Key industries include fishing and fish processing, while the port of Banjul hosts fleets from several West African nations. The main export, groundnut, has been increasing, but there have been marginal declines in cotton and coarse grain exports. Tourism is on the rise despite the temporary dampening effect of the Gulf War; Gambia has become a popular winter resort area for Western Europeans. The IMF has made funds available under both the Enhanced Structural Adjustment Facility and the Structural Adjustment Loan, both geared to reduce the budget deficit, eliminate external debts and increase living standards. An important issue for the government is the growing perception that AIDS is spreading rapidly in Gambia.

Political Rights and Civil Liberties: Despite the PPP's dominance, Gambia is a multi-party, pluralistic system in which citizens over eighteen can vote to change their government by secret ballot. The judiciary is independent of government interference, and the court and general law system is based on the English model. Islamic shari'a law governs marriage, divorce and inheritance for Muslims, while tribal customary law covers these areas for non-Muslims as well as the areas of traditional social and civil relations and local tribal government. In February 1991 the president granted amnesty to 35 prisoners, among them the last of those who were found guilty of complicity in an unsuccessful coup of 1981. Gambians can exercise free speech, and although there are no major newspapers, political party newsletters and other publications can and do criticize the government vigorously. The radio is government owned. There are generally no restrictions on association and assembly, and the secular state protects religious rights. Gambians are free to emigrate and travel is generally unrestricted. There are two main labor federations, and workers have the right to strike.

Germany

Polity: Federal parliamentary democracy
Economy: Mixed capitalist
Population: 79,500,000
PPP: $14,620
Life Expectancy: 75.2
Ethnic Groups: German, Danish

Political Rights: 1
Civil Liberties: 2
Status: Free

Overview: In its first full year of post-World War II unity, Germany faced the spectrum of problems involved in reunifying a nation separated for 45 years by two antithetical economic and political systems. A major issue in 1991 was the economy, particularly in the east. As quickly and powerfully as political change swept across the former East German state, so too was the economic decline of this region throughout 1991 faster and more acute than anticipated. The brief economic boom western Germany enjoyed after reunification resulting from the initial "demand shock" in eastern Germany slowed significantly through the year, while the eastern part of the nation suffered a virtual economic collapse. Related issues were the slumping fortunes of Chancellor Helmut Kohl's ruling Christian Democratic Union (CDU) coalition and increasing violence against foreigners and immigrants by neo-Fascist "skinheads."

On the political front, the year began on a note of triumph and jubilation for Chancellor Kohl, who pushed through the rapid reunification process. On 2 December 1990 Chancellor Kohl's coalition—the CDU, the Bavarian-based Christian Social

Union (CSU) and the Free Democratic Party (FDP)—won overwhelmingly in the first free elections in a united Germany in 58 years. The center-left opposition Social Democratic Party (SPD) garnered only 33 percent of the nationwide vote for seats to the 656-member parliament. Kohl had run on a platform promising a quick economic transition in the east and no tax increases in the west. Oskar Lafontaine, the SPD candidate who stepped down as party chairman after his electoral defeat, had warned of reunification's economic impact.

As 1991 wore on, the government admitted it had underestimated the costs of reunification, declaring that much of the estimated $1-2 trillion needed for reunification over the next ten years actually would be needed in the first year. The expected flood of Western investment in eastern Germany, and in particular from western German business and industry, never fully materialized, as many companies took a wait-and-see approach before sending much needed capital into the area. Though the federal government had originally hoped to earn as much as $6 billion from privatization, the holdings of the *Treuhandanstalt*, the agency administering privatization, were later estimated to be worth only about $530 million. Toward year's end, the agency had disposed of some 4,000 enterprises (transferring some 720,000 jobs to the private sector), but 6,400 companies (employing 2 million), many of them in the heavy industry sector, had yet to be sold.

Western investors worried that the economy in eastern Germany was in too steep a decline to risk large investments. On 1 July, government subsidies for many eastern German companies expired, resulting in the sudden, though anticipated, layoffs of 250,000 workers. Between 30 and 40 percent of the region's inhabitants were either unemployed or were working "short hours." Through its policy of "creative destruc-tion" the government shut down thousands of inefficient businesses and industries and cut the work forces of most of those which remained. In addition to the worsening economy in the region, many western investors were concerned about legal problems involving property claims by former owners who had been forced to hand over land and businesses to the Communist government. With 1.2 million property claims outstanding, the government was slow to implement a system whereby investors could safely acquire property for development while claimants could be assured of equitable compensation.

Adding to these problems was Germany's economic assistance to the multi-national action against Iraq. In addition to pouring billions of Deutschmarks into the east, Germany, under international pressure, donated over $11 billion to the Gulf war effort. Differences over Germany's role sharply divided the public and its political parties.

Chancellor Kohl blamed the unexpected costs of the Gulf crisis for the tax increases contained in the revised 1991 budget. The SPD strongly criticized Kohl for breaking his pledge not to raise taxes and accused the government of being unrealistic and even deceitful in its promise of a smooth and prosperous reunification. Yet, such promises did account for the initial success and popularity of Kohl and the CDU-CSU. In early 1991, the economy was robust, as pent-up consumer demands in the east kept western German factories running at full speed, and the country's trading partners also benefited from a high demand for imported goods. But economic growth was slowed because of higher taxes on income and such essentials as fuel to finance the immense investment needed to integrate the east.

In subsequent months, as euphoria gave way to economic reality, the SPD defeated the CDU in state elections in Hesse, Rhineland-Palatinate (Kohl's home state), and Hamburg, thus taking control of Germany's *Bundesrat*. Although not as powerful as the much larger CDU-CSU-FDP-controlled *Bundestag*, or lower house, the *Bundesrat's* ability to veto various types of legislation made the vote significant. The SPD victories illustrated the decreasing popularity of Kohl and the CDU. In the country as a whole, the combined popularity of the CDU-CSU stood at 34 percent in September; the SPD was well ahead at 45 percent.

The slump in CDU popularity, above all in the east, led to a leadership shake-up. Lothar de Maiziere, the former East German prime minister, who was rewarded after reunification with the post of deputy chairman of the the CDU, resigned after a bitter party squabble and amid rumors of possible involvement with the Stasi, the old East German secret police. And although the economy showed signs of recovery at year's end, the major political parties appeared to be losing members.

A key factor was the emergence of the issue of immigration and a rise in asylum seekers from all over the world, seeking to exploit the country's relatively liberal asylum laws. Some 1,000 refugees a day streamed into Germany from such diverse places as Bulgaria, Yugoslavia, Albania, Turkey, Pakistan, Afghanistan, India, Algeria, Zaire and Angola. By mid-year, anti-foreigner sentiment appeared to spread, particularly in the eastern region, and migrant hostels and immigration centers became targets of violent attacks by neo-Fascist skinheads. The attacks intensified in the fall, with hundreds of incidents of rock-throwing and fire-bombing in which people were injured and at least one killed. In November, eight neo-Nazis were convicted of attacking a home and threatening the occupants, children hurt in the Chernobyl nuclear disaster. On 3 December police in 30 cities throughout Germany raided the homes of suspected rightist radicals.

The CDU advocated tightening up asylum policy, even if it meant changing the constitution. In late November, Cornelia Schmalz-Jacobsen, Chancellor Kohl's chief adviser on matters relating to foreigners, said that she favored an immigration quota system like the one in the United States. The SPD appeared split, between a national leadership which could not contemplate serious restrictions on asylum, and local leaders, like the big city mayors, who had to cope with the influx of refugees and hooligan violence. While most Germans openly deplored the attacks on foreigners and the revival of fascist groups (the neo-Nazi Republican Party failed to win a seat in the 1991 parliament), the issue continued galvanize a xenophobic minority of perhaps 20 or 25 percent of the population. On 29 September the far-right German People's Union won more than 10 percent of the vote in elections for local officials in the western town of Bremenhaven. The same month, there were more than 200 attacks against immigrants and foreign-born laborers in eastern and western Germany.

In other issues, Chancellor Kohl on 25 November realigned his coalition cabinet, promoting Interior Minister Wolfgang Schaeuble to parliamentary leader of the CDU-CSU coalition and raising speculation that he is being groomed as Kohl's successor. The next national elections are set for 1994.

Another contentious matter was whether to move Germany's government from Bonn to Berlin. President Richard von Weizsäcker argued strongly for a complete transfer of government to Berlin, and Chancellor Kohl eventually supported Berlin as well. On 20-21 June the *Bundestag* voted 338-320 to move most of the federal government to Berlin over a 10- to 12- year period.

Political Rights and Civil Liberties:

Germans have the right to change their government by democratic means. Since reunification, former citizens of the GDR have enjoyed the same rights and been protected by the same laws as West Germans. The judiciary is independent; the accused have free access to counsel.

Human rights groups have accused the government of allowing former East German intelligence (Stasi) operatives to work their way back into the German power structure. Prominent anti-Stasi campaigners complained that a secret organization of former agents called Red Fist has been trying to intimidate them. Although the government rejected the request for general amnesty of the approximately 85,000 former Stasi agents and the tens of thousands of informers, many officials complained that Germany's leadership was not taking the Stasi investigation seriously enough. Two senior investigators for the government were dismissed after publicly criticizing the CDU's efforts to rehabilitate former East German Prime Minister and accused Stasi informer Lothar de Maiziére, who eventually resigned his post. A number of former Stasi agents were arrested during 1991 and many more were compelled to resign from government. In the eastern state of Mecklenburg-Pomerania, state-appointed investigators found 10 of the 66 representatives to have had some Stasi connections. Investigations also took place in Saxony, Thuringa, and Saxony-Anhalt. On 2 September four former East German bodyguards went to trial for killing a man who was trying to escape over the Berlin Wall. The case tested whether the new Germany could prosecute members of the old Communist system for violence that occurred before unification.

As a consequence of the Nazi era, Germany's Basic Law, or constitution, requires political parties to be democratic. Although the Communist party and the neo-Nazi Socialist Reich parties were outlawed in the 1950s, the Communist party reorganized and gained strength with the incorporation of former East German officials who still held sway at the local level. Neo-Fascist parties function freely under various names. Although migration from east to west within the nation dropped significantly in 1991, the surge of immigrants from Eastern Europe continued, drawn by Germany's liberal asylum laws, generous social welfare programs, and geographical location. With this surge, the specter of neo-Nazi and other xenophobic extremist groups continued to rise. Incidents of anti-foreign protests grew more frequent and often more violent through 1991, particularly after the lifting of visa restrictions between Poland and Germany in April. Incidents against remaining Vietnamese and Africans also grew in the eastern regions, while guest workers from these areas were restricted in their ability to travel into western Germany. On 1 July a new immigration law ended the right of Germany's 16 states to block the deportation of foreigners whose asylum applications had been rejected by the federal government.

Germans enjoy freedom of religion and freedom of expression, although the use of Nazi symbols is illegal. The press is free, and broadcast media are independent and offer pluralistic points of view. Business, labor and farming groups are free, highly organized, and politically influential. Under Germany's codetermination law, management and labor have equal representation on the boards of major companies.

Ghana

Polity: Military transitional
Economy: Capitalist-statist
Population: 15,500,000
PPP: $970
Life Expectancy: 55.0
Ethnic Groups: Some fifty in number, the majority being Akan (including the Fanti), followed by the Ashanti, Ga, Ewe, and the Mossi-Dagomba

Political Rights: 6
Civil Liberties: 6
Status: Not Free

Overview:

Ghana began a slow process of political change in 1991 which may lead to free multi-party elections and a new regime by the end of 1992. But despite the planned liberalization, Flight Lieutenant Jerry Rawlings, chairman of the ruling Provisional National Defense Council (PNDC), has explicitly reaffirmed his party's leading role in framing the debate on democratization and delayed the legalization of opposition parties.

Rawlings led the military coup which toppled the two-year-old elected government of Dr. Hilla Limann in 1981. He immediately acted to suspend the constitution and dissolve the unicameral National Assembly. In addition, he outlawed political parties, which were only legalized in 1979 after having been banned by an earlier military junta in 1972. In 1982, one year after seizing power, Rawlings disbanded local governments and established a national network of local committees to implement government on a local level. In 1988, elections were held for District Assemblies (DAs), which were designed to supersede the committees. Those who stood for election were nominated by the government; independents and political dissidents were not eligible. The PNDC has asserted that its commitment to the electoral process is displayed through the holding of DA elections in 110 districts, and has said that the process should eventually be extended up to the national level. It has presented no timetable for such an extension, however. The National Commission for Democracy (NCD), created in 1982, participated in developing the DAs and also serves as the government's electoral commission. The opposition has charged that the NCD is unable to operate independently of the regime in its role as the electoral commission.

The NCD is also responsible for the task of developing proposals for realizing a "true democracy" in the country. It submitted its recommendations to the regime in March 1991. By 10 May, the PDNC responded by stating its intention to set up a national Consultative Assembly (CA) to draft a new constitution. The proposed draft constitution, originally intended to be ready by 31 December 1991 but not completed by then, is then to be submitted for ratification by Ghanaians in a referendum. Although the PDNC might have merely reinstated the 1979 democratic Constitution which it abrogated when seizing power in 1982, it apparently preferred the drawn-out process of developing an entirely new constitution. The junta's rejection of the democratic regime it displaced can be seen in its determination to strictly limit opposition participation in the process of re-democratization; opposition groups cannot be legally recognized as political parties and are barred from participating in the drafting of a new constitution. A few independent organizations unaffiliated with the regime, such as the Ghana Bar Association, have refused to send representatives to the CA, charging that the committee and its constituent participants are compromised by their unquestioning acceptance of a process unilaterally defined by the PDNC. The press charged that the behavior of the CA during its tenure showed a preoccupation with maximizing *per diem* allowances for participants and an extreme sensitivity to public scrutiny.

The opposition Movement for Freedom and Justice (MFJ) was founded in August 1990 to "campaign for the restoration of democratic rule in Ghana [in order] to fight for the recognition of the fundamental human and democratic rights of the people of Ghana to decide how they shall be governed and against all forms of dictatorships and domination." The group, led by Professor Adu Boahen, a well-known historian, said it was not a political party, but it planned to campaign for multi-party democracy and civilian rule in Ghana. It criticized the PNDC's insistence on being the sole determiner of the pace and scope of political change. The CA was deemed by the MFJ to be a poor substitute for a national conference which would be made up of independent public bodies as well as the national government and its agents. The MFJ pointed out that the body had received no electoral mandate from Ghanaians to draft or propose a constitution. In response to Rawlings's argument that soldiers had a critical role to play in the political life of the nation, and that strictly civilian rule was merely a "colonial legacy", the MFJ responded that those soldiers with something to contribute to politics should resign their commission and participate as civilians.

In June 1991, the PNDC declared a general amnesty for political exiles, though it was not intended to cover "those who fled the country because of their involvement in subversive activities against the government." In August, the timetable for the transition program was announced; the referendum on the draft constitution was scheduled for January or February 1992 while presidential and parliamentary elections are to be held sometime in the last quarter of 1992. Calls to release political prisoners, however, were ignored.

After six years of substantial average growth of the economy and a pronounced lowering of inflation as the result of an austere, market-oriented recovery program, the Ghanaian economy continued the slide begun in 1990. The program had ended price controls, dropped import restrictions, devalued the currency, tripled prices paid to growers of cocoa (the nation's leading export), and laid off 50,000 civil servants. As growth began to flag the regime was criticized for its sluggishness in divesting state-owned enterprises. Nonetheless, officials remain hopeful that the slow growth may only be precedent to a real economic takeoff. Perhaps fearing the effects of populism by a free-spending, elected civilian government, the PNDC appears to want to constitutionally ensure that its economic program not be tampered with after multi-party elections usher in a new administration.

Political Rights and Civil Liberties:

The citizens of Ghana do not have the means to change their government democratically. The country remains a military dictatorship run by the PNDC in which political parties are illegal and advocates of multi-party democracy are dismissed as "power hungry politicians". Allegations of favoritism toward those of the Ewe ethnic group persist. While most ordinary criminal cases are handled by courts based on the British system, political offenders are tried by "public tribunals" which do not provide assurance of a judiciary free from executive manipulation. In addition, there are reports of a secret tribunal at the military headquarters of the PNDC which detains, interrogates, and tries political opponents of the regime without being required to account for its actions to anyone but the PNDC leadership. Laws such as the Preventative Custody Law provide for indefinite detentions without trial for political cases deemed a threat to national security, and the Habeas Corpus Amendment Law allows prisoners to be held without charge or trial. Local Committees for the Defense of the Revolution are responsible for assisting security agencies in isolating disaffection with the regime; those who refuse to cooperate with the CDRs are deemed counter-revolutionaries and subject to extrajudicial punishment.

The Newspaper Licensing Law is used to muzzle the press; a number of periodicals have been banned. The government-owned media never criticize the government, but some of the few remaining private newspapers have on occasion attacked government economic and foreign initiatives. Publiclyaired allegations of corruption within the military regime bring quick arrest and detention for the offending journalist. The government and local media have attacked Ghanaian journalists who work for the foreign press, accusing them of collaborating with opposition organizations. Since Ghana has no constitution, such rights as freedom of speech, press, assembly, and association are not guaranteed, but merely granted at the discretion of the ruling junta. Nonpolitical professional and civic organizations are allowed to exist and operate, and political associations are tolerated if they behave inconspicuously. In August 1991, eleven opposition groups created an alliance, the Coordinating Committee of Democratic Forces of Ghana, to jointly press their demands for greater and more rapid democratization and political pluralism.

The Religious Bodies Registration Law restricts freedom of religion; Mormons and Jehovah's Witnesses have merited a special PNDC directive which prohibits full practice of their faiths. The ban on Jehovah's Witnesses was lifted in late 1991, but members are still subject to prosecution for refusing to salute the national flag. The Catholic Standard, a religious newspaper, continues to be banned. Ghanaians are generally free to emigrate and travel inside and outside the country. The independent Trade Union Congress (TUC), with seventeen affiliates, is well organized and active.

Greece

Polity: Parliamentary democracy
Economy: Mixed capitalist
Population: 10,100,000
PPP: $6,440
Life Expectancy: 76.1
Ethnic Groups: Greek (98 percent), with Macedonian and Turkish minorities

Political Rights: 1
Civil Liberties: 2
Status: Free

Overview:

In 1991 the major political issues included economic problems, an unprecedented influx of Albanian refugees, difficulties in settling the Cyprus dispute, mounting anti-government protests; terrorism and disputes over its coverage in the media, and the corruption trial of former Prime Minister Andreas Papandreou.

Located on the southern tip of the Balkan peninsula, Greece fought for independence from the Ottoman Empire in the 1820s and 1830s. After its victory, the country became a monarchy in 1835. In a series of wars in the early twentieth century, Greece increased its territory in Europe, and took in Greek refugees from Turkey. After Axis occupation during World War II, civil war broke out between the Communist and royalist forces. With Western aid, the constitutional monarchy prevailed. In 1967 a military junta took control and held power until 1974, when the country became a parliamentary democracy. The Greek parliament has 300 members who serve for a maximum term of four years. There are both single-member and multi-member parliamentary districts. The political party (or coalition) that wins a majority of seats names the prime minister, who then forms the government. The parliament elects the president, who is a largely ceremonial figure. The conservative New Democratic Party controlled the government from 1974 to 1981, when the Pan-Hellenic Socialist Movement (PASOK) took over. Under Prime Minister Papandreou, PASOK renewed agreements for U.S. bases in Greece and reversed its anti-NATO and anti-EEC positions. The New Democracy Party won the last parliamentary elections of April 1990 and Constantine Mitsotakis became prime minister.

Economic troubles became more pronounced in 1991. The poorest member of the European Community (EC), Greece has a foreign debt of $20 billion, high unemployment, and double-digit inflation. Greek officials blame the present economic crisis on the years of Socialist rule, and on the sprawling, overstaffed state bureaucracy. Under the Socialists, the state controlled two-thirds of the economy and employed one out of every five workers. In April 1990 the New Democracy Party and Mitsotakis were elected with a mandate to restructure and privatize the economy, reduce the number of state employees, cut inflation and slash the budget deficit. On 25 February 1991 an EC $3 billion credit for Greece was approved on the condition that, by 1993, Greece will reduce its $15 billion budget deficit, confront tax evasion, start taxing farmers (one third of the work force), bring inflation below 10 percent, cut the number of state employees by one tenth and adopt other austerity measures. In September 1991 the government announced plans to sell thirty-five islands to raise cash. The EC will release money in installments as Greece meets the various targets. The labor movement responded to the austerity policies with several strikes, including a general strike on 24 November 1991.

These economic problems were complicated by the influx of 18,000 Albanians into the country during January and February 1991. The Albanian exodus started in late December 1990 and was, at first, limited to members of Albania's Greek minority. A first-asylum country under the 1951 Geneva Convention on Refugees, Greece found itself ill-prepared to provide the needed assistance and appealed to the Albanians to stay at home and contribute to the democratization of their country. In January 1991, after a meeting between Albanian President Ramiz Alia and Prime Minister Mitsotakis, the Albanian government announced that returning refugees would not be punished. A small number of Albanians eventually did repatriate. By the end of January Greek authorities deported about 1,200 refugees back to Albania, and the government announced that it would provide full protection only for Albanian policemen, soldiers and those with a "well-founded fear of persecution."

In January 1991 President Mitsotakis's support for the allied effort in the Gulf War provoked vocal anti-war and anti-government protests. An indigenous leftist guerilla group, calling itself 17 November, was responsible for terrorist attacks against several targets during the last week of January. The bombings took place in Athens, at five different locations. Student takeovers at Athens Polytechnic and over one thousand high schools, and mass demonstrations in Athens, Thessaloniki and Patras also ended in violence as the police clashed with groups of self-styled "anarchists"; one teacher was beaten to death by rightist elements, and four people died in a building torched during the demonstrations. The students and their teachers were protesting state-imposed control on high school attendance and plans to recognize private universities. They also demanded more government money for education.

The Mitsotakis government got involved in the Persian Gulf conflict in order to score points against the Turkish government on the Cyprus question. The Greek government compared the invasion of Kuwait to the 1974 Turkish invasion of Cyprus, and stressed the need for international support and enforcement of U.N. resolutions (on Iraq and on Cyprus). In 1991 Mitsotakis placed the resolution of the Cypriot problem at the top of his agenda and sought the active diplomatic assistance of the U.S. government. President Bush addressed the Greek parliament in 1991, and pledged to help solve the Cyprus problem in 1991. However, negotiations did not succeed by year's end.

In March 1991 former Prime Minister Papandreou and three senior members of his Socialist Government went on trial on charges of breaching public faith, accepting bribes and receiving stolen money from the owner of the Bank of Crete. The trial was the greatest political and financial scandal in modern Greek history. Papandreou was on trial in absentia, since he refused to attend the trial or have legal representation.

The governing New Democracy Party could not capitalize effectively on Papandreou's problems, due to its own personality disputes. In August Mitsotakis fired his daughter, Dora Bakoyannis, as undersecretary to the prime minister. This followed criticism of his family's role in politics. The premier's wife had feuded publicly with cabinet member Stavros Dimas, who resigned from the government. Problems continued in October when Mitsotakis dismissed Militiades Evert as minister to the Prime Minister's Office. Evert had clashed with the Foreign Ministry over who should promote Greek foreign policy in the international media.

Political Rights and Civil Liberties:

The citizens of Greece have the right to change their government democratically. Freedom of the press is generally respected, but there are some restrictions on expression in the libel laws. For instance, publications which are deemed to be offensive to the president or to religious beliefs may be seized by order of the public prosecutor. Greece also has a controversial law on the press and terrorism, which bans "unwarranted" publicity for terrorists, such as the publication of terrorists' proclamations after bombings. Dora Bakoyannis, the daughter of Prime Minister Mitsotakis, introduced this anti-terrorism legislation following her husband's death in a terrorist incident. In September 1991, the government put nine editors on trial for allegedly violating the Bakoyannis law by publishing terrorists' statements after recent bombings. The court sentenced the editors to five to ten months in prison. After the journalists refused to appeal, they went behind bars. However, the unions representing publishers and journalists paid fines on the editors' behalf, and won their release.

Freedom of association is respected and all workers, except the military and the police, have the right to form or join unions. Unions are linked to political parties, but are independent in their day-to-day operations.

Greek Orthodoxy is the state religion and some 98 percent of the population belongs to this church. The constitution prohibits proselytizing. Greece offers noncombatant military service but does not provide a nonmilitary alternative to the universal conscription of men for national service. Jehovah's witnesses and other conscientious objectors can be tried and sentenced to three to five year terms in military prisons. Greece's Muslim minority, whose religious rights were guaranteed under the 1923 Treaty of Lausanne, objects to the Greek government's insistence on choosing the *mufti* —the leader of the Muslim community. The ethnic Turks also object to the resettlement of ethnic Greeks from the former USSR's Pontic region in Western Thrace, a Muslim area. In February 1991 the Greek government objected to the U.S. State Department's human rights report on Greece, because that document pointed out the discrimination against Muslims and also reported that Macedonians in northern Greece face restrictions on freedom of movement.

Grenada

Polity: Parliamentary democracy
Economy: Capitalist-statist
Population: 100,000
PPP: na
Life Expectancy: 71.5
Ethnic Groups: Mostly black

Political Rights: 1
Civil Liberties: 2
Status: Free

Overview:

Nearly eight years after a bloody power struggle within the Marxist government of Maurice Bishop provoked U.S. military intervention, Grenadians were still struggling to put behind them the events of 19 October 1983 when Bishop and seven of his closest followers were murdered. In 1991 the lengthy appeals process for those convicted of the killings finally ran out. The government of Prime Minister Nicholas Braithwaite decided to commute the death sentences to life imprisonment, but the act of clemency angered many Grenadians, already critical of the government on economic issues.

Grenada is a member of the British Commonwealth. The British monarchy is represented by a governor-general who acts as ceremonial head of state. Grenada became self-governing in 1958 and gained its independence in 1974 as a parliamentary democracy. The state also includes the islands of Carriacou and Petit Martinique.

The government of Prime Minister Eric Gairy was overthrown in a 1979 coup d'état by Maurice Bishop's Marxist New Jewel Movement. In October 1983, Prime Minister Bishop was murdered by New Jewel hard-liners during a factional fight. Bernard Coard and General Hudson Austin took control of the country and declared martial law. Sir Paul Scoon, the governor-general and only duly constituted executive authority in the country, formally asked for international assistance. A joint U.S.-Caribbean military intervention removed Coard and Austin. Scoon then formed an advisory council to act as an interim administration pending general elections.

In free and fair elections held in late 1984 the New National Party (NNP) of Herbert Blaize defeated Gairy's rightist Grenada United Labour Party (GULP). The NNP, a coalition of three parties, won an overwhelming parliamentary majority, taking fourteen of the fifteen seats in the House of Representatives. The bicameral parliament also consists of an appointed Senate, with ten members appointed by the prime minister and three by the leader of the parliamentary opposition.

By mid-1989 the NNP coalition had unraveled, leaving Prime Minister Blaize with the support of only six representatives in the House. In September, Blaize formed The National Party (TNP) from among his six remaining supporters. Opposition parties questioned the constitutionality of Blaize remaining in office without a parliamentary majority, but continued to jockey for position in preparation for elections constitutionally mandated for no later than March 1990.

Blaize died on 19 December 1989 after a prolonged illness and was replaced by his former deputy, Ben Jones. Following the dissolution of parliament eight days later, elections were scheduled for 13 March 1990. The five main contenders in the campaign were: the TNP headed by Jones; the centrist National Democratic Congress (NDC) led by Nicholas Braithwaite, former head of the 1983-84 interim government; the GULP headed by Gairy; the New National Party (NNP) headed by Keith Mitchell; and the leftist Maurice Bishop Patriotic Movement (MBPM) led by Terry Marryshow.

On 13 March the NDC won seven seats, the GULP won four, and the NNP and the TNP two each. After the GULP, NNP and TNP failed to come to terms on forming a coalition government, Braithwaite was appointed prime minister by the governor-general. On 19 March Edzel Thomas, one of the GULP's victorious candidates, defected to the NDC, giving the new government a one-seat parliamentary majority. A week later, Jones and the second TNP candidate also accepted cabinet positions, giving the NDC a 10-5 majority.

GULP Vice President Winnifred Strachan was named official opposition leader after party leader Gairy failed to win in his own constituency. The GULP suffered further blows when two more of its parliamentary representatives left the party, one in 1990 and another in 1991. One GULP defector, Frederick Lawrence Gibbs joined the NDC, restoring its 10-5 majority following the 1991 resignation of the TNP's Jones from the cabinet. The next national elections are due by 1995.

Political Rights and Civil Liberties:

Citizens are able to change their government democratically. Constitutional guarantees were reinstated in 1984 and there are few restrictions on the right to organize political, labor or civic groups. There are numerous independent labor unions and the right to strike is recognized. The exercise of religion and the right of free expression are also generally respected, although some imported leftist publications were banned by the government in early 1989.

The MBPM, founded by former members of the New Jewel Movement after the return to democratic governance, has complained that its representatives have been detained for questioning after returning from conferences in Libya. However, the MBPM was able to participate freely in the 1990 general elections, as it had in 1984, and saw its share of the vote fall from 5 to 2.4 percent.

Newspapers, many of which are weekly political party organs, are independent. Radio is operated by the government but open to independent voices. There have been some complaints that the government has impeded the establishment of independently operated radio. Television is independently operated.

There is an independent, nondiscriminatory judiciary which is generally respected by the police. In 1991 Grenada rejoined the Organization of Eastern Caribbean States court system, with right of appeal to the Privy Council in London. In 1990 the

Braithwaite government set up a five-member committee, including independent public figures, to monitor prison conditions. There are no political prisoners.

After a two-year trial, thirteen men and one woman, including Bernard Coard and General Hudson Austin, were found guilty in 1986 of the 1983 murder of Maurice Bishop and sentenced to death. The proceedings continued into 1991 as the defendants appealed their sentences. In July 1991 the Grenada Court of Appeals turned aside the last of the defendants' appeals, and reports circulated that Coard and four others would be hanged. On 14 August, however, the government decided to commute the death sentences to life imprisonment for all fourteen defendants after a series of appeals by international human rights organizations.

Guatemala

Polity: Presidential-legislative democracy (military influenced)
Economy: Capitalist-statist
Population: 9,500,000
PPP: $2,430
Life Expectancy: 63.4
Ethnic Groups: Ethnically complex, with more than 50 percent Mayan and other Indian

Political Rights: 3
Civil Liberties: 5
Status: Partly Free

Overview:

President Jorge Serrano took office in January 1991 vowing to end the decades-long guerrilla war and guarantee law and order. However, as the end of his first year approached, negotiations with the left-wing guerrillas became deadlocked amid a climate of terror fueled by burgeoning drug traffic, armed civilian patrols controlled by the army, rampant street crime, and military-linked death squads.

The Republic of Guatemala was established in 1839, eighteen years after independence from Spain and following the breakup of the United Provinces of Central America (1824-1838). The nation has endured a history of dictatorship, coups d'état, and guerrilla insurgency, with only intermittent democratic government. After a thirty-year stretch of repressive military rule, Guatemala returned to civilian government in 1985 with the promulgation of a new constitution and the direct election of President Vinicio Cerezo of the Christian Democratic party.

The constitution provides for a five-year presidential term and prohibits reelection. A 116-member unicameral National Congress is also directly elected for five years. The governors of twenty-two departments and the capital, Guatemala City, are appointed by the president. Municipal governments are elected.

Among the leading presidential candidates for the 1990 election were Alfonso Cabrera of the Christian Democrats, Rene de Leon Schlotter for the Social Democratic party, and newspaper publisher Jorge Carpio Nicolle of the centrist National Center Union (UCN). The frontrunner in the opinion polls, however, was former military dictator General Efrain Rios Montt (1982-83), whose law-and-order rhetoric had struck a chord amid a mounting wave of political violence and street crime. But Rios Montt was ruled ineligible by the Supreme Court because the constitution bars former dictators from returning to power.

Serrano, a right-wing businesman and former head of the rubber-stamp legislature during Rios Montt's short but brutal reign, inherited the general's following. In the election held on 11 November 1990, Serrano, with 24 percent of the vote, came a close second to Carpio who received 26 percent. For the 6 January 1991 runoff Carpio conducted a mudslinging campaign engineered by U.S. political operative Roger Ailes that turned off many Guatemalans. Serrano, who like Rios Montt is an evangelical Christian, portrayed himself as an anti-politican and won the presidency by an overwhelming 2-to-1 margin in a vote marked by a 55 percent abstention rate.

Upon taking office, Serrano blasted critics of Guatemala's human rights record, including the U.S. government, and declared that his administration would bring peace to Guatemala through direct negotiations with the left-wing guerrillas of the Guatemalan National Revolutionary Unity (URNG). The URNG had survived the mass repression of the early 1980s and had expanded its activities in the last years of the decade. In 1990, U.N.-monitored talks were held between the URNG and the country's main social, economic and political groups. But the military, which directs the counterinsurgency and controls most of the country's rural administration, refused to permit direct talks with the government until after Serrano became president.

Between April and October 1991, five rounds of U.N.-sponsored talks were held in Mexico City between the government and the URNG. A few agreements were reached in principle, including a commitment that the military operate under civilian authority. But the fifth round ended amid deep distrust and serious differences over holding the military accountable for rights violations.

The military high command, which had appeared to support the negotiating process, was clearly against any concrete agreement on human rights and was under increasing pressure from hardline factions in the officer corps that referred to the negotiations as "treasonous." Groups of junior officers had failed in two coup attempts during the Cerezo administration and, as the URNG carried out a series of offensives in the fall of 1991, there were rumors of a possible third attempt. Meanwhile, levels of political and criminal violence had escalated throughout the year, heightening the state of general lawlessness in the country.

Political Rights and Civil Liberties:

Citizens are able to change their governments through democratic elections, but the powers granted to civilian administrations by the constitution are greatly restricted by the armed forces. In August 1991, the nation's vice-president publicly acknowledged that the military remains the dominant institution in the country.

The constitution guarantees the right to organize political parties, civic organizations and labor unions. There are nineteen legally registered political parties from social democratic left to radical right, most representing small interest groups. Total party membership is less than ten percent of the electorate.

Political expression is severely restricted by an increasing climate of terror reminiscent of the early 1980s. In the last two years there has been a dramatic increase in political and criminal violence including murder, disappearances, bombings and death threats. Political parties, student organizations, street children, peasant groups, labor unions, Indian communities, human rights organizations, and the media are all systematically targeted.

In the early 1980s 200 or more people a month were slain. Under civilian government, dissent and political organizing are no longer tantamount to suicide. However, in the months before the November 1990 elections, the level of violence and the rate of political killings were the highest since the return to civilian government in 1985. During the campaign, over a dozen political party figures were killed, and more than half the presidential and legislative candidates received death threats. According to Guatemalan rights activists, disappearances and political killings occurred at the rate of approximately two a day in 1990, increasing to over three a day in the first eight months of 1991.

The principal human rights offenders are the military, particularly the G-2 intelligence unit, the police and security forces, and a network of death squads-for-hire linked to the armed forces and right-wing political groups.

The civilian government's failure to address human rights violations is most evident in the dysfunctional judicial system and the corruption-plagued police force. The security forces retain a monopoly over criminal investigations, civil courts are intimidated by the military, and military personnel must be tried in military courts, all of which makes the system a black hole for any legal or human rights complaints.

In mid-1990, the Center for Criminal Justice of Harvard University pulled out of a U.S.-sponsored judicial reform project, citing the government's unwillingness to investigate political killings. In August 1991, eight months after President Serrano took office, the official human rights ombudsman elected by the Congress stated, "The reign of impunity goes on." As of November 1991 only two military officers and a handful of soldiers had been convicted of rights abuses, either against Guatemalans or in the cases involving the murders of four U.S. citizens, a foreign journalist, and a prominent Salvadoran politician.

There are a number of independent human rights organizations, the Mutual Support Group (GAM) among the most prominent. However, rights groups regularly receive threats and their offices are frequently raided and bombed. Over two dozen activists have been slain or disappeared since the return to civilian government in 1986—at least seven in the twelve months ending in September 1991—more than in any other country in the Western hemisphere.

The Runejel Junam Council of Ethnic Communities (CERJ) works on behalf of the country's Indians, a majority of the population and probably the most segregated and oppressed indigenous community in the Western hemisphere. Although mass killings of Indians during army anti-guerrilla sweeps have diminished since 1985, they have not stopped. CERJ also reports on the systematic violation by the military of the constitutional article that states no individual can be forced to join any type of civil-defense organizations against his will; the rural civil defense network of nearly half a million members is a key component of the military's counterinsurgency program. Since CERJ was founded in 1988, over a hundred members have received death threats, and over two dozen have been killed or disappeared.

Labor unions have re-established themselves since the return to elected government and often exercise their right to strike. However, dozens of unionists have been killed and labor leaders remain subject to attacks and death threats, particularly in rural areas. In 1990 and 1991 a number of labor leaders fled into exile. Between January 1990 and March 1991, 33 union members were killed, according to the International Confederation of Free Trade Unions, making Guatemala one of the most dangerous countries in the world for trade unionists.

The press and a large portion of the broadcast media are privately owned. There are several independent newspapers offering pluralistic points of view. There are dozens of radio stations, most of them commercial. Five of the six television stations are commercially operated.

Since 1989, however, the media increasingly have been subject to arbitrary detention, torture, bombing attacks and death threats. Nearly two dozen journalists, including the vice-president of the national journalists association, have been driven into exile, and much of the media has been cowed into self-censorhip. A number of radio stations and publications have closed because of threats, and one radio station owner was murdered in October 1990. In 1991 attacks on the media increased, with one journalist arrested and tortured after criticizing President Serrano. The international media also came under attack. In mid-1990, a number of wire service offices and the foreign press club received bomb and death threats. The Mexican news agency NOTIMEX closed its office after a raid by unidentified persons.

Guinea

Polity: Military transitional
Economy: Capitalist
Population: 7,500,000
PPP: $910
Life Expectancy: 43.5
Ethnic Groups: Fulani, Malinke, Soussou, others

Political Rights: 6
Civil Liberties: 5
Status: Not Free

Overview:

Despite government promises to begin democratizing, there was almost no progress towards political liberalization in 1991. Guinea's economy continued to stagnate and, in May, widespread strikes to demand more pay rocked the capital.

Under the leadership of Ahmed Sekou Touré, Guinea declared independence from France in 1958. Touré's dictatorial Democratic Party of Guinea (PDG) ruled the country until his death in 1984. Three days after Touré died, the army overthrew the PDG and has since ruled the country through the Military Committee of National Redressing (CMRN), under the leadership of General Lasana Conté.

During the first years of his reign, Conté strengthened relations with France and opened the country to foreign investment. In October 1989 Conté promised to bring multi-party democracy to Guinea. In December 1990 Guineans approved a new constitution, with a presidential system and a unicameral legislature to be set up within five years. On 16 January in accordance with the new constitution, the CMRN was dissolved and replaced by the Transitory Committee of National Recovery (CTRN). The new committee is composed of both civilians and military personnel, all of whom are appointed by the president. However, little other progress has been made.

On 17 May Alpha Condé, a famous dissident, returned to Guinea, although his stay was short-lived. Upon his arrival, seven political parties and trade unions, along with Condé's Rally of the Guinean People (RPG) immediately announced the formation of the Alliance for the Introduction of Democracy (AID) to press for a national conference on the future of Guinea. However, police broke up an opposition rally on 19 May using tear gas, just as Condé was about to speak. On 21 May the government banned all public meetings and political gatherings, stressing that no political party had yet been recognized. On 16 June Condé was arrested for allegedly importing arms into the country. Police fired on civilians protesting for his release in front of the police station where Condé was being held, killing two and arresting sixty. The government also banned all opposition demonstrations. Meanwhile, Condé took refuge in the Senegal embassy until the Guinean government permitted him to leave the country.

In May 1991 violent mass demonstrations rocked the capital. With the support of students, teachers took to the streets to demand higher pay, and the possibility of promotion. They also wanted the state to pay 50 percent of their health care and to raise the current monthly allowance given to families (the current amount will not even buy a loaf of bread). Guinean bureaucrats, who include teachers, are among the worst paid in all of Africa. Soon, they added a national conference to their list of demands. In response to the protests, Conté promised to raise their salaries 100 percent. He also declared that he would speed up the democratization process, although he made no mention of a national conference, nor did he give a specific timetable. Although the concession was far inferior to the 300 percent raise demanded by the protesters, only the students were willing to reject the proposal and continue striking. Meanwhile, to calm the unrest, security forces closed and occupied the universities until the end of June.

When Conté first took power, he embarked on a massive privatization program in order to make the country accessible to foreign investment. In the process 25,000 people lost their jobs, with only 3,000 of them finding new employment in the private sector. With its enormous store of natural resources, Guinea has the potential of being one of the richest countries in Africa, but corruption, fraud and nepotism have devastated its economy. For example, the two main hospitals of the country receive 3,000 liters of fuel a month, while a government minister receives more than 5,500 liters. Guinea has also lost its credibility in the eyes of the World Bank and the IMF, along with foreign investors. The World Bank is withholding funds until the government cleans up its civil service. Currently there are 1,000 civil servants on the payroll who are not even alive.

Political Rights and Civil Liberties:

In 1991 Guineans did not yet have the right to choose their government democratically. On 10 March the government held the first free municipal elections in thirty years, with 865 candidates vying for 173 seats. However, all candidates were from the single legalized party. Furthermore, the interior minister has stated that no other political parties would be recognized until at least the end of 1991.

The government tolerates major religious groups and does not interfere in their affairs. Although 85 percent of the Guinean population is Muslim, there is no official state religion.

Almost all journalists are state employees. The state-owned weekly, *Horoya*, once under tight control of Touré's party, now enjoys independence. However, it only has a circulation of 2,000. On 13 August an association of newspaper publishers, the Guinean Association of Independent Press Publishers was established in order to develop the press and to defend its freedom. There are currently 7 independent newspapers, although lack of paper makes printing difficult. The government still controls the broadcast media. Radio and television rarely show hard news, concentrating instead on development issues. Although employees say that the atmosphere is considerably more relaxed than under Touré, they still practice self-censorship and rarely criticize the government.

There are over 300,000 Liberian refugees living in Guinea; the government is currently working with the U.N. High Commission on Refugees to repatriate them.

Public gatherings may take place only with government authorization. Public meetings and demonstrations were banned following the unrest in May 1991. The state funds the National Confederation of Guinean Workers (CNTG), which comprises all of Guinea's salaried workers (actually a small proportion of the population, since most Guineans are farmers). Although nominally independent, CNTG has close ties with the government. The teachers demonstrated its ineffectiveness when they took to the streets in order to get a pay raise. The judicial system is erratic, due to inefficiencies, corruption, nepotism and lack of personal qualifications. Some accused have had to languish in jail for up to three years awaiting a trial. Lawyers are provided to those who cannot afford to hire one only in cases involving major crimes. Although those accused of lesser crimes may appeal to the Bar Association for free counsel, few are aware of this fact. Village chiefs still handle much of the local justice system in the traditional manner. The State Security Court handles political crimes. Administrative detention is permitted, though most detainees stay in jail for only a few days.

Guinea-Bissau

Polity: One party (military-dominated) transitional
Economy: Mixed statist transitional
Population: 1,000,000
PPP: $670
Life Expectancy: 42.5
Ethnic Groups: Balanta, Bijogo, Diola, Fulani, Malinke, Mandjague, Nalu, Pepel, as well as mulatto, Moorish, and European minorities

Political Rights: 6
Civil Liberties: 5
Status: Partly Free

Overview:

The most important political event of 1991 was the formal commitment of the long-ruling PAIGC (African Party for the Independence of Guinea-Bissau and Cape Verde) to a transformation from a one-party regime to multi-party democracy. This decision seems to have been a consequence of the Guinean leadership's assessment that a successful economic liberalization must be accompanied by political pluralism if Western investment is to be attracted to the country.

After over a decade of armed struggle, Guinea-Bissau won independence from Portugal in 1973. The current president, Brigadier General João Bernardo Vieira, came to power in 1980 after a coup overthrew the first leader of the independent country, Luis de Almeida Cabral. The 1984 constitution codified the supremacy of the PAIGC to the exclusion of any competing political parties. Members of the unicameral, 150-member National Assembly are designated by eight popularly elected regional councils and elect a Council of State, whose president is also head of state. In elections held in June 1989, Vieira, the only candidate, was elected to another five-year term as president.

In line with Central Committee recommendations and the stated commitment of President Vieira to fundamental change, the PAIGC assembled in late January of 1991 at a party congress in order to formally declare that it no longer considered itself to be the sole legal political force in the country. This action was taken despite a reported lack of enthusiasm from a majority within the Party, who felt that democratization could be best achieved internally without the necessity of giving up its monopoly on political power in the country. Nonetheless, the congress voted to propose both a thorough constitutional revision and the drafting of a new electoral law. Among the rights guaranteed under the new constitution are the right to form independent labor unions, freedom of the press, and the right to form political parties. In addition, the death penalty would be abolished, and the military, security forces, and office of the president would be depoliticized.

The National Assembly passed a law allowing other political parties to legally operate within the country in May of 1991. Among the parties which might participate in the multi-party elections are RGB/MB (Guinea-Bissau Resistance/ Bafata Movement), FLING (Front for the Struggle of Guinea-Bissau Independence), and the United Social Democratic Party.

Both RGB/MB and the FLING may be barred from fielding candidates by the election rules proposed by the PAIGC, which would block the legalization of parties that are regionally or tribally based. In order to qualify for legal recognition by the country's Supreme Court, a would-be party must present at least 1,000 petition signatures, with a minimum of 50 signatures obtained from five of Guinea-Bissau's nine provinces. The RGB/MB is alleged by the government to only represent the Balanta peoples, while the FLING is alleged to represent the interests of the Mandjague. The government seems to fear that the unity of the country would be threatened if such parties were allowed to freely participate in political life. Those movements which do not obtain official recognition as parties will not be allowed by law to demonstrate or meet in public.

The transition to multi-partyism was first proposed by the PAIGC and national leadership as a process that would take as long as three years, with elections coming at the end of 1993. But it now appears possible that elections may be held by the beginning of 1992. The PAIGC maintains sole control over the nature and timing of the transition. Members of the opposition have claimed that their activists have been effectively denied the right to organize within the country.

Some 1,600 refugees from the Casamance region of southern Senegal crossed their national border with Guinea-Bissau in November 1990 to avoid violent insurrection and reaction in their homeland. Senegal has charged that the territory of Guinea-Bissau is used as a rear area by Casamance rebels to mount attacks across the frontier. The government of Guinea-Bissau has asserted in response that it is doing its best to monitor and control the border.

The government claims that its policy of economic liberalization, which dates from the mid 1980s, has had the effect of bringing down inflation, improving the standard of living in rural areas and increasing agricultural productivity, and increasing both the availability of consumer goods and the amount of consumer spending. The government has a new code designed to increase the appeal of direct foreign investment, and it is moving to privatize unprofitable state enterprises.

Political Rights and Civil Liberties: Guinea-Bissau continues to be a state dominated by the PAIGC; citizens cannot yet change their government democratically. Despite ongoing reviews of the political system, the judiciary remains a part of the executive branch. The government retains the power to arbitrarily detain individuals suspected of anti-state activities. Although the leadership has claimed that it has no political prisoners, it has detained those activists from officially disfavored ethnic movements who attempt to distribute their literature. The government controls all media, which generally reflect official policies in its news coverage. However, some criticism of government policy is tolerated. Officials have called for increased impartiality in the dissemination of news. The new economic restructuring and privatization has seen a growth in embryonic associations of engineers, architects, and doctors. Government approval is not required for peaceful, nonpolitical assemblies. Christians, Muslims, and animists can worship freely, and proselytizing is allowed. Travel, both foreign and domestic, is unrestricted. The only union, the National Union of Guinea-Bissau (UNTG), was effectively controlled by the Party until recently. The constitution does not yet provide and protect the right to organize and bargain collectively.

Guyana

Polity: Dominant party
Economy: Mixed statist
Population: 800,000
PPP: $1,480
Life Expectancy: 64.2
Ethnic Groups: Complex, East Indian (50 percent), black (31 percent), mixed (12 percent), Amerindian (4 percent), and the remainder European

Political Rights: 5
Civil Liberties: 4
Status: Partly Free

Overview: Under increased domestic and international pressure, the government of President Desmond Hoyte agreed in 1990 to make significant electoral reforms. After a delay of more than a year, elections were scheduled for 16 December 1991. But after observers, including the Atlanta-based Carter Center, concluded there were serious irregularities in voter registration, elections were postponed again.

A member of the British Commonwealth, the nation has been ruled by the black-based People's National Congress (PNC) since independence in 1966. The 1966 constitution established Guyana as a parliamentary member of the Commonwealth, but the monarchical structure was abandoned in 1970.

Under President Forbes Burnham, Guyana was redesignated a "cooperative republic" in 1970, attesting to Burnham's commitment to socialism. Since the 1970s, the PNC has retained power through fraudulent elections. In 1980 the PNC installed a new constitution which formalized the "paramountcy" of the PNC in all government spheres. It provides for a president with virtually unlimited powers and a 53-seat National Assembly to be directly elected for five years. Twelve more Assembly seats come from elected regional councils. After Burnham's death in 1985, he was succeeded by Hoyte who was elected for a full term in an election that was fraudulent in virtually every respect.

In 1986 the opposition formed the Patriotic Coalition for Democracy (PCD), composed of the Marxist, East Indian-based People's Progressive Party (PPP), the social democratic, mixed-race Working People's Alliance (WPA), and three small centrist parties. Hoyte rejected the PCD's demands for electoral reform.

In 1990 the Guyanese Action for Reform and Democracy (GUARD), a civic movement for electoral reform, was established with the backing of the Anglican and Catholic churches, the Guyanese Human Rights Association (GHRA), independent labor unions and media, and business and professional groups. The GUARD pressed for an independent electoral commission, new voter registration rolls, vote counting at polling places, and international monitoring. By the summer, GUARD was attracting thousands to weekly rallies, the largest opposition gatherings under PNC rule.

At the same time the PCD obtained international support for free elections. Since 1988, Hoyte has been implementing an economic liberalization program and seeking Western assistance. In 1990, key U.S congressmen and international human rights organizations pressed Washington to tie economic assistance to political reform.

In mid-1990, Hoyte began making concessions, inviting electoral observation missions from the British Commonwealth and the Council of Freely Elected Heads of Government led by former U.S. President Jimmy Carter. Then, during a visit to Guyana by Carter in October, Hoyte conceded on two of the opposition's main demands—vote counting at polling places, and a complete revision of the voter registration rolls. Hoyte also agreed to an independent electoral commission.

In 1991, negotiations between the government and the PCD led to the formation of a new electoral commission with opposition representation. After numerous delays, the commission finally produced a new voter list at the end of September, and Hoyte dissolved the parliament, meaning elections had to be held within ninety days.

However, the new list was seriously flawed, with approximately 25 percent of the electorate left off and another 10 percent placed in the wrong polling districts. At the beginning of November a delegation from the Carter Center concluded that it would take two to three months to clean up the list and advised the government to reinstate parliament and adopt a constitutional amendment to extend the date for elections to March 1992.

The government rejected the recommendation and scheduled elections for 16 December 1991. The election commission, minus opposition representatives who had resigned in protest, initiated a hurried attempt to fix the voter list. The Carter Center then informed the government that without a clean and complete list, it would send no observers to the vote. Because the government needed the Carter Center's validation of the electoral process to secure foreign economic assistance, particularly from the U.S. and the United Kingdom, Hoyte announced in early December that the vote was being postponed until some time in 1992, and reconvened the parliament to validate his decision.

Meanwhile, the PCD had failed to unite around a consensus candidate, and the main contender against Hoyte appeared to be the PPP's Cheddi Jagan. A poll sponsored by the independent *Stabroek News* in September showed Jagan leading Hoyte 35 percent to 27 percent, with four other candidates sharing 13 percent, and 24 percent undecided.

Political Rights and Civil Liberties:

Because of the ruling party's continued domination of the state and the compilation of a seriously flawed voter registration list in 1991, citizens remain unable to change their government through democratic elections.

The constitution grants the right of free expression, freedom of religion and the right to organize political parties, civic organizations and labor unions. However, although the pervasive fear and intimidation that existed under Burnham have diminished significantly, political rights and civil liberties rest heavily on government tolerance rather than institutional protection. There is little evidence that institutions such as the judiciary, the police and the military are able to withstand pressure to promote the ruling party's political interests.

The government has taken steps to professionalize the police, but opposition supporters and independent labor are still on occasion subject to harassment, violent intimidation, and torture during interrogation, and the right of habeas corpus is not consistently respected. The police also were lax in providing security for opposition organizers against violent provocations by the ruling party during the 1991 election campaign. And the government has used the police to interrupt organizational efforts by the 40,000 Amerindians residing in the interior of the country.

The judicial system, while nominally independent, is influenced by the government and understaffed. In recent years the courts have tended to display greater neutrality, but the government often ignores judgments made against it. Prisons are overcrowded, with deplorable conditions leading to numerous deaths by starvation and AIDS.

There is an independent and well-respected Guyana Human Rights Association (GHRA) which is backed by independent civic and religious groups. The government has tried to impede its work through a series of libel actions, but attempts at outright intimidation have diminished.

Under Burnham, labor unions were either co-opted through the Trade Union Council (TUC) or subject to repression. However, in recent years, the TUC has suffered splits, with a number of factions joining independent labor unions in protesting the government's economic austerity program. Since 1990, there have been a number of strikes in the vital bauxite and sugar industries. Strikes are legal, but often lead to violence during clashes with the police and the arbitrary dismissal of public sector workers.

In 1986, the Hoyte administration permitted a new independent newspaper, the *Stabroek News*. But the government continues to make excessive use of libel suits and controlled access to hard currency to curb the independent press, particularly the *Catholic Standard*, an outspoken church weekly. Political party publications are similarly affected. Public radio is primarily an instrument of the ruling party. The two television stations are nominally independent, but program content is heavily influenced by the government.

Haiti

Polity: Military
Economy: Capitalist-statist
Population: 6,300,000
PPP: $970
Life Expectancy: 55.7
Ethnic Groups: Black and mulatto

Political Rights: 7
Civil Liberties: 7
Status: Not Free

Overview:

President Jean-Bertrand Aristide, the first freely elected leader in Haiti's history, fled the country following a military coup on 30 September 1991. The Organization of American States (OAS) denied recognition to the puppet government installed by the army and imposed severe economic sanctions. In mid-November, the *de facto* government and the OAS agreed to hold negotiations for the restoration of constitutional rule, but many obstacles stood in the way of Aristide's possible return.

Since becoming independent following a slave revolt in 1804, the Republic of Haiti has endured a history of poverty, violence, instability and dictatorship. A February 1986 military coup ended twenty-nine years of rule by the Duvalier family, but it did not end the corruption, repression and terror. The military ruled directly or indirectly for the next five years, often in collusion with remnants of the *Tontons Macoute*, the sinister paramilitary organization of the Duvaliers.

Under heavy international pressure, the military allowed for the election of a constituent assembly that drafted Haiti's twenty-third constitution. The document was approved in a March 1987 referendum, but a campaign of terror by the military and the *Tontons Macoute* culminated in a bloodbath that aborted national elections eight months later.

In March 1990 General Prosper Avril left the country during a nationwide protest, handing power over to General Herard Abraham. Abraham yielded to a coalition of political parties and civic groups and accepted Supreme Court justice Ertha Pascal-Trouillot as interim president. The provisional government reinstated the constitution and formed a new electoral council to prepare for a new election.

The 1987 constitution provides for a president directly elected for five years, a directly elected parliament composed of a 27-member Senate and an 83-member House of Representatives, and a prime minister appointed by the president. It establishes a strict separation of powers among the executive, the legislature and the judiciary, but gives the incoming president wide powers to implement reforms during the first six months in office.

The election was scheduled for November but postponed to 16 December 1990 because of mounting political violence. During voter registration, conditions improved after the arrival of hundreds of observers from the OAS, the United Nations and the Atlanta-based Carter Center. The two main presidential contenders were Marc Bazin, a former World Bank official, and Rev. Jean Bertrand Aristide, an enormously popular radical priest whose outspoken opposition to dictatorship had made him the target of numerous assassination attempts.

President Aristide was elected in a landslide, taking nearly 70 percent of the vote. A month before Aristide's 7 February 1991 inauguration, Roger Lafontant, former chief of the *Tontons Macoute*, seized the national palace and declared himself president. With a popular insurrection brewing in the streets, General Abraham ordered an assault on the palace and Lafontant and his henchmen were jailed.

In his inaugural speech, Aristide praised the military for defending democracy and declared a "marriage" between the soldiers and the people. Abraham retired soon after, and Aristide appointed General Raoul Cedras in his place. Cedras had received high marks from international observers as head of the military commission in charge of electoral security, and for the first time in Haitian history, there appeared to be a chance for establishing a rule of law.

Aristide's record during his brief tenure was mixed. Article 295 of the constitution gives the president authorization for six months to "carry out any reforms deemed necessary in the Government administration and the judiciary." Aristide opted for the broadest interpretation of this article and formed a government from among his most trusted if politically inexperienced associates. He then forged ahead with a program to strengthen the judicial system, establish civilian authority over the military, and end pervasive official corruption. One result was a dramatic decrease in political violence.

By August, Haitian elites, who feared and hated Aristide from the beginning, were furious over the anti-corruption campaign which threatened their control over the economy—0.5 percent of the population enjoys 46 percent of the country's income, much of it illicit. When their representatives in parliament initiated a no-confidence vote, it was supported by many legislators who had originally supported Aristide but were angered by being left out of his government. However, instead of addressing the challenge politically, Aristide, like many charismatic leaders before him, succumbed to the temptation to exceed his constitutional authority by inciting his legions of supporters to violence. Under siege by thousands of angry demonstrators, the legislators shelved the no-confidence bill.

At the same time, Aristide's effort to set up a new police force, trained by Swiss experts and under the control of the justice ministry as required by the constitution, rankled the military, long accustomed to enriching itself through graft, contraband activities, and drug trafficking. At the end of September, Aristide returned from abroad amid rumors of a coup. In his absence the army had sent the Swiss security advisors packing. As in August, Aristide responded with an incendiary speech, attacking the military and the wealthy and calling upon his supporters to take action. He concluded with a transparent reference to lynching with a burning tire around the neck.

On 30 September army units assaulted Aristide's residence. He escaped the country due to the intervention of the French and U.S. ambassadors. Gen. Cedras, who was either an instigator or a willing bystander, condoned the coup. But it was clear he did not control the hardline factions that carried it out and installed a puppet government at gunpoint. The *de facto* government—headed by Joseph Nerette, an aging Supreme Court judge, as president, and Jean-Jacques Honorat, a lawyer and former director of tourism under Jean-Claude Duvalier, as prime minister—was denied recognition by the 33-nation OAS, which voted to impose an economic blockade on Haiti to pressure for the restoration of Aristide's government.

The initial reaction of the new rulers was defiance. By mid-November, however, with the blockade threatening to shut down the country, an OAS delegation convinced General Cedras and the *de facto* government to allow members of parliament to meet with Aristide's representatives outside Haiti to find a way to restore civilian rule in line with the constitution. The accord stopped short of calling directly for Aristide's return, but did not rule out the possibility.

For his part, Aristide appeared willing to make concessions in order to restore his government, tacitly admitting that he had overstepped his authority in the months before the coup. But even if an agreement were to be reached, the question was whether the OAS could guarantee its implementation, given the volatile atmosphere in Haiti and Cedra's uncertain control over hardline army factions whose leaders vowed to kill Aristide if he returned. There also was the question of how the military could accept an agreement in which it were held accountable for the massive human rights violations committed after the coup.

Political Rights and Civil Liberties:

The 1987 constitution guarantees the right of free expression, freedom of religion and the right to organize political parties, civic organizations and labor unions. Although President Aristide incited his followers to acts of political intimidation toward the end of his brief administration, political rights and civil liberties were respected more during his tenure than in any other period in Haitian history. And while the justice system remained largely ineffectual, some efforts were made to hold rights violators accountable and rural section chiefs were placed under the control of the justice ministry, resulting in a dramatic decrease in political violence. Also, journalists and international rights organizations were given unprecedented access to the prison system.

The constitution was not formally suspended after the coup, but Haiti returned to the absolute lawlessness of the past as the military relied on savage repression to control the country. In the first days, there were over 300 confirmed killings, and the numbers will rise steeply if international rights monitors are ever allowed to investigate. According to reports by Haitian rights activists, the military, in order to mask the toll, had disposed of bodies itself, rather than taking them to the central morgue in Port-au-Prince. Also, the international media was denied access to most of the countryside, where some of the worst repression took place under prior military rule. Among the dead and missing were an undetermined number of children at an orphanage founded by Aristide, and Sylvio Claude, head of the Christian Democratic party, possibly killed by Aristide supporters.

After the coup, political dissent became tantamount to suicide, and the independent media was either silenced or allowed to operate only under a high degree of self-censorship. State-run Radio National was taken over and its director arrested. At least four other stations were destroyed and a number of others damaged by marauding soldiers. Most of the Creole radio broadcasts, the main source of news for the predominantly non-Frenching-speaking population, were repressed, and a number of station managers and journalists killed. Those that returned to the air were forced to broadcast statements by the military and the *de facto* government. Radio Metropole, usually an objective source for local news, said it had canceled news programs under pressure from both "the extreme left and the extreme right." For information, most Haitians depended upon a Creole broadcast from a station in the neighboring Dominican Republic or Voice of America broadcasts in Creole from Washington.

Honduras

Polity: Presidential-legislative democracy (military influenced)
Economy: Capitalist-statist
Population: 5,300,000
PPP: $1,490
Life Expectancy: 64.9
Ethnic Groups: Relatively homogeneous, approximately 7 percent Indian

Political Rights: 2
Civil Liberties: 3
Status: Free

Overview:

In 1991 the Honduran armed forces came under increasing domestic and international pressure for corrupt practices and human rights violations. Reform-minded officers appeared to be gaining the upper hand over hardliners, but prospects for a military more responsive to elected civilian government remained uncertain.

After achieving independence from Spain in 1821, and after the breakup of the United Provinces of Central America (1824-1838), the Republic of Honduras was established in 1839. Its history has been marked by armed rebellions, coups d'état, military rule and only intermittent democratic government. A democratic trend began with the election of a constituent assembly in 1980, the election of President Roberto Suazo of the Liberal Party (PL) in 1981, and the promulgation of a democratic constitution at the time of his inauguration in January 1982.

The 1982 constitution provides for a president and a 130-member, unicameral National Congress directly elected for four years. In the 1981 and 1985 presidential races, parties could nominate more than one candidate; the winner was the leading candidate of the party with the highest total aggregate vote. Thus, Jose Azcona, one of three PL candidates, was elected to succeed President Suazo in the November 1985 vote with only 27 percent of the vote, less than the 43 percent received by Rafael Leonardo Callejas of the National Party (PN), the country's other major political party. Smaller parties received collectively less than 5 percent.

In 1988 the independent electoral tribunal instructed the parties to hold primary elections. Roberto Flores won a four-way race to become the PL candidate and Callejas was selected to run again for the PN. Two smaller, left-leaning parties also nominated candidates. The key campaign issues were government corruption and the declining economy. Honduras remains one of the hemisphere's poorest nations; over half the population is either unemployed or active in the informal economy.

In the internationally monitored general elections held on 26 November 1989, Callejas defeated Flores, taking just over 50 percent of the vote. The PN also won a majority of the congressional seats and control of over two-thirds of the country's 283 municipal governments. The governors of the country's eighteen regional departments are appointed by the executive. The inauguration of President Callejas in January 1990 marked the third consecutive peaceful transfer of government to an elected civilian administration since 1982, and the first ballot-box transfer of power to an out-party in 57 years. The next elections are scheduled for 1993.

In the last two years, Callejas has initiated a sweeping economic restructuring program and succeeded in restoring portions of the U.S. and international development assistance cut off during the Azcona administration. However, this bold approach, including massive layoffs and government spending cuts, has alienated the well-organized labor sector, private business and the Catholic church. A number of crippling labor strikes have been staged since 1990.

Since the return to civilian rule, the 24,000-member military has retained influence over civilian governments on security, budgetary and land reform issues. By law, the National Congress elects the chief of the armed forces, who commands for a three-year period, from a list of nominees provided by the military. In reality, however, the military's first choice is routinely approved. The influence of the military appeared to be enhanced in 1990 after Callejas resorted to the use of troops during labor confrontations.

However, following a series of grisly, military-linked slayings in 1991, the armed forces came under increasing domestic and international pressure—including a 50 percent cut in U.S. military aid—to be held accountable for corrupt activities and rights violations. In an unprecedented concession, the military submitted to the authority of civilian courts to try two officers implicated in the murder of a student. Also, reform-minded officers succeeded in establishing an internal commission to investigate military misconduct and demoting a number of known human rights offenders. Further civil-military showdowns were expected, however, as momentum gathered for a constitutional reform that would eliminate the job of armed forces chief and place the military under a civilian defense minister.

Political Rights and Civil Liberties:

Citizens are able to change their governments democratically, but civilian authority over the military is still limited.

Constitutional guarantees regarding free expression, freedom of religion and the right to form political parties, labor unions and civic organizations are generally respected. There are a half dozen legal political parties ranging from the right to social democratic left.

The Honduran Communist Party (PCH) gained legal status in 1981, but until 1991 remained underground because of its support for a handful of small, left-wing guerrilla groups. However, since a 1990 government amnesty implemented with the cooperation of the United Nations, a number of radical groups have disarmed and resurfaced as political organizations.

Political expression has been restricted, however, by an increase in political violence since 1988. Sporadic left-wing guerrilla violence continued in 1991, accompanied by several political killings carried out by right-wing extremist groups, particularly against the unionists, students, and peasant groups. Several of these clandestine extremist groups have issued public death threats. The military and security forces also have been responsible for extra-judicial killings as well as systematic torture during confinement, although there have been no reports of disappearances in recent years. Independent rights activists also have been targeted; at least one was killed in 1991.

The government human rights office has acknowledged a pattern of abuses by the armed forces. The Callejas administration has invited the United Nations Human Rights Commission to conduct investigations, and submitted legislation to repeal an oppressive anti-terrorist law, which has provided a legal pretext for the military's crackdowns against peasant groups in rural land disputes. In 1988, the government cooperated on a case brought against Honduras at the Inter-American Court of Human Rights, but has yet to pay monetary damages assessed by the Court for two killings committed by security forces. The military has also yet to be held accountable for more than one hundred disappearances dating back to the early 1980s.

The Honduran judicial system, headed by a Supreme Court, remains weak, although in 1991 a number of civilian judges asserted themselves in unprecedented fashion in cases involving human rights violations by the military. Most cases against the armed forces, however, remain in the purview of military investigators, away from the public eye, and normally result in dismissal of charges.

Labor unions are well organized and permitted to strike. The government, however, has resorted on occasion to mobilizing the military and hiring scab workers to break streaks, particularly in the key banana and mining industries. Labor leaders, religious groups and indigenous-based peasant unions pressing for land reform, have been subject to official repression and violent attacks. At least one agrarian reform activist was killed in 1991.

The press and broadcast media are largely private. There are several daily newspapers representing various political points of view. In recent years, however, several of the approximately one hundred radio stations and a number of print journalists have been threatened with suspension by the government for interviewing independent human rights monitors and labor activists. Nonetheless, the media has become more emboldened in covering human rights issues and criticizing the armed forces.

Hungary

Polity: Parliamentary democracy
Economy: Mixed statist transitional
Population: 10,400,000
PPP: $5,920
Life Expectancy: 70.9
Ethnic Groups: Hungarians (95 percent), Slovak, German, Romanian minorities

Political Rights: 2
Civil Liberties: 2
Status: Free

Overview:

In 1991 Hungary continued solidifying its transition to multiparty democracy, clarifying such key constitutional issues as the division of power between Prime Minister Jozef Antall, who was directly elected in May 1990 as head of the Hungarian Democratic Forum (MDF), and President Arpad Goncz of the Alliance of Free Democrats, the largest opposition party, elected by parliament. Other major issues were the power of the Constitutional Court, passage of a compensation law for the recovery of property confiscated by the Communists, the escalating civil war in Yugoslavia, and growing unemployment resulting from economic restructuring.

Hungary has a unicameral 386-member parliament. After free elections in May 1990, the MDF held 165 seats; the Free Democrats, 92; the Independent Smallholders, 43; the Christian Democrats, 21; the Hungarian Socialist Party (formerly the ruling Communist Hungarian Socialist Worker's Party), 33; and FIDESZ, a former student group, 21. Other smaller parties won 11 seats. The ruling coalition includes the MDF, the Smallholders and the Christian Democrats.

On 23 September the Constitutional Court imposed limits on President Goncz powers in an attempt to end an intensifying dispute between the prime minister and the defense minister, on the one hand, and the president, on the other. The court reviewed three aspects of the president's power: his position as commander-in-chief, his right and duty to appoint public officials, and his immunity. The court ruled that Goncz restrict himself to giving guidelines to the armed forces and not interfere in their day-to-day operations. It also ruled that the president approve candidates for state positions nominated by the government, unless those appointments endanger the democratic functioning of the institutions involved. As for the president's immunity, the court ruled he was immune from political accountability to parliament and could not be made to account for his political decisions.

The dispute arose from ambiguities in the constitution. Article 29 states that "the president of the republic is the commander-in-chief of the armed forces." Yet, Article 40 states that the command of the armed forces is "the exclusive province of the parliament, the president, the National Defense Council, the government, and the competent minister as laid down in the constitution or a separate law." Both the MDF and the Free Democrats disagreed about the interpretation of the court's ruling.

The Constitutional Court, which under Hungarian law has more power than the U.S. Supreme Court, was itself at the center of controversy. At the core of the debate over the extent of the court's power was its right to review draft legislation both prior to and after its passage by parliament. Many viewed this right as a serious impediment to the legislative process, because Hungary's constitution was not yet fully revised to reflect the country's political transformation, it still contained inherent contradictions. On several occasions the court had to decide somewhat arbitrarily which articles to uphold over others.

In an important decision, the court on 29 May overturned a compensation law passed in April, temporarily stalling land privatization and the development of a real estate market. The court first became involved in the issue in 1990. The Smallholders' party ran on a platform that would restore confiscated land and pushed the MDF, its coalition partner, to submit a law that returned land to original owners on the basis of the 1947 land register. Prime Minister Antall, reluctant to face the complexities such a bill would cause, submitted the measure to the Constitutional Court. In October 1990, the court upheld the rights of agricultural cooperatives by ruling that their land could not be repossessed without full compensation. It took several months to frame the new draft law that would compensate 800,000 former landowners and 40,000 real estate holders. Owners of large factories, banks and businesses that were nationalized in 1947-8 were excluded from the bill. The Free Democrats criticized the draft law, mainly because it gave a clear advantage to landowners over other property owners. The bill was passed on 24 April and turned over to President Goncz to sign into law. However, as a Free Democrat, Goncz took advantage of his right to ask the Constitutional Court for a review.

On 29 May the court ruled (with nine judges in favor and one abstaining) that to compensate landowners fully but other property owners only partially was unconstitutional. Nor did the court accept the choice of 8 June 1949 as the decisive date in compensation cases. On 4 July Goncz signed an amended version of the law, which took effect 10 August.

There were several differences between the two compensation laws. The second version, for instance, included the requirement that a second law be passed in November to address the illegal confiscation of private property between 1 May 1939 and 8 June 1949. The date 1 May was chosen because the so-called Jewish law, which restricted property ownership by Jews, was enacted on 5 May 1939. The second version also provided that land owned by agricultural cooperatives would be auctioned off to the highest bidder. By the end of the year, implications of the compensation law remained unclear, including the effect of land privatization on agricultural output, and to what extent the new law would increase the budget deficit.

The economy continued to be a crucial issue in 1991. Hungary's $21 billion foreign debt remained the largest per capita in Eastern Europe. By September, unemployment stood at 294,000, but was projected to hit 300,000 out of a workforce of 4.6 million by year's end. Production was down by 10-12 percent in the first half of 1991, and bankruptcies became more common. Inflation hovered between 30 and 40 percent. In late July the Organization of Economic Cooperation and Development (OECD) concluded that Hungary's economy was buffeted by the abrupt loss of major markets in the Soviet Union and other former East Bloc countries after the dissolution of COMECON. In the first half of 1991, 75 percent of Hungary's trade was with the OECD, and 50 percent with the European Community (EC) members. The OECD said that the economy, which shrank by 5 percent in 1990, would shrink by another 5 to 8 percent. And while Hungary had outpaced other former East Bloc nations in adopting market-oriented policies, problems such as taxation, property rights and restructuring the public sector still had to be addressed. In August Finance Minister Mihaly Kupa told the state media the country needed to concentrate on reducing unemployment rather than raising revenues by privatization. Higher prices and plant closings contributed to an increase in the number of homeless to an estimated 55,000.

Despite these problems, the economy showed signs of vitality in some sectors. Even after debt payments, Hungary showed a surplus in its account balance. The finance minister announced that Hungarian currency would be ready for convertibility by 1992. The country's private sector expanded, with the number of small companies tripling from 10,000 to 30,000, including new shops and services. The output of companies with fewer than 50 employees increased by nearly 200 percent. Exports to hard-currency markets grew by 17 percent, slowly replacing crumbling trade with former COMECON partners. More than 150 state industries were scheduled to be sold during 1992. Foreign investment was expected to double from 1990's $900 million.

Another important issue in 1991 was the civil war in neighboring Yugoslavia. On 23 August Hungarian military officials announced that Yugoslav military jets violated Hungarian air space three times and fired missiles at targets in Croatia. By late September, an estimated 20,000 refugees, mostly Croatians, had crossed the border into Hungary to escape the fighting. The flow of refugees put a further strain on the economy and relief efforts. A refugee camp in Mohac designed to hold 1,700 had swelled to 8,000 in one August weekend. Hungary had already accepted between 30,000 and 35,000 Romanian citizens before October 1989.

The dissolution of the Warsaw Pact and the war in Yugoslavia prompted Hungary to seek closer ties to the 16-nation NATO alliance. At a 10 October NATO meeting in Brussels, Prime Minister Antall expressed concern about the lack of political control over armies in Eastern Europe, and cited the troubles with the military in Yugoslavia. He also implied that Hungary desired to have more formal links with NATO, perhaps as an associate member.

Another significant event was the withdrawal of the last Soviet troops from

Hungary on 19 June, ending more than four decades of sometimes bloody Red Army occupation. A March 1990 agreement mandated the withdrawal of more than 50,000 troops, 860 tanks, 600 pieces of mobile artillery and an unknown number of short-range rockets, some with nuclear warheads.

Political Rights and Civil Liberties:

Hungarians can change their government democratically. Constitutional amendments and new laws guarantee the integrity and impartiality of the judiciary. Public confidence in the judiciary returned, and a number of citizens sought judicial help in civil courts against the state authorities. Nevertheless, after more than four decades of Communist rule, the dearth of judges with training and experience in a society based on the rule of law remained a serious handicap. The security apparatus is no longer an intrusive arm of state repression. Citizens are free to express their views, the state media offers diverse viewpoints, and there are hundreds of independent publications. Freedom of assembly and association are guaranteed and respected.

Freedom of conscience and religion is viewed as a fundamental liberty not granted by the state or any other authority. In 1991, the state increased financial aid to Hungary's largest churches, the Catholic, the Reformed (Calvinist) and the Lutheran. In June, the government submitted a draft law stipulating that church buildings confiscated by the state after 1 January 1948 be returned over a period of ten years if the churches use them for religious or social purposes. Hungary's major opposition parties—the Free Democrats, FIDESZ and the Hungarian Socialists (the former Communists)—opposed the draft law on the grounds it violated the principle of the separation of church and state. They also accused the government of pursuing a "Christian course."

Hungarians are free to travel abroad and there are no internal travel restrictions. Workers are organized in the independent Confederation of Hungarian Trade Unions (MSzOSz), the Democratic League of Independent Trade Unions and Workers' Solidarity, a blue-collar coordinating group. There are several nonaffiliated unions. Most workers have the right to strike, excluding judicial and military personnel and police.

Iceland

Polity: Parliamentary democracy
Economy: Capitalist
Population: 300,000
PPP: $16,820
Life Expectancy: 77.8
Ethnic Groups: Icelander

Political Rights: 1
Civil Liberties: 1
Status: Free

Overview:

In 1991, the major news stories from Iceland were parliamentary elections and the formation of a new coalition government, a debate over domestic tax policy, and early diplomatic recognition of Lithuania.

Iceland began the year with a center-left coalition government, which included the rural-oriented Progressive Party, the Social Democratic Party, and the left-wing People's Alliance. In April parliamentary elections, the conservative, pro-Europe Independence Party obtained 26 seats in the legislature to become the strongest party in parliament. It formed a new coalition government with the Social Democrats, who hold 10 seats. The new prime minister is David Oddsson of the Independence Party. With 13 seats, the Progressive Party went into opposition after nearly 20 years in government. The left-wing People's Alliance and the Women's List hold the remaining 14 opposition seats.

Iceland's parliament, the *Althing*, is a bicameral legislature composed of 63 members elected to four year terms. Forty-nine members of the Althing are selected on the basis of proportional representation from eight districts: the remaining 14 are chosen based upon parties' percentage of the national vote. The Althing divides itself into two houses after elections: an upper house composed of 21 members selected by and from the Althing's representatives, and a lower chamber. Every four years, voters elect a president, the ceremonial head of state, who chooses the prime minister from the party or coalition able to command a parliamentary majority. The current president is the non-partisan Vigdis Finnbogadóttir, who announced in June 1991 that she would run for another four-year term in 1992.

Iceland has a parliamentary tradition which dates from the tenth century. After disaffected Norsemen settled Iceland in the tenth century, Iceland flourished as an independent republic until the thirteenth century, when it came under Norwegian rule. In the fourteenth century, Iceland came under Danish rule and remained under rigid colonial control until 1874, when it received limited autonomy within the Kingdom of Denmark. However, it was not until 1944, when British and American forces occupied Denmark, that Iceland achieved full independence. Icelanders are a racial mixture of Nordic and Celtic elements which has over the centuries become a homogeneous linguistic and ethnic group unto itself. In addition to almost no existing ethnic and racial cleavages in Iceland, there are virtually no economic or social cleavages. The language spoken is Icelandic, which is derived from old Norse.

A major issue in Icelandic politics is Iceland's relationship with the European Community. A major obstacle to Iceland's entrance into the European Community concerns Iceland's fishing industry. Most European Community members have subsidized fishing industries. Iceland fears competition with heavily subsidized fishing industries in the European Community and therefore seeks a compromise with the rest of the European states before entering into the Community. The Independence Party supports tax reform to make the economy more competitive, and the Social Democrats back more market-oriented policies to advance the economy.

Iceland offered diplomatic recognition to Lithuania in January 1991, well ahead of most other countries.

Political Rights and Civil Liberties: Icelanders have the right to change their government democratically. There is freedom of association. Freedom of assembly, expression and assembly are generally respected.

The newspapers are a combination of independent and party-affiliated publications. There is a public broadcasting service, which is run by an autonomous board. The U.S. Navy also broadcasts from its NATO base in Iceland. The constitution forbids censorship. Over 95 percent of the population belongs at least nominally to the state-supported Lutheran Church. There is freedom of worship for non-established churches. It is illegal to discriminate on the basis of language, race, gender and social status in Iceland. However, the Women's List alleges that there are cases of unequal pay for women. Workers have the right to organize and to strike.

India

Polity: Parliamentary democracy
Economy: Captialist-statist
Population: 838,000,000
PPP: $870
Life Expectancy: 59.1
Ethnic Groups: Indo-Aryan (72 percent), Dravidian (25 percent), other

Political Rights: 3
Civil Liberties: 4
Status: Partly Free

Overview:

In 1991 India was plagued by the worst electoral violence in recent history, including the assassination of former Prime Minister Rajiv Gandhi. Sectarian strife, direct federal rule over five of India's 25 states, and persistent religious and caste polarization further eroded the foundation of the world's most populous democracy.

Although the murder of Mr. Gandhi, leader of the Indian National Congress (Congress Party), during the May elections shocked the world, campaign violence, corruption, attacks on candidates and voter intimidation had been commonplace throughout the election. In the state of Bihar, for example, armed private gangs hired by politicians regularly seized polling stations and stuffed ballots; fourteen of a bloated 74 ministries in this impoverished state were headed by reputed criminals.

The 1991 elections were called after the 6 March resignation of Prime Minister Chandra Shekhar, who had assumed power in November 1990 with the support of the Congress Party. Shekhar had replaced Prime Minister V.P. Singh of the the the left-wing Janata Dal Party. During his 13 months in office, Prime Minister Singh promised to implement bold political changes, but by mid-1990 he appeared stymied by some of the country's most ancient problems—caste warfare, factionalism, and separatism. In August, his proposal that 27 percent of government and public sector company jobs be set aside for "intermediate" castes—over half the population—touched off months of rioting. Dozens of students committed suicide by self-immolation. The proposal also angered the prime minister's two key political allies: the radical Hindu Bharatiya Janata Party (BJP), which had been trying to unite Hindus of all castes under a single banner, and the two Communist parties.

On 5 November 1990, less than forty-eight hours before Prime Minister Singh was to face a confidence vote in parliament, dissidents formed the Janata Dal-Socialist coalition led by Chandra Shekhar, who took a quarter of Singh Janata Dal parliamentary support with him. The split damaged the party's image as an alternative to the Congress Party. The following day, Gandhi gave a guarded pledge of support to Mr. Shekhar, and on 7 November the government of Prime Minister Singh collapsed after losing the confidence vote. Days later, Mr. Shekhar, an old-guard socialist, assumed the prime ministership.

As 1990 ended, Hindu-Muslim violence in the northern state of Punjab had killed 3,800 people. Indian troops began a crackdown on separatists in the eastern state of Assam, as Prime Minister Shekhar ousted its government and placed the state under direct federal rule. Tensions remained high over a disputed religious site at Ayodhya in Uttar Pradesh state, where Hindu militants' plans to build a shrine on the site of a 400-year-old mosque led to clashes that left thousands dead and injured. Moreover, the prime minister faced the formidable challenge of reforming a badly slumping economy.

On 11 January 1991 eight lawmakers of Prime Minister Shekhar's Janata Dal-Socialist party were expelled from parliament under an anti-defection law, which forbids any faction from breaking away from a party unless it carries one-third of the party's members. The disqualifications brought down to 54 the strength of Shekhar's party in the 511-member house. The government retained power because it was also supported by the 211 members of Gandhi's Congress Party.

On 30 January Prime Minister Shekhar dismissed the elected government of Tamil Nadu, a large southern state, ostensibly for helping Tamil Tiger guerrillas fighting for a separate state in Sri Lanka. Tamil Nadu became the fifth Indian state under direct federal rule, joining Assam, Punjab, Pondicherry and Jammu-Kashmir (*A separate essay on Kashmir appears in the section on Related Territories.*). Administrations were also replaced in Andhra Pradesh and Goa. Although India's constitution allows the prime minister to impose direct rule, he may do so only if the state's governor (an appointee of the central government) certifies that law and order have broken down. Tamil Nadu's governor refused.

The takeover sparked riots in Madras, capital of Tamil Nadu, and the government sent in federal troops. On 5 February authorities rounded up 23,000 people to forestall a general strike. The prime minister's actions were widely criticized by the opposition, and non-partisan analysts were virtually unanimous in interpreting the takeover as part of the political strategy of Gandhi and the Congress Party.

On 9 February, in a move to strengthen its image as an alternative government for India, the BJP—the leading opposition party—named a shadow cabinet in preparation for a crucial session of parliament later that month. By March it was clear that the Congress Party and Gandhi were seeking any means to regain power, particularly in the face of the rising popularity of the BJP among middle class, urban Hindus. Former Prime Minister Singh's mainstream Janata Dal continued to enjoy the support of lower-caste Hindus, Muslims and other less privileged groups. In the south, local council elections in Kerala showed a shift away from Congress to leftist groups nationally aligned with Janata Dal. On 6 March, Prime Minister Shekhar, aware that Congress was no longer willing to support his government and tired of being manipulated by Gandhi, resigned.

On 10 March Gandhi formally requested new elections. Three days later, after parliament passed urgent budget legislation and extended the central government's direct rule in the Punjab, President Ramaswamy Venkataraman dissolved the legislature, ordering that it be reconstituted by 5 June. Shekhar was asked to continue as caretaker prime minister, pending elections on 20, 23 and 26 May. On 12 April the country's Election Commission confirmed the dates of the national vote, but announced that balloting would not be held simultaneously in the insurgent-shaken states of Assam, Punjab, and Jammu-Kashmir. The three states had 33 seats among them, a crucial amount if no party or alliance gained a majority. The commission decided that Assam and Punjab would vote in June, and Muslim-majority Jammu-Kashmir would not vote at all.

The campaign focused on religious and caste issues, with clear-cut distinctions between the centrist Congress vision of a secular India and the two main contenders: the BJP and former Prime Minister Singh's Janata-Dal. The Hindu-nationalist BJP, led by Lal Krishan Advani and backed by several militant Hindu organizations, called for making Hinduism the national culture. Mr. Advani pledged to dismantle the Muslim mosque at Ayodhya and build in its place a gigantic temple dedicated to the Hindu warrior-god Rama. The BJP also appealed to Hindu nationalism and anti-Muslim sentiments by raising fears about Muslim secessionists in Kashmir and Sikh separatists in Punjab. Mr. Singh's center-left alliance advocated a social revolution "against the thousands of years of injustice" inflicted on the backward and untouchable castes, estimated to represent 52 percent of the population.

The Congress Party tried to stake out a middle ground, appealing to the traditional core of its support—Brahmins and other upper castes, numbering about 10 percent of the population, the former so-called untouchable castes and various tribal peoples, about 15 percent in total, and Muslims, another 12 percent.

The campaign for 511 contested parliamentary seats and five state assemblies was extraordinary violent. The chief election commissioner designated more than 300 of the country's 567 parliamentary constituencies as "sensitive," or prone to violence. Nearly 2 million police officers and paramilitary personnel were sent to troublesome states. Nevertheless, by the closing days of the campaign, over 300 people had died in political violence, including at least 10 candidates at national or state level.

On 20 May, the first day of voting, killings, allegations of voter fraud and riots were reported throughout the country. Violence forced the closing of polling stations and several cities were placed under curfew. The Election Commission invalidated results from 5 of the 204 districts where voting was held. New voting was ordered in 64 other districts. Communists and Congress Party supporters battled in Calcutta with guns and bombs. In Uttar Pradesh, 20 people were confirmed killed and hospitals reported many wounded before a curfew was established and the army sent in. The bloodshed made the election the most violent since independence and resulted in a turnout of barely 50 percent, the lowest in independent India's history.

The escalating violence did not prepare the country or the world for the assassination of Rajiv Gandhi on 21 May, while he was campaigning in Sriperumpudur, near Madras in Tamil Nadu. A Tamil separatist woman set off a bomb strapped to her body that killed her, 14 others and decapitated the former prime minister. The sophistication of the bomb placed suspicion on the Tamil Tiger rebels of Sri Lanka. (In August, seven suspects in the Gandhi murder committed suicide as the police closed in on their hideout.)

The assassination threw the Congress Party and the election into turmoil. The final phase of the voting was postponed until 12 and 15 June. Sonia Gandhi, the former prime minister's Italian-born widow, rejected Congress efforts to have her succeed her late husband as party leader. On 30 May the struggling Congress Party chose 69-year-old former foreign minister P.V. Narasimha Rao to succeed Mr. Gandhi. The ailing Mr. Rao was expected to serve for an interim to carry the party through the elections. Meanwhile, Prime Minister Shekhar and his caretaker government continued to rule and violence continued to plague the elections.

On 7 June it was reported that at least 400 candidates had gone into hiding two weeks before elections in Punjab, the first since 1985. Others were in protective custody. Nineteen were killed by Sikh militants, and campaign violence was behind some 600 violent deaths in Punjab since April. Two thousand candidates were contesting the 13 parliamentary seats and 117 seats in the state legislature that were at stake in the vote scheduled for 22 June, a week after the rest of the country went to the polls. On 16 June, Sikh militants killed 74 Hindu passengers in two trains.

As voting resumed on 12 June, exit polls suggested that no one party would claim a parliamentary majority. After results from 90 percent of the 511 contested seats were in, the Congress Party with 217 seats—and some 20 from its declared allies—was still short of the 256 needed for a majority. The BJP, which swept Congress from the northern, Hindi-speaking states of Uttar Pradesh and Bihar, became the largest non-Congress Party force in parliament by increasing its seats from 86 to 121. The Janata Dal-National Front coalition and the Left Front coalition that included the Communist Party of India-Marxist (CPM) controlled 126 seats; the All-India Anna Dravidia Munnetra Kazhagam (AIADMK), a Congress ally, 11; and smaller parties, the remaining seats.

On 20 June, after much speculation, P.V. Narasimha Rao was chosen by the Congress Party to be India's next prime minister. Rao, suffering from heart disease and other ailments, was sworn in on 21 June.

In early July, Prime Minister Rao surprised the nation with a bold economic reform plan intended to transform India's inward looking, control-bound economy into one favoring free markets and foreign trade. The government devalued Indian currency; announced a new trade policy to reduce discrimination against exporters; and promised an austerity budget on 24 July which would cut the budget deficit from 9 percent of GNP to 6.5 percent. The radical moves were necessitated by several factors: India had drawn down its reserves below the $1.8 billion lent by the International Monetary Fund in January; although its total foreign debt of $71 billion was not serious, its short-term debt of $6.5 billion and the $10 billion in high-interest deposits collected from Indians living oversees were causing concern. Worried by the possibility of India defaulting on its debt, bankers had cut off lines of short-term credit.

By November the government's tough economic stabilization measures began to pay off. From a high of 15.7 percent in early September inflation fell to 13.4 percent by mid-October.

On the political front, the government faced 16 by-elections in November. Prime Minister Rao won his seat by an astonishing majority of 580,000 votes. Initial results indicated that Congress had won seven seats. Predictably, violence marred polling. There were reports that Rao supporters captured booths and stuffed ballot boxes. In Bihar, many people died and new balloting was ordered in hundreds of polling stations.

Toward year's end, Hindu-Muslim tensions remained potentially explosive. While the government's new Places of Worship Act technically barred Ayodhya-like campaigns elsewhere in India, Hindu militants continued their agitation. On 11 December, the BJP's new president, Murli Manohar Joshi, embarked on a 14,000-kilometer "unity pilgrimage" from the southern tip of India to Kashmir. The mission was to convince Hindus to close ranks against the Muslims.

The year also saw continued violence in Assam and Punjab. In February 1991 a separatist insurgent group in Assam—the United Liberation Front of Asom (ULFA)—which had been terrorizing tea plantations, said it was ready to negotiate a peaceful settlement after a three-month crackdown by Indian Army troops. The move was seen to be a result of a relentless government campaign that included the arrest of 2,000 people accused of aiding the rebels. But in July, separatist guerrillas in eastern Assam kidnapped a Soviet engineer and 14 Indian government officials. The following month, tribal guerrillas from the Bodo tribe murdered a former state minister, his son and a bodyguard. On 16 September Indian soldiers captured 136 guerrillas and smashed 12 training camps in Assam. On 2 November, ULFA rebels killed at least 18 people in a fresh wave of violence. Dozens were wounded. On 16 December the

ULFA released 20 hostages. One day later, in the face of an Indian Army crackdown, the ULFA announced, as a prelude to negotiations, a cease-fire and an end to its uprising.

On 18 September parliament extended the four-and-a-half year federal rule over the Punjab. Killings continued unabated through October, and in November a car bomb nearly killed a BJP vice-president. On 2 December police arrested a Sikh militant for allegedly planting a bomb on an Air India plane bound for New York. Shootings, lynching and bombings continued in December, bringing the total number of those killed during the year in Punjab alone to over 5,000.

Political Rights and Civil Liberties:

Indian citizens can change their government democratically, but endemic corruption, patronage, graft and widescale political violence seriously undermine India's democratic system. In 1991, the country experienced the most violent election campaign in the 44 years since independence. In some states, such as Bihar, corruption has become institutionalized and accepted, as armed gangs routinely attack polling stations and reputed criminals serve as state ministers. Entire regions of the country remain under a feudal system, and five states—a fifth of the total—are under direct rule by the central government.

Political killings, sectarian and separatist unrest and police actions cost thousands of lives and resulted in murders, kidnappings, massacres and torture. A National Security Act permits detention of persons judged to be security risks, and police are allowed special powers; in Assam, Punjab and Kashmir police have powers to detain, interrogate, or shoot on sight suspected terrorists. Abuses by security forces are common, particularly in Kashmir and Punjab, where Amnesty International reported in May that 10,000 Sikhs were being held under sweeping anti-terrorist laws without any chance to be brought to trial.

The judiciary is independent, and civil and criminal proceedings are free and generally open, but the legal system continues to be hopelessly backlogged.

Free speech is protected and generally respected, and India has a lively independent press that publishes diverse opinions. But during the year, the government and Sikh militants inflicted considerable duress on journalists in Punjab. In January and February, authorities in the Punjab issued orders to the press not to print militants' statements and raided newspaper offices on several occasions. The papers included the *Tribune*, *Indian Express* and Ajit. Militants threatened journalists with death if they published government releases or complied with the official ban on separatist statements. On 23 April, Mohammad Shabaun Vakil, editor of the daily *al-Saf*, was killed by two unidentified gunmen in Kashmir.

Peaceful protests and demonstrations are generally allowed, though they sometimes require routine permits. India is nominally a secular state. But violent tensions between religious groups led to massacres and injuries in 1991, as Hindus, Muslims and Sikhs clashed throughout the year.

Despite an official ban on the caste system, the 3,000-year-old hierarchical structure is very much alive in India. In 1990, a government plan to set aside 27 percent of public sector jobs for lower castes led to upper-caste student riots. In India's villages, caste-based violence is commonplace. In a village 100 miles from Delhi, villagers in March hanged and then burned a girl and two boys; as their fathers were forced to watch the boys were castrated and tortured before they were hung. The girl, from the powerful Jat caste, allegedly tried to elope with the boys, both outcaste members of the Chamaars, leather workers born to handle dead animals. In another example of caste-based violence, in three villages in Bihar, huts of over 400 families of untouchables were burned down by gangs working for the local landowning caste because they were demanding the legal minimum wage, 16 rupees (78 cents) a day.

Despite laws on sexual equality, women are clearly second-class citizens in much of the country and frequent targets of dowry murder and burnings by dissatisfied spouses. Hundreds of women died this way in 1991. In Kashmir, women were the target of gang rapes and beatings by Indian troops.

Private civic, business, special-interest and human rights groups are free to operate. Domestic travel is generally free, except in some security areas. Emigration and foreign travel are allowed.

Child labor, though outlawed for certain hazardous jobs, is widespread. Western organizations estimate that millions of children are bonded laborers in India, although India banned debt bondage 14 years ago. Indian workers can join a wide range of trade unions, though strikes are forbidden in certain essential industries.

Indonesia

Polity: Dominant party (military-dominated)
Economy: Capitalist-statist
Population: 186,644,000
PPP: $1,820
Life Expectancy: 61.5
Ethnic Groups: A multi-ethnic state—Javanese (45 percent), Sundanese (14 percent), Madurese (7.5 percent), Coastal Malays (7.5 percent), other (26 percent)

Political Rights: 6
Civil Liberties: 5
Status: Partly Free

Overview:

In 1991, major developments in Indonesia, an archipelago of 13,500 islands and the world's fifth most populous nation, included preparations for upcoming general elections and the proliferation of independent democratic groups. Indonesia also faced international criticism of its repressive policies in the annexed territory of East Timor (*see Related Territories for reports on East Timor and Irian Jaya*), and charges of human rights abuses in Aceh, a region in Sumatra with a long-time separatist movement.

Executive power is vested in President General Suharto, who assumed emergency powers in 1966. Named acting president in 1967, Suharto was elected in 1968 by the 1,000-member People's Consultative Assembly (MPR), the highest state body and sole arbiter of the constitution. Suharto ensures the certainty of his re-elections through a complex system of political controls. The 1,000 members of the MPR choose the president and vice-president by unanimous consensus at their two-week meeting in March of every fifth year. The MPR is made up of 500 members of the nation's other legislative body, the People's Representative Council (DPR); the other 500 members are appointed by the military and Golkar, President Suharto's political organization. Though technically not a party, Golkar is the coalition that supports Suharto's government and is funded almost exclusively by the *Dakab yayasan*, a foundation funded by Suharto himself. Of the 500 members of the DPR, 400 are elected every five years and 100 are appointed by Golkar. It is forbidden to campaign for the presidency more than two weeks before the MPR makes its choice; candidates for the DPR cannot run on a platform promising to oppose Suharto at the next MPR. Suharto, 71, was elected to a fifth term in 1988 and is expected to win easily in 1993.

Other parties include the United Development Party (PPP), a merger of Islamic groups which won 15 percent in the 1987 election, and the Indonesian Democratic Party (PDI), an amalgam of five parties, including the Indonesian National Party of long-time president Sukarno. It won only 10.8 percent in the 1987 vote. Both parties are funded by the government and support the president. The 1985 Law on Mass Organizations requires that all parties accept the state ideology, the *pancasila*, based on monotheism, national unity, humanitarianism, social justice and democracy by consensus.

1991 opened with all three of the country's major political groupings planning for general elections scheduled for June 1992, and speculation about presidential elections the following year. Both regional and Indonesian analysts predict that Golkar, which won 73 percent of the vote in 1987, and President Suharto are virtually guaranteed victory, partially because electioneering is carefully controlled and tempered by intensified monitoring of political expression. In early 1991, the government adopted new election rules aimed at ensuring that campaign rallies would be even more rigidly controlled than in previous years. On 18 June 1991, Home Affairs Minister Rudini announced that political party insignias would be the only pictures allowed to be used in the 1992 campaign. Frustrated by the government's refusal to open up the political process, Indonesian intellectuals organized a series of pro-democracy mass organizations (*ormas*) that began to overshadow the existing, traditional non-governmental organizations. In March, four new political organizations were formed: the Democratic Forum, the League for Restoration of Democracy (LRD), the National Democratic Alliance (Aliande) and the All-Indonesian Alliance of Democratic Forces (AKSI). In August, a group of dissidents led by a retired general announced the creation of Forum for Purification of People's Sovereignty. The Democratic Forum was formed by a loose coalition of 45 Muslim and Christian scholars, businessmen and human rights lawyers to challenge official dominance of political debate. Although the Forum's proclaimed purpose was to promote dialogue and discussion, it came under intense government pressure. The LRD, whose leader was the director of the Institute of Human Rights and a board member of a free trade union, attacked election laws which, aside from banning the participation of any new unauthorized parties, also gave the government broad powers in selecting candidates.

On 4 July Indonesia's most prominent dissident organization, Petition 50, accused the government of making unjust allegations against the group. Petition 50 takes its name from 50 leading Indonesian dissidents who signed a 1980 statement denouncing President Suharto. Speaking at a parliamentary hearing, the group's leader said the government had intimidated mass media into not publicizing the group's positions. On 20 August police attempted to disrupt a meeting of the group in Jakarta, the nation's capital, after it had called for a change in national leadership. In April the government had banned all members of the group and other dissidents from traveling abroad.

On 16 September, Indonesia's three main parties submitted their lists of nominees for the 1992 legislative elections. The early submission was to allow for screening by

a government-appointed committee. The lists, submitted to Home Affairs Minister
Rudini, also the chairman of the General Election Committee, included the maximum
800 candidates from the governing Golkar, 800 from the PDI and 762 from the PPP.
On 10 October PDI announced that it was prepared to back President Suharto for a
sixth term in 1993.

In 1991 Indonesia faced international condemnation for its continued repression of
East Timor, which Indonesia invaded and annexed in 1976. Between 1975 and 1979,
some 100,000 to 200,000 East Timorese starved to death, allegedly after Indonesian
forces destroyed crops and livestock. In November 1991, Indonesian forces massacred
some 100 people attending a funeral in East Timor. There were also reports from
East Timor that Indonesian armed forces were beating and arresting people suspected
of taking part in protests against Indonesian rule. A February report by Amnesty
International said that over 100 people had been detained and possibly tortured in East
Timor during the previous six months. The same month, the European Community
presented a statement to the U.N. Commission on Human Rights accusing Indonesia
of torture and widespread killings in East Timor.

In the province of Aceh, situated at the northern tip of Sumatra with a population
of 3 million, Indonesian forces were accused of torture, kidnapping and murder in
their 18-month campaign against the separatist Aceh-Sumatra Liberation Front. Aceh
won special provincial status in 1959 after a six-year uprising against central government control. Human rights groups charged that the 18,000 elite troops deployed in
May 1990 to fight the rebels committed atrocities against civilians that left thousands
dead. An Indonesian human rights group reported that 1,197 people were killed in
Aceh during a two-week period in August.

In 1991 Indonesia's economy continued the export-led economic boom which
began in 1987. In 1970 over 60 percent of the population lived below the poverty
line. By 1987 that figure had dropped to 17 percent.

Political Rights and Civil Liberties:

Continued political dominance by President Suharto and the
lack of a formidable opposition effectively precludes
Indonesians from changing their government democratically.
The judiciary is made up of civil servants employed by the executive branch.
Although appeals are permitted, initial judgements are rarely overturned. The state
convicted a large number of citizens under Indonesia's Anti-Subversion Law in 1991.
Defendants were denied the right to choice of counsel, and many "confessions" were
obtained under torture. Some executions of "subversives" took place without a
judicial hearing for the accused, particularly in Aceh and East Timor. The police,
who are officially part of the armed forces, abuse and often torture prisoners during
interrogation.

Freedom of speech and press are often curtailed. All newspapers are members of
the National Press Council, which is chaired by the Minister of Information. On
8 April 1991, a court sentenced a former editor of the popular *Monitor* to five years
in prison for publishing a reader's poll in 1987 of most admired figures; President
Suharto finished first and the prophet Mohammad placed eleventh. In June 1991 press
officials urged the government to review regulations allowing the information minister
to revoke publication licenses without appeal. Boundaries of acceptable reporting are
arbitrary and change without notice. Broadcasts are government supervised. The

government banned six books on religious topics in 1991. Early in the year, authorities arrested and tried two men for insulting public officials after they released a calendar that caricatured government leaders. The Home Affairs Minister announced in 1991 that the government would forbid parties from using pictures other than party insignias during the 1992 DPR campaigns. Indonesia also constrains freedom of association. All groups must honor the official state ideology, and there are especially tight restrictions on association for public servants.

Indonesia holds the world's largest Muslim population and recognizes Islam as one of four officially permissible religions, along with Buddhism, Hinduism, and Christianity. A group of Indonesia's most prominent Muslim thinkers established the Association of Muslim Intellectuals (ICMI) in December 1990. The ICMI accepted as members many prominent government critics in 1991, despite accusations that Suharto desired to use the group to gain support within the Muslim community.

In April 1991, the Indonesian weekly magazine *Tempo* quoted the country's director general of immigration as stating that at least 15,000 Indonesians were banned from travelling abroad. Large numbers of refugees have attempted to seek asylum in neighboring Malaysia, many to avoid political persecution. Particularly severe human rights abuses have been reported in Aceh. The small Chinese minority, which dominates much of the country's business, faces discrimination.

Government influence on the All Indonesian Workers Union (SPSI) keeps international labor from recognizing it as a free trade union. The government maintains the illegality of Setia Kawan, a rival union created in late 1990 by the Institute for the Defense of Human Rights. In 1990 the government lifted a 27-year ban on strikes for workers in strategic industries. There were several strikes in 1991.

Iran

Polity: Presidential parliamentary (clergy-dominated)
Economy: Capitalist-statist
Population: 58,600,000
PPP: $3,560
Life Expectancy: 66.2
Ethnic Groups: Persian, Turkic, Arab, other

Political Rights: 6
Civil Liberties: 5
Status: Not Free

Overview:

In 1991, after more than a decade of war and revolution, Iran emerged from international isolation as an important post-Gulf War Middle Eastern power. President Ali Akbar Hashemi Rafsanjani, a so-called moderate, clashed with the conservative elements of the Islamic Republic, as he attempted to reconcile broken ties with the West.

The Islamic Republic of Iran, established in 1979 following the overthrow of the monarchy led by Shah Reza Pahlavi, is a theocratic state based on the late Ayatollah Khomeini's interpretation of Shi'a Islam. While Ayatollah Sayed Ali Khamenei replaced Khomeini as the country's supreme religious leader, Rafsanjani in effect wields control over the country. Since the death of Ayatollah Khomeini in 1989, the President has led so-called moderates in a a power struggle against radical Islamic elements of the Iranian leadership.

As 1991 began, the President reaffirmed Iran's neutrality in the Persian Gulf crisis, despite calls from radicals to join the *jihad* (holy war) against the "Great Satan" (the U.S.). Reasserting his condemnation of the Iraqi invasion of Kuwait, Rafsanjani vehemently rejected the notion of allying with Iraqi dictator Saddam Hussein, stating that to do so would be "suicide." While consistent in demanding Iraqi withdrawal from Kuwait, Iran continued normalizing relations with Iraq, a process which began in 1990. On 8 January, the two countries agreed to create a half-mile-wide buffer zone by pulling back forces remaining from the 1980-88 Iran-Iraq war. Through newly reopened diplomatic channels, Iranian leaders tried to persuade Saddam to withdraw his troops from Kuwait. But, according to some reports, Iran supplied Iraq with food and medicine, in violation of the U.N.-sanctioned trade embargo. Iran also sharply criticized the Western military presence in the Gulf and the Arab nations that sanctioned it. Iran's neutrality was called into question in late January, when more than 80 Iraqi warplanes flew to Iran in search of refuge from the allied air strikes. Though it did not destroy the planes, Iran reaffirmed neutrality and impounded the aircraft, rejecting appeals from Baghdad for their return to Iraq.

Iran's position during and after the Gulf War was part of President Rafsanjani's campaign to bring his country out of world isolation and portray Iran as a responsible regional force. During the crisis, Tehran received emissaries from France, Algeria, Yemen, the Soviet Union, Turkey, and even Iraq. At the beginning of February, Rafsanjani offered to serve as mediator between the U.S. and Iraq in order to end the Gulf war. Though dismissed by the U.S., the offer reflected Rafsanjani's pragmatic line and marked the first time the Iranian government has alluded to possible direct talks with Washington since diplomatic ties were severed in 1979. Iran also played a role in Soviet and French attempts to coordinate a peace settlement.

After the Gulf War, as a Shiite revolt in Iraq began to spread, President Rafsanjani denounced Iraqi dictator Saddam Hussein and called on him to resign. Relations between Iran and Iraq abruptly froze when Saddam had one of the most revered Shiite leaders, Ayatollah Abolqassem al-Khoei, appear on Iraqi television to express support for the repression of Shiite rebels. Iran intensified its support to the Shiite and Kurdish uprisings in Iraq, abandoning its former policy of dealing with Iraq—on the one hand encouraging peace and on the other undermining the Iraqi leadership by covertly supporting the Shiites, mostly under control of the Tehran based Supreme Assembly of the Islamic Revolution of Iraq (SAIRI). President Rafsanjani denied reports of aiding the rebels.

In April, Iran opened its doors to over 1 million mostly Kurdish refugees fleeing Saddam Hussein's troops, and stationed them in camps and hospitals built during the Iran-Iraq war. Iran made numerous appeals for international aid from the U.N. High Commission on Refugees and the Red Cross. President Rafsanjani ridiculed the initial amounts of Western aid pledged for the more than 1 million refugees, underestimated at 35,000 by the U.N. Disease spread among the refugees amassed on the border, and by May the death rate had reached some 2,000 per day.

In the spring, reports suggested that Islamic militancy in Iran was on the wane. In Tehran, for example, the once omnipresent pictures of Ayatollah Ruhollah Khomeini, the leader of the 1979 Islamic revolution, have largely disappeared except in Government buildings. At the end of March, an inflammatory political monthly noted for criticizing the West, especially the United States, was suspended for "technical reasons." In April, the Komiteh (religious police assigned with the enforcement of Islamic norms) were merged with the regular police; earlier the Revolutionary Guards were merged with the regular army.

Despite these changes, Iran remained a major violator of human rights. Rafsanjani and the ruling clerics tolerate little political opposition. However, in a remarkable sign of liberalization, Tehran television broadcast a Jewish religious service and a *seder* marking the start of the Passover holiday, the first such broadcast since the revolution. In the post-Gulf War period, Rafsanjani continued to incite storms of criticism from radicals for re-establishing diplomatic ties with several European nations, including the leaders of the European Community, in addition to countries once on Iran's hate list, such as Britain (in late 1990), Morocco and Jordan. Anti-Westernism remained strong among sectors of the population as well as the ruling clerics. In April protesters carried placards saying "Death to America, Death to Israel" during a march on behalf of the Palestinian cause. Throughout the year, leading radical clerics charged the government with plotting a conspiracy to undermine Ayatollah Khomeini's revolution by seeking rapprochement with the West.

Rafsanjani hoped to boost Iran's slumping economy by attracting foreign investment through a reform program of privatization and economic liberalization. Iran has a per capita income of $100 and 40 percent inflation. In March Iran's international diplomatic and economic-reform efforts paid off in the form of a $250 million loan from the World Bank, the first since the 1979 revolution. In April, Iranian delegates participated in joint spring sessions of the International Monetary Fund (IMF) and the World Bank. Rafsanjani's administration sought a total of $27 billion for a 5-year reconstruction plan. On May 27, in the largest international conference held in Iran since 1979, President Rafsanjani, addressing 250 Western, Asian and Arab oil officials, called for increased economic and political cooperation with the West and Gulf states. But the Bush administration would not relax the trade embargo on Iran or release the estimated $10 billion frozen in the U.S. since 1981 hostage crisis until 12 Western hostages held in Lebanon were released.

In May Rafsanjani stepped up a campaign to encourage educated Iranian professionals residing abroad to return and participate in Iran's economic reconstruction. Early in the month, the Iranian Minister of Finance and the governor of the Central Bank met with 400 Western-based Iranian businessmen, most of whom had been condemned *in abstentia* for being monarchists and dispossessed of all their property by the revolutionary regime. The government acknowledged its "unjust behavior" and urged the businessmen to repossess their properties and help reconstruct the nation. The government created a list of about 37,000 Iranians, many of them industrialists, free to travel in and out of Iran. Hardliners feared the return of Westernized, and therefore morally corrupt, Iranians.

Also in May, radical fundamentalists assailed the Rafsanjani administration when a member of Iran's National Security Council acknowledged the possibility of aligning with Washington "in a marriage of convenience" to pursue shared interests in the Gulf, such as stability and reliable oil markets. The official noted, however, that domestic political pressures precluded formal diplomatic ties with the U.S. In a May night raid on a Tehran University campus, police evicted fundamentalist students from their headquarters. Following the raid, about 400 students marched chanting "Death to American-style Islam." The students belonged to the Bureau for the Consolidation of Islamic Societies of

University Students, which has frequently opposed the president's policies. Earlier in the year, Rafsanjani encouraged the formation of a new, more moderate student group.

In addition, the Majlis (Iran's General Assembly) enacted an election law requiring at least two candidates to run for each vacancy, making it harder for Rafsanjani to bar the candidacies of radicals he would like removed. Earlier in the year, the regime prevented radicals from winning control of the Assembly of Experts (the body that elects the Revolutionary Leader's successor) by denying ballot applications, in many cases leaving only one candidate. In June, however, the Majlis re-elected its radical speaker Mehdi Karrubi by a wide margin—193 votes, verses 37 for a moderate candidate. The numbers suggested, however, that Karrubi was also supported by moderates, who view him as an important bridge between the president and radicals.

Throughout 1991, Iran sought to strengthen ties with its Arab neighbors, publicly insisting that its days of encouraging Islamic fundamentalism abroad were over. In March diplomatic ties were renewed with Saudi Arabia for the first time in four years. In June Egypt allowed the re-opening of its Iranian Embassy, which had been closed since 1987. Iran also participated in the international effort to reconstruct Kuwait. American fire fighters battling the Gulf emirate's blazing oil fields worked alongside Iranian experts, who in May won a $100 million contract to help put out the flames.

Despite these developments, Iran was somewhat unsuccessful in its attempts to be part of a regional security arrangement, which it had hoped would not include foreign powers. Arab states excluded Iran from negotiations of the "6 plus 2" countries (the six Gulf Cooperation Council states plus Syria and Egypt) on the peacekeeping arrangement. In September, Iran vehemently denounced Kuwait's signing of a bilateral pact with the United States, a move which also angered Egypt and Syria. Iran also rejected the creation of a U.S.-led rapid deployment force in Turkey.

In July a series of extrajudicial killings and assaults of opponents of the Iranian regime cast doubt upon Iran's newly moderate image. In Milan, the Italian translator of *The Satanic Verses*, by Salman Rushdie, was near-fatally stabbed. In Tokyo, the Japanese translator of Rushdie's book was stabbed to death. An Iranian dissident group later reported that the Iranian government had a squad of assassins stalking the author, on whom the late Ayatollah Khomeini had placed a death sentence for writing the *Satanic Verses*. In early August, Mr. Shapur Bakhtiar, the Shah's last prime minister and leader of a secular and liberal opposition group, was found with his throat slit at his Paris home. Bakhtiar's aid was also found stabbed to death. U.S. intelligence reported that Iran's mission to the U.N. in Geneva helped direct the attack.

In July the government cracked down on "bad *hejab*," or deviations from the Islamic dress code for women, in a reversal of a trend perceived just months earlier that the *hejab* rules had begun to loosen. Earlier in the year, enforcement of *hejab* was decidedly lax and "guidance" reportedly replaced whipping as the judgement handed down to women whose clothing failed to meet the standards of the regime. At the end of the month, a riot involving hundreds of people erupted in Isfahan, when authorities attempted to enforce the Islamic dress code on women. After stopping women in the city square, Komiteh police fired into the air and reportedly detained 300 people. In September the government's renewed efforts to enforce the dress code continued. The Tehran police shut down 12 offices, 224 beauty salons and 335 clothing shops for violations.

Social unrest and public protest, which began in late summer, reached unprecedented levels and continued through year's end. During the summer, hundreds of students at the

Open University in Teheran and Karaj held sit-ins over a doubling of tuition. On 7 July a protest reportedly escalated into a violent clash between students and police. Another riot erupted when Iranian security forces tried to raze a tenement neighborhood reportedly built without permits. As economic conditions deteriorated in August, demonstrations, bombings, arson attacks, and violent clashes between citizens and police posed a serious challenge to the Tehran Government. The incidents were unusual, given that most organized opposition groups went into exile ten years ago. The Iranian government continued to face threats by the People's Mujaheedin, an exiled opposition group and armed insurgency based on the Iran-Iraq border. Women comprise 30 percent of the Mujaheedin army.

In October radical elements led by militant MP Hojatoleslam Ali Akbar Montashemi and the Ayatollah Khameini vehemently rejected the U.S.-sponsored Middle East peace conference in Madrid. On October 19, Iran invited delegates from over 60 countries to its own conference to counter the one held in Madrid. Iran reportedly offered radical Palestinian organizations up to $2 million per month to openly oppose the direct negotiations between Israelis and Arabs. Though Rafsanjani criticized the Madrid conference and the Arab nations that attended, the president reportedly opposed the "anti-conference" in Tehran. The president promised to help the Palestinian cause "within the limits of Iran's resources." The Tehran conference drew angry reactions from the PLO.

Political Rights and Civil Liberties:

Iranians do not have the right to change their government democratically. Although there are elections for president, parliamentary deputies and the Assembly of Experts, a small group of Islamic clergymen and politicians wield effective control over the country. A stringent religious test and the absence of organized, legal opposition prevents voters from having a free choice.

The regime exercises strict control over the media. While the state tolerates some criticism of government mismanagement, it represses attacks on the regime, Islam, Islamic government and the mistreatment of minority groups. Independent journalists may be arrested and publications shut down for disseminating anti-regime information or views. The Ministry of Information scrutinizes and censors books before publication. Nine signers of a 1990 critical open letter to Rafsanjani were given prison sentences in 1991 after being held for 14 months.

In 1991 there were over 1,000 announced executions. Many political prisoners reportedly have been executed on false drug trafficking charges. Officially-sanctioned physical and psychological torture is common in prison. Arbitrary, indefinite, incommunicado detention is frequent and not prohibited by law. Extrajudicial executions also continue. In 1991, the Iranian government was implicated in a series of assaults and killings of political opponents residing abroad. Iran's court system is comprised of civilian and revolutionary courts. The latter try all political cases, and may override civilian court decisions. Iran's legal system is based on an extreme Shiite interpretation of Islamic law (*Sharia*).

The Khomiteh, the religious police apparatus, enforces religious discipline and has wide police powers. Strict Islamic dress code for women is still strictly enforced. Women not covered from head to foot with the *chador* may face prison sentences, whip lashings, fines or even death.

Non-Shiite religious groups face severe social and legal obstacles. International pressure forced Iran to stop executing members of the Baha'i faith. The government reluctantly tolerates other minority religions.

Freedom of association is circumscribed. Private, independent organizations are rare. The Islamic Union, the main trade union confederation is run by the Labor Ministry. Travel abroad is difficult because of a high exit tax. Politically suspect persons are unable to leave the country.

Iraq

Polity: One-party	**Political Rights:** 7
Economy: Statist	**Civil Liberties:** 7
Population: 17,100,000	**Status:** Not Free
PPP: $3,510	
Life Expectancy: 65.0	
Ethnic Groups: Arabs (75 percent), Kurds (15 percent), Turks and others	

Overview:
After Iraq's defeat in the Gulf War and its forced withdrawal from Kuwait on 26 February 1991, President Saddam Hussein faced mounting anti-government uprisings, a devastated infrastructure, international condemnation of Iraq's nuclear weapons program, and a continued international trade embargo. Hussein maintained ultimate control over the country by violently crushing Kurdish and Shiite uprisings and promoting a revisionist view of Iraq's Gulf War "victory" in the government-controlled media.

On 2 August 1990 Iraq invaded and declared the annexation of its tiny, oil-rich neighbor, Kuwait. Within days the U.N. Security Council condemned the invasion, ordered a total trade embargo of Iraq, and called for Iraq's unconditional withdrawal. By January 1991, Iraqi forces faced a U.N.-sanctioned military force in Saudi Arabia that included 500,000 American troops, the largest U.S. military deployment since the Vietnam War.

Hussein attempted to appeal to religious and pan-Arab aspirations by portraying the war over Kuwait a "symbol for the whole Arab nation" and tried to divert international attention from Iraq's occupation of Kuwait to Israel's occupation of Palestinian territory. But several Arabs nations joined the allied coalition condemning the Iraqi invasion. The U.N. Security Council declared a deadline of 15 January 1991 for Iraq's withdrawal from Kuwait. Diplomatic efforts to resolve the crisis before 15 January proved to be futile. On 9 January, in a six-hour meeting between U.S. Secretary of State James Baker and Iraqi Foreign Minister Tariq Aziz, Iraq refused to give any indication that it would withdraw from Kuwait in compliance with the 12 U.N. resolutions passed since the invasion. In an eleventh hour plea on 15 January, U.N. Secretary General Javier Perez de Cuellar pledged that if Hussein showed readiness to comply with the U.N. resolutions, Iraq would not be attacked, and "every effort would be made to address...the Arab-Israeli conflict, including the Palestinian question." In the days before the war, the international trade embargo against Iraq (dependent on imports for three-fourths of its food) caused long—sometimes over-night—bread lines and skyrocketing food prices.

On 17 January, the U.S.-led allied forces began a bombing campaign that targeted

Iraqi military installations and devastated much of the country's infrastructure. While Hussein took refuge in a luxurious, nuclear-proof underground bunker, Iraq's 4.5 million people either fled or hid in mosques, bomb shelters or basements, enduring drastic shortages of food and medicine.

On 18 January, Iraq fired scud missiles at Israel, apparently in an attempt to reassert linkage of the Kuwait crisis to the Israeli-Palestinian dispute. Iraq fired a total of 37 Scuds at Israel. On 22 January, Iraqi troops began setting fire to Kuwaiti oil refineries and oil fields. On January 21 and 22, Hussein released videotapes of ten captured allied pilots. The men appeared severely mistreated, in violation of the Geneva Convention provisions on prisoners of war. Iran denied the International Committee of the Red Cross access to the allied prisoners. On January 29 one of the allied prisoners, apparently used as a "human shield," died in an allied air raid on a government building.

Iraqi citizens reportedly rallied in support of Hussein during the first weeks of the war; thousands participated in pro-Hussein and anti-American demonstrations. But as the war progressed, reports suggested that Hussein's popular support plummeted. In February, a few cases of graffiti were found stating "Down with Hussein." Iraqi news did not portray the success of the allied forces and continually described Hussein as the liberator of "the Arab nation." Iraqi radio called Western leaders "war criminals" and said the allies were targeting civilian areas like houses, mosques and medicine warehouses. On 15 February Iraq's Revolutionary Command Council proposed a highly conditional acceptance of U.N. Security Council Resolution 660, which called for Iraqi withdrawal of Kuwait. The Iraqi conditions included the abrogation of all resolutions adopted after 660 (including those calling for war reparations), a withdrawal of all foreign forces and weaponry within one month of a cease-fire, and Israeli withdrawal from its occupied territories. President Bush called the offer a "cruel hoax," and urged Iraqi military leaders and the civilian population to "take matters into their own hands" and force Hussein from power. Iraqi citizens' jubilation at hearing the announcement of a possible end to the war was quickly dampened by the resumption of allied bombing.

On 23 February the U.S. began its full-scale ground offensive into Kuwait. Tens of thousands of hungry and demoralized soldiers, in some cases entire battalions, surrendered to allied forces in the first two days of the ground assault. On 26 February Hussein announced Iraq's withdrawal from Kuwait. Soldiers in Baghdad celebrated the end of the war by firing guns into the air. On 28 February President Bush ordered a cease-fire as allied troops solidified full control of Kuwait and some Iraqi territory. Iraq agreed to comply fully with all U.N. resolutions on Kuwait, but Hussein proclaimed victory. In a Baghdad radio address on 26 February he invoked the Koran and referred to the war as "an epic struggle between right and wrong." Hussein declared a victory for the Iraqis for fighting "thirty countries and all the evil and the largest machine of war and destruction in the world."

On 3 March cease-fire terms were set at a desert meeting between between Iraqi and allied commanders. The agreement included prompt release of POWs and Iraqi compliance with all U.N resolutions, including the acceptance of liability for war damages. Meanwhile, the U.N. Security Council pledged to exempt food and humanitarian aid from its trade embargo against Iraq.

On 1 March an Iraqi soldier returning from Kuwait fired on a portrait of Saddam Hussein in the port city of Basra, igniting an armed anti-government insurrection. Soldiers who refused to surrender their arms or join this Shiite revolt were reportedly shot. Government officials were dragged through the streets, burned and hanged. Over the next 10 days, the uprising spread across southern Iraq, reaching the suburbs of Baghdad. On 13 March massive street protests were reported in Baghdad. Meanwhile, a Kurdish insurrection raged in northern Iraq and, by 14 March, Kurdish rebels claimed control of wide areas of Iraqi Kurdistan.

On 11 March Iraqi opposition groups met in Beirut to formulate a credible alternative to Hussein's regime. Delegates included secular Kurdish resistance generals, radical Shiites, Communists, dissident Baathists, and representatives of smaller minorities. The opposition's plans included a coalition government to represent Iraq's various interests. Shiite groups, representing 55 percent of Iraq's population, pledged a commitment to democracy and affirmed that the uprising in southern Iraq was not a fundamentalist Shiite revolution. The Kurds, a non-Arab, Sunni Muslim people, have been fighting for autonomy since Iraq's creation in 1921. The 1991 crisis had its origins in the failure to implement a 1920 Treaty providing for an independent Kurdish state. During the Iran-Iraq war, Baghdad blasted Kurdish areas with chemical weapons, razed villages, and forced thousands to relocate.

In an all-out assault, forces loyal to Hussein swiftly quelled the uprising. Using tanks, heavy artillery, rockets and helicopter gunships, Hussein's military machine moved from city to city, killing an estimated 30,000 Iraqi civilians and bulldozing mass graves. By 4 April, Hussein's troops crushed the Shiite rebellion in southern Iraq and, within a few days, recaptured all of the main towns in Iraqi Kurdistan. Despite U.S. encouragement of the rebellion, the allied forces remaining in the Gulf took no action to prevent Hussein's deadly repression of the uprisings. During the war, U.S. President George Bush repeatedly said, "The Iraqi military and the Iraqi people should take matters into their own hands to force Saddam Hussein the dictator from power." This message was reinforced by Voice of America and U.S.-supported "Voice of Free Iraq" broadcasts to Iraq. But at the height of the insurrections, the Bush administration announced its refusal to "interfere with Iraq's internal affairs."

On 10 April Washington ordered Baghdad to stop all military operations north of the 36th parallel. But the Shiite and Kurdish rebellions had already been crushed. Two million refugees amassed on Iraq's borders with Turkey and Iran, driven from their homes by the genocidal backlash of Hussein's forces. Enduring sleet, hail, and zero temperatures, the refugees amassed in the mountains, without food, shelter or proper sanitation. Iran accepted over 1 million Iraqi refugees, but thousands more were left on the border. Turkey refused to take in the 700,000 refugees on its border. In mid-April, after mounting international pressure and 18 days after the mass exodus began, the U.S. sent 7,000 troops to join British, French and Dutch troops in securing and building refugee camps inside Iraq.

By June, most of the refugees had returned to the camps inside Iraq. On 7 June all humanitarian functions in the 3,600 square mile security zone were officially turned over to the U.N. High Commission on Refugees. Despite demonstrations and pleas by Kurdish leaders asking them to stay, on 12 July allied forces began withdrawing from northern Iraq, leaving only international relief workers and U.N. guards operating the camps. To deter further attacks on the Kurds, an eight nation rapid-deployment force of 2,500 troops was formed in southeastern Turkey.

In April, dialogue began between Hussein and Kurdish leaders Jalal Talabani of the Patriotic Union of Kurdistan (PUK) and Massoud Barzani of the Kurdish

Democratic Party (KDP). On April 24, Iraq announced that Hussein had agreed in principle to grant a measure of autonomy to the Kurds based on the implementation of a 1970 autonomy agreement. In June a draft autonomy accord between the Kurds and the Iraqi government included provisions for free elections. However, these promises never materialized.

Kurdish negotiations with Baghdad were accompanied by tensions in the Iraqi opposition coalition. Shiite leaders accused the Kurds of "selling out" to Hussein; Kurdish leaders insisted it was their only hope for establishing a safe zone for their people. In late October, tensions heightened between rival Kurdish groups. Massoud Barzani challenged Jalal Talabani to a referendum to let Kurds settle the question of how to achieve Kurdish goals. While Barzani advocated continued negotiations with Baghdad, Talabani was in favor of setting up a provisional government in Kurdistan and using northern Iraq as a base of attack against government forces. In the fall, Iraqi forces resumed their attacks on the Kurds north of the 36th parallel. In the last months of 1991, the government disrupted food and energy supplies to the Kurdish region.

Economic sanctions against Iraq had serious consequences. In July, Prince Sadruddin Aga Khan, the chief coordinator for the U.N.'s humanitarian efforts in Iraq, confirmed reports that Iraq was suffering from severe famine. Prince Sadruddin and his mission recommended that sanctions be eased enough to allow Iraq to import a minimum amount of food, drugs and equipment to get the water supply, sanitation and telecommunications systems back in working order. In November an 87-member international team of health experts, engineers and economists cited 900,000 malnourished children and over 100,000 at immediate risk of starvation.

After accepting the U.N. cease-fire resolution which required Iraq to provide the U.N. with detailed information about its nuclear program and allow for the destruction or removal of nuclear weapons, Iraq denied that it had a nuclear weapons program. On several occasions Iraq obstructed U.N. inspection teams, prompting the U.S. to threaten military action. The U.N. teams eventually seized thousands of documents on Iraq's nuclear program.

Political Rights and Civil Liberties:

Iraqis do not have the right to choose their government democratically. President-for-Life Saddam Hussein wields virtually absolute authority. He serves also as prime minister, head of the Baath Socialist Party and chief of the Revolutionary Command Council (RCC), a top executive body composed of the leaders of the Iraqi wing of the Arab Socialist Renaissance (Baath) Party. Head of state since 1979, Hussein has been effectively in power since a 1968 coup. Most high-level officials are related to Hussein or come from his village of Tikrit.

President Hussein and the RCC have never been elected. All 250 members of the unicameral National Assembly, a rubber stamp for RCC decisions, are either Baath candidates or pre-screened "independents." The government suppresses all forms of political opposition, and subjects political dissidents to deportation, arbitrary arrest, torture and execution. Torture is reportedly employed against children of political dissenters. After the Gulf War, Hussein's forces used heavy weaponry in a sweeping and bloody campaign to quell popular uprisings, killing thousands of civilians, and driving 2 million from their homes.

The government has violated several autonomy agreements with the Kurds. In

March 1988, the government launched poison gas attacks on Kurdish villages, killing over 5,000 Kurds and forcing 400,000 to relocate.

All Iraqi media are state owned and strictly controlled by the state. The Iraqi government controlled all news about the Gulf War and on 6 March expelled all Western correspondents from Baghdad. Members of Iraqi media are severely punished for even the slightest form of dissent.

Trials of ordinary cases are held in civil, criminal and religious courts and are normally open. In a move to promote a reformist image, the government abolished the Revolutionary Courts established by the RCC for specific incidents such as political crimes. The Revolutionary Court was exempt from all constitutional safe-guards of the rights of defendants.

Iraqis may hold public meetings only under the auspices of the Baath party. The government bans public sector unions. The Baath party controls all trade union activity through the General Federation of Iraqi Trade Unions. Freedom of religion is generally recognized and Iraqi citizens practice their faith but may not proselytize. More than 1,000 Egyptians who had been living in Iraq were reportedly murdered by the government during the Gulf War.

Ireland

Polity: Parliamentary democracy
Economy: Capitalist
Population: 3,500,000
PPP: $7,020
Life Expectancy: 74.6
Ethnic Groups: Irish (Celtic) majority, Anglo-Irish minority

Political Rights: 1
Civil Liberties: 1
Status: Free

Overview:

Major developments in Ireland in 1991 concerned several scandals linked to the government, failed talks with England on the future of Northern Ireland, the rise of small parties and independents in local elections and the poor economy and austerity measures.

Following centuries of British domination and occupation, twenty-six of Ireland's thirty-two counties won home rule within the British Commonwealth in 1921. In 1948 Ireland proclaimed itself a republic independent of the Commonwealth. The six counties of Northern Ireland have remained part of the United Kingdom, but the Irish constitution lays claim to sovereignty over Northern Ireland. Under the terms of the Anglo-Irish Accord of 1985, the Irish government has a consultative role in the administration of the North. The Unionist parties, which represent the Protestant majority in the North, oppose the Anglo-Irish Accord, because they fear that the mostly Catholic republic's involvement in the six counties could lead to Irish unifica-tion. In 1991 the Irish and British governments and Northern Ireland's major parties (except Sinn Fein) held preliminary "talks about talks" concerning the North's future. Some Dublin politicians proposed giving up the Irish constitutional claim to the North in exchange for a Protestant-Catholic power-sharing arrangement in the six northern counties. However, the Irish government never had the opportunity to make a formal proposal because the talks among the Northern parties broke down in July.

The head of government is Prime Minister Charles Haughey, the leader of the

Fianna Fail (Soldiers of Destiny) Party. When Haughey failed to secure a majority in the Dail (lower house of parliament) in the general election on 15 June 1989, he was forced to form a coalition with the small Progressive Democrats Party. The largest opposition groups are the Fine Gael (Family of the Gaels) and the Labour Party. Other parties include the Workers Party and the Greens. The Dail has 166 members elected by proportional representation for a maximum term of five years.

The largely ceremonial, popularly elected President of the Republic is head of state and appoints the prime minister from the party or coalition able to command a majority in the Dail. In 1990, Labour Party and Workers Party candidate Mary Robinson won the first contested presidential election in seventeen years. A former senator, Robinson supports women's rights and liberal social legislation. Her election has caused major party politicians to advocate changes in laws on lifestyle and morality issues such as divorce, birth control, and homosexuality. Future reform legislation is likely to trigger clashes with the Catholic hierarchy.

The upper house of parliament, the Senate, consists of sixty members, who serve the same term as the Dail. The prime minister fills eleven seats, universities name six senators, and occupational panels elect the remaining forty-three. The Senate is relatively powerless, but it can delay Dail legislation.

The two major parties lost ground in 1991 as Fianna Fail suffered major defeats in numerous municipal and county elections. Several small parties (Labour, the Greens, the Progressive Democrats, the Workers Party) and local independents (such as the anti-pothole Cavan Roads Action Group) gained significant ground. John Bruton, the leader of Fine Gael, the traditional number-two party, tried improving his party's image with a conference designed for televised entertainment. However, the plan flopped when Adele King (alias Twink, the comedienne) embarrassed the party with jokes in questionable taste.

In 1991 several scandals involving businessmen with ties to the government raised questions about the integrity of Prime Minister Haughey and his associates. The first scandal involved the Irish-based Goodman companies, which a television documentary charged with off-the-books dealings and fraudulent practices, including selling falsely labelled beef as complying with Islamic dietary laws to the Muslims. The companies' owner, Larry Goodman, is a major Fianna Fail contributor. Subsequently, another corrupt company, Greencore, assumed control of the Goodman assets. Greencore, the recently privatized firm known previously as Irish Sugar, was the subject of conflict-of-interest charges involving its chief executive. Other major scandals involved Dermot Desmond, wealthy broker, airport authority executive, and friend of Haughey. In one case, Desmond was allegedly involved in selling land at an inflated price to the state telephone firm. The prime minister also faced charges that his government had pressured local authorities to install a new sewer line in a neighborhood where he owns property. The media dubbed the scandal "Sewergate."

Despite the scandals, the Progressive Democrats renewed their coalition with Fianna Fail, and gave Haughey the votes to defeat a Fine Gael no-confidence motion in October 1991. Led by Finance Minister Albert Reynolds and Environment Minister Padraig Flynn, Haughey's opponents in his own party tried removing him, but he survived by a 55-22 vote in the parliamentary caucus. Haughey fired Reynolds and Flynn, and named a new cabinet, which included Jim McDaid as defense minister. After photographs surfaced which showed McDaid celebrating with a former IRA member, opposition parliamentarians attacked the nominee, and McDaid had to step down.

The Haughey government has instituted austerity measures to deal with Ireland's severe debt. In 1991 unemployment rose to 20 percent, and wages remained low. These factors have led more than 130,000 people (especially young workers and graduates) to emigrate since 1986. A dramatic drop in emigration during 1990-91 caused a rise in unemployment figures. In January 1991 the government reached a ten-year accord with civil servants, trade unions, and farmers. The agreement promised tax cuts and social welfare increases in return for wage restraint. However, by year's end civil service unions grew worried that the cabinet would renege on the deal and impose employment cutbacks in 1992. The government also began selling off controlling interests in several state companies.

In early 1991 the government decided to permit U.S. military aircraft to land and refuel in Ireland en route to the Persian Gulf. Supported by the Dail, this policy marked a break with traditional Irish neutrality in the view of the small left-wing parties. The Irish also debated whether the country's membership in an increasingly stronger European Community implied an Irish role in a common continental defense.

Political Rights and Civil Liberties: Irish voters can change their government democratically. In 1990 the Irish Labour Party proposed granting voting rights to Irish citizens who have emigrated in recent years, but the government defeated such legislation in the Dail in April 1991.

Due to occasional spillovers from the violence in Northern Ireland, the police have special powers to detain and question suspected terrorists. The Irish Republic and the United Kingdom have an extradition agreement which allows accused terrorists to be tried in Britain for crimes allegedly committed in the U.K.

Terrorist organizations, such as the Provisional IRA, are illegal, but Sinn Fein, the IRA's political wing, is legal. The press is generally free, but there is censorship on moral grounds, affecting pornography, for example. The state uses the anti-terrorism laws to exclude Sinn Fein representatives and members of paramilitary and "subversive" groups from the broadcast media. However, broadcast journalists may report Sinn Fein's views and quote from its publications. In 1991 the Dublin City Council voted to exclude a Sinn Fein convention from Mansion House, a municipal building. This measure was a protest gesture against the IRA bombing of a hospital in Northern Ireland. An autonomous public corporation operates television and radio outlets. Independent Century FM Radio had economic problems, and shut down in November 1991.

There is no legal divorce. Voters rejected it in a 1986 referendum. However, leading politicians expect the Dail to allow divorce within the next year. Ireland expanded the autonomy of the family in 1991 when it legalized the adoption of Romanians and other foreign children. However, restrictions remain on artificial methods of birth control. The authorities fined the Irish Family Planning Association for selling condoms at a record shop in Dublin, but the rock group U2 paid the fine for them. The European Court of Human Rights ruled in 1990 that Irish statutes outlawing homosexual acts were a denial of human rights. Reforming these laws is on the government's legislative agenda. The influence of the Roman Catholic Church remains strong, but freedom of religion is respected. There have been Protestant presidents and a Jewish mayor of Dublin.

Business is generally free, and free trade unions and farming groups are influential. The Irish government has taken steps toward pay equity between the sexes, including fines for wage disparities.

Israel

Polity: Parliamentary democracy
Economy: Mixed capitalist
Population: 4,622,000
PPP: $10,860
Life Expectancy: 75.9
Ethnic Groups: Jewish majority, Arab minority

Political Rights: 2
Civil Liberties: 2
Status: Free

Overview:

Iraqi scud missile attacks terrorized the Israeli population and pushed Israel to the brink of war in early 1991, but the American-led coalition's defeat of Iraq in the Persian Gulf War neutralized Israel's most heavily armed enemy. After the war, increased calls for a negotiated peace settlement between Israel and its Arab neighbors led to talks in Madrid and Washington. Meanwhile, disputes over loan guarantees to settle Soviet Jews led to a major rift with the Israel's closest ally, the United States.

Israel was formed in May 1948 out of less than one-fifth of the original British Mandate Palestine. Much of its short history has been marred by war with its Arab neighbors. Israel fought Egypt in 1956 and, in June 1967, went to war for six days after Egypt closed the Gulf of Aqaba to its ships, taking the Gaza Strip, West Bank, Golan Heights and East Jerusalem. After repulsing an Arab attack in 1973, Israel signed a peace treaty with Egypt in 1979, and returned the Sinai in 1982. In 1982, Israel invaded Lebanon to neutralize Palestine Liberation Organization guerrillas operating there.

A major development which will shape Israeli politics for decades has been the influx of Jews from the Soviet Union, which could reach 1 million by the mid-1990s. The economy has been strained by the introduction of these well-educated newcomers, many of whom have been placed into cramped housing and given menial jobs. In addition, in May over 14,000 Ethiopian Jews emigrated to Israel in a single day, adding to the over 20,000 already in the country. These new citizens are expected to push unemployment above the 1991 rate of 10 percent. The economy is also by slowed inefficient state enterprises, price controls covering one-quarter of all goods and 20 percent inflation.

The country faced the specter of war after Iraq attempted to draw Israel into the Gulf conflict and disrupt the American-led coalition by launching 39 Scud missile attacks on Israel beginning on 18 January 1991, mostly targeted towards the coastal cities of Tel Aviv and Haifa. The missiles caused several deaths, injuries and destroyed thousands of apartments. For weeks, schools were closed and the population repeatedly donned protective gas masks out of fear that Iraq might top the missiles with chemical warheads. Hard liners such as Defense Minister Moshe Arens warned that Israel would be forced to launch military strikes into western Iraq to eliminate the Scud launchers. To keep Israel out of the war and hold the coalition together, the United States sent anti-missile Patriot missile batteries, and later provided $650 million in emergency relief to cover the damages. Israel also received $670 million in German aid amidst reports that German firms had assisted in building Hussein's military and chemical warfare capabilities.

The apparent destruction of Saddam Hussein's army and the end of Soviet aid to the Arab states brought international and domestic calls for Israel to "trade land for peace." During the summer, the United States repeatedly warned that new housing settlements for Jews in the occupied territories would jeopardize U.S. guarantees for $10 billion in loans from commercial banks to house the newly arrived Jews from the Soviet Union. Prime Minister Yitzhak Shamir's government insisted the loan guarantees were needed for humanitarian purposes and should not be tied to other issues. Finance Minister Yitzhak Modai warned of huge tax increases and drastic cuts in social services if the country could not borrow the money. In September, U.S. President George Bush indicated he would veto any Israeli request for the loan guarantees prior to the start of peace negotiations for fear of the Arab states backing out of the conference. Veteran Israeli statesman Abba Eban called the loan dispute the worst U.S.-Israeli rift ever. In late September, Shamir said he doubted the U.S. could be an impartial mediator at the peace conference, and suggested it might be time for his country to look for new supporters.

With plans for a conference being set, hard-line Housing Minister Ariel Sharon called for Shamir's resignation on 19 October, saying the prime minister had "led Israel on a mistaken path and continues to anesthetize the public against the truly terrible dangers Israel faces." Despite Sharon's warning and the lingering issue of the loan guarantees, on 21 October the Israeli cabinet voted 17-3 in favor of Israel participating in a peace conference. Thousands demonstrated in Tel Aviv in favor of Israel's participation. The historic conference opened on 30 October in Madrid with the presence of both President Bush and Soviet leader Mikhail Gorbachev, along with delegations from Israel, Syria and Lebanon and a joint Jordanian-Palestinian team. Shamir led Israel's delegation and assured the right-wing members of his coalition that he would not make any territorial concessions. On 9 December, the groups met for inconclusive talks in Washington D.C., where they largely haggled over the Palestinian insistence they be treated as a separate delegation, and on 22 December, the groups agreed to meet again in early 1992. In an effort to stimulate the peace process, the United Nations repealed the 1975 "Zionism Equals Racism" resolution.

Among the contested issues is the presence of Israeli troops in southern Lebanon. The government says they are necessary to prevent Arab attacks on Jewish citizens in northern Israel and the occupied territories, and refuses to withdraw its troops until the Syrian army fully withdraws from Lebanon. In July, three Israeli soldiers in Lebanon were killed in a gun battle with Hezbollah guerillas. The army is also seeking either the return or remains of seven soldiers captured by Arab guerillas. In September Israel released 51 Lebanese army soldiers after receiving evidence that one of the seven had died.

The peace process had significant ramifications for Israel's domestic political affairs. The 120-member Knesset is elected via proportional representation from national party lists. The 1 percent cutoff for a seat allows small parties to play a critical role in shaping governing coalitions. Currently, Likud holds 41 seats and Labor 39, while thirteen parties hold six seats or fewer. Smaller parties often hold extremist views. On 3 February, the government voted to include the far-right Moledet Party in the ruling coalition despite the opposition of senior ministers who called the party's demand for the expulsion of all Arabs from the occupied territories racist. Shamir said he disagreed with Moledet's Arab plan but needed the party in his coalition. After some hesitation, the right-wing Tehiya party ultimately remained in the coalition after threatening to pull out if Shamir went ahead with the peace talks. Although right-wing parties often blend religious and political viewpoints, the two major parties are secular and differ primarily over the Palestinian situation. Likud has offered elections in the West Bank and the Gaza Strip as a first step to greater Palestinian autonomy, but refuses to relinquish ultimate Israeli control over the West Bank for reasons of both national security and religious ideology. Likud has also urged stronger measures to quell the *intifada*, an uprising by Palestinians in the West Bank begun in 1987. Labor has been split by internal disagreements over whether Israel should support the formation of a Palestinian state. In November, the party voted to support Palestinian "national rights" but stopped short of calling for self-determination. Parliamentary elections will be held by November 1992.

Political Rights and Civil Liberties:

Israeli citizens can change their government democratically. Arabs have the right to vote, and minor parties representing Arabs as well as extremist Jewish views are represented in parliament. However, the right-wing Kach party has been banned from parliament for what the High Court considered racist views. The judiciary is independent of the government. In July, an extensive ninth-month investigation into the October 1990 Temple Mount incident, which left 17 Arabs dead, concluded that the police had initially provoked the violence. No disciplinary action against the police has been taken. The Israeli security service (Shin Bet) has been accused of practicing psychological and physical torture on Arabs and Arab sympathizers.

The country's press features over 600 publications printed in several languages, many of which are critical of government policies. However, publications deemed to be dealing with security matters must be cleared by a military censor. It is illegal to display Palestinian flags or express open support for the Palestine Liberation Organization (PLO). Television and radio are government owned but have independent editorial boards. There is freedom of association, although contacts with outlawed groups are illegal. In separate incidents in 1991, peace activists Abie Nathan and David Ish-Shalom were given jail sentences of 15 and 9 months respectively for meeting with members of the PLO.

There is full freedom of religion in this predominantly Jewish state. Recognized religious communities have authority over their members in matters such as marriage and conversion, and the government does little to promote religion. Religious Jews often sharply disagree with government policies in this largely secular society. However, Orthodox Jews do retain significant influence in politics because the support of small religious parties is often critical to holding governing coalitions together. There is freedom to travel both domestically and abroad, although certain domestic areas may be off-limits for security reasons. An equal opportunity law requires employers to pay women equal wages for equal work. Most Arab citizens are not subject to the military draft and thus often are disadvantaged when seeking subsidies and jobs for which veterans receive preferences. Some 80 percent of workers belong to unions under Histadrut (General Federation of Labor), which provides social insurance benefits and collective bargaining arrangements. Non-resident workers, who are predominantly Palestinian, cannot join Histadrut but are entitled to representation.

Italy

Polity: Parliamentary democracy
Economy: Capitalist-statist
Population: 57,700,000
PPP: $13,000
Life Expectancy: 76.0
Ethnic Groups: Italian (Latin), various immigrant groups, and a small Austro-German minority

Political Rights: 1
Civil Liberties: 1
Status: Free

Overview:

Major developments in 1991 included debates over constitutional reform, a huge influx of Albanian refugees, the collapse of the forty-ninth postwar government and the formation of the fiftieth.

Modern Italian history dates from the nineteenth-century movement for national unification. Most of Italy had merged into one kingdom by 1870. Italy began World War I on the side of Germany and Austria-Hungary, but switched to the Allied side. As a consequence, Italy won territory that had belonged to Austria. The country lived under the fascist dictatorship of Benito Mussolini from 1922 to 1943 and was allied with Germany once again during World War II. A referendum in 1946 ended the monarchy of the House of Savoy, banished the royal family and established a republican form of government.

Since the abolition of the monarchy, the head of state has been a largely ceremonial president elected for a seven-year term by an assembly of members of Parliament and delegates from the Regional Councils. The president chooses the prime minister, who is often, but not always, a member of the largest party in the Chamber of Deputies, the lower house of Parliament. Members of the 630-member Chamber are elected directly by proportional representation for terms of up to five years. There are 315 senators elected regionally for five-year terms. The president can appoint five senators for life and becomes one himself upon leaving office. In 1991, President Francesco Cossiga, a Christian Democrat, pleaded for major constitutional reform under which government would be more decisive and less the captive of narrow, partisan interests. Many public and private sector institutions allocate jobs on the basis of a party quota system.

Most prime ministers since World War II have been Christian Democrats, and have headed multi-party governments of short duration. Although cabinets come and go frequently, many of the same Christian Democrats and their coalition partners are back in government repeatedly. For example, six-time Prime Minister Giulio Andreotti has held senior cabinet posts in twenty-nine of Italy's fifty postwar governments. The forty-ninth postwar government, which broke up in March 1991, included the Christian Democrats, the Socialists, the Social Democrats, the Liberals, and the Republicans. That cabinet fell apart when the Socialists demanded the creation of a strong presidency and a new electoral system to weaken the smaller parties. The same parties from the previous government formed the fiftieth postwar cabinet, and agreed to take up major reforms after the 1992 parliamentary election. Within days of joining the new government, the Republicans walked out in a disagreement over cabinet posts.

Until 1990, the largest opposition group was the Communist party. At a party congress in 1990, Communist leader Achille Occhetto proposed that the party adopt a new name, symbol, and philosophy. He argued that the Communists had to break with the past, and become a broader party of the left, possibly as an affiliate of the Socialist International. Occhetto had a tough struggle with party traditionalists, and won a pro-NATO resolution by a tiny majority. At a follow-up congress in 1991, the party adopted a new name, Party of the Democratic Left and a tree symbol. Hard-line traditionalists left the party and started the Communist Refoundation Party. Anticipating the Communists' name change, the Socialist Party became the Socialist Unity Party, in order to suggest that it is the party to unify the left.

Italian voters endorsed electoral reform in a referendum in June 1991. This measure cut the number of ranked preferences for candidates voters could make on party slates from four to one. Critics had charged the old system was subject to party manipulation and fraud, especially in the southern regions. Voters used to indicate their preferences by writing a number by a candidate's name on the ballot paper. In some cases, vote fraud changed a preference for candidate "3" to candidate "8." Under the new system, voters must write out the name of their choice.

The party system has been fragmenting along regional lines in recent years. In the North in 1991, five regionalist parties formed a bloc under the leadership of the Lombardy League, which is hostile to the economically backward South.

The problems of neighboring Albania and Yugoslavia visited Italy in 1991. Thousands of Albanian refugees came to Italy by ship, seeking relief from the collapsing economy and political instability of their homeland. Italy sent most of the Albanians back, but also sent food aid to Albania. Many refugees got involved in violent confrontations with police who attempted to deport them. Italians expressed concern about the Italian minority in Yugoslavia, which underwent civil war in 1991. There was tension and a decline in cross-border trade in the city of Trieste, which borders Yugoslavia. Many Italians were outraged when their government suggested that it would allow Yugoslav federal troops to retreat through Italy. The government changed its position and such a retreat never took place.

Political Rights and Civil Liberties:

Italians have the right to change their government democratically. However, Italy often gets a new cabinet between elections as a result of the shifting pattern of political deals rather than as a consequence of changing public opinion. Elections at the national, regional, and local levels are competitive. There is some friction between the Italians and the Austro-German minority in the northern area of Alto Adige, which was part of the Austro-Hungarian Empire until World War I. Some of the German-speakers demonstrated for independence in 1991.

The media are generally free and independent, but there are some minor restrictions on the press in the areas of obscenity and defamation. Broadcasting is a mixture of public and private companies. There was controversy in 1991 when RAI, the state broadcasting corporation, refused to broadcast an interview with Iraqi President Saddam Hussein. Freedom of assembly is respected. The Italian court system is notoriously slow, but the government instituted trial reform in 1989 with the hope of getting speedier justice.

Freedom of association is respected. There are competing labor federations with differing ideological orientations. In 1991, the left-wing General Confederation of Italian Labor (CGIL) broke its ties with the former Communists. After several episodes of friction between Italians and foreign workers in 1989, pressure to control immigration has grown. There is freedom of religion. Although the Catholic Church is still the dominant one, it is no longer the state church. Organized crime and corruption remain threats to free political expression and other liberties, especially in the South and in Sicily. On 1 March 1991 the cabinet closed a loophole in criminal law, thereby causing several recently released Mafia lead-ers to be re-arrested. Lawyers in Palermo protested this decision with a one-day strike. About 17,000 public officials are under investigation for corruption and Mafia ties.

Ivory Coast

Polity: Dominant Party
Economy: Capitalist
Population: 12,500,000
PPP: $1,430
Life Expectancy: 53.4
Ethnic Groups: Baule, (23 percent), Bete (18 percent), Senufo (15 percent), Malinke (11 percent), over 60 tribes

Political Rights: 6
Civil Liberties: 4
Status: Partly Free

Overview:

In its treatment of new opposition parties and suppression of public demonstrations in 1991, the Ivory Coast government continued to cast doubt on its expressed willingness to convert to a democratic multi-party system.

A former French colony, Ivory Coast has been ruled by President Félix Houphouët-Boigny since its independence in 1959. Houphouët-Boigny was also one of the founders of the African Democratic Rally (RDA), an international political party, and currently leads its Ivoirian branch, the Democratic Party of the Ivory Coast (PDCI).

In response to large-scale anti-government demonstrations in early 1990, President Houphouët-Boigny authorized the creation of opposition parties. He also had the National Assembly create the post of prime minister to which he appointed Alassane Dramane Ouattara. Ouattara, who was the former head of the Central Bank of the West African States, immediately reduced the government from twenty-nine to twenty ministries, replacing several aging Houphouët-Boigny loyalists with new technocrats. He also began the painful task of compliance with the IMF structural adjustment program, a function which is certainly going to test his popularity with the people. In November, Ouattara created a Ministry of Industry and Commerce to create new economic reform policies.

One of the first of more than 25 new parties to register in 1990 was the Ivoirian Popular Front (FPI) led by Laurent Gbagbo, one of Houphouët-Boigny's most outspoken critics. On 25 October, Gbagbo ran against President Houphouët-Boigny in the first multi-party election since independence. Gbagbo officially received only 20 percent of the vote, but the elections were marred by widespread electoral fraud by supporters of the victorious Houphouët-Boigny. Although the government admitted that the elections were "poorly organized", there were no large protests amid charges that the government had rigged the election.

In late April the FPI decided to hold a "liberty week" rally on 1 May, to celebrate the party's first anniversary. Although other political parties roundly objected to the celebration—because the citizens of the country were still not free—thousands of people attended, with surprisingly no interference from the military. The split in the opposition widened further over the issue of a national conference. While most opposition parties have put a national conference on their platforms, the FPI, while not being totally opposed to the idea, has declined to make it its principle goal. The ruling PDCI has refused even to consider the notion, fearing that a national conference could turn into a public trial of the current regime, as it has in several other African countries.

On 15 May, when the Student and Scholar Federation of the Ivory Coast (FESCI) tried to hold a press conference, *loubards,* or government-employed vigilantes, entered the conference room and beat up the students. On the following day, the university teachers' union meeting on the Cocody campus to address the incident was blocked for "security reasons." The union responded with a two-day strike. On 17 May the students were meeting at a stadium when government troops turned out the lights, stormed the structure, beat up the students, and raped some of the women. According to the Ivoirian League of Human Rights (LIDHO), nineteen students were sent to the hospital with injuries. Newspapers published the names of five students who have been missing. The action was roundly condemned by all political parties. A demonstration on 5 June organized by the LIDHO to protest against the 17 May incident was broken up by security forces. On 17 June a mob of students killed a fellow student, accusing him of being a *loubard.* Following the incident, the government dissolved the FESCI, and arrested eleven students for the lynching. In response, the teachers union declared a strike. Although the government ordered the teachers back to work, 80 percent of the union remained on strike. In August, amid rumors of a pending coup d'état, an unknown number of military officers were arrested. Two officers reportedly died during interrogation. In October President Houphouët-Boigny declared an amnesty which freed 5,000 detainees.

Despite Prime Minister Ouatarra's efforts to revive the economy, farmers' income has fallen by as much as 75 percent in the last two years. Out of 575,000 children born each year, only 80,000 reach the age of five. Only 19 percent of the population has access to fresh water and 70 percent have no access to health services. Currently, the interest due on the public debt is equal to the entire annual revenue of the state. But Ouatarra has reduced government expenditures by 25 percent by trimming the excess civil servants off the payroll, privatizing the water and electricity companies and cutting customs duties. Ouatarra's reform efforts have won Ivory Coast $113 million in credits from the International Monetary Fund, two World Bank loans and a $23 million aid package from the U.S.

Political Rights and Civil Liberties: In 1990 Ivory Coast held its first multi-party presidential elections, but they were widely believed to be rigged by the government.

Radio and television are controlled by the government, but with the authorization of opposition parties, private newspapers have been allowed to circulate. However, the government has set up a commission "for the transparency and the pluralism of the press," a group with the power to make unannounced visits to press enterprises and impose random fines. No press can benefit from foreign capital. The official media does not criticize the government. The government expelled the regional director of the AFP for having reported negatively on the 17 May attack by the army on the students. Jacques Kacou, editor of the independent weekly *Liberté*, was sentenced to three months in prison and required to pay a fine for "insulting" the president in an article entitled "Beware, Houphouët has lost his senses."

Although freedom of assembly is guaranteed in the constitution, in 1991 peaceful demonstrations were broken up by police or army units on several occasions. Freedom of religion is respected. Freedom of movement is also generally respected, although there are still reports of citizens being harassed at roadblocks. The nominally independent judicial system is generally fair in ordinary criminal cases, but justices generally follow the lead of the government in cases involving national security. In rural areas, justice is still administered at the village level through the traditional forum of debate.

Workers have the right to organize, but almost all union activity takes place within the government-sponsored General Union of Ivory Coast Workers (UGTCI). The university teachers' union is one of the only independent unions. Although the constitution guarantees the right to strike, the UGTCI rarely gives permission to do so.

Jamaica

Polity: Parliamentary democracy
Economy: Capitalist
Population: 2,500,000
PPP: $2,630
Life Expectancy: 73.1
Ethnic Groups: Black majority; mixed race, European and Asian minorities

Political Rights: 2
Civil Liberties: 2
Status: Free

Overview:

The health of Prime Minister Michael Manley of the ruling People's National Party (PNP) continued to deteriorate in 1991, sparking rumors of a possible snap election by year's end. Opinion polls conducted in the fall showed the opposition Jamaica Labour Party (JLP), led by former prime minister Edward Seaga, with a slight edge.

Jamaica, a member of the British Commonwealth, achieved independence in 1962. It is a parliamentary democracy, with the British monarchy represented by a governor-general. The bicameral parliament consists of a sixty-member House of Representatives elected for five years, and a twenty-one-member Senate, with thirteen senators appointed by the prime minister and the remaining eight by the leader of the parliamentary opposition. Executive authority is invested in the prime minister, who is the leader of the political party commanding a majority in the House. Since independence, power has alternated between the social democratic PNP and the conservative JLP. Manley was prime minister from 1972 to 1980. Seaga held the post from 1980 until February 1989 when the JLP was defeated by the PNP in general elections.

The 1989 election campaign was marked by a significant reduction in political violence, owing in large part to an Agreement and Declaration on Political Conduct signed by Seaga and Manley, and supported by civic and religious organizations. More than 750 people died in election-related violence in 1980; 13 died in 1989. Overseen by an independent electoral commission, and with security provided by the police and military, voting proceeded for the most part in orderly fashion. With 57 percent of the popular vote, the PNP won forty-four seats in the House; the JLP took the remaining sixteen.

In local elections held in March 1990, the PNP won all but one of the twelve disputed municipal councils. Only about half of the electorate turned out to vote. The PNP vowed to restore meaningful functions to local governments, which have weakened over the last decade. Meanwhile, the JLP's heavy defeat led to a severe rift between JLP leader Seaga and five top party officials who threatened to break away to form a new party.

To general surprise, the Manley government has kept to the economic program initiated by the JLP deregulation, spending cuts, tax reform, tariff reduction and privatization of state-owned enterprises. But falling income and continuing unemployment problems caused a decline in the the PNP's popularity in 1991, and chronic medical problems appear to have deprived Manley of his old fire. If Manley decided to step down or call snap elections, his most likely successor would be his deputy prime minister, P.J. Patterson. Although opinion polls showed that the JLP had recovered ground since its 1989 election loss, Seaga was still preoccupied with trying to restore unity within the JLP and seemed unenthusiastic about the prospect of an early election. Constitutionally, the next national elections are not due until 1994.

Political Rights and Civil Liberties:

Citizens are able to change their government democratically. Constitutional guarantees regarding the right to free expression, freedom of religion and the right to organize political parties, civic organizations, and labor unions are generally respected. While the JLP and PNP dominate the political scene, there are a number of small parties ranging from radical left to radical right. Labor unions are politically influential and have the right to strike.

Newspapers are independent and free of censorship and government control. Broadcast media are largely public but open to pluralistic points of view. For over a decade, public opinion polls have been an integral part of the political process. There is one television station which is state owned. However, in September 1990, the government announced it would grant two new broadcast licenses—one for a commercially operated television station and another for an island-wide radio station.

An independent judicial system is headed by a Supreme Court and includes several magistrate's courts and a Court of Appeals, with final recourse to the Judicial Committee of the Privy Council in London. However, the legal system is slow and inefficient in responding to charges of police brutality and severe prison conditions. There is a mounting backlog of cases due to an increase in violent crime, a shortage of court staff at all levels of the system, and a general lack of resources. The Jamaica Council for Human Rights, the country's main human rights organization, reports that allegations of police brutality, including apparent cases of extra-judicial executions, have been on the increase since 1989. Some cases have been successfully prosecuted, with victims receiving court-ordered monetary reparations, but officers guilty of abuses go without punishment and many cases remained unresolved.

In response to a resurgence of gang violence (mostly drug related but with political overtones), the government re-introduced the controversial Suppression of Crime Act in August 1990. The act, first introduced in 1974 but phased out by the Manley government in 1989, gives the security forces sweeping powers of search and arrest. The reinstatement of the anti-crime act was criticized by the Human Rights Council and legal groups who claim it is unconstitutional.

Japan

Polity: Parliamentary democracy
Economy: Capitalist
Population: 123,800,000
PPP: $13,650
Life Expectancy: 78.6
Ethnic Groups: Japanese, Korean, and small immigrant groups

Political Rights: 1
Civil Liberties: 2
Status: Free

Overview:

Huge financial scandals and a failed electoral reform package were the leading developments in Japan in 1991. Meanwhile, Kiichi Miyazawa's replacement of Toshiki Kaifu as prime minister signified a full political rehabilitation for leaders implicated in past scandals.

Modern Japan was established as a constitutional monarchy in 1947, two years after its defeat in World War II. Although the nominal leader is Emperor Tsugunomiya Akihito, Japan is a multi-party parliamentary democracy. The ruling Liberal Democratic Party (LDP) has controlled the lower house of parliament and the prime ministership since 1955 and dominated postwar Japanese politics. The party is split into five factions, which are driven more by influence and patronage than ideology. Party bosses named the obscure Toshiki Kaifu prime minister in August 1989 in the wake of the Recruit shares-for-favors scandal which brought down then prime minster Noburo Takeshita and numerous other top politicians. Takeshita's successor, Sosuke Uno, lasted a mere fifty-three days before being implicated in a sex scandal. The bosses expected Kaifu, dubbed "Mr. Clean," to be a caretaker until temporarily disgraced politicians such as Miyazawa could be re-elected to parliament.

Kaifu's popularity grew in 1991 after more politicians became linked to new scandals, leading to speculation he might be able to win a second term. Currently, Japan's bicameral parliament, or *Diet*, consists of a directly elected House of Repre-sentatives, whose 512 members are chosen from 130 electoral districts for 4-year terms, and a 225-seat upper House of Councillors. The LDP has a solid 280 seat majority in the lower house, but lost its control of the upper house in the July 1989 elections when it won only 110 seats.

Prime Minister Kaifu pegged his political future to the issue of electoral reform. The high cost of contesting elections in multiple-seat districts is said to foster corruption. Kaifu proposed replacing 130 multiple-seat districts with 300 single-seat districts, 171 of which would be elected through proportional representation. The opposition favors the multiple-seat districts, since they can win seats by coming in third or fourth in a district. The LDP leadership also opposed the changes because their party would lose seats if the parliament shrunk to 471 members. Kaifu had also wanted to change the way the districts are drawn. The Supreme Court has declared the current system unconstitutional since some rural districts have less than a quarter the population of urban ones, but are represented by the same number of MPs.

The prime minister's re-election bid came to a halt on 30 September when a parliamentary committee scrapped his electoral reform bill, and decided not to roll it over to the next session. That evening, Kaifu told reporters he would "strive to the best of my ability in a last ditch stand for reform", interpreted by many as a threat to dissolve the parliament. His critics attacked him both for making the threat and lacking the courage to carry it out. His second threat to dissolve the parliament, on 4 October, caused the Takeshita faction to withdraw its support for him. At the time, polls showed over 56 percent of the Japanese supported Kaifu. In his place, the LDP elected 72-year old Kiichi Miyazawa as party president.

Kaifu's clean reputation had added to his popularity as a wave of financial scandals hit Japan in 1991. The most notorious involved the revelation in June that the Big Four securities firms, including Nomura, the world's largest, had compensated top clients over $1 billion for losses suffered in stock crashes of 1988 and 1990. Up to twenty small and medium-size firms had compensated clients an additional $150 million. Although such payments are technically legal if the clients are not guaranteed compensation beforehand, the magnitude of the dealings angered the public and fueled speculation that politicians may have been among those compensated. However, in December Miyazawa's failure to push a bill through parliament authorizing the Japanese Self-Defense Force to participate in U.N. peacekeeping missions, and continuing questions about his role in the Recruit scandal, raised doubt as to whether he would last to serve out his two-year term. Nomura also allegedly manipulated the price of stock in a company after selling shares in it to an underworld figure, and employees at several banks were accused of using fake deposit certificates to arrange several billion dollars worth of loans.

Taking a cue from party elders, Kaifu refused to call for an independent commission to regulate the securities industry. Finance Minister Ryutaro Hashimoto, whose ministry nominally monitors the securities industry, came under increased pressure to resign after he admitted that three close friends had received $2 billion worth of fraudulent loans arranged by a top aide. With public outrage at a peak, the tiny, fanatical right-wing Shokonjuko group took matters into their own hands. For weeks in July, they verbally harassed Big Four firms by driving vans equipped with mobile loudspeakers past their offices. They then rammed a van through the window of a Nomura office and attacked two employees, and in August held a Nomura official hostage for over an hour and fired a bullet into an electronic stock-ticker board. On September 27, parliament approved a bill outlawing loss compensation. Hashimoto finally offered to resign in early October, but remained in the cabinet several weeks longer to attend the World Bank meetings in Bangkok.

Meanwhile, several smaller scandals competed for attention. In July, reports surfaced that Japan Aviation Electronics Ltd. had secretly funnelled military parts to Iran via Singapore. The same month, the chairman of the Japan Broadcasting Corporation (NHK) resigned after lying to parliament about his whereabouts the day a rocket carrying an NHK satellite exploded. In separate incidents, two top politicians, factional leader Hiroshi Mitsuzuka, and Shintaro Ishihara, the co-author of "The Japan That Can Say No", admitted taking contributions from fraudulent businessmen.

The LDP's largest opposition failed to capitalize on the public's anger over the scandals. The Social Democratic Party of Japan (SDPJ) —which added the word "Democratic" to the English version of its name while keeping the Japanese version "Japanese Socialist Party"—holds 73 seats in the upper house. Takako Doi resigned as party head after the party's weak showing in the April local elections. Voters have been intimidated by the overtly Marxist tone of some of the party's public statements, and were turned off by its extreme pacifist position. Makoto Tanabe, who promised to modify some of the party's more extreme views, took over for Miss Doi in July.

Overseas events played a large role in the domestic political maneuvers. Critics pounded Kaifu for his waffling over support for the allied forces in the Persian Gulf. Nearly all Japanese agree that Article Nine of the constitution, which renounces war and prohibits the country from maintaining military forces, prevented the country from sending combat troops to the region. But some MPs claimed the clause prohibited Japan from assuming any role in the Persian Gulf conflict, including sending non-military aid, while others said Japan would be shirking its responsibility as a leading economic power by failing to provide any assistance.

Shortly after Iraq invaded Kuwait, Japan approved $4 billion in aid for the allied effort, but under pressure from opposition parties, it shelved a plan to send 2,000 non-combat troops to the Gulf. In late January 1991, the LDP won approval of an additional $9 billion in non-military aid to the region. Two months after the fighting ended, Japan sent a naval unit of minesweepers to clear shipping lanes for Japanese oil tankers in the Persian Gulf, the first overseas assignment for Japanese forces since World War II.

Japan's reluctance to contribute to the war effort, and its refusal to open its markets to rice imports, threatened its relations with the United States, but in 1991 Japan agreed to provide U.S. businesses greater opportunity to bid for public works programs and to end large-scale drift net fishing. Kaifu met with U.S. President George Bush five times to discuss issues which had led to "Japan-bashing" by Americans. A CIA-funded report describing Japan as an "amoral, manipulative culture" and the publicity surrounding the fiftieth anniversary of the bombing of Pearl Harbor added to American anxiety. The negative sentiments flowed both ways—a June 1991 survey showed that 24 percent of Japanese consider the United States to be the top threat to their nation.

Japan has also engaged in a futile attempt with the Soviet Union to get control over the southern Kurile Islands, which it claims were illegally seized at the end of World War II. The islands were the main topic of discussion during Soviet leader Mikhail Gorbachev's visit to Tokyo on 16-19 April. Prior to the talks, there had been reports of exorbitant sums which the Japanese were prepared to pay for the islands— figures up to $30 billion had been mentioned—but in the end only minor agreements were signed on unrelated issues. Japanese hopes were boosted by the aborted Soviet coup in August and by the Russian republic's need for hard currency. Top aides to Russian leader Boris Yeltsin agreed in September to accelerate talks on the islands. Kaifu also visited China in August amidst speculation that Japan would trade foreign aid for support for a seat on the U.N. Security Council.

Political Rights and Civil Liberties: The Japanese can change their government democratically. Although the Liberal Democratic Party (LDP) has controlled parliament for most of the postwar period, elections are free and several opposition parties exist. However, the LDP reportedly pays off opposition MPs in return for crucial votes. During a February 1991 debate, an LDP member chastised an opposition MP for challenging the ruling party, considering he receives $3,800 "as many as twenty times a year."

In January 1991 the government formally agreed to end the practice of finger-printing the country's 680,000-strong Korean minority. However, Koreans are not automatically granted citizenship at birth, and must submit to an official investigation of their backgrounds and adopt Japanese names if they wish to become citizens. Both the Koreans and the Burakumin community, who are descendants of a feudal-era untouchable class, are discriminated against in housing and employment opportunities. Foreigners of Japanese descent also claim discrimination in jobs and services.

The judiciary is independent of the government, and strong procedural safeguards exist for the accused. Freedom of speech and association are guaranteed by the constitution and respected in practice. There is complete freedom of religion; Buddhism and Shintoism have the most adherents. Japanese citizens have the right to travel domestically and abroad. Concern over the country's declining birthrate prompted a government program which will pay subsidies to families for each pre-school child and expand child-care programs. The constitution guarantees the right for workers to bargain collectively, and approximately one-quarter of the work force is unionized. A shortage of skilled labor has brought up to 300,000 illegal aliens into the country, and some foreign women imported for menial work have been unwittingly caught in brides-for-sale swindles.

Jordan

Polity: Monarch and limited parliament
Economy: Capitalist
Population: 3,400,000
PPP: $2,570
Life Expectancy: 66.9
Ethnic Groups: Palestinian and Bedouin Arabs, small minorities of Circassians, Armenians, and Kurds

Political Rights: 4
Civil Liberties: 4
Status: Partly Free

Overview:

In 1991 the Persian Gulf War shook the tiny Hashemite Kingdom of Jordan, ruled by King Hussein since 1953. In the postwar period, Jordan played a major role in the Arab-Israeli peace conference. In the face of rising tensions among political groups over negotiations with Israel, and economic decline exacerbated by the influx of refugees from Iraq and Kuwait, King Hussein continued to pursue democratization.

When Iraq invaded Kuwait on 2 August 1990, King Hussein tried to maintain a position of neutrality by both condemning the invasion and assailing the military troop presence in Saudi Arabia. Attempting to retain his long-time alliance with the U.S., King Hussein agreed to abide by the international embargo against Iraq, but he maintained ties with Iraqi President Saddam Hussein and allowed some goods to flow to Iraq through Jordan.

Up until the eve of the U.N.-sanctioned 15 January deadline for Iraqi withdrawal from Kuwait, King Hussein met with several Arab and Western leaders in an unsuccessful attempt to bring about a peaceful solution to the crisis. King Hussein became increasingly embittered by what he called the embargo on dialogue by the U.S. and advocated the linkage of the Iraqi invasion of Kuwait and the Israeli occupation of Palestinian territory. On 10 February, three weeks after the start of the allied bombardment of Iraq, the king made a televised speech calling for a cease-fire. The king sharply attacked the U.S.-led coalition of forces, accusing them of seeking to destroy Iraq and put the entire area under foreign hegemony. The strongly worded speech, swiftly condemned in Washington and Tel Aviv, amounted to a cutting of the decades-long ties with the U.S.

In Jordan thousands of Palestinians and members of the Muslim Brotherhood marched in support of Iraq. Both the Lower House of Parliament, in which the Muslim Brotherhood forms the largest bloc, and the Senate, urged support for Iraq.

The Persian Gulf war had far-reaching effects for Jordan, which had to deal with a continued influx of refugees long after the 28 February cease-fire. The invasion and the war sent almost 1 million people to Jordan from Iraq and Kuwait. Most of those who entered were citizens of other countries who were later repatriated, staying in Jordanian camps only temporarily. The influx of almost 300,000 Palestinians from Kuwait put the greatest strain on the Jordanian economy, already damaged by the trade sanctions against Iraq, Jordan's main trading partner. The Palestinians settled in poor refugee camps and slums. The migration was the third largest in the history of the Palestinian people.

As U.S. efforts to convene an Arab-Israeli peace conference got under way, Jordan hoped its cooperation would win back the economic and diplomatic ties with the U.S. and the Gulf that it had lost by supporting Iraq. In April, U.S. Secretary of State James Baker's visit to King Hussein paved the way for renewed ties and coordination on the peace process. On 26 September Washington renewed military aid to Jordan.

King Hussein's agreement to participate in the U.S.-sponsored peace talks had serious implications at home. Fierce opposition came from the Muslim Brotherhood, which holds 26 out of 80 seats in the lower house of parliament and rejects any negotiations with Israel. On 18 June the king dismissed the Cabinet and replaced conservative Prime Minister Mudar Badran with Taher Masri, a liberal democrat of Palestinian origin who favors negotiations with Israel. Mr. Badran's government was associated with strong support for Iraq and attempts to enforce Islamic social values. The Cabinet change, however, was not enough to stave off mounting political tensions. On 22 July, just hours after King Hussein officially told Secretary Baker that Jordan would attend a peace conference and support Egypt's proposal to end the boycott of Israel, parliament issued a tough statement condemning the peace process.

On 19 October the government officially announced its acceptance of an invitation to the peace conference. The king used his constitutional powers to delay the opening of parliament until December, to defer dealing with internal opposition. However, a coalition of conservatives, Islamic fundamentalists, extreme nationalists and radical leftists called for Prime Minister Masri's resignation. In addition to the peace talks with Israel, at issue were controversial International Monetary Fund (IMF) austerity measures, and delay in repealing martial law. Five Cabinet ministers who opposed the peace talks resigned. In November Prime Minister Masri stepped down. King Hussein, in a move away from liberal politics, appointed his cousin, Sherif Zaid Ben Shaker, as prime minister. In 1989 Shaker led the transitional government which oversaw Jordan's first parliamentary elections. The Shaker government accommodated Jordan's Constitutional bloc conservatives, the king's traditional allies, but not members of the Muslim Brotherhood opposed to the Middle East peace talks. Underscoring the government's campaign against Islamic extremism, in October security forces arrested 150 Islamic militants. The government tried 18 Islamic fundamentalists on charges of using terrorism to set up an Islamic regime.

PLO Chairman Yassir Arafat gave King Hussein his blessing for Jordan to lead a joint Jordanian-Palestinian delegation in the bilateral negotiations between Israel and its Arab neighbors. The talks opened in Madrid on 30 October and resumed for a second session in late December in Washington. Jordan remained firm in its support for complete Israeli withdrawal from the occupied territories. In addition, Jordan hoped to solve its water shortages by negotiating a share of Jordan River water, which Jordan claims is virtually all taken by Israel.

Jordan's democratization has set an important precedent for the Arab world. In 1989 after anti-government rioting, Jordan held its first parliamentary elections, in which the Islamic Fundamentalist Party, the Muslim Brotherhood, gained over one-quarter of the seats of the lower house. In 1991 Jordan's democracy was strengthened by the signing of the national charter, which legalized political parties in exchange for the opposition's recognition of the constitutional legitimacy of the monarchy. On 7 August Jordan lifted most of the martial law provisions in effect since the 1967 Arab-Israeli war.

Political Rights and Civil Liberties:

Jordanians have limited means to change their government democratically. Though formally an absolute monarchy, in 1991 Jordan continued on its course toward democratization begun in 1989 when Jordan held its first parliamentary elections. On 9 June the Jordanian government adopted the National Charter, a document formulated by a commission made up of all major political groupings. The Charter legalizes political parties in exchange for the opposition's recognition of the constitution, which stipulates that Jordan is a Hashemite Monarchy.

On 7 July King Hussein abolished martial law provisions in effect since the 1967 Arab-Israeli war. Martial law had banned public meetings, but had not been thoroughly enforced since 1989. Freedom of the press and public expression continued on their expanded course, but met with some government interference in 1991. In October members of the Muslim Brotherhood were not allowed to stage a rally to protest the Middle East peace conference. Though by law the cabinet can suspend or abolish the publishing licenses, self-censorship continued to decline and bans on journalists have been lifted. In October 1991 the government censored two leftist newspapers. However, King Hussein demonstrated a commitment to free press when he publicly defended a Jordanian journalist expelled by his union for giving an interview to Israeli television. Television and radio are controlled by the government.

The government generally does not restrict movement within or travel outside the country. However, a married woman must present the written consent of her husband to obtain a passport. Most political detainees were released from prison in 1990. Jordan generally adheres to laws guaranteeing humane treatment of prisoners. Most criminal cases are tried in civilian courts. However, crimes involving state security are tried in military tribunals, where 18 Muslim militants were tried in October.

Jordan, which is 90 percent Muslim, generally respects freedom of worship. Islamic influence in Parliament has resulted in legislation which restricts personal freedoms, such as segregation of the sexes in schools. Jordanians are free to join trade unions, but foreigners, representing one-third of the work force, are not.

Kenya

Polity: One-party
Economy: Capitalist
Population: 25,200,000
PPP: $1,010
Life Expectancy: 59.7
Ethnic Groups: Kikuyu (21 percent), Luhya (14 percent), Luo (13 percent), Kalenjin (11 percent), Kamba (11 percent), Kisii (6 percent), Meru (5 percent), Somali (2 percent), other

Political Rights: 6
Civil Liberties: 6
Status: Not Free

Overview:

Following more than 20 years of one-party rule, in December 1991 President Daniel arap Moi announced the end of the Kenya African National Union's (KANU) legal monopoly on power. The move came days after Western governments pressured the regime to make political reforms or lose financial aid. However, opposition leaders expressed doubt that the current KANU-appointed electoral commission will hold free and fair elections. Prior to the move, the government had arrested and detained prominent individuals for their non-violent challenge to the authoritarian system.

In 1978, President Daniel Teroitich arap Moi took office after the death of the first president of independent Kenya, Jomo Kenyatta. The president heads KANU, formed in 1969 and established by constitutional amendment in 1982 as the only legal party. The unicameral National Assembly, whose 200 representatives are all associated with KANU, redesignated President arap Moi to successive five-year terms in 1983 and 1988. In this multi-ethnic country bordering on the Indian Ocean and Lake Victoria in East Africa, arap Moi's political power is based on alliances with various provincial barons and an inner circle whose members consist primarily of his own minority Kalenjin tribe. The main opposition party, as of December 1991, is the newly formed Forum for the Restoration of Democracy (FORD).

As multi-partyism has swept Africa over the past few years, calls for democracy in Kenya have increased considerably. Until December 1991, the regime's response had been one of intransigence and aggressive counter-measure. Claiming to speak on behalf of a *wananchi* (citizenry) which had rejected multi-partyism, the regime asserted that such a political system would cause social fragmentation along tribal lines, threatening Kenyan national stability. What the government had termed political reforms were carefully crafted so that their ultimate impact on the *status quo* was minimal. At a KANU party congress in June 1991, delegates voted to support the president's proposal to allow all candidates to contest elections. However, candidates had to be life members in good standing of KANU, and the leadership retained the right to clear them.

Citizens who have spoken out for political change have been warned against "straying into politics", which a government minister asserted ought to be left to those who have received a "mandate from the public" in the one-party elections. Ever less tolerant of free expression, the regime has gone beyond issuing warnings to clamping down through the repeated arrest and detention of individuals who dissent. The president publicly directed security officers to deal "firmly" with those who were found to be spreading rumors that general elections were to be held sometime in 1991. Asserting that only he could set the electoral timetable, arap Moi's concern appeared to arise from what such rumors might imply about his control of events.

Several prominent individuals pushed for change in 1991. Former vice president Jaramogi Oginga Odinga was rebuffed when he attempted to launch a new political party in late February, the National Democratic Party (NDP). For the second time in seven months, the editor-in-chief of the *Nairobi Law Monthly* was arrested in early March for publishing Odinga's NDP party platform and an editorial charging that the regime explicitly favored those of the president's own Kalenjin tribe for top government positions. Gitobu Imanyara joined in prison Charles Rubia and Kenneth Matiba, two former government ministers who had been arrested in 1990 after calling for multi-partyism. Denied bail, all four were eventually released on medical grounds after months of pre-trial detention. Four others accused of holding a seditious meeting in a cafe and possessing seditious publications, including a former member of parliament, were convicted and sentenced in mid-1991 to seven years in prison. Koigi wa Wamwere, leader of the outlawed opposition Kenya Patriotic Front, remained in prison charged with treason after having reportedly been kidnapped in Uganda by Kenyan security agents and forcibly transported across the border. A confession subsequently produced by Kenyan authorities, in which he admitted to subversive activities under the sponsorship of the Libyan, Norwegian, and Ugandan governments as well as the human rights group Africa Watch, was admitted into evidence after a ruling by the High Court, despite an affidavit by wa Wamwere alleging that the statement was the product of torture.

In their own public pronouncements, arap Moi and members of KANU preferred to focus on the turmoil in Somalia and Liberia rather than the numerous peaceful processes of political liberalization being experienced in other multi-ethnic countries throughout the continent. Citing the threat of an imminent invasion from Uganda, the Kenyan government called for the citizenry to loyally rally behind it. In addition, the government media has characterized Amnesty International's claims of human rights abuses as "extravagant", and warned of the danger of subversion under the auspices of foreign organizations such as the BBC.

Western governments moved to cut the regime's financial support at a meeting in Paris on 25 November. In an unprecedented move, the lenders froze new aid for six months pending political reform. The United States announced that it had been prepared to give Kenya $47 million in economic and social assistance in 1992, but would instead only grant a previously agreed $9 million to non-government humanitarian agencies. U.S. ambassador Smith Hempstone has been particularly outspoken against the regime. The government accused Hempstone and others in the diplomatic community of sponsoring a peaceful opposition rally in support of multi-partyism in November which was forcibly broken up with tear gas.

The 1990 murder of former Foreign Minister Robert Ouko also put pressure on the regime. Government minister Nicholas Biwott, President arap Moi's closest aide and also a Kalenjin, allegedly threatened Ouko's life when the foreign minister seemed likely to go public with Biwott's history of receiving kickbacks from private contractors. Although the president had received a report to that effect a year before from a special Scotland Yard investigation, it was not until the investigators publicly testified before the commission that the evidence pointed to the Biwott's involvement in the murder, that arap Moi acted. He first fired Biwott and then had him arrested with three others implicated in the crime. However, the president also quelled the inquiry as testimony brought to light his own involvement and that of Vice President Saitoti in the receipt of kickbacks. Many Western aid donors specifically cited the Ouko affair as part of their decision.

Another top issue in 1991 has been the civil war and anarchy in neighboring Somalia, which has created a flow of refugees into Kenya. The Kenyan government has agreed to grant them temporary asylum, even though Kenyan-born Somalis continue to face harassment and summary deportation. However, up to 1,000 Rwandian and Ugandan refugees have been forcibly deported to their countries of origin, while others are harassed by security forces and militants of the KANU youth wing.

Political Rights and Civil Liberties:

Despite President Daniel arap Moi's December 1991 decision to legalize parties other than the ruling Kenya African National Union, citizens cannot change their government democratically. With the constitution yet to be formally amended, dissident members of the ruling party were frequently subject to suspension and imprisonment in 1991. Freedom of assembly for political purposes is strictly curtailed. Those attending unauthorized meetings are subject to beatings and arrest. Professional associations exist, but those whose members speak out on public issues in a manner deemed provocative by the government are subject to de-registration.

The independence of the judiciary is now theoretically greater since the power to fire judges merely at his "pleasure" was surrendered by the president in 1991 to a special panel. However, the panel consists of members appointed by the president. On the order of government officials, the High Court has issued injunctions restraining political dissidents. The court has also allowed government officials to avoid repaying private bank loans. Kenyan courts regularly reject without investigation affidavits filed on behalf of jailed dissidents alleging torture and other ill-treatment by the Directorate of State Security Intelligence. The Preservation of Public Security Act allows for the unlimited detention of suspects in political cases.

Sedition laws restrict expression which the authorities determine tends to "excite disaffection against the Government of Kenya," and by their provisions cover possession of publications criticizing the regime, audio recordings with political lyrics and, apparently, even the private notes and the unpublished letters of dissidents. In 1991 the government continued its campaign of harassment against the *Nairobi Law Monthly*, again shutting it down and imprisoning its editor. Television and radio are controlled by the government and reflect official positions and policy, though the end of 1991 saw some reporting critical of the government. The regime is able to force the media to adopt a blackout on certain news stories, such as the NDP's announcement of its founding at a press conference. Journalists were beaten in 1991 at the scene of a number of news events. In an incident that seized international attention at mid-year, a mob of boarding school boys killed 19 girls and raped 71 in a rampage one night in a rural area of the country. Commentators asserted that it was only the deaths that set the episode apart from similar attacks on boarding school girls, and was symptomatic of the oppressed condition that the vast majority of women experience in today's Kenya. Religious denominations need government approval to operate in the country. Authorities have frequently harassed and restricted the activities of Protestant churches and implicitly threatened the lives of outspoken ecclesiastics who have called for multi-partyism. Domestic travel is generally unrestricted, but there are some regulations on foreign travel. The leadership of the Central Organization of Trade Unions (COTU), the only legally recognized federation, has close ties with the arap Moi regime and has supported the president's stand against multi-partyism.

Kiribati

Polity: Parliamentary democracy
Economy: Capitalist-statist
Population: 65,000
PPP: na
Life Expectancy: 52.0
Ethnic Groups: Kiribatian (Micronesian, 84 percent), Polynesian (14 percent), other (2 percent)

Political Rights: 1
Civil Liberties: 2
Status: Free

Overview:

The Republic of Kirabati consists of thirty-three islands with a total land area smaller than New York City, scattered over 2 million square miles of the Pacific Ocean. It has been an independent member of the British Commonwealth since it gained independence on 12 July 1979. Its founding president, Ieremia Tabai, began his fourth term in parliament after winning his seat in the May 1991 elections. However, because the constitution prevents him from a holding a fourth presidential term, Tabai threw his support behind his friend Teato Teannaki, who won the July presidential election.

The unicameral parliament is composed of thirty-five members elected directly from twenty-three constituencies, along with a representative nominated from the Banaba Island community by the Banaban Rabi Council of Leaders. The president, a member of parliament, is directly elected from a list of three to four candidates nominated by the parliament. Local Island Councils are established on all inhabited islands. Politics are generally conducted on a personal rather than political level, although three parties exist—the ruling National Progressive Party, the Christian Democratic Party, and the United Kirabati Party.

The economy is supported through fishing, copra production, and farming. License fees from countries which fish in its waters provide a major source of revenue. In 1991, the government pledged to help the 400 residents of Banaba Island, whose economic development came to a standstill after phosphate mining ended there in 1979, to modernize their agricultural and fishing methods.

Political Rights and Civil Liberties:

The citizens of Kirabati can change their government democratically. Political parties play a relatively minor role, and generally coalesce around timely issues. Freedom of assembly, press and speech are enumerated in the constitution and respected by the government. The radio station and newspaper are government-run but offer pluralistic viewpoints. The independent judiciary system is modeled on English common law. Freedom of religion is guaranteed by the constitution, and people of all faiths can freely practice. A minor dispute arose a week before the 1991 parliamentary election when the Catholic magazine *Te Itoi Ni Kirabati* ran an editorial asking Catholics to vote for candidates of their own religion, but this had no apparent effect on the election. Workers are free to organize into unions and conduct strikes. The Kirabati Trade Union Congress is composed of seven trade unions and has approximately 2,500 members.

Korea, North

Polity: Communist one-party
Economy: Statist
Population: 21,800,000
PPP: na
Life Expectancy: 70.4
Ethnic Groups: Ethnically homogeneous—Korean

Political Rights: 7
Civil Liberties: 7
Status: Not Free

Overview:

In 1991 the Democratic People's Republic of Korea, one of the few remaining bastions of Stalinist orthodoxy and increasingly isolated after the collapse of Communist regimes in the Soviet Union and Eastern Europe, took some tentative steps toward integration into the international community. North Korea's breakthrough rapprochement with archenemy South Korea and its reluctant bid for admission to the United Nations seemed to augur the possibility of greater cooperation with the West. But North Korea's open development of nuclear weapons raised serious questions about its commitment to easing regional tensions.

Established 9 September 1948, North Korea is a one-party Communist dictatorship ruled for 43 years by 79-year-old Marshal Kim Il Sung, general secretary of the Korean Workers' (Communist) Party who was installed by the Soviet Union. In 1990, after some speculation that he would turn over power to his son, Kim Jong Il (known as "Dear Leader"), Marshal Kim began a new four-year presidential term, defiantly lauding communism as he kept his iron grip on power.

In 1991 North Korea continued the on-again, off-again talks with South Korea that in 1990 saw the first set of high-level negotiations between the two governments since Korea was partitioned in 1945. In early February, North and South Korea agreed to enter united Korean teams in international sporting events. But on 18 February 1991, North Korea called off a round of high-level talks with South Korea scheduled for later in the month, blaming what it called military provocation by Seoul and the United States. The focus of the complaint was annual joint military exercises carried on by South Korea and the U.S., which had 43,000 troops stationed in the south. Earlier in the month, North Korea announced that it had crushed a plot within the ruling Korean Workers' Party to thwart the planned transfer of power from President Kim to his son, but the report could not be confirmed. It is known that Kim Il Sung, known as "Greater Leader" in keeping with his deliberate creation of a cult of personality, had been grooming his son to succeed him. As part of the mythical image-building, the North Korean propaganda machine even went so far as to change Kim Jong Il's birthday (he turned 50 on 16 February), so that celebration of his fiftieth birthday would coincide with his father's eightieth birthday in 1992. Other facts were also changed to fit the official leadership myth. In reality, Kim Jong Il was born in the Soviet Siberian city of Khabarovsk; official sources insist he was born on Mt. Paekdu, Korea's highest and most sacred mountain. Despite attempts at deification, rumors persisted throughout 1991 that the military and younger party cadres were not satisfied with the possibility of Kim Jong Il as leader.

On 28 May, in a major policy reversal intended to end its diplomatic isolation, North Korea announced it "had no choice" and would apply for separate membership in the United Nations. The move was seen as a reluctant response to South Korean

President Roh Tae Woo's courting of China and the Soviet Union (which established diplomatic relations with Seoul in September 1990), the North's chief patrons. For decades, both Koreas, which had observer status at the U.N., resisted membership because it would amount to international ratification of the 46-year partition of the Korean peninsula. The UN General Assembly voted on 17 September to accept the two Koreas as members.

In July there were unconfirmed reports that both Koreas had been studying proposals for a new peace treaty and non-aggression pact. On 16 July, North Korea released a proposal for a conference by 50 delegates from each side. Three days later, officials from both countries confirmed that their prime ministers would re-open talks in late August on easing tensions and on unification, a resumption of the fourth-round negotiations suspended in February. A breakthrough came during prime ministerial meetings in late October when both sides began drafting a historic agreement incorporating all proposals on reconciliation, non-aggression and exchanges. North Korea for the first time agreed to call for efforts to reunite 10 million families separated by the 1945 partition; it dropped demands that South Korea repeal all laws restricting contact with the North; and it accepted language banning terrorist activities and attempts to overthrow each other's government. The two sides differed on the non-aggression draft, with the North insisting that a simple statement of intent would suffice and the South demanding specific measures to monitor activity of the 1.7 million troops on either side of the border. On 13 December, during the fifth prime ministerial meetings in Seoul, both sides signed a historic non-aggression pact. The result was a pledge not to interfere in each other's internal affairs. The agreement provided for a military hotline to cut the risk of accidental war; restored rail, road, postal and telephone links; the reunion of divided families; free movement of people and ideas; and liberalized trade and investment. Final details were to be spelled out in early 1992.

The end of 1991 saw greater U.S. pressure on North Korea to stop developing a nuclear bomb. In June, North Korea told the International Atomic Energy Agency it would sign an agreement allowing international inspection of nuclear sites. Later in the month, South Korean intelligence reported finding traces of a North Korean test explosion for devices that could detonate nuclear weapons. In July, a report said that North Korea was building long-range SCUD missiles and had produced 1,000 tons of chemical warheads. In London, *Janes Intelligence Review* confirmed that the North had the capability to produce an atomic bomb. In September, a ranking North Korean diplomat who defected to the South confirmed that his country had an underground nuclear research center. On 13 September, North Korea, which had earlier announced it would allow international inspection of its nuclear facilities without conditions, said it would do so only if "the U.S. threat" were removed. The same month, Japan announced it would not consider having diplomatic relations with the North until inspectors were let in.

In late October, North Korea presented another set of tough conditions for inspection, five days after the Bush Administration made public U.S. intentions to remove all nuclear weapons based in South Korea. On 13 November, Secretary of State James Baker told leaders in Seoul that Washington considered the North's atomic development a matter of global urgency and that the U.S. was actively exploring with China, Japan and the Soviet Union ways to curtail the program. One week later, American and South Korean defense officials stepped up warnings to North Korea, declaring after a day of high-level talks that Pyongyang's "nuclear program must be stopped in advance without fail."

The following month the U.S. and South Korea said they would allow North Korea to inspect any civilian or military sites in the South in return for reciprocal rights in the North and an agreement that neither Seoul nor Pyongyang would produce weapons-grade plutonium. On 11 December, at the start of the fifth round of prime ministerial negotiations, North and South Korea made surprising proposals for a nuclear-free Korea calling for the elimination of weapons of mass destruction and an end to Cold War hostilities. Both sides had provisions to allow inspections, but North Korea continued to insist on a ban on U.S. nuclear umbrella protection for South Korea. On 19 December, Marshal Kim again denied his country was making nuclear weapons.

In 1991 the North Korean economy was a shambles. Most of its trading partners in the former Communist bloc, including the Soviet Union, refused to barter or accept Korean currency. They demanded hard, convertible currencies for the goods, including Soviet oil, on which North Korea depends. Under Marshal Kim's three-year policy of *juche*, or self-reliance, the economy had become autarchic, with almost no foreign currency reserves. By the end of the year, it was years behind on several billion dollars of foreign debt. Poor harvests caused North Korea to purchase 5,000 tons of rice from a South Korean company, a striking admission that it could not feed its own people. Throughout the year, there were credible reports of hunger in the North. Virtually all food was rationed, and one-third of all factories were reported shut down, with half the remaining ones operating part-time because of fuel and raw materials shortages.

Political Rights and Civil Liberties: Citizens do not have the means to change the one-party system through democratic means. The judiciary is completely subservient to the state-party apparatus. The penal code outlines several "political crimes," and prescribes the death penalty for forty crimes. The number of political prisoners is believed to be over 100,000, housed in at least 12 special labor camps, re-education centers and prisons.

All media are strictly controlled by the government and external publications are excluded. Citizens are subject to security ratings that determine access to employment, party membership, food, health care and higher education. Foreign travel is severely restricted. In 1991, a North Korean citizen was allowed to visit his ailing mother in the U.S., the first time an ordinary citizen was given a visa in recent memory.

Religious believers have suffered official discrimination, and Christians and Buddhists are routinely persecuted. The government interferes in family life by forcing children and young adults to attend indoctrination camps, and babies as young as three months are placed in state nurseries so mothers may be allowed to work. There are no free trade unions.

Korea, South

Polity: Presidential-legislative democracy
Economy: Capitalist-statist
Population: 43,200,000
PPP: $5,680
Life Expectancy: 70.1
Ethnic Groups: Ethnically homogeneous—Korean

Political Rights: 2
Civil Liberties: 3
Status: Free

Overview:

Major developments in South Korea during 1991 included a corruption scandal involving members of the ruling Democratic Liberal Party (DLP), the first local elections in 30 years, weeks of often bloody clashes between student protesters and police, membership in the United Nations and a breakthrough non-aggression agreement with Communist North Korea.

The Republic of Korea was established in August 1948. Intermittent, unpopular martial-law regimes and social unrest led to amendments of the 1948 constitution in 1987 and the acceptance of sweeping political reforms. Full executive power is vested in a president, directly elected for a single five-year term. The president appoints a prime minister and cabinet. Three-quarters of the 299-member, unicameral National Assembly are directly elected, 38 seats are allocated to the party winning the largest number of elections, with 37 divided among all parties in proportion to seats gained.

In 1990 President Roh Tae Woo, who in 1987 became the first president elected directly by the people since 1971, announced that his ruling Democratic Justice Party (DJP) was merging with two opposition parties—the Reunification Democratic Party (RDP), led by Kim Young Sam, and the New Democratic Republican Party (NDRP), headed by Kim Jonh Pil. The new party was named the Democratic Liberal Party (DLP). The merger left the Party for Peace and Democracy (PPD), led by Kim Dae Jung, a prominent dissident during the country's long period of military rule, as the sole opposition. The merger gave the DLP 217 of 299 Assembly seats.

In February 1991 three legislators from the DLP and two from the PPD were arrested in February on charges of taking $1.3 billion in bribes from a building firm to help it gain a lucrative housing deal in Seoul. The scandal further eroded the government's popularity, even after President Roh publicly apologized to the nation. In March, partly to deflect attention from the corruption scandal, the government announced that the first local government elections in 30 years would be held on 26 March. The new councils, together with mayors and governors, would assume some of the power held by the central government. The elections were scheduled for two phases—the first for 4,304 councillor seats in small towns, municipalities and counties, and the second, to be held in June, for larger cities and regions. Even though the elections for the small authorities were to be non-partisan, both the DLP and the opposition viewed them as a barometer of the public's attitude toward the government.

The elections were marred by charges of vote buying and an unexpectedly light turnout, as only 55 percent of eligible voters went to the polls, far fewer than the 89 percent who voted in the December 1987 presidential election. Supporters of the DLP won a resounding victory, claiming more than half the posts. The PPD won only

18 percent, and the vast majority were in Kim Dae Jung's home province. Partly as a result of its poor showing, the PPD merged with the small dissident Party for New Democratic Alliance to form a new opposition, the New Democratic Union (NDU). The new party's platform was similar to that of the PPD; it included commitments to a market economy, independent diplomacy and the restoration of morality within the political sphere. The merger was seen as the first step toward a unified opposition in preparation for the 1992 legislative elections and the 1993 presidential vote to replace President Roh, who under the constitution is prohibited from seeking another term.

Before the June local elections the government faced another serious crisis as the worst student riots since 1987 rocked the country. The unrest was sparked by the 26 April beating death of a student demonstrator by riot police. Even though President Roh responded quickly by firing Interior Minister Ahn Eung Mo, the violent demonstrations escalated through May, as tens of thousands of students battled police and seven committed suicide by self-immolation. The rioting also reflected a seasonal regularity of demonstrations leading to the 18 May anniversary of a 1980 massacre of protesters in Kwangju by the military. In an attempt to quell the protests, President Roh released several dozen prisoners, most of whom were convicted under the stringent National Security Law. But unlike 1987, the country's growing and prosperous middle class, generally satisfied with Roh's record on diplomatic achievements and democratization, opted for political stability and did not back the students.

Nevertheless, the severity of the protests led President Roh to further reshuffle his cabinet, the eleventh shake-up since he took office. On 22 May, Prime Minister Ro Jai Bong resigned after assuming responsibility for triggering the unrest. He was replaced by Chung Won Shik, considered a hardliner who helped smash the National Teachers' Union in 1989. By mid-June, with university exams due to start, the protests subsided.

The campaign for the 20 June local elections was rife with charges of libel, corruption and vote buying, as well as election-eve clashes between small groups of students and police. President Roh's government party scored a smashing victory in the nationwide poll. Final tallies showed that the DLP swept 564 seats, or 65 percent, of the 866 local council seats at stake in six large cities and nine provinces. Kim Dae Jung's NDU won 165 seats, the splinter Democratic Party won 21 and the dissident People's Party won one. The DLP managed to secure the traditional opposition stronghold of Seoul. But independent candidates won an impressive 115 seats, a sign of growing public distrust of faction-ridden political parties. Election turnout was a low 58.9 percent. The NDU's poor showing led Kim Dae Jung to offer his resignation, but the offer was overwhelmingly rejected by the party leadership. On 10 September, in order to further consolidate the opposition, the NDU merged with the small Democratic Party, led by Lee Ki Taek, to form a new Democratic Party. The merger gave the new party control of 80 seats in the 299-seat Assembly.

In foreign affairs the paramount issue in 1991 was the often tortuous process of diplomatic maneuvering to normalize relations with Communist North Korea, with the ultimate goal of unification. The collapse of Communist regimes in Eastern Europe and the Soviet Union, coupled with President Roh's skillful courting of Moscow and Beijing, the North's long-time patrons, had forced North Korea to seek greater integration with the West and a rapprochement with its southern neighbor. High-level prime ministerial talks begun in 1990 continued through the year, despite several setbacks. In February, North Korea cancelled talks, blaming what it called military provocation by the U.S. and South Korea, which were holding regularly scheduled joint military exercises. In April, South Korea warned that further negotiations were seriously jeopardized by the North's development of atomic weapons at a facility in Yongbyon. The North had promised to allow International Atomic Energy Agency officials to inspect its facilities, but later said permission was conditional on the U.S. withdrawing all its nuclear weapons from the South. North Korea later demanded that the South forswear any nuclear umbrella protection by the U.S.

Negotiations resumed in August. The same month, South Korea formally applied for membership in the United Nations after the North had yielded to the idea of having two Koreas represented in the international body. In October, North Korean officials welcomed President George Bush's pledge to eliminate short-range nuclear weapons from the South, but insisted they would not allow international inspections of nuclear plants until all such weapons were withdrawn. On 8 November President Roh declared for the first time that his country would no longer possess or store American or any other nuclear weapons on its soil. But North Korea's nuclear weapons program led U.S. Defense Secretary Dick Cheney to halt a long-planned American troop reduction.

On 13 December, after last-minute wrangling, North and South Korea signed a historic non-aggression accord, though doubts remained over whether the North's orthodox Stalinist regime of Marshal Kim Il Sung was actually committed to reconciliation or was merely looking for ways to salvage a bankrupt economy. Under the agreement, rail and telephone lines would be reconnected between the two countries, family visits would be permitted, and economic exchanges would be expanded. On 18 December, in a move intended to increase pressure of the North to halt its nuclear weapons program, President Roh announced on national television that there were no nuclear weapons on South Korean territory.

Political Rights and Civil Liberties:

South Koreans can change their government democratically. While civil and criminal cases are generally adjudicated fairly, security provisions continue to curtail legal rights and civil liberties. Although the widely feared National Security Law (NSL) was amended in May, it still allowed the prosecution of people who "praise or encourage, communicate or meet with anti-state organizations" or their representatives "knowing that to do so would endanger the state's security or the basic order of free democracy." While President Roh granted amnesty to hundreds of political prisoners in February and during the student unrest in May, the nation's largest church group reported on 15 July that South Korea had 1,630 political prisoners, an all-time high since President Roh assumed office.

Dozens of newspapers have been started since 1987, and many take strident anti-government positions. But National Security Law restricts freedom of expression, and government influence over radio and television remains strong. Freedom of assembly, though having some restrictions, is generally respected. Throughout 1991, students and political groups held massive rallies and demonstrations. Although freedom of religion is guaranteed, politically active churches occasionally run into difficulties with authorities. Freedom of movement is generally unrestricted, except for visits to North Korea.

Unions continue to play an increasingly political role, and the government has responded with repressive measures. In February 69 labor activists meeting to consider support for strikers at South Korea's second-largest shipyards were detained by police. The government continued its two-year repression of the independent teachers' union. The independent, 2 million-strong Federation of Korean Trade Unions (FKTU) continued to fight for greater workers' rights, including rescinding a constitutional clause that explicitly bans trade unions from collecting funds for or otherwise supporting specific political parties or candidates.

Kuwait

Polity: Traditional monarchy **Political Rights:** 6
Economy: Mixed capitalist-statist **Civil Liberties:** 5
Population: 1,400,000 **Status:** Not Free
PPP: $9,310
Life Expectancy: 73.4
Ethnic Groups: Kuwaitis and other Arabs, and various foreign workers

Overview: After allied victory in the Persian Gulf War forced Iraq to withdraw from Kuwait on 26 February 1991, Kuwaitis began the mammoth task of rebuilding a country devastated by Iraqi troops. In the war's aftermath, suspected Iraqi collaborators faced martial law tribunals and an emboldened opposition pushed for democratic reform.

On 2 August 1990, following a month of threats by Iraqi dictator Saddam Hussein, Iraqi forces invaded and occupied Kuwait, seizing the emirate's oil fields, sending the Kuwaiti leadership into exile, and setting up a proxy government composed of Iraqi military officers. During the occupation, Iraqi soldiers committed atrocious human rights violations, such as execution of unarmed civilians, rape, torture, and forced evacuation of civilians. Human rights groups reported that thousands of Kuwaitis—soldiers, police and civilians—were killed or held in prison camps. The Iraqis looted billions of dollars worth of valuables, including $500 million worth of gold.

The Kuwaitis who remained to fight the Iraqis organized their own underground resistance. Some were assigned to American units in Saudi Arabia and trained to help American-led ground forces identify Iraqis in Kuwait. The Kuwaiti resistance published a clandestine newspaper, patrolled neighborhoods, provided food to people in hiding, executed collaborators and secretly filmed Iraqi soldiers attacking civilians.

In early January 1991 some 600,000 Iraqi soldiers in Kuwait faced approximately the same number of allied troops on the Saudi Arabian border. Shattered by over one month of intense allied bombardment, on February 26 Iraq announced withdrawal from Kuwait. In March Iraq agreed to U.N. cease fire terms requiring Iraq to rescind its annexation of Kuwait, accept liability for war damages, return the thousands of Kuwaiti prisoners and billions worth of stolen property, and recognize a 1963 Iraq-Kuwait border agreement.

In less than a month after the Iraqi evacuation, the Al-Sabah's unhurried return from comfortable exile, slowness in restoring basic services to citizens, and failure to rein in pro-government vigilantes in possession of confiscated Iraqi weapons sparked bitter criticism of the royal family. On 20 March the government banned the country's leading newspaper *"February 26"* for commentaries criticizing official incompetence. On 22 March, in violation of martial law, Kuwaitis held an outdoor rally to demand a new coalition government. For the first time since 1962 opposition members called for the crown prince to step down.

The main strands of the Kuwaiti opposition—the Democratic Forum (leftist Arab nationalists), the Constitutional Alliance (merchants), the Popular Islamic Congress (Sunni Muslim), the Islamic Constitutional Movement (Sunni Muslim Brothers), the National Islamic Coalition (Shia Muslim)—are together referred to as the Constitution-alist Movement. The Iraqi occupation gave birth to a new and intensely demanding political grouping. Mainly city-dwelling Sunnis and Shia Muslims, the 230,000 Kuwaitis that stayed in Kuwait to fight the Iraqis emerged from the occupation as an emboldened political force.

The opposition groups' list of demands includes the restoration of the National Assembly and the reinstatement of the 1963 constitution, both of which had made Kuwait one of the freest Gulf states until their abolition by royal decree in 1986. They also called for the lifting of press restrictions. Women's involvement in the resistance led to increased pressure on the Emir to allow women the right to vote. Following a petition signed by 96 opposition leaders demanding democratic reform, in early April the Emir announced that elections would be held within a year. He did not, however, take steps to create a government of national unity. The formation of a new Cabinet in mid-April amounted to nothing but a cosmetic reshuffle. Shocking many Kuwaitis, the Government retained the defense and interior ministers in power at the time of the invasion. Furthermore, the government took no steps towards the restoration of the National Assembly or the reinstatement of the constitution. Opposition groups demanded the abolition of the National Council, a royally appointed governing body. The Council, formed in June 1990 is considered a "toothless substitute" for the original national assembly. In the last months of 1992 the Emir allowed the open formation of an opposition party, the Democratic Forum. However, in the face of a highly restricted press, and uncertainty about the fate of parliament and the 1963 constitution, Kuwaiti democracy remained elusive.

In other issues, brutal and indiscriminate collective reprisals against non-Kuwaitis, especially Palestinians, for possible collaboration with the Iraqis attracted international attention. Following the Iraqi evacuation, vigilante groups and the Kuwaiti police force set out to punish anyone suspected of collaborating with Iraq. The Kuwaiti leadership largely ignored the widespread use of extrajudicial killings, torture, unlawful detention and deportation. The Kuwaiti authorities also set up martial law tribunals to try alleged collaborators. Human rights groups assailed the trials for severe procedural shortcomings, such as the extraction of confession through torture, lack of an appeals court, trials in absentia, denial of legal counsel, and the use of martial law to try petty crimes. The government used a vague definition of collaboration that shocked even Kuwaitis. Some who remained during the occupation reported they were labeled quasi-collaborators for not fleeing. From 19 May to the end of martial law on 26 June, 118 people were convicted on charges of collaboration. In some cases, harsh sentences were meted out for small transgressions: one youth received a 15-year prison sentence for wearing a Saddam Hussein T-shirt. Under international pressure, the government commuted the 29 death sentences to life imprisonment.

One of the earliest post-liberation decisions was to "Kuwaitize" the country, and get rid of half of Kuwait's pre-invasion population of 2 million, 70 percent of which were non-Kuwaitis. Palestinians, who for decades provided the core of the country's professionals, technicians and middle managers, were the main target; Kuwaiti authorities barred the return of hundreds of 180,000 Palestinians, regardless of property and homes left behind. The remaining 150,000 Palestinians faced eviction or deportation by November 1. Also targeted were the Bedouins, who are stateless Arabs descended from nomadic tribes born and living in Kuwait all their lives, but who could not qualify for citizenship or simply did not apply, as their allegiances were traditionally tribal. Kuwait barred the re-entrance of about 5,000 Bedouins; the remaining 200,000 faced continued harassment, and were forced to leave the country by 1 November or face deportation.

The task of reconstruction was enormous. The Iraqi scorched earth strategy destroyed water, electricity, sanitation and communications and petrochemical facilities. Five-hundred (or more) burning oil wells, set ablaze by Iraqi troops, cast a dark smoke cloud over Kuwait city. Though within four months basic services had been restored and some public buildings repaired, complete recovery will take an estimated 2 years.

Political Rights and Civil Liberties: Kuwaitis do not have the right to change their government democratically. The Al-Sabah family has ruled Kuwait exclusively since 1756. Sheikh Jabir al-Ahmad al Jabir, the Kuwaiti emir, has virtually absolute power, although Kuwaiti males may discuss policy with emir in traditional meetings, called *diwaniya*. The emir promised parliamentary elections for 1992. Kuwait's opposition forces called for the reinstatement of the National Assembly and the 1963 constitution, both abolished by royal decree in 1986. In 1991 Kuwait reconvened the National Council, a government-dominated substitute for the original assembly.

Though Kuwaiti law tightly restricts political activity, authorities allowed Kuwaiti opposition groups to organize and meet in *diwaniya,* with little interference, even during martial law, which lasted from 26 February until June. In October, the government allowed the formation of the first open political party in Kuwait, the Kuwaiti Democratic Forum. The Government continues to deny women the right to vote, but the emir pledged to consider women's suffrage for the 1992 election.

Government strictly controls the press. In March, Kuwaiti authorities banned an independent post-liberation newspaper, *February 26*, for criticizing the government's delay in restoring basic services. Kuwait's main newspaper after liberation was *New Dawn*, a pro-government daily.

Martial law awarded wide powers to the emir and the police. After liberation, Kuwaiti security forces and pro-government vigilante groups committed serious human rights violations against non-Kuwaitis. Most victims were Palestinian and Iraqi; others included Egyptian, Sudanese and Bedouin. According to Middle East Watch, abuses included torture, unlawful detention, deportation and scores of extrajudicial executions. In June, 54 victims of post-liberation killings were found in a mass grave. By year's end 3,000 detainees remained in Kuwaiti prisonrs, most without charge. Most of 1,500 of those who were forcibly deported to Iraq were prisoners, many of them Iraqi, but others included Palestinians and Bedouins, deported to Iraq against their will.

The state religion is Islam. The ruling family and most prominent citizens are

Sunni Muslim. Kuwait's largely underprivileged Shia Moslems comprise 30 percent of the population.

Kuwait recognizes but highly restricts the right to strike. Foreign workers can join a union after five years of residency but have no union voting rights. Kuwait barred hundreds of thousands of non-Kuwaiti workers, mostly Palestinians, from returning to their jobs and homes after liberation.

Laos

Polity: Communist one-party
Economy: Mixed statist
Population: 4,100,000
PPP: na
Life Expectancy: 49.7
Ethnic Groups: Multi-ethnic—Lao (50 percent), Thai (20 percent), Phoutheung, Miao (Hmong), Tao and others

Political Rights: 6
Civil Liberties: 7
Status: Not Free

Overview:

Finding itself among the last of the the world's Communist nations, in 1991 the ruling Lao People's Revolutionary Party (LPRP) in Laos strengthened its one-party system while continuing its program of economic reform and decentralization.

The Supreme People's Assembly adopted the country's first constitution under Communist rule on 15 August 1991. The constitution formally makes the LPRP the "leading organ" of the political system and establishes an expanded presidency. It also requires the state to protect private ownership "by domestic capitalists and foreigners who make investments" in Laos. The assembly elected premier and party leader Kaysone Phomvihane to the new presidential office, which had previously been a ceremonial post. Kaysone now officially has the power to remove the premier, is the head of the armed forces, and can ratify and abolish all treaties signed with other countries. General Khamtay Siphandon, also a veteran Marxist revolutionary, succeeded Kaysone as premier.

Laos became a French protectorate in 1893. Occupied by the Japanese during World War II, it won complete sovereignty from the French on 23 October 1953. Neutralist, Communist and conservative factions formed a coalition government in 1962 after several years of fighting. Fighting resumed after the Communist Pathet Lao forces withdrew from the coalition in 1964. The United States engaged in an intensive bombing campaign in the late 1960s and early 1970s within Laotian territory against North Vietnamese and Pathet Lao forces. In May 1975 the Pathet Lao overran the capital, Vientiane, and established the Lao People's Democratic Republic in December 1975.

In 1986, the LPRP's Fourth Party Congress enacted the New Economic Mechanism (NEM), designed to transform the centrally planned economy into a freer system. It has resulted in some decentralized economic decision-making, privatization of many state enterprises, and stricter standards for those industries still under government control. Prices for many goods have been deregulated. Government economists report that gross domestic product has increased by 30 percent since the NEM began.

Kaysone continued to champion economic reform at the LPRP's Fifth Congress held 27-29 March 1991, where he blamed many of the country's economic shortcomings on the party itself. Kaysone announced plans to speed up the replacement of agricultural cooperatives with family farms, to increase exports, and to reform the banking and monetary systems in order to attract more foreign investment. As a sign of the times, several private businessmen and religious figures were consulted on economic issues, and Western diplomats were invited to ceremonial meetings before the congress.

However, the LPRP showed no sign of giving up its monopoly on power. The Congress re-elected Kaysone as party chairman, and changed his party title from secretary general to "President of the Party" in honor of his "great virtue and tireless devotion" in leading the party since its inception in 1955. In a surprising move, the central committee removed Kaysone's wife to make room for his son, Saysomphone. The party also abolished its nine-member secretariat, through which provincial party officials often dealt with the central government. Observers said the central party leaders felt the secretariat had allowed local party power to increase too much under the new economic decentralization.

The economic changes have helped Laos attract aid and investment from several Western nations, as well as Thailand and China, although GNP remains less then $200 per capita. The World Bank and the United Nations Development Program signed agreements with Laos in 1991 to provide aid for economic reform and development. But major obstacles stand in the way of further economic development. Nearly one-third of the population is illiterate, and only 10 percent of the villages are served by roads. Some 60,000 Laotians remain in refugee camps in Thailand, many of whom will eventually have to be repatriated. The government also ordered local officials to control the rampant illegal timber logging which has caused widespread destruction to forest areas. In August, it claimed corrupt officials were largely responsible for logging enterprises being run beyond the scope of state regulations.

A reduction in Soviet and Vietnamese economic aid has sparked a foreign policy shift towards neighboring Thailand in recent years. In 1987 and 1988 the two countries fought a series of brief but bloody battles over small areas of land. In March 1991 Thai army commander General Suchinda Kraprayoon visited Laos and reached an agreement calling for both sides to withdraw their forces from disputed areas along their common border. Laos has held discussions with Thailand on building a dam on the Mekong River along the border which would provide Lao farmers with much needed irrigation. The two countries have also increased their trade and economic ties. One result of the new cooperation is that the Thai government may be turning its back on Laotian guerrillas who had previously sought sanctuary in their country. In June, the *Bangkok Post* quoted sources saying that Thailand had ordered anti-Communist Hmong rebels at clandestine bases inside the Thai border to return to Laos or disarm and go to refugee camps. Thailand had previously aided the Hmong tribesmen, who were recruited by the CIA in the early 1970s to fight the Laotian Communists. There were also unconfirmed reports in June that Laos had used chemical weapons against the Hmong.

Political Rights and Civil Liberties:

Citizens of Laos cannot change their government democratically. The Lao People's Revolutionary Party (LPRP) is the only legal party. The Supreme People's Assembly contains only LPRP candidates or those approved by the party under the Lao Front for National Reconstruction. The judiciary is not independent of the government and defendants have limited procedural rights. Although most political re-education camps have been closed, there are reportedly at least thirty-three political prisoners. All media are state owned and reflect only party views. Public criticism of the regime is not permitted. Freedom of assembly is limited to pro-government or religious and sporting activities. Unspecified "de-stabilizing subversive activities" are illegal and can be punished by death. All associations, including labor unions, are government controlled. The Ministry of Interior watches society closely, and the LPRP has its own network of informants. Reportedly, the government has relaxed monitoring of individuals, but it appears determined to maintain tight control. Citizens must often obtain government permission for internal travel, and opportunities for travel abroad remain limited.

Nearly all Lao are Buddhists, and the government officially recognizes freedom of religion. The government monitors the activities of Roman Catholic and Protestant churches.

Latvia

Polity: Presidential-parliamentary democracy
Economy: Statist transitional
Population: 2,667,000
PPP: na
Life Expectancy: na
Ethnic Groups: Latvians (52 percent), Russians (34 percent), Ukrainians, Poles, Byelorussians, Lithuanians and Jews

Political Rights: 2
Civil Liberties: 3
Status: Free

Overview:

A year that began with Soviet violence against this small Baltic republic ended in triumph, as Latvia regained sovereignty it had lost over 50 years ago under the Hitler-Stalin Pact.

Although nationalist movements have existed in Latvia since the 1940 Soviet takeover, the republic's recent road to independence gained momentum in July 1989 when the Latvian Supreme Council (legislature) adopted a "declaration of sovereignty" and amended the Latvian constitution to assert the supremacy of its laws over those of the Soviet Union. Later that year, the legislature abolished the Communist party's monopoly on political power and legalized a multi-party system.

On 15 February 1990, a stormy session of parliament ended with the adoption (by a vote of 177 to 48) of a declaration condemning the 1940 "request" to enter the USSR. A month later, in the first competitive elections since 1940, Latvians voted for candidates to the 201-member Supreme Council. The Popular Front of Latvia (PFL), formed in 1988 as an umbrella group for a wide range of pro-independence opposition groups, won 116 of the 170 seats in the first round, and an additional five in run off races on 25 March and 1 April. The PFL ran on a platform that called for Latvian independence and the implementation of market reforms. PFL leader Ivars Godamis was named prime minister and Anatolijs Gorbunovs was named president. The Interfront, a pro-Moscow group claiming to represent some 300,000 of Latvia's 800,000 Russian-speakers, won 39 seats in the first round, and the Agricultural Union (AU), founded in 1989 to represent peasant and farmer interests, won 6 seats. Nine unaffiliated deputies were also elected.

The PFL endorsed a number of "reform" Communists. By late February, the Latvian Communist Party (LaCP), which included some 70,000 Latvians among its 175,000 members, broke into three factions: the conservatives, who did not favor secession from the USSR; the independents, among them many Latvians who favored an independent LaCP; and a so-called "Third Way" group, which supported greater autonomy but not complete independence. Other pro-independence groups included the Latvian Social Democratic Workers Party, founded in 1905 and the largest party during Latvia's inter-war independence, the Latvian Green Party, an environmental-ecological group, the Democratic Union of Latvia, representing Russians supporting Latvian sovereignty, and the National Independence Movement of Latvia (LNNK), an uncompromising and openly anti-Communist group established in 1988. Twenty-three LNNK candidates ran under the PFL banner, but some LNNK members refused to take part in the vote, arguing the elections would legitimize what they considered a structure of a hostile foreign power. The Republican Party of Latvia (RPL), formed in 1989 to uphold the pre-war constitution, boycotted the votes.

1991 opened with a crisis in the Baltics, as the central Soviet government under President Mikhail Gorbachev unleashed a violent crackdown. On 2 January Interior Ministry MVD Black Berets, or OMON, attacked a publishing center in Riga, Latvia's capital. On 15 January, Soviet commandos stormed a Latvian police academy and seized weapons from cadets. Five days later, four people were killed and 11 wounded when Black Beret commandos stormed the Latvian Interior Ministry. Another threat to the government came from the so-called All-Latvian Public Salvation Committee, which on 17 January declared it was in charge of Latvian political life, noting that "Soviet Latvia must remain in a renewed USSR." The shadowy committee was linked with hard-line Communists in Latvia and Moscow who hoped to intimidate Latvia's non-Communist government. Following international concern about the violence in the Baltics, President Gorbachev tried to distance himself from the events, implying that the OMON forces could have acted without the knowledge of central authorities in Moscow.

Undaunted by Soviet tactics, the Latvian parliament voted on 12 February to hold a referendum on the creation of "a democratic Latvia as an independent state." One-hundred-one of the 105 deputies present in the 201-seat parliament reportedly supported the proposed vote, which was scheduled for 3 March, just two weeks before the national referendum on Soviet unity organized by President Gorbachev. On 3 March, 73 percent voted "yes" to the question, "are you for a democratic and independent Latvian republic?" Three days later, the Supreme Council ruled that the 17 March all-union referendum had "no legal effect on Latvia."

Black Beret intimidation flared up again in July when four commandos broke into the customs post at the main railroad station in Riga. There were at least three similar attacks during the month. OMON forces also seized and interrogated two policemen unloading cartridges, and confiscated the ammunition. On 17 July, a mysterious blast caused by explosives placed in a lavatory rocked the procurator's office in Riga. The same month, the Council of the PFL discussed a "transitional constitution" that would replace the Latvian SSR document.

The August coup attempt against President Gorbachev greatly accelerated the independence process. On 23 August, Latvia joined Estonia and Lithuania in declaring independence. Four days later, the European Community recognized the breakaway republics. Moscow and Washington soon followed. On 17 September, the United Nations General Assembly voted to accept the applications of the new Baltic states. On October 24 the three were admitted as associate members of the North Atlantic Treaty Organization (NATO).

On 10 September the Latvian Supreme Council banned the LaCP and its related organizations including the Komsomol, the Council of Labor Collectives, and the Council of War and Labor Veterans. On 3 October the Supreme Council voted to end all participation in parliamentary bodies in the USSR. The decision withdrew all deputies from the USSR Supreme Soviet and the Congress of People's Deputies. The Supreme Council decided that as of 1 November the council's official documents and proceedings would no longer be translated into Russian.

The citizenship question was perhaps the most controversial and complex issue faced by the state, primarily because some 40 percent of the population is non-Latvian. In mid-September, some 3,000 Latvian nationalists protested in Riga against proposals to allow Soviet immigrants the right to vote. On 15 October the Latvian Supreme Council adopted a decision "On the Restoration of the Rights of Citizens of the Republic of Latvia and Regulation for Naturalization." The legislation set forth guiding principles for attaining Latvian citizenship. The citizenship requirements included conversational knowledge of Latvian, knowledge of the Latvian legal structure, 16 years residence in Latvia, an oath of allegiance, and the renunciation of citizenship from another state. Only those who were Latvian citizens on 17 June 1940—when the Soviets invaded— and their descendants were automatically granted citizenship.

The decision was criticized by both pro-Moscow factions and Latvian nationalists. The first group, opponents of Latvian independence, charged that the legislation would bring a type of apartheid to Latvia and violate widely accepted norms of human rights. Only 21 percent of the nation's Russians speak Latvian. Latvian nationalists argued that the Supreme Council had no authority to pass legislation, since it had been elected by Soviet citizens at a time when Latvia was not independent. The situation was further complicated because none of the country's five leaders— including the president and prime minister—participated in the citizenship resolution. All were either out of the country or abstained from voting, reportedly because they feared the explosive issue could be politically damaging. In the past, President Gorbunovs supported the so-called "zero option," in which all people living in Latvia when it declared independence would automatically have become citizens. The PFL also supported "zero option," but since independence, politics had become more radically nationalist. By the end of 1991 the citizenship issue had not been resolved. Latvia's demographic dilemma was complicated by the fact that its cities are over-whelmingly Russian. Riga is only one-third Latvian and Daugavpils, the second largest city, is only 13 percent Latvian. In addition, more than 80 percent of Latvia's private capital is controlled by non-Latvians. Latvia's skilled laborers are also primarily Russian. A large exodus of non-Latvians could have a profound impact on Latvia's economy.

The citizenship controversy virtually paralyzed privatization and other market reforms, because property ownership was tied to citizenship. Leaders feared that the perception of political instability threatened Western investment. On 4 September Latvia opened the way for the return of foreigners' property seized after the Soviet annexation. On 15 September the Bank of Latvia announced that it would no longer be able to complete transactions with banks in Estonia, Lithuania and the USSR owing to a shortage of rubles. The problem was created by the refusal of Soviet central authorities to ship rubles to Latvia after its independence was recognized. Despite these problems, most Western experts predicted that Latvia and the other Baltic states would receive substantial Western investment because of their skilled work force, established international banking links, high productivity and a comparatively developed infrastructure. On 6 November Radio Riga announced that the Supreme Council had established a monetary reform committee to oversee the introduction of the *lats* as Latvia's official currency. On 21 November, President Gorbunovs announced that prices would be freed by December 1991, adding that price reform was the only way to carry out the transition to a market economy. As of 1 November, Russia decided to restrict its gasoline and oil shipments to the Baltic states. On 5 December, all Russian energy shipments to Latvia were cut to force the return of Interior Ministry Commander Sergei Parfyonov, a Black Beret officer who took part in the January crackdown.

Another major issue was the removal of the KGB and Soviet troops from Latvia. At the end of September, the deputy chairman of the KGB told Moscow radio that the KGB would be dissolved in the Baltics by early 1992. On 5 November the Supreme Council adopted a resolution laying claim to all property occupied by the Soviet armed forces, border guards and Interior Ministry troops and invalidating any commercial transactions involving such property that took place after 24 August. The Soviets, who have over 100,000 troops stationed in the Baltics, said they would withdraw by 1994, a position unacceptable to Latvia.

Political Rights and Civil Liberties:

Latvians can change their government democratically under a new multi-party system. Parliamentary elections were held in 1990, before Latvia became an independent state, and a new vote is expected in 1992. Since independence, the process to make the judiciary truly independent has accelerated. There is a varied independent press which no longer faces the strictures of Soviet law. Freedom of assembly and association are generally respected and there are several well-organized political parties, but the government banned the Communist Party and its affiliated organizations. The final citizenship law may yet prove to discriminate against the non-Latvian minority. Since 1989 freedom of religion has been respected in this largely Lutheran country. In 1990 Easter and Christmas were made official holidays, a theological faculty was established at Riga University, and the first Jewish school in the Baltics was opened in Riga. Although freedom of movement is generally respected, there were some restrictions. In late October, the deputy prime minister signed a government decision to limit trips to Poland by residents of Latvia until 1 January 1992. The reason was based on the fact that many people traveled to Poland to engage in speculative economic transactions. Otherwise, Latvians are free to travel abroad. Since independence, a free trade union confederation has been established.

Lebanon

Polity: Presidential-parliamentary (military and foreign-influenced)
Economy: Mixed statist
Population: 3,400,000
PPP: na
Life Expectancy: 66.1
Ethnic Groups: Eastern Hamitic (90 percent), Greek, Syro-Lebonese

Political Rights: 6
Civil Liberties: 4
Status: Partly Free

Overview:

In 1991, after 16 years of civil war, Syrian-brokered peace began to take hold in Lebanon under terms of the 1989 Arab League-sponsored Taif Accord. Following reunification of Beirut last December, the Syrian-backed Lebanese Army disbanded and disarmed the country's major militias, including the PLO, and asserted control over most of its territory, except Lebanon's south, where Israel, facing hardline Shia guerillas, maintained its self-proclaimed "security zone." While the government of President Elias Hrawi moved ahead on reconstruction plans and announced that elections would take place by spring of 1992, Syrian hegemony over Lebanon cast doubt on prospects for sovereignty and democracy.

In 1990 the Lebanese Army, with Syrian backing, defeated the forces of Michel Aoun, who refused to relinquish power to the central government formed in accordance with the Taif accord. Aoun fought to expel Syrian forces, which still number over 40,000 on Lebanese territory. Lebanon first invited Syria in 1976 to help quell Muslim groups seeking accomodation in the Maronite-dominated government.

The present Lebanese government was formed in December 1990, in accordance with constitutional changes (stipulated by the Taif accord) nullifying guarantees of Christian dominance. The president, a Christian, shares power with an eqully divided Christian-Muslim Cabinet led by a Sunni Muslim prime minister. Christians and Muslims are to have equal representation in Parliament, which formerly had a Christian majority. The Parliament speaker should also be a Muslim.

As 1991 began, reverberations of the Gulf War, such as bank runs and explosions at banks with Western and Saudi interests, were overshadowed by changes taking place in Lebanon. In late 1990, the disbanding of the private Christian and Muslim militias and dismantling of the barricades which had divided Greater Beirut into a Christian East and Muslim West for 16 years had ushered in feelings of optimism among Lebanese.

Prime Minister Omar Karami's Muslim-Christian cabinet, formed last Christmas Eve after the resignation of former Prime Minister Selim al-Hoss got off to a late start due to a boycott by three key Christian ministers—Samir Geagea, leader of the Christian Lebanese Forces, George Sa'adah, former leader of the Phalange Party and Micheal Sassin, labor minister—in protest of Syria's heavy influence in Lebanese affairs.

The government resumed in March when Sassin and Sa'adah agreed to take up their posts in the Cabinet, which includes nine ministers to represent the nine main Christian, Druze and Muslim militias. Citing personal security reasons, Samir Geagea resigned, and was replaced by Roger Dib, secretary-general of the Phalangist Party. On March 28, the Cabinet met for the first time to decide plans for reconstruction and complete reunification. Among the decisions made was a deadline of April 1 for the disbandment and disarmament of all the militias. The government also decided to increase the number of Parliamentary seats to 108 from 98. The government needed to nominate 30 already missing members plus the additional ten. Maronites contended that the already existing members of Parliament, not the pro-Syrian Cabinet, should do the nominating.

Part of the government's truce with the militias is the integration of some 20,000 out of 50,000 militia members into the national armed forces and the police. Militia members would first undergo 6 months of rehabilitation and training. What to do with the other 30,000 militia men, largely from underprivileged backgrounds, remained controversial, as the civil war has destroyed most economic opportunity.

After closing down illegal ports, formerly a main source of the militias' revenue, Lebanese authorities opened Beirut port and smaller ports in the Greater Beirut area. For the first time in 16 years, citizens moved about safely in most of the country. Lebanese, many of them visiting or returning from exile, flocked to archeological sites, beaches and mountain resorts. Businesses began to revive and foreign airlines resumed flights to Beirut, while bankers came to Lebanon to explore possibilities of reopening offices and investing in Lebanon's reconstruction efforts.

The issue of Syrian hegemony over Lebanon remained a source of concern for many Lebanese. On 22 May Syria and Lebanon signed a "Treaty of Brotherhood, Cooperation and Coordination," which gives Syria a voice in all major areas of Lebanese affairs, including foreign policy and security, and allows indefinite deployment of the Syrian army in all areas of the country. According to some reports, candidates for the legislature must be approved by Syria.

Not much progress in the way of peace was made in south Lebanon, where a mini-war has raged among rival factions of the PLO; two Shiite groups, the Iranian backed Party of God and pro-Syrian Amal; and Israel, which occupies a 9-mile wide security zone north of the Israeli border and backs the South Lebanese Army (SLA). During the Gulf war in early 1991, Israel and the PLO exchanged heavy fire; Israeli commandos moved beyond the security zone to raid PLO bases in Sidon, near two camps where thousands of Palestinian guerrillas are entrenched.

In February the Lebanese army moved into the area for the first time in 13 years in an attempt to extend the authority of the Lebanese Government. Its goal was to stop PLO strikes against Israel, in order to remove Israel's reason for maintaining its security zone. All the armies of south Lebanon failed to comply with the 1 April deadline. The PLO claimed it was not a militia, but the national army of Palestine facing the Zionist enemy. Hizbullah cited waiting for orders from Teheran. Israel maintained it would never leave until Syria withdraws its troops.

In May, Lebanese troops took up positions at entrances to Palestinian refugee districts and areas close to Israel's security zone. In July, after a 4-day battle, Lebanese forces succeeding in dismantling the power base of Yassir Arafat's PLO, comprised of an estimated 6,000 guerillas, as well as the radical breakaway group led by the world-renowned terrorist Abu Nidal. The battle ended with peaceful agreement from both sides. The Beirut government announced the lifting of job restrictions on the 400,000 Palestinians living in Lebanon.

After destroying the PLO bases, President Hrawi began to appeal to the international community, especially the United States, for implementing UN Security Council Resolution 425 calling for Israeli withdrawal from south Lebanon. For the remainder of the year, fierce fighting continued between Israel and Shiites and remaining Palestinians; Israel continued bombing Shia villages from the air.

In other matters, pressure by Iran and Syria on Hizbollah and Amal led to the release of Western hostages seized in Lebanon in the 1980s. In late 1991, the Shiite groups released all the American hostages. Two German hostages remained in Lebanon. The Shiite groups demanded Israel's release of Palestinian and Lebanese prisoners and Party of God cleric, Sheik Abdul Karim Obeid. Israel pressed for the return of seven missing Israeli servicemen.

Political Rights and Civil Liberties: Lebanon has not had direct parliamentary elections since 1972. In 1991 Lebanon's new government announced plans to hold elections in 1992. According to the constitution, direct elections should be held every four years for the Parliament, which in turn elects a president every six years. The president appoints the Cabinet which must obtain the confidence of Parliament.

The present Lebanese government is based on the rules of a 1989 Arab League peace plan called the Taif Accord, which establishes political equality between Christians and Muslims. Syrian dominance in Lebanese affairs casts a shadow over the country's right of self-determination. A 1991 cooperation pact between the two countries allows indefinite occupation of Lebanon by Syrian troops, which number 40,000.

Once an Arab bastion of law and civility, Lebanon protects fredom of press, speech, religion and assembly. Many other basic rights which had been circumscribed by the country's civil war have been returned to Lebanese citizens, who are now able to move about the country freely and safely. Freedom of movement however did not improve in south Lebanon, where fighting continues.

Private armies, such as Hezbollah and the South Lebanese Army, detain suspects arbitrarily for indefinite periods. Goverment forces are also responsible for arbitrary detention. Detainees are often held incommunicado. The legal system is formally independent and Lebanese law and custom provide for the right of fair trial. Fair judicial procedure, disrupted by the breakdown of central authority over the past years, is still lacking. Militias often intervene on behalf of their supporters.

With fourteen radio stations, several TV companies and eight daily newspapers, Beirut is one of the liveliest publishing and broadcasting centers in the region. The Lebanese population receives Arab and Western music and news in French, English and Arabic. *Es Safir*, one of the country's major newspapers, is banned in Israeli-controlled Southern Lebanon.

The country has no official religion and there are no restrictions on religious groups. Yet the politico-religious civil war fostered religious hostilities. Neighborhoods and villages continue to be separated according to religion, but the segregation is no longer enforced by the private militias. Conversion to a religion other than that of one's birth is complicated and leads to ostracism, except in the case of women, who normally adopt the religion of their spouse.

Lesotho

Polity: Military transitional
Economy: Capitalist
Population: 1,800,000
PPP: $1,390
Life Expectancy: 57.3
Ethnic Groups: Sotho (99 percent)

Political Rights: 6
Civil Liberties: 4
Status: Partly Free

Overview:

In 1991 the major news stories in Lesotho involved the struggle for control of the state and the outbreak of inter-ethnic violence. On 30 April troops forced the ruling military strongman, Major General Justin Metsing Lekhanya, to announce his government's resignation after his refusal to grant a pay raise to enlisted men.

Lesotho, a traditional monarchy in which real political power rests with the head of the Military Council, has been an independent state within the British Commonwealth since 1966. The present head of state is King Letsie III, while Lekhanya's successor as commander-in-chief of the military is Colonel Pitsoana Ramaema. Major General Lekhanya had ruled the country at the head of a military council since 1986, when he overthrew Prime Minister Chief Leabua Jonathan of the Basotho National Party (BNP). After this coup, widely believed to have been engineered by South Africa, the ruling Council dissolved the parliament, which had been appointed by Chief Jonathan in 1983. The military banned all political activity after taking power, and both legislative and executive power were conferred on the Council by the former king. The major political conflict in Lesotho in the past few years has been between King Moshoeshoe II (King Letsie III's father) and Lekhanya. In 1990 Lekhanya stripped the king of his powers for continuing to oppose the political will of the major general. The throne was offered to Letsie. Presently, Moshoeshoe lives in exile in London. Lekhanya was placed under house arrest after an alleged attempt was made to return him to power three months after he was overthrown.

Inter-ethnic violence erupted in May 1991 after a Sotho woman who allegedly shoplifted from an Asian-owned store was beaten to death by security guards. In the rioting that followed, hundreds of shops were looted and vandalized, some factories were burned down, and 34 rioters and bystanders were reportedly killed by security forces. Many residents of Indian and Chinese descent, the majority involved in the country's small-scale commercial sector, fled to nearby South Africa. Gangs of Sothos created roadblocks and reportedly beat some of the fleeing Asians, although only one non-African was said to have been killed in the unrest. The government imposed a curfew to control the situation, and some Lesothans accused the government of directing the police to use deadly force in order to pacify the business sector.

Before he was ousted Lekhanya set up a National Constituent Assembly to rewrite the nation's constitution and provide for multi-partyism. After the coup, the NCA submitted the finished product to Ramaema and the Military Council for approval. The new military government has promised that civilian rule will be restored in Lesotho as planned by Lekhanya, and that the military will return to the barracks. In May 1991 Ramaema lifted the five-year-old ban against political parties. Parties have begun to form in preparation for elections. Significant popular sentiment exists in the country in favor of restoring Moshoeshoe to the throne.

Lesotho's economy is heavily dependent on the Republic of South Africa for employment and energy; a major source of foreign exchange is remittances from migrant gold and diamond miners working in South Africa. There is indication that some 40,000 Basothos may lose jobs in South African gold mines due to industry difficulties. In addition, ANC activists reportedly resent the Basotho migrants, who tend to work hard, spend little, live quietly in substandard hostels, and keep out of South African politics. Earlier, Lekhanya had worked closely with South African security and intelligence forces and expelled the anti-apartheid African National Congress (ANC) from Lesotho, long a haven for exiled opponents of apartheid and guerrillas.

Political Rights and Civil Liberties: Lesothans cannot yet change their government democratically. In May, the new government repealed the ban on political parties and continues to prepare for a 1992 election. The judiciary is relatively independent in civil and criminal cases. The 1984 Internal Security act allows the government to hold individuals without charge. The private press is able to criticize the government. Although overwhelmingly Christian, other faiths have the right to practice. Non-political associations are free to organize and meet. Domestic and foreign travel is generally unrestricted. Workers formally have the right to organize in practice and strike. There are two labor federations, the Lesotho Confederation of Free Trade Unions (LCFTU) and the Lesotho Federation of Trade Unions (LFTU).

Liberia

Polity: Transitional (military and foreign influenced)
Economy: Capitalist
Population: 2,700,000
PPP: $890
Life Expectancy: 54.2
Ethnic Groups: Sixteen major tribes, including the Krahn, Mandingo, Gio and Mano (95 percent), Americo-Liberians (5 percent)

Political Rights: 7
Civil Liberties: 6
Status: Not Free

Overview: Liberia's civil war continued in 1991, although peace appeared close with the signing of an accord in November. The war has left at least 10,000 dead, destroyed most of the nation's infrastructure, and sent hundreds of thousands of refugees fleeing to neighboring countries.

Liberia was established in 1847 by freed American slaves, whose descendants are known as Americo-Liberians. The present conflict has its origins in the ten-year brutal reign of General Samuel Doe, who overthrew the elected government of William Tolbert in 1980. The Tolbert government had been led by an Americo-Liberian elite, which has dominated the country's politics since 1878. A member of the Krahn, the most rural and deprived of Liberia's ethnic groups, Doe became the first indigenous African to rule the country. Promoting himself to general, he consolidated his power by establishing and heading the National Democratic Party of Liberia (NDPL) and forming a hand picked Interim Assembly, dominated by his Krahn tribe. Giving a large proportion of government positions to members of Krahn, (they make up 4 percent of Liberia's population), Doe was accused of oppressing ethnic groups.

In December 1989 the National Patriotic Front of Liberia (NPFL), composed in large part of Gio and Mano tribesmen and led by Charles Gankary Taylor, an Americo-Liberian and former Doe cabinet member, began to attack government troops. In February 1990 a second rebel faction, the Independent National Patriotic Front of Liberia (INPFL), was created by Taylor's former second in command, Prince Yormie Johnson. By mid-1990, the capital, Monrovia, became a city under siege, with shortages of food, water and medicine. Government soldiers looted shops, warehouses and restaurants. The INPFL gained control of Monrovia on 23 July, and subsequently tortured, dismembered and killed Doe, capturing his final moments on videotape.

Fearing the effect the war could have on their own countries, members of the Economic Organization of West African States (ECOWAS) decided to intervene in August by sending an armed Monitoring Group (ECOMOG). By the end of 1990, the warring groups arrived at a stalemate. The ECOMOG, which had the support of the INPFL and the remnants of the Armed Forces of Liberia (AFL), controlled the capital, while the NPFL controlled the rest of the country. An ECOWAS-sponsored interim government, with Amos Sawyer as President, was set up in November 1990. The INPFL eventually left the interim government in August 1991, accusing it of economic mismanagement.

Sawyer attempted to involve the NPFL in the interim government, appointing an NPFL representative as speaker of the interim legislature and offering to have Taylor pick two out of the five Supreme Court seats. Sawyer also began reconstituting the Liberian Armed Forces to fairly represent the country's ethnic groups. In May, the entire cabinet resigned two weeks after a national conference had re-elected Dr. Sawyer as interim president, in accordance with his promise to share power with the NPFL and the INPFL. The members of the reconstituted cabinet had to resign any party affiliation.

Throughout 1991, the factions attempted to end the civil war, with Johnson's loyalty wavering between the NPFL and Sawyer's government. With an initial cease-fire on 18 January, all factions agreed to cease hostilities and to draw up buffer zones. However, they deadlocked over issues concerning disarmament and confine-ment of troops. During another cease-fire conference on 13 February in Togo, the warring parties finally agreed to confine their troops and disarm them in time for a national conference on 15 March, although neither side kept its pledges. Charles Taylor also announced his candidacy for the presidency, although the cease-fire agreement expressly forbade him from doing so.

Participants in the March national conference included representatives of all warring factions and political parties. Taylor sent representatives to the conference but refused to attend himself, believing that Prince Johnson would attempt to assassinate him. Eventu-ally, the NPFL delegation walked out, declaring the entire process illegal and unaccept-able. The conference affirmed Sawyer's presidency and set an October date for new elections. The latest peace efforts have been a round of talks in Ivory Coast among the 5 states that make up ECOMOG. At the final meeting on 29 October, Taylor agreed to disarm and encamp his troops under supervision of a larger ECOMOG force, on condition that Senegal increase its representation in the peacekeeping force and that Nigeria reduce its contingent. The NPFL further agreed to allow ECOMOG to control the country. The disarmament was to begin 60 days from the signing of the accord, with elections to follow in six months. One notable feature of the peace talks was the fact that the INPFL was not invited to participate. In retaliation, Prince Johnson initially stated that he would not disarm his troops, but on 8 November he agreed to rejoin the government in return for several key ministerial posts, including the Ministry of Defense. By the end of 1991, Taylor had not yet begun to disarm his troops.

During 1991 the conflict spread to neighboring countries. In late March, reports surfaced that members of the NPFL were attacking villages over the Sierra Leone border, which had allegedly been used as conduits for trade between the rebels and Sierra Leonean border guards. Although Taylor denies have anything to do with the attacks, many people believe that he is encouraging the de-stabilization of neighboring countries who have contributed to the ECOWAS efforts. In September an armed group of Liberian refugees and former government soldiers, under the name of ULIMO (United Liberation Movement for Democracy), began attacks on the NPFL from bases in Sierra Leone. ULIMO is also comprised of members from two other exile groups, the National Defense Force and the Guinea-based Movement for the Redemption of the Muslims. Heaviest fighting occurred in Cape Mount County, with ULIMO claiming control in November. With the signing of the peace accord, ULIMO agreed to cease hostilities unilaterally, but insisted that it would not disarm until the NPFL had completely laid down their arms. The civil war has created a huge refugee problem. Nearly half of the country's 2.5 million people have fled the country or were displaced internally. Currently there are over 300,000 displaced persons in Monrovia, who have come from the Taylor-held territories, complaining of harassment by hungry and disgruntled rebels. Others have fled to Guinea, Sierra Leone and Burkina Faso.

Despite the almost complete destruction of civil society, political activity increased in 1991. A group of prominent Liberians formed the "People to People Contact for Peace" to assist in the search for a solution to the country's problems. The True Whig party, which had governed the country for over a century until Doe's coup in 1980, reactivated itself in May. Other parties include Doe's own National Democratic Party, Sawyer's Liberian People's Party, the United People's Party, the Unity Party, the Liberian Action Party and the Liberian Unification Party.

Although the situation in Liberia is still bleak, there have been signs of renewal, notably in Monrovia. Brigades of youths have been cleaning up the capital, while other groups have been working to restore basic necessities. Electricity has been restored to the center of the city, but clean water remains scarce.

Political Rights and Civil Liberties:

Liberians do not have the right to choose their government democratically. However, the latest round of talks in 1991 has slated the first post-civil war elections for early 1992.

As the civil war progressed, any respect for political rights and civil liberties broke down completely. Until February 1991, Taylor forbade Muslims from worshipping in their mosques in NPFL territory and accused the Mandingos, who make up the mainstream of Muslims in Liberia, of siding with Doe's Krahn ethnic group. Even after Taylor lifted the ban, there were still reports of Muslims being harassed or even executed. Taylor did not interfere with Christian worship. Religious organizations, both Christian and Muslim, were active in trying to find peace and in helping to bring aid to displaced people.

Before the war, the government-controlled radio and television stations dominated the media. Several independent newspapers and three independent radio stations were permitted to operate, although there was some censorship and occasional harassment. However, by the end of the civil war, most media had been shut down. Both the interim government and the NPFL control their own radio stations. Just before Christmas 1990, the first newspaper to resume publishing, *Torchlight,* appeared. A couple of weeks later, another newspaper, the *Enquirer*, also resumed publishing. Monrovia has enjoyed freer speech and assembly than the NPFL areas. Although ECOMOG did ban demonstrations and nonreligious public gatherings in December 1990, this was not rigidly enforced. Freedom of speech is severely restricted in NPFL territory. Only one newspaper, *The Patriot,* is allowed. Dissenters are beaten and imprisoned. Personal letters are often confiscated and their carriers jailed if the letters are critical of the NPFL. Freedom of movement is restricted within Liberia, especially between the capital and the other counties. According to escapees from NPFL territory, people who admitted they were travelling to Monrovia were given twenty-five lashes and sent back. Although some of the major roads were opened for the national conference in March, most still remain closed. In Monrovia, small independent businesses are allowed, but the NPFL keeps tight control over the economy in the rest of the country. Most, if not all, of the revenue from the NPFL-controlled ports goes to the rebel organization. NPFL commandos themselves make up the bulk merchants, selling stolen goods to supplement their paltry salaries.

Libya

Polity: Military
Economy: Mixed statist
Population: 4,400,000
PPP: na
Life Expectancy: 61.8
Ethnic Groups: Arab and Berber

Political Rights: 7
Civil Liberties: 7
Status: Not Free

Overview:

In 1991 Libyan dictator Colonel Mu'ammar al-Qadhafi attempted to forge better ties with the international community, taking a neutral stance in the Persian Gulf War and renouncing international terrorist activity. However, amidst evidence suggesting Libyan involvement in the 1988 bombing of Pan Am flight 103, resumption of ties with the West, especially the United States, remained elusive.

In 1991, Libya, emphasizing the goals of Arab unity, established closer ties with its North African neighbors. Qadhafi and Egyptian President Mubarak met several times during the Gulf crisis. As part of an economic cooperation agreement, Libya imported nearly 1 million Egyptians to till land irrigated by the new Great Man-Made River (GMR) project in Libya. In return for Libya's new cooperation, Egypt made overtures to the United States for a more open policy toward Libya. In mid-February, Libya held a special meeting of the Maghreb Union—Libya, Algeria, Tunisia, Morocco and Mauritania—to discuss the Gulf War. In March, Libya destroyed the gate separating Egypt and Libya, announced the lifting of travel restrictions and customs and duties on goods flowing between the two countries, and excluded Arabs from a ban on hiring foreign workers. Qadhafi also called for lifting the ban on some Egyptian newspapers and magazines.

Libya's 15-year-old war with Chad remained unresolved but appeared nearing an end. In late 1990, Libyan-backed rebels overthrew Hissein Habre's regime and brought to power Idriss Deby, favored by France. However, Chad and Libya still could not agree on a peaceful solution to their dispute over the mineral-rich Aouzou strip border region.

Another source of discord was the Chad government's decision to force 600 members of the National Front for the Salvation of Libya, a United States-backed Libyan opposition force, into uncertain exile rather than hand them over to Libya. In early 1991, the United States brought the Libyan dissidents to Kenya, then to Zaire. In May the United States agreed to accept 350 of the homeless dissidents. In March 1991, the exiled Libyan Prince Idris declared that he would take charge of the dissident group and organize its fight against the Qadhafi regime.

Toward the end of 1991, the United States and Great Britain accused Libya of orchestrating the bombing of Pan Am Flight 103 in 1988. The Western powers demanded the extradition of two Libyans said to be responsible for the incident. Colonel Qadhafi denied Libya's involvement in the affair and called on Britain and the United States to present their evidence to a neutral international tribunal or the United Nations. Qadhafi appealed to the Arab League for support and announced Libya would begin its own investigation. The issue foiled Libya's efforts to improve relations with the West. In June, Qadhafi said he hoped for a "period of Arab-U.S. cooperation." Pursuant to this Libya has distanced itself from renowned terrorist Abu Nidal and vowed to sever relations with other terrorist groups. In an attempt to appease Britain, Qadhafi promised to cease relations with the Irish Republican Army. Libya stressed that it would continue to support what it deemed liberation movements struggling for self-determination, such as the PLO, but would not "help them take hostages or hijack planes." Earlier in the year, the U.S. accused Libya of developing poison gas facilities.

Political Rights and Civil Liberties:

Libyans do not have the right to democratically choose their leaders. Theoretically a socialist *Jamahariya*, a community based on mass support, Libya is actually a dictatorship of Col. Mu'ammar Qadhafi. In power for twenty-one years, Qadhafi is the "revolutionary guide" who, along with very few associates, makes all effective decisions. Political parties are outlawed and no opposition is tolerated.

Nominal power lies with the general secretary of the General People's Congress. The GPC is indirectly elected by popularly elected municipal committees called People's Committees, which monitor the populace. The Revolutionary Committees oversee the People's Committees and screen all of their candidates. Libya's multi-layered surveillance network is coupled with an extensive security apparatus.

Only groups supportive of the regime are allowed to organized and demonstrate. Independent trade unions and vocational groups are banned. The Libyan press lauds the regime; criticism of the government is impossible. Though the People's Committees provide some leeway for discussion, citizens generally do not express political views for fear of discovery by the revolutionary committees and a huge informer network. At least one hundred political prisoners are believed to be held incommunicado in secret detention centers. Political dissidents living abroad risk regime-sponsored assassination attempts. The right to fair trial is often not provided by Libya's arbitrary judiciary system. Detainees are frequently beaten and deprived of counsel, and are sometimes sentenced without trial. The death penalty is applied for many offenses. In

1991, around 500 Nigerians deported from Libya reported "barbaric torture" of Nigerians in Libya, which worsened after Nigeria resumed ties with Israel in August.

Predominantly Sunni Muslim, Libya cracks down on Islamic fundamentalist activity and the state closely monitors all mosques for potential political agitation. In 1990, all bearded males were subject to round ups and detention on suspicion of being members of fundamentalist groups. Foreign workers have been forcibly drafted into the Libyan military. Travel abroad, especially throughout the Maghreb, has recently been made easier.

Lithuania

Polity: Presidential-parliamentary democracy
Economy: Statist transitional
Population: 3,673,000
PPP: na
Life Expectancy: na
Ethnic Groups: Lithuanian (80 percent), Russian, Ukrainian, Byelorussian, others (20 percent)

Political Rights: 2
Civil Liberties: 3
Status: Free

Overview:

A year that began with Soviet military violence against this breakaway republic ended with international recognition of Lithuania as a fully independent state. Among key issues facing the newly independent country in 1991 were negotiating the withdrawal of Soviet troops and implementing comprehensive economic reform.

In early January, Moscow sent troops into the Lithuanian capital of Vilnius to intimidate the republic's independence-minded government, whose President Vytautas Landsbergis, had led the pro-independence Sajudis popular front to victory in the February 1990 parliamentary (Supreme Council) elections. Lithuania had proclaimed independence in March shortly after the vote.

The crisis began on 8 January with the resignation of Prime Minister Kazimiera Prunskiene and her cabinet after months of growing tensions between the prime minister and President Landsbergis on how to deal with Moscow and reshape the economy. She stepped down after parliament suspended her government's decision to raise retail prices of food sharply in an attempt to move the republic to a market economy. The same day, some 5,000 demonstrators, organized by the pro-Moscow Interfront group, an umbrella for Russian minorities and orthodox Communists, marched in Vilnius to protest the pro-independence policies of the government and the proposed price hikes. Gediminas Vagneris was named prime minister. The next day, Soviet troops surrounded Lithuania's television tower and positioned themselves near the republic's parliament building. Thousands of Lithuanians gathered around the parliament after President Landsbergis called on citizens to defend the legislature. On 10 January, President Gorbachev warned Lithuanian leaders that he might impose direct rule on Lithuania if it did not comply with national laws. Later in the week, representatives of Lithuania's Russian, Polish, Jewish, German and other minorities issued a statement supporting the Lithuanian government's position on autonomy.

Peace was shattered on 13 January, as Soviet tanks and soldiers killed 14 and wounded over 400 Lithuanians who had gathered to protect the television facility in Vilnius. At the same time, a self-styled National Salvation Committee announced that it had seized power and that a Red Army major general had been named commandant of Vilnius. The shadowy committee installed by Moscow declared a curfew, banned public gatherings, outlawed the possession of television cameras or tape recorders and imposed a "social regime" of personal searches and random document checks.

President Gorbachev blamed the Lithuanian separatist government and leadership for bringing on the violence and said the troops were called in without his knowledge to protect the National Salvation Committee. He insisted that no one in Moscow had issued orders to the troops in Lithuania. Meanwhile, the army, which had gained control of broadcast facilities in Vilnius, announced that the killing of the demonstrators was a defensive action. A similar line was taken by newspapers and television news from Moscow. While Lithuanians continued to guard the heavily fortified parliament building, ignoring Soviet assurances, the Lithuanian government resumed broadcasting from the city of Kaunus.

On 16 January, the day the USSR Supreme Soviet decided the scheduling of the all-union referendum, the Lithuanian Supreme Council passed a resolution calling for a referendum on Lithuania's independence. Lithuania announced that it would boycott the all-union referendum scheduled for 17 March. Amid increased tension, the Lithuanian government went ahead with the plebiscite on national independence on 9 February, ignoring President Gorbachev's warning that the vote was "without legal foundation." Voters were asked, "Are you in favor of the Lithuanian state being an independent, democratic republic?" According to official results announced two days after the vote, the turnout was over 84 percent, and 90.5 percent voted "yes." The Supreme Council also voted in a special session to describe Lithuania as "an independent, democratic republic" in a new constitution being drafted.

After Lithuania's plebiscite, the Soviet central government continued to use force to pressure Vilnius. On 24 and 25 April, special interior ministry "Black Berets," or OMON, stormed 12 buildings throughout the besieged republic, including the Central Republic Bank and two airports. Several border posts were also seized by marauding Black Berets. In all, there were 400,000 enlisted men, and several divisions of special forces paratroopers in Lithuania. On 15 May, Soviet troops bombed a Lithuanian post on the Byelorussian border. Several days later, two men were killed in an attack on another border post.

In June, the crisis continued as Soviet troops appeared in the streets of Vilnius and conducted identity checks. Late in the month, the Black Berets seized Lithuania's central telephone and telegraph exchange and cut off the republic's communication for two hours before withdrawing. The raid was believed to have been an attempt by Lithuanian Communists to further intimidate the independence drive and embarrass President Gorbachev less than a month before he was to travel to London for a meeting with Western leaders to ask for aid.

On 31 July, as President Gorbachev was meeting with U.S. President George Bush in Moscow, six Lithuanian border guards were murdered execution-style on the Byelorussian border. In previous raids on customs points the attackers had been identified as Soviet troops or forces loyal to Moscow.

The 19 August coup attempt against President Gorbachev led to more violence in Lithuania. On 21 August, one man was killed and another wounded as Lithuanian security guards and Soviet troops exchanged gunfire at a checkpoint near the parliament building in Vilnius. The clash occurred well after it had become clear that the coup against Gorbachev was collapsing. Other Soviet forces began withdrawing from Vilnius and other Baltic cities. On 26 August, President Landsbergis vowed to take control of Soviet troops in Lithuania; two days later, Lithuania took control of its borders and began issuing visas. The same day, the USSR Supreme Soviet said it would view Lithuania and the other Baltic states as independent. Almost immediately, several nations formally recognized Baltic sovereignty. By 28 August, 23 nations had extended formal recognition to Lithuania. On 17 September Lithuania and the two other Baltic republics were admitted to the United Nations General Assembly.

On 7 September a senior Lithuanian official reported that under an agreement with Moscow, Soviet troops were to begin withdrawing from Lithuania by the end of the year. On 9 October, Western news agencies reported that Lithuania and the USSR had agreed that 10,000 Internal Ministry troops (MVD) would start to leave the country in March 1992. However, on 28 October, the USSR Ministry of Defense said Lithuania had to provide material and financial aid and help with the construction of new installations to house Soviet troops being withdrawn from Lithuania. A Soviet official also said that USSR forces would not leave Lithuania completely until the end of 1994.

A citizenship law passed in 1989 granted citizenship to all persons who had been citizens and residents of Lithuania prior to 15 June 1940, and all of their descendants living permanently in Lithuania. Citizenship was also automatically granted to current permanent residents of the republic who had been born in Lithuania or could show that at least one parent or grandparent had been born there, provided they were not citizens of any other country. Persons residing in the republic at the time of the passage of the law were given two years to decide whether they wanted to become Lithuanian citizens.

On 10 September, some 200 Poles demonstrated in Vilnius against the dissolution of two regional councils in predominantly Polish-inhabited areas of Lithuania. A member of one of the councils maintained that their dissolution was unjust because they had been legally elected. The leader of the Polish faction in parliament said that some Poles felt threatened by Lithuanian independence. The councils were disbanded in connection with accusations that they had supported the August coup attempt. On 19 September, a Polish delegation that visited Vilnius demanded that Poles living in Lithuania be given citizenship automatically. Other demands were the establishment of a Polish university in Vilnius and guarantees that the boundaries of the Polish-speaking regions would not be changed.

In economic affairs, Lithuania continued efforts to attract foreign investment to assist the transition to a market economy. By July, some 200 joint ventures had been registered, but most were involved in small-scale commercial and consultative activities. One clear impediment to reform was Lithuania's long-established links with the Soviet command economy. Privatization laws passed in 1990 allowed Lithuania to proceed faster in this area than other republics. But the new country's reliance on the inflationary ruble held up reforms. On 5 November, the Supreme Council voted to start preparations for the introduction of the *litas* as Lithuania's official currency. A committee was established to decide when the currency would be introduced and to determine an official exchange rate against the ruble.

Political Rights and Civil Liberties: Even before independence, Lithuanians had the means to democratically elect a government. The judiciary is being restructured to conform to democratic principles. Lithuanians have and exercise the right to speak freely. There is a wide range of independent papers and periodicals, but the chairman of the Lithuanian Journalists Union said in August that after the coup attempt there were "serious assaults on the principles of press freedom." The government seized the country's largest rural newspaper on the grounds that its editors were former Communists.

Freedom of assembly and association are guaranteed and respected in practice. The Roman Catholic Church, the predominant denomination, is thriving. There was some concern among the Polish and Russian minorities that their rights would not be guaranteed and that they would face discrimination in an independent Lithuania. Several cases have been reported, but the government has pledged to guarantee minority rights. There are no domestic or international travel restrictions. Independent trade unions have been established, including the Lithuanian Workers Union.

Luxembourg

Polity: Parliamentary democracy
Economy: Capitalist
Population: 400,000
PPP: $14,290
Life Expectancy: 74.9
Ethnic Groups: Luxembourger, other European

Political Rights: 1
Civil Liberties: 1
Status: Free

Overview: The Grand Duchy of Luxembourg received international recognition as an independent neutral country in 1867. However, Germany occupied the country during both world wars. Since World War II, Luxembourg has been a major advocate of European unity, and belongs to both the European Community and NATO.

Grand Duke Jean is head of state. He appoints the prime minister from the party or coalition able to command a majority in the 60-member Chamber of Deputies. Voters elect deputies by proportional representation for a maximum term of five years. There is also an appointive Council of State, whose 21 members have life terms. The Chamber can overturn the Council's decisions. In the general election held 18 June 1989, the center-right Christian Social Party won 22 seats, the Socialist Workers' Party 18, and the liberal Democratic Party 11. The growing Green Alternative won four seats, and the Communists captured one. Winning four seats, a new single-issue force, the Five-Sixths Party, advocates pensions worth five-sixths of the final salary for all workers. The prime minister, Jacques Santer, heads a Christian Social-Socialist coalition government. The future of the European Community and NATO and the decline of the steel industry are major concerns in Luxembourg.

Political Rights and Civil Liberties: Luxembourgers have the right to change their government democratically. About one-quarter of the residents are foreign. Non-Luxembourgers have no right to vote in national elections, but they are free otherwise. There is freedom of speech and of the press.

Print journalism is private and uncensored, except for restrictions on pornography. Broadcast media are state-chartered and free. The country has freedom of association. The steel industry, agricultural interests, and small businesses all have lobbying groups. Affiliated with the Socialist and Christian Social parties, two competing labor federations organize workers. The population is mostly Catholic; there is religious freedom and no state church. The productive economy is largely private.

Madagascar

Polity: Dominant-party (military-dominated)
Economy: Mixed statist
Population: 12,400,000
PPP: $670
Life Expectancy: 54.5
Ethnic Groups: Antaisaka, Bara, Betsimisaraka, Merina, Sakalava, Sihanaka, Tanala, Tsimihety, other

Political Rights: 4
Civil Liberties: 4
Status: Partly Free

Overview:

President Didier Ratsiraka, who has led the country since 1975, hung on to power in 1991 despite vigorous but pacific attempts to dislodge him. By year's end the political impasse was finally resolved as the opposition received sought-after concessions before joining a transitional government leading to new elections.

Madagascar, a large island and five small isles located off the south-eastern coast of Africa, won independence from France in 1960. Ratsiraka has led the country as leader of the ruling Vanguard of the Malagasy Revolution (Arema), one of the political associations that make up the loosely knit National Front of the Malagasy Revolution (FNDR). He was re-elected to a seven-year term as president by universal suffrage in March, 1989, receiving 62.7 percent of the votes in defeating candidates of two other political associations. Legislative elections were held two months later, with the ruling coalition winning 120 of 137 seats at stake. Both the opposition associations fielding presidential candidates were then part of the FNDR. Until March of 1990, when a High Constitutional Court decree permitted multi-partyism, political associations had to operate within the FNDR as the nation's sole legal political entity. Since then, a number of ideologically diverse parties have been either newly created, reconstituted from earlier associations, or re-emerged from illegality. Notwithstanding the form and pace of any reforms, Ratsiraka himself would not have to face the voters again until 1996 according to ground rules he set down for political change.

In August 1990 a meeting of various new opposition political parties, labor unions, and non-political organizations called for the immediate dissolution of the existing government and the formation of a multi-party transitional government to organize new elections for a constituent assembly. The parties in the governing coalition refused to attend the meeting, and its recommendation for the immediate dissolution of the government was ignored.

But the regime's legitimacy was more forcefully challenged in 1991. The year began with the regime's announcement that the constitution would be amended to transform the Supreme Revolutionary Council, heretofore the "guardian of the Malagasy Socialist Revolution" into a upper house in a new bicameral parliamentary system. The opposition had called for the abolition of the Council the year before. At the beginning of May, the opposition set a deadline for the convening of a national conference, but the government let the deadline pass without reply. Instead it submitted a draft bill to the National Assembly in early June specifying amendments to the existing constitution. The amendments fell short of opposition demands, including that any reference in the constitutional text to the guiding inspiration of the principles of Ratsiraka's "Malagasy socialist revolution" be expunged. The constitution itself decrees that "the socialist option of the regime cannot be revised." The largely non-Marxist opposition has argued that only a national conference can suspend operation of the provision by creating a new regime and a new constitution. The opposition also called the National Assembly itself unrepresentative, and alleged that the 1989 elections were rigged.

The campaign for a new constitution was soon taken to the street. In June opposition had begun to organize marches and then declared a general strike. The protests were peaceful, although four people reportedly died during the first ten weeks of sustained protest in Madagascar. Protesters called for Ratsiraka's resignation, accusing him of secreting away a substantial amount of state funds for personal use in overseas bank accounts.

As the stalemate continued, Ratsiraka proclaimed a state of emergency. Despite its requirements of an overnight curfew, press censorship, a ban on public gatherings, and unrestricted access to private premises for searches, the state of emergency was not enforced by the military and police. Opposition politicians of the sixteen-party "Gallant Forces" movement and hundreds of thousands of their supporters rallied daily in the streets of the Malagasy capital of Antananarivo for over three months. Civil servants went on strike and brought national administration to a halt while the opposition named a shadow cabinet and occupied government ministry buildings in what amounted to a ceremonial takeover of the state. Albert Zafy was designated "prime minister," while Jean Rakotoharison was named by the opposition coalition as the new "president." The Movement for Proletarian Power (MFM) broke with the Gallant Forces coalition in opposition to the parallel government.

On 28 July, Prime Minister Victor Ramahatra and his cabinet resigned. Ratsiraka offered to re-initiate talks with the opposition, form a coalition government of "reconciliation," and hold a national referendum on a new constitution. In the absence of an electoral repudiation, however, he again stated his refusal to step down from power, and made no concession with regard to a national conference. The opposition rejected his offer and again demanded his resignation. Meanwhile, Guy Razanamasy, a non-aligned former mayor, accepted appointment by the president to head a new cabinet after the government of reconciliation was stillborn. Razanamasy formed a cabinet without any major element of the opposition, and Ratsiraka retained significant power in the new administration.

The continuing demonstrations were met by violence from the presidential security force on 10 August. A march of an estimated half million people on the presidential palace resulted in the death of as many as 100 and injury to 300 when the presidential security force fired on the crowd as it pushed through security barriers and neared the premises. Another 20 died that weekend in political clashes elsewhere on the island. In contrast to the security force, the military and regular police did little to obstruct opposition activities. The opposition has proposed that the military join it in displacing Ratsiraka and, in late October, the defense minister issued a veiled warning that if the regime and its opposition were unable to reach agreement, the military would "shoulder its responsibility."

A power-sharing agreement between the government and opposition in October was aborted when Zafy rejected it. The MFM accepted posts in a new administration. Finally, an agreement was reached in mid-December between Zafy and the prime minister. A transitional government was formed with minsterial portfolios almost equally divided between the opposition and those pro-Ratsiraka. A national conference, a constitutional referendum, and elections are planned for 1992.

Political Rights and Civil Liberties: While a multi-party system was formally introduced in Madagascar in 1990, a government/opposition stand-off has delayed the realization of democracy. An independent judiciary functions without government interference. There is a vibrant private press, and a law abolishing censorship of the written media was adopted in 1990. When the government attempted to re-impose censorship under the state of emergency in 1991, the private press refused to cooperate. Radio and television are government controlled. Religious freedom is respected, and there are few restrictions on travel. Workers have the right to join unions and strike. There are nine national labor organizations, most affiliated with political associations.

Malawi

Polity: One-party
Economy: Capitalist
Population: 9,400,000
PPP: $620
Life Expectancy: 48.1
Ethnic Groups: Chewa, Gomani, Lomwe, Mombera, Nyanja, Tao, Tumbuku

Political Rights: 7
Civil Liberties: 6
Status: Not Free

Overview: The major issues in Malawi during 1991 included the continued presence of nearly 1 million refugees from Mozambique and an emboldened opposition's calls for democratic reform.

A densely populated, landlocked country in southeast Africa, the Republic of Malawi has been ruled since independence in 1964 by President Hastings Kamuzu Banda, head of the ruling Malawi Congress Party (MCP). The 91-year-old ruler, designated president-for-life in 1971, wields dictatorial power. Increasingly, however, governing responsibility is shifting to both John Tembo, of the MCP Executive Committee, and Mama C. Tamanda Kadzamira, Tembo's niece and the country's Official Hostess. The unicameral National Assembly is elected, but all candidates are MCP-approved.

Several opposition groups—including the Socialist League of Malawi (Lesoma), the Malawi Socialist Labour Party (MSLP), the Congress for the Second Republic (CSR), and the United Front for Multi-party Democracy—continue to push for political reform. Recent opposition demands include the release of political prisoners, suspension of the authoritarian constitution, and creation of a government of national unity. MSLP claimed in 1991 to be organizing a guerrilla struggle against the Banda regime. In response to calls for the introduction of multi-partyism, the speakers at the MCP convention in September 1991 asserted that one-party rule was chosen by the citizenry during the last multi-party elections in 1964.

The continued presence of nearly 1 million refugees from Mozambique put a strain on Malawi's economy, one of the poorest in Africa. Refugees now make up nearly 10 percent of the population. Although the government has taken ambitious steps to improve living conditions by privatizing parts of the economy, inflation and debt continue to be serious problems. European aid donors have warned that development assistance will be reduced or eliminated if the human rights situation does not improve. Continued disruption of transportation routes by Mozambique's RENAMO guerrillas has also had an adverse impact on the economy.

Political Rights and Civil Liberties:

Malawians cannot change their government democratically. The Malawian one-party regime remains one of the most repressive in Africa. Authoritarian power is vested in chief-of-state Hastings Banda and the Malawi Congress Party. All political activity outside the MCP is deemed criminal. Dissidents residing in exile are reportedly subject to assassination or kidnapping by Malawian government agents.

The judiciary is not independent and the president appoints all judges. Those tried in the "traditional courts" for political and other crimes have no right to call witnesses. The security apparatus is pervasive and intrusive. Criticism of the president and the ruling party are crimes that can lead to arrest and detention without charge under the 1965 Public Security Regulations. Some political prisoners have been released due to the pressure of foreign aid donors. The country's leading poet, Jack Mapanje, was detained without charge for nearly four years until he was released on Banda's birthday in May 1991. The government maintains the right to revoke the property rights of those suspected of "economic crimes." There are severe restrictions on the press. A 1973 law makes sending "false information" out of the country punishable by life imprisonment. An exiled dissident journalist was murdered in 1989. Malawi's tight visa restrictions for foreign journalists have made it one of Africa's most under-reported countries.

Religious groups must register with the government. Those of the Tumbuku ethnic group and of South Asian origin suffer government-sanctioned discrimination. There are few restrictions on domestic travel, but government employees and civil servants must obtain written permission to travel abroad. The independent Trade Union Congress of Malawi is small, and unions are weak.

Malaysia

Polity: Dominant party
Economy: Capitalist
Population: 18,300,000
PPP: $5,070
Life Expectancy: 70.1
Ethnic Groups: Multi-ethnic state—Malays, Chinese, non-Malay indigenous, Indians and others

Political Rights: 5
Civil Liberties: 4
Status: Partly Free

Overview:

In 1991, a year after national elections and the emergence of a fragile Malay-led opposition to the ruling United Malays National Organization (UMNO) of Prime Minister Dr. Mahathir Mohamad, the government faced an influx of refugees from Vietnam and the Aceh region of Indonesia, a dispute with Indonesia over two islands, and the country's continued economic development.

Present-day Malaysia was established on 16 September 1963, with the merger of the Independent Federation of Malaya (formed in 1957) and the states of Sarawak and Sabah which border Indonesia on the island of Borneo. (Singapore was included but withdrew in 1965.) A constitutional monarchy, the country is nominally ruled by King Azlan Muhibuddin Shah. The ruling UMNO party is the largest party in a National Front (NF) coalition that currently includes ten ethnically based parties, and has won two-thirds or better of majorities in the Dewan Rakayat (lower house of parliament) in all eight general elections since 1957. The Senate (upper house) is partially appointed and has little power. Administration of the 13 states is carried out by rulers or governors. Each state has a constitution and unicameral State Assembly that shares legislative powers with the federal parliament.

In the October 1990 elections, the UMNO-dominated National Front won easily. But tensions in the once monolithic UMNO and the emergence of a Malay opposition changed the character of national politics. In 1988, former trade minister and Mahathir ally Razaleigh Hamzah organized a splinter party, and filed for recognition of a new party (UMNO-Malaysia) after the country's High Court ruled on 4 February 1989 that the UMNO had contravened the Societies Act and was therefore illegal. On 13 February, however, Prime Minister Mahathir managed to legally reconstitute his party as the UMNO-Baru. In June 1989, Razaleigh formed the Semangat '46 (Spirit of 1946, the year the UMNO was established) as a legal, secular party which explored the possibility of joining with the PAS (*Parti Islam*), whose support was overwhelmingly Malay, and the Chinese Democratic Action Party (DAP). Semangat '46 and the PAS formalized their cooperative relationship within the framework of "Muslim Unity," namely the Angkatan Perpaduan Ummah (APU). With the formation of the APU, the strength of the Malay opposition was roughly equal to that of UMNO-Baru. A pact with DAP was finalized in December 1989.

The alliance ran into several difficulties, as rank-and-file members of the PAS were reluctant to support a secular-based Malay Party that had links with the DAP. Similarly, the Malaysian Chinese Association (MCA), a member of the ruling National Front, exploited Chinese fears of an Islamic state by drawing attention to the PAS-DAP alliance. A string of losses in by-elections convinced Semangat '46 and its allies of the need to de-emphasize the links with the PAS and the DAP. This was achieved with the formation of the eight-member Gagasan Rakyat, a confederation of parties with secular ideologies that began to function alongside the Muslim-based APU.

Shortly before the 1990 federal elections, the largely Christian United Sabah Party (PBS) withdrew from the National Front and went into opposition. Nevertheless, the National Front won 127 of the 180 seats (UMNO, 71; MCA, 18; Malaysian Indian Congress (MIC), 6; Malaysian People's Movement, 5; United Sabath National Organization (USNO), 6; Sarawak affiliates, 21). The remaining seats went to the DAP, 20; PBS, 14; Semangat '46, 8; Pan-Malaysian Party, 7; independents, 4.

In 1991, relations worsened between Sabah state and the government in Kuala Lumpur. The PBS's withdrawal from the National Front coalition was interpreted as a reflection of anti-federal sentiment in the state. During 1990, several Sabahans were detained under the Internal Security Act (ISA) for trying to "take Sabah out of Malaysia." On 5 January 1991, Prime Minister Mahathir appeared to take his revenge against PBS when the Chief Minister of Sabah and president of PBS, Datuk Joseph Pairin Kitingan, was arrested and charged with three counts of corruption.

Among key economic developments was the adoption in June 1991 of the National Development Policy (NDP) that replaced the 1971 New Economic Policy (NEP), the stated purpose of which was the redistribution of economic power from the Chinese minority to Malays using severe and strictly enforced racial quotas. The NEP was launched one year after ethnic riots, and influenced all aspects of Malaysian life, from corporate structures, investment and employment patterns, to daily attitudes. Its twin policy pillars were the eradication of poverty and economic restructuring. It set a target of 1990 by which time 30 percent of the country's corporate sector would be in the hands of the *Bumiputras* (literally, "sons of the soil"). These were Malays and small, diverse groups of natives who represented less than 10 percent of the population. The NEP also called for 40 percent of the corporate sector to be in Malaysian, non-*Bumiputras* hands by 1990 and 30 percent controlled by foreigners. The NDP, while essentially a copy of its predecessor, carried no deadlines and no explicit emphasis on target quotas for ownership of the corporate sector. It also acknowledged that the previous policy goals had suffered from excesses of implementation. The NDP put emphasis on training *Bumiputras* to manage and develop the wealth they had gained as a result of the NEP. Overall, Malaysia's economy continued its double-digit growth, but inflation was on the rise. In announcing its 1992 budget in October, the government pledged to continue its fast-track growth strategy, despite negative factors such as the current account deficit and a decline in the country's international reserves.

In August, the parliament, in a controversial move, gave the government absolute powers to develop land belonging to individuals. Opposition groups charged that the bill would allow the Malay-dominated government to forcibly obtain land owned by ethnic Chinese, who controlled much of the country's economy. The bill allowed the state governments to acquire land for any purpose "deemed beneficial to the economic development of Malaysia."

In other issues, Malaysia sought to deal with a growing refugee problem. The government ordered the closure of the Pulau Bidong refugee camp in Trengganu, which housed 13,000 Vietnamese refugees. The year also saw the influx of Acehnese refugees fleeing turmoil in the Aceh region on the northern tip of the Indonesian island of Sumatra. Malaysia returned these asylum seekers to Indonesia, stating that it had no wish to encourage a separatist movement in another state.

In foreign affairs, the establishment in July of a joint commission with Indonesia indicated that Malaysia was moving toward a settlement of a long standing dispute over the Sipadan and Ligitan islands. Relations with Thailand deteriorated when Malaysia announced in July that it was planning to build a wall across a 60-mile stretch along the Thai border in an attempt to stop smuggling of illegal goods such as narcotics and taxable goods such as cigarettes.

Political Rights and Civil Liberties: Ethnic Malay and UMNO domination of national politics hinders Malaysians in exercising their legal rights to change their government democratically. There are restrictions on campaigning and freedom of speech. The October 1990 elections were generally fair, and it is doubtful whether irregularities played a major part in the National Front's two-thirds majority in the legislature. However, the government called the elections with little warning and allowed only an eleven-day campaign period. Opposition parties represent many different political and ethnic groups, and the government declared on 12 February that it would not stop the Communist Party of Malaya (CPM) from participating in Malaysian politics if it did so legally. The media are largely state-owned, and exhibit a strong bias toward government policies. There are many small, independent publications in the several languages that often criticize the government.

Three laws enable the government to detain suspects without trial: the 1960 Internal Security Act (ISA) the Emergency (Essential Powers) Ordinance of 1969, and the Dangerous Drugs Act of 1985. The government claims that as of January 1991, 143 people were being detained under the ISA, including 117 former Communist Party of Malaya guerrillas. Detention under the Dangerous Drugs Act is particularly unrestricted, and suspects can be held for repeated two-year periods with only perfunctory "judicial review." The death penalty is mandated in Malaysia for drug offenses, and even small-scale trafficking is frequently punished by death.

Though predominantly Muslim, Malaysia generally allows religious minorities to practice their faith. Laws ban criticizing Islam and proselytizing Muslims. There are disputes over Muslim conversions of children of other religions. There are no government restrictions on emigration and Malaysians generally face no strictures on domestic and foreign travel. Malaysians are generally free to organize in unions, though in some industries the government has prevented the establishment of national unions, restricting organization to in-house groups.

Maldives

Polity: Non-party presidential-legislative (elite clan-dominated)
Economy: Capitalist
Population: 200,000
PPP: na
Life Expectancy: 62.5
Ethnic Groups: Mixed Sinhalese, Dravidian, Arab, and Black

Political Rights: 6
Civil Liberties: 5
Status: Not Free

Overview:

The poor, Islamic, Republic of Maldives is a 500-mile-long string of nineteen mostly uninhabited coral islands in the Indian Ocean. Unrest following President Maumoon Abdul Gayoom's re-election to a third term in September 1988 triggered a coup attempt by a band of Maldivian and foreign mercenaries which Indian troops quickly suppressed. In response, the government boosted the National Security Service, which is in charge of internal security as well as territorial defense, to 2,000 troops, and Gayoom appointed more family members to high government offices. A small, hereditary elite controls the state.

The February 1990 elections for the unicameral Citizens Assembly (majlis) brought in a crop of younger activists who sought to enact the first significant reforms since a 1968 referendum ended 815 years of rule by the ad-Din sultanate. Gayoom himself spoke of sharing some powers with parliament. But by April, protests against official corruption and nepotism led to the arrest of several activists and journalists. After briefly allowing a free press, the government banned all non-sanctioned publications. In March 1991 Gayoom's brother-in-law, Ilyas Ibrahim, returned to the cabinet as Minister of Atolls administration less than a year after he fled the country after being charged with embezzlement. Ibrahim allegedly operates an elite police unit, the Bimbi Force, which conducts surveillance on critics of the government.

Political parties are not forbidden by law, but they are strongly discouraged and none exist. The forty-eight seat majlis is popularly elected, except for eight seats appointed by the president. Every five years, the majlis selects the president, who is subject to a popular referendum for approval, and who appoints top officials. The Special Citizens Council advises the president on political and economic issues.

In May 1991 violent storms pummeled the islands. Flooding left almost one-tenth of the population homeless and caused $30 million in property damage. The country's location and lack of resources makes it heavily dependent on fishing and tourism for revenues. Gayoom has sought to increase regional economic integration through the South Asian Association For Cooperation.

Political Rights and Civil Liberties: Maldivians cannot change their government democratically. Citizens hold only indirect influence over the government and its policies. The government has successfully discouraged organized opposition, and although political parties technically are legal, none exist. A police crackdown in 1990 led to the arrest of several activists and journalists who were campaigning for political reform. Government pressure forced two independent newspapers, *Sangu* and *Hukuru*, to close in 1990. State-owned media reflect official views. Although citizens can lodge complaints through accepted channels, such as petitioning members of the majlis, the law prohibits actions which would "arouse people against the government." Freedom of assembly is guaranteed by the constitution, but citizens rarely gather for political purposes. The president appoints and can remove judges, and the legal system is based on Islamic law. Criminals can be flogged and banished to remote islands. Clubs and associations are permitted if they do not violate Islamic or civil laws. The constitution defines all citizens as Muslims, and conversion to other religions could lead to a loss of citizenship. Women have assumed a greater role in public affairs in recent years, have equal divorce rights, and generally receive wages equal to men. The government does not recognize the right of workers to form unions or strike.

Mali

Polity: Military-civilian transitional
Economy: Mixed statist
Population: 8,300,000
PPP: $500
Life Expectancy: 45.0
Ethnic Groups: Arab Bedouin, Bambara, Berabish Berber, Bozo, Dialonke, Dogon, Fulani, Kagoro, Kasonke, Masina, Malinke (50 percent), Minianka, Songhai, Soninke, Tuareg (Aullimiden, Antesar, Udalan), other

Political Rights: 6
Civil Liberties: 4
Status: Partly Free

Overview: The arid, landlocked Republic of Mali took significant steps away from one-party rule on 26 March 1991, when the country's ruler of twenty-three years, General Moussa Traoré, was overthrown by a military coup. The country also faced continuing unrest among ethnic groups in the north.

The nation's only legal party since 1979, Traoré's Mali People's Democratic Union (UDPM) was abolished by military decree after the March coup, which capped two months of sporadic and often violent public demonstrations against the regime. Traoré himself had ousted leftist Modibo Keita in a bloodless military coup in 1968, and was reelected in 1985 to a second six-year term as president after running unopposed under the UDPM banner.

In a 1991 New Year's message to the nation, Traoré stated that there would be a debate on democracy within the single-party system at the March congress of the UDPM, but asserted that political pluralism outside of the UDPM was unnecessary given both the party's ability to encompass all shades of opinion and the danger to national unity that multi-partyism posed to a multi-ethnic state. Believing the scope of the debate to be inadequate, thousands took to the streets in cities and towns throughout the country in the midst of a general strike to demand a multi-party system, continuing a series of protests that had begun toward the end of 1990. A government ban on opposition activities was soon announced.

In an attempt to further stifle organized opposition among young Malians, the regime arrested Oumar Mariko, general secretary of the independent Mali Pupils and Students Association (AEEM), in January of 1991. Hundreds of people, including children as young as eleven, were also arrested and imprisoned for their participation in anti-government demonstrations. Young detainees were reportedly beaten and deprived of food. Despite domestic and international pleas for an end to ill treatment of all those held as prisoners, and speedy release of those who had not participated in rioting and looting, the regime professed to have no knowledge of either the use of torture in its detention facilities or the identities of the many whose release was sought.

The repeated anti-regime marches and demonstrations in early 1991 were generally well-organized and pacific. However, in early February, the justice minister called for citizens "to eradicate passionate behavior from Mali." A state of emergency and curfew were announced.

On 22 March the protests degenerated into destructive sprees directed against government buildings and the properties of officials and their relatives. The government response ranged from tear gas and beatings to machine gunfire resulting in numerous injuries and an estimated 160 or more deaths. Peaceful meetings of the membership of legally registered opposition organizations were also forcibly disrupted by security forces. At the same time, the UDPM mobilized its activists to march in public demonstrations against multi-partyism.

Calling for immediate dialogue, the political opposition denounced both the use of violence by the authorities and the rioting, which it blamed on the government and its strategy of repression. The advocates of multi-partyism, demanding Traoré's resignation, scorned the regime's call for patience until the UDPM's next party Congress in March. Ignoring the fact that he had never faced an opponent in a election, Traoré stated that he would not resign because he "was elected not by the opposition but by all the people of Mali." The government had taken no action to open up a substantive dialogue with the opposition by the time of its overthrow in the 26 March military coup.

The leader of the all-military "National Reconciliation Council," Amadou Toumani Toure, pledged soon after the coup that the junta's role would be limited to ensuring multi-party elections, and that the soldiers would return to the barracks by 20 January 1992. The Council dissolved itself within the week, ceding power to a twenty five-member Transitional Committee for National Salvation (CTSP), which had a mixed civilian-military composition. A civilian, Soumana Sacko, was named interim prime minister. Traoré and leading members of his regime were jailed in anticipation of trials for murder and corruption.

A critical task of the CTSP was the organization of a national conference of all newly-constituted political parties in order to draw up plans for a new electoral code and constitution which would ensure multi-partyism. The various pro-democracy groups united in a Coordinating Committee of Democratic Associations and Organizations (CCAOD) in order to better cooperate with the interim government. The two-week conference, which opened 29 July, adopted a draft constitution that included the established judicial independence and the guarantee of civil liberties. The constitution was approved in a national referendum on 1 December.

Some two weeks before the national conference was convened, an attempted military coup was put down near the capital of Bamako. The leader, a former governor of the Timbuktu region, was imprisoned along with his principal co-conspirators. Tens of thousands of Malians gathered in the streets to demonstrate their solidarity with the transition administration. The reasons for the mutiny were variously speculated to have been dissatisfaction with low wages and fear of trials for human rights abuses during the Traoré regime.

Another key issue has been the rebellion which broke out during the summer of 1990 among the Tuareg ethnic minority of northern Mali. Attempts by Traoré's troops to extinguish it by force had met with limited success by the end of the year, and negotiations between the government and the Popular Front for the Liberation of the Azawad (FPLA) resulted in a peace agreement on 7 January 1991. However, Tuaregs of the FPLA rejected the agreement after the government delayed the grant of greater autonomy to the north and the withdrawal of army troops from the region. The Tuareg rebels began a series of attacks in May 1991 on government facilities and black Malian population centers in the area around Timbuktu and elsewhere, resulting in deaths and injuries. Vigilante committees of self-defense consisting of non-Tuaregs have been used by military officials in villages to control Tuaregs who may be sympathetic to the rebellion. Units of the Malian military reportedly extrajudicially executed Tuareg community leaders and merchants for alleged complicity in rebel attacks. Other Tuaregs have been detained incommunicado by authorities. In addition, bandits have raided villages in the north. A special all-parties conference was scheduled in Timbuktu to grapple with the "Problems of the North" in mid-November, but it was postponed due to the difficulty of ensuring the FPLA participation.

Political Rights and Civil Liberties:

Although Malians do not yet have the means to change their government democratically, municipal, legislative, and presidential elections are scheduled for early 1992. There are reportedly some fifty political parties planning to compete for municipal and legislative seats.

A number of independent newspapers have sprung up since the fall of Traoré. The press has participated freely in the national debate about the transition to democracy and the continuing unrest in the north of the country. The new constitution guarantees freedom of the press.

International human rights organizations have expressed concern over the Malian army's torture and extrajudicial execution of innocent Tuaregs and Moors in retaliation for armed attacks by rebels in the north of the country. The prime minister has given assurances that those responsible for abuses have been punished. Amnesties for all those detained for political offenses allegedly committed before the fall of the Traoré regime were decreed in mid-July 1991. The new constitution promises trade union independence.

Malta

Polity: Parliamentary democracy
Economy: Mixed capitalist-statist
Population: 400,000
PPP: $7,490
Life Expectancy: 73.4
Ethnic Groups: Maltese (mixed Arab, Sicilian, Norman, Spanish, Italian, and English)

Political Rights: 1
Civil Liberties: 1
Status: Free

Overview:

The major development in Malta in 1991 was the privatization of radio. The government licensed several new private stations and allocated stations to the ruling Nationalist Party, the opposition Malta Labor Party and the Roman Catholic Church. In 1992 Malta will also have an American-led cable television consortium.

Located in the central Mediterranean, Malta was under foreign rule for most of its history. The British occupied the island in 1800, and later made it a British colony. Malta gained independence from Britain in 1964. The socialist Malta Labor Party ruled from 1971 to 1987 and followed left-of-center economic policies and a neutral foreign policy. It also ordered some confiscations of church property and restricted private financing for Catholic schools. Labor turned to Libya for aid and support in the early 1980s. The socialists lost control to the Nationalist Party in the 1987 general elections. Nationalist Prime Minister Edward Fenech Adami advocates a more Europe-oriented foreign policy while maintaining neutrality. Malta applied to join the European Community, and hopes for full membership after 1992. The Nationalists are attempting to reverse Labor's restrictions on the Roman Catholic Church. On a visit to Malta in 1990, the Pope asked the government to do more to make the Church "free from undue pressures, obstacles, and manipulation." The Nationalists are also carrying out a gradual privatization of the state sector.

The parliament, called the House of Representatives, has 65 seats and a maximum term of five years. Voters choose the representatives by proportional representation. Elected by parliament, the largely ceremonial president serves for five years, and appoints the prime minister from the parliamentary majority party. Under a constitutional amendment adopted in 1987, a party getting a majority of the popular vote gets a majority of the seats in parliament. In the previous elections, it was possible for a party to receive a majority of votes while winning only a minority of seats.

Political Rights and Civil Liberties:

The Maltese have the right to change their government democratically. The privatization of the major media should increase the variety of broadcast political opinion. The government is lifting rules which mandated "balanced" opinion at each station. Malta's constitution guarantees freedom of speech and press. The only exception is a law passed in 1987 which forbids foreign involvement in Maltese election campaigns. The press is free, and many newspapers are politically affiliated. Religion is free for both the Catholic majority and for religious minorities. All groups have freedom of association. Many trade unions belong to the Labor Party's General Union of Workers, but others are independent.

Marshall Islands

Polity: Parliamentary democracy
Economy: Capitalist-statist
Population: 43,000
PPP: na
Life Expectancy: na
Ethnic Groups: Marshallese (Micronesian)

Political Rights: 1
Civil Liberties: 1
Status: Free

Overview:

The Marshall Islands' admission to the United Nations and the international acceptance of the country's independence were the major developments for the islands in 1991.

Located in the Pacific Ocean, the Marshall Islands were independent until the late 1800s, when the Germans established a protectorate. After World War I Japan governed the islands under a League of Nations mandate until the U.S. Navy occupied the region in 1945. The U.S. administered the islands under a United Nations trusteeship after 1947. The Americans recognized a distinct Marshallese constitution in 1979, thereby causing a *de facto* change in the Marshalls' legal status. However, the Soviets and others waged an international legal dispute for several years over the islands' trusteeship. In 1986, the U.S. notified the U.N. formally that the trusteeship was over, and that the Marshalls had implemented a Compact of Free Association with the U.S. Under the Compact, the Marshalls had self-government, but still depended on American defense. Following changes in Soviet policy and the international political climate, the U.N. recognized the dissolution of the trusteeship in December 1990.

The Marshallese government sought and received diplomatic recognition as an independent country in 1991. Britain granted recognition on 1 August 1991, and the U.N. seated the Republic of the Marshall Islands as a full member on 17 September.

The Marshalls have a parliamentary system. Voters choose the thirty-three member parliament from twenty-four election districts. The legislators elect a president and cabinet who are responsible to them. There is also an advisory body of Micronesian chiefs. Having won re-election in 1988, President Amata Kabua is serving his third term.

The economy depends heavily on U.S. and other foreign assistance. The U.S. carried out extensive nuclear testing on the islands from 1946-58. America has faced numerous lawsuits from residents who cited the nuclear activity as the cause of their illness and other problems. In 1990, a panel of judges ruled that plaintiffs could receive $45 million in compensation from the U.S. for illness caused by the American nuclear tests.

Political Rights and Civil Liberties: The Marshallese have the right to change their government democratically. A bill of rights protects most civil liberties. There are some minor restrictions on freedom of movement, due to defense installations and nuclear contamination. The cabinet can deport aliens who take part in Marshallese politics, but it has never done so. There is freedom of the press. The islands have private and public broadcast media and a private newspaper. The government respects freedom of association, but there are no trade unions.

Mauritania

Polity: Military transitional
Economy: Capitalist-statist
Population: 2,100,000
PPP: $960
Life Expectancy: 47.0
Ethnic Groups: White and Black Moors, various black sub-Saharan African ethnic groups (Tuculor, Hal-Pulaar, Soninke, Wolof)

Political Rights: 7
Civil Liberties: 6
Status: Not Free

Overview: During 1991 the Mauritanian government announced a democratic transition, the credibility of which is in question both in light of continuing human rights violations perpetrated by authorities against black Mauritanians, and highly restrictive requirements for would-be candidates to enter multi-party elections.

Mauritania has been under military rule since 1978, when officers ousted President Ould Daddah and established a Committee for National Recovery, later renamed the Military Committee for National Salvation (CMSN). Daddah and his Mauritanian People's Party (PPM), supported by the Moorish elite, had run the country as a constitutional one-party state since independence was won from France in 1960. Upon taking power, the military suspended this constitutional arrangement and abolished the PPM, but despite early promises, failed to act for some thirteen years on a proposed constitution establishing multi-party democracy. Colonel Ould Taya currently is the country's president, prime minister, and head of the CMSN. National legislative elections are scheduled for 1992.

Mauritania has been beset by severe animosity between its black African tribes, which are located largely within and adjacent to the Senegal River valley along the country's southern border, and its politically and economically dominant Moors of the north and center. The Moors, both white and black, are culturally Arab-Berber and make up about three-fourths of the population. In 1980 the officers of the CMSN, as part of a general effort at extending Moorish hegemony throughout society, attempted to impose Muslim fundamentalism in Mauritania by establishing Islamic courts applying particular interpretations of religious law (*shari'a*).

Beginning in May 1989, the government forcibly expelled 45,000-55,000 of its own non-Moorish citizens into Senegal. Reports from those expelled, independent refugee officials, and Amnesty International indicate the victims have often been falsely denounced as Senegalese illegally resident in Mauritania or sympathizers of indigenous anti-Moorish guerrilla movements. The victims have had their shops looted, property confiscated, and identity cards destroyed before being driven across the border into Senegal and Mali. Some of those refusing expulsion have been tortured, beaten or raped.

In 1991 expulsions of non-Moorish citizens continued at a reduced intensity. Official security forces and armed militias largely composed of black Moors have reportedly raided unarmed villages, burning them and terrorizing their inhabitants. As a consequence of these raids, many not actually expelled have in fact fled to Senegal and Mali. This seems to indicate that there is an unofficial government policy of forcing out those considered by the Moorish leadership as not being Mauritanian by definition—black Africans not speaking Arabic as their first language. The government denies that it is acting against Mauritanian citizens.

The government has accused the government of Senegal of sponsoring forays by "Senegalese" (i.e., returning Mauritanian expellees) who have attacked military posts and attempted to reclaim their property in Mauritania. Sporadic border clashes, such as one on 2 March, also have occurred between the military forces of Senegal and Mauritania. The Mauritanian government has demanded the repatriation of all Moors resident in Senegal. In addition, Mauritania claims that some 240,000 Moors were forced from Senegal and claim that they are owed some one billion dollars in compensation. Whenever Mauritanian officials are confronted with accusations and evidence of the abuse of their non-Moorish citizens, they attempt to deflect the charge by alleging persecutions of the sizable Mauritanian Moor shopkeeper population in Senegal.

As many as 3,000 members of the Hal-Pulaar and Soninke ethnic groups were arrested and imprisoned incommunicado as of November 1990 without being charged with any crime. The government has claimed that a certain number of these detainees—primarily civil servants and members of the military—were involved in a conspiracy to overthrow the government. In March 1991 an amnesty for political prisoners was declared; after the release of detainees, it was discovered that some 200 of those arrested were unaccounted for and possibly victims of extrajudicial execution. After bread riots in June, there were more arrests, notably of various prominent figures of the just-formed United Democratic Front of Forces for Change (FDCU), a coalition of internal political opposition movements led by a minister in the prior civilian regime.

President Taya announced in mid-April of 1991 that there would be a constitutional referendum by the end of the year, to be followed by multi-party legislative elections sometime in 1992 to fill positions in a new Senate and National Assembly. The constitution, which provides for a strong-president system, was voted upon by mid-July. Although the government claimed close to 100 percent approval, independent reports suggest that the turnout was one-fifth or less of the official percentage. Both professionals and trade unionists have demanded a transitional civilian government and amnesty for opponents in exile. Among those who were expected to compete for legislative seats if permitted by the regime are pan-Arab nationalists, Muslim fundamentalists, Marxists, black nationalists and liberals such as those of the National Democratic Movement (MND). Muslim fundamentalists or regional movements with the goal of secession may be barred by law from legally organizing. Black non-Moors who are Mauritanian citizens are often unable to update their identity cards, and hence cannot vote. A law passed in October required that candidates for multi-party elections obtain the signatures of 30 mayors or 400 municipal councilors, even though almost all were members of the President's Republican Democratic Party (PDR). After an outcry from opposition parties, signatures of only 50 councilors were required. The opposition responded with demands for new municipal elections and new electoral districts which did not over represent areas of PDR strength.

Three illegal armed movements of opposition operate from outside the country. The African Liberation Force of Mauritania (FLAM) was begun 1989 by black military officers dismissed in a 1987 purge. In mid-1991, FLAM announced that it was suspending its armed struggle following a general amnesty decreed by the government. More recently, the Resistance Front for Unity, Independence, and Democracy in Mauritania (FRUIDEM) and the United Front of Maurtianian Armed Resistance (FURAM) have formed. The government has responded by further terrorizing the natural constituencies of these armed groups, namely the black non-Moors.

Political Rights and Civil Liberties:

Despite the promise of free and fair elections in 1992, Mauritanians are still ruled by the unelected Military Committee for National Salvation (CMSN) which came to power in 1978. Though allowed to form political parties, citizens are prevented by onerous registration requirements from freely choosing national level representatives. Municipal elections, believed by some to be unfair, took place in 1986 and 1989, with the debate strictly confined to local issues.

According to the new constitution, the source of law in Mauritania is Islam. Islam is the official and only recognized religion. Conversion to a non-Muslim faith is prohibited. In 1980, Islamic law, the *shari'a,* was imposed as national law and Islamic courts were established, though the actual rigor of enforcement is in question.
The constitution provides for freedoms of expression, association, and the equality of all citizens. A law on freedom of the press was adopted by the regime in July 1991; however, it is illegal to promote "national disharmony." Material construed by officials as "insulting the President" can be punished by fine and imprisonment. Privately-owned publications exist, though they are loyal to the regime. The government owns and operates a daily paper and both the radio and television stations.

Slavery, long practiced in the country, was formally abolished in 1980, but the United Nations Human Rights Commission estimates there are still 100,000 Mauritanians in slavery. The use of torture by the authorities against political prisoners reportedly continued in 1991. Detainees are held without criminal charge for pro-longed periods, often with inadequate food and water. Extrajudicial execution of those detained has reportedly become more common. Some dissident military officers remain in internal exile, without trial or formal charge. Other opposition figures have been expelled. Courts are under the sway of the military rulers in political cases; State Security Court decisions are non-appealable. The Mauritanian League for Human Rights has been tolerated.

All unions must belong to the government-controlled general labor confederation, the Mauritanian Workers' Union (UTM). Although strikes and political involvement are severely discouraged, the UTM announced that it favored multi-partyism over a week before the president announced that elections would be held. All associations require government approval.

Mauritius

Polity: Parliamentary democracy
Economy: Capitalist
Population: 1,100,000
PPP: $5,320
Life Expectancy: 69.6
Ethnic Groups: Indo-Mauritians (68 percent), Creole (27 percent), Sino-Mauritian (3 percent), and Franco-Mauritian (2 percent)

Political Rights: 1
Civil Liberties: 2
Status: Free

Overview:

The governing coalition of Prime Minister Sir Anerood Jugnauth scored a stunning victory in the September 1991 parliamentary elections, winning 59 of 62 seats at stake in the 70-member, unicameral Legislative Assembly. The Gulf War, and the supporting role of the American airbase on the Diego Garcia atoll claimed by Mauritius, were particular preoccupations of the Mauritius government during the early part of the year. The government announced its intention to adopt a republican form of government in March 1992.

This crowded multi-ethnic island nation east of Madagascar gained independence from Britain in 1968. Mauritius has had one of the longest operating multi-party systems in post-colonial Africa. The transfer of power to a victorious political opposition after a free and fair election, a rare phenomenon in Africa until 1991, was a democratic milestone passed almost a decade ago in Mauritius.

The 1991 parliamentary elections were preceded by shifting political alliances. In mid-1990 Paul Berenger's opposition Mauritian Militant Movement (MMM) joined the governing coalition led by Prime Minister Jugnauth's Mauritian Socialist Movement (MSM), a revival of an old partnership. Meanwhile, the Labor Party (TP) moved into political opposition after Jugnauth fired his deputy, Sir Satcam Boolell of the PT, and all other government ministers opposed to a governing coalition with the MMM. The PT went into the September elections leading an opposition alliance that included the PMSD (Mauritius Social Democratic Party), which quit the government in 1988, the CAM (Muslim Action Committee), and the PSM (Mauritian Socialist Party).

Jugnauth asserted before the election that "our enemies will end up like salted fish drying in the sun"; in fact, the 82 percent voter turnout gave the opposition only three out of 62 elected seats in the new parliament. Alleging the danger of election fraud, the opposition had called for strict international supervision of voting before the election. After their crushing defeat, they demanded that the Supreme Court declare the election null and void. The Court refused.

Under the republican arrangement to go into effect in March 1992, Mauritius is to have a president as titular head of state, instead of the present arrangement in which a governor-general represents the British crown.

The claim of Mauritian sovereignty over the British-held Chagos archipelago, to which the atoll of Diego Garcia belongs, seemed no closer to vindication in 1991. Indigenous Ilois people from Diego Garcia, who were displaced from their island by the American airbase, have demonstrated at the U.S. Embassy in Mauritius to demand greater compensation from the U.S. Meanwhile, the Mauritian government favors speedy removal of the American base, suspecting that the facility is used to store nuclear arms. Mauritius's goals are the creation of a nuclear-free zone in the Indian Ocean and assertion of Mauritian jurisdiction over the Chagos. However, the 50-year American lease of Diego Garcia that the British government signed will not lapse until 2016. Mauritius also continues to press its claim to the Indian Ocean island of Tromelin, presently a French colony.

Political Rights and Civil Liberties:

Citizens have the right to choose their government democratically in a vibrant multi-party system. A special provision is made for assuring legislative representation of Mauritian ethnic and religious minorities through operation of a so-called "best loser" system. This requires that a determined number of seats always be set aside for ethnic minorities regardless of election returns. The judiciary, modelled after the British system, is independent of government. Some sixteen privately-owned newspapers are free to print diverse viewpoints. Freedom of assembly and association is guaranteed, and there are no restrictions on religious freedom. There are nine trade union federations encompassing 300 unions, and workers have the right to strike.

Mexico

Polity: Dominant party
Economy: Capitalist-statist
Population: 85,700,000
PPP: $5,320
Life Expectancy: 69.7
Ethnic Groups: Mestizo (60 percent), Indian (30 percent), Caucasian (9 percent), other (1 percent)

Political Rights: 4
Civil Liberties: 4
Status: Partly Free

Overview:

Although President Carlos Salinas de Gortari has carried out a remarkable opening of the Mexican economy, Mexico remains the most authoritarian state in Latin America outside of Cuba. The mid-term elections held on 18 August 1991 were inherently unfair and marked by flagrant fraud, indicating that the basis of rule in Mexico is still power, not law.

Mexico achieved independence from Spain in 1810 and established a republic in 1822. Following the Revolution of 1910, a new constitution was promulgated. Under the 1917 constitution, the United Mexican States is a federal republic consisting of 31 states and a Federal District (Mexico City). Each state has its own constitution and elected governors and legislatures. The chief executive of the Federal District is appointed by the president. The president is directly elected for a six-year term. A bicameral Congress consists of a 64-member Senate directly elected for six years, and a 500-member Chamber of Deputies elected for three years—300 by direct vote, and 200 through a system of proportional representation. Municipal governments are elected.

The near total domination of the executive, Congress, and state and local governments by the Institutional Revolutionary Party (PRI) since 1929 has been challenged in recent years. Despite systematic electoral fraud and manipulation, the PRI's presidential vote has declined by nearly half since 1976.

According to official results, Salinas won with 50.36 percent of the vote in the July 1988 presidential election, taking only one of every four votes in Mexico City.

The main challengers were Manuel Clouthier of the right-wing National Action Party (PAN) with 17 percent, and a coalition of leftist parties and former PRIistas led by Cuauhtemoc Cardenas who received 31.3 percent. With most Mexicans believing he actually lost the election to Cardenas, Salinas was inaugurated in December 1988 with the weakest mandate of any PRI president. The PRI also failed for the first time to win a two-thirds legislative majority.

In the first half of Salanas's six-year term, economic modernization has far outpaced political reform. In 1989, the PRI conceded defeat in a gubernatorial race for the first time ever, to the PAN in Baja California Norte. But the nearly two dozen state and municipal elections held between 1988 and 1990 were marked by blatant fraud and violent crackdowns against opposition protests. Less than ten percent of Mexico's nearly 2,400 municipalities are governed by opposition parties.

In effect, the PRI functions as the electoral arm of the state, and the national election commission, despite opposition representation, is dominated by the PRI and subordinate to the president. In 1991, opposition parties were powerless to prevent the PRI's manipulation of the new voter registration list. The PRI also exercised an enormous financial advantage in the August mid-term election campaign. The PRI's use of state resources for political purposes is legendary and illegal; without an independent electoral body to conduct a comprehensive audit of campaign financing, fair competition is impossible. Finally, fraud was widespread on election day itself; duplicate voter IDs, repeat voting, ballot-box stuffing and voter intimidation marred the election. Opposition observers frequently were denied access to polling stations.

The PAN and Cardenas's Democratic Revolutionary Party (PRD), with little legal recourse because the electoral authorities are dominated by the party committing the fraud, mobilized major demonstrations, particularly in the states of Guanajuato and San Luis Potisi. President Salinas, concerned by the intensity of the protests and critical coverage by the international media, ordered the PRI's winning gubernatorial candidates in those states to resign in favor of interim governments and repeat elections in 1992. His actions, however, confirmed the president's final and arbitrary authority in electoral matters.

According to official results, the PRI won a nearly two-thirds majority in the Chamber of Deputies and all but one of the 32 contested Senate seats. It is true that Salinas has enhanced his popularity with the promise of a North American free trade agreement, economic reform, and a $4-billion public works, anti-poverty program. But the dubious nature of the PRI "landslide" has been acknowledged even by top party operatives, some of whom promised a more level playing field in the future. But until the structures of government and the electoral system are overhauled, Mexicans will remain unable to express freely their political will through the ballot box.

Political Rights and Civil Liberties:

Because of the ruling party's domination of the state, citizens are unable to change their government through free and fair elections. Constitutional guarantees regarding political and civic organization are generally respected, and there are over a dozen political parties occupying the spectrum from right to left. However, political expression is often restricted by repressive measures taken by the government during elections, labor strikes, and rural land disputes.

In 1990 the government created an official human rights commission. But minimal progress has been made in curtailing the systematic violation of human rights—including false arrest, routine torture, disappearances, murder and extortion—by local police and federal security forces. Targets include political and labor figures, journalists, human rights activists, criminal detainees and, with regard to extortion, the general public. Over the last decade nearly 500 people have disappeared.

In 1991 the government appointed a new attorney general who declared an "end to the policy of official impunity," and ordered the arrest of a Federal Judicial Police commander implicated in the 1990 murder of human rights activist Norma Corona. The government has also enacted new rules of evidence to curb police torture, and dismissed dozens of security agents. However, corruption and rights violations remain institutionalized within the judicial police—which routinely makes political arrests under the pretext of drug enforcement—and Mexico's other law enforcement agencies.

The judiciary is headed by a Supreme Court whose members are appointed for life by the president with the approval of the Senate. Although it is nominally independent, the judicial system is weak, politicized and riddled with corruption. Relatively few corrupt government officials ever spend time in jail, and when they do, it is often for minor offenses that serve to cut short investigations of serious crimes. In many rural areas, respect for laws by official agencies is nonexistent. Lower courts and law enforcement in general are undermined by widespread bribery, as is the state bureaucracy. Drug-related corruption is evident in the military, police, and security forces, as well as in a number of state and local governments.

Labor unions are powerful, notoriously corrupt, and traditionally allied with the ruling PRI. Salinas has removed some of the most corrupt labor officials, often by force. But the government refuses to recognize unions unaffiliated with the PRI, denying them collective bargaining rights and the right to strike. Independent unions and peasant organizations are subject to intimidation and violent crackdowns, and dozens of labor and peasant leaders have been killed in ongoing land disputes, particularly in southern states, where indigenous Indian groups comprise over a third of the population.

The press and broadcasting media, while mostly private and nominally independent, are largely controlled by the government through regulatory bodies, dependence on the government for advertising revenue and operating costs, and frequently, outright intimidation. The PRI's domination of the broadcast media was evident in 1991 in the blanket uncritical coverage by the television networks of the party's electoral campaign. Most newspapers and magazines normally derive over half of all advertising revenues from official sources, which explains how Mexico City's thirty-odd newspapers can survive with an estimated circulation of less than half a million. Over twenty journalists have been killed or disappeared in the last four years, with most cases still unresolved. Dozens of others or their employers have been detained or otherwise threatened.

At the end of 1991, the Salinas government instituted a series of constitutional changes giving legal recognition to religious institutions for the first time since the Mexican Revolution. The measures, culminating a three-year reconciliation between the government and the Roman Catholic Church, included restoring the clergy's right to vote and legalizing parochial education, access to media, and the presence of foreign priests.

Micronesia

Polity: Federal parliamentary democracy
Economy: Capitalist
Population: 114,000
PPP: na
Life Expectancy: na
Ethnic Groups: Micronesian

Political Rights: 1
Civil Liberties: 1
Status: Free

Overview:

In 1991 Micronesia joined the United Nations, elected a new president and received a major new development grant.

Located in the Pacific Ocean, the Federated States of Micronesia was a U.N. trust territory under American administration from 1947 until 1979. Previously, the islands had been successively under a German protectorate and a Japanese League of Nations mandate. In 1982 the U.S. and Micronesia signed the Compact of Free Association, under which the U.S. retains responsibility for defense. In 1990 the U.N. Security Council voted to recognize the end of American trusteeship. When the United Kingdom extended diplomatic recognition to Micronesia on 1 August 1991, it paved the way for U.N. membership in September.

The unicameral legislature consists of one senator-at-large from each island state elected for a four-year term, and ten senators elected on the basis of island populations for two-year terms. The senators elect the president for a two-year term from among the four at-large senators. After legislative elections in 1991, the legislature voted to replace President John Haglelgam with Bailey Olter. Three of the four island states still have traditional leaders and customs.

Agriculture, tourism, forestry, and fishing are major industries. U.S. economic aid and public sector employment are substantial. In 1991 the government received a $450,000 grant from the Asian Development Bank to study the country's agricultural potential. The grant assisted the government's policy of encouraging economic diversification.

Political Rights and Civil Liberties:

Micronesians have the right to change their government democratically. Micronesia has a bill of rights and provisions for respecting traditional rights. Land is not sold or transferred to non-Micronesians. Otherwise the country respects cultural diversity. Islanders speak eight separate native languages. There is freedom of the press and association. Governmental authorities operate some media, while private enterprise and religious groups operate others. Trade unions are legal, but none exist.

Mongolia

Polity: Presidential-parliamentary democracy
Economy: Statist transitional
Population: 2,200,000
PPP: na
Life Expectancy: 62.5
Ethnic Groups: Khalkha Mongols (75 percent), other Mongols (8 percent), Kazakhs (5 percent)

Political Rights: 2
Civil Liberties: 3
Status: Free

Overview:

In 1991 Mongolia continued its fast but rocky transition to a democratic, market-oriented society. Fear of a Communist resurgence prompted a law barring government officials from party membership, while foreign aid donors moved in to prevent the economy from collapsing.

China controlled this vast central Asian area for over 200 years until 1921. The Mongolian People's Revolutionary Party (MPRP) established a Communist state in 1924 following three years of nominal rule by aging Buddhist lamas. In the wake of the anti-Communist revolutions in Eastern Europe, a group of dissidents formed the Mongolian Democratic Union (MDU) in December 1989. MDU-organized street protests and hunger strikes led to the resignation of much of the MPRP leadership in March 1990. Free elections were held four months later. They were contested by the Mongolian Democratic Party (an offspring of the MDU), the Social Democratic Party (SDP), the Progressive National Party (PNP), and a host of smaller parties and independent candidates in addition to the MPRP.

Although the MPRP won 357 of the 430 seats in the directly elected Great People's Hural, few of the party's standing deputies were re-elected. In the newly-created Little Hural, set up to draft, amend, and abolish laws, the Communists won thirty-three of the fifty-three seats via party preference balloting. Despite the MPRP's call for a coalition administration, it largely excluded the two leading opposition groups, the MDU and the PNP, from top posts. In September 1990, the Great Hural voted the MPRP's Punsaalmagiyn Orchirbat as president and the SDP's Radnaasurenjiyn Gonchigdorj as vice-president. Legislation in 1991 shaped the presidency, which can issue decrees, declare martial law, and advance policy proposals to parliament.

Despite its control of the government, the MPRP's influence continued to fade in 1991. At its Twentieth Congress in late February, the party replaced its commitment to Marxism-Leninism with a vague affirmation of "scientific socialism," and named moderate Budragchaagiyn Dash-Yondan as the new party leader. However, citizens continued to be wary of a remaining core of hard liners. Thousands rallied in the capital on 25 August to express concern that radical elements in the MPRP might follow their Soviet comrades and attempt a coup. Some carried "Smash the MPRP" banners and called for the government to be purged of Communists. Three days later, the Small Hural passed a law banning top government and military officials, as well as police, diplomats, and journalists from belonging to political parties. On 10 September, President Orchibat and other top government officials resigned from the MPRP to comply with the law. Over a thousand others in the government, including opposition leaders, followed their lead and resigned from political parties.

Mongolia's biggest challenge is in dismantling nearly seventy years of central economic planning. Since January 1991, it has been forced to pay for Soviet goods with hard currency at market prices. Staple food items are rationed, and meat is in short supply in a country where livestock outnumber people by ten to one. Electricity shortages are frequent, particularly in the capital, Ulan Bator, which is home to one in four Mongolians. Lack of spare parts and railroad breakdowns have caused the closing of numerous factories and mining works, while those that remain open are operating at less than 50 percent capacity. Monetary reserves have dwindled, making it doubtful Mongolia will be able to pay a controversial $16 billion debt to the Soviets. The government says the true size of the debt is much smaller, since for years the Soviets forced their country to buy expensive, inefficient equipment and sold its raw materials at market prices after receiving them as bartered goods.

The government launched an ambitious free-market reform program in 1991. In early June, it unveiled a plan to convert 70 percent of the state's assets to private ownership. The first stage of the plan placed small shops and services on the auction block. Later, large enterprises are to issue stock which could be bought by citizens and foreigners alike. All Mongolians born before 31 May 1991 will be given coupons to purchase shares in enterprises of their choice. The government also devalued its currency (the tugrik) by nearly 600 percent in June with a goal of making it convertible in several years, and in July slashed the 1991 budget by 30 percent. The government also plans an unprecedented bond issuance to raise money and mop up excess cash reserves; a stock market is in the works. Efforts to free 300 agricultural collectives have proceeded much more slowy.

The government's commitment to economic reform and the country's natural resource potential have prompted a host of foreign investment overtures. Japanese and South Korean companies have taken the lead in providing technical assistance and establishing joint ventures, and China agreed to let the landlocked nation use the Chinese port of Tianjin for foreign trade. President Orchirbat visited the United States in January 1991 to negotiate aid agreements. Fourteen nations, along with the World Bank and the International Monetary Fund, pledged $150 million at a conference in Tokyo in September, allowing decentralized banks to provide credit to small enterprises. Over 60 foreign firms are interested in establishing joint ventures with the state oil firm Mongol Gazryn Tos to extract what could be vast amounts of oil lying beneath the Gobi Desert.

Political Rights and Civil Liberties:

As a result of the bloodless 1990 revolution, Mongolians can change their government democratically. Opposition leaders agree that the inaugural elections in 1990 were generally free, but claim they did not have adequate time to campaign against the established Mongolian People's Revolutionary Party (MPRP). In addition, the electoral system favored rural areas, still an MPRP stronghold. The laws require 10,000 urban votes but only 2,000 rural votes for a seat in parliament.

Fundamental freedoms, suppressed by the Communists, are now generally respected by the government. The press plays an important role in framing economic and political policy issues. While several independent newspapers exist in Mongolia, newsprint is rationed, and opposition leaders say they cannot publish as frequently as the government does. The judicial system, long an MPRP fiefdom, is being reformed. Since the 1990 revolution, there are no reported political prisoners. The state security apparatus has been reduced, but it is still allowed to use surveillance measures "when necessary."

Mongolians can travel freely within the country, and a 1989 law liberalized rules for traveling abroad. Freedom of religion has been introduced in this largely Buddhist nation, and monasteries are being refurbished and reopened. In September 1991, the Dalai Lama received a rousing reception during a three day visit. Unions in Mongolia are no longer required to be affiliated with the Federation of Mongolian Trade Unions.

Morocco

Polity: Monarchy and limited parliament
Economy: Capitalist-statist
Population: 26,200,000
PPP: $2,380
Life Expectancy: 62.0
Ethnic Groups: Arab-Berber

Political Rights: 5
Civil Liberties: 5
Status: Partly Free

Overview:

Opposition to the country's involvement in the Persian Gulf War, declining living standards and rising Islamic fundamentalism all put pressure on Moroccan King Hassan II's conservative, pro-Western government in 1991. An economic austerity program has limited the government's options in dealing with growing resentment towards the country's small, wealthy elite.

The 60-year-old King has ruled the country since March 1961. He is commander-in-chief of the armed forces, can dissolve parliament, and appoints provincial governors, all judges, and the prime minister. The current constitution was ratified by a popular referendum in 1972. The King has weathered two attempted military revolts in the early 1970s as well as severe unrest in Casablanca in June 1981 over economic conditions. While opposition leaders call for Hassan to transfer more power to the parliament, ordinary citizens have been increasingly concerned with rising food prices and high unemployment. Public discontent has been exacerbated by a March 1990 austerity program which included a 9 percent currency devaluation and cutbacks in state spending aimed at reducing the country's $21 billion foreign debt and satisfying World Bank and IMF lending conditions.

The frustration felt by much of the country's youth turned to violence in mid-December 1990 after two of the country's largest trade unions called a general strike to win a doubling of the minimum wage (currently $111 per month). As the police braced for violence, thousands rioted in Fez, attacking symbols of wealth including banks, jewelry stores and the five-star Les Merinides Hotel. Soldiers fired on the crowd, and by some accounts over 100 soldiers and civilians were killed. Within days, the King raised wages by 15 percent, but further alienated unions by not first consulting with them. Hundreds were arrested, with some eventually jailed for up to fifteen years.

Early in 1991, the Persian Gulf War threatened to combine with economic dissatisfaction to bolster the opposition. In a show of support for the American-led coalition, Hassan sent 1200 troops to Saudi Arabia and 500 to the United Arab Emirates, and initially attempted to suppress popular support for Saddam Hussein and

Iraq. Seeking to balance his close economic relationship with the West against popular support for Iraq, Hassan later declared his support for the Iraqi people and allowed a pro-Iraq march on 3 February. Organized by opposition parties, the rally ballooned to 300,000 people who burned American, British, Israeli and French flags. Several thousand Islamic fundamentalists participated. Although the march marked one of the most aggressive displays by both the opposition and the fundamentalists, the crowd was orderly and both groups obeyed the king's ban on further demonstrations.

Another divisive internal issue has been the country's attempt to claim the mineral-rich Western Sahara, abandoned by Spain in 1975 and annexed by Morroco in 1976. The government's battle with the Polisario guerrillas for control of the territory is estimated to cost up to $2 million per day. Economic problems have reportedly weakened support for the Saharan policy, although speaking out against it is illegal. A United Nation's sponsored referendum on the issue is slated for early 1992.

Citing the upcoming U.N. referendum on Western Sahara, King Hassan has delayed parliamentary elections until October 1992. Currently, 206 members of the unicameral Chamber of Representatives are directly elected and 100 seats are chosen by a body of business and government leaders. Governing parties holding seats are the Constitutional Union with 83, the National Assembly of Independents with 61, the Popular Movement with 47, and the National Democratic Party with 24. Opposition parties tend to be Arab ultra-nationalists and range across the left-wing spectrum. Those in parliament are the Independence Party with 41 seats, and the Socialist Union of Popular Forces (USFP) with 36, along with six parties holding a total of 14 seats. There have been recent signs of growing cohesion among opposition groups. In November 1991, the Independence Party and the USFP agreed to coordinate their economic and political positions. In a joint statement, the pair called for a national program of youth employment and said it would be necessary to re-draft the constitution to "consolidate institutions' power and the state of law, democratize and modernize state bodies and build a strong and developed Morocco." The Independence Party has also increasingly embraced Islamic fundamentalist causes, including a call for a ban on alcohol.

The key issue in foreign affairs has been deteriorating relations with France, which along with Spain, granted Morocco independence in 1956. The October 1990 publication in France of Gilles Perault's "Our Friend the King", which outlined scandals and human rights violations during the king's reign, led the government to denounce what it called an "anti-Moroccan campaign." Hassan is also angered by French President François Mitterand's wife's open support for the Polisario guerrillas.

Political Rights and Civil Liberties:

Despite the direct election of roughly two-thirds of the parliament, Moroccans are limited in their ability to change or influence their government. King Hassan II, the hereditary ruler, has broad authority over virtually all sectors of society. The king asserted at the opening session of parliament in October 1990 that "there are no breaches of human rights in Morocco", but widespread violations are reported. There are reportedly hundreds of political prisoners and a dungeon-like facility is said to exist in Tazmamet in the Atlas Mountains. Upon his release in September 1991 after 17 years in jail, 65-year-old Abraham Serfaty, a founding member of the Moroccan Communist Party, told interviewers in France that many political prisoners spend up to 23 hours per day in cells so small they cannot lie down, and "some keep their sanity only by smoking hashish, otherwise they would kill themselves."

The judiciary features secular courts based partly on French legal precepts and an Islamic system which deals with family and inheritance issues for Islamic Muslims. All judges are appointed by the king, and in political trials the accused enjoy few procedural safeguards. Dissidents are often tortured and coercively interrogated prior to trial. Freedom of speech does not extend to criticism of the king, Islam, or the government's claim to Western Sahara. In September, the government banned a new left-wing weekly published by former political prisoners, *El-Mouaten,* after just two issues. Freedom of press is limited and self-censorship practiced. The government owns the Maghreb Arab Press news service as well as the nationwide television service. Foreign publications are allowed, but are often censored when they contain articles critical of the government. Freedom of association is also limited and permits are required for large demonstrations.

Islam is the official religion, and although the 10,000-strong Jewish community and Christians are allowed to practice, other groups, such as the Baha'i community, are forbidden to worship together. The government resists calls for a fundamentalist Islamic society. In 1991, a series of clashes broke out at several universities between fundamentalists and Marxist students armed with knives and spiked clubs. A leftist group said the fundamentalists sought to foster "an atmosphere of fear and terrorism" on the campuses.

Citizens are free to travel inside the country, but political activists and former political prisoners are often denied permission to travel abroad. Women must have permission from their fathers or husbands to leave the country. Workers have the right to organize and bargain collectively. The three top unions are independent of the government and have democratically-elected leaderships.

Mozambique

Polity: One-party transitional
Economy: Mixed statist
Population: 16,100,000
PPP: $1,070
Life Expectancy: 47.5
Ethnic Groups: Lomwe, Makonde, Makua, Ndau, Shangaan, Thonga, Yao, others

Political Rights: 6
Civil Liberties: 4
Status: Partly Free

Overview:

Important developments in Mozambique in 1991 included the country's movement towards a multi-party system, the inconclusive efforts to end the civil war between the ruling Mozambique Liberation Front (Frelimo) and the rebel Mozambique National Resistance (Renamo), and an abortive coup by disaffected military and civilian members of Frelimo.

After more than two decades of fighting Portuguese colonial occupation, Frelimo successfully established the People's Republic of Mozambique in 1975. Samora Machel led the Marxist-Leninist one-party state, located in southeastern Africa, until he was killed in an airplane crash in 1986. Joaquim Chissano succeeded him as both president and Frelimo party leader. Frelimo had preempted all legal political activity in the country from independence until it allowed for non-violent political opposition under a new constitution in 1990. A unicameral people's assembly had been indirectly elected by provincial assemblies as recently as 1991, but all candidates had to be approved by Frelimo.

Almost since independence, the country has been torn by civil war and lawlessness. In rebellion against the government since the mid 1970s, Renamo was allegedly sponsored by the Ian Smith regime in Rhodesia in response to Frelimo's support for the armed insurgency against white minority rule in Rhodesia. Since 1980, when South African private and public sources reportedly began providing Renamo's financial support, the 25,000-member guerrilla force has carried on extensive activities throughout the country, controlling large areas of rural territory.

Traditional tribal leaders and religious figures, as well as peasants located in the center and north of the country, provided a measure of willing support for the Renamo insurgency. This support was largely due to the government's rural modernization program, which often forced peasants off their traditional lands and into communal villages where they could be conveniently organized into production brigades. Under the direction of Frelimo cadres, traditional political structures and social customs were dismissed in favor of new revolutionary organizations and values. Renamo has committed atrocities against civilians, including kidnapping peasants to serve as forced labor in the guerrilla war. Deserters from both the army and from Renamo have taken to banditry or set themselves up as warlords in local fiefdoms independent of outside control.

The government extended implicit recognition to Renamo as a political force by meeting in Rome with the insurgents for direct talks during 1990. On 1 December 1990 a limited cease-fire agreement was reached, the first accord between the two sides since the beginning of the insurgency. This "Rome Accord" eventually broke down amid Renamo's allegations of cease-fire violations.

Talks regarding a permanent and total cease-fire broke down several times in 1991. Meanwhile, in the absence of peace, President Chissano in April postponed the elections until sometime in 1992. He had said in late 1990 that elections would be held sometime between June and September of 1991. The government also arrested sixteen Frelimo "hardliners" in June for plotting a coup d'état. The interior minister was later linked to the coup plot and arrested in August. The plotters were reportedly dissatisfied with the weakening position of Frelimo and the military resulting from increasing political pluralism and economic liberalization over the past few years. In 1991 legislation was passed to end formal Frelimo party influence in the military.

Renamo has rejected the 1990 constitution as the product of an illegitimate regime and its non-democratic legislature. It has demanded that it be accorded a special enhanced status which would legally set it apart from the various new political parties springing up to contest the proposed multi-party elections. Renamo leader Dhlakama has further called for a joint national military of both Frelimo and Renamo elements, the abolition of private (anti-Renamo) militias, international supervision of political party registration, and U.N. governance of the country during the period leading up to multi-party elections. He has stated that he intends to run for the presidency.

Political Rights and Civil Liberties:

Mozambicans have not yet been given the opportunity to democratically choose a government. A new constitution introduced on 30 November 1990 formally provides for universal suffrage, direct legislative and executive elections, and a powerful executive branch. The new constitution abolishes the requirement that candidates for office be members of Frelimo. It also provides for free association, the right to own private property, the right to strike, religious freedom, and the independence of a depoliticized legal system. There has been some criticism of the degree to which the constitution concentrates power in the hands of the chief executive of the country.

Although special revolutionary tribunals hearing national security cases have been abolished, official misconduct during trials of political prisoners reportedly continues. This includes inadequate representation by court-appointed attorneys, placing the burden of proof on the accused, and conviction, both based on uncorroborated and coerced confessions. There is a right of appeal, although according to Africa Watch many convicted of national security violations appear to be unaware of this. The new constitution establishes the presumption of innocence for criminal defendants. Members of militia units, soldiers, and military counterintelligence agents continue to violate basic human rights; there are persistent reports of torture, rape, summary execution, and other abuses of those taken into custody.

Renamo has continued its methods of terrorizing the citizenry. Massacres of civilians are common. Hundreds of thousands of lives have been lost since the beginning of the civil war. According to human rights reports, a substantial majority of them are due to Renamo actions.

The personal behavior of citizens in government-controlled areas has largely continued to be monitored by Frelimo-organized "popular" organizations and security forces. A new security force will replace the People's National Security Service (Snasp), which was abolished in July of 1991 and had a poor human rights record. Opposition political demonstrations have been prohibited in the past, but are formally permitted under the new constitution. Private education has recently been allowed for the first time since independence.

Freedom of the press is still somewhat restricted, with foreign journalists subject to expulsion from the country for reporting the news unfavorably. The government is opposed to any licensing of private broadcasting facilities within Mozambique. Government-controlled media reflect official policy, with occasional tactical criticism. Religious publications discuss sensitive issues and foreign radio and TV broadcasts from South Africa are received without interference.

All trade unions have had to belong to the Organization of Mozambican Workers. Workers have the right to strike, provided that 3 to 4 day advance notice is given.

Namibia

Polity: Presidential-legislative democracy
Economy: Capitalist
Population: 1,500,000
PPP: na
Life Expectancy: 57.5
Ethnic Groups: Ovambo (50 percent), Kavango (9 percent), Herero (7.5 percent), Damara (7.5 percent), Baster and Colored (6.5 percent), White (6 percent), Nama/Hottentot (5 percent), Bushman (3 percent)

Political Rights: 2
Civil Liberties: 3
Status: Free

Overview:

On 21 March 1991 the southwest African country of Namibia celebrated its first anniversary of independence as one of a growing number of African nations with a function-

ing multiparty political system. The leader of the South West Africa Peoples'
Organization (SWAPO), Sam Nujoma, assumed office as the nation's first president in
1990. SWAPO, an former insurgency movement which had contested South African
control of Namibia since the sixties, gained a majority of the votes as a political party
in free and reasonably fair pre-independence elections in early November of 1989.

The 1989 elections were contested by ten political groups that vied for the
seventy-two seats up for grabs in a national constituent assembly. Because no party
won a two-thirds majority needed to dominate subsequent proceedings to write a
constitution, a one-party system could not be adopted. Even before Namibians went to
the polls, however, SWAPO reversed earlier statements indicating a preference for a
one-party state by issuing public reassurances that it would respect democratic
principles should it win. President Nujoma's first 16-member cabinet, consisting of
representatives of the major parties in the Assembly as well as the diverse ethnic and
racial groups in Namibia, represented a visible commitment to pluralism. There are
presently representatives of six political parties in the National Assembly, with
SWAPO having 41 seats and the center-right Democratic Turnhalle Alliance (DTA)
21. Regional elections are to be held during the first half of 1992.

Two issues which could be controversial in the future are the status of the
Pretoria-controlled enclave of Walvis Bay and the heavy South African presence in
the vital diamond, coal, and uranium extractive sectors in Namibia. Walvis Bay, the
only deep-water port in the region and physically encircled by Namibian territory, is
claimed by Namibia in its constitution, as are a number of small uninhabited offshore
islands. South Africa, which also claims the Bay and islands, negotiated in 1991 with
Namibia over the disputed territory, but no agreement was reached. The government
has explicitly called for private Western investment in order to spur national development and to lessen Namibia's economic dependence on South Africa, its southern
neighbor. All significant transportation and communications links are with South
Africa, a legacy of the League of Nations mandate relationship which placed Namibia
under Pretoria's control in 1920. Namibia has created an investment code to facilitate
such Western activity but foreign investment in Namibia is likely to be predominantly
South African for some time to come.

Underdevelopment of water supply systems limits further expansion of farming; most
foodstuffs must be imported from South Africa. There is marked inequity in ownership of
land and income between the black majority and the white minority. Land redistribution
policies to favor the black majority by opening up underused farmland often owned by
absentee white landlords, a major plank in SWAPO's pre-independence program, were
addressed at a special advisory conference in 1991. Among the resolutions adopted at the
conference were that single ownership of multiple commercial farms or of very large
farms ought to be prohibited. Under-utilized farmland and land owned by absentees is to
be expropriated and redistributed for productive use.

Namibian economic problems have been compounded by the influx of an estimated
100,000 refugees who have fled from drought, famine and war in neighboring Angola.
Unemployment, at some 35 percent, is a major problem, and it has only been mitigated
slightly by the new government's hiring of a number of SWAPO supporters to serve in
an already bloated public sector. The government has been running a substantial deficit
and will soon be forced to trim the public payroll. Meanwhile, there is frustration among
SWAPO supporters who had hoped that electoral victory and independence would mean

quick and substantial results in view of the leadership promises of land, jobs, health care, and improved educational opportunities.

Political Rights and Civil Liberties: Namibians can change their government democratically. An executive president was initially elected by the National Assembly and will later attain office by direct popular vote. The president will be limited to two five-year terms. Constitutional provisions establish regular elections for a bicameral parliament; members of the upper house of the National Council will be chosen through equal regional representation in 1992, members of the lower Assembly through proportional representation in 1995. White Namibians, a tiny minority in the country, are represented in the multi-ethnic government from the Cabinet level down.

There is a bill of rights, and an independent judiciary is mandated by the constitution. The right of private property is constitutionally recognized. The press freely expresses diverse points of view, including those critical of the relatively swank lifestyles which officials of the new government were alleged to have attained upon gaining power. The broadcast media are owned by the state, and some sectors of the SWAPO administration have reportedly put pressure on radio journalists to avoid critical reporting of the government. SWAPO's official weekly party newspaper, *New Era,* is state subsidized, a privilege apparently not extended to periodicals not affiliated with the party. The National Union of Namibian Workers, with links to the International Confederation of Free Trade Unions, has worked to organize mining, industrial, commercial, and public employees unions since 1986.

Nauru

Polity: Parliamentary democracy **Political Rights:** 1
Economy: Mixed capitalist-statist **Civil Liberties:** 2
Population: 8,100 **Status:** Free
PPP: na
Life Expectancy: na
Ethnic Groups: Indigenous Nauruans (mixture of Polynesian, Melanesian, Micronesian (58 percent), other Pacific islanders (26 percent), Chinese (8 percent), European (8 percent)

Overview: In 1991, Nauru, the world's smallest nation, remained locked in a legal dispute with Australia, its giant neighbor to the southwest. Australia administered Nauru and sold its phosphate below world market prices before granting it independence in 1968. The ravages of over eighty years of phosphate mining have forced the Nauruans to the fringes of their island, most of which is a scarred wasteland. Preliminary hearings before the International Court of Justice opened on 11 November 1991 on the country's claim against Australia for $60 million to rehabilitate the island. Nauruans currently have one of the highest per capita incomes in the world, but that will end in the mid-1990s when the last of the phosphate is mined. Contrary to Australia's original expectations, the Nauruans have refused to leave their island unless they are given legal sovereignty over another island. The government of President Bernard Dowiyogo is looking for new sources of revenue to supplement the phosphate income. It is particularly interested in developing a tuna processing industry, which would require training the largely unskilled workforce and building a desalinization plant; all of the country's water currently must be imported.

Both the eighteen-member parliament and the Nauru Local Government Council (NLGC) are popularly elected. The president is elected by the parliament from among its members. President Dowiyogo began his three-year term in December 1989. The NLGC, representing fourteen districts, provides local government services. While there are no organized political parties, candidates representing a wide variety of viewpoints contest the parliamentary seats.

Political Rights and Civil Liberties: Nauruans can change their government democratically. Voting is compulsory, and individuals run for the parliamentary seats according to specific issues or ideas rather than parties. The judiciary is independent of the government and procedural safeguards protect the rights of the accused. Freedom of speech and of press are respected, although there is no independent newspaper on the nine-square-mile island The country's only publication, the *Government Gazette*, reports official notices and announcements, while the government-owned radio station broadcasts Radio Australia, the BBC, and local news. Several foreign publications are available. In May 1991, the country's first television station began broadcasting. Freedom of association is provided for in the constitution and is respected in practice. There are no restrictions on foreign travel, and any domestic point can be reached on foot. Females may not marry non-Nauruans, and males must get permission from the government to marry foreigners. The government has been slow to address the problem of physical abuse of women, which is generally alchohol-related. Although the constitution allows workers to bargain collectively, the government discourages trade unions and none exist. Any foreign worker who is fired must leave the country within sixty days. Most of the phosphate miners are foreign, many of them from other Pacific countries.

Nepal

Polity: Constitutional monarchy
Economy: Capitalist
Population: 19,600,000
PPP: $770
Life Expectancy: 52.2
Ethnic Groups: Newar, Indian, Tibetan, Gurung, Magar, Tamang, Bhotia, others

Political Rights: 2
Civil Liberties: 3
Status: Free

Overview: In 1991, this Himalayan nation continued the democratization process begun last year when King Birendra, faced with escalating social unrest and violence, lifted a twenty-nine year ban on independent political activity and agreed to a draft constitution that calls for a constitutional monarchy and a popularly elected parliament.

The 1990 constitution calls for a parliament consisting of a 205-member House of

Representatives (lower house) elected from 75 districts, and a 60-member National Council (a third of whose members must be rotated every two years) to be determined by party strength in the lower house. Under the constitution the king is to nominate 10 percent of the members in the upper house on the advice of the prime minister. Earlier in the year, Krishna Prasad Bhattarai, president of the Nepali Congress Party (NC) was named interim prime minister. The NC, which held power briefly in 1959, joined with a seven-member coalition of leftist and Communist groups—the United Left Front (ULF)—to form the Movement for the Restoration of Democracy led by Ganesh Man Singh, a member of the NC. The new constitution meant the end of the traditional, non-party "panchayat system" (which gave the king holding near-absolute power as head of state). Bhattarai's 11-member coalition cabinet included four ministers from his party. Three members came from the ULF and one labor organization. There were two palace representatives and two independents.

The key development in 1991 was the parliamentary elections held on 12 May. In January, the two major factions of the Nepal Communist Party (NCP) agreed to merge to form the United Nepal Communist Party (UNCP). A total of 47 parties registered by 21 January for the general election, the first multi-party vote in more than 30 years. Of the myriad parties, the NC and the leftist NCP-UNCP coalition were the best organized. To preclude campaign violence, interim Prime Minister Bhattarai inducted 42,000 retired police and ex-servicemen for temporary duty, and announced that the 35,000-strong army was also ready to secure the election process. Nevertheless, the independent Human Rights Organization of Nepal expressed concern about reported election-related killings in the Terai region near the Indian border, where approximately 38 percent of the people live. The Terai, who call themselves *medhesiya* (midlanders), are heavily Indianized and grossly under-represented in Nepalese institutions, including the army and the police. The regions proximity to and cultural affinity with India had allowed political thugs from Indian states to cross the border and, for a price, intimidate voters. At least nine people were reported killed in pre-election violence.

During the campaign, the major parties ran on platforms that promised more resources to education, health, and village development. In light of India's 1989 trade blockade, which virtually cut off Nepal from the outside world, some parties raised the historic connection between the Nepali Congress Party and the Indian Congress Party.

On election day, the Nepali Congress won 110 seats; the UNCP 69; the People's Front (*Jana Morcha*), 9; Nepal Friendship Party, 6; National Democratic Party (Chand), 3; Nepal Workers' and Peasants' Party, 2; Communist Party of Nepal (Democratic-Manandhar), 2; National Democratic Party (Thapa), 1; independents, 3. Leftist parties won overwhelmingly in the capital, Kathmandu, and other developed areas. Interim Prime Minister Bhattarai lost to Madan Bhandari, general-secretary of the NCP-UNCP. Post-election analysts in Nepal suggested that the NC was hurt by allowing itself to be identified with former "panchayat" leaders and a pro-Indian foreign policy. International observers reported that the vote was essentially free and fair.

To counter Communist influence, the NC chose Girija Prasad Koirala, a staunch anti-Communist, as prime minister. On 29 May, the 65-year-old leader of the 1990 mass movement for democracy was formally asked by King Birendra to form a government.

The most pressing challenge for the government was improving the economy and the life of the kingdom's citizens, nearly half of whom live in rural poverty.

On 4 September, Prime Minister Koirala gave an upbeat assessment of his government's first 100 days, saying it maintained law and order and strengthened democracy. He said the government's top priorities were improving general adminis-tration, implementing rural development projects and getting parliament to approve a new budget. Since taking office, the prime minister faced an inflation rate of 25 to 35 percent (brought on partly by a devaluation of the Nepalese currency) and a 56-day civil servants' strike in August that brought the state administration to a virtual standstill. The strike ended only when the Nepalese Communist Party withdrew its support. On 20 September, the government dismissed 47 pro-panchayat civil servants and promoted 44 others to the vacated posts.

To ease financial burdens, the government announced plans to privatize much of the business sector, gradually withdrawing from 64 enterprises. The finance minister said the government would hand over total management of its jute, sugar and paper mills, as well as four agricultural operations, to private entrepreneurs.

On 29 November, several Communist parties held an anti-government rally in Kathmandu that attracted more than 10,000 demonstrators. Students were protesting a rise in admission and tuition fees at universities and spiralling inflation, particularly a 61 percent hike in electricity and a 50 percent jump in telephone rates.

On 3 December, the government unveiled a five-year economic plan which relied heavily on the private sector to generate 1.4 million jobs and boost gross domestic product to 5.1 percent annually. About 60 percent of the funds are expected to be provided by the private sector in the form of investment in industries such as textiles, clothing, handicrafts, and carpets. A government spokesman said that Nepal would take measures to encourage foreign investment.

Political Rights and Civil Liberties:

Under the 1990 constitution, citizens can elect a government under a multi-party system, a right that was exercised in largely "free and fair" parliamentary elections in May. There were isolated reports of election-related violence. The constitution provides for an independent judiciary. On 5 November, King Birendra appointed 67 judges to nine appellate courts in a bid to speed up the judicial process and make it impartial and independent. A justice ministry source said that the country's zonal, regional and special courts "would be closed forever," doing away with the fourth tier of the judicial system. The three levels of the system will be judicial courts, district appellate courts, and the Supreme Court headed by the chief justice. Under the 30-year *panchayat* system most civil servants with legal knowledge were appointed as district or zonal judges, creating the fourth tier which delayed the legal process. The legal system provides the right to counsel, protection from double jeopardy and open trials. The constitution also endorses freedom of the press. For its size, the country has an unusually large number of newspapers—nearly 400 dailies and weeklies. The govern-ment owns and operates radio and television.

On the question of religious freedom, Article 19 of the new constitution contains identical language to Article 14 of the old document providing that "every person... may profess and practice his own religion as handed down from ancient times," but that "no person shall be entitled to convert another person from one religion to another." The legal code provides prison terms for any Hindu in this predominantly Hindu nation who converts to another religion and stiffer sentences for anyone trying to proselytize a Hindu. There is a large Buddhist minority and a smaller group of Muslims and Christians. Nepal has over a dozen non-governmental human rights groups.

Domestic travel is generally unrestricted, as are emigration and foreign travel. The new government abolished the official Nepal Labor Organization and the constitution provides the right of workers to join unions, associations and other groups. There are several independent trade unions.

Netherlands

Polity: Parliamentary democracy
Economy: Mixed capitalist
Population: 15,000,000
PPP: $12,680
Life Expectancy: 77.2
Ethnic Groups: Dutch (99 percent), Indonesian and others (1 percent)

Political Rights: 1
Civil Liberties: 1
Status: Free

Overview:

The top news stories in 1991 included losses by the Labor Party and the Christian Democrats in provincial elections, disputes over social welfare policy, and controversies over asylum policy.

The independence of the Netherlands dates from the late sixteenth century, when the Dutch provinces rebelled against Spanish rule. Located in Western Europe, the country has long-established traditions of representative government and constitutional monarchy. The Netherlands held its most recent parliamentary election in 1989. Christian Democratic Prime Minister Ruud Lubbers called the election after his right-wing Liberal coalition partners objected to his tough environmental proposals. The issues in the campaign were the environment, the economy, and the welfare state. The Christian Democrats emerged the leading party in the lower house with fifty-four seats. They formed the current center-left coalition government with the Labor Party, led by Wim Kok.

The coalition's original governing accord called for limiting defense spending, increasing expenditures on social welfare and the environment, and cutting the value-added tax rate. However, in 1991 inflationary pressures led the government to adopt austerity measures, including higher rents and fares and changes in unemployment and disability payment policies. As of 1991, 14 percent of the workforce was out of work and on disability payments. In addition, the austerity plan called for delinking unemployment benefit levels and worker pay increases. Marjanne Sint, chairwoman of the Labor Party, suggested pulling her party out of the coalition over the disability plan. Labor feared that its participation in austerity policies would undermine the party's working-class base. Both the Federation of Dutch Trade Unions and the Christian National Trade Union staged strikes and other industrial actions to protest the austerity plan.

Both Labor and the Christian Democrats lost ground in the provincial elections on 6 March 1991. Democrats '66, a center-left party, and the right-wing People's Party for Freedom and Democracy made gains at their expense. The Dutch Communist Party voted to dissolve itself in June. It members joined the Green-Left coalition, an amalgam of left-wing and environmentalist groups. Prime Minister Lubbers has announced that he will retire in 1993.

Political Rights and Civil Liberties: The people have the right to change their government democratically. Power shifts back and forth between center-left and center-right coalitions with the Christian Democrats playing the pivotal role. The bicameral parliament, the States General, is divided into a 75-member First Chamber, which the eleven provincial councils elect indirectly for four-year terms, and a more powerful 150-member Second Chamber, which the voters elect by proportional representation for a maximum term of four years. Due to the electoral system, the Second Chamber includes many parties from right to left.

Civil liberties are generally respected. The press is free, but it generally observes unofficial limits in writing about the royal family. Broadcasting is state owned but autonomously operated, and offers pluralistic points of view on social and political issues. Traditionally, commercials have been restricted, and are banned on Sundays for religious reasons.

The Netherlands has accepted immigrants from its former colonies, Suriname and Indonesia, and granted asylum to various refugees from other developing countries and Eastern Europe. However, the newcomers have encountered some discrimination in housing and employment. The Dutch government tightened admissions standards in 1991. For example, it expelled hunger-striking Vietnamese who had arrived from Czechoslovakia. In retaliation for the new immigration rules, the terrorist group, Revolutionary Anti-Racist Action (Ra Ra) bombed the Interior Ministry and the minister's home in November 1991.

Religious freedom is respected. The state subsidizes church-affiliated schools based on the number of registered students. The extensive public sector regulates the private economy, and provides generous social welfare benefits. Organized labor is free. Only civil servants lack the right to strike, but they strike sometimes anyway. The Dutch have tolerated euthanasia for twenty years. The hospitals employ guidelines requiring the patient's expressed consent, but critics charge that health professionals violate this guideline by taking lives without such consent.

New Zealand

Polity: Parliamentary democracy
Economy: Capitalist
Population: 3,500,000
PPP: $11,310
Life Expectancy: 75.2
Ethnic Groups: Predominantly Anglo-Saxon, Maori and Polynesians (12 percent)

Political Rights: 1
Civil Liberties: 1
Status: Free

Overview: In the face of mounting opposition, New Zealand's ruling National Party plunged ahead in 1991 with highly controversial reforms of the country's social welfare programs.

The National Party has been in power since its landslide victory over the labor party in the October 1990 elections. Labor's six-year reign had been marked by vigorous attempts to liberalize the country's economy, and, more recently, by recession and high unemployment. The Labor Party reduced or eliminated most tariffs and export subsidies, deregulated the banking system, floated the currency, and privatized several state-owned enterprises. Experts said such changes were necessary since agricultural export revenues could no longer prop up an inefficient economy.

Prime Minister Jim Bolger launched even deeper reforms. In July 1991, Finance Minister Ruth Richardson unveiled a $16.9 billion budget which slashed $570 million in spending. The government seeks to reduce unemployment and healthcare benefits and target them to a more limited group. Under a new pension scheme, universal benefits will be phased out and the eligibility age raised. Prior to the cuts, welfare payments had accounted for nearly one-third of the government's budget. Richardson called financial austerity critical to keeping inflation down and maintaining the country's credit rating, but opposition leaders quickly blasted the budget for doing nothing to create new jobs.

The first casualties of the new budget were two National Party members of parliament, Gilbert Myles and Hamish McIntyre, who quit the party in August to protest both the government's policies and the opposition's weak response. In early September, Myles claimed two-thirds of the National Party's rank-and-file members across the country had left the party in 1991, and the pair proceeded to revive the Liberal Party, which had disbanded back in 1927. The defections left the Nationals with 66 seats in parliament to Labor's 28, with one New Labor MP in addition to the two new Liberal Party members. A poll on 4 September showed Prime Minister Bolger's popularity had nose-dived to 7 percent, with support for the Nationals as a whole at 20 percent. Nearly 40 percent supported neither major party. Reports of a serious rift in the cabinet between Finance Minister Richardson and Commerce Minister Philip Burdon over tariff reductions contributed to the public's discontent with the National Party. Burdon and others said cutting tariffs would leave industries unprotected and further increase unemployment, which hit 10 percent in September. However, Richardson pointed to the inflation rate, down to 2.2 percent the same month, as a sign her policies were working.

After a stormy National Party crisis meeting on 7 November, Bolger announced the government would reintroduce an unpopular tax surcharge despite complaints it should be focusing on economic growth instead. 70-year old Sir Roger Muldoon, who served as prime minister from 1975-1984, announced on 17 November during a radio talk show he would leave the parliament, saying the divided party's deregulatory plans had gone too far and a by-election for his seat would "give the government a fright." As prime minister, Muldoon had strongly supported the programs now being cut.

In other domestic issues, 300 Maoris, led by 96-year old wheelchair-bound Dame Whina Cooper, marched on the capital on 10 October to protest Prime Minister Bolger's dismissal of popular Maori Affairs Minister Winston Peters, who had repeatedly criticized the government's economic policies. The country announced a new immigration policy in November aimed at attracting young, skilled people, which featured regional quotas favoring people from Europe and the Americas. The government also planned to privatize the retail electricity system by allocating shares to all adults.

In foreign relations, New Zealand reassessed its defense and foreign affairs policies in 1991 and sought to improve relations with the United States. A white paper published in May called for a "new internationalism" and stressed regional defense partnerships, particularly with Southeast Asian countries, based on economic interests in addition to defense requirements. In a major shift, the government announced it would review a 1985 law prohibiting nuclear-powered ships and ships with nuclear weapons at New Zealand ports. The policy has led to a major split with the United States, and jeopardized the country's inclusion in a possible future free trade alliance with Australia and the North American countries.

Political Rights
and Civil Liberties:
New Zealanders can change their government democratically. Freedoms of speech, association and press are respected. The independent media feature over 700 newspapers and magazines. In August, the largest evening paper, *The Auckland Star*, closed due to financial problems and declining circulation. Free political advertising is granted to parties with at least ten seats in Parliament. The independent judicial system affords substantial procedural safeguards for the accused. New Zealand has no official religion, and all faiths have the right to practice freely. The 1991 Employment Contracts Act broke the system under which unions had exclusive bargaining rights for workers. There are now contracts between individual workers and employers. Unions may represent workers, but management is not legally bound to recognize them.

New Zealand's indigenous Maori citizens make up 12 percent of the population. By Maori request, four Maori MPs are selected from separate electoral rolls. The Waitangi Tribunal hears grievances from the Maoris against the government, while the Iwi Transition Agency is charged with transferring some government programs to Iwi (tribal) authorities. By some estimates, Maoris claim up to 70 percent of the land. Roughly half of New Zealand's prison population is made up of Maoris and other Polynesian groups.

Nicaragua

Polity: Presidential-legislative democracy (military influenced)
Economy: Capitalist-statist
Population: 3,900,000
PPP: $2,660
Life Expectancy: 64.8
Ethnic Groups: Complex, with mestizo (approximately 70 percent), Caucasian (16 percent), black (9 percent), and indigenous (5 percent)

Political Rights: 3
Civil Liberties: 3
Status: Partly Free

Overview:
Many Nicaraguans hoped the 1990 election of President Violeta Chamorro would break the cycle of violence and instability that has run throughout Nicaraguan history. But her administration continues to be overmatched by the extortionist tactics of the Sandinista National Liberation Front (FSLN), which remains in control of the military and the police, and the country continues to be threatened by further upheaval.

The Republic of Nicaragua was established in 1838, seventeen years after it gained independence from Spain. Fierce power struggles between the Liberal and Conservative parties dominated politics until General Anastasio Somoza Garcia came to power in 1937. Authoritarian rule under the Somoza family lasted until the 1979 revolution that brought the Sandinista National Liberation Front (FSLN) to power.

The Marxist FSLN suspended the 1972 constitution and ruled by decree until

1985. In 1984, elections for president, vice-president, and a National Assembly were held in what was little more than a state-controlled plebiscite. FSLN Comandante Daniel Ortega was elected president and the FSLN took 61 seats in the 96-seat Assembly.

The Assembly drafted a constitution that was promulgated in January 1987. Provisions on civil liberties were automatically suspended under state-of-emergency regulations decreed because of the Contra insurgency. The 1987 constitution provides for a president, vice-president, and National Assembly directly elected for six-year terms, and institutionalizes the Sandinista army as the national military.

In August 1987, President Ortega and the other four Central American presidents signed the Arias peace accord. A year later, Ortega agreed to move up the November 1990 elections to February 1990. In 1989, the FSLN agreed to allow the National Opposition Union (UNO), a coalition of fourteen political parties ranging from left to conservative right, to review voter lists and monitor votecounting.

UNO nominated Violeta Chamorro, the publisher of opposition newspaper *La Prensa*, to run for president against Ortega. The FSLN attacked UNO as a U.S. puppet and Contra front and, despite substantial U.S. funding for UNO, used state funds to outspend UNO by at least five to one. Chamorro emphasized freedom and democracy, promised open government, and pledged to end the military draft. On 25 February 1990, monitored by observers from the U.N. and the OAS, 55 percent of the electorate voted for Chamorro, 40 percent for Ortega. UNO won 51 Assembly seats, with the FSLN taking 39, and two seats going to smaller parties. UNO also won in nearly two-thirds of the municipal races.

Before Chamorro's inauguration, Antonio Lacayo, her son-in-law and campaign chief, negotiated a transition agreement with General Humberto Ortega, Daniel's brother and commander of the Sandinista military. With Daniel threatening the FSLN would "govern from below," Lacayo agreed, over the heads of UNO leaders, to let Humberto remain as military chief. In exchange, Humberto agreed the defense and interior ministries would be headed by civilians, and the state security apparatus would be dismantled.

After the new government took office, however, it was evident the interior minister would have limited authority, and the defense minister, President Chamorro herself, practically none. Before leaving office, Daniel Ortega had secretly decreed a military law, made public in mid-1990, which makes it virtually impossible to remove General Ortega from his command and grants him complete control over the military's internal and external affairs. The national police, while part of the interior ministry, remained under the direct command of a longtime Sandinista militant. Also, General Ortega secretly transferred the state security apparatus from the interior ministry to the army. In sum, the new government took office with no control over the military, the police, or state security forces.

If Lacayo, the minister of the presidency and power behind the throne, believed the transition agreement would allow the new administration to establish itself on the strength of a market-oriented, economic reform program, he miscalculated. In 1990, the FSLN exercised veto power over government policy through violent extortion. The government, with the stated goal of "national reconciliation," regularly caved in to FSLN demands in order to stop the seizure of state enterprises and government ministries by armed FSLN militants. By the end of 1990, the FSLN had leveraged the Chamorro administration into a power-sharing arrangement officially known as the National Concordance. Left on the sidelines were UNO, private business and independent labor—the three pillars of the coalition that had supported Mrs. Chamorro for president.

In 1991, angry UNO leaders, wielding a majority in the Assembly, passed a bill requiring the return of an estimated $1 billion in government property appropriated by the FSLN before leaving office. The so-called "Pinata," enormous even by Latin American standards, included homes, cars, land, businesses, and media outlets, and practically overnight made the FSLN business empire the largest in Nicaragua.

When UNO demanded that President Chamorro back the anti-Pinata legislation, Daniel Ortega called for a popular uprising and FSLN militants carried out a series of bombings, attacks and armed labor strikes. In line with the pattern established in 1990, Antonio Lacayo was able to temporarily appease the FSLN with a presidential veto of UNO's bill. But in October, under increasing pressure from UNO and polls showing popular opinion against the Pinata, President Chamorro agreed to negotiate a new property law. That, plus plans by a number of municipal governments to create independent police units, led to renewed calls by Daniel Ortega for armed rebellion.

In early November, FSLN cadres occupied farms and factories and attacked independent labor unions. After unknown persons bombed the tomb of a former FSLN leader, FSLN supporters went on a rampage in Managua and three other cities, burning, looting, stoning, and shooting. City halls, UNO-linked media outlets, and dozens of government vehicles were destroyed. The police stood by and watched. UNO leaders demanded that the Chamorro administration finally stand up to the FSLN and called for Daniel Ortega to be charged with terrorism.

The Chamorro administration responded the same way it had during previous FSLN rampages: by inviting the FSLN leadership for private meetings. The first round was inconclusive, but Antonio Lacayo stated afterward that "national reconciliation" remained the government's goal. But the reality was that he and President Chamorro had little room to maneuver between the extortionist FSLN and furious former backers in UNO.

The return to guerrilla actions by a number of Contra bands added to the instability. Because of the devastated economy, the Chamorro administration has had difficulty providing economic aid to former Contras, part of the 1990 demobilization agreement mediated by the OAS. Former Contras in the rural north also have been subject to abuse by the FSLN-controlled army and police. Hundreds took up arms again in 1991 to demand the removal of General Ortega and a new, independent police force. In response, former Sandinista soldiers formed paramilitary units, vowing to crush the "Re-Contras." OAS efforts to defuse the threat of renewed conflict in the countryside appeared to run aground during the general upheaval in November.

Many in Nicaragua refer to the co-governing arrangement between the Chamorro administration and the FSLN as "Kupia-Kumi," a Miskito Indian phrase meaning "beating with one heart." The phrase refers to the historical pattern of feuding elites making deals to end civil strife and guarantee each others's economic interests. One side or the other has invariably tried by hook and crook to dominate the arrangement, setting off a new round of conflict. Many Nicaraguans hoped the the election of President Chamorro would break the cycle, but the FSLN and Antonio Lacayo appear intent on continuing it.

Political Rights   Citizens are able to change their government democratically.
and Civil Liberties: The 1987 constitution permits the organization of political
                          parties, civic groups and labor unions. However, the FSLN
prepared the document with the expectation of holding power indefinitely; the legal
existence of independent organizations is contingent on, among other things, their
contribution to "the construction of a new society." Individual rights, civil liberties, and
the right to free expression are so narrowly defined and qualified as to often make them
inapplicable in practice. In effect, the 1987 constitution does not guarantee political
rights and civil liberties; it guarantees the right of the government to restrict them.

The Chamorro government has committed itself to the full respect of political
rights and civil liberties, notwithstanding the constitution. But even if the government
were able to muster the two-thirds majority in the Assembly to amend the document,
it would be unable to guarantee full respect for these rights and freedoms because the
military and the police remain under FSLN control and operate with impunity.

Since the new government took office, there have been continuing reports by
Nicaragua's independent human rights organizations of intimidation, false arrest, and
torture during interrogation. Abuses are directed primarily against demobilized Contras
and UNO supporters. Many violations are committed by former members of state
security transferred to the national police in 1990. More than 200 people have been
killed as a result of political violence—over 50 demobilized Contras, with the
remainder including FSLN supporters, UNO sympathizers, peasants and independent
labor leaders. There also have been abuses by the army during the campaign to
disarm the civilian population of tens of thousands of weapons left over from the
Contra war. Prisons are overcrowded and conditions deplorable, with hundreds of
detainees held for months and in some cases years before being brought to court.

The police rarely protect people and property from the armed actions of FSLN
labor unions or rural paramilitary units. In nearly two years, there have been virtually
no arrests in response to the bombings, takeovers of government buildings and other
incidents of FSLN violence. The judiciary, headed by a Supreme Court and appellate
courts stacked by the FSLN before leaving office, provides little recourse. The judicial
system also has been ineffectual against a surging crime wave fueled by a decade of
economic deterioration.

The FSLN, however, has demanded full freedom for its own activities, and
frequently justifies the action or inaction of police as necessary for the protection of
its rights. The FSLN claims the police do not intervene during the armed occupation
of ministries and state enterprises because it would impinge on the right to strike.
Under FSLN rule, labor strikes were outlawed.

International and Nicaraguan human rights organizations are investigating long-
standing charges of systematic, summary executions by FSLN government forces.
Since 1990, at least twelve clandestine mass graves have been uncovered, but as of
1991 the army had refused to cooperate with investigations. According to the new
military law, the army alone is responsible for investigating charges of rights violations against its members.

The army also has stonewalled the investigation of the 28 October 1990 murder
of Jean Paul Genie who, according to a group of Venezuelan jurists working at the
request of UNO, was killed on a highway south of Managua by members of General
Humberto Ortega's armed escort. Similarly, the police investigation into the

16 February 1991 murder in Managua of former Contra leader Enrique Bermudez remained stalled nearly a year later.

The Chamorro government has committed itself to full freedom of expression, and all voices are represented in the print and broadcast media. Before leaving office, the FSLN dismantled the 17-station state radio network and "privatized" it to mostly FSLN loyalists, part of the massive, illegal transfer of state resources to the FSLN party. They left behind two television channels which are operated by the government.

FSLN cadres frequently attack non-FSLN media. During armed strikes in 1990, they blew up the transmitting tower of Radio Corporacion, orchestrated mob assaults on independent media outlets, and invaded the government broadcast center. Similar incidents continued in 1991, with a number of bombings and takeovers during the summer and fall when FSLN mobs destroyed Radio Corporacion and Radio Dario.

There are no restrictions on religious expression under the Chamorro government. The Catholic church has been outspoken in its concern over the Chamorro government's inability to carry out its legal mandate.

Niger

Polity: One-party military
Economy: Capitalist
Population: 8,000,000
PPP: $610
Life Expectancy: 44.5
Ethnic Groups: Adarawa, Arab Bedouin, Daza, Djerma, Fulani, Hausa, Kanuri, Kawar, Kurfei, Manga, Mauri, Songhai, Tazarawa, Teda, Tuareg (Asben, Aullimiden), Zerma, other

Political Rights: 6
Civil Liberties: 5
Status: Partly Free

Overview:

In 1991 the Nigerien political system began its formal transformation into a multi-party democratic regime, though not without some difficulties.

A large, landlocked West African country, Niger gained its independence from France in 1960. A civilian, one-party government was overthrown in 1974 by the military. General Ali Seibou was named head of state by a supreme military council in 1987. In late 1988, President Seibou announced plans to return Niger to constitutional rule by formalizing one-party rule. A few months later Seibou was re-elected without electoral opposition to a seven-year term. In December 1989, the government reported that voters overwhelmingly adopted a constitution providing for institutionalization of a one-party regime, with governing National Movement of the Society for Development (MNSD) as the sole legal political party. Nonetheless, the president announced in November 1990 that the country would adopt a multi-party system based on the recommendations of special commissions set up earlier in the year to assess the country's political structure. He indicated that a national conference would be convened sometime in 1991 to determine the parameters of multi-partyism, with elections likely to take place during the first three months of 1992. The president's announcement was preceded by a general strike called by the USTN (National Trade Union Federation) to press for multi-partyism and the end of austerity measures.

In accord with the regime's plans, during early 1991 political parties were allowed to apply for provisional legal recognition by the Ministry of the Interior. In March President Saibou was re-designated chairman of the MNSD at a party congress despite reports that his support among delegates was waning. Also in March, the Army withdrew from a partisan affiliation with the MNSD and the National Assembly approved a new constitution which established civilian authority over the military and formalized the new multi-party political system. Both the original date for convening the national convention, and the organizations who were to attend, were unilaterally determined by the government, but later modified after pressure from the opposition. President Saibou terminated his MNSD party membership prior to the national convention in line with his desire to detach the office of the presidency from any particular political party.

The national convention was convened in July. Before it was adjourned, the constitution was suspended, the legislature dissolved, and most of the president's powers, including formal control of the armed forces, were transferred to a transitional prime minister appointed by the conferees. Senior Army officials responded by asserting an overriding loyalty to Saibou. The conference removed the two top Army officers from their positions, while junior officers pledged support for the sovereignty of the conference. Amadou Cheiffou was chosen to be prime minister. While some Malians saw the conference as an opportunity to air old grievances about corruption, economic mismanagement, and human rights abuses against authorities, government officials and the official media cautioned that the conference should not be made into a tribunal.

Sporadic problems between the government in Niamey and the nation's Tuareg population in the north continued, including hit-and-run attacks mounted by rebels on public facilities. Demands from the Tuareg population include greater regional autonomy as well as more government spending in their drought-stricken portion of the country.

Niger has been struggling with the effects of an economic austerity program involving a severe pruning of its large public sector workforce. Faced with the threat of a general strike in April, the government agreed to discontinue privatization, staff reduction, and the freeze of promotions in its public sector.

In foreign affairs, Niger sent a 491-man contingent to participate in the American-led international coalition fighting Iraq in the Persian Gulf War. Although the role of Nigerien forces was ostensibly to protect Saudi Arabia from Iraqi attack, the action provoked domestic opposition among among many in Niger's largely Muslim population. Representatives of the newly-formed political parties signed a joint statement demanding the Nigerien soldiers be withdrawn from the Gulf.

Political Rights and Civil Liberties: Despite the legalization of 37 political parties in 1991, Nigerien citizens have not yet been given the opportunity to change their government democratically. There is some concern that multi-party democracy will rapidly become clientalist in rural areas where traditional chiefs still hold sway. The national conference has tried to anticipate the problem by limiting the degree to which the influence of chiefs will be allowed to affect the make-up of political parties.

Civil and criminal cases are generally conducted fairly, while security cases have in the past been tried by the State Security Court, which functions outside the normal legal framework. Special courts handle civil servant corruption cases. Political detainees, particularly Tuaregs, have been held indefinitely without charge or trial after dozens were arrested in 1990. Almost all media are controlled by the government, although there are two small independent publications that do criticize the government. The political opposition has protested its inability to gain adequate access to the official media, although the problem seems to be easing. Freedom of religion in this overwhelmingly Muslim country is generally respected.

The USTN trade union federation, consisting of twenty-eight unions, is partly funded by the government and has long been linked with the ruling party. It has recently detached itself from the ruling MNSD and become a significant political force on the national scene, despite warnings from the government that it should limit its activities to labor issues. There are two unions not affiliated with the USTN. The federation has been able to organize paralyzing national strikes in support of wage demands.

Nigeria

Polity: Military transitional
Economy: Capitalist-statist
Population: 122,500,000
PPP: $1,030
Life Expectancy: 51.5
Ethnic Groups: Hausa, Fulani, Ibo, Yoruba, Kanuri, other

Political Rights: 5
Civil Liberties: 4
Status: Partly Free

Overview:

In 1991, Africa's most populous country continued to implement President Ibrahim Babangida's plan to create a two-party system. Despite some indication to the contrary, the president vowed that the transition to democratic civilian rule would be completed by October 1992.

After taking power in 1985, Major General Babangida established and became chairman of the Armed Forces Ruling Council (AFRC), serving as both head of state and chief executive. A ban on political parties was lifted in May 1989, but with substantial restrictions. The government banned all would-be politicians of the "old breed"—anyone who had participated in prior elective politics—from running for office again. Meanwhile, the junta allowed the registration of only two parties: the National Republican Convention (NRC) and the Social Democratic Party (SDP). The president described the two as a "little right of center, and a little left of center," but their party manifestos differed little. There was a sense among some Nigerians that the regime must see ideology as much as ethnicity, regionalism, religion, and political corruption as a threat to the stability of a multi-party system.

The local elections in December 1990 were generally judged as fair and relatively non-violent, but the voter turn-out rate was reportedly no more than 10 percent. In response to complaints concerning the fairness of the open balloting system, in which voters line up behind the name or picture of their desired representative, the National Electoral Commission (NEC) conducted a study of the problem. Critics charged that the voters' fear of intimidation by powerful local chiefs and politicos, as well as apathy due to the lack of real choice, had resulted in the low turnout. In March 1991, however, the NEC concluded that although voter participation had been low, the open ballot system helped prevent the violence and ballot box stuffing which had marred past elections, and would thus continue to be used in future elections. Much of the

Nigerian media expressed outrage at the continuation of the open ballot system, while the SDP supported the system as long as the process was "fine tuned." The NRC called for an "open-secret" ballot, in which the ballot could be marked in secret but be dropped into an outside box and counted outside.

The struggle between the two political parties became more lively as nation-wide campaigning continued. This was manifested in part through violence at political rallies and meetings. Elections using open balloting for state assemblies and state governors were held in November and December. Reports of irregularities were much more common than in the earlier local elections. Presidential primaries and final elections for President Babangida's civilian replacement were scheduled to take place in 1992. The president's announcement of the creation of nine new states and local government jurisdictions sparked riots in some areas aggrieved that their region had not merited a separate state. More than poverty, unemployment, or the population, the most important campaign issue for most Nigerians was corruption. Despite calls by the current leadership for self-sacrifice and honesty in government, corruption persisted in 1991. Domestic and international observers brought numerous accusations of fraud and bribery against the military government and even against Babangida himself.

Since independence in 1960, the country has been polarized by an underlying conflict: co-existence of the relatively wealthy, largely Christian south and the poorer but politically dominant Muslim north. Muslims make up about half of the population and run both the army and the national government. Religious tension erupted into violence in three major incidents during 1991. Demonstrations by relatively small groups of Muslims led to violent riots and confrontations with Christians and the police. The radical Islamic group "Muslim Brothers" collided with the Katsina state government in April after the group attacked a newspaper office which they asserted had published a blasphemous article. Also in April, Muslim accusations of Christians butchering hogs in a municipal slaughterhouse erupted into a riot; churches were burned down and as many as 1,000 were killed. In October, riots in the Islamic stronghold of Kano followed fundamentalist Muslim opposition to the holding of a public Christian revival meeting. An estimated 300 people were killed. The government arrested hundreds during the riots and later set up a judicial inquiry to investigate the unrest.

In October 1991 Nigeria conducted its first census since 1973. Attempting to avoid fraud or violence, questions dealing with respondents' ethnicity or religion were deleted from the population count. Nigeria's birthrate continues to grow at 3.5 percent per year, a rate which would give Nigeria a higher population than all of Western Europe in only 30 years.

In 1991 Cameroon moved to annex several Nigerian fishing villages. Regional Nigerian politicians and the media called for firm action against Cameroon by the national leadership, but Babangida continued to insist on maintaining peaceful negotiations.

The military government relaxed its economic austerity plan, the Structural Adjustment Program (SAP), early in 1991 but continued to remain strictly within IMF and World Bank guidelines. Despite initially higher oil revenues due to the Gulf crisis, Nigeria's economy continued to suffer under the weight of its massive international debt and an unemployment rate of 20 percent.

Political Rights and Civil Liberties: In 1991 Nigeria continued to be ruled at the national level by a military regime, and citizens could not change their government democratically. But national elections are scheduled for 1992 and two-party elections were held at the local and state levels in 1991. Political activity centered on the establishment of two parties, the NRC and the SDP, which were supposed to form the basis for the promised return to civilian rule by 1992. "Discredited" former politicians were denied full rights of democratic participation by being liable to prosecution for political activity, but the regime suddenly dropped this prohibition in late December.

Military tribunals have jurisdiction over drug trafficking, armed robbery, embezzlement, sedition, and other offenses. Defendants before the tribunals are not guaranteed either a public trial, legal counsel of their choice, or the right to appeal a conviction. Officials habitually ignore court orders, and the government has eliminated judicial review of some of its actions.

Early in 1991, the regime amended its dreaded State Security Decree No. 2, reducing the allowable time of detention without charge from six months to six weeks. Detentions still remain indefinitely renewable, however. Human rights groups have reported incidents of arbitrary arrest, long-term detention without trial, and excessive violence (including torture) by security forces. The regime has commonly incarcerated innocent relatives of suspected political offenders in order to draw the suspects out of hiding. Prison conditions are generally horrific. Lack of drinkable water and primitive methods of disposing of human waste pose serious health hazards.

In April 1991 police broke up a press conference held by independent student leaders. Meanwhile, the National Association of Nigerian Students (NANS) ignored government warnings against student disturbances. Protests turned into riots in May when two students were killed. Other demonstrations in July were followed by the arrest of the NANS leader and two former NANS officials.

Nigeria has a lively and independent press which frequently prints articles critical of government policy, but is often subject to government intimidation and sometimes restrictions on the coverage of topics such as military corruption, demonstrations, and riots. The government owns and operates radio and television media, which rarely air points of view critical of the government.

Freedom of religion is guaranteed, although all religious groups must be sanctioned by either the Christian Association of Nigeria (CAN) or the Supreme Council for Islamic Affairs. Religious tensions between Muslims and Christians in the northern half of the country continued to sporadically erupt into violence in 1991.

In general, Nigerians may travel without restrictions both inside and outside the country. All labor unions belong to the Nigeria Labor Congress (NLC), created in 1978 by government decree. The NLC, which is closely monitored by the government, has nevertheless organized a number of strikes over the past few years. Attempts by the NLC to forge links with the Social Democratic Party were blocked by the government through the National Electoral Commission, which stated that organizations could not endorse candidates.

Norway

Polity: Parliamentary democracy
Economy: Mixed capitalist
Population: 4,300,000
PPP: $13,820
Life Expectancy: 77.1
Ethnic Groups: Norwegian, Finnish, Lappic, and small immigrant groups

Political Rights: 1
Civil Liberties: 1
Status: Free

Overview:

Important developments in 1991 included a banking crisis, a reflationary budget proposal, a fishing dispute with the European Community and an intelligence scandal.

The Kingdom of Norway is a constitutional monarchy established in 1905 with the dissolution of the union with the Swedish crown. The present monarch, King Harald V, ascended the throne in 1991 following the death of his father, King Olav V. He is a largely ceremonial head of state. The government is a multi-party parliamentary system based on the 1814 constitution known as the Eidsvold Convention, one of the oldest written constitutions in Europe.

Executive power is exercised by the prime minister, who heads the Council of Ministers *(Statsrad)*. The *Statsrad* is responsible to the 165-seat parliament *(Storting)*, elected every four years by universal suffrage. The parliament elects one-fourth of its members to the upper house *(Lagting)*, and the rest serve in the lower house *(Odelsting)*.

In 1989 a center-right coalition consisting of the Christian People's Party, the Center Party, and the Conservative Party took control after the general election. Conservative party leader Jan P. Syse became prime minister, replacing Gro Harlem Brundtland of the Norwegian Labor Party, who had headed a minority government in coalition with the Socialist Left Party since 1986. The center-right minority government lacked a parliamentary majority and depended on the libertarian Progress Party.

The Conservative-led government had to resign in October 1990, because the parties could not agree over trade negotiations. The agrarian-based Center Party opposed plans for Norway to join a proposed European Economic Area (EEA), because joining would have changed Norway's laws which limit foreign ownership. The EEA would have involved both European Community (EC) members and non-members. Syse and the Conservatives favor Norwegian membership in the EC, but agreed not to press for it.

Under Norwegian law, it is now unconstitutional for a government to dissolve parliament between general elections. After the trade dispute, this rule forced the parliamentary parties to try to form a new governing coalition to hold office until 1993. The Center Party announced its willingness to back a Labor government since that party had not committed itself to the EC.

When Labor Prime Minister Gro Harlem Brundtland took office again in late 1990, he faced growing economic crises. The government bailed out the second largest bank in 1991 and financial panic led to a run on the bank, despite government assurances of security. The government responded to the recession with a reflationary budget plan for 1992. The plan would freeze defense spending and invest more in offshore oil and gas fields.

Trade disputes continued in 1991. Norway and other non-EC countries negotiated a trade deal, but disagreement arose over fishing rights. Norwegian fishing fleets blockaded harbors to protest competition from foreign fleets.

Norway had a major intelligence scandal in 1991. From January to August, the intelligence service allowed Israeli agents to interrogate Palestinians seeking asylum in Norway. No Arabic-speaking Norwegian was present during these un-taped sessions. British agents also questioned the Palestinians. Following these revelations, the intelligence chief resigned in October.

Political Rights and Civil Liberties: Norwegians can change their government democratically through general elections every four years.

The government subsidizes the culture of the Lappic (Sami) minority. The Finnish area in the North has a regionalist party, the Finnmark List. There are no significant restrictions on speech, press, assembly or association. The government film board has some little-used power to censor or ban films that are extremely violent, pornographic, or blasphemous. The state church is the Evangelical Lutheran Church (to which 93 percent of Norwegians belong). The king and half the cabinet must belong to the Church. Other religions are free to practice and proselytize. There is no official discrimination based on sex, language, social status, and race, but there has been some public concern over the immigration of non-Nordic peoples such as Asians, Africans, and Latin Americans. Both domestic and foreign travel are unrestricted. Some 60 percent of the work force is unionized, and there is a right to strike.

In 1991 Norway ratified an addition to the International Convention on Civil and Political Rights which outlaws the death penalty. The country had already eliminated capital punishment in civilian cases. The ban now extends to cases of wartime treason.

Oman

Polity: Traditional monarchy
Economy: Capitalist-statist
Population: 1,600,000
PPP: $9,290
Life Expectancy: 65.9
Ethnic Groups: Arab, Baluchi, Zanzibari, Indian

Political Rights: 6
Civil Liberties: 6
Status: Not Free

Overview: A small, oil-rich country, the Sultanate of Oman has been led by Sultan Qabus ibn Sa'id Al Sa'id since 1970, when he overthrew his isolationist father in a palace coup. Oman is one of the most politically undeveloped Arab states, with no constitution, legislature or political parties or elections. The Sultan rules in consultation with his appointed cabinet. A 55-member Consultative Assembly that meets quarterly was created in 1981. Governors of districts are appointed by the sultan.

On 18 November 1990, Sultan Qabus announced that a new consultative council would be established within a year. He said the new council would include representatives from Oman's 42 counties, and would be more representative than the existing council, which is made up of government officials and private citizens appointed by the sultan. The new council, he said, would exclude government officials, but it remained unclear how the council would be chosen. One official said it would be a popularly elected parliament, while others said the method of choosing members had yet to be determined. By the end of 1991, the consultative council had not yet been set up.

Although the Gulf War provided a temporary boost in oil revenues, declining prices and reports that the country may only have twenty years of reserves left have caused the government to concentrate on diversifying the economy. The Sultan called 1991 the "year of industry" and encouraged Omani citizens to work harder and be less dependent on foreign labor. Currently, about 45 percent of the sultanate's work force are foreigners. The Sultan has implemented an "Omanization" aimed at repatriating a majority of the sultanate's foreigners. The government also unveiled a five-year diversification plan. The plan will concentrate on the industrial, agricultural and fisheries sectors of the economy. Despite dwindling oil reserves, Oman has increased production as new deposits are found. Also, the government is encouraging natural gas drilling after huge reserves were discovered in 1991. For the first time in the country's history, the state has issued government bonds to cover the country's deficit.

Political Rights and Civil Liberties: Citizens of Oman cannot change their government democratically. Legal protections are generally underdeveloped, but in practice the criminal code applies Islamic law (*Shari'a*) by impartial Islamic judges. Some of the more severe punishments of Islamic law, such as stonings and amputations, have not been used in several years. Defendants have no right to a jury, counsel or public trial. Alongside the civilian courts are Shari'a courts which handle family matters. The government owns and operates radio and television, and controls two of three newspapers. All printed material is subject to censorship. Criticism of the sultan or the legitimacy of the regime is not tolerated. An Islamic state, Oman forbids proselytizing by non-Muslims but allows non-Muslims to worship at specified sites. Since 1986, Omani men have been barred from marrying foreign women. Unions are prohibited, as are strikes. Workers may, however, file grievances.

Pakistan

Polity: Parliamentary democracy
Economy: Capitalist-statist
Population: 117,500,000
PPP: $1,790
Life Expectancy: 57.7
Ethnic Groups: Punjab, Baluchi, Sindhi, Pathan, Afghan

Political Rights: 4
Civil Liberties: 5
Status: Partly Free

Overview: In its first full year in office, Prime Minister Nawaz Sharif's Islamic Democratic Alliance (IDA) beat the Pakistan People's Party (PPP) in the March 1991 Senate elections, began an ambitious privatization program and passed legislation placing the country under Islamic law. Sharif's plans to modernize the country have been jeopardized by near-anarchy in the Sindh province and violence in other areas, scaring investors and raising the threat of a military crackdown.

Formed in 1947 through the partition of India, Pakistan became an Islamic republic in 1956. The country went to war with India over the Kashmir province in 1947-1948 and again in 1965. In 1971 East Pakistan separated to form Bangladesh, leading to a third war in which India soundly defeated Pakistan. In 1970 Ali Bhutto became president, but was deposed in a 1977 military coup led by General Zia ul-Haq. General Zia imposed martial law and outlawed political parties. Bhutto was hanged in 1979 on charges of complicity in a 1974 political murder. In 1985, political parties were again allowed to function and martial law was repealed. Zia died in August 1988 in a mysterious airplane crash, and elections in November 1988 brought Bhutto's daughter, Benazir, to power as prime minister.

President Ghulam Ishaq Khan dismissed Benazir Bhutto on 6 August 1990 for alleged corruption, nepotism and abuse of authority, and dissolved the 237-seat National Assembly. In the October 1990 elections for a new Assembly, the conservative IDA coalition soundly defeated Bhutto's PPP and formed a new government under Sharif. Of the 217 directly-elected seats, the IDA won 105, while the PPP, in a coalition called the People's Democratic Alliance, won just 45. Despite Bhutto's claim of massive vote-rigging, in January 1991 an international team released a report concluding that the election was generally free and fair. But the international observers also urged reforms in the electoral process, including the removal of corrupt officials.

In 1991 the IDA also strengthened its control of the 87-seat Senate, which has 76 members chosen by the country's four provincial assemblies, and eleven members chosen by the National Assembly from the tribal region and the capital, Islamabad. The Senate has the power to block lower-house legislation. In March elections for 46 Senate seats the IDA took 23 seats, the PPP took 5 and smaller parties and independents took 18. Prior to the election, Bhutto had accused Sharif of running a "brutal dictatorship" and warned that the IDA would attempt to sabotage the vote, although no evidence of large-scale vote-rigging was produced.

In addition to the PPP's decline, Bhutto herself has been under investigation by a special one-judge court on eight counts of corruption and mismanagement during her 20 months in office. Her husband, Asif Ali Zardari, is being investigated by a similar tribunal on charges of kidnapping, extortion and murder stemming from an August 1990 political hit which turned into a massacre killing 22 people. In June a report released by the Canadian High Commission in Islamabad called the tribunals biased, saying neither court meets even "the minimum standards of due process of law." If convicted, Bhutto could lose her parliamentary seat and be barred from politics for seven years, while her husband faces the gallows. Days after the release of the Canadian report, the PPP released a study claiming the October 1990 election was rigged in 70 out of the 217 races. The report also said the caretaker government that succeeded Bhutto had contributed to the result by being partisan towards the IDA through misuse of the state-run media and arrests and intimidation of PPP candidates. The PPP accused President Khan of creating an "election cell" which created "ghost" polling stations, issued fake identity cards, and stuffed ballot boxes.

The PPP's troubles increased on 18 June when the judge trying Bhutto's husband's case was killed in an early morning ambush. Jam Saddiq Ali, a leading Bhutto foe and the chief minister of the Sindh province where the PPP is based, immediately blamed the PPP and vowed revenge. Within days, 750 PPP supporters were rounded up for questioning. The arrests in the Sindh province spread fear among

PPP members of parliament. By early August, some 27 MP's defected to the IDA, and Bhutto claimed the arrest total had reached 5,000. On 3 August, Naved Malik, an IDA defector, said he had been a member of the IDA's "election cell" which had rigged the October 1990 election by adding 20,000 fake votes in each constituency. His assertion could not be verified. The next day, Bhutto staged a 12-hour hunger strike outside parliament, calling for Jam Saddiq's dismissal and an end to the government's harassment of her supporters.

In addition to opposition from the PPP, Sharif's most serious problem in 1991 was growing lawlessness in the Sindh province. The province has been terrorized by bandits armed with Kalashnikov rifles and rocket launchers who have been responsible for extortion of landlords and peasants. Those who refuse to give money have been abducted, had their their crops destroyed and had their electricity transformers blown up. One police officer complained, "There are 12,218 criminal cases pending with the courts in Sindh and the legal system has collapsed." In Hyderabad alone, 3,000 have been killed since 1985. Streets are deserted at night throughout the province. In one northern region of the Sindh, criminals have organized into a federation which divides gains and coordinates information about the police, and several gangs have formed public affairs offices in Hyderabad. In addition to the criminal violence, in June and July the Sindh experienced fighting between the PPP and the separatist Muhajir Qaumi Movement (MQM), as well as between rival MQM factions. Gun battles in June and July claimed several lives. In 1991 several foreign workers and tourists were kidnapped in the Sindh, and a Swede was killed in a shootout between his kidnappers and police. In late June the violence spread into the Punjab province, which had already been experiencing a wave of bank robberies, when 22 people were massacred, several of them beheaded. In addition, violence in Kashmir surrounding the June election took 20 lives.

Sharif responded to the unrest by proposing a constitutional amendment that would give him the power to declare a state of emergency and suspend any constitutional provisions. An accompanying ordinance would allow low-level police officials to fire on crowds without a magistrate's approval. After many in his own party rejected the proposal, the parliament eventually adopted an amendment providing for special anti-terrorist courts where judgements could only be appealed once.

In another crisis, on 6 November Sharif went on national television to defend his government against charges of wrongdoing in the collapse of financial cooperatives which had robbed more than 600,000 people of their life savings. The prime minister pledged to reimburse the depositors and set up a judicial commission to investigate.

Another top domestic issue has been the country's growing Islamic fundamentalism. In April the government introduced legislation which would make the *shari'a*, or Islamic law, the supreme law of the country. Claiming "I am not a fundamentalist" but needing the support of several small Islamic parties which are critical to his coalition, Sharif proposed changes that would shape the schools, courts and the economy along fundamentalist lines. In May, parliament passed the law by voice vote, and in August it made the death penalty mandatory for anyone who defames the Prophet Mohammed. By the fall, many fundamentalists accused Sharif of not implementing the bill fast enough. Under the law, several men convicted of rape have been flogged by Islamic scholars in stadiums jammed with spectators.

Sharif, a former businessman, has taken large steps towards increasing investor confidence in the economy through privatization and reform. Early in 1991, he outlined a program to end controls on foreign currency entering the country, cut import duties to a maximum of 50 percent, and streamlined trade and tax rules. All industrial ventures set up before June 1995 in urban areas will be free of income tax and other duties for five years, and a no-questions-asked policy will apply to investment income in order to draw money from the black market. The government also slated several banks and upwards of 160 businesses for privatization, possibly including Pakistan International Airlines. In March Sharif said 90 percent of the government's economic functions will be transferred to the private sector. The International Monetary Fund has withheld a $240 million aid package until the country reforms its economy. The founder of the scandal-plagued Bank of Credit and Commerce International, Agha Abedi, received assurances from Sindh Chief Minister Jam Saddiq that he would not be extradited abroad. Citing "a hegemonic control of the Jewish lobby on the world's financial institutions," Sidiq said Abedi was "a great benefactor of the wretched of the Earth and ailing humanity in the present century" who deserved protection.

The country's top foreign affairs issues involved the continuing standoff with India over nuclear non-proliferation and Kashmir. A 1949 cease fire divided the territory into Pakistani and Indian sectors despite Pakistan's claims to the entire territory owing to its Moslem population. The largest of several clashes in 1991 along the disputed Kashmir frontier occurred on 26 September, when several soldiers died after 100 Pakistani soldiers allegedly attacked an Indian border post. The two countries also moved to ease nuclear tensions on 27 January when a treaty pledging that neither country would attack the other's nuclear facilities came into effect. However, on 29 July the government placed its intelligence agencies on heightened alert and tightened security around its largest nuclear reactor in response to what one newspaper termed the threat of "a joint India and Israeli attack" on nuclear facilities. Pakistan's alleged nuclear program has led to a rift with the United States, which cut off $580 million in aid in October 1990 because Congress could not "certify" that the country does not possess a "nuclear explosive device."

Political Rights and Civil Liberties:

Pakistanis can change their government democratically. Despite claims by the opposition of substantial vote rigging, an international team of election monitors said the October 1990 National Assembly elections were generally free and fair.

Political killings occur frequently among rival groups, particularly in the Sindh province among native-born Sindhis and those who immigrated with the 1947 partition of India. Legislation passed in 1991 nominally places the country under the *shari'a*, or Islamic law, although few changes have actually been implemented. The Hadood Ordinances, passed in 1979, mandate punishment for those violating various Islamic norms and are used most frequently against women. Special Islamic courts try cases under the Ordinances and decide whether civil laws contravene Islamic law. The current civil judicial system provides for open trials and the right to an attorney, although a shortage of judges has created a severe backlog. Persons suspected of threatening public safety can be detained for up to 90 days by court order. Police often torture suspects to elicit confessions, and human rights groups allege that prisoners are occasionally beaten to death and reported as suicides. Special "speedy courts" set up for high profile criminal cases have meted out death sentences in less than five days. In 1991 the IDA used the Maintenance of Public Order Ordinance to arrest hundreds, if not thousands, of PPP activists.

Although Pakistanis generally enjoy freedom of speech, a law passed in 1991 mandates the death sentence for anyone defaming Mohammed, and laws prohibit strong criticism of the armed forces and the constitution. The government owns electronic media and controls their news content. CNN is broadcast live, although portions are often blacked out. Four large newspapers are run by a government-operated trust, but their circulation is exceeded by privately-owned papers. Although editors frequently practice self-censorship, they do print statements critical of the government. Freedom of association is generally respected, although magistrates can ban gatherings if they suspect violence. The population is 97 percent Muslim, and while non-Muslims are generally allowed to practice freely, Hindus complain of harassment by fundamentalists. Ahmadis, who are considered "non-Muslims," also complain of harassment and discrimination in education and employment. Citizens are generally free to travel internally and abroad, although students and government officials must obtain special permission to leave the country. Many of the country's Afghan refugees, estimated at over 3 million, reside outside of refugee camps and are permitted to hold jobs. Large sectors of the labor force are prohibited from bargaining collectively, union activity in state-run sectors is restricted, and strikes are often banned under the pretext of community or national interest.

Panama

Polity: Presidential-legislative democracy
Economy: Capitalist-statist
Population: 2,500,000
PPP: $3,790
Life Expectancy: 72.4
Ethnic Groups: Mestizo (70 percent), West Indian (14 percent), white (10 percent), Indian (6 percent)

Political Rights: 4
Civil Liberties: 2
Status: Partly Free

Overview:

Two years after the U.S. ousted the government of General Manuel Antonio Noriega, the economy has rebounded and political freedoms have expanded. However, the government of President Guillermo Endara is weak, increasingly unpopular, and dependent on the presence of 10,000 U.S. troops to defend it against rebellious former members of Noriega's Panama Defense Force (PDF), many of whom remain in the revamped national police.

Panama was part of Colombia until 1903, when a U.S.-supported revolt resulted in the proclamation of an independent Republic of Panama. Until World War II, the government was dominated by small groups of family-based, political elites. The next two decades, however, saw mounting popular discontent over U.S. control of the Panama Canal. A 1968 military coup resulted in the coming to power of General Omar Torrijos and a renegotiation of the treaty that originally granted the U.S. control of the Canal Zone in perpetuity. A year after the 1977 canal treaties were signed,

Torrijos announced that Panama would become a democracy with the direct election of a president in 1984.

However, after Torrijos' death in 1981, General Noriega emerged as PDF chief and rigged the 1984 election that brought to power the Democratic Revolutionary Party (PRD), the political arm of the PDF. The 1972 constitution, after substantial revision in 1983, provides for the direct election of a president and a Legislative Assembly for five-year terms.

The May 1989 elections were controlled by the government and unfair in every aspect. Nonetheless, Guillermo Endara, the presidential candidate of the Democratic Alliance of Civic Opposition (ADOC), defeated Carlos Duque of the Noriega-controlled Coalition for National Liberation (COLINA) by nearly three to one, according to international observers. But Noriega annulled the election, and violently repressed ADOC protesters. After the failure of a three-month effort by the Organization of American States (OAS) to effect a transfer of power, Noriega abolished the 67-member Legislative Assembly and declared himself head of state.

On 20 December 1989, after a U.S. military invasion removed the Noriega government, Guillermo Endara was sworn in as president. His running mates, Ricardo Arias Calderon and Guillermo "Billy" Ford were sworn in as first and second vice-presidents. On 23 February 1990, the electoral tribunal, working on the 7 May 1989 returns, confirmed the winners of 58 of 67 legislative seats. Fifty-one seats went to the ADOC coalition; 27 to Arias Calderon's Christian Democrats, 15 to Ford's Molirena party, 5 to Endara's Arnulfista party and 4 to the Authentic Liberal party. Seven seats went to the PRD. With the assembly in place, the government filled out cabinet and judicial positions requiring legislative confirmation.

After Noriega's ouster, the military was restructured and renamed the Public Force (PF). Over a hundred PDF officers were retired and a civilian was appointed as PF chief. The PF assumed responsibility for public order after the U.S. invasionary forces left Panama. In 1991, by a vote of the legislature, the constitution was amended to formally abolish the military and establish the PF as a national police force.

The PF, however, remained weak, poorly disciplined, and retained within its ranks former PDF members with questionable loyalties. A coup attempt led by a retired officer in December 1990 was put down only because of the intervention of U.S. troops. Meanwhile, hundreds of rebellious former officers still remained underground and were linked to the sporadic terrorist activity against the government in 1991. The government reported it had uncovered a number of coup plots. The PF was also ineffectual against the drug trade as Panama continued to be a major cocaine transshipment point.

In 1991 the economy was growing again after a decline of nearly 20 percent in 1987-89, but there were few benefits for the majority of the population. Unemployment remained close to 25 percent, fueling unrest and violent crime. The government's free-market economic program, undermined by corruption and general mismanagement, led to a series of paralyzing labor strikes in 1991. Popular discontent was also evident in the January 1991 elections for the nine legislative seats left in dispute in 1990. Five of the seats were won by the PRD and other opposition parties, four by ADOC.

In April, the government was weakened further as the ADOC coalition split apart. The Christian Democrats went into opposition after clashing with Endara over control of government policy, leaving the president with minority support in the legislature. Soon after, opinion polls showed that Endara's popularity had plunged from nearly 80 percent when he took office to less than 15 percent. By mid-year, the Endara government found itself in a lame-duck situation with the next presidential election still more than two years away.

The polls also revealed little popular confidence in the government's ability to stand on its own. In a June 1991 survey, nearly two-thirds of Panamanians said that the ten U.S military bases—with a contingent of 10,000 U.S. troops—should remain after 1999 instead of being dismantled in accord with the 1977 treaties.

Political Rights and Civil Liberties:

Despite the ouster of Noriega, the first real test of citizens' ability to change their government through democratic means will not take place until the national elections scheduled for 1994. After the removal of Noriega, decrees restricting the constitutional rights of freedom of expression, organization, assembly and religion were rescinded. The government did not impose limitations on political parties or media that supported the former regime. The PRD, formerly the ruling party and political arm of Noriega's PDF, was allowed to take the Legislative Assembly seats it had won in the 1989 election, and has been free to sponsor its own publications.

All media shut down under Noriega were allowed to reopen. Three private newspapers seized two decades ago under the rule of General Torrijos were returned to their owners. Since 1990, the media, both public and private, have been a raucously critical assortment of daily newspapers, weekly publications, and talk shows. Broadcast media includes live coverage of Legislative Assembly debates. A number of restrictive media laws dating back to 1978 remain on the books. Although the government has vowed to have them repealed, at least two journalists were brought up on charges in 1991.

Labor unions, including those associated with the previous regime, are well organized and free to strike. But the government has suspended the collective bargaining rights of workers in free trade zones. Government attempts to modify the unwieldy labor code as part of its economic restructuring program bogged down in the face of a divided legislature and a series of paralyzing strikes in the second half of 1991.

The judiciary, cowed into submission under Noriega through bribery and intimidation, was revamped in 1990, and many new judges known for their integrity were appointed. President Endara replaced all nine Supreme Court judges, who in turn appointed thirteen new members to the 19-seat Superior Court and replaced two-thirds of the 48 lower court justices. But the judicial system, despite a U.S. assistance program, has been overwhelmed, its administration in a near-state of collapse. During the U.S. invasion, the Supreme Court building was sacked by looters and hundreds of thousands of court records destroyed. The burdens caused by missing records were compounded by a sudden influx of cases, most of them grievances against PDF officers accumulated over two decades of military rule.

In 1991, there were over 17,000 court cases pending, with the number climbing due to a surging crime wave. Less than 15 percent of the nation's prison inmates had actually been tried and convicted, and the penal system has been marked by a rash of escapes and violent disturbances in decrepit facilities packed with up to four times their intended capacity.

There are at least four human rights organizations that operate without interference, including one linked with the opposition PRD which works on behalf of PRD members charged with crimes committed during the Noriega years. The government has shown a tendency to arrest civilians and former Noriega officials on vague evidence. It also has been slow in responding to reports of missing persons and charges of summary executions from the time of the U.S. invasion. However, it has been open to investigations by international human rights organizations, and has accepted the jurisdiction of the Inter-American Human Rights Court.

Papua New Guinea

Polity: Parliamentary democracy
Economy: Capitalist
Population: 3,900,000
PPP: $1,960
Life Expectancy: 54.9
Ethnic Groups: A multi-ethnic, multi-tribal state—some 1,000 indigenous tribes

Political Rights: 2
Civil Liberties: 3
Status: Free

Overview:

In 1991 the Papua New Guinean government regained control of much of Bougainville Island, which has been under siege by rebels demanding independence. The country also faced a constitutional crisis and escalating lawlessness in urban areas.

Consisting of the eastern half of New Guinea and several islands, Papua New Guinea received its independence from Australia in 1975 and is a member of the British Commonwealth. The unicameral parliament currently has 109 members, of which 89 are elected nationally and 20 from provincial electorates. A six-party, 57-seat ruling coalition is headed by Prime Minister Rabbie Namaliu's Papua New Guinea United Party, which holds 26 seats. The leading opposition group is the People's Democratic Movement led by Paias Wingti which holds 18 seats.

The government's biggest challenge since independence has been the takeover of Bougainville, located 450 miles east of the mainland in the country's North Solomons Province. The crisis grew out of the islanders' long standing grievances over a huge Australian owned copper and gold mine at the town of Panguna. Demanding compensation for environmental damages and a 50 percent share of the profits, a group led by former army officer Sam Kauona and ex-miner Francis Ona began a series of sabotage attacks on the mine in December 1988. The guerrilla tactics forced the closure of the mine in May 1989, but the rebels then called for complete secession of Bougainville.

In January 1990, the government launched "Operation Footloose" to crush the newly-formed Bougainville Revolutionary Army (BRA). The offensive bogged down in the rugged Bougainville terrain, and the BRA retaliated by attacking government facilities on the island and forcefully closing major plantations. Following a March cease-fire, the rebels pronounced the independent "Republic of Bougainville" in May 1990. The government blockaded the island, home to 160,000 people, and in late July the rebels agreed to negotiations aboard the New Zealand supply ship Endeavour. The so-called Endeavour Accords called for a lifting of the blockade, restoration of essential services to the island, and an agreement that government security forces would not return pending the outcome of further talks. However, the blockade continued as talks stalled over the presence of government troops on nearby Buka Island.

Faced with an increasingly desperate situation due to the blockade, the secessionists sent representatives to a peace conference in the Solomon Islands on 22-24 January 1991. The rebels were granted immunity from prosecution in return for a surrender of their weapons to a Multi-national Supervisory Team (MST). The government agreed to end the blockade and promised not to launch another military offensive. By various estimates, the blockade caused up to 3,000 deaths due to food and medicine shortages.

Throughout the spring of 1991, the government searched in vain for regional nations willing to participate in the MST. The BRA insisted that any nation sending MST members must agree to eventually accept Bougainville's independence. They also refused to allow Australia, which continues to supply the country with financial aid and military equipment, to contribute to the MST. Faced with a stalemate, 300 government soldiers captured the northern reaches of Bougainville in an unauthorized dawn raid on 13 April, which the government later sanctioned.

Security forces and rebel soldiers engaged in sporadic gun battles on both Buka and Bougainville throughout the summer. Further peace talks were repeatedly postponed because of disagreements over their location. Prime Minister Namaliu threatened to open talks with non-BRA leaders on the island if the rebels refused to negotiate. On 23 October the government and provincial officials agreed to set up an interim authority in the southern part of Bougainville, which is not under BRA control. Similar agreements were later reached with local authorities in the northeast and northwest as well as on Buka. However, the BRA continued to control part of the island. On 4 November, fifteen rebels were killed in an attack on security forces in the north, and by year's end, no peace talks were scheduled.

Another leading domestic issue involved deputy prime minister Ted Diro. In September a leadership tribunal found him guilty of 81 charges of official misconduct, fined him $3,300 and recommended his dismissal. The charges included accepting illegal campaign contributions and obstructing justice. Under the constitution, only governor-general Sir Serei Eri had the power to carry out the dismissal. Eri touched off a constitutional crisis by refusing to dump Diro. Both are members of the People's Action Party, which Eri founded and is part of the governing coalition. On 1 October Eri resigned after the government asked head of state Queen Elizabeth II to fire him. An acting governor-general dismissed Diro, and opposition leaders have called for criminal charges to be brought against both men.

Disorder and economic problems have also plagued the country. A severe crime wave, which included an attack on the German ambassador and the killing of an Australian defense officer, prompted a government crackdown on the country's criminals, known as "Rascals." Measures announced on 14 March included an 8 PM to 5 AM curfew in four cities including the capital, Port Moresby. On 28 August, with "our place going to the dogs" according to one politician, parliament voted to restore the death penalty for violent crime. Despite the new measures, over 1,000 people rioted in Daru in October, demanding an accounting of municipal funds.

The economy has suffered from the closure of the Panguna mine, which had provided 40 percent of the country's export earnings. The government's economic planning revolves around the country's natural resource base, which continues to attract foreign investment. A recent oil discovery at Kutubu promises a 200 million barrel yield and a huge copper discovery has recently been announced by CRA Limited, formerly the indirect owners of the Panguna mine.

Political Rights and Civil Liberties: Despite the ongoing secessionist revolt on Bougainville, citizens of Papua New Guinea can change their government democratically. The ethnically diverse nation includes roughly 1,000 tribes and over 600 distinct linguistic groups, and an extreme social dichotomy exists between the urban areas and the rural, tribal-dominated regions. The country's judicial system is based on English common-law traditions, and is independent of the government. Freedom of speech, press, and assembly are provided for in the constitution and respected in practice. All religions may worship freely, and missionaries often provide social services in highly inaccessible areas. Citizens may travel freely both internally and abroad, although parts of Bougainville remain under BRA control. Workers have the right to bargain collectively, although unions must be registered with the government to be legally recognized.

Paraguay

Polity: Dominant party
Economy: Capitalist-statist
Population: 4,400,000
PPP: $2,590
Life Expectancy: 67.1
Ethnic Groups: Mostly mestizo; small Indian, white, black minorities

Political Rights: 3
Civil Liberties: 3
Status: Partly Free

Overview: The May 1991 election of labor leader Carlos Filizzola as the mayor of Asunción, the capital city, indicated that democracy was making headway against authoritarian traditions that date back to the Republic of Paraguay's independence from Spain in 1811. And the December election of a constituent assembly to replace an anti-democratic constitution—a legacy of the thirty-five-year dictatorship of General Alfredo Stroessner—enhanced the prospect for free and fair presidential elections in February 1993.

Following the 3 February 1989 overthrow of Stroessner by General Andres Rodriguez, the new government initiated a dramatic period of liberalization. Rodriguez has promised a transition to full democracy by 1993. Rodriguez, hailed as a hero, was easily elected on 1 May 1989 to finish Stroessner's last presidential term. But the enormous advantage exercised during the electoral process by Rodriguez and the ruling Colorado Party demonstrated that the traditions of authoritarianism, militarism and corruption continued to weigh heavily against democratic reform.

Despite the wide open electoral campaign, authoritarian structures remained intact. The main opposition groups—the Authentic Radical Liberal Party (PLRA), the Febrerista Revolutionary Party (PRF), and the Christian Democratic Party (PDC)—threatened to boycott the election unless constitutional and electoral reforms were made first. But realizing that Rodriguez would win on popularity alone, they decided to participate.

The bicameral Congress has a 32-seat Senate and a 72-seat Chamber of Deputies.

Under Stroessner's electoral law, the party with the most votes, even if only a plurality, automatically receives two-thirds of the seats in both bodies. Remaining seats are divided proportionally between other parties based on percentage of vote. With over 70 percent of the congressional vote, the Colorados obtained 24 seats in the Senate and 48 seats in the Chamber. The center-left PLRA obtained eleven seats in the Senate and 21 in the Chamber. The social democratic PRF obtained one seat in the Senate and two in the Chamber.

Acknowledging the glaring irregularities and structural deficiencies in the political system, President Rodriguez moved to make the changes necessary for a democratic transition. Colorado moderates, backed by Rodriguez, passed significant electoral reforms in 1990. The new law mandates a direct-vote system for selecting political party leaders and prohibits members of the military from joining political parties. It also calls for a second round if no presidential candidate secures an absolute majority in the first round of voting and a new system of fully proportional representation in the Congress.

In 1991 electoral authorities modernized the old voting list in preparation for the 26 May municipal elections, the first in the nation's history. One-third of voter names were purged, largely the dead, and a system of multi-party ballots and the practice of inking voters' fingers to prevent repeat voting were introduced. Voting day was marked by a number of administrative foul-ups, but observers from the Organization of American States (OAS) concluded the irregularities did not invalidate the process.

In a stunning upset, 31-year-old Carlos Filizzola, a political independent who ran at the head of an anti-corruption movement, was elected mayor of Asunción. It was the first time the ruling party had lost a major election since 1947. The Colorados did win a majority of the over two hundred municipal races, but their share of the national vote fell to 43 percent from 74 percent in the 1989 election. The PLRA saw its share nearly double to 33 percent. President Rodriguez countered agitation among Colorado hard-liners by inviting Filizzola to the presidential palace and declaring his election a victory for democracy.

Seven political parties registered candidates for the December constituent assembly election. The Colorados appeared poised for a comeback after Rodriguez leaned on the various factions to present a common front. The other main contenders were the PLRA and the Constitution for All Movement (CPT), an offshoot of Filizzola's group. On 1 December the Colorados won 55.1 percent of the vote and 123 seats in the 198-member body. The PLRA won 57 seats and the CPT, with little organization outside of Asuncion, came in third with 16. The PRF and the PDC each won a single seat.

In accordance with Latin American juridical tradition, the constituent assembly is deemed sovereign—it is able to write an entirely new constitution and even replace the sitting Congress. However, for Paraguay to complete the transition to democratization, the new constitution must curtail the power of the presidency, establish a separation of powers in government, and clearly define the military as subordinate to civilian rule. The question was whether President Rodriguez could keep hard-line officers and recalcitrant Colorados at bay while the assembly conducted its business.

Political Rights and Civil Liberties: Citizens are able to change their government through elections at the local level. However, pending constitutional reform and presidential elections scheduled for 1993, the ruling party continues to exercise inordinate political control at the national level.

After the February 1989 coup, Rodriguez decreed full freedom of expression, association and assembly. Since then, all independent press and radio closed under Stroessner have operated freely. New and independent publications have also appeared. Passionate political debate occurs regularly in all media, including on state-run television. However, with the media pressing investigations of pervasive corruption within the government and among the economic elite, a number of journalists have been subject to intimidation and violent attacks. The case of Santiago Leguizamon, murdered in April 1991, was still unresolved at the end of the year.

Since 1989, political parties and civic groups have operated in relative freedom in urban areas. Political prisoners were freed in 1989 and political exiles invited to return home. The previously banned Paraguayan Communist Party and other leftist parties now have legal status. Meetings, rallies and marches are held regularly. However, violations of labor rights continue. Under the Rodriguez government, over a hundred trade unions and two major union federations have been legalized. But reform of the restrictive labor code has proceeded slowly. Public sector workers are denied the right to strike, the military intervenes to break up labor actions, and labor leaders are frequently detained.

In the countryside, peasant organizations demanding land have met with violent police crackdowns, mass detentions, and forced evictions by vigilante groups in the employ of large landowners. Nearly a dozen peasants have been killed in the ongoing dispute. The government's promise of land reform has been a non-starter, as nearly 80 percent of farm and ranch land remains in the hands of foreign companies and a few hundred Paraguayan families.

The judicial system offers only limited recourse. It remains subject to the influence of the ruling party and the military, compromised by corruption, and generally unresponsive to human rights groups presenting cases of rights violations committed either before or after the overthrow of Stroessner. Current allegations include illegal detention by police and torture during incarceration. The government, hoping to counter criticism of continuing abuses, established an official human rights commission in 1991.

Peru

Polity: Presidential-legislative democracy
Economy: Capitalist-statist
Population: 22,000,000
PPP: $3,080
Life Expectancy: 63.0
Ethnic Groups: Complex, Indian of Inca descent (46 percent), Caucasian (10 percent), and mixed (44 percent)

Political Rights: 3
Civil Liberties: 5
Status: Partly Free

Overview: As President Alberto Fujimori entered his second year in office, the nation's institutions were buckling amid severe economic recession, drug-related corruption, the systematic violation of human rights, and the onslaught of the Shining Path (Sendero Luminoso) guerrilla organization.

The independent Republic of Peru was proclaimed in 1821. Its history has been marked by periods of civilian rule and military dictatorship. The military ruled most recently between 1968 and 1980. The transition to democracy began with the 1978 election of a constituent assembly and the drafting of a new constitution in 1979. The 1980 elections were won by Fernando Belaunde Terry of the right-wing Popular Action (AP) party. Alan Garcia of the center-left American Popular Revolutionary Alliance (APRA) won the 1985 elections.

The 1979 constitution provides for a president and bicameral Congress directly elected for five years. The Congress consists of a 60-member Senate elected on a regional basis and a 180-member Chamber of Deputies elected on the basis of proportional representation. In 1987, the country's 25 departments were redivided into 15 regions, each to have a popularly elected assembly. Regional assembly elections were held in seven regions at the time of the municipal elections in November 1989.

Alan Garcia presided over five years of fiscal chaos and economic collapse. In 1988, novelist Mario Vargas Llosa formed a free-market reform movement, the Democratic Front (FREDEMO), with the support of the AP and the Christian Popular Party (PPC). As the April 1990 elections approached, Vargas Llosa led nine other presidential candidates in the opinion polls.

In the campaign, economic issues were matched by concern over the mounting strength of the Maoist Shining Path, one of the most virulent, tightly organized insurgencies in the history of guerrilla warfare. The Shining Path is self-financing, with earnings estimated at $40 million a year from Peru's cocaine trade, and now challenges the military for control of half of Peru's national territory. The Marxist Tupac Amaru Revolutionary Movement (MRTA), less of a threat, also regularly carries out urban guerrilla attacks and kidnappings.

In February 1990 Fujimori, an agricultural engineer, was a political unknown. But his Change 90 movement gained momentum as he promised economic renewal without the shock measures advocated by Vargas Llosa. The surge in support also reflected the disdain among citizens for traditional politicians, who generally are viewed as inept and corrupt. In addition, the nation's poor majority, primarily Indian and mixed race, began to view Vargas Llosa as part of the predominantly white political class.

The 8 April 1990 election was held in an atmosphere of generalized violence. In the last two weeks of the campaign, the Shining Path and MRTA killed four congressional candidates, occupied radio stations to threaten voters and, in over 200 actions, dynamited power pylons, party offices, banks, police posts, hotels, government offices, movie theaters and factories.

Despite the conditions, and prodded by compulsory voting laws, nearly 80 percent of the electorate turned out, Vargas Llosa received 27.6 percent of the vote and Fujimori 24.6 percent. In the June 1990 run-off, Fujimori won by a landslide with 56.5 percent of the vote. However, he had only minority backing in the Congress; in April, Change 90 had won just 14 of 60 Senate seats, and 29 of 180 seats in the Chamber of Deputies.

After taking office, Fujimori stunned the nation by decreeing a drastic economic austerity program—exactly what he promised not to do. Lacking an organized political party, he turned to the armed forces to shore up his government. The army was given control of the national police and troops were called into the streets to prevent food riots. The army was also given a free hand to step up counter-insurgency measures against the Shining Path. Four more provinces were put under martial law, leaving over half the country under army control. In absorbing the police, the military took control of the anti-drug effort. But in Peru, the world's largest coca producer, the military is the institution most often implicated in drug-related corruption.

By 1991 Fujimori had succeeded in halting hyper-inflation, which had reached an annual rate of over 10,000 percent. But the shock program, coupled with an outbreak of a cholera epidemic, also resulted in economic depression, a wave of paralyzing labor strikes, and a growing exodus abroad of many in the professional class. Fujimori bulled ahead nonetheless, decreeing laws to attract foreign investment and renew Peru's standing with international creditors. Nearly all of his reforms have been by executive order, leaving an already weak Congress to go after his predecessor on corruption charges.

In 1991 the Shining Path—with 5,000 soldiers and a highly disciplined national underground support network—continued to gain ground. It controlled most of the Upper Huallaga Valley, the main area of coca leaf production and home to a quarter million people who depend on the crop for a livelihood. Having established a virtual state-within-a-state in the highlands, the Shining Path initiated a concerted attack on urban centers and by mid-year dominated a growing number of teeming shantytowns in Lima itself. The offensive, according to Shining Path declarations, was the beginning of the "final stage" of revolution. The 120,000-man army, poorly trained, ill-equipped and demoralized, seemed to be overmatched and feared mainly by the civilian population. While the Shining Path was not necessarily on the verge of victory, the state appeared to be edging closer to defeat.

Political Rights and Civil Liberties:

Citiznes are able to change their government democratically. The constitution guarantees free expression, free exercise of religion and the right to organize political parties, labor unions, and civic groups. However, political expression is severely restricted by the climate of violence and terror caused by the Shining Path and MRTA guerrilla insurgencies, and the repressive, indiscriminate counter-insurgency measures taken by the military, security forces, and associated paramilitary death squads. In Fujimori's first year in office, political violence caused ten deaths per day, up from four a day in 1989; and the rate appeared to be climbing in the second half of 1991.

In September 1990 the Fujimori government admitted that it could not guarantee the security of elected officials or government functionaries, let alone average citizens. The Shining Path has assassinated dozens of political candidates and more than 300 town mayors in the last decade. It has also assassinated priests and nuns, foreign missionaries and aid workers, human rights activists, and journalists—in short, it is committed to destroy anyone associated with the established order.

Constitutional guarantees remain suspended for over half the population by the state of emergency that covers more than 40 percent of the national territory. Since the military took control of the police in 1990, mass arrests have been common in urban areas. Lima and the neighboring port city of Callao are under virtual martial law. Civilian killings and torture by the military and security forces occur with a frequency that reveals such practices are integral to counter-insurgency policy. For the fifth year in a row, the number of disappearances reported to the United Nations was the highest in the world, nearly 400. Peru's three dozen human rights groups are also subject to violent attacks from all sides. International rights organizations are threatened and their offices bombed.

In 1991, in response to pressure from the U.S. Congress which held up a U.S. aid package because of Peru's rights record, the government established an official human rights commission and agreed to cooperate with the Organization of American States in an effort to diminish abuses. At the same time, however, Fujimori infuriated local rights groups by publicly accusing them of "playing the game of subversion."

The judicial system is headed by a Supreme Court whose judges are appointed by the president with the approval of the Senate. There are also eighteen district courts. Virtually all of Peru's institutions are in crisis, but none more than the judicial system. It is overwhelmed by cases, riddled with corruption, and subject to intimidation by drug dealers, the Shining Path, the armed forces and paramilitary groups. Judges are attacked, at least ten lawyers were killed in 1991, and a growing number of government prosecutors have been driven into exile by death threats. Less than five percent of people arrested on terrorism charges are convicted. The prisons are overflowing, an estimated 70 percent of prisoners still await trial, and a number of jails are controlled by Shining Path detainees. And, because military courts generally exonerate officers and soldiers charged with rights abuses, the armed forces operate with impunity.

Despite the war, a wide array of political parties and well-organized labor unions remain active. Nearly two dozen political parties, ranging from Marxist to far-right, ran candidates in the 1990 elections. Labor unions are permitted to strike and do so regularly, but strikes frequently result in violent clashes with police and security forces. The trade unions, however, like the political parties, are targeted by the Shining Path. Leftist unions and student groups are subject to abuses by security forces.

The press is largely private. Numerous daily and weekly newspapers reflect the wide political spectrum. There are even publications linked with the Shining Path and the MRTA. Radio and television are both private and public. Journalists, however, are targets of political violence; over 30 have been killed in the last ten years and at least five in the first ten months of 1991. Radio stations are frequently attacked and occupied by both the Shining Path and the MRTA. Journalists are banned from emergency zones and prohibited from giving the names of military personnel stationed there. Most of the media, under pressure from the government, practices self-censorship in reporting the war.

Philippines

Polity: Presidential-legislative democracy
Economy: Capitalist-statist
Population: 62,300,000
PPP: $2,170
Life Expectancy: 64.2
Ethnic Groups: Christian Malay (92 percent), Muslim Malay (4 percent), Chinese (2 percent)

Political Rights: 3
Civil Liberties: 3
Status: Partly Free

Overview:

Major issues in this island nation in 1991 included speculation over who would succeed lame-duck President Corazon Aquino in the May 1992 elections, negotiations with the United States over the closing of U.S. naval bases, and two devastating natural disasters. During the year, the government also sought to deal with mutinous elements in the military, an ongoing Communist insurgency, persistent charges of official corruption, the growing influence of provincial barons with private armies and the controversial return of Imelda Marcos, widow of the late Philippine strongman Ferdinand Marcos.

In 1991 the country's fragile democracy continued to be hit by daunting structural and social problems that have plagued President Aquino since the "people power" revolution swept her into power in 1986. Under the 1987 constitution, the Philippines scrapped the parliamentary system and created a two-tiered Congress consisting of a House and Senate. Although Aquino supporters won about 80 percent of 200 directly elected seats in the House and 22 of 24 in the Senate in the May 1987 elections, the president never joined the pro-government Lakas ng Demokratikong Pilipino (LDP) coalition, choosing instead to stay out of party politics.

The "people power" movement did little to break the political domination of oligarchies and businessmen who had long controlled the reins of power and whose commitment to national rather than parochial interests remained questionable. Forty-four of the 200 congressmen elected in 1987 were also successful candidates in 1984, 18 were members of Marcos's 1978 Interim Batasan Pambasa and another 30 ran in the 1984 elections and lost. According to the Institute for Popular Democracy, 130 had pre-1987 experience as local or national politicians. Many new congressmen came from traditional ruling elites. Apart from a large percentage of traditional clan leaders, 39 members, or 19.5 percent, were relatives of traditional clans. Researchers found only 31 congressmen or women, or 15.5 percent, who had no electoral history going back to 1971 and did not appear directly related to any of the past traditional clan leaders.

The weakness of President Aquino (she survived seven coup attempts), combined with anemic political party structures and deeply-rooted nepotism and patronage, led one Philippine analyst in 1991 to describe the political system as "mafiosi democracy" funded by "shadowy figures such as smugglers or gambling lords."

In 1991 the central political preoccupation was the presidential campaign for the May 1992 vote. At least 10 candidates declared or suggested that they would run for the post. Early in the year, the front-runner appeared to be Defense Secretary Fidel Ramos, an LDP stalwart who helped quell seven coup attempts. But a 30 November

LDP straw poll picked House Speaker Ramon Mitra, suggesting that Ramos would likely run as an independent. Factionalism also split the Nacionalista Party (NP), led by presidential contender and Aquino Vice President Salvador Laurel. On 8 November, Laurel, who announced his candidacy in August, expelled his two rivals for the NP's nomination, party general-secretary Juan Ponce Enrile, a former defense minister and Aquino ally who was charged in 1990 for allegedly being part of a coup attempt, and Eduardo "Danding" Cojuangco, Aquino's cousin and rival.

Both men, who will likely run in 1992, are associated with the old corrupt power structure. In the last two years, Enrile's Jaka Investments Corp. quietly gobbled up real estate, bought out two manufacturing firms and increased its stake in the second-biggest industrial project in the country, controlled by a former colleague in the Marcos government. "Danding" Cojuangco was given control of the nation's biggest industry (coconuts) by Marcos and built a broad patronage base. Cojuangco, who went into exile with Marcos, was charged by the Aquino government with stealing control of more than $1.5 billion of corporate assets. However, in May the Supreme Court, in a setback to Aquino, gave him back control of a huge food and beer conglomerate. Earlier, Cojuangco associates applied to the Commission on Elections to register the Partido Pilipino (PP), a newly formed party he was expected to use as a vehicle for a presidential bid.

Other key contenders were likely to be Miriam Defensor Santiago, a former judge who became popular for her anti-corruption campaign; Joseph Estrada, a movie actor and senator; Jovito Salonga, the Senate president; Chief Justice Marcelo Fernan, who had the backing of the powerful Roman Catholic Church; and former congressman Oscar Orbos, who unexpectedly resigned as President Aquino's successful executive secretary in July.

A bitter issue in 1991 was the fate of six U.S. naval bases, which symbolized U.S. presence in the Philippines dating back almost 100 years and whose lease expired in September 1991. In 1990 the U.S. announced that it was withdrawing planes from Clark Air Base. The Philippine government offered to grant the U.S. more time to withdraw from the huge Subic Bay facility. On 16 February, what had been expected to be the final round of negotiations over the bases concluded without an agreement, with the U.S. maintaining that it wanted to keep the bases for 10 to 12 years and offering $400 million. The Philippines wanted compensation of $825 million, with the bases remaining for seven years. On 17 July the U.S. and Manila announced agreement on a new lease under which the U.S. would remain at the Subic Bay installation for at least 10 years, paying $203 million a year for rent. The lease needed approval by two-thirds of the 23-member Philippine Senate, but despite intense lobbying efforts by President Aquino, the legislature rejected the agreement on 9 September. When the president said she would defy the Senate and seek a national referendum on the future of the base, which employed tens of thousands of Filipinos, several opposition leaders called for impeachment. On 2 October, after the president withdrew her support for a referendum, the Senate agreed on a three-year withdrawal of U.S. forces. But on 27 December, an aide to President Aquino announced the U.S. would leave Subic Bay by the end of 1992.

In 1991 the government also sought ways to rein in an often mutinous military. At the end of 1990, in what was the most severe warning to those plotting to overthrow the Aquino government, a military court sentenced 81 officers and men to prison terms up to 32 years for their part in an August 1987 rebellion. The government was sending a strong message to the rebel Reform the Armed Forces Movement (RAM), which had attempted a 1989 coup, and the Young Officers Union (YOU), made up of self-styled nationalists who also played a role in the 1989 coup attempt. On 6 February, two officers who led attempts to overthrow the government—Lieutenant Colonel Victor Batatc, a member of RAM, and Major Abraham Puruganan of YOU—were captured by military agents. RAM founder and coup-plotter Gregorio Honasan remained a fugitive. In April, President Aquino appointed a chief of staff and army commander known for military professionalism.

During the year, the government intensified operations against the New People's Army (NPA), the armed wing of the Communist Party of the Philippines. On 19 July, clashes between government forces and NPA guerrillas left at least 11 dead in northern Philippines. Three rebels were also shot by soldiers in the south. In an important victory, the government captured Romulo Kintanar, NPA chief of staff, and his wife, Gloria Jopsan, also a party functionary, on 6 August. The arrests weakened the 23-year insurgency movement, which had seen the previous arrests of 13 key leaders. On 12 September, Communist rebels announced a unilateral cease fire as the Senate moved to reject a new lease for the American base at Subic Bay. The NPA also called for the government to hold peace talks. On 13 December, police killed four Communist guerrillas north of Manila.

A continuing problem in 1991 which undermined the democratic transition was the power of provincial land barons, many with competing private armies. There were fears that a downturn in the economy had strengthened an already deeply rooted patronage system under which rural oligarches dispense largesse in the form of jobs, education expenses, food aid and even birth and funeral costs. President Aquino's brother, Jose Cajuangco, brought a string of oligarches and former Marcos stalwarts into the LDP, and it has long been rumored that he maintains a private army on the family's Hacienda Luisita. With some 800,000 unregistered weapons in the country, some analysts expressed concern about the possibilities of campaign violence in 1992.

In November, Imelda Marcos, widow of the late dictator, came back to the Philippines after President Aquino overturned a ban on her return. The former first lady, who was charged with tax fraud shortly after her arrival, denied that she had any political ambitions for 1992, but some speculated that her reputed wealth would make her a force in the elections.

Political Rights and Civil Liberties:

Filipinos can change their government democratically. The political system remains in the hands of traditional clans and oligarches, and political parties are weak. Corruption, graft, patronage and nepotism continue to be an integral part of the political culture, although there have been signs of greater pluralism and fragmentation in the political and business elite since the fall of Marcos in 1986. One cornerstone of political pluralism is an uninhibited media. There are 32 daily newspapers and 240 weeklies, 56 operating television stations and 321 radio stations. Many take positions adversarial to the government. The judiciary is independent, and civil and criminal trials are open and generally fair. But political statutes give authorities leeway that infringes on due process. In 1990, the Supreme Court expanded the instances under which a person can be arrested without a warrant. Human rights monitors, lawyers, church workers, labor and community activists continued to be vulnerable to security statutes. In February the International Commission of Jurists issued a report that faulted the Aquino government on human rights, concluding that the legal system and a government-appointed human rights commission "have not been effective in redressing most abuses." Throughout the year, Amnesty International reported scores of cases of disappearances, torture and illegal detention by police and the military.

Freedom of assembly and association are generally respected, and there is a broad range of private and professional organizations. Freedom of religion is respected in this predominantly Roman Catholic country. Travel is generally unrestricted. Workers are allowed to join unions and most unions belong to the Trade Union Congress of the Philippines (TUCP).

Poland

Polity: Presidential-parliamentary democracy
Economy: Mixed statist transitional
Population: 38,200,000
PPP: $4,190
Life Expectancy: 71.8
Ethnic Groups: Polish , Ukrainian, Byelorussian, German, and others

Political Rights: 2
Civil Liberties: 2
Status: Free

Overview:

In 1991, Poland became the last former Soviet-bloc country to hold a fully democratic parliamentary election. But elections came only after months of bitter wrangling between President Lech Walesa and the outgoing 460-member parliament (Sejm). Two-thirds of the Sejm was controlled by former Communists and their allies because of a 1989 compromise that led to a Solidarity-led coalition government. The October election, contested by 67 parties, left the Sejm badly fragmented. By year's end, it was unclear if Prime Minister-designate Jan Olszewski would be able to form a government.

In January 1991, a month after former Solidarity union leader Walesa was overwhelmingly elected president, the government of Prime Minister Krzysztof Bielecki, leader of the Gdansk-based Liberal Democratic Congress, was sworn in and pledged to continue the pioneering free-market reforms launched in 1990. Leszek Balcerowicz, the former finance minister and architect of the controversial "shock therapy" economic restructuring program, was retained to oversee the plan after several foreign ambassadors hinted that aid and possible debt relief were dependent on Balcerowicz's presence.

The following month, President Walesa told a convention of Solidarity, the union he co-founded and molded into a political force that brought down the Communist regime, that he was committed to wage restraints as a check against inflation, even in the face of threatened work stoppages. The president's position reflected the insistence of international financial organizations that the country pursue an austerity plan as the price for supporting reduction of Poland's $42 million debt.

President Walesa also pressed parliament to adopt an election law and schedule voting for the end of May. He called for scrapping the deal made by Solidarity in

1989 with the former Communist party, under which 65 percent of 460 Sejm seats were guaranteed to Communists and their allies. The 100-seat Senate, which was democratically elected in 1989 and included 99 Solidarity-backed candidates and one independent, would not be dissolved. On 9 March, after a three-day debate, parliament voted overwhelmingly to delay action on a draft electoral law and reject the May election date. The rebuff set off a power struggle between the president and parliament that dragged on for months. Elections were ultimately set for late October.

In June, sharpening his confrontation with the Communist-dominated parliament, President Walesa asked legislators to empower the cabinet to rewrite the nation's economic laws by decree. The move was a reaction to parliament's foot-dragging on 90 bills crucial to economic reform. On 14 June, the president appeared to gain an important political victory after parliament failed to over-rule his veto of an election law draft he said would lead to unstable government. The crisis worsened the following day when the Sejm approved a measure to regulate the elections, but refused to satisfy the president's complaint that the legislation, which stipulated that people must vote for individual candidates rather than party lists, would favor minor political groupings and would lead to a weak, fragmented parliament. On 11 July the Sejm rejected a third attempt by President Walesa to tighten the election law. The vote was significant because the Communists were joined by a group of deputies that were once prominent Solidarity leaders.

The political deadlock culminated with Prime Minister Bielecki's attempted resignation in the face of parliament's threat to block his economic reform plan. On 31 August, the government survived a tense parliamentary confrontation with ex-Communists when parliament refused to accept Bielecki's resignation by a vote of 211 to 114. The vote temporarily boosted the Bielecki government and eased a three-day standoff that had threatened Poland with its worst political crisis since the overthrow of the Communist regime in 1989. In the end, the ex-Communists withdrew their motion to dismiss Bielecki after the Sejm rejected his resignation. But the political paralysis continued.

The 27 October elections did little to break the gridlock and showed the public's growing disillusionment with the political process. Barely 40 percent of Polish voters bothered to go to the polls in the first fully democratic parliamentary elections since 1928. With 67 of 120 political groups contesting the elections, no one party got more than 12 percent of the vote. The so-called post-Solidarity parties, former members of the Citizens' Parliamentary Caucus, won less than half the vote, while the former Communists finished a strong second.

The Democratic Union led by former Prime Minister Tadeusz Mazowiecki, who lost the 1991 presidential campaign to Walesa, won 12.1 percent of the vote and 62 seats; the Democratic Left Alliance (SLD), made up of former Communists and their allies, won 11.98 percent and 60 seats.

Catholic Action, a coalition dominated by the Christian National Union, a fiercely traditionalist party, was third with 8.73 percent and 49 seats, while the Polish Peasant Party, once an ally of the Communists, took 8.67 percent and 48 seats. The conservative Confederation for an Independent Poland (KPN), a former underground organization with a long history of anti-Communism, won a surprising 7.5 percent, and 46 seats.

The biggest losers appeared to be the major post-Solidarity parties, which were expected to do well. The Center Citizens' Alliance won 8.7 percent and 44 seats; the Liberal Democratic Congress, 7.48 percent and 37 seats; the Peasant Alliance, 5.46 percent and 28 seats; the Solidarity Trade Union, 5.05 percent and 27 seats; and Labor Solidarity, 2.05 percent and 4 seats. The outlandish Polish Beer Lovers' Party polled 3.27 percent of the vote and 16 seats, making it the tenth largest party in parliament. In all, 29 parties were represented in the new Sejm. Prime Minister Bielecki, whose Liberal Democratic Congress only got 7 percent of the vote and 37 seats, said the elections were "a vote against the market economy."

President Walesa was quick to blame the fragmentation on an electoral law with a complex proportional system that excessively helped small parties. By dividing Poland into 37 multi-member districts, the law gave local groups the chance to elect candidates without having to compete on a nationwide basis. But elections to the 100-member Senate, which were not included in the law, also resulted in fragmentation, with only the Democratic Union (21 seats) and the Solidarity Trade Union (11) gaining double digits. The rest of the 68 seats were split among 10 parties and six independents.

The results left President Walesa, who, under the constitution (a holdover from communist days), was empowered to name a prime minister, with the difficult task of choosing someone who could form a coalition government. On 6 November, five center-right parties announced they had reached a preliminary agreement on forming a government: Catholic Action, the Center Citizens' Alliance, the KPN, the Peasant's Party and Prime Minister Bielecki's free-market Liberal Democratic Congress. Together they commanded 176 votes in the Sejm. They proposed that long-time activist lawyer Jan Olszewski, a critic of radical free-market reforms, be named prime minister. But on 8 November, Walesa, in a surprise move, ignored the coalition's request and asked Bronislaw Geremek, a former ally and recent critic whose Democratic Union controlled the most Sejm seats, to form a government.

The stalemate continued through November, as talks broke down between Walesa and the coalition, which itself was having difficulties reconciling different factional interests and working out a coherent economic program. On the eve of the first session of the new Sejm, the Bielecki government formally decided to resign. In an 11th-hour letter to the prime minister, Walesa asked him not to step down, arguing "that the country cannot remain without a government." During the Sejm's opening session on 25 November, the coalition pushed through its candidate for speaker, Wieslaw Chzranowski.

In early December, Walesa finally relented and nominated Olszewski as prime minister. He was approved by the Sejm on 6 December. But the president also continued to press for changes in the constitution that would allow him to pick the cabinet. On 12 December, the Liberal Democratic Congress withdrew from the coalition because they disagreed with Olszewski's economic program. The KPN also threatened to withdraw if the prime minister did not appoint its leader, arch-conservative Leszek Moczulski, as defense minister.

On 12 December, Prime Minister Olszewski gave up an attempt to form a new government from center-right parties that wanted to slow Poland's move to a market economy. He blamed President Walesa for failing to support his efforts. The following day, the Sejm gave the new prime minister a vote of confidence to continue efforts in forming a government.

The murky political picture at the end of the year made it difficult to predict the future of Poland's radical market reforms. Throughout the year, the economy was bleak. By September, unemployment stood at 8.4 percent. After almost vanishing in 1990, the budget deficit in 1991 headed toward 2.5 percent of GNP, far beyond the target agreed to by the IMF. In the first five months of the year, GNP fell by 14.9 percent. The 1990 near $4-billion hard-currency trade surplus became a $1 billion deficit in 1991. During the year the United States and the Paris Club agreed to write off half the $30 billion Poland owed them, but only if reform continued and IMF targets were met. The government took a big step toward establishing a capitalist economy when it announced plans to transfer a fourth of all state-owned industry into private hands within six months.

Looming unemployment and social pressures led the Solidarity union and other former Walesa allies to urge the government to loosen wage controls, which limited pay raises in the state sector to 60 percent of inflation, and lift the stringent fiscal and credit controls set forth by the IMF. The government countered that reflation in the face of unemployment was not a long-term, market-oriented solution.

A divisive social issue in 1991 was the question of abortion, which had been readily available in this predominantly Roman Catholic country since 1956. In May, weeks before Pope John Paul II was to visit his homeland, the legislature faced a difficult choice when it took up a bill that would have banned abortion. Public opinion polls indicated that a majority of voters opposed the bill, while the Church supported the measure. The rift eroded public support for the Church, once the only repository of Polish nationalism and anti-Communism. Parliament did not pass the bill.

Political Rights and Civil Liberties:

Poles can change their government democratically. However, this year's legislative elections, the first fully democratic contest since 1928, resulted in a badly fragmented parliament and a rift between President Lech Walesa and the prime minister. On several occasions President Walesa warned that he would dissolve parliament or suggested that he would assume the role of prime minister or rule by decree.

In 1990 a National Judiciary Council was created to "protect the independence of the judiciary and the freedom of the courts." Poles are free to express their views openly. There is a vibrant free press. During the year, there were frequent charges that the government was using television to further its own political agenda.

Freedom of association and assembly are respected, and freedom of religion is guaranteed. There were several localized incidents of attacks on Gypsies, who number about 15,000.

Domestic and foreign travel is unrestricted. Independent trade unions are allowed, and workers staged several work stoppages in various industries to protest the government's tight-money policies and rising unemployment.

Portugal

Polity: Presidential-
parliamentary democracy
Economy: Mixed Capitalist
Population: 10,400,000
PPP: $5,980
Life Expectancy: 74.0
Ethnic Groups: Portuguese and Africans from former Portuguese colonies

Political Rights: 1
Civil Liberties: 1
Status: Free

Overview:

1991 was a year of increased economic growth as Portugal continues to reap the benefits of membership in the European Economic Community. Portugal has also been instrumental in ending the civil war in Angola and has been active in protesting Indonesia's treatment of East Timor.

This small, homogeneous, Catholic country on the Atlantic coast of the Iberian peninsula was a monarchy until it was declared a republic in 1910. One of the first countries to conduct overseas exploration, Portugal eventually built one of the largest and most far-reaching empires in the world. From 1932 to 1968, Portugal was ruled by the fascist dictator, António de Oliveira Salazar. His slightly more liberal successor, Marcello Caetano, held power until 1974 when the leftist Armed Forces Movement overthrew the regime. The military, exhausted by its constant effort to retain Portugal's African colonies, decided to overthrow the dictatorship. In 1975, Portugal adopted a new democratic constitution.

In the first of two major elections of 1991, Dr. Mário Soares, a Socialist ex-prime minister, was re-elected for a five-year term as President by an overwhelming majority. As head of state, Dr. Soares appoints the head of government from the largest party or coalition in Parliament. Anibal Cavaço Silva, a Social-Democrat, is the current prime minister. Mr. Silva benefited from his country's rapid growth during legislative elections in the fall of 1991. His Social Democratic Party received 50.4 percent of the vote, again giving it an absolute majority of seats. The main challenger, the Socialist Party, won only 29.4 percent. Although over 14 candidates competed, none was able to tarnish Silva's record of leading his country through unparalleled economic growth during the past four years. The Portuguese Communist Party, which was receiving 18 percent of the vote as late as 1983, saw its popularity continue to slide, winning only 8.8 percent in this last election. Silva kept his government largely intact, except for the surprise replacement of his Economic Minister. Miguel Beleza, who was known for his experience with the EC's intricate moves towards unity, was replaced by Braga de Macedo, an outspoken free-marketeer.

Other political parties include the Portuguese Socialist Party, the Democratic Renewal Party, the People's Monarchist Party, the Unified Democratic Coalition (includes the Portuguese Communist Party, the Democratic Intervention and the Greens), the Portuguese Democratic Movement (leftist), the Popular Democratic Union (leftist), and the United Workers' Organization. There are several minor parties, mostly of leftist orientation.

Portugal has come out strongly against Indonesia's treatment of Portugal's former colony, East Timor. Indonesia forcibly annexed the territory in 1976. President Soares declared a national day of mourning on 19 November 1991, after Indonesian government troops massacred dozens of pro-independence demonstrators. At the World Court, Portugal accused Australia of undermining the right of self-determination of the East Timor people by negotiating with Indonesia for oil-exploration off the East Timorese coast in 1989. The Portuguese government also called for the suspension of trade with Indonesia.

Portugal has also been intensely involved in mediation efforts to resolve the 16-year old Angolan civil war by bringing together representatives of the Communist MPLA government and the U.S.-backed UNITA rebels. After a false start at the beginning of 1991, the two parties finally signed a cease-fire agreement on 1 May 1991.

Portugal's economy is increasingly oriented towards the EEC, which accounts for 70 percent of its foreign trade. Despite rapid economic growth, Portugal still has the highest illiteracy and infant mortality rates in the European Community. Furthermore, the Portuguese are the lowest paid workers in Europe, earning an average of only $3.40 per hour. This is unlikely to get better as Portugal faces increasing competition from Eastern Europe in its primary industry, textiles. Overall, Portugal's economic and social situation has improved considerably with generous subsidies from the EEC for structural development.

Political Rights and Civil Liberties:

The Portuguese have the right to change their government by democratic means. Both the president and the parliament are chosen through direct, competitive elections.

In 1991, the last government-owned newspaper was privatized. Many newspapers are directly affiliated with political parties or labor unions. There are three television stations, two are government-owned and one church-owned. The state does not practice censorship, and the broadcast media presents a diversity of viewpoints. In 1989 the government authorized the operation of private radio stations and more than 250 are now on the air. There is still a law on the books making criticism of certain government entities illegal, but it has not been enforced recently. All political organizations are allowed except those of a fascist nature. Although Portugal is largely Catholic, there are no official restrictions on religious affiliation. Citizens may organize protest marches as long as they give the government 24-hour notice.

In September 1991 railroad and port workers staged a series of strikes that paralyzed the country. Union leaders accused the government of backtracking on an earlier agreement for wage increases of between 8 and 18 percent. They also demanded shorter working hours, greater protection from dismissal and an earlier retirement.

Qatar

Polity: Traditional monarchy
Economy: Capitalist-statist
Population: 500,000
PPP: na
Life Expectancy: 69.2
Ethnic Groups: Arab, Pakistani, Indian, Iranian

Political Rights: 7
Civil Liberties: 5
Status: Not Free

Overview:

In 1991 the major news event for this small, wealthy sheikdom in the Persian Gulf concerned an ongoing territorial dispute with neighboring Bahrain. Also in 1991 Qatar joined other Gulf countries in making its military installations available to multi-national forces after Iraq's invasion of Kuwait in August.

The dispute with Bahrain concerns ownership of a series of tiny islands and two shoals in the Persian Gulf. Qatar never accepted the British ruling that the islands belonged to Bahrain. In July, Qatar unilaterally brought the case to the International Court of Justice. However, it later withdrew the petition, and called for the establishment of a tripartite committee consisting of Bahrain, Qatar and Saudi Arabia to work out a settlement between the two countries or find a way to submit their differences to the World Court in a joint application.

Qatar gained its independence from Great Britain in 1971. Since 1972 Qatar has been ruled by Sheikh Hamad ibn Khalifa al Thani, who came to power after deposing his cousin in a palace coup. He rules the country as head of state and prime minister. A provisional constitution provides for a Council of Ministers and an Advisory Council of 30 members, 27 of whom were to be elected. These elections have never taken place.

Expatriate laborers, mainly from South Asia, outnumber Qataris four to one, and this disparity has been a cause of concern for local authorities. The regime has beefed up its internal security forces and offered jobs only to native Qataris in certain government-owned industries.

A government reshuffling in 1990, however, introduced some young reformers into cabinet posts. Because of this, expatriate workers had an easier time switching jobs and Qatari men have been allowed to bring foreign wives, previously excluded, into the country.

Political Rights and Civil Liberties:

Under the absolute rule of the emir, Qataris cannot change their government democratically. The constitution provides that an emir be selected from adult males of the Al Thani family. There are no elections and political parties are banned. The 30-member Advisory Council, appointed by the emir, is powerless. The emir rules by decree, but governs within limits set by the royal family. The judiciary is not truly independent, since many judges are non-citizens who hold their residence at the whim of the monarch. The rights of the accused or detained in security cases are not respected. Non-Muslims may not bring suit, and only Muslims may ask for a change of forum to a traditional court.

Because a large proportion of laborers in Qatar are foreign (approximately 85 percent), the government has established an extensive security apparatus to guard against subversion. One arm of this structure, Mubahathat, is almost completely independent from the rest of the security apparatus and is known for its occasional use of severe force during investigations.

The government owns both radio and television stations and prohibits public criticism of the regime as well as political demonstrations. Although the government has issued statements calling for greater free speech, non-Qatari journalists avoid testing its limits for fear of getting their residence permits revoked. Private associations, though permitted, are carefully watched. Non-Muslims may not worship in public and cannot proselytize. Workers are not allowed to join unions, but may associate based on professional or private interests.

Romania

Polity: Dominant party transitional
Economy: Statist transitional
Population: 23,400,000
PPP: na
Life Expectancy: 70.8
Ethnic Groups: Romanians (88 percent), Hungarians, Germans, Gypsies

Political Rights: 5
Civil Liberties: 5
Status: Partly Free

Overview:

In 1991, amid increasing factionalism in the ruling National Salvation Front (NSF), Prime Minister Petre Roman's government fell after repeated clashes with President Ion Iliescu over economic reform. Romania also became the second East European country after Bulgaria to adopt a new post-Communist constitution, which voters approved overwhelmingly in a December referendum.

In other issues, the country's deepening economic crisis led to massive labor unrest throughout the year, the opposition Center Alliance and other groups remained essentially fragmented, convictions of several leading Communists were overturned and right-wing, nationalist groups continued to foment ethnic tensions. Corruption remained pervasive among bureaucrats, state employees, private entrepreneurs, peasants and professionals. The dreaded Securitate (secret police) was resurrected under a new name—the Romanian Intelligence Service—which was used by the state as a vehicle of repression.

In January, thousands rallied to support anti-government strikers in Timisoara, site of the first large anti-government demonstrations in 1989. Rallies were organized by the opposition Civic Alliance, an umbrella group for the extraparliamentary opposition founded in November 1990. Forty thousand striking workers and 22,000 striking students demanded the resignation of President Iliescu and the NSF government, which had led the coup that overthrew the 24-year regime of Nicolae Ceausescu in 1989 and won two-thirds of the seats in the bicameral parliament in 1990.

On 1 April Romanians confronted their biggest food-price increases in almost half a century. Staples like bread, eggs and meat doubled in price as the government ended four decades of Communist subsidies on basic foods.

In May nationwide protests mounted against the NSF, and by June the government was considering calling a general election before the end of the year. Polls indicated a sharp drop in the popularity of Prime Minister Roman after the government adopted radical economic reforms urged by Western creditors. The government estimated that inflation would soar to 200 percent before the end of the year. During the month, the Senate passed a national security law which contained references to threats of "separatist action," a clause that caused senators from the Hungarian Democratic Union (HDUR) to walk out in protest.

On 10 June, the deputy head of the Romanian Intelligence Service was dismissed after journalists discovered a cache of secret police documents which indicated that the RIS had continued the Securitate practice of spying on the opposition.

The threat of broad strikes continued in the summer. On 17 June, unions representing health workers and pharmacists joined tens of thousands of other strikers, urging their members to strike for increased government funding for the decrepit health system. Over 40,000 teachers and 13,000 industrial workers also went out on strike. On 18 June, railway workers walked off the job for the second time in 1991.

Partly to assuage its rapid decline in public opinion polls, parliament on 19 June passed the draft of a new constitution aimed at ensuring liberal democracy. The new constitution, which was initially backed by the parliamentary opposition, promised freedom of speech and assembly, "no censorship of any kind," and the rights of minorities to study in their native language—a key demand of the Hungarian-speaking minority, about 10 percent of the population. However, the HDUR said that the draft "restricts the use of the mother tongue in local administration." The new constitution separated the legislative, judicial and executive branches of government. Under the 1965 Communist constitution, laws dictated by the party were handed down from the government to a rubberstamp parliament.

Political uncertainty and economic collapse also led to the proliferation of ultra-nationalist, right-wing groups, among them Romania Mare, or "Greater Romania." The party's newspaper, *Romania Mare*, reportedly the most widely read in the country, published anti-Semitic, anti-Hungarian and anti-Gypsy commentaries. The year also saw an escalation in the desecration of several Jewish synagogues and cemeteries, attempts by some groups to rehabilitate World War II leader and Nazi ally Ion Antonescu, and repeated calls from mainstream opposition groups for the restoration of the monarchy under exiled King Michael.

On 5 July the Civic Alliance movement began a three-day congress by announcing that it would become a political party. The alliance, which claimed several million backers and was supported by the independent newspaper *Romania Libera*, was formed by some 200 intellectuals in 1990 to promote "civil society" and democratic values.

Civil turmoil continued into September. On 6 September 5,000 anti-Communist protesters thronged the main square of Bucharest, the capital, calling for the outlawing of the Communist party and the resignation of President Iliescu, a prominent former-Communist with a long history of ties to the Ceausescu regime. On 25 September, several thousand angry miners, upset over price hikes and demanding the resignation of the prime minister and President Iliescu, stormed government headquarters in Bucharest and fought riot police. Ironically, miners were used by the government to brutally attack opposition parties and students in June 1990. The following day, as more miners descended on the capital, Prime Minister Roman resigned. President Iliescu, also a target of protest, announced on radio that consultations had begun to form a new government. On 27 September, a third straight day of rioting continued, with protesters clearly bouyed by the resignation of Roman. Three people were killed.

On 1 October President Iliescu asked former Finance Minister Teodor Stolojan, a 48-year-old economist who pledged to support tough reforms and a broad-based government of national unity, to form a new government. On 15 October, the NSF daily *Azi* published the list of cabinet members, mainly technocrats, NSF members and representatives from the National Liberal Party, a party with roots in pre-Communist Romania. Despite Stolojan's consultations with leaders of all parties in parliament, including those grouped in the National Convention for the Establishment of Democracy (NCFED), the last word on the new government came from the ruling NSF. On 26 September, a statement by the government had in fact specified that the new government should reflect "the outcome of the 1990 parliamentary elections." The announcement indicated that the extraparliamentary Civic Alliance would be left out of the government. The National Peasant Party (NPP), another historical party, was the only organization in parliament to reject the idea of joining any coalition that included the NSF. The Civic Alliance, also a member of the NCFED, adopted a stance similar to the NPP. The ultra-right Romania Mare openly advocated the creation of an authoritarian "predominantly military government, capable of ensuring peace, order, reconstruction, real democratization, sovereignty and territorial integrity."

The 21-man list of ministers presented to the parliament on 16 October consisted of nine NSF representatives, seven independents (most of whom, including the prime minister, had actually belonged to the NSF's team of technocrats and even been part of the former cabinet), three Liberals, one member of the Ecological Movement of Romania (EMR) as Environment Minister and one member of the Democratic Agrarian Party (DAP) as Agricultural Minister. The NLP got the finance and economy portfolio as well as the ministry of justice.

In his inaugural speech, Prime Minister Stolojan said that his cabinet's main goal was to pave the way for free and fair elections in 1992. He also pledged to go ahead with economic reforms initiated by his predecessor, including plans to privatize state-owned industries and make the Romanian currency convertible. He also warned that the government was considering food-rationing in the winter.

On 21 November parliament ratified the new constitution, which paved the way for general elections, probably in April 1992. Opposition parties and most deputies from the NLP, which joined the ruling coalition, voted against the new constitution, arguing that it gave the president too much power and ruled out a return to monarchy. The month also saw the emergence of a wider rift between former Prime Minister Roman, who remained head of the NSF, and President Iliescu, whom the former accused of supporting "neo-Communists" in the ruling party who opposed democracy and free-market reforms. He said the NSF would not support Iliescu in upcoming elections.

On 9 December, Romanians went to the polls and endorsed the new constitution by a wide margin. The Hungarian minority, however, rejected the document, with 85 percent and 78 percent voting "no" in two predominantly Hungarian areas. Two-thirds of Romania's 16 million voters turned out for the vote, in which they were asked to accept or reject a new constitution that made the country a presidential multi-party republic. Over 77 percent voted "yes." One week later, approximately 20,000 demonstrated in Timisoara demanding President Iliescu's resignation and the return of King Michael.

In economic matters, the country continued to suffer through the throes of restructuring. Early in the year, Romania was hit with energy shortages, exacerbated by severe winter conditions and a reduction of Soviet gas imports to 35 percent of their early 1990 levels. The shortage forced the government to stop production at several key industrial installations. The number of unemployed people was expected to hit anywhere from 500,000 to 1 million. In December, in a move to placate public unease, Prime Minister Stolojan said he would concentrate on the economy and not run for public office in 1992.

Political Rights and Civil Liberties: Romanians nominally have the right to choose their government democratically, but the 1990 parliamentary elections were marred by intimidation and violence against an opposition not given adequate time or resources to campaign effectively. In 1991 Romanians approved a new constitution containing impressive safeguards on political rights and freedoms, but the extent of its implementation remained to be seen; the next elections are tentatively scheduled for April 1992. The president will be elected by direct vote.

The judiciary is not free from NSF influence. Preventive detention and arbitrary arrests were still common in 1991. On 12 December, the military section of the Supreme Court acquitted 15 former Communist Party leaders, overturning a lower-court decision under which they were jailed for their role in the attempted suppression of the 1989 revolution. No reason was given by the court. On 20 June, parliament passed a national security law that defined the Romanian Intelligence Service as apolitical, but the measure included a controversial provision requiring all Romanians to cooperate with the secret police.

Freedom of the press is limited. In March, the government proposed legislation that could send journalists to jail for up to five years if they are found guilty of insulting authorities. A draft law signed by Prime Minister Roman in February proposed that "defamation of the president of Romania" in the media be punished by imprisonment and/or fines. On 11 December, the dailies *Adevarul*, *Romania Libera* and *Tineretul Liber* called a warning strike to protest what they regarded as the government's indifference to huge increases in the price of newsprint and other printing and distribution costs, which favored the pro-government press. The same day, Romania's first independent national television station, SOTI, went on the air for the first time. The authorities had previously rejected SOTI's demands for an independent national television station, claiming that the costs would be too high. The government-owned media reflects government policies and a pro-NSF bias.

The government exercises control over religious activities and churches, the largest being the Romanian Orthodox Church. Domestic and foreign travel restrictions have been eased.

Workers are organized in independent trade unions, and represent an important opposition force despite NSF efforts to monitor union activities and co-opt union leadership.

Rwanda

Polity: One-party
(military dominated)
Economy: Mixed statist
Population: 7,500,000
PPP: $730
Life Expectancy: 49.5
Ethnic Groups: Hutu (84 percent), Tutsi (15 percent), Twa
pygmy (1 percent)

Political Rights: 6
Civil Liberties: 6
Status: Not Free

Overview:

In late 1990 the Rwanda Patriotic Front (FPR), a force of
Rwandan refugees lately resident in Uganda, invaded their own
country. The effects of that invasion were felt throughout 1991.

Meanwhile, the outlines of a multiparty system, promised in 1989 by President
Juvenal Habyarimana in a major break with past policies in this military-dominated
one-party state, began to emerge. The government created a new constitution and
legislation that allowed opposition political parties.

Rwanda, which gained independence from Belgium in 1962, is a poor, landlocked
country in central-east Africa, with the highest population density of the entire
continent. It is led by Maj. Gen. Habyarimana, head of the National Revolutionary
Movement for Development (MRND), who seized power in a bloodless coup in
1973. The MRND, established in 1976, was the only legal party under the 1978
constitution. Running unopposed in 1988 as the candidate of the ruling MRND,
Habyarimana was re-elected to a third five-year term as president with a claimed 99
percent of the vote. The unicameral National Development Council consists of
members nominated by the MRND and elected every five years.

In October of 1990, a force of five to ten thousand RPF under Ugandan Maj. Gen.
Fred Rwigyema invaded the country from neighboring Uganda. Many of the insurgents
were from the Tutsi tribe and were serving in the Ugandan army during their exile. The
invasion was another episode in an often violent inter-tribal rivalry between Rwanda's
numerically dominant Hutus and the minority Tutsis, who had traditionally dominated
national life until 1959, when the Tutsi king was overthrown by insurgent Hutus. The
Rwandan refugees and their descendents, numbering today as many as a half million,
have been the source of manpower for those dedicated to the overthrow of the successive Hutu-dominated regimes that have governed Rwanda since the '59 coup. In 1963 a
country-wide blood-letting took place, precipitating the flight of many thousands of
Tutsis to neighboring Uganda, Burundi, Tanzania, and Zaire. Further communal killings
in the tens of thousands occurred over the next three decades. A portion of the RPF
forces is made up of Hutus from southern Rwanda who resent the monopoly on power
wielded by Habyrimana and his coterie of northern Hutus.

A short time before the October 1990 invasion was launched, President
Habyarimana publicly requested countries harboring Rwandese refugees to naturalize
them, saying that Rwanda was too crowded to take them back. The RPF has
demanded that all in the Rwandese diaspora be allowed to return freely, that institutionalized ethnic and regional discrimination cease, and that a government of national
unity replace the existing regime and its leader.

Although the October invasion was beaten back with the aid of Zaïrois troops, the RPF has mounted repeated guerrilla attacks and occasional offensives against government forces in northern Rwanda throughout 1991. Negotiated ceasefire agreements between the parties have failed to keep the peace for long. The Rwandan government has charged that the Ugandan military has actively aided the insurgents, a charge that has been denied by the Ugandan president. The Rwanda government regime now asserts that refugees are free to peacefully return to Rwanda and participate in multiparty politics, and offers an amnesty to insurgents.

In November of 1990, the president announced his intention to move Rwanda toward multipartyism. By the end of 1990, a government-appointed committee recommended certain democratic reforms, including limitation on the president's term in office, creation of the post of prime minister, abandonment of the MNRD's special relationship with the state, and requirement that political parties in a multiparty system not be ethnically based. A new constitution went into effect in mid-1991.

There are at least nine newly legalized political parties as well as the re-baptized National Republican Movement for Democracy and Development (formerly the MNRD). Opposition political parties have called for a transitional government of national unity with representatives of all the parties and a prime minister chosen by consensus. Some government critics have demanded that a sovereign national conference be convened, but the president rejected that option in December 1991. On 19 December representatives of four opposition parties walked out of an all-party meeting with the regime, objecting to the president's opposition to a national conference, the requirement that the prime minister be of the ruling MNRD during the transition to multi-party elections, and the weak authority of the prime minister. Although municipal and legislative elections were scheduled for the last quarter of 1991, the government stated that electoral change will be limited until the RPF is disarmed and hostilities cease.

Like neighboring Burundi, which it resembles ethnically and geographically, Rwanda faces severe economic problems due to low coffee prices, underdeveloped transportation system, land erosion, and overpopulation on arable land. The invasion has further weakened an already disastrous situation. The spread of AIDS continues as a problem in this densely populated country.

Political Rights and Civil Liberties:

Although the constitution now allows for democratic multipartyism, and political opposition to the regime has been allowed to organize, in the absence of openly contested elections Rwanda remains a military-dominated one-party state. Its citizens have not yet been allowed to determine democratically the make-up of their national and local governments. It is still not known in detail to what extent the formal political opening will allow for an expansion of civil liberties in what has been an environment of repression and severely circumscribed human rights. There are reports that members of recently-legalized political parties have been harassed by government authorities.

The security apparatus in Rwanda is pervasive and intrusive. Security laws allow for the preventative detention of persons suspected of undermining national interests and public safety. Some 8,000 alleged RPF "accomplices" were rounded up from the Tutsi population after the October 1990 invasion. Though the government has since released most of them, often there was nothing more to justify their detention than mere suspicion of active complicity based on possession of anti-government documents, or their passive support for the insurgency based on their ethnicity. Among the over 1,000 not released, some have been sentenced to extended prison terms for allegedly knowing of the impending invasion and not acting to warn the government. Many of those detained were beaten, some were tortured, and a few were extrajudicially executed. Trials in the separately constituted security courts have been characterized by a lack of official interest in allegations of confessions induced by torture, the absence of legal counsel for most defendants, criminal charges inadequately supported by the evidence, and judicial predisposition toward conviction. A general amnesty was declared in early October by the regime.

There are continuing reports of atrocities and murders committed against Tutsi noncombatants by government troops as well as by Hutu militiamen and civilians. The regime continued to deny direct responsibility for a February massacre in northwestern Rwanda until mid-August; the international media reports that as many as 1,200 Tutsis were slaughtered by militiamen operating under government auspices. Meanwhile, the RPF denies any responsibility for civilian deaths suffered as a consequence of its own armed activities. The number of casualties is said to mount into the thousands.

Discriminatory quotas have limited the level of Tutsi participation in public employment and education. Hutu hard-liners, who are present in the government, demand the continuation of discriminatory measures. In the face of government harassment the independent Rwandan Association for the Defense of Human Rights, founded in September of 1990 pursues its mission of publicizing abuses and demanding official respect for the rights of *all* Rwandans.

There is a measure of press freedom for privately published periodicals that support the political line of the government, which is implicitly pro-Hutu. The nation's penal code has not yet been revised to reflect a greater tolerance for diversity of opinion and criticism of officialdom appropriate to a democracy. Journalists of the independent press have been detained and charged with sedition for various political offenses, including contacts with the RDF and publication of articles criticizing the regime's discriminatory policies. Those who accuse the authorities of corruption, economic mismanagement, and of giving preference to citizens of their own region in the country have been arrested and imprisoned.

Prior to the invasion, there had been some official restriction of stridently anti-Tutsi publications. Since the invasion, however, Amnesty International reports that the media have advocated revenge and violence against the Tutsi. The regime controls broadcasting, and presently allows opposition parties only fifteen minutes of air time a week.

Freedom of religion is constitutionally guaranteed in this predominantly Christian country where 30 percent of the people practice traditional African religions and 1 percent are Muslim. Nonetheless, the government continues its harassment of some religious sects, particularly Jehovah's Witnesses.

Until the recent legislation permitting multiple political parties, freedom of association was curtailed with only those private organizations registered with and approved by the government allowed to function. Freedom of assembly has been severely restricted in the past, but the first opposition party demonstration to be held in Rwanda took place without incident on 17 November. The Central Union of Rwandan Workers has been controlled by the ruling MRND, and all worker associations have had to belong to it. Strikes had to be approved by the government-controlled executive committee.

St. Christo- pher and Nevis

Polity: Parliamentary democracy
Economy: Capitalist
Population: 40,000
PPP: na
Life Expectancy: 67.5
Ethnic Groups: Black, mulatto, other

Political Rights: 1
Civil Liberties: 1
Status: Free

Overview:

This island nation, consisting of the Caribbean islands of St. Kitts and Nevis, became an independent state with a federal constitution in 1983. The British monarch is represented by a governor-general who appoints a prime minister as leader of the parliamentary majority. The governor-general also appoints a deputy governor-general for Nevis.

There is a unicameral National Assembly, whose members are directly elected for five years from single-member constituencies, eight on St. Kitts and three on Nevis. Senators, not to exceed two-thirds of the elected members, are appointed, one by the leader of the parliamentary opposition for every two by the governor-general.

Nevis is provided with an island Assembly currently consisting of five elected and three appointed members. The governor-general appoints a premier and two other members of the Nevis Assembly to serve as a Nevis Island Administration. Nevis is also accorded the right to secession from St. Kitts if approved by two-thirds of the elected legislators and endorsed by two-thirds of those voting on the matter in an island referendum.

The current People's Action Movement (PAM) government of Prime Minister Kennedy Simmons came to power in the parliamentary election of 1980 with the support of the Nevis Reformation Party (NRP) and led the country to independence in 1983. The center-right PAM-NRP coalition increased its majority in early elections in 1984, the PAM winning six of the eight seats on St. Kitts and the NRP taking all three on Nevis. The Labour Party (LP), a left-leaning party that once dominated the political scene, lost all but two of its seats.

Simmons was sworn in for a third term after the PAM retained its six seats in the 1989 elections. The NRP retained two seats on Nevis, losing one to the Concerned Citizens' Movement (CCM). The LP retained its two seats. Denzil Douglas, a parliamentary newcomer, was elected the LP leader following the elections and replaced Lee Moore as the parliamentary opposition leader. In 1991, Douglas and the LP conducted an anti-corruption campaign against the government, an apparent effort to gear up for the next elections, constitutionally due by the end of 1992.

Political Rights and Civil Liberties:

Citizens are able to change their government through free and fair elections. Constitutional guarantees regarding the right of free expression, the free exercise of religion and the right to organize political parties, labor unions and civic organizations are respected. The main labor union, the St. Kitts Trades and Labour Union, is associated with the opposition LP. The right to strike, while not specified by law, is fully recognized and respected in practice.

Television and radio on St. Kitts are owned by the government but offer different points of view. There is no daily newspaper but each of the major political parties publishes a weekly or bi-weekly newspaper. The opposition publications are free to criticize the government and do so vigorously. There is a religious television station and a privately owned radio station on Nevis.

Rule of law, based on the 1983 constitution, is respected. The judiciary is independent and the highest court is the West Indies Supreme Court (based in St. Lucia) which includes a Court of Appeal and a High Court. In certain circumstances, there is right of appeal to the Privy Council in London.

St. Lucia

Polity: Parliamentary democracy
Economy: Capitalist
Population: 200,000
PPP: na
Life Expectancy: 70.5
Ethnic Groups: Black, mulatto, other

Political Rights: 1
Civil Liberties: 2
Status: Free

Overview:

St. Lucia, a member of the British Commonwealth, became internally self-governing in 1967, and achieved independence in 1979. The British monarchy is represented by a governor-general whose emergency powers are subject to legislative review. Under the 1979 constitution, there is a bicameral parliament consisting of a seventeen-member House of Assembly elected for five years, and an eleven member Senate, with six senators appointed by the prime minister, three by the leader of the parliamentary opposition, and two by consultation with civic and religious organizations. The prime minister must be a member of the House and command a majority therein. Since 1985, the island has been divided into eight regions, each with its own elected council and administrative services.

The leftist St. Lucia Labour Party (SLP) won a landslide victory in the 1979 elections, but factional disputes between SLP radicals and moderates led to new elections in 1982. The left-wing faction led by George Odlum broke off to form the Progressive Labour Party (PLP). The 1982 elections saw the return to power of the United Workers' Party (UWP) led by Prime Minister John Compton.

In the 1987 elections, the UWP won a narrow 9-8 victory over the SLP which had declared a social democratic orientation under the new leadership of Julian Hunte. The SLP refused unity proposals from the PLP, which ended up winning no seats. Prime Minister Compton, hoping to increase the UWP majority, called new elections a few weeks later, but there was no change in the distribution of seats. However, an SLP representative switched parties later in the year, giving the UWP a 10-7 majority.

The next elections were constitutionally due by July 1992, but when Prime Minister Compton officially launched the UWP campaign at the party convention in August 1991, it was believed elections might be called earlier. The SLP began its campaign soon after, targeting the government on economic issues, particularly unemployment and the national budget.

Political Rights and Civil Liberties:

Citizens are able to change their government through free and fair elections. Constitutional guarantees regarding free expression and the right to organize political parties, labor unions and civic groups are generally respected as is the exercise of free religion.

Opposition parties have complained of difficulties in getting police permission for demonstrations and charge the government with interference. Newspapers are mostly private or sponsored by political parties. In 1991 the government was charged with trying to influence the press by withholding government advertising. Television is privately owned; radio is both public and private.

Civic organizations are well organized and politically active. The labor unions, which represent a majority of wage earners, are free to strike. The competition among political parties and allied civic groups is heated, particularly during campaign periods when there is occasional violence and mutual charges of harassment.

The judicial system is independent and includes a High Court under the West Indies Supreme Court (based in St. Lucia), with ultimate appeal under certain circumstances to the Privy Council in London. Personal security is generally respected under the rule of law, although the recent appearance of drug-related violence has become a cause for concern.

St. Vincent and the Grenadines

Polity: Parliamentary democracy
Economy: Capitalist
Population: 100,000
PPP: na
Life Expectancy: 70.0
Ethnic Groups: Black, mulatto, other

Political Rights: 1
Civil Liberties: 2
Status: Free

Overview:

St. Vincent and the Grenadines have the status of "special member" of the British Commonwealth, with the British monarchy represented by a governor-general. St. Vincent became internally self-governing in 1967 and achieved independence in 1979, with jurisdiction over the northern Grenadine islets of Beguia, Canouan, Mayreau, Mustique, Prune Island, Petit St. Vincent, and Union Island.

At the time of independence, the constitution provided for a unicameral House of Assembly with thirteen members directly elected for five years. Six senators are appointed, four by the government and two by the opposition. The prime minister is the leader of the party or coalition commanding a majority in the House. In 1986, the House approved a constitutional amendment raising the number of elected members to fifteen.

In the May 1989 elections, Prime Minister James Mitchell won a second term when his centrist New Democratic Party (NDP) swept all fifteen seats. The three opposing parties were the moderate socialist St. Vincent Labor Party (SVLP), which had held power in 1979-84, and two leftist parties, the United People's Movement (UPM) and the Movement for National Unity (MNU). Despite failing to win any seats in the "first past the post" system, the opposition garnered over 30 percent of the vote.

In 1991 charges of misconduct by the national police commissioner, and a scandal involving the seizure by U.S. authorities of a St. Vincent-registered vessel allegedly carrying a large quantity of hashish, led the three opposition parties to form the National Council in Defence of Law Order. The council, backed by trade unions and some private sector and civic groups, became the main opposition vehicle for criticizing the Mitchell government, and previewed a possible coalition for the next elections, due by 1994.

Political Rights and Civil Liberties: Citizens can change their government democratically. Constitutional guarantees regarding the right to free expression, freedom of religion and the right to organize political parties, labor unions and civic organizations are respected. Labor unions are active, politically involved, and permitted to strike. Political campaigns are hotly contested, with occasional charges from all quarters of harassment and violence, including police brutality. In 1990 the government admitted during United Nations Human Rights Committee hearings that prison conditions were poor, but denied allegations by the St. Vincent and the Grenadines Human Rights Association of prisoner beatings.

The press is independent and uncensored, with one privately owned independent weekly, *The Vincentian*, and two weeklies and a fortnightly run by political parties. *The Vincentian* has been charged with government favoritism by the opposition and the Caribbean Association of Media Workers. Radio and television are government owned. Differing points of view are presented, but there is evidence of government interference in radio programming.

The judicial system is independent. The highest court is the West Indies Supreme Court (based in St. Lucia), which includes a Court of Appeal and a High Court, one of whose judges is resident on St. Vincent. The Human Rights Association has criticized judicial delays and the large backlog of cases caused by a shortage of personnel in the local judiciary.

Sao Tome and Principe

Polity: Presidential-legislative democracy
Economy: Mixed statist (transitional)
Population: 100,000
PPP: na
Life Expectancy: 65.5
Ethnic Groups: Black, mulatto, Portuguese

Political Rights: 2
Civil Liberties: 3 .
Status: Free

Overview: After sixteen years of post-independence one-party rule, on 20 January 1991 São Tomé and Príncipe became the second former Portuguese colony in Africa to hold multi-party elections. The long-ruling Movement for the Liberation of São Tomé and Príncipe (MLSTP), gained some 30 percent of the vote and 21 seats in the 55-seat national assembly, coming in second place to the opposition Democratic Convergence Party-Group of Reflection (PCD-GR), which received 55 percent and 31 seats. In third place was the Democratic Opposition Coalition (CODO), with 5 percent and 3 seats. On 3 March Miguel dos Anjos Trovoada was elected president of the republic after the incumbent chief of state, Manuel Pinto da Costa, and two other aspirants withdrew from the race. Trovoada gained 80 percent of the vote, although only 40 percent of those registered.

Located in the Gulf of Guinea some 130 miles off the coast of Gabon, the

Republic of São Tomé and Príncipe consists of two main islands and several smaller islets. Until 1991 Manuel Pinto da Costa served as president of the republic and and also as leader of the sole legal party, the Movement for the Liberation of São Tomé and Príncipe (MLSTP). The transformation of the state from a leftist, single-party political structure into a multi-party democracy formally began at the end of 1989 following the national MLSTP conference which recommended constitutional amendments to allow for multi-party elections and term limitations for the office of the presidency. Opposition figures were granted amnesty and opposition movements were legalized.

Opposition leader Afonso Dos Santos, sentenced to a long prison term after having been convicted of leading a coup attempt against President da Costa in March 1988, won amnesty in April 1990. Dos Santos sought the lifting of a ban against his conservative São Tomé National Resistance Front opposition party so that it could organize in advance of any multi-party elections. Former prime minister and MLSTP leader Miguel dos Anjos Trovoada returned from exile in order to run as an independent candidate whose candidacy was supported by both the PCD-GR and CODO. Former Defence Minister Guadalupe de Ceita also announced his decision to seek election as an independent leftist. The MLSTP renamed itself the MLSTP-PSD (Social Democratic Party) and nominated President da Costa for re-election. Elections were scheduled for 20 January 1991.

Less than a week before the presidential polling, de Ceita and dos Santos pulled out of the race after a petition to the High Appeals Court to postpone the election was turned down. Accusing Trovoada of a record of corruption that ought to act to disqualify his candidacy, they sought judicial recourse. He refused to respond to their accusations that he had embezzled millions of dollars of foreign assistance while he served as São Tomé's prime minister in the 1970s. Though the challengers withdrew in alleged response to the failure of their appeal, Trovoada asserted that, like Pinto da Costa, they had dropped out to avoid defeat. As the only candidate left in the race, Trovoada won 80 percent of the vote.

In the months after the elections, the change in administrations produced frictions between the MLSTP-SDP and the new regime. Trovoada objected to the "golden parachute" which out-going officials provided for themselves in the last session of the National Assembly. Pinto da Costa was legislatively slated to receive his full salary, official vehicles, bodyguards, and various other perquisites. The new PCD-GR majority in the Assembly resolved that all members of the prior regime must return formerly state-owned vehicles and dwellings which they had sold to themselves before the elections at bargain-basement prices. In response to PCD-GR charges of corruption and demands for the return of public property, the MLSTP-PSD repeatedly boycotted the legislative session.

A leading world producer of cacao, the country has faced an economic crisis since the price of the commodity began to drop in 1980. This has led to hiring freezes and preliminary moves toward cuts in the number of employees in the public sector, as well as reduced public spending. The new government under Prime Minister Daniel dos Santos Daio has continued the prior administration's efforts to de-nationalize some businesses, encourage foreign investment, and privatize cacao plantations. Daio's first stated economic objective after taking office was to re-establish links with the World Bank, suspended by the institution as a result of the MLSTP regime's failure to meet certain conditions of a structural adjustment program.

Political Rights and Civil Liberties: For the first time since independence in 1975, new constitutional provisions permitted citizens to change their government democratically in 1991. In August 1990 an overwhelming majority of voters approved a new constitution which called for a multi-party system, a mixed economy, freedom of expression, and the right to strike. The MLSTP regime seriously limited rights of assembly and association in the past, but allowed political organizing by the opposition before multi-party elections. Until quite recently, the judiciary has not been fully independent from executive interference, particularly in security and political cases. The secret security police of the prior regime are to be disbanded. Radio, television, and a periodic newspaper are government-controlled, but there is now more latitude to criticize government policies. Although the new constitution recognizes labor rights, there is doubt as to how a state-linked trade union which exists mainly on paper could exercise such rights. Leaders of the new regime have explicitly promised to respect freedom of association and religion, allow diverse opinions in the media without government interference, respect judicial independence and depoliticize the military.

Saudi Arabia

Polity: Traditional monarchy
Economy: Capitalist-statist
Population: 15,500,000
PPP: $9,350
Life Expectancy: 64.5
Ethnic Groups: Arab tribes, other Arab and Muslim immigrants

Political Rights: 7
Civil Liberties: 6
Status: Not Free

Overview: In 1991 the Persian Gulf War brought an American-led international military force of over 500,000 troops to Saudi Arabia and had far-reaching effects on Saudi society. The crisis atmosphere and the presence of Westerners and liberal Arabs ignited unprecedented public debate which lasted, and even gained momentum, through the end of the year.

In anticipation of the 17 January start of the Gulf war, Saudi Arabia stepped up civil defense and began selling gas masks, for fear of an Iraqi chemical weapons attack. Many Saudis fled Riyadh to places like Jidda, beyond the range of Iraq's Scud missiles, and to Mecca and Medina, Islam's holiest cities. At the end of January, Saudi troops backed by American marines successfully battled Iraqi soldiers for the town of Kafji on the Kuwaiti border. The 36-hour battle was the war's first ground battle. Eighteen Saudi soldiers were killed.

During the Gulf crisis reform-minded Saudis at all levels of society became more vociferous. In a rare display of dissent, many Saudis questioned the war and the king's decision to allow such a massive foreign military presence. For the first time, there were public demands for increased participation in political life and for greater accountability in government.

Well-educated but underemployed Saudi liberals, known as technocrats, were especially bold in voicing dissent. They demanded an end to censorship and corruption, and the reestablishment of the *Majlis al-Shura*, a consultative assembly which was established when the state was founded but was later abandoned. King Fahd has been promising to re-establish the *shura* since 1953. At the end of the Gulf War, a group of intellectuals distributed a petition outside the kingdom suggesting a change to a constitutional monarchy with guarantees of freedom of expression, freedom of the press, and the right to organize parties.

The Islamic clergy also petitioned the king for change. While advocating respect for human rights and political participation through the *shura*, the clergymen countered the efforts of the intellectuals by advocating strict Islamization of the nation's social, economic, administrative and educational systems. They demanded the strengthening of the Islamic media and the use of propaganda in the service of Islam, social justice based on Islamic laws, and the preservation of the Islamic nation's purity by "keeping it out of non-Islamic pacts and treaties." The last demand was seen as a criticism of Saudi Arabia's alliance with the West.

The Gulf War accentuated the failings of the censored local media, which in August 1990, didn't mention the Iraqi invasion of Kuwait until three days after it occurred. During the war, many Saudis relied on western news sources like Voice of America or BBC; Saudi government officials and businessmen watched CNN by satellite. Saudi Arabia's internal debate continued after the withdrawal of Western troops and the defeat of Saddam Hussein in late February. Liberals and Islamic conservatives continued throughout the year to petition King Fahd by fax machine, as Saudi Arabia does not tolerate political criticism in the press. On 17 November the king announced plans to implement significant changes by January 1992, including the formation of the *Majlis al-Shura*, the introduction of a constitution-like written body of laws, and greater local autonomy for provinces. Sparking the ire of liberals, Islamic clergymen immediately claimed the right to screen candidates for the planned *shura*.

In foreign affairs, Saudi Arabia sought to minimize its role in postwar Middle East politics. Saudi Arabia strongly opposed the idea of hosting foreign troops—Arab or Western—as part of a postwar security arrangement, and declined involvement in the Arab-Israeli peace conference in Madrid.

Saudi Arabia resumed relations with Iran in 1991 and agreed to allow Iranians not only to participate in the June pilgrimage (*hajj*) to Mecca and Medina but also to hold a peaceful rally in the holy cities for the "disavowal of the infidels." Saudi Arabia had severed ties with Iran in 1987, after Saudi security forces clashed with Iranian *hajj* demonstrators, leaving 400 dead. Saudi Arabia has long been wary of the spread of Shia Islam: The kingdom's 400,000 underprivileged Shiites have been the most serious source of opposition to the monarchy. Shiites object to the regime on economic and political grounds and view the royal family rule as corrupt and un-Islamic.

Political Rights and Civil Liberties: Saudi citizens cannot change their government democratically. The royal family, led by Kind Fahd and Crown Prince Abdalah, rules the country almost exclusively. There are no elections, no written constitution, no political parties and no public demonstrations. A formal system of consultation exists, however, in the form of the *majlis* or daily audiences held by Saudi family princes to which citizens may bring complaints or express opinions on matters of state. The influx of Westerners and other more liberal Arabs during the Persian Gulf War led to more open debate and public requests for greater political participation. In 1991 the king promised to reestablish the official *Majlis al-shura* or consultative assembly, and to introduce a written body of laws.

Public criticism of Islam or the Saudi regime is not tolerated. There is a private press, but it must adhere to 1982 government press guidelines. The regime may dismiss newspaper editors. Foreign publications are frequently censored. Television and radio are government owned and operated. Freedom of thought and artistic expression is severely limited; the study of Freud, Marx, philosophy and music, for example, is forbidden. Nonpolitical organizations may form with government permission, but education and cultural institutions are strictly regulated by the government. Professional groups are discouraged from maintaining contact with their international counterparts.

Saudi Arabia is an Islamic state. Non-Muslim religions are not recognized; converts from Islam to another religion may be sentenced to death; all Saudi citizens must be Muslim. The majority of the population, including the ruling family, is Sunni Muslim. Saudi custody over the Grand Mosque in Mecca and its quotas for national pilgrimages has caused friction with Iran.

Saudi Arabian law, based on *shari'a*, codified Islamic law, prescribes punishments considered cruel, unusual or disproportionate by international standards. The death penalty, usually by beheading or stoning, is applied for murder, apostasy, adultery and narcotics smuggling. Other penalties for lesser crimes include flogging and amputations. After the Gulf War, Saudi Arabia's appalling human rights record attracted international attention when Saudi authorities publicly beheaded 16 men. According to human rights monitors, the General Directorate of Investigations routinely tortures detainees, often to extract confessions. The GDI regularly holds suspects incommunicado and without charge for lengthy periods.

The sometimes undisciplined religious police who enforce Muslim precepts regarding food, alcohol, dress, and behavior, reportedly carry out beatings and whippings of suspects. The religious police may detain suspects for up to 24 hours. The discretion of authorities, including religious police, to search private residences is more limited, however. The Saudi judiciary is generally regarded as independent in common civil and criminal trials. All trials, however, are closed and counsel is permitted before but not during proceedings.

Christian and Jewish troops stationed in Saudi Arabia during the Gulf War were prohibited by United States policy from openly practicing their religion in order not to offend the Saudis. Troops were not allowed to receive rosaries, Stars of David or other religious objects.

Discrimination in Saudi society is pervasive. Women may not marry non-Saudi; they cannot travel alone or without the permission of a male relative; they must wear the black chador; they must study separately from men; and they cannot drive cars. In late 1990, 40 women were arrested and lost their jobs for driving their own cars. Under Islamic law, widowed or divorced women do not retain custody of children older than seven. Men may divorce women by repudiation, but not vice-versa. Non-Saudi female domestics are subject to sexual abuse by their patrons.

Royal family members occupy most important government posts and can evade legal regulations. Social mobility for Shiites is limited. Expatriate workers, with some exceptions cannot be accompanied or easily visited by family. Saudi officials refused to renew Yemeni work permits on account of Yemen's sympathy to Iraq. Amnesty International reported the arrest and torture of large numbers of Yemeni nationals.

Saudi Arabia prohibits labor unions, strikes and collective bargaining. There is no minimum age for child labor.

Senegal

Polity: Dominant party
Economy: Mixed capitalist
Population: 7,500,000
PPP: $1,250
Life Expectancy: 48.3
Ethnic Groups: Diola, Fulani, Malinke, Moor, Serer, Tukulor, Wolof, other

Political Rights: 4
Civil Liberties: 3
Status: Partly Free

Overview:

The coastal West African republic of Senegal, independent from France since 1960, has one of the continent's liveliest (if not always the most competitive) multi-party systems and is firmly under civilian control. Legislative elections are held every five years, with presidential elections to be held every seven years under a recent constitutional amendment. The broad-based Socialist Party (PS) established by Leopold Senghor, the country's renowned poet and first president, continues to dominate political life, with strong intra-party factionalism. Senghor, who led the country from independence until his retirement in 1980, was succeeded by his prime minister, Abdou Diouf, as president and head of the PS. Elections have consistently given the PS large majorities, but these contests have historically sparked opposition charges of fraud, episodes of unrest, and high voting abstention rates. This was particularly the case in the 1988 elections.

Despite new electoral laws passed in 1989, undemocratic electoral practices persist which fuel the charges of fraud. Examples of such practices include the absence of a national electoral commission to oversee elections and impartially process complaints and the lack of private polling booths. Because voters are not required to show identification cards at polling places, repeat voting is common in rural areas. In January 1991, however, the government announced that it intended to draw up a voters' register and provide identity cards before elections in February 1993.

Among the sixteen opposition parties, two are currently a part of the government coalition: the liberal Senegalese Democratic Party (PDS) and the leftist Independence and Labor Party (PIT). Remaining in the opposition are the Revolutionary Movement for a New Democracy and some associated minor parties of the Left, as well as a number of other small parties. Nine of the parties had joined together as the National Conference of Opposition Party Leaders (COMACPO), calling for a sovereign national conference, a new constitution, and a transition government prior to new elections. Asserting that multi-party democracy was already a *fait accompli* in Senegal, the government dismissed talk of a "transition" leading to early elections.

The leadership of the PS, as well as that of the PDS and PIT surprised their respective memberships and other political players in Senegal when they announced that leaders of the two latter parties would shed their association with COMACPO and join the government in the capacity of ministers. This was the first government in post-independence Senegal to include members of parties other than the PS. Abdoulaye Wade of the PDS, who had long denied legitimacy to the Diouf government, joined the national unity government as Minister of State. Prior to his switch, he had led the opposition boycott of the 1990 municipal elections, consistently charging that he had lost the 1988 presidential election because of fraud. Some domestic commentators said that the lack of intra-party consultation with the grassroots prior to formation of the new administration showed that the participating parties were merely vehicles for their respective leaderships. The government also appointed Habib Thiam to the newly re-established post of prime minister.

The separatist rebellion in the fertile southern Casamance province continued in 1991. Armed attacks by the Casamance Democratic Forces Movement (MFDC) on military and security forces have led to a high-profile counter-insurgency campaign. Thousands of citizens from the region, which has a population of some 400,000, have reportedly fled to neighboring Guinea-Bissau and the Gambia in the face of military repression that has included torture, extrajudicial executions, beatings, and indefinite detentions of guerrillas and anyone suspected of having separatist sympathies. The MFDC was formed in 1982 after a Christmas day confrontation with the police in which the Senegalese flag was burned.

Other groups are also believed to be involved in guerrilla activity, since a number of attacks have been against civilians, which is not said to be characteristic of the MFDC. The MFDC itself is largely made up of members of the Diola tribe, which forms a majority in the Casamance region. The Diolas are mostly Catholic, although Catholics make up only five percent of the Senegalese population. The Diola are said to resent the dominance in national political life of the northern Wolof elite, who are generally Muslim.

The administration in Dakar announced in May 1991 that it had entered into a cease-fire accord and dialogue with representatives of the MFDC. The truce was soon breached by armed bandit gangs preying on civilians, as well as members of separatist factions which had not entered into agreement with the government. The truce had been preceded by the release of separatist detainees and Dakar's decision to end the prosecution of those with separatist sentiments. In the last quarter of the year, the government and the MFDC agreed to form a peace commission to implement the May accord. According to the accord, the insurgents are to turn over arms to Guinea-Bissau officials and the government is to withdraw its security forces from Casamance.

In the past, Senegalese officials have accused Mauritania of supplying logistical support to the rebellion. Senegal and Mauritania have fought sporadic border skirmishes since April 1989 and Mauritania has expelled both native-born non-Moorish Mauritanians and resident Senegalese. In 1991, however, tensions appeared to be easing between the two countries as they have resumed diplomatic relations.

Senegalese armed forces participated in the American-led coalition fighting Iraq in the Persian Gulf War. Senegal also sent troops to join the ECOMOG peace-keeping effort in Liberia in late October.

Political Rights and Civil Liberties:

Although the country has a multi-party system and the political opposition is quite vocal, the ruling Socialist Party (PS) has never faced a serious challenge to its hold over Senegalese political life. The opposition has repeatedly charged that elections are not fair. The press is diverse and free. However, radio and television are government-controlled and tend to favor the PS in their coverage.

Though public demonstrations require government authorization, freedom of assembly is generally respected. Unionized workers, a small percentage of the work force, are politically important. The leadership of the largest labor organization, the National Confederation of Senegalese Workers (CNTS), coordinates with government policy.

Criminal suspects have been reportedly abused by the police in the past, and there have been confirmed reports of army torture and extrajudicial executions of suspected separatists in Casamance. Arbitrary arrest is, however, formally prohibited by law. The judiciary is considered independent, despite allegations of sensitivity to government pressure.

Senegalese have complete freedom of religion; Islamic law does not apply except by consent, and discrimination based on religion does not normally occur. Citizens are largely free to travel within and outside the country and are free to emigrate.

Seychelles

Polity: One-party
Economy: Mixed-statist
Population: 100,000
PPP: na
Life Expectancy: 70.0
Ethnic Groups: Mixed African, South Asian, European

Political Rights: 6
Civil Liberties: 6
Status: Not Free

Overview:

This archipelago of 115 islands situated in the Indian Ocean east of Tanzania remained a one-party state in 1991, dominated by President France Albert Rene's Seychelles People's Progressive Front (SPPF).

The country gained independence from the British in 1976. Prime Minister Rene installed himself as head-of-state after overthrowing President Sir James Mancham in 1977 and declared the SPPF the only legal party in June 1978. Only SPPF-approved candidates stood for the 25 seats in 1987 National Assembly elections. As president, Rene was re-elected to a third five-year term in June 1989, once again without facing an opponent. In 1991 the SPPF and the state became more intertwined when the regime transformed local Party sections into branches of local government. In these new district councils (DCs), eligibility for positions is also limited to SPPF-approved Party members. Eligible candidates compete for the six seats in each DC, and chairmen automatically become members of the National Assembly.

Despite a system structured to minimize the participation of non-Party members in the country's political life, many attendees at the SPPF Party Congress in 1991 called for the next congress to organize an internationally-supervised referendum on multi-partyism. President Rene has stated his preference for one-party rule. Addressing the Congress, the president asserted that because Seychellois socialism was unique, there was no need to abandon it simply because other countries are abandoning their forms of socialism. Nevertheless, Rene said that the question of the referendum would be taken up some time after DCs were chosen by voters in the last quarter of 1991.

Political opposition to the regime has been fragmented until recently due to disagreement over opposition leadership. Among the most prominent opponents are Dr. Maxime Ferrari, founder of the Rally of the People of Seychelles for Democracy; David Joubert, leader of the Seychelles Democratic Party; Edmond Camille, head of the Seychelles National Movement; and former Seychellois President Mancham, leader of the Crusade for Democracy. Since all opposition groups are illegal on the islands, those which exist operate either clandestinely or outside the country. Meeting in Europe in July 1991, opposition representatives formed the United Democratic Movement opposition front to press for democratization.

Despite opposition charges of economic mismanagement and corruption, there is little poverty on these naturally endowed islands. Per capita income exceeds $2,000 and there is free health care and education as well as a public housing program. Tourism is a major industry, though the government has sought to preserve the natural beauty of the islands by allowing only 100,000 visitors per annum. With the help of the United Nations and the World Bank, the government has drawn up a $600 million environmental management plan which it hopes donor countries will finance.

Political Rights and Civil Liberties: Citizens of the Seychelles cannot change their government democratically. The socialist Seychelles People's Progressive Front is the only legal political party. Freedoms of expression, assembly and association for those opposed to the regime are severely restricted. A pamphleteer distributing anti-regime tracts in 1991 was arrested and detained. Nonpolitical groups can exist, but must be registered with the government. Civil and criminal cases are adjudicated fairly, but the executive has special judicial powers in political cases. Under security provisions, persons can be detained indefinitely and incommunicado without charge or trial. The government says there are no political prisoners, but the Public Security Act of 1981 allows the president to indefinitely detain people on security grounds and serves to intimidate dissidents. The state and SPPF control all media and laws provide for jail sentences for anyone accused of oral or written criticism of the regime or its policies.

Freedom of religion is respected. There are no restrictions on internal travel, but there are restrictions on citizens travelling abroad. The National Worker's Union (NWU) is the only union authorized by the government and is controlled by the state and party. Strikes are permitted by law, but other regulations inhibit workers from exercising that right.

Sierra Leone

Polity: One-party transitional
Economy: Capitalist
Population: 4,300,000
PPP: $1,030
Life Expectancy: 42.0
Ethnic Groups: Temne (30 percent), Mende (30 percent), Krio (2 percent), other including Bulom, Limba, and Sherbro

Political Rights: 6
Civil Liberties: 5
Status: Partly Free

Overview: The two major developments in 1991 in the Republic of Sierra Leone were the official decision to move toward multi-partyism after thirteen years of official one-party rule, and the violent conflict in the eastern portion of the country.

In August 1990, a constitutional review committee was appointed by President

Joseph Momoh to study the much-criticized 1978 constitution. The constitution enshrined the All People's Congress (APC) as the sole legal party in the country. The APC came to power in 1967 when it defeated the Sierra Leone People's Party (SLPP) in the general elections. The SLPP never won another general election and, in 1978, former President Siaka Stevens declared Sierra Leone to be a one-party state.

President Momoh, Stevens' anointed successor, made it clear as late as 1990 that he opposed a multi-party system, asserting that it would only spell doom for the country. His creation of the constitutional review committee was preceded by press reports of voter-registration irregularities and a public chorus of demands led by university students for a switch to multi-partyism. Demands for multi-partyism arose out of growing popular dissatisfaction both with the APC and the deteriorating state of the economy.

In March 1991 the constitutional review commission released recommendations including the adoption of a multi-party system. Although national elections were held in May under the one-party constitution, the government endorsed the switch to multi-partyism on 23 May. Other notable recommendations by the constitutional review commission that were accepted by the government included the prohibition of parties associated with a particular ethnic group, elimination of the president's power to appoint members of Parliament, and the limitation of a president's tenure in office to two terms of five years each. The government rejected recommendations which called for creation of a bicameral legislature and the necessity of obtaining parliamentary consent to presidential judicial appointments. Parliament approved a draft multi-party constitution in July and it was approved by national referendum in August.

Meanwhile, in the face of evidence of a long-term and systematic voter-registration fraud, there was increased public pressure for a re-registration of voters before national multi-party elections. Other opposition leaders called for a transitional government and international observers to oversee the elections.

The civil war in Liberia spilled over into Sierra Leone with an initial incursion in late March by armed forces of Charles Taylor's National Patriotic Front of Liberia (NPFL). With the assistance of Guinean and Nigerian troops, Sierra Leonean troops were eventually able to contain the invasion in the eastern portion of the country. By the end of 1991, all but a few territorial gains of the attackers had apparently been reversed. A central controversy was over whether the attackers were in fact primarily or solely invaders from Taylor's NPFL, as the Momoh government, or from an indigenous Sierra Leonean force of insurgents. The native Sierra Leone Revolutionary United Front (RUF) declared itself to be responsible for the attacks, stating that its intention was to overthrow Momoh. Taylor likened Momoh's position to that of Liberian ex-dictator Samuel Doe, allegedly refusing to come to terms with a "people's revolution" until it was too late.

Political Rights and Civil Liberties:

Citizens of Sierra Leone have not yet been given the opportunity to change their government democratically. However, the government legalized opposition parties and adopted a democratic constitution in 1991. Even after official approval of multi-partyism, however, opposition party supporters have been harassed by local authorities for openly displaying their party affiliation and expressing disaffection with the ruling APC.

The judiciary is generally free from executive interference, and local chiefs administer customary law. In 1991, however, Sierra Leonean authorities indefinitely imprisoned the wife and children of the leader of the insurgent RUF, Foday Saybana Sankoh, though they were apparently guilty of nothing illegal.

Numerous independent newspapers and journals print diverse views, but are subject to arbitrary government censorship and harassment. Journalists have been imprisoned and reportedly personally threatened by the Ministry of Information. Public meetings require government approval. Freedom of religion is respected. There are some restrictions on domestic travel, but foreign travel is generally permitted. Trade unionism is an integral part of society, and workers have the right to strike. Most unions belong to the Sierra Leone Labor Congress (SLLC).

Singapore

Polity: Dominant party
Economy: Mixed capitalist
Population: 2,800,000
PPP: $10,540
Life Expectancy: 74.0
Ethnic Groups: Ethnic Chinese (76 percent), Malay (15 percent), Pakistani and Indian (7 percent)

Political Rights: 4
Civil Liberties: 4
Status: Partly Free

Overview:

In August 1991 parliamentary elections, the ruling People's Action Party (PAP) had its worst showing since 1968. Nevertheless, the PAP only lost three seats and retained its near-monopoly control of parliament.

Goh Chok Tong became prime minister in November 1990, replacing the venerable Lee Kuan Yew. Lee had ruled Singapore for 31 years before retiring in 1990 and remains head of the PAP. He guided the tiny island-nation from its status as a self-governing colony within the British Commonwealth in 1959, through its break with the Malaysian Federation in 1965 which brought Singapore formal independence, to its brilliant economic rise of the 1970s and 1980s. The PAP has been at the forefront of the country's rapid industrialization through its rigid control of politics, education, and cultural norms.

During his first nine months in office, Goh sought to offer an alternative to Lee's paternalistic, authoritarian leadership style. Calling for a more consultative government, the prime minister frequently discussed politics face to face with citizens during weekend walkabouts. However, critics charged that Goh had, in effect, done little more than ease some forms of censorship, most notably on pornographic films. Significantly, no effort was made to repeal the Internal Security Act (ISA), which the government has used to detain political prisoners for years without trial under the pretext of national safety.

Seeking a popular mandate for his more open style, and riding the tail end of an economic boom which saw 7 percent growth in the second quarter, on 14 August Goh called for a snap election on 31 August. Workers Party leader J.B. Jeyaretnam claimed the election was being held before November to prevent him from running. The former opposition MP had been convicted in a controversial 1986 court case of irregularities in collecting party funds and barred from office until November 1991.

His victory in a 1981 by-election had broken a fifteen year PAP monopoly in parliament.

By the 21 August filing deadline, opposition parties had fielded candidates for only 40 seats in the 81 seat unicameral parliament, thus clinching a victory for the PAP before the elections were even held. However, since the PAP held all but one of the seats going into the election, Goh clearly needed an overwhelming victory to get his popular mandate. By his own admission, he would need slightly more than the 63.2 percent share of the popular vote which his party received in the 1988 election. Meanwhile, Chiam See Tong, secretary-general of the Singapore Democratic Party (SDP) and the lone elected opposition MP in parliament, said that his party would treat the vote as a by-election, allowing anxious voters to give Goh his mandate while the SDP would hope to pick up a few seats.

The final tally showed the PAP winning 77 seats with 61 percent of the votes cast, its worst showing since 1968. The SDP won three seats and the Worker's Party won one. Days later, Goh said a tiny country like Singapore did not need political opposition or confrontational politics, which would "divide the country." The PAP later admitted its policies had not focused enough on low-income, Chinese-speaking citizens.

Mid-summer changes to the electoral law may have prevented the opposition from winning even more seats. The government increased the number of Group Representation Constituencies (GRC) from thirteen to fifteen, and increased the number of seats in each GRC from three to four. Opposition parties often have trouble contesting GRCs since one of the seats must be filled by a minority candidate, and they often have trouble finding credible minority candidates.

Also influencing the political situation was the January parliamentary decision to adopt an elected presidency with expanded powers. Under the existing system, the president, currently Wee Kim Wee, is nominated by the parliament and performs largely ceremonial duties. The new office will have power to veto parliamentary decisions regarding Singapore's financial reserves and top civil service and judiciary appointments. Presidential candidates will be screened by a three-person panel of which two members will be government appointees. Candidates for the office must be at least 45 years old, have sufficient financial management skills, and may be be rejected by the committee on the basis of poor or improper character, a clause that opposition leaders fear will be used to bar them from office. Although former Prime Minister Lee told the BBC in an August 1991 interview that he will not seek the expanded presidency, many Singaporeans feel that either he or his son, Lee Hsien Song, will contest the presidential election in 1993.

Political Rights and Civil Liberties:

Citizens of Singapore nominally have the right to change their government, although the ruling People's Action Party has utilized various mechanisms for maintaining its virtual political monopoly. The PAP infuses society with its values and policies through the media, public advertising campaigns, labor associations, local organizations and the military, even though organized political activities within non-political organizations are prohibited. The Internal Security Act (ISA) allows the government to indefinitely detain people deemed to pose a threat to national security, and has often been used to jail opposition figures. Those held under the ISA are not entitled to a public trial, and judicial review in such cases is limited to procedural matters. Subordinate court judges can be transferred to other government positions, and higher judges are closely aligned with the government. In 1990 former Prime Minister Lee Kuan Yew asked Singapore's lawyers to consider the needs of society before those of individuals, and in recent years several lawyers who championed opposition or human rights causes have been detained under the ISA.

The constitution provides for freedom of speech and of press, although in practice these rights are curtailed. The state-owned Singapore Broadcasting Corporation runs all electronic media and only disseminates the PAP's views. While the country's newspapers print articles from foreign sources, their editorials cannot deviate from the government line. In 1991 the government lifted a circulation limit on the Hong Kong-based *Asiaweek* magazine which had been imposed in 1987, after the magazine printed articles allegedly interfering with Singapore's politics. Former Prime Minister Lee Kuan Yew settled a longstanding legal dispute with the Dow Jones Company in 1991, and in October the government allowed the *Asian Wall Street Journal* to circulate on a limited basis. However, the ban on the Dow Jones's *Far Eastern Economic Review* remained in effect. In November the government ordered *Woman's Affairs* magazine to stop publishing after it printed an article critical of PAP female MPs. Public educational institutions have refused tenure to professors who criticize the PAP's policies. The government formed a committee in 1991 to consider relaxing certain censorship laws, particularly those relating to the arts. Restrictions on certain forms of censorship such as pornographic movies were relaxed but then partially restored in 1991 after the election. Freedom of association is limited by the Societies Act, which requires any organization of more than ten people to be registered with the government. The Act gives the government wide discretion in banning groups. Public assemblies of more than five people require police permission.

The constitution guarantees freedom of religion, and while this is generally respected, the government has used the Societies Act to ban or restrict some religious sects. The Maintenance of Religious Harmony Act of 1990 prohibits religious proselytizing when it would create tensions between religious groups and limits the right of religious groups to engage in political activities. Singaporeans have the freedom to travel both internally and abroad, although citizens over the age of thirteen must carry an identification card, and the government has denied passports and restricted internal travel for some dissidents under the ISA. Chia Thye Poh, a former MP who was detained for 23 years under the ISA, lives on an adjacent island and can only visit Singapore proper during daylight hours. A group of aging left-wing activists were allowed to return to Singapore in 1991 after being barred since the 1960s. Younger exiles have not been permitted to return. Workers have the right to bargain collectively and strikes are legal. Nearly all unionized workers are affiliated with the umbrella National Trade Union Congress, which is ideologically aligned with the government.

Solomon Islands

Polity: Parliamentary democracy
Economy: Capitalist
Population: 300,000
PPP: $2,540
Life Expectancy: 69.5
Ethnic Groups: Melanesian (93 percent), small Polynesian, Micronesian and European minorities

Political Rights: 1
Civil Liberties: 1
Status: Free

Overview:

A collection of ten large islands and four groups of smaller islands in the Western Pacific Ocean, the Solomon Islands has been an independent member of the British Commonwealth since 1978. The 38-seat unicameral parliament is elected by universal suffrage for a term of up to four years. Solomon Mamaloni has been prime minister since March 1989, a month after his People's Alliance Party won an 11-seat plurality to form the country's first one-party government. Other parties taking seats were the Nationalist Front for Progress with 5, the Liberal Party with 4, the United party with 3, and the Labor Party with 2 seats. Thirteen seats went to independents. Accused by opposition leader Andrew Nori, as well as by some PAP members, of ruling in a non-consultative fashion, Mamaloni resigned from the PAP in October 1990, remaining as prime minister to form a government of "national unity." His new cabinet featured four opposition members and a PAP backbencher, while seven Alliance members shifted to what is currently a sixteen-member opposition.

In November 1991 Joses Tuhanuku replaced Nori as the leader of the opposition, and called for Mamaloni's resignation in an 8 November article in the *Solomon Star,* because of his failure to deal with a slumping economy. The same day, the Solomon Islands Council of Trade Unions also called for Mamaloni's resignation and a repeal of the pay raises given appointed officials earlier in the year. Meanwhile, economic indicators continued to plummet. In October, foreign reserves dropped from $13.6 million to $9.2 million. The government surpassed the $21.4 million borrowing limit it has with the Central Bank of Solomon Islands. Opposition leaders said the government would be headed for "financial disaster" if it borrowed from commercial banks. To cut costs, the government cancelled all overseas trips in December by government officials and cut back on overtime for non-essential workers.

Political Rights and Civil Liberties:

Citizens of the Solomon Islands can change their government democratically. Party affiliations tend to be based on personal loyalties rather than ideology. In August 1991 Prime Minister Solomon Mamaloni called for the country to leave the British Commonwealth and draw up a new constitution, calling the old one "lousy and very inadequate." The judiciary is independent of the government and provides procedural protection for the accused. Freedoms of speech and press are respected in practice. The country has two private weekly newspapers and several government publications. State radio provides diverse viewpoints. The country does not have a television broadcast system, and the government controls the use of satellite dishes because it feels that outside programming containing sex and violence could have a negative effect on the population. Permits are required for demonstrations but they have never been denied on political grounds. Christianity is the established religion, but there are no restrictions on other groups. Citizens may travel freely inside the country or abroad. The Trade Disputes Act of 1981 provides for collective bargaining, but only private sector workers can strike. However, public school teachers did successfully strike in 1989.

Somalia

Polity: Military
Economy: Mixed-statist
Population: 7,700,000
PPP: $1,330
Life Expectancy: 46.1
Ethnic Groups: Somali (Hawiye, Darod, Isaaq, Isa, other), Gosha, Bajun.

Political Rights: 7
Civil Liberties: 7
Status: Not Free

Overview:

As 1991 ended, rebel forces continued a bloody, prolonged assault on the Somalian government holed up in a section of the capital city of Mogadishu. With the fall of the 22-year dictatorship of Siad Barre, the country faced widespread disorder, tribal conflict and a breakdown in national unity.

After being dislodged from the capital by the insurgent United Somali Congress (USC) of the Hawiye clan, remnants of the Siad Barre regime fled in late January 1991 to its traditional Marehan stronghold near the Kenyan border. The Marehan are a sub-clan of the Darod clan, which is one of the six clan families all Somalis trace their lineage through. During the rest of the year, various ethnic Somali clans and sub-clans forcefully struggled to expand their enclaves. Northern Somalia declared its independence from the rest of the country as the "Republic of Somaliland" in May. In December the guerrilla forces of one USC faction sought to overthrow Ali Mahdi Mohamed, transitional Somalian president and chief of another USC faction.

Upon winning independence in 1960, British Somaliland and Italian Somaliland merged to form Somalia. Major General Siad Barre seized power in a bloodless coup in 1969. Over the years, his rule devolved into a repressive and dynastic form of crypto-Marxism which strongly favored his own minority sub-clan, alienating majority clans and fueling several clan-based insurgencies.

Three principal armed movements, all founded in rebellion against the Siad Barre regime, currently operate in separate parts of Somalia. Operating in the north is the Somali National Movement (SNM), composed mainly of members of the Isaaq clan. Formed in 1981, the SNM did not substantively intensify its insurgency efforts until after April 1988. In its attempt to stifle rebellion in the north, Siad Barre's army devastated much of the region. Operating in the far south since 1989 is the Somali Patriotic Movement (SPM), largely composed of Ogadenis and others of the larger Darod clan. The United Somali Congress (USC), which was formed in 1989 and ousted Siad Barre and his troops from the capital city, finds support among the Hawiye clan of central Somalia.

In 1990 Siad Barre called for a referendum to determine whether Somalis wanted a constitutionally guaranteed multi-party system. The armed oppositions characterized the proposal as a hoax designed to buy the hard-pressed regime time. They pointed out that Siad Barre, whom they ridiculed as the "mayor of Mogadishu," could only conduct a vote in the limited area still under government control and asserted that they would rather work toward the regime's overthrow than agree to any referendum. Until he fled the capital in January 1991, Siad Barre, who had been elected for a seven-year term in 1986 running unopposed, refused to heed calls that he step aside before his latest term of office ended.

From the moment the guerrillas of the USC first attacked Mogadishu in early December 1990 until Siad Barre and his coterie fled the city, the situation was virtually anarchic. Government troops, armed insurgents and mere bandits all partici-pated in an orgy of wild gunfire, killing and looting, which led to widespread destruction in the capital. Law enforcement officials were unable to maintain control and contributed to the breakdown of law and order by indiscriminately pouring mortar fire down upon neighborhoods of the city controlled by the USC. Two-thirds of Mogadishu's inhabitants fled. The city was littered with the dead bodies and was without water and electricity and short of food and medicine.

Within a few days of Siad Barre's flight, the USC appointed Ali Mahdi Mohamed, a Hawiye businessman and former member of parliament, as "interim" Somalian president. Mahdi Mohamed named Umar Arteh Ghalib, a respected former foreign minister and an Isaaq, to his caretaker administration as interim prime minister. The USC announced that these appointments were temporary until a broad-based democratic government of national unity was formed. A national conference of reconciliation was called for late February to allow all clans and insurgent movements to discuss the outlines of such a future government. Some USC leaders, however, reportedly claimed the national presidency for their own organization.

The SMN immediately denounced the USC's creation of a caretaker government without consultation with other armed groups as premature and unacceptable. The SMN refused to participate in the February conference or any other subsequent multi-lateral gathering. It moved to organize an independent administration in the area of northern Somalia under its control. In May 1991 the SMN unilaterally abrogated the 1960 act of union which had united the British and Italian portions of colonized Somaliland by declaring a new and independent "Republic of Somaliland" which incorporated the territory of the former British colony.

The response of the new USC government in Mogadishu was moderate, calling for talks with the SMN on the subjects of reconciliation and regional autonomy within a united Somalia and asserting that it would not use force in reunifying Somalia. The response from Hargeysa, the "capital" of Somaliland, was that the Republic of Somaliland was a *fait accompli,* and that any relations between it and the administration in Mogadishu would henceforth be on a state-to-state basis. The SNM has promised a democratic constitution and multi-party elections in its Somaliland within two years, and its territory remained peaceful in 1991, even while what remains of Somalia has suffered continuing turmoil. However, the Organization of African Unity has reiterated that it stands opposed as a matter of policy to the secession of portions of established countries in Africa.

The government of Djibouti hosted two all-party conferences of reconciliation in its capital in June and July for the armed movements in Somalia/Somaliland. The SNM boycotted both. Ali Mahdi Mohamed was confirmed at the July conference as transitional president for two years. A cease-fire was also formally agreed to, but was observed only sporadically. General Mohamed Farah Aidid, whose USC troops ousted

Siad Barre from Mogadishu in January, was elected chairman of his movement at mid-year.

In September, the rival USC forces of the president and General Aidid clashed in heavy fighting in the capital. In the naked power struggle, Aidid demanded Ali Mahdi's resignation as interim president. As each man was from a separate sub-clan of the Hawiye, most saw it as simply the latest manifestation of long-traditional feuds. An uneasy peace prevailed for a few months but fighting broke out again in late November between the two USC factions. Gunfire ripped through Mogadishu, with mortars devastating civilian dwellings and snipers indiscriminately killing noncombatants. The level of violence was so high that the United Nations agency charged with relief services finally refused to jeopardize the lives of its personnel to provide emergency food or medical assistance for those in the city.

Political Rights and Civil Liberties: The Somalian people cannot change their government democratically. Since fighting first broke out in 1988 between the former Siad Barre government and the northern SNM, over 85,000 combatants and civilians have been killed. Thousands have been either dislocated within Somalia or forced to flee into Kenya, Ethiopia and Djibouti. The mainly Isaaq SNM has been accused of killing the less numerous Isas, whose traditional base is close to the Djibouti border, as well as Somali refugees of the Ogadeni clan from Ethiopia. Meanwhile, Hawiye and Darod militiamen have subjected each other and civilians to summary execution during 1991 for being associated with another clan.

Within areas under their control, the various armed movements prohibit dissent against their rule. The USC, SNM and SPN control the media in areas they control. The Republic of Somaliland has declared that Islamic shari'a law will form the basis of its jurisprudence.

South Africa

Polity: Presidential-legislative democracy (whites only) transitional
Economy: Capitalist-statist
Population: 40,600,000
PPP: $5,480
Life Expectancy: 61.7
Ethnic Groups: Black (Xhosa, Zulu, Sotho, Lovedu, other; 69 percent), white (Afrikaner, English; 18 percent), coloured (10 percent), Indian (3 percent)

Political Rights: 5
Civil Liberties: 4
Status: Partly Free

Overview: Despite continuing black-on-black violence, 1991 ended on a hopeful note: the opening round of negotiations at the "Convention for a Democratic South Africa" (Codesa) in December produced progress towards a new, non-racial regime by the end of 1992. In 1991 the government repealed discriminatory laws considered the "pillars of apartheid," prompting several nations to end sanctions against South Africa.

The Union of South Africa became a self-governing dominion within the British

Empire in 1910 and a republic outside the British Commonwealth in 1961. This mineral-rich, highly industrialized nation is ruled by a white minority under the system of apartheid which disenfranchises the country's black majority. It remains a *de facto* segregated society despite recent dismantling of laws which required separate development of the races. A third of blacks, and most mix-raced Coloureds and Asians, live in racially segregated areas in and near large cities. Some 10 million blacks live in ten so-called tribal homelands.

Black-on-black violence continued in 1991, usually pitting supporters of the Zulu-based Inkatha movement led by Chief Mangosuthu Buthelezi against partisans of the African National Congress (ANC), mostly young 'comrades' of the Xhosa ethnic group. Since the fighting flared in 1984, the ANC has alleged that the South African police and security forces were instigating and abetting Inkatha attacks. The government denied the intervention of this so-called "third force" in the violence. The ANC has demanded that Zulu spears and fighting sticks be barred from political rallies to curb factional fighting, while Inkatha has rejected the demand on the basis that the weapons are a necessary expression of an individual's ethnic identity. The fighting, which has taken an estimated 12,000 lives, intensified in early 1991 and led to the first meeting between Buthelezi and the ANC's Nelson Mandela since Mandela's release from prison in February 1990. The 29 January meeting resulted in a joint call for peace and an agreement to take concrete steps to defuse hostility at the local level.

But massacres and pitched battles continued and thousands fled urban townships and rural settlements torn by the conflict. A peace accord was reached by Mandela and South African President F.W. de Klerk on 10 May after the ANC threatened to boycott further negotiations on an all-party conference unless the government acted to stop violence in black communities. This was preceded in March by another Mandela-Buthelezi meeting, and followed by the signing of a peace accord by the ANC, Inkatha and the government on 14 September. None of the measures were effective in halting the killing, however. President de Klerk formed a commission in October to look into the problem, while Amnesty International reported that an important cause of the violence was revenge attacks by both sides for earlier deaths.

In a related matter, a South African newspaper revealed in July that the security police had in fact been covertly funding Inkatha in order to strengthen its position *vis-á-vis* the ANC. The exposé, which disclosed that funds had been given to run an Inkatha-linked black trade union and to allow Buthelezi's organization to hold rallies, undercut the government's claim of impartiality toward the ANC and Inkatha. Undercut also was a measure of Inkatha's credibility as an independent movement opposed to the apartheid regime. The "Inkathagate" scandal cost two Cabinet Ministers their jobs, and President de Klerk pledged to stop all secret financing of political groups.

Throughout 1991 the ANC continued to insist on the replacement of the de Klerk government with a multi-racial interim government to lead the nation to direct elections. On 8 January the ANC proposed an all-party conference (ultimately to be held in December and attended by representatives of 19 organizations, including the government) which would create a broad framework for South Africa's future political system. As the ANC developed its proposal during the year, it called for the transformation of the conference within eighteen months of its first meeting into a transitional administration having authority over the existing Parliament. This interim government would oversee elections to a constituent assembly, which would draft a new, non-racial constitution replacing the existing document. Parliamentary and presidential elections would follow.

Though rejecting calls that it immediately stand aside in favor of an interim "government by decree", the de Klerk government eventually embraced the all-party conference proposal. For de Klerk's National Party, the conference was a critical means to ensure that all participating political parties would bind themselves to respect minority rights, multi-partyism, and judicial independence before any constituent assembly was convened. The government emphasized that an extended period of power-sharing (ten years or more) among all groups would be key in any new political arrangement, and that it would not bow to a simple majority formula obliterating the power of the white minority.

The conference itself was not convened until December due to intervening crises, such as "Inkathagate", and differences of opinion that hindered negotiations. Some movements on the political fringe rejected the conference from the start. The right-wing, pro-apartheid Conservative Party saw it as the occasion for a sell-out of white interests, and condemned the government's willingness to consider it. The neo-Nazi Afrikaner Resistance Movement rejected any negotiations with non-whites and leftists in pursuit of its demand that an independent white state be carved out of a post-apartheid South Africa.

At the other end of the political spectrum, the radical Azanian People's Organization (Azapo) rejected any conference in which the apartheid regime could avoid simply handing over power to representatives of the black majority. The black-consciousness Pan-Africanist Congress (PAC) attempted to form a "Patriotic Front" with the ANC before the conference convened in December, but the PAC decided at the last moment not to attend. It accused the ANC of colluding with the government and rejected a South African site for the negotiations.

Although the two-day start of the Codesa in December 1991 adjourned without tackling the most substantive issues, it was a confidence-building session that appeared to set a tone of mutual accommodation for the more difficult sessions to be held in 1992. Working groups were formed to discuss the thorniest issues of contention between the parties, and to present their findings to the conference within three months. The specifics and compromises on transitional administrations, referenda, and constituent assemblies are to be negotiated in the coming year.

The South African Communist Party (SACP), legalized in February 1990, has been a vocal critic of apartheid and is still closely linked to the ANC. In 1991 the SACP reiterated its goal of a Marxist-Leninist South Africa even while nervous spokesmen of the ANC attempted to publicly distinguish their organization's own objectives.

One of the economic issues which held center stage in 1991 was the lifting of sanctions, despite ANC protests, by the governments of most industrialized countries including the U.S. There was continued controversy over the ANC's history of anti-capitalism; the organization softened its advocacy of nationalizing much of the South African economy.

Political Rights and Civil Liberties:

Only minority white South Africans have the power to democratically change the government. Blacks do not yet have the vote, but the government continued negotiations aimed at drafting a democratic constitution and power-sharing for a future, non-racial society.

The judiciary is independent of the executive, and most civil and criminal cases are handled fairly. In the most celebrated criminal prosecution of 1991, Winnie

Mandela was found guilty and sentenced to six years in prison for kidnapping and being an accessory to the assault of four young men. Despite strong evidence against her, supporters charged that the trial amounted to harassment of the ANC.

Although over 1,000 political prisoners have been released since 1990 by the government, critics charge that the same number remain in detention, a claim the regime disputes. An internal security law allows people to be indefinitely detained without trial for purposes of interrogation. A Supreme Court judge issued a finding in January 1991 that security police organized "death squads" which murdered anti-regime activists with government knowledge. Allegations of human rights abuses in ANC-controlled refugee camps located in the "Frontline States" surrounding South Africa continued in 1991, with public charges by victims in August that the ANC's "Imbokodo" security forces were responsible for repeated cases of torture, illegal detention and the disappearance of up to 500 dissidents in the host countries.

The first group of exiles repatriated to South Africa by the U.N. arrived in mid-December 1991. Of the estimated 25,000 to be brought home under the auspices of the High Commissioner for Refugees, 750 were expected to arrive by the end of 1991. They were allowed back into the country after selectively being granted amnesties by the Pretoria regime, which rejected the ANC's call for a blanket amnesty.

In June 1991 the white-dominated Parliament repealed most of the discriminatory laws long considered the "pillars of apartheid." Significant laws repealed included: the Group Areas Act, which segregated housing; the Land Acts, which limited the property non-whites could own to 13 percent of the national territory; and the Population Registration Act, which required that all South Africans be classified and registered by race at birth.

Although the government no longer strictly controls the movement of blacks and other non-whites, pervasive poverty still limits residential opportunities for the vast majority of South Africans and results in *de facto* segregation. The government has no plans to offer reparations or restoration of seized property to the 3.5 million non-whites dispossessed from their lands and residences by apartheid laws.

Those South Africans already classified by race will continue with the same status, at least until a new constitution is approved. The government introduced a proposed law in mid-November 1991 which would give everyone over 18 with an identity card the right to vote in a referendum on a new constitution. Blacks will not be able to vote in elections before the constitutional referendum is presented to the electorate.

The educational system remains largely segregated. However, the government has provided that if 72 percent of white parents at a school vote for integration, their school can be integrated. More than 200 of South Africa's 2,000 white schools have decided to integrate.

Freedom of assembly was expanded in 1991 when a restrictive law limiting opposition meetings was not renewed. Direct censorship and restrictions on reporting unrest have ended, but freedom of the press is limited by regulations giving police powers to bar reporters from covering street clashes. Black journalists working for the dozens of independent black publications face severe intimidation by militants from Inkatha and the ANC.

Legalized in 1979, black trade unions play an increasingly important role in political, social, and economic life. The two main black labor federations are the pro-ANC Council of South African Trade Unions (COSATU) and the National Council of Trade Unions (NACTU).

Spain

Polity: Parliamentary democracy
Economy: Capitalist
Population: 33,846,500
PPP: $8,250
Life Expectancy: 77.0
Ethnic Groups: Spanish (Castilian, Valencian, Andalusian, Asturian, 72.8 percent), Catalan (16.4 percent), Galician (8.2 percent), Basque (2.3 percent), Gypsy

Political Rights: 1
Civil Liberties: 1
Status: Free

Overview:

Major developments in Spain in 1991 included a feud within the governing Socialist Workers Party (PSOE); conservative, leftist, and regionalist gains in local and regional elections; Spanish assistance to the anti-Iraq coalition; the country's increasing involvement in the European Community; a surge in regionalist and separatist sentiment; a police scandal; and an anti-Gypsy boycott in the schools.

Spain is a constitutional monarchy which has had democratic government since 1977. The country returned to monarchy in 1975 following four decades of right-wing dictatorship by Generalissimo Francisco Franco and a brief transitional government headed by Adolfo Suarez, a moderate conservative. King Juan Carlos, the largely ceremonial head of state, used his personal prestige to support the transition to democracy in the 1970s.

The Socialists have been in power nationally since 1982, having won re-election in 1986 and 1989. In the general election in 1989, the Socialists won 176 of the 350 seats in the lower house of parliament. That was just enough for an absolute majority for Prime Minister Felipe Gonzalez. The Communist-led United Left won 17 seats, a gain of 10, while the right-wing Popular Party garnered 106 seats, a gain of one. The balance of the lower house is held by various centrist, regional, and nationalist parties. The government has a four-year mandate. The less powerful upper house, the Senate, has 208 directly elected members who serve for four-year terms. Each province sends four members. Outlying territories send from one to three members each. Spain has seventeen regions with varying degrees of autonomy.

In 1991 the Socialists' radical and technocratic tendencies clashed over policy. Deputy Prime Minister Alfonso Guerra, a supporter of left-of-center policies, resigned in January following allegations that his brother was involved in campaign finance corruption. Gonzalez reshuffled his ministers in March, and selected a government team more in tune with Finance Minister Carlos Solchaga, a moderate technocrat. This development continued the party's recent move toward the center. Damaging the PSOE's image, Solchaga and Guerra feuded over a major housing program during the campaign for local and regional elections. Although the Socialists emerged as the leading party in the elections, the right-wing Popular Party, the United Left, and various regionalist parties made significant gains. The voting practically wiped out the center-right Democratic and Social Center, and Adolfo Suarez resigned as its leader.

In foreign affairs, Spanish bases served as staging areas for the allied bombing of Iraq during the Gulf War. The United Left coalition and some other opposition groups criticized the government for its support of the war. As one of the poorest members of the European Community, Spain benefited from EC subsidies and experienced the consequences of competition from other EC members in 1991. The EC began major investments in the Spanish and Portuguese infrastructures in 1991. The Community hopes that both countries will benefit from such regional economic development projects. At the same time, Spain's traditional sherry industry has been suffering a decline in recent years, due to rival products from elsewhere in Europe. Spanish sherry workers went on strike in September 1991, in order to keep their pension fund in existence. During EC negotiations over eliminating economic barriers, Spain and Britain clashed over Gibraltar, the British colony which borders Spain. Spain wanted Gibraltar excluded from the new European Community border policy on the grounds that it is not part of the EC. Other Community members proposed allowing both Britain and Spain to supervise the Gibraltar border.

Internally, Spain experienced increasingly vocal regionalist demands. Of Spain's seventeen regions, four (Andalucia, the Basque country, Catalonia, and Galicia) have more autonomous rights than the others. In September 1991, the central government began talks with the thirteen other regions about expanding their rights. Catalans, who are concentrated in the northern and eastern parts of Spain, have become increasingly assertive about advancing Catalan as a language distinct from Spanish. Moved by the largely peaceful changes in East Europe, *Terra Lliure*, a Catalan terrorist group, disbanded in July 1991, and its members turned to non-violent means to achieve Catalan independence. In contrast, the terrorist group, Basque Land and Liberty (ETA), remained active in 1991. It carried out bombings of hotels and consulates across Europe. There was a major scandal in 1991 which resulted from unofficial counter-terrorism against Basque separatists. An investigation revealed that elements of the police had formed the Anti-Terrorist Liberation Group (GAL), and had murdered twenty-three Basque nationalists in the 1980s. Prime Minister Gonzalez issued a statement at the trial of the police in which he stated he had "no knowledge of its (GAL's) creation, organization or aim." Despite GAL's activities in the 1980s, Basque terrorists suffered no loss of influence in 1991. With successful bombings, they backed environmentalists' plans to re-route a proposed highway in a border region.

Spain's Gypsy (Rom) minority suffered organized shunning incidents in 1991. In several localities, Spanish parents kept their children out of school to protest the presence of Gypsies in the student body. Many Spaniards associate the Gypsies with the distribution of illegal drugs.

Political Rights and Civil Liberties:

Spanish voters have the right to change their government democratically. Regional cultures have significant autonomy, but Basque separatist terrorism remained a problem in 1991. Basque prisoners have charged the government with mistreatment. Ethnic minorities, especially immigrants, have complained about discrimination, but Spain still lacks a law dealing with racial discrimination.

Under new rules, Spain requires visas for visitors from North Africa; the government punishes employers for hiring illegal aliens; and immigration quotas now favor the groups the state believes are easiest to integrate.

The print media are free and competitive, but the opposition has charged that state television has a pro-government bias. There are two competing labor federations, one traditionally Socialist, the other Communist. They co-operated in a general strike in 1988. The General Union of Workers (UGT) broke its formal ties to the Socialists in late 1990. Enterprise is increasingly free and modern as Spain becomes more closely linked with the more advanced countries of the European Community.

Religious freedom is guaranteed under the 1978 constitution. Roman Catholicism is the majority faith, but there is no state religion. Since the government signed a religious accord in 1990, Protestantism and Judaism have been on par with Roman Catholicism. The agreement recognizes the legitimacy of Protestant and Jewish weddings, allows for Jewish and Protestant religious education in the schools, and mandates the armed forces to respect the rights of these minority faiths to observe their holy days. The Roman Catholic Church still benefits from contributions designated on tax returns. However, as the government's liberal proposals on birth control indicate, the influence of Catholicism on the state has declined sharply since Franco's death. In 1991, the Catholic hierarchy and the government clashed over public distributions of condoms to young people.

Sri Lanka

Polity: Presidential-parliamentary democracy
Economy: Mixed-capitalist statist
Population: 17,400,000
PPP: $2,120
Life Expectancy: 70.9
Ethnic Groups: Sinhalese, (74 percent), Tamil (18 percent), Moor (7 percent), others

Political Rights: 4
Civil Liberties: 5
Status: Partly Free

Overview:

Sri Lanka's civil war between the Sinhalese-dominated government and Tamil separatist forces witnessed its heaviest fighting in the summer of 1991.

The Liberation Tigers of Tamil Eelam (LTTE) have been waging a brutal struggle for an independent homeland in the country's northern and eastern provinces since 1983. The Hindu Tamil minority claims the Buddhist Sinhalese majority discriminates against them in jobs, housing, and education. The battle took on a surprising dimension following the government's May 1987 recapture of the main rebel stronghold on Jaffna Peninsula; India began airlifting humanitarian aid supplies to the Tamils. Facing pressure from the Indian government, Sri Lanka signed a treaty which brought in a peacekeeping force of Indian troops (IPKF), ostensibly to protect Tamils, and merged the country's Tamil-dominated northern province and ethnically-mixed eastern province into a single legislative council. The presence of the IPKF, which eventually mushroomed to 80,000 troops, aroused the ultra-nationalist left-wing Sinhalese Janatha Vimukthi Peramuna (JVP) group, which launched a bloody terrorist campaign against the government in the southern part of the island nation which lasted until 1989.

The LTTE boycotted the 1988 election in the newly merged northeastern province because of Indian support for its rival, the Eelam People's Revolutionary Liberation Front (EPRLF), which won control of the council. Meanwhile, the LTTE temporarily abandoned its war against the government and fought the IPKF to a standstill. In March 1990 the last Indian troops were withdrawn, and the EPRLF leadership withered away, many of them fleeing on departing Indian troop ships. Efforts to prepare for a second round of council elections fell through, and in June 1990 fighting resumed with a series of attacks by the LTTE against the government.

Except for a brief cease-fire at the beginning of the year, the civil war in the north continued nearly unabated in 1991. The government suffered a major loss in a 17 February ambush by the LTTE which killed 44 army soldiers. On 4 March a car bomb killed deputy Defense Minister Ranjan Wijneratne, who had led the government's battle against the rebels. The government announced that over 1,000 soldiers, civilians, and rebels died in war-related incidents in the month ending 21 April. In June, government troops slaughtered in excess of 200 Tamil civilians near the town of Batticaloa after a land mine explosion killed three army soldiers. The government took the unusual step of issuing its condolences and promised that an inquiry would take place.

The heaviest fighting of the eight-year-old civil war occurred in the summer as the government fought to break a rebel siege of the strategic army base at Elephant Pass, which straddles the causeway between the mainland and Jaffna Peninsula. Government forces broke through to the camp on 3 August after a 25 day battle which claimed the lives of over 2,000 rebels and soldiers. Shortly afterwards, the government lifted a curfew in much of the north and east except in the Jaffna and Kilinochchi districts where the rebels were said to be regrouping.

Prospects for peace rose and fell after the Elephant Pass battle. On 22 August, the government appointed Mangala Moonesinghe of the opposition Freedom Party to chair a committee charged with recommending a peaceful political settlement of the conflict. However, the LTTE launched another of its frequent attacks on Muslims, whom they accuse of supporting the government. On 19 September, the LTTE killed eleven sleeping Muslims in the town of Palliyagodella. In late September, LTTE leader Vellupillai Prabhakaran invited government tourism minister Sauumiamoorthy Thondarman, a Tamil, to Jaffna for negotiations. But in November, the government began a heavy aerial attack on several rebel targets, and by year's end no solution appeared in sight.

During the year, the LTTE lost the critical support of India's southern state of Tamil Nadu, which had been used as a staging and resupply area for numerous attacks on government forces. In February, the Indian government dissolved the pro-LTTE Tamil Nadu state assembly for its links to the rebels. India later blamed the LTTE for the May assassination of former Indian Prime Minister Rajiv Gandhi. Meanwhile, conditions in the northern areas controlled by the LTTE continued to deteriorate. Many villages lacked electricity, and severe food shortages have been reported.

In other domestic issues political attention has been focused on the unpopularity of President Premadasa, who critics claim is too authoritarian. The 1978 constitution established a "Gaullist" presidential-parliamentary system, with the president appointing the prime minister. Many MPs have claimed the presidential office has grown too strong, and that top bureaucrats often have more influence than the ministers to whom they report. On 28 August parliamentary speaker Mohamed Haniffa Mohamed received a petition calling for Premadasa's removal. It accused him of blocking inquiries into human rights violations committed against political opponents and of abusing his power. The following day, Premadasa received a boost from his 27 member cabinet, which gave him a unanimous vote of confidence. The no-confidence motion ended on 7 October, when Mohamed ruled some of the signatures on the petition were invalid.

Eight MPs from the president's United National Party (UNP) were thrown out of the party because they signed the petition. Led by Lalith Arthulathmudali, the group joined a new party, the Democratic United National Front. The UNP is left with 117 seats in the 225-member parliament, with former Prime Minister Sirima Bandaranaike's Sri Lanka Freedom Party (SLFP) holding 67 seats and the remainder split among several smaller parties and independents. The UNP had a strong showing in the May 1991 regional elections, putting it into control of 190 of the country's local authorities as opposed to 36 for the SLFP.

The large-scale fighting in the north and fallout from the Persian Gulf War wiped out the effects of a 6.5 percent GDP growth in the southern part of the country in 1990. Over 100,000 Sri Lankans who worked in the Middle East and sent home remittances were forced to return to Sri Lanka. The country also lost one-quarter of its tea export market after economic sanctions were imposed upon Iraq. In November, the government said it would resort to foreign and domestic borrowing to close an expected 1992 budget gap of $1.63 billion.

Political Rights and Civil Liberties: Citizens of Sri Lanka can change their government democratically. Political killings are carried out by several parties, including the government security forces, the police, and various separatist groups. The suppression of the JVP has returned much of the southern and western portions of the island nation to normal, although vigilante groups continue to kill suspected JVP operatives. By some estimates, there have been up to 30,000 executions in the anti-JVP campaign. The Prevention of Terrorism Act (PTA) and Emergency Regulations (ER), which grant security forces extra powers, remained in effect in 1991 in the northern province, which is largely controlled by the Liberation Tigers of Tamil Eelam (LTTE). The LTTE serves as the *de facto* government in areas it controls, extorting taxes and levies. Both the government and the LTTE have used civilians in their military campaigns, including reports of army units marching villagers through minefields. Disappearances of both Tamils and Sinhalese number in the thousands. Although non-political trials are conducted with procedural safeguards, trials under PTA or ER jurisdiction are conducted with less stringent protections for the defendant.

The constitution provides for freedom of expression, but allows this right to be restricted by the government in times of national emergency. The government controls the country's largest newspaper chain, as well as the radio and television services. Several independent newspapers carry pluralistic views. Journalists for these newspapers report being threatened by anti-government groups for refusing to carry certain articles. Freedom of association can be restricted under the PTA and ER. Buddhism, which the government must "protect and foster," is the official religion, but the rights of other groups to practice their religion are protected. Citizens are free to travel both internally and abroad, although movement in the contested northeast is often restricted by curfews or fighting. Workers have full rights of association, although public employees are not permitted to strike. The government reserves the right to ban strikes in what it considers "essential services."

Sudan

Polity: Military
Economy: Mixed capitalist
Population: 25,900,000
PPP: $970
Life Expectancy: 50.8
Ethnic Groups: Arab, sub-Saharan African (Dinka, Nuer, Shilluk, Nuba, Fur, other)

Political Rights: 7
Civil Liberties: 7
Status: Not Free

Overview:

Sudan continued to be embroiled in a civil war in 1991; government troops and tribal militias of the predominantly Arabic-speaking North continued fighting insurgents of the non-Arabic-speaking South and West. Based in the South, the Sudan People's Liberation Army (SPLA), led by Colonel John Garang, has been fighting since 1983 to replace the existing government, establish greater autonomy for its own region, and abolish the universal application of Islamic law.

In an atmosphere of growing governmental corruption and inefficiency as well as economic breakdown, a junta headed by Brigadier General Omar al-Bashir overthrew the democratically elected prime minister, al-Sadiq al-Mahdi, on 30 June 1989. Al-Bashir has asserted that the cause of the 1989 coup was the increasing movement by the non-fundamentalist al-Sadiq government toward the "slaughter of the *shari'a*" (Islamic law) and destruction of "Sudan's Arab, Islamic cultural identity" to appease the SPLA. Since coming to power, al-Bashir has suspended the constitution, dissolved Parliament and banned all opposition political parties, trade unions and professional associations. He has also closed down all newspapers except the Army's and certain selective publications controlled by Muslim fundamentalists associated with the National Islamic Front (NIF), a group advocating the imposition of Islamic law for the entire country. Curfews are periodically declared under a continuous state of emergency, giving the regime extraordinary powers to stifle dissent. The regime's notorious security committee has purged the military and civil service of most non-fundamentalist Muslims and non-Muslims and installed NIF loyalists to the vacated positions.

After the fall of the Ethiopian dictator Mengistu in May 1991, an ally of the SPLA, the SPLA and Sudanese refugees were expelled from their havens in southern Ethiopia. The SPLA, which holds all of southern Sudan except for a few besieged cities held by the Sudanese army, was easily able to relocate much of its training and leadership back into the country.

The regime announced in early June that it was establishing a federal system of nine states in order to provide a greater measure of self-rule to the various regions making up the country. Because Khartoum would appoint the leadership of all states, the change would not address the SPLA demand for increased regional autonomy. The political opposition making up the National Democratic Forces—composed of labor unions, professional associations and banned political parties—dismissed the changes as cosmetic. The charter of the National Democratic Forces, which the SPLA leadership subscribes to, calls for the restoration of a secular, multi-party democratic system.

The regime announced in August that it had foiled a coup attempt, but opponents charged that the "coup" was a sham to justify the arrest of former military officers and ex-politicians who were unsympathetic to the NIF dictatorship. That same month, three SPLA officials said that they intended to depose John Garang as SPLA leader. Calling him a warlord and human rights abuser, the dissidents called for replacing Garang's objective of overthrowing the al-Bashir government with the goal of independence for a separate state in southern Sudan. The power struggle, which pitted Southerners of different ethnic groups against each other, turned violent with reports of fighting between armed supporters of the two factions. Negotiations between the parties were announced in late November.

The effects of crop failure due to the worst drought in Sudan since 1985 were worsened by a scarcity of grain reserves; the grain had reportedly been sold by the government for foreign exchange in order to buy arms. The regime has killed farmers resisting the requisition of their crops for use by the military, and foreign food aid is also commonly confiscated by the military. The government continues to bomb concentrations of refugees created by foreign relief organizations for famine victims.

Despite the prevailing conditions of famine, until late February the government in Khartoum refused either to declare that a food emergency existed in Sudan or to formally make a request for assistance from international donors. Because foreign relief organizations feared that food aid would be diverted if the regime controlled distribution, the potential donors demanded control as a condition of any relief program. Before it temporarily relented in March to permit food relief, the regime continued to assert that Sudan would reach self-sufficiency in food production shortly and charged that the purpose of Western relief efforts was to defame the country. The government again forced the suspension of relief efforts in late August. Estimates are that the cost of this extended reluctance to accept aid will be at least hundreds of thousands of Sudanese lives.

Political Rights and Civil Liberties:

The Sudanese do not have the power to change their government democratically. The military regime forcibly curtails the activities of all political parties but the NIF. Under the state of emergency, arrest without a warrant is permissible. Defendants are no longer permitted representation in court by a lawyer. Many political opponents jailed by the al-Bashir regime at the time of the coup in June 1989 were freed in spring 1991. It is believed, however, that many more still remain incommunicado without charge or trial in "ghost houses" under the control of a relatively new militia made up of NIF sympathizers called "Security of the Revolution." Extrajudicial execution of prisoners is still common. The death penalty has been enacted and carried out against those striking illegally.

Suspended in 1985 by the preceding democratic government, the Muslim *shari'a* law was re-established in 1991 by the current Islamic fundamentalist regime. It is to be enforced on both Muslims and non-Muslims. *Shari'a*-prescribed punishments include amputation of the limbs for theft, public flogging for consuming alcohol, and stoning to death for adultery. Christians and animists in the North are subject to serious physical punishment for infractions of *shari'a* such as drinking beer.

Government-sponsored Arab militia have rampaged through Southern villages in the past, massacring suspected rebels and members of the Dinka and Shilluk tribes and taking children as slaves. Such raids have decreased in the past few years as the SPLA has managed to consolidate its control over 90 percent of the Southern Sudan. Regular military forces also have regularly engaged in atrocities.

Some Southern Sudanese have complained about both SPLA attacks on civilians and the detention, torture and execution of SPLA dissidents from non-Dinka ethnic groups. Now-abandoned refugee camps for Sudanese in southern Ethiopia reportedly included prison camps for SPLA dissidents. Surrendering government troops have been summarily executed by the SPLA and the group reportedly confiscates relief aid destined for civilians for use by its guerrillas.

Pursuant to a "new information order" publicly heralded by al-Bashir, the regime has declared it illegal to broadcast or publish anything deemed damaging to the "reputation of the Sudan." The maximum penalty now prescribed by law is death. The regime has attempted to ensure favorable coverage by eliminating all but official government and NIF publications and by imprisoning unsympathetic journalists.

Suriname

Polity: Parliamentary democracy (military-influenced)
Economy: Capitalist-statist
Population: 400,000
PPP: $3,830
Life Expectancy: 69.5
Ethnic Groups: East Indian (approximately 40 percent), Creole (approximately 30 percent), followed by Javanese, Bush Negroes, Amerindians, Chinese and various European minorities

Political Rights: 4
Civil Liberties: 4
Status: Partly Free

Overview:

Ronald Venetiaan of the New Front for Democracy and Development (NF) was elected president in a process that began with parliamentary elections in May 1991 and concluded with an electoral college vote in September. Venetiaan vowed to strengthen civilian rule, but Commander Desi Bouterse's 3,000-member, which overthrew the last elected government in December 1990, remained a major obstacle to democratic rule.

The Republic of Suriname achieved independence from the Netherlands in 1975 and functioned as a parliamentary democracy until a military coup in 1980. Bouterse emerged as the strongman of the ruling National Military Council that brutally suppressed all civic and political opposition. In 1985, Bouterse announced a program for a "return to democracy," appointed an assembly to draft a new constitution, and lifted the ban on political parties.

The 1987 constitution provides for a system of parliamentary democracy, but gives the military the right to intercede in political affairs. A 51-member National Assembly, elected for a five-year term, selects the nation's president. The president is nominally the head of the armed forces, but civilian authority is undercut by the Military Council, which by law retains a tutelary role as the "vanguard of the people."

The Front for Democracy and Development, a three-party coalition, won the November 1987 general elections, taking forty of 51 seats in the Assembly. Bouterse's National Democratic Party (NDP), the army's political front, won three seats. The assembly elected Ramsewak Shankar president.

During its three years in office, the Shankar government was perpetually hamstrung by the military on most policy issues, including its efforts to negotiate a peace agreement with the Bush Negro-based Jungle Commando insurgency. At the same time, the military deepened its involvement in cocaine trafficking and remained unaccountable for human rights violations. In 1990 the government made noises about investigating rights violations and drug trafficking. But in December 1990, two months after it announced the creation of a constitutional reform committee, the government was ousted in a bloodless coup and replaced by a puppet government controlled by Bouterse's NDP.

Under intense international pressure, both political and economic, the government scheduled elections for 25 May 1991 and invited the Organization of American States (OAS) to observe. The leader in the opinion polls was the NF, essentially the same coalition of Hindustani, Creole and Javanese parties that had been ousted in 1990. Also contending were the NDP, and the newly formed Democratic Alternative 91 (DA 91), an ethnically mixed coalition led by young professionals who campaigned for establishing a commonwealth-type relationship with the Netherlands as a means of limiting the power of the military.

In the May election, which was validated by the OAS, the NF won 30 seats in the National Assembly, the NDP 12, and DA 91 nine. But the NF lacked the two-thirds majority needed to elect its presidential candidate, educator Ronald Venetiaan. After it failed to receive the backing of DA 91, an electoral college was convened, formed by members of the Assembly and representatives of district and municipal councils. Venetiaan won 80 percent of the 817 electoral college votes.

President Venetiaan took office in September and vowed to amend the constitution to bolster civilian rule (amendments require a two-thirds majority vote in the Assembly), and to strengthen ties with the Netherlands, the U.S. and neighboring Venezuela as a means to preclude a recurrence of military interference. With an OAS observation team still posted in the country, Bouterse kept a low profile during the inauguration. But a confrontation with the military seemed inevitable if Venetiaan tried to fulfill his commitments. Because of his reputation for toughness, Venetiaan appeared better suited to standing up to Bouterse than the ousted Shankar. The military, however, after more than a decade of controlling the country, frequently in brutal fashion, remains an unrepentant, outlaw force, still capable of cowing a society rooted in the gentler traditions of the Caribbean. It therefore appeared that the strength of civilian rule would depend primarily on continued international pressure.

Political Rights and Civil Liberties:

Citizens are able to choose their governments in relatively free elections, but the military remains the dominant power in the country. The 1987 constitution gives the military virtually unlimited right to intervene in political affairs. The military used the constitution to justify the 1990 coup, on the false grounds of ensuring national stability.

The constitution guarantees the right to organize political parties, civic organizations and labor unions. Aside from the parties in the government coalition, there are at least a half dozen other parties, including a number of labor-based organizations. Labor unions are well-organized and legally permitted to strike, but remain subject to pressure by the military.

The constitution also guarantees the right of free expression. Radio is both public and private, with a number of small commercial radio stations competing with the government-owned radio and television broadcasting system. All broadcast in the various local languages and offer pluralistic points of view. There are a number of independent newspapers. However, government and independent media practice self-censorship because of intimidation by the military.

The constitution provides for an independent judiciary but the military does not respect its authority and, in a continuing climate of a climate of fear and insecurity, the judicial system remains weak. Stanley Rensch, leader of the main Surinamese human rights organization, Mooiwana '86, has frequently been arrested and was driven into exile in 1989. After returning to Suriname in October 1990, he and other activists remained targets of intimidation and death threats, particularly in the wake of the December 1990 coup.

Most of the country's interior remains under the direct control of the military. Bouterse made a deal in 1991 with Ronny Brunswijk, leader of the Bush Negro-based Jungle Commando guerrilla group, to end hostilities, possibly in exchange for a share in drug-trafficking operations. But most of the 10,000-plus Bush Negro refugees in neighboring French Guiana do not trust the arrangement and are afraid to return. Also, the military finances the Tucayana Amazonas, a paramilitary group which dominates the Amerindian community. George Pierre, an Amerindian human rights activist, was driven into exile in 1991 after reporting the disappearances of a number of Amerindians who refused to submit to the military's control.

Swaziland

Polity: Traditional monarchy
Economy: Capitalist
Population: 800,000
PPP: $2,110
Life Expectancy: 56.8
Ethnic Groups: Swazi, European, Zulu

Political Rights: 6
Civil Liberties: 5
Status: Partly Free

Overview:

The most important development in Swaziland in 1991 was the March release of five political dissidents who had been in police custody since November 1990. Despite calls in 1990 by King Mswati III for a national dialogue on modifying the political system, the state has not yet made any significant steps toward political reform. On the occasion of his nationally celebrated 23rd birthday in April, the King warned the country to guard itself against "subversive" elements, referring to those citizens actively favoring a multi-party regime.

Swaziland is a small, land-locked monarchy tucked into an eastern corner of South Africa whose population is almost entirely ethnic Swazi. In 1968, it became an independent state with a Westminister-style parliament. However, in 1973 the first monarch in independent Swaziland, King Sobhuza II abolished the multi-party system.

In 1978 Sobhuza set up a *tinkhundla* legislative system based on tribal councils. Two members of each council are selected by chief's committees and elected via a public head count form an 80-member electoral college. The college, in secret session, designates 40 of the 50 members of the legislative House of Assembly. The King appoints the remaining ten members of the House. In turn, the House and the King each appoint 10 members to the Senate. The king also designates the prime minister.

The bicameral legislature passes legislation that must be submitted to the king for approval. Hence, the king retains ultimate political power. Responding to criticism of the *tinkhundla,* King Mswati declared in 1990 that he would appoint an advisory council to assist him in evaluating it, but he has not yet formed such a council.

The political trial against alleged members of the underground anti-*tinkhundla* PUDEMO (The Peoples United Democratic Movement) ended in late October 1990. Their links with South Africa's African National Congress through a Nelson Mandela reception committee and allegations of their membership in the PUDEMO were deemed by the government to be evidence of high crimes. Over half of the defendants were convicted of violating a law prohibiting the organization of any meeting of a political nature. The defendants were not, however, convicted of the considerably more serious charges of sedition and treason. Stymied by the court's refusal to convict on the greater charges, the government arrested five of the defendants after the conclusion of the trial and held them in prison under successive sixty-day administrative detention orders indefinitely renewable at the prime minister's discretion. Finally, in March 1991 they were released during the last of a series of debilitating hunger strikes.

In November 1990 a number of students sustained severe injuries and three were reportedly killed when police violently invaded two college campuses. The invasions were in response to protests over substandard campus conditions and the academic expulsion of two defendants after the recently concluded "PUDEMO" trial. At the same time, two 'PUDEMO' defendants sought refuge at the U.S. Embassy in the capital of Mbabane in fear of re-arrest after their just-concluded trial. They were reportedly pressured out within days by the Embassy, and after attempting to enter South Africa, were delivered by South African border officials to Swaziland authorities and imprisoned.

Political Rights and Civil Liberties:

Swazis cannot change their government democratically. Political parties are prohibited by the King's Decree No. 12 (1973), which also prohibits the organization or attendance of political meetings. The government has warned citizens to limit political expression to the *Tinkhundla* gatherings. The legislature tends to function as an rubber-stamp for the king, and the prime ministership is always filled by someone from the Dlamini princely family. Some five opposition organizations operate clandestinely; most of them are committed to the establishment of a constitutional monarchy with multiple political parties.

A state of emergency, declared in 1973, is still in effect. There is an independent judiciary composed of a High Court, a Court of Appeal, district courts and several other courts for tribal and customary issues. Special tribunals hear cases dealing with offenses against the king. Police may hold prisoners incommunicado without charge or trial for a renewable sixty-day period under a 1978 detention law. In 1991 the Ministry of the Interior and Immigration refused to allow the registration of an independent human rights organization, reportedly basing its decision on "the public interest".

The media practice a measure of self-censorship, but the private press increasingly presents diverse views on controversial issues. The Sedition and Subversive Activities Act prohibits the printing, publishing and distribution of literature considered to be "subversive." The media are required to funnel all inquiries touching on government operations through a director of information, who may respond at his discretion. The police allow gatherings, although anti-government demonstrations and meetings are not tolerated and dealt with harshly. Although unofficially a Christian country, other religions are tolerated. Professional and business associations function openly. Workers can freely organize unions. The leading labor federation is the Swaziland Federation of Trade Unions.

Sweden

Polity: Parliamentary democracy
Economy: Mixed capitalist
Population: 1
PPP: $14,940
Life Expectancy: 77.4
Ethnic Groups: Swedish (99 percent), Finnish, Lappic, and small immigrant groups

Political Rights: 1
Civil Liberties: 1
Status: Free

Overview:

In 1991 Sweden's Social Democratic Party, which had ruled for most of the last 59 years, lost to a conservative coalition promising a radical break from Sweden's socialist polices.

Sweden is a constitutional monarchy governed by a parliamentary democracy. Its economy has a well-developed private sector, and heavy taxes support a comprehensive social welfare system. The public sector employs one-third of the work force. Swedes built their prosperity on forestry, mining and metals, but recent international economic trends are undermining such traditional economic sectors.

The head of state is King Carl Gustaf XVI. Executive power is invested in the prime minister, who heads the majority party or ruling coalition in a unicameral, 349-member parliament (*Riksdag*). Voters elect 310 parliamentarians directly, and 39 seats are distributed among parties that receive at least 4 percent of the nationwide vote. There is a three-year term.

In the parliamentary election in September 1991, a four-party, non-socialist coalition defeated the Social Democrats, who had governed Sweden for 53 of the previous 59 years. The conservative Moderate Party, the Liberals, the Center Party and the Christian Democrats captured a combined 170 of the 349 parliamentary seats. The coalition depends on the new right-wing populist New Democracy Party, which gained 25 seats. The New Democracy Party had campaigned to make life "simpler, cheaper, and more fun," and called for cheaper alcohol, lower immigration and no foreign aid to Africa. This platform was too harsh for some of the other center-right politicians, so the new party stands outside the coalition. Losing nineteen seats, the Social Democrats took only 138. The Left Party, the successor to the Communists, lost five seats, holding sixteen.

The Moderate Party leader, Carl Bildt, is the new prime minister. His government program includes lowering taxes, encouraging private business, lifting restrictions on foreign ownership, allowing private child care facilities and selling off state holdings in 35 companies. In addition, he proposes making convicted criminals serve longer prison terms and stopping aid to Cuba and Vietnam. All of this represents a sharp reversal of the Social Democrats' traditional policies.

Although the Social Democrats had campaigned for their welfare state and interventionist economic policies, they had adopted more market-oriented policies in recent years. The last Social Democratic budget sought to halt public sector expansion and contained cuts in benefits for sick, absent workers. Following implementation of the latter policy, the number of those reporting sick fell by 20 percent within two months. Between 1989 and 1991 the Social Democrats instituted a major reform of the income tax. Faced with low economic growth, the government cut the top national income tax rate from 72 to 50 percent, reduced the number of tax brackets from 21 to two, and exempted low income households. As of 1991, about 57 percent of gross domestic product went to taxes. The party also postponed the start of the phaseout of nuclear power until after 1995.

Under the Social Democrats, Sweden applied to join the European Community in 1991. This was a significant break from the country's previously cool attitude towards the EC, which neutral Sweden had identified with NATO. With the end of the cold war, Sweden pegged its currency, to the EC's ECU (European Currency Unit), the forerunner of a common European currency.

In 1991, Sweden also conducted negotiations with Denmark about the possibility of building a bridge and tunnel link between the two countries. Like membership in the EC, such a link would subject Sweden to more competition with goods and service from the heart of Europe.

Political Rights and Civil Liberties: Swedes can change their government democratically. Parliamentary elections take place at least once every three years. Aliens resident for three years have the right to participate in local elections.

The judiciary is independent. The rights of the accused are generally well respected. Some suspected Kurdish terrorists have not been deported, because they would be executed back in the Middle East. They are confined to their local municipalities in Sweden. Sweden granted humanitarian asylum to some Iranians in 1991, but reportedly deported Mohammed-Sadeq Pourmozafari, a sympathizer of the Iranian opposition group, the People's Mojahedin. With a few minor exceptions, freedom of expression is guaranteed, and the press is free. The government subsidizes daily newspapers regardless of their politics. Publications or videotapes that contain excessive violence or national security information are subject to censorship. Following the success of private satellite television channels, the Social Democratic government agreed to license a land-based commercial television station in 1991. Freedom of assembly and association are guaranteed and respected in practice. Lutheranism is the state religion, and the church gets public funding. However, other religions are free to practice.

Emigration and domestic and foreign travel are unrestricted. Workers have the right to form and join trade unions and to strike. Although the government proposed some restrictions on the right to strike in 1990, the measures lost in parliament. The labor movement has been traditionally strong and well-organized.

In late December 1991 Sweden experienced at least one terrorist bombing and several bomb threats. The neo-Nazi Aryan Resistance Front claimed responsibility for the bombing of a pizzeria on 20 December. Anonymous callers followed this with threats to bomb airports and other crowded places. After one such anonymous call, police detonated a bomb at Stockholm's central rail station on 30 December.

Switzerland

Polity: Parliamentary democracy
Economy: Capitalist
Population: 6,800,000
PPP: $17,220
Life Expectancy: 77.4
Ethnic Groups: German, French, Italian, Romansch

Political Rights: 1
Civil Liberties: 1
Status: Free

Overview:

Switzerland faced the most serious challenges to its definition of neutrality during its 700th anniversary in 1991. Other major issues of 1991 included the rise in anti-immigrant sentiment and government secrecy.

Switzerland has stood as an example of how democracy can make a multi-ethnic society work. This small country is a patchwork of cultures, principally French, German, Italian and Romansch. Swiss history dates back to 1291, when three cantons signed an "eternal alliance" against the Hapsburgs. Since then, Switzerland avoided becoming involved in conflicts. The European powers confirmed Swiss neutrality at the Congress of Vienna in 1815.

Switzerland has guarded its neutrality up to the present day, going so far as to refuse admission to the U.N. However, the Gulf War has sparked a debate about what form its neutrality should take in an increasingly interdependent world. On 7 August 1990, three days after the U.N. Security Council announced its embargo on Iraq for invading Kuwait, the Swiss government announced it would participate in the sanctions, the first time Switzerland has taken an action of this nature. There is now discussion on whether Switzerland, in order to respect instruments of international law, should have a "differential" neutrality—participating in economic sanctions, but continuing to refuse any military action.

Fear of economic isolation and decline have also caused the Swiss to rethink its policy of neutrality. In October 1991, Switzerland joined its partners of the European Free Trade Agreement in signing a treaty with the European Community (EEC) for the creation of a "European Economic Area." Also, following a poll declaring that for the first time a significant majority of Swiss citizens favored belonging to the European Community, and a declaration by the economics minister that joining the EEC must be Switzerland's long-term goal, the government announced its intention to apply for full membership. This step was taken with the knowledge that by joining the EEC, the Swiss may be forced to make painful changes in their unique political structure and customs.

Switzerland has also been known for its liberal treatment of refugees. As of July 1991, there were 64,000 applicants for asylum. However, even this has been challenged this year. In 1990, due to a huge influx of refugees, the Swiss government modified its policy, making it more difficult to obtain political asylum. On 9 May 1991, Switzerland authorities deported twenty-four Kurdish refugees back to Turkey, declaring that there was insufficient evidence that they would be in danger in their homeland. The U.N. High Commission on Refugees concurred. In July, the Federal Council issued a highly criticized report that recommended focusing humanitarian aid on those areas from which most asylum applicants come from. Critics point out that this would disadvantage many of the world's poorer countries, from which no one emigrates to Switzerland. Still even with these steps, the numbers reached a record high in 1991 of 1.14 million, or 16.9 percent of the total.

The combined trends of increasing attacks on neutrality and the influx of foreigners produced a backlash during the parliamentary elections in October 1991. The center-right Radical Democrats, the key to the four-party coalition which has ruled Switzerland since 1959, lost seven seats, bringing its mandates to a record low of 44. However, it still remains the largest influence in the lower house. The centrist Christian Democrats lost six seats, while the other two coalition partners, the center-left Social Democrats and the conservative Swiss People's Party experienced no change in influence. Despite their losses, the governing coalition still has enough seats to stay in power. However, the biggest gain in the elections went to the rightist Auto Party, which won eight seats, up from two received in the last elections four years ago, giving it major party status. Originally created in 1985 to protect motorist rights, the party's original platform opposed "idiotic speed limits." This year the party began a campaign against the flood of immigrants entering the country. Left-wing parties, including the Greens,. also did well in the elections. Parties on both ends of the political spectrum oppose entry into the EEC. Other parties participating in the elections include the liberal Independents' Alliance, the Liberal Party, the conservative Protestant Evangelical People's Party, the Communist Workers' Party, and the leftist Progressive Organizations of Switzerland.

Two other significant events concerning suffrage happened in 1991. On 3 March 1991, the Swiss government lowered the voting age from twenty to eighteen years of age. This action added 100,000 new voters to the electorate. Also, the last half canton in Switzerland, Appenzeller-Inner Roden, finally began to allow women to vote this year. 1991 was the twentieth anniversary of the year that suffrage for women was established in most of the country.

The military was touched by scandal after it narrowly escaped abolition in a referendum in 1990. A published report exposed several "secret" activities of the military. These included the creation of a secret service for military counterespionage and a secret resistance organization. The Federal Council ordered both groups disbanded. The study also showed that certain Swiss organizations with links to the USSR have been kept under secret surveillance and files have been kept on some citizens suspected of anti-army activities.

Switzerland has a bicameral Federal Assembly. The voters elect the 200-member lower house, the National Council, to four-year terms by proportional representation. The cantons use various methods to elect two members each of the forty-six in the Council of States. The Federal Assembly chooses the seven members of the Federal Council, Switzerland's executive branch. The presidency is rotated annually between the members of the Federal Council. Currently, the Interior Minister, Flav͘ Cotti, a Christian-Democrat, is the head of state. There are twenty full and six half cantons, with a large degree of autonomy vis-à-vis the central government.

Political Rights and Civil Liberties:

The Swiss have the right to change their government by democratic means. However, with a system based on consensus and coalition governments, it is difficult to make radical change in policy. The voters have substantial powers of initiative and referendum. (In fact in one half-canton, the whole voting population acts as the legislature.) Because of the autonomous nature of the cantonal system, cultural heritage is preserved. There is no official religion and all religions are permitted to operate freely. Although Switzerland does not exempt conscientious objectors from military service, Swiss voters approved in July a revision of the Military Penal Code permitting the courts to sentence conscientious objectors to community service in such areas as environmental protection, health care or mountain rescue instead of prison. The term of service would be one and a half times the normal period in the military. No longer are conscientious objectors to be considered as criminals. The scandal concerning the military has raised questions as to how much information the government is allowed to keep on its citizens.

Switzerland has complete freedom of the press and media. Although television and radio receive government money, no censorship is imposed. There is freedom of association. Groups that are determined to be a potential threat to the state may have restrictions placed upon them; however, no such group is currently affected. Although there is no official state church, many cantons do support various churches with public funding. However, there are no restrictions imposed on worship. There are no restrictions placed on labor federations; however, a unique agreement between the government and the unions since the 1930s has resulted in fewer than 20 strikes per annum since 1975. There is no national minimum wage; salaries are negotiated for each individual industry through collective bargaining. Workers' rights are protected by extensive legislation.

Although women were declared equal under the law in 1981, many women complain that the Swiss social security laws do not recognize housewives' work, that there is a lack of day-care facilities and that women pay higher medical insurance. Furthermore, it is alleged that women earn one-third less than men. On 14 June 1991, an estimated 500,000 women staged a one-day work stoppage to protest inequalities between the sexes.

Syria

Polity: Dominant party (military-dominated)
Economy: Mixed statist
Population: 12,800,000
PPP: $4,460
Life Expectancy: 66.1
Ethnic Groups: Arab (90 percent), Kurdish, Armenian and others (10 percent)

Political Rights: 7
Civil Liberties: 7
Status: Not Free

Overview:

In 1991 Syrian president Hafez al-Assad continued to court Western nations by backing the American-led coalition in the Persian Gulf war and agreeing to peace negotiations with Israel. Meanwhile, the ruler established a virtual protectorate over Lebanon through a supposedly equal treaty of cooperation, moved closer to restoring ties with the mainstream faction of the Palestine Liberation Organization, and demonstrated his control over the country by running unopposed in a show election.

The French declared Syria a republic in September 1941, with full independence coming in January 1944. The country merged with Egypt as the United Arab

Republic in February 1958, but withdrew in September 1961 to re-establish itself as an independent state. A March 1963 military coup brought the pan-Arab, socialist Baath party to power. Leadership struggles within the Baath party continued until November 1970, when the party's military wing took power under Assad, who became president in February 1971. The party's greatest internal threat has been from the Moslem Brotherhood, a fundamentalist group from the Sunni Moslem majority which began a series of anti-government attacks in the late 1970s. In February 1982, soldiers killed approximately 20,000 of these militants and civilians after an armed rebellion in Hama. The government justifies spending upwards of 60 percent of the national budget on state security by citing this fundamentalist unrest as well as an alleged threat of an Israeli attack. Syria has fought Israel three times, losing the strategic Golan Heights in 1967.

Assad serves as head of state and government, commander in chief of the armed forces and secretary general of the Baath party. A former fighter pilot and a member of the Alawite Muslim minority, he has shrewdly given key government positions to members of the Sunni majority and played up his devotion to Islam, while using the army and up to a dozen intelligence and security units to keep a close watch on the population. A 250-seat People's Assembly is elected for four-year terms and nominally approves legislation and the budget but holds little actual power. In the May 1990 elections, the National Progressive Front, dominated by the Baath Party, won 166 seats with the remainder going to state-approved independents. On 2 December 1991 Assad, running unopposed after being nominated by the Assembly, won a fourth seven-year term with a reported 99.982 percent of the popular vote. Government officials closely watched the voters, who had a "yes" or "no" choice.

The Persian Gulf War afforded Syria an opportunity to find new supporters in the face of the collapse of its Communist patron, the Soviet Union. Despite years of anti-Western vitriol and the risk of Sunni Moslem and Palestinian unrest, Syria quickly supported the American-led coalition against Iraq. The decision involved Assad's personal animosity towards Iraqi leader Saddam Hussein, who heads a rival wing of the Baath party. Some 20,000 troops were sent to the Gulf while state-run newspapers ran anti-American articles to pacify the population. The main public outburst occurred in late August 1990 in villages near Damascus; it reportedly ended with army units killing dozens of pro-Iraqi Syrian and Palestinian demonstrators. During the war in 1991, diplomats noted the arrest of students and other citizens who spoke out against Syria's position, although no major protests occurred. For its relatively minor military contribution, Syria received over $3 billion in aid from Western countries and Gulf states, much of it reportedly going towards the purchase of new weapons, including Scud missiles from North Korea. After the war, Syraia tentatively agreed to send upwards of 40,000 troops to the Iraqi-Kuwait border on a peacekeeping mission in return for further financial aid; it later reduced this commitment allegedly because the Gulf states preferred Western protection.

In July 1991 Assad agreed to face-to-face peace negotiations with Israel. Although clearly seeking the return of the Golan Heights, the Syrian president said he would push for a comprehensive Arab-Israeli agreement rather than sign a separate deal with Israel. In October Assad said his country would not attend later talks on regional problems such as disarmament and water rights until Israel agreed to give up all territory occupied after the 1967 war. But Syrian representatives attended the Madrid conference which began on 30 October and appeared likely to attend further talks in an effort to procure Western aid and avoid being left out should a settlement with Israel be reached.

Syria's strategic shift resulted in the restoration of diplomatic ties with several Western countries after they had been broken off in the mid-1980s due to the country's links with terrorism. Assad has also attempted to get his country off the United States State Department's list of countries that sponsor terrorism. In recent years he has expelled noted terrorists. In 1991 he played a role in the release of Western hostages from Lebanon and demoted General Muhammed al-Khouli, who allegedly planned the 1986 bombing of an El Al flight out of London's Heathrow Airport. However, Assad still safeguards some terrorists as well as radical Palestinian factions and the German Red Army. Syria is also said to harbor the Nazi war criminal Alois Brunner. On 9 December, the government expelled Nazi-hunter Beate Klarsfeld as she attempted to track down Brunner in Damascus. The government also moved to heal a rift with Fatah, the mainstream PLO faction, hinting in November the group would soon be able to reopen offices in Damascus.

The other top regional issue has been the country's involvement in Lebanon, where it has maintained a presence since 1976 when troops were sent in to mediate a civil war. In October 1990 the army helped Lebanese troops overthrow General Michel Aoun, installing the parliamentarily-elected, pro-Syrian President Elias Hrawi. On 22 May 1991 Syria and Lebanon signed a "Treaty of Brotherhood, Cooperation, and Coordination" which provides for binding economic and strategic policy decisions for the two countries to be jointly made under a council comprised of their heads of state and other top officials. Syria continues to base 40,000 troops in two-thirds of Lebanon, and while the treaty stressed equality, many regional experts see it as a vehicle for further Syrian hegemony.

Political Rights and Civil Liberties:

Syrians cannot change their government democratically. President Hafez al-Assad has run the country virtually according to his whim since November 1970. His son Basil is his designated successor. All political parties essentially must be aligned with the Baath-dominated National Progressive Front. In a rare public statement against the regime, former cabinet minister Jamal Atassi told the *New York Times* after Assad's 1991 re-election that "Those who rule this totalitarian state see people as objects to be manipulated, and they use these spectacles to justify their hold on power. The public has no real say and no real knowledge of the inner workings of the regime. This gives the bureaucrats a free hand to engage in corruption." There are reportedly 7,000 or more political prisoners, and torture is said to occur frequently. Several thousand Palestinians were reportedly released in 1991 in a gesture of goodwill. Jewish, Kurdish and Palestinian minorities are frequently the targets of government and civilian persecution. The government generally does not involve itself in routine criminal and civil cases, but controls all aspects of political trials, which are held in the State Security court. A near-continuous state of emergency is used to justify arbitrary searches and arrests. Freedoms of speech, press and association do not exist, with all media reflecting state views and foreign media frequently banned or censored. All groups and public meetings must be approved by the state.

There is no state religion, although the president must be a Muslim. Minorities such as Jews and Christians are generally allowed to practice their religions but face severe restrictions and are closely monitored by the state police. Teaching about Israel or Jewish history is forbidden. Jews often must post a sizable bond before traveling abroad, and a close family member is generally required to stay behind. Workers are not free to organize outside of the official Syrian General Federation of Trade Unions. The government employs some 40 percent of the labor force, and strikes in all sectors are discouraged and rarely occur.

Taiwan (Republic of China)

Polity: Dominant party
Economy: Capitalist-statist
Population: 20,500,000
PPP: na
Life Expectancy: 71.5
Ethnic Groups: Chinese (native majority, mainland minority, 98 percent) Aboriginal (2 percent)

Political Rights: 3
Civil Liberties: 3
Status: Partly Free

Overview:

In 1991 Taiwan's transition to democracy continued as President Lee Teng-hui proceeded to further overhaul an authoritarian political system established by the late General Chiang Kai-shek over 40 years ago when his forces fled mainland China and established a government under the Nationalist Party, the Kuomintang (KMT), which has ruled ever since.

During the year, President Lee oversaw an end to the 1948 state of emergency that granted the president broad powers to override constitutional guarantees in the interest of national security. In so doing, he abolished the legal grounds for freezing in office members of the National Assembly, a 693-member part of a tricameral parliament composed mainly of aging China-born legislators elected by mainland constituencies before the Communist victory in 1949. In December, Taiwanese went to the polls to freely elect a new National Assembly under a 1990 court ruling that those legislators, who had not faced elections in over 40 years, had to resign by the end of 1991.

Under Taiwan's complex political structure, the National Assembly has the power to elect and recall the president and amend the constitution. The president, elected to a six-year term, appoints officials, can declare war and mediate between the five government branches (*yuans*)—Executive, Judicial, Legislative, Control and Examination—each of which has its own president. The Executive branch is headed by the premier; the popularly elected Legislative Branch enacts laws; the Judicial Branch implements the constitution; the Examination Branch is in charge of civil service exams and the Control Branch has several mainly administrative functions.

In 1989, two new laws—the Civic Organization Law governing registration of political and social groups, and the Electoral Law setting out rules for elections and election campaigns—created an institutional framework within which the *de facto* parties and other opposition groupings could coexist legally and compete with the KMT. That year, the main opposition party, the Democratic Progress party (DPP), captured 22 seats in the Legislative *yuan*, two more than needed to initiate bills.

In March 1990, President Lee, who had managed to rebuff conservatives and was nominated by the KMT, was easily re-elected to a six-year term. Before the election, the National Assembly, which is also the electoral college, moved to upgrade itself from a rubber-stamp organization that convened to elect the president every six years to a powerful legislative body.

Early in 1991, there were disagreements in the government and KMT over several critical aspects of the emerging political system—namely the powers of the president and premier, and whether the president should be elected directly. To appease KMT conservatives, the party called for revising the constitution through amendments and leaving the original articles in tact. Thus, the National Assembly would continue to elect the president indirectly. KMT hardliners also wanted to retain the National Assembly to legitimize the party's claim to sovereignty over all of China, including not only Taiwan but the 1.1 billion Chinese on the mainland. Under a KMT plan, from 25 to 50 percent of new National Assembly members would be appointed as mainland representatives of the KMT and other parties. Seats would be allocated according to the percentage of the vote each party received. The new Assembly would amend the constitution, act as an electoral college and vote by referendum on constitutional amendments submitted by the legislative *yuan*. The opposition DPP and some younger KMT reformers overwhelmingly favored a direct presidential election.

In early April, President Lee faced a rebellion by old-guard KMT conservatives who feared that constitutional amendments would undermine Taiwan's historic claim of sovereignty over all China. Moreover, an ongoing hunger strike by university students and massive demonstrations by DPP supporters protested articles of a proposed constitutional amendment that granted the president continued emergency powers and retained three security and intelligence agencies set up by Chiang Kai-shek. Fist fights erupted in the National Assembly and the Legislative *yuan* .

The president managed to weather the storm, and on 1 May more than four decades of civil war between Taiwan and mainland China ended officially—at least as far as Taiwan was concerned—when President Lee signed a decree terminating the "period of communist rebellion" on the mainland. The presidential decision eased legal and ideological constraints on official policy toward mainland China. Lifting the period of rebellion also abolished the "temporary provisions" under which Taiwan had been ruled since the 1940s and which had blocked full exercise of constitutional government on the island. With the anti-Communist provisions removed and the constitution amended by the National Assembly, President Lee completed the first phase of domestic political reform. As chairman of the KMT, Lee also acknowledged officially for the first time the existence of the Communist government in Beijing 43 years after the KMT retreated to Taiwan.

In September, the DPP, citing the disintegration of the Soviet empire, openly expressed what had been official heresy: that Taiwan should not worry about reuniting with the Chinese mainland, but should forge an independent future, including separate membership in the United Nations. The abandonment of a one-China policy led the Communist regime in mainland China to warn that it would use force if Taiwan declared its independence. The debate intensified as part of the campaign for the 21 December elections, in which nearly two-thirds of National Assembly seats would be contested. But polls indicated that only 12 percent of Taiwanese supported independence.

On 27 September, DPP chairman Hunag Hsin-chieh, who in 1980 was convicted of sedition and sentenced to 14 years' imprisonment before being paroled in 1986, resigned to encourage elderly legislators to retire. "Let us resign and use this symbolic move to end the unjust and distorted period of the past," he said.

On 25 October, some 30,000 opposition supporters marched to demand independence. The protest came a week after the government arrested 11 pro-independence activists in a crackdown following the issuance of a DPP manifesto demanding a plebiscite to establish an independent Republic of Taiwan. In November, the government backed away from prosecuting the DPP for sedition, choosing to postpone any decision until after the December elections. On 12 December, six opposition county executives quit their posts as heads of local election committees to protest a government ban on candidates' calls for Taiwanese independence. The Central Election Committee had ordered the six counties to delete pro-independence calls from election bulletins.

The December vote marked a significant step in the democratization process. The old-guard KMT legislators had retired and a quarter of the 325 seats were designated to represent the mainland, no longer with the pretensions to represent any specific constituencies. Direct elections from Taiwanese constituencies accounted for 225 seats, with the other 100 allotted proportionately according to each party's share of the vote. On 21 December, the governing KMT won a major victory in the country's first full election in more than four decades, as voters rebuffed opposition calls for independence from China. The KMT won 71 percent of the vote, while the DPP got 24. The rest of the votes were cast for smaller parties. Of the 325 Assembly candidates, 254 were from the KMT and 66 from the DPP. Five were independent or non-aligned. Including 78 members who were elected in 1986 and who would also participate in the constitutional conference, the KMT would have 79 percent of the seats, giving it the three-quarters control necessary to approve a revised constitution. Less than 22 percent of the new legislators were originally from the Chinese mainland.

In other issues, the Taiwanese economy remained robust, and prospects of greater economic relations with mainland China appeared auspicious. In early 1991, Taiwan had the 25th largest economy in the world and was the 13th largest trading entity. Taiwan had $74 billion in official foreign exchange reserves, more than any other country except Japan. The government planned a $300 billion, six-year project to develop infrastructure, which led to a jump in foreign investment. In June, the government also announced plans to speed up privatization of state-run enterprises. Gross Domestic Product (GDP) was expected to grow by a healthy 6.2 percent in 1991, and per capita income was projected to jump to $14,000 by 1996.

Political Rights and Civil Liberties:

In 1991 the government continued its democratic reforms, with direct elections to the National Assembly. Direct elections for other branches of government are expected in 1992. The judiciary, based on European and Japanese models, is not fully independent, and some Taiwanese dissidents remain jailed under various sedition statutes. On 17 May, the legislature approved a resolution to scrap a draconian sedition law. Although Taiwan retained other sedition-related laws in the criminal code and the 1987 National Security Law, none were as ferocious as the abolished law, which mandated the death penalty for those convicted under vaguely defined charges involving attempts to overthrow the government. On 7 December, a Taiwanese dissident returning home after 20 years of exile in the U.S. was arrested under sedition charges filed in 1970 for advocating independence from China. While it remains technically illegal to challenge the regime's policy of anti-communism or its claim to represent mainland China, the DDP openly advocated Taiwanese independence in the December election campaign, and by the end of the year the government had yet to take any legal action against the opposition party or its members.

Television and radio stations are still run by the government or KMT, but open debate has increased after martial law was lifted in 1987. The press is subject to restrictions, but private newspapers are relatively free and often critical of government policies. Freedom of association and assembly are generally respected, political parties are legal and numerous demonstrations have taken place without interference. Freedom of religion is observed in practice, and in 1990 parliament abolished exit and entry requirements for citizens travelling off the island.

Trade unions are closely regulated, and most of the country's over 3,000 unions are KMT-controlled. The Chinese Federation of Labor is the only legal confederation in Taiwan.

Tanzania

Polity: One-party
Economy: Statist
Population: 26,900,000
PPP: $570
Life Expectancy: 54.0
Ethnic Groups: African (Sandawe, Kindiga, Iraqi, Goroa, Masai, Nyamwezi, Ngoni, other), with significant South Asian and Arab minorities

Political Rights: 6
Civil Liberties: 5
Status: Not Free

Overview:

In 1991 Tanzania continued to publicly consider ending the institutionalized one-party rule of the Revolutionary Party of Tanzania, or Chama Cha Mapinduzi (CCM). But when dissidents created two opposition parties to protest the slow and uncertain pace of reform, they were quickly arrested.

The East African United Republic of Tanzania was formed in 1964 with the merger of Tanganyika and Zanzibar and functions as a "cooperative-socialist" system. President Ali Hassan Mwinyi, running as the only candidate, was re-elected in 1990 to a second five-year term. He succeeded to the leadership after Julius Nyerere, the still-influential first president of post-independence Tanzania, decided to step down in 1985.

Nyerere, considered one of Africa's leading elder statesmen, was the architect of *ujamaa,* a Swahili word for a system which stresses self-reliance and socialism. Launched in the famous Arusha Declaration of 1967, *ujamaa* was characterized in part by the establishment of communal villages practicing collectivized agriculture and the creation of state-owned marketing boards. Vast domestic industries were set up in pursuit of an import-substitution scheme and private banks, commerce and factories were nationalized. Although there were some gains in social equity, the economy as a whole experienced inefficiency, bureaucratic mismanagement, and rampant corruption.

In early 1990, after regimes in Eastern Europe had toppled, Nyerere made several statements criticizing the CCM's stagnation and corruption. In July 1990 however, he reaffirmed his commitment to the Arusha Declaration, and in mid-August, at the opening of the annual CCM congress where he stepped down as Party chairman, he urged the continuation of the country's one-party system. CCM officials have warned that the national unity of the one-party system is necessary because the West conditions debt relief and aid on developing nations allowing interference in their internal political affair.

Amidst continuing national discussion and intra-Party debate about introducing multi-partyism, Mwinyi appointed a presidential commission in March 1991 to formally investigate the matter. The Commission was assigned to move through the country for one year, taking public testimony and proposals and presenting its findings to the president in March 1992. However, Commission members reportedly used the interviews to re-enforce the government position that political pluralism would lead to social unrest.

An independent seminar on multi-partyism was planned for April by a group of citizens opposed to continued one-party rule. Self-designated as the "Steering Committee for the Seminar on the Course of the Transition to Multiparty Democracy in Tanzania," its chairman dismissed the government's efforts as an attempt to ride out the growing public interest in a multi-party system. These dissidents called for a general amnesty for political prisoners and exiles and the creation of a national conference to draft a new constitution.

The seminar was postponed a few months after its sponsor, an education trust registered with the government, was banned on grounds that it was illegally involved in politics. When it finally took place in June, participants took the opportunity to denounce the government's record of human rights abuse and undemocratic practices.

In November 1991 frustrated opposition leaders founded two parties: the Civic Movement and the Union for Multiparty Democracy. Both party leaders, Chief Abdalah Fundikyera and James Mapalala, were arrested and charged with attempting to form unconstitutional political organizations.

Some Zanzibaris continued in 1991 to call for the separation of Zanzibar from its current political union with Tanganyika. The island's government has rejected the possibility of holding a referendum on independence. Seif Shaffir Hamad, charged with plotting to overthrow the island administration in 1989, was released from detention in November 1991 after 30 months' imprisonment.

There are an estimated 270,000 refugees in Tanzania. Over half of them are Burundian ethnic Hutus living in refugee camps in the northwestern portion of the country. The Tanzanian government has attempted to control the organizing activities of Hutu movements of political and armed opposition to the Burundi government. The second largest displaced group in Tanzania consists of the 72,000 Mozambicans, who have fled the civil war between their government, the RENAMO rebels, and various warlords.

Political Rights and Civil Liberties:

Tanzania in 1990 remained a one-party state monopolized by the CCM. Candidacy for elections is limited to members of the Party. Zanzibar enjoys a measure of political autonomy, with a directly-elected president and House of Representatives. Those Zanzibaris opposed to a continued union between Zanzibar and the Tanganyikan mainland are barred from open political activity. Tanzania's legal system is based on the British model, with changes to accommodate Islamic and customary law. The judiciary is generally free from government interference, but security provisions under the Preventive Detention Decree allow for indefinite detention without bail for persons considered a threat to national security and public order. Under the Deportation Act, political offenders may also be internally exiled.

Restrictive laws made it difficult to establish private publications in the past, although independent newspapers such as the *Business Times* and the *Family Mirror* have appeared in the last few years. Reportage in government-owned periodicals has begun to reflect a greater diversity of opinion; during the on-going national debate on political liberalization, the viewpoint of multi-party advocates have been accurately reported in the government-owned *Daily News*. Nevertheless, in late 1991 government officials warned that publications which allegedly "flouted professional ethics" were subject to banning, asserting that the dissemination of "dangerous lies" and "unfair comments" would not be tolerated. The president is permitted by law to require that any periodical cease publication if he determines that it is not "in the interest of the people."

Freedom of association and assembly is limited. Apart from the ban on political parties other than the CCM, police have arrested and detained demonstrators for unlawful assembly. Independent non-political organizations are allowed to function as long as they avoid politicization. Freedom of religion for the country's Muslims, Christian, and animist citizens is respected. Travel is generally unrestricted, but in an effort to prevent mass migration to the cities there are residency and employment requirements. All unions must belong to Juwata, the government-controlled labor federation. Workers have and use the right to strike.

Thailand

Polity: Military
Economy: Capitalist statist
Population: 58,800,000
PPP: $3,280
Life Expectancy: 66.1
Ethnic Groups: Thai (84 percent), Chinese (12 percent), Malaysian, Indian, Khmer, Vietnamese minorities

Political Rights: 6
Civil Liberties: 4
Status: Partly Free

Overview:

Thailand's army, a powerful domestic political force for the past six decades, ousted the elected government of Prime Minister Chatichai Choonhaven in a bloodless coup in February 1991. Accusing the Chatichai administration of excessive corruption and interference with the army, the generals quickly returned the country to civilian rule.

The military has considered itself a check on the government ever since it transformed the country from an absolute to a constitutional monarchy in a bloodless 1932 coup. The monarchy is still revered, in part for its diplomatic success in keeping Thailand free of European colonization in the nineteenth and early twentieth centuries. A succession of civilian and military governments has ruled since the 1932 coup, and Thailand has maintained its pro-Western, anti-communist stance since the end of World War II. The 1991 military action was the country's seventeenth coup attempt, although the first successful one since 1977. A group of middle-ranking officers attempted two coups in the 1980s, but they were blocked by more senior officers.

Major General Chatichai took office in 1988 as the first directly-elected prime minister since 1976. The first sign of a military challenge to Chatichai came in March 1990 when General Chaovalit Yongchaiyudh resigned as commander of the armed forces and joined the cabinet as deputy prime minister and defense minister. Ten weeks later Chaovalit resigned from the cabinet after being accused of corruption by fellow cabinet member Chalerm Yoobamrung, whose comments were considered by many officers to be directed at the military establishment as a whole. Despite pressure from the army, Chatichai refused to drop Chalerm from the cabinet even after he criticized the army's seizure of a radio truck which the government had allegedly used to monitor military communications. In December 1990, Chatichai resigned for one day, coming back to form a new five-party coalition, led by his Chart Thai party, in the lower house of parliament.

Early in 1991, Chaovalit began campaigning under the populist banner of his newly-formed New Aspiration Party (NAP) for a general election which many felt Chatichai would have to call before the end of the year. Meanwhile, an investigation into the murky details of a string of assassination attempts on former prime minister Prem Tinsulanond and former army commander Arthit Kamlang-ek in 1982 began to gain momentum. The swiftly moving situation emphasized the power dynamics between both the military and the civilian government, and between Chulachomklao Royal Military Academy's Class Five, from which much of the current military elite comes from, and Class Seven, from which some of the suspected assassination plotters hailed. Also suspected in the 1982 assassination attempts were members of the outlawed Communist Party of Thailand, assorted left-wing academics, and, according to anonymous leaflets, Prime Minister Chatichai's son Kraisak Choonhavan.

With the assassination investigation reportedly gaining momentum, Chatichai transferred the investigations director, police Lieutenant-General Boonchu Wangkanond, a Class Five graduate, to a higher but less influential position. Chatichai had already elevated Class Seven member Manoon Roopkachorn, a suspect in the assassination plot as well as the alleged ringleader of the failed coups in the 1980s, to the defense ministry. Many in the military resented Manoon's political revival and viewed Chatichai's moves as a check on Class Five military leaders. The naming of former army commander Arthit as deputy defense minister on 20 February without the consent of army leaders proved to be the fatal blow to Chatichai's government.

Armored vehicles rolled across Bangkok on 23 February, securing broadcast facilities and government buildings without firing a shot. Led by Army Supreme Commander General Sunthorn Kongsompong, the military junta, calling itself the National Peacekeeping Council (NPC), immediately dissolved the government, imposed martial law, and abolished the 1978 constitution. The coup leaders said rising government corruption and attempts to "destroy" the military and "distort" the assassination investigation in order to protect Manoon had necessitated Chatichai's overthrow. That night, in an apparent attempt to win popular support as the protector of the monarchy, the NPC aired a videotaped confession by a Class Seven assassination plot suspect, who claimed as fact the startling rumor that Queen Siskirit had also been a target in the 1982 attempts. On 24 February Suchinda said the NPC intended to amend the constitution and hold elections within six months. However, the next day Sunthorn admitted elections might take longer then six months to organize, but would be held as soon as possible because "We don't want the public to get bored."

Within days the troops returned to the barracks and the average Thai in the street appeared unfazed by the situation. Many agreed with the coup leaders that the government had been corrupt, although some analysts said given the spectacular advances in Thailand's economy over the past several years, the level of corruption had been relatively unchanged. King Bhumibol Adulyadej issued a limited endorsement of the coup, saying "it is apparent that administration by the government with General Chatichai Choonhavan as prime minister has failed to gain the people's confidence and has also failed to maintain peace and order in the country." Public negative reaction was largely limited to demonstrations at Bangkok's Ramkhamhaeng University in which fifteen students were arrested.

The military chose former diplomat Anand Panyarach to be prime minister of a transitional civilian government on 2 March. He quickly reassured investors that much-needed infrastructure projects already underway would continue. The King approved an interim constitution giving military leaders a supervisory role in the interim government's affairs, and allowing the NPC to remove the interim prime minister at its discretion. It also called for a national assembly to draft a new constitution, with elections being held 120 days into 1992 at the latest. Pro-democracy groups were particularly concerned with Article 27, which gave the NPC and the interim prime minister broad powers to "do what is necessary" against any individual or group considered to be a threat to national security, public order, or public morals. The army appointed 292-member interim national assembly, composed mostly of active or retired military officers, along with businessmen, bureaucrats or journalists who had openly supported the coup.

NAP leader Chaovalit warned the junta that stalling the re-introduction of full civilian rule could have grave consequences. Sensing broad popular support for his candidacy, and apparently attempting to distance himself from the junta, Chaovalit called for holding elections before drafting the new constitution.

The army lifted martial law in early May. The interim government set up a rural development fund as part of an effort to decentralize control of spending and rural management, and to address the substantial income polarization between the Bangkok area and the outer regions. Local governments were also given greater discretion in collecting revenues. However, critics charged that true decentralization could not occur until district heads and village chiefs, who generally have lifetime appointments, are elected on a regular basis.

In the fall, the interim government released a draft of a constitution to replace the 1978 document. While the proposed constitution gave the military no specific role in a new government, the army appeared to be planning for a political role with the emergence of the Samakkhi Tham party, which openly stated it is supported by Class Five officers. The Samakkhi Tham party has been endorsing junta leader Suchinda for prime minister. The new party also allied itself with the Chart Thai party, whose government had been overthrown by the junta, reportedly because corrupt Chart Thai politicians were hoping to avoid prosecution by siding with the generals. In addition to the NAP, opposition to a military influence in a new government has come from the recently-formed Pracha Dhamma party, composed of former student activists.

The national assembly approved the final draft of the new constitution on 7 December. Protest rallies by pro-democracy groups in late November and early December had convinced the assembly to remove a clause which would have allowed the electorate to vote for party slates rather than individuals, which could favor military-led parties having strong financial support but few well-known candidates. It also removed a clause which would have allowed civil servants and military officers to join the cabinet. In addition, the assembly reduced the number of Senate seats from 360, the same number as the House of Representatives, to 270, and the withdrew the Senate's power to jointly choose a prime minister with the lower house.

However, the assembly refused to change the most controversial provision, which will allow the NPC, rather than the prime minister, to appoint the Senate in the next elected government. Pro-democracy groups fear that if the military controls all 270 seats in the Senate, it would only take 46 MP's in the lower house from the Samakkhi Tham/Chart Thai alignment to form the majority needed to dismiss the government. The assembly also refused to remove a provision giving the speaker of the lower house the option of recommending to the king a non-elected prime minister, who could be drawn from the army or elsewhere.

The economy appeared unaffected by the coup. The government released Thailand's seventh five-year plan in September, which aims for 8.2 percent growth over the period. It calls for further deregulation in finance, trade and industry, and for improvements in education and environmental protection. The down side of Thailand's prosperity has been a torrent of refugees from hardline regimes in neighboring Burma, Cambodia, Laos, and Vietnam. Some 330,000 Cambodians live in Thai camps. Human rights groups were concerned in 1991 with the treatment of Burmese refugees, whose peaceful protests in Bangkok prompted authorities to announce a crackdown on Burmese asylum-seekers. Thailand, which has received lucrative logging concessions in Burma, considers the asylum-seekers to be illegal immigrants.

Political Rights and Civil Liberties: Citizens of Thailand currently lack the democratic means to change their government as a result of the February 1991 military coup. The interim government has promised elections by 30 April 1992.

The judiciary is considered to be independent of the government and adequate procedural safeguards exist in criminal and civil cases, although in recent years there have been reports of police beatings of prisoners. The government can detain suspects under the Anti-Communist Activities Act without charging them for up to 480 days. Although martial law placed overt restrictions on the press for only one day, many journalists reportedly practiced self-censorship afterwards for fear of reprisal. While freedom of expression is largely protected, various laws limit the right to criticize the monarchy, advocate communism, or publish materials deemed to be a threat to internal or national security. Freedom of assembly has been restored with the lifting of martial law, which had forced political parties to suspend their activities and banned political gatherings of more than five people. Political groups, with the exception of the outlawed Communist Party of Thailand, can organize freely. Citizens may travel externally and within the country, except in areas allegedly used as bases by communist rebels. While Theravada Buddhism has a pervasive influence on the country, freedom of religion is respected and observed.

The interim national assembly passed two bills on 15 April 1991 breaking up state enterprise unions and replacing them with collective associations having no right to strike or bargain collectively. Some Thais supported the crackdown because they resented the high wages and power of the state enterprise unions, which represented roughly one-quarter of a million workers and had formed the vanguard of the labor movement. Labor leader Thanong Pho-arn disappeared in June after criticizing the NPC's actions; some fear he was kidnapped and murdered. Civil servants cannot unionize but can form associations, while private sector workers can unionize but there are some constraints on their right to strike.

Togo

Polity: Military-civilian cabinet (military-dominated)
Economy: Mixed statist
Population: 3,800,000
PPP: $700
Life Expectancy: 54.0
Ethnic Groups: Aja, Ewe, Gurensi, Kabyé, Krachi, Mina, Tem

Political Rights: 6
Civil Liberties: 5
Status: Not Free

Overview:

After an auspicious start in 1991, Togo's path to democratization was slowed late in the year by violent street demonstrations by citizens demanding faster change. The military moved to protect the 24-year old regime of General Gnassingbe (originally Etienne) Eyadéma and a transitional government was dissolved in favor of a less independent "national unity government."

This West African country in the Gulf of Guinea became independent in 1960, and has been ruled from 1967 by President Eyadéma as a one-party state under the Rally of the Togolese People (RPT) Togo was a multi-party democracy until 1963, when Eyadéma assassinated the president in the first military coup in post-independence West Africa to overthrow an elected civilian government. Most positions of power in Eyadéma's regime have been held by the northern Kabyé ethnic group, a departure from earlier governments dominated by southern Ewes.

Following pro-democracy protest in October 1990 in which government troops fired on a crowd and killed 34 people, the president set up a 109-member commission to draft a multi-party constitution. Completed that December, the draft constitution provided for a system with a strong president who could serve a maximum of two seven-year terms, a judiciary which could pass on the constitutionality of laws, and a legislature with the ability through a vote of no confidence to topple an administration headed by a prime minister. The military regime announced that no political organizations or parties other than the RPT would be allowed to function until a referendum was held at the end of 1991.

Asserting that the president's electoral timetable was too slow, the opposition called for immediate legalization of additional parties and a general amnesty. A strike begun on 12 March by high school and university students in support of a national conference to speed the democratic transition led to violent clashes with security forces and pro-regime students in the capital, Lomé. By mid-march 1991, the president agreed to permit the formation of opposition parties, issue a full amnesty, and allow for a "national forum of dialogue" (i.e., a national conference) to be convened.

The important step toward political pluralism was marred by the discovery in mid-April of 26 Ewe corpses in a Lomé lagoon, victims of street executions by soldiers during the continuing demonstrations. Meanwhile, the "dialogue of the streets" between radicalized Ewe protestors and Kabyé soldiers was carried on with truncheons, tear gas, Molotov cocktails and rocks.

In May ten opposition groups set up the Front of Associations for Renewal (FAR) coalition. Its demands included a general amnesty, a sovereign national conference, a transition government led by a prime minister charged with leading the country to multi-party elections, and greater access to the national broadcast media.

Eyadéma temporarily resisted a transferral of sovereignty to a conference, arguing that his government had democratically won the popular mandate in the repeated one-party elections of the past. When the conference finally opened in July, speakers accused the regime of a history of human rights abuses and corruption; it was the first time such charges were freely expressed before a national audience. The president responded with a call for a "national conciliation." The conference voted at the end of August to form an interim High Council of the Republic (HCR) to assume national authority during the transition to elections and barred Eyadéma from running for re-election. The president of the Togolese League of Human Rights, Kokou Koffigoh, was appointed as transitional prime minister.

Up to and during the national conference, the military seemed on the verge of derailing the democratic transition. The army refused to participate in the proceedings as delegates. As conference participants proceeded to pass resolutions that the size of the military be cut and that a civilian serve as defense minister, troops surrounded the hall and demanded that proceedings be suspended. One group of soldiers occupied the radio station in the capital and demanded pay increases promised by Eyadéma. Another group broadcast a demand that the transitional government resign and a third group sought to arrest the prime minister. Nevertheless, President Eyadéma signed a decree ratifying the decisions of the conference. He was allowed to stay on as head of state with ceremonial powers and disavowed involvement in any plots to reassert military power over the nation.

While Koffigoh was in Paris at the end of November, the HRC voted to ban the RPT, reportedly because its partisans were attempting to block opposition party rallies. In the midst of violent clashes between supporters and opponents of the RPT, on 2 December army troops surrounded the prime minister's palace to which Koffigoh had returned from France. Demanding Eyadéma's restoration to full power and the end of the HCR, they temporarily abandoned their siege but returned a day later to launch an attack on the palace. At least a dozen members of the palace guard were killed as the soldiers captured the prime minister and delivered him to the president. Under duress, Koffigoh agreed to dissolve his transitional administration and announced a new 25-member "national unity government" on 31 December which Eyadéma and his supporters are expected to control.

Political Rights and Civil Liberties:

Citizens of Togo cannot democratically change their government. Voting has been compulsory by law in the past and citizens were only able to vote "yes" or "no" for one candidate.

Dissidents have been subjected to indefinite detention without charge, and torture of political prisoners has been common. Nonetheless, the president asserted in January 1991 that there was not a single political prisoner in Togo.

With the passage of a more liberal press code, a flood of condemnations of the regime were published in 1991. The broadcast media, still in government hands, has been exhibiting greater independence, but the regime has emphasized that freedom of expression does not give license to "slander" the head of state. Early in 1991, the regime attempted to restrain coverage of turmoil, dissent and corruption within the country by the many independent periodicals which were springing up in the capital and elsewhere. Journalists stood trial for honest reportage and outspoken editorializing.

Freedom of assembly has been guaranteed under the new constitution, but military troops sporadically continue to shoot and kill demonstrators. Religious activity is no longer hindered as a matter of official government policy. Restrictions on travel abroad have been loosened. All wage-earners must pay dues to the government-linked National Confederation of Workers of Togo (CNTT), which holds a virtual monopoly on union activity.

Tonga

Polity: Monarchy and partly elected legislature
Economy: Capitalist
Population: 108,000
PPP: na
Life Expectancy: 59.0
Ethnic Groups: Tonga (98 percent), other Pacific Islanders and Europeans (2 percent)

Political Rights: 3
Civil Liberties: 3
Status: Partly Free

Overview:

The major story of 1991 for this island nation concerned the ongoing scandal stemming from the sale of passports to foreigners. Tonga also saw the largest pro-democracy demonstration in its history.

This South Pacific Kingdom of 200 Islands (45 inhabited) gained independence within the British Commonwealth in 1970. It has been ruled since 1965 by King Taufa'ahua Tupu IV, a 72-year old monarch, who succeeded his mother. The constitution grants the king broad political powers independent of the unicameral Legislative Assembly; he selects the prime minister and the Privy Council, which makes major policy decisions. The 30-member Legislative Assembly consists of nine nobles selected by the 33 hereditary nobles of Tonga, nine people's representatives elected by universal suffrage, and twelve cabinet ministers. On 21 August 1991, Prince Fatafehi Tu'ipelehake, prime minister for over 25 years, resigned due to poor health.

The passport scandal began in 1981 when Tonga started secretly selling passports to non-citizens through the Tongan consulate in Hong Kong and the Tongan Ministry of Police for prices up to $35,000. Most customers were Hong Kong citizens looking to leave the country before China gets control of it in 1997. Customers also included South Africans, Libyans, and Filipinos. Even Imelda Marcos was the recipient of a Tongan passport. After Akilisi Pohiva, a people's representative in the Legislative Assembly, publicly exposed the sales of the passports, they were declared unconstitutional in 1988. In response, the King called a special session of Parliament in February 1991 to change the constitution, granting citizenship to all current holders of Tongan passports, estimated at 426, and taking out the clauses in the Constitution which interfered with the selling of passports.

This action sparked the largest demonstration in Tongan history. Organized by Representative Pohiva, approximately 2,000 people, including opposition leaders, protested against the King's tinkering with the Constitution. The demonstration also set the stage for demands of more democratization. The nine people's representatives in Parliament asked the king to increase the number of people's representatives to equal the nobles' representatives. There have also been increasing calls for an accounting of the proceeds that Tonga earned from the passport sales. The Tongan Justice Minister, Tevita Tupou, insisted that the $14.7 million made from the sales had been fully audited and placed in a trust to be used only for the benefit of the Tongan people. However, the government refuses to release the audits to the deputies in Parliament.

Political Rights and Civil Liberties:

Tongans cannot change their government democratically. Political life is dominated by the nobles and the king through their control of large landholdings. The constitution allows the king broad powers that supersede legislative. Nine members of the Legislative Assembly are elected, but the unelected nobles, combined with the cabinet ministers who sit *ex officio,* retain a permanent majority. There are currently no formal parties, although an informal grouping has formed around people's representative Akilisi Pohiva.

Freedom of the press is guaranteed by the constitution, but the island radio station and largest newspaper, *Kalonikali Tonga/Tonga Chronicle* are government owned. Pohiva publishes a monthly opposition newsletter. A "pirate" television station, ASTL-V3, began transmission in 1984.

In 1990, Tonga began to reorganize its justice system with the creation of a Court of Appeal. This court is completely separate from the judicial system. This took the role of appeals court away from the Privy Council. The right of a fair trial is respected and no one may be summoned before the court without first seeing a written indictment.

Freedom of religion is provided for in the constitution and observed in practice. There are no significant restrictions on freedom of assembly or travel.

Trinidad and Tobago

Polity: Parliamentary democracy
Economy: Capitalist-statist
Population: 1,300,000
PPP: $4,580
Life Expectancy: 71.6
Ethnic Groups: Complex, black (41 percent), East Indian descent (41 percent), mixed (16 percent), white (1 percent)

Political Rights: 1
Civil Liberties: 1
Status: Free

Overview:

The strength of Trinidad and Tobago's democratic institutions was evident in the nation's recovery from the bloody coup attempt by a small group of Muslim extremists in July 1990. In 1991 attention turned to electoral politics, as the opposition People's National Movement (PNM) headed by Patrick Manning, taking advantage of difficult economic conditions, returned to power with a decisive victory over the government coalition of Prime Minister A.N.R. Robinson in elections held on 16 December 1991.

The Republic of Trinidad and Tobago, a member of the British Commonwealth, achieved independence in 1962. The state is composed of two islands, with Trinidad accounting for nearly 95 percent of the country's area and population. Under the 1976 constitution, Trinidad and Tobago became a republic with a president, elected by a majority of both houses in parliament, replacing the former governor-general. Executive authority, however, remains invested in the prime minister.

The political system is a parliamentary democracy. The bicameral parliament consists of a 36-member House of Representatives elected for five years, and a 31-member Senate, with 25 senators appointed by the prime minister and six by the leader of the parliamentary opposition. The prime minister is the leader of the party or coalition commanding a majority in the House. Local government (counties and major municipalities) is elected.

In the December 1986 general elections, the opposition National Alliance for Reconstruction (NAR) led by A.N.R. Robinson decisively defeated the black-based People's National Movement (PNM), which had ruled for 30 years. The NAR took 33 seats in the House. The PNM, led by outgoing Prime Minister George Chambers, took only three. Robinson was credited with forging the first solid opposition coalition, including both black and East Indian elements, against the PNM. The NAR was composed of Robinson's Democratic Action Congress (DAC), the East Indian-based United Labour Front (ULF) led by Basdeo Panday, Karl Hudson-Phillip's Organization for National Reconstruction (ONR), and the Tapia House Movement.

In 1980 the House approved a bill establishing a fifteen-member House of Assembly for Tobago, with twelve members directly elected for four years and three named by the majority party. In January 1987 Tobago was granted full internal self-government. In elections held in November 1988, the NAR retained eleven of its twelve seats.

After assuming office in 1986, Prime Minister Robinson contended with key defections from his ruling coalition. By 1988 the Tapia House Movement had withdrawn and Panday, the NAR deputy leader, and three other NAR members of parliament had been expelled. Panday formed a new East Indian-based party, the United National Congress (UNC) in 1989, and became the official opposition leader in 1990. Robinson also encountered a series of labor strikes as powerful unions protested the government's economic austerity program and the declining standard of living. By mid-1990 polls showed a sharp decline in support for the government.

On 27 July the radical Moslem group Jamaat-al-Muslimeen, led by Yasin Abu Bakr and numbering less than 300 members, seized the nation's parliament and the state-run television facility. A five-day stand-off marked by rampant looting in the capital city Port of Spain left at least 23 people dead and more than 300 wounded according to official sources. The siege ended when the government tricked Bakr into believing the insurgents would receive amnesty if they surrendered.

In the aftermath, Bakr and 112 others were arrested and charged with treason, murder and kidnapping, among other charges. In 1991 defense lawyers challenged the validity of the charges, claiming that Bakr had given up the rebellion in exchange for amnesty. However, the High Court and Court of Appeal ruled in 1991 that an amnesty does not negate the process of law. The trial was expected to continue into 1992.

The coup attempt delivered a shock to the country's already ailing economy, causing tens of millions of dollars in damages and setting back an anticipated tourist boom that the government had hoped would soften the effects of its austerity program. It also left the Robinson government struggling to restore confidence amid increasing animosity between the roughly equal black and East Indian communities.

In fall 1991, Robinson called for new elections. On 16 December the PNM won 21 of 36 parliamentary seats and Manning became the prime minister. Panday's UNC became the official opposition by winning 13 seats. The election was a crushing defeat for Robinson, whose NAR won only two seats.

Political Rights and Civil Liberties: Citizens are able to change their government through free and fair elections. Constitutional guarantees regarding the right to free expression and the right to organize political parties, civic organizations and labor unions are respected.

There are a number of human rights organizations. Traditionally active in addressing allegations of police brutality, in 1989 they criticized government anti-narcotics initiatives that would give power to the police to conduct searches without a warrant. Following the 1990 coup attempt, these groups reported scattered charges of harassment by security forces against the Muslim community, which comprises six percent of the nation's population. Freedom of religion, however, is generally respected.

Labor unions are well organized, powerful and politically active. They have the right to strike and have done so frequently in recent years. Since 1988 organized labor has spearheaded a campaign against the government's austerity programs. An independent industrial court plays a central role in arbitrating labor disputes.

Newspapers are privately owned, uncensored and influential. There are independent dailies as well party publications. Radio and television are both public and private. Trinidad and Tobago's new media giant, Caribbean Communications Network (CCN), launched the country's second television station in 1991. The other station is run by the state-owned Trinidad and Tobago Television Company.

An independent judicial system is headed by a Supreme Court, which consists of a High Court and a Court of Appeal, with district courts operating on the local level. Under the constitution, there is a right of ultimate appeal to the Privy Council of the United Kingdom.

Tunisia

Polity: Dominant party
Economy: Mixed capitalist
Population: 8,400,000
PPP: $3,170
Life Expectancy: 66.7
Ethnic Groups: Arab

Political Rights: 5
Civil Liberties: 5
Status: Partly Free

Overview: The leading issue in Tunisia in 1991 was the government's increasing repression of the Islamic fundamentalist opposition. Unrest during the Persian Gulf war led to a crackdown in which several hundred were arrested, and violence spread to the country's universities.
President Ben Ali continues to ban Tunisia's strongest opposition group, the

Islamic Al- Nahda, or Renaissance Party. In a concession early in 1990, Ben Ali allowed Al- Nahda to start its own newspaper, *Dawn*, but the government banned a special election week issue of the paper in June 1990 and threatened its editor. The government accused the party of forming a clandestine group in 1988 that was responsible for increasing acts of violence in the capital.

In February 1991 the government faced unrest from groups of pro-Iraq fundamentalists and leftists opposed to the country's neutral stance in the Persian Gulf War. On 6 February, security forces fired at demonstrators who were attacking National Guard headquarters in the south. Eight people, including three National Guardsmen, were wounded. On 17 February the offices of the Ruling Constitutional Rally (RDC) in Tunis were set on fire by protestors, killing at least one security guard and wounding three others. Following these attacks, the president named Abdallah Kallel as the new Interior Minister, charging him with taking a more hardline approach in suppressing Al-Nahda. Over 800 people connected with the group were arrested following the 17 February attack, leaving only three members of the executive committee free. Eventually, five of the fundamentalists arrested were sentenced to death and seven others given life sentences for participating in the attack on the offices.

After the attack on the RDC bureau, remaining members of Al-Nahda's executive committee announced they were suspending the group's activities and issued a statement declaring that the attack appeared to be instigated by younger members of the movement. Many saw the statement, which reiterated a commitment to peaceful means, as a rebuff to the exiled Al-Nahda president, Rashid Ghannouchi, a staunchly pro-Iraq hardliner. Mouru also announced the possible formation in the future of a new, more moderate Islamist party, an act cautiously welcomed by the government.

The disbanding of Al- Nahda did not stop the violence, which shifted from the streets to the campuses. The government closed the fundamentalist General Union of Tunisian Students (UGET) on 29 March following a series of raids during which the police claimed to have found anti-government tracts and materials to make petrol bombs. In reaction, a series of clashes erupted at various universities, with students attacking university administration offices and attempting to burn down campus police stations. After the government began to require students to show their identity cards in order to enter campus, fundamentalists held a demonstration on 6 May, demanding that the UGET be reinstated. In the clashes with police that followed, at least two students were killed with dozens injured.

In a startling announcement on 22 May, the government claimed that the violence was all part of a coup plot hatched by Ghannouchi and his hardline fundamentalist followers. New Interior Minister Kallel detailed a five-stage plan through which the Islamists planned to take power by force and establish a theocratic state, including: 1) distribution of anti-government tracts; 2) demonstrations; 3) violent attacks on symbols of authority; 4) unrest in schools and universities; and, 5) with the spread of anarchy, a call for popular uprising, with Islamist agents in the military taking over the government. The scant evidence given included a videotape of a military man giving details of the plot and a display of captured weapons, mostly knives, irons bars and material to make gas bombs. Over 300 militants, one-third from the army, were arrested in connection with the alleged coup plot.

Following the arrests, the Tunisian League of Human Rights (LTDH) issued a communiqué condemning the "serious penalties" (torture) which have accompanied the operations to restore order and announced the creation of a team to investigate the death of two members of Al-Nahda while in detention. On 20 June, Amnesty International accused the government of holding "more than seventy people" incommunicado for more than the ten-day limit prescribed by Tunisian law and torturing some of them. A senior official at the U.S. State Department also criticized the Tunisia human rights record. In contrast to the contempt the government has often shown when faced with such charges, it appointed a commission headed by prominent politician Rachid Driss to investigate the accusations of human rights abuses and to determine the cause of death of the two Al-Nahda members. Furthermore, the government promised the LTDH access to detention centers.

The virtual elimination of Al-Nahda means the elimination of real opposition. The "legal" opposition parties—including the Democratic Socialist Movement (MDS), Tunisian Communist Party (PCT), the Popular Unity Party (PUP), the Progressive Socialist Assembly, the Progressive Social Party (PSP) and the Unionist Democratic Union—are weak and dependent on the government. Wary of alarming Western aid donors and trading partners, President Ali renewed his attempts towards strengthening the opposition, offering parties financial support along with funds for printing newspapers. He also promised additional access to the media. Most significantly, President Ali offered to not present any candidates during the legislative by-elections in October, which would guarantee the opposition at least nine seats in the 141-seat Chamber of Deputies. The Chamber has been composed exclusively of RDC members since its inception in 1959. The offers pitted the opposition's need for financing against their desire to be considered independent of the government. The largest groups, the MDS and the Progressive Socialist Assembly, rejected the offer, claiming the elections would not be credible without the participation of all parties.

In foreign affairs, the country's refusal to firmly support the coalition against Saddam Hussein caused the United States to eliminate all military aid and reduce economic aid by 76 percent. However, during a July visit French head of state François Mitterand renewed his commitment to repairing relations with Tunisia.

Political Rights and Civil Liberties:

Though Tunisia is constitutionally a parliamentary democracy, in practice the right of its citizens to democratically change their government is limited. The ruling RCD holds a monopoly on power and the parliament essentially reaffirms policy made by the president. Political parties other than the RCD have been allowed to form, but the leading opposition movement, the fundamentalist group Al- Nahda, is still denied recognition. All political parties require government authorization, and only groups which are authorized may be allowed to hold public meetings, which call for further government approval. Islamic fundamentalists are subject to government harassment, delays in passport renewal, phone taps, mail opening, searches without warrant, arbitrary arrest and detention and physical abuse by unidentified plainclothesmen. Several civil servants have been fired and transferred on the basis of their enthusiasm for Islam. The government has maintained a heavy police presence in universities to oversee student demonstration and Islamic groups. The government also runs the mosques and may appoint and dismiss all imams.

Cases of torture against political dissidents, mainly Islamic fundamentalists, were reported in 1991. Under the law, suspects may be held incommunicado for up to ten days before being brought before a judge. According to Amnesty International, incommunicado detention often exceeds the statutory time limits. Tunisian law permits arrests and searches without a warrant. President Ben Ali has publicly endorsed an independent judiciary, but the executive wields influence over judges by having the authority to grant them tenure and by assigning them to different districts. Special security courts were abolished in 1988.

The Tunisian press is both privately and publicly owned; and in 1991 there were approximately 115 domestic newspapers. Self-censorship is frequently practiced as most printing houses are dependent on government money and all written material must have prior authorization to be published. Specific issues of newspapers have been confiscated for articles critical of the government. The press is not allowed to print communiqués from the Al-Nahda. During the Gulf War, censorship increased for articles judged to be "inflammatory." Writers, editors, and publishers are often arrested, imprisoned or fined on charges of defamation. Television and radio are state-owned and operated and coverage heavily favors the government, although President Ali has promised air time to the opposition. *Le Maghreb,* a private newspaper, was forced to close in early 1991 when its government-owned printing house refused to publish the paper. The newspaper's staff believes that the action was taken in retaliation for the paper's critical reporting. In February 1991 the government closed Al-Nahda's weekly, *Al-Fajr,* for the third time since it was first published in April 1990.

Islam is the state religion, and while the small Christian and Jewish communities are generally free to practice, the Baha'i may not worship. Tunisians are relatively free to travel within and outside the country, but the Tunisian Human Rights League is concerned about the withholding of passports from fundamentalists. Twenty percent of workers are unionized and almost all belonging to the General Union of Tunisian Workers (UGTT), which has become increasingly independent. The government has instituted a series of reforms to improve the lot of women.

Turkey

Polity: Presidential-parliamentary democracy
Economy: Capitalist-statist
Population: 58,500,000
PPP: $3,900
Life Expectancy: 65.1
Ethnic Groups: Turks (85 percent), Kurds (12 percent), others (2 percent)

Political Rights: 2
Civil Liberties: 4
Status: Partly Free

Overview:

In 1991 the major issues for Turkey were the Persian Gulf war and the resulting influx of Iraqi Kurdish refugees, its own Kurdish separatist movement and parliamentary elections which ended Turgot Ozal's eight-year domination of politics.

Mustafa Kemal Ataturk proclaimed the Turkish republic in 1923. The country has maintained a pro-Western foreign policy and has been a member of NATO since 1952. Free elections were first held in 1950, although the military has intervened several times to maintain public order. A military coup ousted an elected government in 1980 and imposed martial law until 1983. One month after the November 1983 elections, the Motherland Party formed a government under prime minister Ozal, who used a parliamentary majority to become president in 1989. The 1982 constitution provides for a unicameral National Assembly which elects a president. The president appoints the prime minister and can dissolve the Assembly with the concurrence of two-thirds of Parliament or if faced with government crisis of more than 30 days. President Ozal supported the U.S.-led allied coalition against Iraq in the Persian Gulf war. Immediately after the August 1990 Iraqi invasion of Kuwait, the President shut an important pipeline carrying Iraqi oil and sent troops to its southeastern border with Iraq. On 17 January, as the allies began their intense bombardment of Iraq, Turkey authorized the use of Incirlik Air Base for American air strikes.

Islamic fundamentalist as well as mainstream opposition parties assailed the President for siding with the American-led coalition. In January, there were several anti-war demonstrations, including one which attracted an estimated 40,000 people. The government attempted to conceal the extent of the country's involvement in the war: CNN television news coverage of air strikes launched from Turkish bases was interrupted by soft waterfall scenes and commercials. In addition, the lack of gas masks caused widespread alarm about the possibility of Iraqi retaliation.

In the aftermath of the war, over 500,000 Iraqi Kurds fled to Turkey's southeastern border to escape the backlash of Iraqi dictator Saddam Hussein. Under international pressure, on 15 April the government lifted the ban on refugees entering the country, which had been in place out of fear the influx would heighten the problem of containing its own Kurdish separatist movement, the Marxist Kurdish People's Party (PKK).

President Ozal made some attempts to resolve the domestic Kurdish problem. In February Ozal called for the lifting of the restrictions on the Kurdish language—a move strongly opposed by Turkish nationalists. The military took steps to suppress Kurdish separatist activities. Throughout most of 1991, fierce battles occurred between Turkish forces and the 8,000-strong PKK, which has been waging its campaign for an independent Kurdistan since the mid-1980s. In August Turkish forces set up a three-mile buffer zone into Iraq from which it launched attacks on PKK bases. In the fall, Turkish forces napalm bombed and strafed PKK-controlled Kurdish villages. Ozal supported the idea of an independent Kurdistan in Iraq and secretly met with Iraqi Kurdish leaders, but rejected any compromise of Turkish borders.

The country experienced major domestic political shifts in 1991. In June, the ruling Motherland Party (Anap) elected Mesut Yilmaz as chairman, thus ousting Prime Minister Yidrim Akbulut. It was the first time a sitting prime minister had lost his post through a party congress. On 20 October Turkey held parliamentary elections in which a variety of political parties participated, due to the nullification of the much-reviled penal code articles banning Communist, Islamic or Kurdish separatist parties. In a significant reversal, Ozal's Anap Party—with only 24 percent of the vote—lost to the True Path Party, led by Suleyman Demirel, which won 27 percent of the vote and 180 of 450 seats in parliament. In order to attain a parliamentary majority, the True Path formed a coalition with Erdal Inonu's left-of-center Social Democratic Populist Party and a tripartite alliance of union-linked liberal democrats, remnant Ataturkists and pro-Kurdish lobbyists. The coalition claimed 48 percent of the vote and 57 percent of the seats in parliament. The Welfare Party, the country's main Islamic group, won 17 percent of the vote. According to polls, Turkish citizens had been disenchanted with the Anap party, particularly the perceived nepotism within the

Ozal clan—Ozal's wife Semra became chairperson of Anap in Istanbul—and the inability of the government to curb the 66 percent inflation rate.

Demirel has been premier six times previously and ousted twice by the army in military coups. He and Inonu, stating democratization as the new government's top priority, immediately agreed upon a sweeping political reform program, including a new constitution to replace the one promulgated by the generals who ruled from 1980 to 1983. The government promised to restore the right of students, academics and labor unions to take part in political activities, grant the state-owned radio and television network autonomy, and improve the country's human rights situation. The prime minister vowed to have Parliament examine the legality of Ozal's presidency, which he claims is unconstitutional.

Demirel also emphasized a commitment to resolving the Kurdish problem "with compassion," while maintaining Turkey's territorial integrity. The new government proposed granting the Kurds cultural and social rights, including publication of Kurdish newspapers, and suggested enabling Kurds in the southeast to administer their own affairs.

Economists estimate the Persian Gulf war cost Turkey $5 billion in lost revenue from the Iraqi pipeline and tourism. In addition, the country has a $49 billion foreign debt and a 60 percent inflation rate which has led to union discontent over wage restrictions. President Ozal began a virtual economic revolution in Turkey in the 1980s, which included opening Turkey's external markets, privatization of state-run companies and reducing subsidies. However, the government-sector, of which only one-third was profitable, remained overwhelmingly and inefficiently large. The European Economic Community, of which Turkey is an associated member, continued to deny Turkey full membership, citing that Turkey still imposes charges on EC exports. The issue was further complicated by Turkey's intransigence on Cyprus, which prompted Greece to continue to veto Turkish membership in the EEC.

Political Rights and Civil Liberties:

Turks have the right to change their government democratically, but the country's history of military intervention has limited the scope of democratic politics. In April Turkey nullified the constitutional ban on Islamist and communist political activity; the move commuted death sentences given before April 1991 and amnestied about 40,000 prisoners. The government simultaneously passed the Anti-terror act, which human rights groups assailed for broadening the definition of terrorism, lengthening prison sentences, adding restrictions on press and political activity and making it difficult to bring legal action against police for torture.

The Turkish police force is known to carry out serious human rights abuses. In 1991 human rights organizations reported widespread torture of detainees by security forces and scores of suspicious deaths of detainees. Defendants generally have the right to an open trial, free counsel is provided to indigents and cases are heard by a judge or panel of judges. Certain cases are heard by martial law and state security courts, which try those charged with terrorism, drug smuggling and other crimes against the state.

Although privately-owned media criticizes the government and reflects a variety of opinions, there are significant restrictions on speech and press. The criminal code provides penalties for those who "insult" the president, parliament or army. The government frequently harasses and arrests left-wing journalists and often confiscates left-wing written material. There are tight restrictions on media coverage of events in southeastern Turkey. Despite a 1991 law allowing the use of the Kurdish language—previously one could receive a prison sentence for speaking Kurdish in public—there are no Kurdish media outlets. Turkey continues to suppress expression of Kurdish cultural identity.

Turkey allows Jews and Christians to practice their religions, but there are some restrictions on Christian missionaries. The official secularism of the regime restricts the religious expression of Islamic fundamentalists, but Islamic religious instruction is compulsory for Muslims. Turkey has seen an upsurge in Islamic fundamentalism since the 1980s. The government severely restricts trade union activity.

Tuvalu

Polity: Parliamentary democracy
Economy: Capitalist
Population: 9,000
PPP: na
Life Expectancy: 58.1
Ethnic Groups: Polynesian

Political Rights: 1
Civil Liberties: 1
Status: Free

Overview:

A series of nine atolls in the South Pacific, Tuvalu is one of the smallest countries in the world; the country's total land area is approximately 10 square miles. Formerly part of the British empire, Tuvulu became a "special member" of the Commonwealth in October 1978. The British crown is still represented by a governor-general.

The legislative branch consists of a unicameral Parliament with members elected by the public for four year terms. Executive control is in the hands of the prime minister, elected from among the members of Parliament, and the cabinet. On the advice of the prime minister, the governor-general officially forms the cabinet. The current prime minister is Bikenibeu Paeniu.

The biggest news for Tuvalu in 1991 was the discovery that the country was actually sinking into the Pacific Ocean. Most of the islands which make up Tuvalu are very flat and only a few feet above sea-level. In recent years, the tide has been reaching farther up the beaches and typhoons have had a more damaging effect on the interiors of the islands. Numerous experts have been to the islands to figure out what could be done with this problem that also threatens neighboring Pacific Island nations, such as Tonga and Kiribati. A coral sea wall held together by wire netting was constructed at Funafuti, the capital atoll, but the wire rusted and the wall disintegrated. A concrete wall was put in its place.

Political Rights and Civil Liberties:

Tuvaluans have the right to change their government democratically. Elections are freely contested and the judiciary is free from government control. The Parliament is composed of twelve members, two from each of the four islands with populations in excess of 1,000. Both the biweekly newspaper, *Tuvalu Echoes/Sikuleo o Tuvalu,* and radio are government-controlled. There is no television. The constitution guarantees freedom of religion and assembly.

Uganda

Polity: Military
Economy: Capitalist statist
Population: 18,700,000
PPP: $410
Life Expectancy: 52.0
Ethnic Groups: Acholi, Alur, Baganda, Chiga, Gisu, Jie, Karamojong, Labwor, Lango, Lugbara, Madi, Nkole, Nyoro, Soga, Teso, Turkana, and Toro

Political Rights: 6
Civil Liberties: 6
Status: Not Free

Overview:

In 1991 this East African nation continued to be plagued by rebel violence, human rights abuses by government forces, a stagnating economy, and the rampant spread of AIDS.

Uganda is ruled by the unelected President Yoweri Museveni. In early 1986 Museveni seized control of the state as leader of the guerrilla National Resistence Army (NRA) and then retained power as the head of the purportedly "interim" National Resistence Council (NRC). In 1990, Museveni announced the extension of the life of the NRC and his own term in office until at least 1995.

Inter-ethnic warfare, insurrection, intermittent coups, and brutal dictatorships have been a sad fact of life in Uganda virtually since its independence in 1962, and have led to the deaths of an estimated 800,000 Ugandans. After the ouster of strongman Idi Amin by Tanzanian troops in 1979, the country was ruled by Milton Obote, whose re-installed regime was marked by military atrocities, further economic disintegration, corruption, and civil strife. In July 1985, Obote was deposed by Liutenant General Tito Okello, who six months later was overthrown by Museveni at the head of the NRA.

Since taking control as commander-in-chief of the NRA and chairman of the NRC, President Museveni has become one of the most powerful leaders in Uganda's history. The President has asserted that chief among his political goals is the restoration of democracy, but has made clear that while "democracy" may mean respect for human rights as well as regular and open elections, it does not necessarily mean multi-partyism. Rather, Museveni has said that a mass democracy without any parties is more appropriate until the country is economically developed. The NRM has organized "Resistance Council Committees" on the local and regional levels to administer their respective jurisdictions and to encourage popular participation in support of the regime.

The NRM regime has worked to undermine Uganda's traditional political parties, declaring them suspended. The government dismisses the parties as antiquated and only representing narrow, elite interests. In October 1991 former President Godfrey Binaisa announced in London the formation of the Uganda Democratic Reform, a political organization committed to democratization and demilitarization of politics in the country. There have been calls both within and outside the country for a national referendum on multi-partyism or formation of a transition government leading to multi-party elections after a national conference is held. The president said in November that the opposition would be allowed to contest the 1995 elections.

The NRM formed a constitutional review committee in 1989 to travel throughout the country and consult with Ugandans on the type of political system they preferred. Nonetheless, the political opposition has charged that the NRM concept of "democracy" means codification of NRM rule in a new constitution. Moreover, at a constitutional seminar organized in 1991 by the NRA, military commanders emphasized that they would intervene to overthrow the constitution in case of conflict if the government "represents the minority interest" when, at the same time, "the army represents the majority interests." The constitution is not to be completed until 1995.

In what has come to be the tradition in Uganda the president has given key jobs in government, the military, and the security apparatus to those from the same region of the country as himself, consequently antagonizing Ugandans from other regions. Because President Museveni comes from southern Uganda, his government has continued to face insurgencies in the north, west, and east of the country. The rebel Uganda People's Christian Democratic Army, continued its abductions and violent assaults in north-central Uganda in 1991. Although it was alleged by the government of causing most civilian casualties there, press reports indicate that the majority of deaths in 1991 were in fact the result of army excesses. The military has rarely hesitated to use brutal tactics in its war against rebels and their unarmed civilian supporters. Meanwhile, another rebel group, the rebel National Army for the Liberation of Uganda, operating in the Ruwenzori Mountains of the west and led by an ex-minister in the Obote regime, also fought the NRA during counter-insurgency operations in 1991.

In late 1990 a force of several thousand Rwandan refugees invaded Rwanda from Uganda. They were led by a Rwandan national who was one of Uganda's top army officer. Rwanda charged that the Ugandan government had been aware of the insurgent intentions of many Rwandan nationals serving in the NRA and of the massing of forces on the border in preparation for the invasion. In 1991 the beleaguered Rwandan regime charged that the Ugandan government was assisting the rebels in plans to mount another attempt to topple it. The Ugandan government denied the charges. The continuing tension at the border led to some brief clashes between Ugandan and Rwandan troops during the year. There are some 300,000 Rwandan refugees in Uganda.

Another serious crisis facing the country is the rapid spread of AIDS, which has devastated significant areas of the country, particularly in the south.

In economic affairs, the country continues to feel the effects of debt servicing, low coffee prices, slow capital inflow, a poor transportation and distribution infrastructure, unemployment, and inflation. The military accounts for nearly 50 percent of the budget. There are also charges that government troops engage in large-scale cattle rustling in northern and eastern Uganda, deriving extra income from the illegal trade in hides and meat.

Political Rights and Civil Liberties:

Ugandans cannot change their government democratically. Political parties are suspended, though not banned, and they face government intimidation and harassment. The judicial system is based on the British model, and defendants in most non-political civil and criminal trials enjoy fundamental legal rights. The government manipulates the legal system to intimidate and punish non-violent political opponents; those charged with seditious activity can be detained for years without charge or trial. Freedom of assembly is curtailed for political groups and the government frequently breaks up demonstrations and party meetings. The press has covered a broad range of topics, including guerrilla fighting, human rights abuses by the army, and other politically sensitive issues. Journalists do face harassment, however, and their ability to cover counter-insurgency activities in 1991 were severely limited by the regime's efforts to avoid damaging international publicity about illegal army violence. President Museveni denounced "those in the habit of putting out seditious publications or statements against the state and the army."

There have been numerous instances of such violence against civilians in rebel areas, particularly in the northern and eastern regions of the country. During an army campaign to root out insurgency in spring 1991 in northern Uganda, thousands of people were arrested and "screened" to uncover rebels or their sympathizers. Many suffered beatings at the hands of soldiers during interrogation. Rapes and extrajudicial executions of prisoners during these operations were also alleged by residents of this region. A government minister, two members of parliament, and a number of local civilian officials who lodged protests with the army against such abuses were formally charged with treason. Rebel groups have also been responsible for slaughtering and kidnapping civilians, including women and children.

Nonpolitical associations and independent human rights groups must register with the government. Their members are often subject to official intimidation. The government does not interfere with religious practice. Rebel activities have put certain restrictions on domestic travel. Workers are organized under the National Organization of Trade Unions (NOTU).

Ukraine

Polity: Transitional
Economy: Statist-transitional
Population: 51,449,000
PPP: na
Life Expectancy: na
Ethnic Groups: Ukrainian (72.6 percent) ; Russian (22 percent); others (5.4 percent)

Political Rights: 3
Civil Liberties: 3
Status: Partly Free

Overview:

Ukraine, the former Soviet Union's second-largest republic and a major agricultural-industrial power, became an independent state on 1 December 1991, effectively triggering the final collapse of the 69-year Union of Soviet Socialist Republics (USSR). The proclamation, recognized by 25 nations before year's end, culminated seven decades of struggle that included: the forcible incorporation of most of Ukraine into the USSR after a civil war and a period of independence in 1918-1919; the death of 7 million Ukrainians during Stalin's man-made famine; anti-Soviet insurgencies during and after World War II; the suppression of human rights activists in the 1960s-70s; and the emergence of a democratic opposition movement in the mid-1980s spearheaded by former political prisoners.

By December 1991 leaders of Ukraine, Russia and Belarus, the three Slavic former Soviet republics, met in Minsk, the capital of Belarus, and established a Commonwealth of Independent States (CIS), later joined by eight former republics (Georgia and the three Baltic Republics did not join). Before the end of the year, Ukraine and Russia were wrangling over such issues as Ukraine's insistence on nationalizing detachments of the Soviet Navy and armed forces on its territory. Ukraine's wariness of its neighbor stemmed from 300 years of Russian and Soviet occupation of large parts of Ukraine (western Ukraine was annexed under the 1939

Hitler-Stalin Pact) marked by paternalism, Russification of Ukrainian culture, and the suppression of Ukraine's Uniate (Eastern Catholic) and Orthodox churches.

While independence was a long-time aspiration of strongly nationalist western Ukraine, the impetus for greater autonomy in eastern Ukraine was the 1986 Chernobyl nuclear disaster north of Kiev, Ukraine's capital. The accident, and Moscow's subsequent indifference, spurred the formation of independent ecological and political associations which called for a greater voice in managing the republic's affairs. By September 1989, independent groups meeting in Kiev established *Rukh* (the Popular Movement of Ukraine for Perestroika), an unlikely amalgam of former political prisoners, newly elected deputies to the all-Union Congress of People's Deputies, reform Communists, and members of the intelligentsia who, unlike the dissidents, had chosen to remain in state/party organs. Unlike similar groups in the Baltics and elsewhere, *Rukh* guaranteed the rights of minorities living in Ukraine. Russians, Jews and other non-Ukrainians held visible positions in the movement, precluding the inter-ethnic and anti-Semitic extremism and violence in other republics.

In March 1990 elections to the 450-member Ukrainian Supreme Soviet (parlia-ment), candidates from nascent political parties under the *Rukh* umbrella ran as the Democratic Bloc against the well organized and orthodox Ukrainian Communist Party (CPU). Given Ukraine's historic restiveness and strategic-economic importance to the USSR, leaders from Stalin to Gorbachev kept a tight rein on Ukrainian politics. Even with glasnost and perestroika, Gorbachev waited until 1989 to purge hardline Ukrai-nian party boss and Politburo member Vladimir Shcherbitsky, a Brezhnevite holdover appointed in 1972 to quell dissident intellectuals. *Rukh* was not permitted to register until 9 February, about a month before elections.

The elections were marred by electoral violations, but the Democratic Bloc did win 90 seats, mostly from the nationalist western Ukraine and Kiev. They represented several parties: the Ukrainian Republican Party, a nationalist group of former dissi-dents and human rights activists from the disbanded Ukrainian Helsinki Union; the Party of the Democratic Rebirth of Ukraine, based on the former Democratic Platform of the Communist Party; the Democratic Party of Ukraine; and the Green Party. A total of 15 parties were established in 1990. Parliament held its first session from 15 May to 3 August. Ideological lines soon became clear: the conservative Communist bloc, called the Group of 239; the Democratic Bloc, which evolved into the National Council with 125 deputies; and the centrists, who voted either way depending on the issues. Live television broadcasts exposed millions for the first time to the Democratic Bloc's positions on democracy and autonomy, speeding the radicalization of a nation that for decades had been essentially forced or deceived into passivity and fear. Media exposure was behind the Democratic Bloc's decision to run 12 candidates for parliament chairman, as each got an hour of TV time to express his views.

On 4 June 1990 parliament elected Communist Party leader Volodymyr Ivashko, the hardline successor to Shcherbitsky, as chairman, with 100 opposition deputies boycotting the vote. Ivashko agreed to relinquish his party post, and was replaced by Stanislav Hurenko. Ivashko subsequently resigned the Supreme Soviet chairmanship to become deputy general secretary of the Communist Party of the Soviet Union (CPSU). On 23 July Leonid Kravchuk, the CPU deputy secretary, was elected Supreme Soviet chairman. Democratic Bloc members were named to several standing committees.

On 16 July 1990, in a development that stunned Ukrainians and the Kremlin, the republic's Supreme Soviet voted 355-4 to adopt a far-reaching Declaration of State Sovereignty. Though falling short of full independence, it proclaimed sovereignty "as supremacy, independence, fullness and indivisibility of the republic within the boundary of its territory, and its independence and equality in external relations." Several factors led to the historic event: growing politicization of citizens manifest in escalating demonstrations and strikes, the departure of hardliner Ivashko as party leader and dwindling party membership, opposition pressure, and Boris Yeltsin's dramatic resignation from the CPSU, which seriously undermined the party's and Gorbachev's power.

Parliament's second session convened on 1 October amid mass demonstrations in Kiev calling from the resignation of Kravchuk and Prime Minister Vitaly Masol, a holdover for the previous regime. When the hardline Group of 239 voted to uphold a ban on public gatherings in parliament square, National Council deputies walked out. Hundreds of students went on a hunger strike in Kiev demanding multi-party elections, nationalization of CPU property and the return of Ukrainian soldiers stationed outside Ukraine. On 17 October Prime Minister Masol resigned. In a blow to President Gorbachev, parliament voted to abstain from consideration of the new union treaty until after the sovereignty declaration was officially implemented. As 1990 ended, Ukraine had signed bilateral agreements of cooperation with eight republics, including Russia. Ukrainian and ethnic Russian coal miners in the Donbas coalfields had held their second national congress, confirming their antagonism toward central authority and establishing their own union.

In 1991 key developments in the independence drive included the unlikely transformation of Supreme Soviet Chairman Leonid Kravchuk, the CPU's former ideological secretary, from a colorless apparatchik to an ardent pro-independence nationalist. He was overwhelmingly elected president of Ukraine in December. Other issues were the 17 March referendum on preserving the Soviet Union, Ukraine's declaration of independence following the abortive coup against President Gorbachev, a national independence referendum, the increasing complexity and importance of the Russian-Ukrainian relationship and economic reform.

In February, more than 500,000 miners in the Donbas coalfields threatened a 24-hour strike to press for wage increases. Ukrainian authorities, who took over the administration of the mines in January, agreed to a 40 percent increase and other benefits. In 1989 the miners joined their counterparts in the Kuzbass and Vorkuta regions in Russia in a series of strikes that paralyzed Soviet energy supplies. The miners became a powerful vanguard for workers' rights.

A crucial test of President Gorbachev's leadership was the all-Union referendum on preserving the "Union of Soviet Socialist Republics as a renewed federation of equal sovereign republics." Kravchuk, pressured by the Kremlin and Ukrainian Communists to back the referendum and by the opposition to boycott the vote, cleverly proposed that in addition to the Soviet referendum, a republican question be included on the ballot: "Do you agree that Ukraine should be part of a union of Soviet sovereign states on the principles of the (1990) declaration of state sovereignty of Ukraine?" His success in having the proposal approved (more than one-third of Communist deputies voted with the Democratic Bloc) revealed that the parliamentary majority was no longer a monolithic Communist-controlled voting bloc and that the sovereignty declaration was being accepted by Communists.

On 17 March, 70.2 percent of voters in Ukraine approved the Gorbachev referendum. But 80.2 percent also approved the republican question, which qualified precisely the kind of agreement Ukrainian citizens preferred.

Kravchuk's emerging national assertiveness was confirmed the following month. Although Ukraine had signed the "nine-plus-one" agreement hailed as a breakthrough in the standoff between the center and republic leaders, Kravchuk skipped the signing ceremony, visiting Germany instead. Once back, he declared the agreement had no juridical force in Ukraine.

Further indication of Kravchuk's position toward the center came at the end of June, when Ukraine's parliament voted overwhelmingly to postpone all discussion of the draft treaty until September. In July, Ukraine used its industrial and agricultural strength to reject all central government-led economic programs. Ukrainian Prime Minister Vitold Fokin rejected an all-union denationalization and privatization plan conceived by Soviet Prime Minister Valentin Pavlov and accepted by the USSR Supreme Soviet. The Ukrainian parliament overwhelmingly voted to reject seven central government laws on foreign currency, taxation and imports-exports. Ukraine also launched substantial efforts to establish a separate currency. These moves were supported by the industrial establishment, as factory managers voted for economic sovereignty in parliament and asked for help in enforcing republican legislation transferring control of their enterprises from Moscow to Kiev.

August was a pivotal month for the independence movement: U.S. President George Bush visited Ukraine, hardliners briefly seized power from President Gorbachev and Ukraine declared independence after the failed coup. During his visit, President Bush, who hoped to relay his willingness to deal with the republics, angered Ukrainians when he warned against "suicidal nationalism" in a speech before the Ukrainian Supreme Soviet. What galled nationalists and reform Communists was that Ukraine's measured progress toward self-determination was largely democratic and free from violent unrest and inter-ethnic confrontation.

Although Kravchuk's initial hesitation to condemn the 9 August coup against Gorbachev angered the opposition, others saw it as a deft ploy to keep all options open. On 24 August, days after the coup, the Ukrainian Supreme Soviet proclaimed independence subject to a referendum (and presidential election) on 1 December. Legislators voted to disband the CPU, temporarily seize Communist property, and amnesty political prisoners.

The independence declaration raised strains between Ukraine and Russia. Russia's President Yeltsin, whose courage during the coup allowed him to eclipse Gorbachev as leader, said Russia reserved the right to review its borders with other republics. Of particular concern were the Crimea and other heavily Russian areas. Delegations from the USSR and Russia rushed to Kiev on 28-29 August to resolve what was described as an "emergency situation." The talks resulted in a document that confirmed the articles of a 1990 Ukraine-Russia treaty regarding territorial integrity of the two states and minority rights. Ukraine also agreed to maintain economic ties with Russia. For the first time, the phrase "the former USSR" was introduced into the political lexicon.

On 5 September opposition deputies gained effective control of Ukraine's parliament. Communist members had attempted to overturn the government's earlier decision to disband the party. But although nominally 324 of 450 deputies were communists before the failed putsch, the party could only muster 50 votes.

Another key issue was the presence of nuclear weapons in Ukraine. Although in its 1990 sovereignty declaration the republic pledged to be a "nuclear-free zone," new political realities, particularly Russia's proposal to have all nuclear weapons transferred to its soil, raised speculation Ukraine would use the weapons as a bargaining chip.

On 17 September plans to create a new economic union from the shambles of the Soviet Union were jeopardized when Ukraine's parliament rebuffed Kravchuk's attempts to ratify an economic compact. After first boycotting an economic cooperation treaty signed by eight republics on 18 October, on 6 November Ukraine signed the pact, partly to assure voters it did not want to cut vital economic links with Russia.

In October Ukraine's parliament began discussing and adopting a legislative package designed to form a 400,000-member army from Soviet military units already in the republic, a national guard and its own border guards. In November Kravchuk announced that Ukraine would never sign a treaty that had the slightest hint of an "administrative central organ." Ukraine did not attend a mid-November meeting to resume work on a draft union treaty. In late-November the Ukrainian leader accused Russia of breaching the economic agreement and declared the agreement was dead.

On 1 December, 90 percent of voters voted "yes" to independence. Kravchuk was elected president with 62 percent of the vote, defeating six candidates. Second was *Rukh* candidate Vyacheslav Chornovil, a dissident journalist who spent 12 years in a labor camp in exile. Even in heavily Russian areas like Donetsk and the Crimea, the pro-independence vote was 77 and 54 percent, respectively. Unlike Russians in the Baltics, most Russians in Ukraine have deep historical roots and territorial loyalty, and with such factors as high rates of intermarriage and the similarity of the two languages, felt less threatened by Ukrainian independence.

In mid-December, President Kravchuk joined President Yeltsin and the leader of Belarus in forming the Commonwealth of Independent States (CIS). Ukrainians emphasized that the CIS, headquartered in Minsk, was a true commonwealth and not a supra-state structure. The year ended amid renewed tensions between Russia and Ukraine over President Kravchuk's plans to nationalize Soviet military and naval forces in Ukraine. Details of the CIS and its ultimate functions had yet to be finalized.

USSR (former) through December 1991

Polity: Transitional
Economy: Statist transitional
Population: *See individual republics*
PPP: na
Life Expectancy: 70.6
Ethnic Groups: *See individual republics*

Political Rights: 4
Civil Liberties: 4
Status: Partly Free

Overview:

In 1991, after over 70 years as the flagship of communism, the Soviet Union unraveled, sundered by the centrifugal forces of nationalism, economic chaos, structural decay, a last-ditch coup attempt, and the vacillating leadership of President Mikhail Gorbachev who, paradoxically, failed to understand that his liberalization policies, far from galvanizing the Soviet people to revitalize the Communist state, would accelerate impulses toward dissolution of the last, forcibly maintained multinational empire.

Almost from the onset of glasnost and perestroika in 1985-86, republics from the Baltics to Russia itself began to assert their sovereignty over political and economic affairs, seizing the opportunity to become masters of their destiny. By 1990, President Gorbachev found himself walking a tightrope between orthodox Communists and reformers, free-marketeers and command economy bureaucrats, separatists and statists, stubbornly searching for a middle road that wasn't there. His unwavering commitment to communism blinded him to the political, economic and social realities of a huge country rapidly spinning out of control and prevented him from fully abandoning the Marxism-Leninism that was the core of its plight.

All these factors coalesced in 1991, with the collapse of the nuclear superpower that once controlled much of Europe, and for decades defined the context of global relations. Its historic demise, however, left a volatile situation at year's end, with newly independent republics facing inter-ethnic strife, crippled economies, and the specter of a resurgent, imperialist Russia. In the latter half of 1990, amidst intense political, economic, ethnic and social upheaval a frustrated Gorbachev improvised from crisis to crisis as the central government's control over national events gradually weakened. Abandoned by his democratic-liberal allies for his reluctance to fully embrace radical reforms and for consolidating his presidential power, Gorbachev also faced resistance from the conservative Soyuz (Union) parliamentary block. Straddling an increasingly untenable middle-ground, Gorbachev had to chose a power base to maintain initiative and authority.

In January 1991, he seemed to side with hardliners, among them Vice President Gennady Yanayev, Defense Minister Dimitri Yazov, KGB Chairman Vladimir Kryuchkov, Prime Minister Valentin Pavlov, and Interior Minister Boris Pugo. Soviet forces were sent to intimidate the democratically elected governments of three Baltic republics (Latvia, Estonia, Lithuania) which had declared independence. On 13 January, Soviet OMON Black Berets opened fire on a group of unarmed civilians guarding the television station in Vilnius, Lithuania, killing 14 people. Earlier, President Gorbachev had threatened to impose direct rule on Lithuania. His decision to place himself firmly in the ranks of those advocating strong central rule to keep the Soviet Union in tact put him on a collision course with Russian leader Boris Yeltsin, his chief rival, who supported an alliance of nationalist governments among the republics as an alternative power structure.

The killings touched off a wave of angry protests. In Moscow, thousands marched to denounce Gorbachev as a fascist for ordering deadly force. On 20 January more than 100,000 people, organized by Democratic Russia, a coalition of reformers, marched to the Kremlin to protest the bloodshed. Many called for Gorbachev's resignation. Gorbachev's endorsement of the army action, and subsequent calls for renewed controls of the press, rallied the opposition. Demonstrations were also held in Leningrad, Kiev, Sverdlovsk, Donetsk and Kishniev. Yeltsin flew to the Baltics, warning that the possibility of a dictatorship extended far beyond Lithuania.

Another indication of Gorbachev's shift towards the hardliners was a Kremlin plan that gave sweeping investigative power to the KGB and authorized the use of the army to police major cities and regions, ostensibly to combat economic crime. The measure caused protests around the country. In the face of price rises in non-government markets and food shortages Gorbachev also slowed free market economic reform and again seemed to embrace economic communism.

The Communist Party of the Soviet Union (CPSU) renewed attempts to win back control, which had been rapidly eroding in the last several years. At an angry 31 January party plenum, Central Committee members condemned perestroika as a failure, attacked press freedoms and blamed the Kremlin leadership for abandoning Marxist-Leninist principles in favor of a "bourgeois morality." Gorbachev went on television to press voters to support the 17 March referendum on national unity, even as several republics vowed to boycott the vote. In Russia, Yeltsin, in a clear challenge to Gorbachev, had put a second question on the referendum, asking Russians if they favored a direct presidential election.

On 19 February, in a dramatic television interview, Yeltsin called for Gorbachev's immediate resignation for amassing "absolute personal power" and "deceiving the people" with a failed plan for national renewal. He urged public support for his demand to transfer power to the new Federation Council, a consultative body composed of republic leaders. Five days later, 40,000 demonstrators rallied in Moscow to support Yeltsin, who had come under blistering attack in the Communist press for his remarks. A special session of the Russian parliament aimed at ousting Yeltsin was called, but he deftly split the party and, after a weeklong deadlock, won a strong endorsement of his plan for direct presidential elections. He was also granted interim expanded "extraordinary powers" as head of the Russian legislature.

By 17 March, six republics—Armenia, Estonia, Georgia, Latvia, Lithuania and Moldavia—had opted to boycott the referendum. Instead, Lithuania, Latvia, Estonia and Georgia held independence referendums, which were overwhelmingly adopted. While the other republics, particularly in Central Asia, overwhelmingly voted "yes," Ukrainians approved a second question on upholding the republic's 1990 declaration of "sovereignty" and Russian voters affirmed Yeltsin's plan for direct republican presidential elections.

Later in the month, as demonstrations intensified in Moscow, Gorbachev decreed a ban on street demonstrations in the capital and placed the city's police force under the control of the Kremlin's Interior Ministry. Democratic Russia announced it was ignoring the ban and on 27 March, thousands rallied in Moscow.

Another problem facing Gorbachev in the spring was growing labor unrest. A strike by miners in the coal regions of Kuzbass, Karaganda, Vorkuta and Donbas launched in 1 March had paralyzed the industry. In late March, the Supreme Soviet invoked emergency legislation to order an end to coal strike for the next two months, but the measure was ignored. The Donbas miners were demanding pay increases and better living conditions, but the Kuzbass strike was more political, with miners demanding Gorbachev's resignation, dissolution of the USSR Congress of People's Deputies, and the transfer of power to the Federation Council. In early April, coal ministry officials met with leaders of the Independent Union of Miners (IUM) to negotiate an end to the strike which by then involved some 200,000 miners and had stopped production in 150 mines, one-third of the total. Although agreement was reached on wage and productivity issues, the IUM said it would not suspend strikes until its political demands were met. By 15 April the number of mines effected nationwide had grown to 163.

Labor unrest was not limited to the coal mines. In early April, workers in the normally quiescent republic of Belarus staged a spontaneous series of strikes in several factories in Minsk, demanding higher wages to offset price hikes. By 10 April,

100,000 demonstrators jammed the streets of the capital. Strikes continued all month. On 26 April, an estimated 50 million workers in Russia responded to a call by the Federation of Independent Russian Trade Unions by joining a one-hour warning strike or holding meetings at their workplaces to protest against falling living standards.

In early May, Yeltsin dealt a serious blow to Gorbachev's prestige when he returned from the Russian coalfields with a deal to end the two-month strike. The Russian President announced that the coal mines would be transferred to the Russian republic. In a similar move, Ukraine later agreed to transfer control of the Donbass mines to republican jurisdiction.

Two other major issues in April were the ongoing "Nine-Plus-One" talks between the center and nine republics over decentralization, and the announcement of the so-called "anti-crisis" economic program. On 22 April the government announced an economic plan that angered both liberals and hardliners, combining a measure of privatization with stern government discipline, including a ban on strikes. Prime Minister Pavlov described the plan as a "third variant" between the extremes of returning to the old command system and a total embrace of the free market, both of which he said would lead to large scale unemployment and social chaos. Two days after the plan was announced, the CPSU Central Committee blamed Gorbachev for economic stagnation.

On 23 April, a day after parliament endorsed the "anti-crisis" program, President Gorbachev met leaders of nine republics (excluding the three Baltic states, Georgia, Armenia and Moldavia). What emerged was a declaration broadly supporting the anti-crisis program, but altering it in several crucial respects. Some of the price rises were to be reconsidered. The republics were permitted to proceed with economic reform plans of their own. The declaration suggested that President Gorbachev was acknowledging the need to share authority with the republics.

On 21 June, confronted with competing economic plans from the left and right, President Gorbachev declared he would combine the two. He decided not to support the radical plan worked out by liberal economist Grigory A. Yavlinsky, in collaboration with Harvard economists. Rather, he would merge it with the more conservative "anti-crisis" program supported by his prime minister. Gorbachev commented on his plans during a stormy session of parliament, in which he tangled with Soyuz-bloc conservatives, who chided him for giving into the republics and Western institutions such as International Monetary Fund (IMF). Yavlinsky insisted that the two programs were not compatible, a view supported by Yeltsin.

In mid-June a new union treaty draft was sent to republican parliaments. The draft would give the republics, now described as "sovereign states," control over land and natural resources and the right to establish direct diplomatic, consular, trade and other relations with foreign states. The federal center would command the armed forces, foreign economic activity, and the union budget. The draft also included a two-tiered taxation system with a direct federal tax, a provision instantly rejected by Yeltsin and Ukrainian leader Leonid Kravchuk. Kazakhstan also objected to the proposed system.

Politically significant developments in June included the creation of a new opposition coalition, the Democratic Reform Movement (DRM), launched by former Foreign Minister Shevardnadze and Gorbachev senior advisor Aleksandr Yakovlev, and the Ukrainian parliament's decision to postpone all discussion of the draft union treaty until September.

On 28 June, on the eve of the Soviet-U.S. summit, Yakovlev, a leading liberal reformer, resigned as the president's senior advisor because of a deepening rift over the need to force change in the CPSU. Before the resignation, President Gorbachev had sought to alleviate fears among CPSU stalwarts by promising to overturn an order by Russian President Yeltsin barring the party from workplaces and Russian state institutions.

Ukraine's decision to postpone consideration of the union treaty came a few weeks before Gorbachev was to meet leaders of the G-7 industrial nations in London, where he hoped to show a semblance of national unity. In July, Ukraine rejected all central government-led economic programs, including Prime Minister Pavlov's "anti-crisis" program passed by the USSR Supreme Soviet. It also rejected seven central government laws on foreign currency, taxation and imports-exports.

In July, Gorbachev launched an attack on CPSU conservatives, warning that the CPSU was on the brink of demise (it had lost 4.2 million members in two years) and accused hardliners of destroying the Party. He also gave his blessing to the DRM and other progressives in a clear overture to regain liberal support. On 25 July, the start of a two-day meeting of the CPSU Central Committee, Gorbachev lashed out at hardliners, proposing a new charter for the party that rejected some of its key principles, including the sanctity of Marxism-Leninism. He criticized party "fundamen-talists," and sided with reformers seeking to replace militant utopianism with a broad social-democratic platform. The proposed program also stood to bolster Gorbachev's reformer credentials before President George Bush's visit in early August. On 26 July the CPSU leadership overwhelmingly approved Gorbachev's proposed new charter, which embraced such previously heretical ideas as private property, a market economy and a pluralism of views. Nevertheless, liberals outside the party thought the changes were too tame, noting that they were quietly accepted by the Central Committee without the expected backlash from conservatives.

In early August, as food shortages continued, President Gorbachev issued an emergency decree seeking to secure supplies of food and basic consumer goods in the face of falling productivity and warnings of harvest shortages. Meanwhile, hardliners continued to lash out at republican attempts at greater sovereignty. On 14 August, less than a week before an all-union treaty was due to be signed and five days before the coup, Prime Minister Pavlov accused the republics, especially Russia, of sabotaging proposals to tighten monetary discipline. He warned of shortages and the "disintegra-tion of the USSR." The urgency was spurred by President Yeltsin's insistence that most enterprises and resource controlled by the center—including oil and gas—would be transferred to the republics signing the union treaty on 20 August. On 16 August the CPSU expelled Yakovlev, who warned of an impending coup.

On 19 August, one day before the union treaty was to be signed, the Soviet Union and the world were stunned when hardline members of Gorbachev's govern-ment announced the ouster of the vacationing Soviet president and the transfer of power to an Emergency Committee for the State of Emergency headed by Vice President Gennady Yanayev. The key players were Defense Minister Yazov, Prime Minister Pavlov, KGB head Kryuchkov and Interior Minister Pugo. Within two days of the coup, it became apparent that the plotters had not adequately coordinated a national action—telephone lines to the West remained opened, airports were not secured, and the military had not seized key posts in Moscow. On 21 August a defiant President Yeltsin, holed up in the Russian parliament complex, called for nationwide resistance. Three people were killed defying the military curfew, as crowds gathered around parliament to protect Yeltsin. By 22 August, the coup had collapsed and Gorbachev returned to Moscow. But the attempted takeover accelerated forces that were to seal the final collapse of the Soviet Union.

In the coup's immediate aftermath, the CPSU was banned, Ukraine and Belarus declared independence, and the West recognized the independence of the Baltic republics. Russian President Yeltsin, by his heroic stand in the face of the coup, eclipsed President Gorbachev and became *de facto* leader overseeing the dismantling of the USSR. Even as President Gorbachev called an emergency session of the all-union parliament, Armenian President Levon Ter-Petrossyan told a television audience: "The center is dead."

Gorbachev, however, renewed efforts to hold the union together. On 27 August, he announced that Russia and Kazakhstan had agreed with him and the president of Kirgizia on the need for an early signing of a revised treaty between the Kremlin and those republics willing to stay in the union. He proposed the formation of a new economic union. Even as he announced the agreement, Moldavia declared independence.

On 2 September, in a last-ditch effort to prevent fragmentation of the union, President Gorbachev and leaders of ten republics stunned the opening session of the all-union parliament by proposing to transfer all central authority to the republics and an appointed legislative council until a new union could be formed. The interim ruling structure would include a State Council made up of Gorbachev and heads of the republics, a Legislative Council of 20 deputies from each republic, and an Economic Council of republican representatives. The plan called for collective security, details of which would be negotiated separately, the right of each republic to join the United Nations, and the formulation of a new union treaty. In effect, the announcement meant the end of the Congress of People's Deputies, the first and highest authoritative assembly elected by the entire Soviet Union in 1989.

On 5 September the all-union legislature voted to surrender power to the new government largely controlled by the republics, essentially confirming the collapse of central authority. Even as the new emergency government took over, the republics were steadily moving to consolidate their new-found power with little regard for Moscow. Ukraine continued to refuse to participate in any talks of a new union, and scheduled a public referendum and a presidential election for 1 December. On 17 September, Ukraine rebuffed attempts to ratify a new economic compact. Russia continued to expand its own powers at the expense of the center. In November, as Western creditors rescheduled the Soviet debt, four republics, including Ukraine, did not sign the agreement. The same month, Ukraine did not attend a meeting to resume work on a draft union treaty.

A major blow to any final hope of cobbling together a new union was Ukraine's declaration of independence after over 90 percent of the republic's citizens, including a majority of the large Russian population, approved a 1 December independence referendum and elected Leonid Kravchuk president. Just a few days earlier, Russian President Yeltsin assumed control over Kremlin purse strings by agreeing to finance the Soviet payroll and guarantee Soviet state bank credits.

On 8 December leaders of Russia, Ukraine and Belarus—the three former Slavic republics—declared that the Soviet Union had ceased to exist and proclaimed a new Commonwealth of Independent States (CIS). The following day, President Gorbachev rejected the right of the three to dissolve the Soviet Union, but was powerless to stop it. Within days, as other republics suggested they would support the CIS, it was clear that the Gorbachev era was over. On 21 December, eleven former republics formally constituted the CIS in Alma-Ata, capital of Kazakhstan. Only the Baltic nations and Soviet Georgia, embroiled in an uprising against its government, did not join the new commonwealth.

On 25 December, President Gorbachev resigned.

By year's end, the actual function of the CIS remained unclear. There were indications that several republics remained wary of possible Russian hegemony, particularly after Russia insisted it control strategic and tactical forces. It was impossible to predict if the new body would be a true commonwealth of equals, a vehicle for Russian domination or a prototype for a new confederation.

Political Rights and Civil Liberties:

Before the disintegration of the USSR, citizens had only a limited right to change their government democratically.

Gorbachev never faced a popular election for the presidency and the all-union Congress of People's Deputies, which also did not face voters, still reserved 750 seats for CPSU and affiliated organizations. Several republics held presidential elections; some were generally free, while others were uncompetitive and marred by irregularities. The move toward decentralization by the republics substantially weakened formerly authoritarian structures such as the CPSU and the KGB. In January, Soviet forces cracked down in the Baltics, leaving 14 dead in Lithuania. Ethnic violence led to the use of federal troops in South Ossetia, an autonomous region in Georgia, and along the border between Armenia and Azerbaijan. Although steps were taken toward judicial reform in the last few years, in 1991 persons continued to be detained on charges that would be inadmissible in the West. People remained in prison as conscientious objectors or for trying to leave the country or returning after an illegal trip abroad. Some prisoners continued to be held under Article 64 of the Criminal Code, embracing "crimes against the state." Human rights groups both in and outside the Soviet Union continued to raise cases of some 90 people detained in mental hospitals for dubious reasons. Some 12,000 prisoners, sentenced under the old regime for commercial activities, remained imprisoned, though the types of business activities they engaged in were no longer illegal. Human rights abuses and jailing political dissidents did go on in several republics experiencing social unrest, particularly Georgia.

Early in the year, Gorbachev tried to ban demonstrations in Moscow and issued an edict authorizing the army and the KGB to police major cities to prevent economic crimes. The decrees were roundly criticized and largely ignored.

Throughout the year, political parties and associations were free to operate, although most republics barred many CPSU activities. After the coup, the CPSU was banned. An all-union Islamic Renaissance Party was banned in many Central Asian republics.

Early in the year, President Gorbachev attempted to curb press freedoms due to increasingly strident criticism of his policies and the crackdown in the Baltics. His attempts were largely ignored, and newspapers continued to offer diverse views and commentary. There were scores of independent publications in most republics, but press restrictions existed in the Transcauceses and Central Asia. Soviet citizens could express their views freely and openly. Although the short-lived post-coup junta tried to curb civil liberties, it was ignored.

There was increased religious freedom in 1991. The formerly outlawed Ukrainian Orthodox and Uniate (Catholic) Churches were allowed to function and Western clerical leaders of the formerly banned religions traveled to Ukraine and were allowed to say liturgies. There was a resurgence of the Russian Orthodox Church. Despite instances of organized and open anti-Semitism by such groups as Pamyat and the Liberal Democratic Party, more synagogues and schools were open.

Freedom of movement also improved. In May the Supreme Soviet approved a long-awaited law giving citizens the right to emigrate and travel abroad freely. In September Foreign Minister Boris Pankin told the Commission on Security and Cooperation in Europe (CSCE) meeting in Moscow that the law would become fully operational in 1993.

In 1991 the labor movement continued to grow in strength. In March, coal miners from the Independent Union of Miners (IUM) staged a two-month strike that resulted in the Russian Federation and Ukraine taking over control of the mines from the central government. Workers also struck in Belarus and Russia, where the Federation of Independent Trade Unions led a one-day slowdown strike by 50 million workers. During the year, President Gorbachev tried to implement measures that would curb strikes, but the steps went nowhere.

Overviews of what transpired in the republics in 1991 and provisional ratings of political rights and civil liberties are provided below.

Armenia

Population: 3,304,000
Ethnic Groups: Armenian, (93 percent), others

Political Rights: 5
Civil Liberties: 5
Status: Partly Free

In 1991 the non-Communist government of Armenia, a small republic located along the borders of Turkey and Iran, faced a number of serious challenges: ongoing conflicts with republican and central Communist Party leaders in Moscow over the nationalization of party assets; criticism from Communists and Armenian radical nationalist groups for its advocacy of rapprochement with Turkey; renewed violence along the republic's border with Azerbaijan; the resolution of the three-year impasse with Moscow and Azerbaijan over Nagorno-Karabakh, a predominantly Armenian enclave in Azerbaijan; and an economy devastated by the 1988 earthquake, intermittent rail blockades by Azerbaijan, and the influx of 300,000 refugees fleeing ethnic pogroms in Azerbaijan.

The government, headed by Levon Ter-Petrossyan, chairman of the umbrella Armenian National Movement (ANM), was formed in 1990 after a series of tumultuous Supreme Soviet (parliament) elections and runoffs in May, June and July marked by irregularities and violence. Frustrated by Moscow's intransigence on Nagorno-Karabakh's three-year effort to join Armenia, only 50 percent of eligible voters turned out for the first-round in May and candidates obtained an absolute majority in only 74 of 259 electoral districts. After subsequent runoffs in June and July, no single political organization had a clear majority in the new parliament. On 20 July, with only 195 of 259 seats filled, the Supreme Session convened in a session marked by procedural wrangling. 72 percent of the deputies were Armenian Communist Party members, although some had been elected as representatives of the ANM. On 2 August six candidates were proposed for the office of chairman, among them Communist Party First Secretary Vladimir Movsisyan. Leader of the nationalist Union for Self-Determination, Paruir Hairikyan, who was elected to parliament while in exile in the U.S. (he returned in November) said he would not run against Ter-Petrossyan. After three inconclusive rounds of voting, Ter-Petrossyan was elected chairman of the new Supreme Soviet on 4 August.

On 25 August parliament adopted a declaration of sovereignty that called for the establishment of a depoliticized armed forces, the supremacy of the Armenian constitution, a national currency and national bank, civil liberties guarantees and a multi-party system. To the consternation of both Communists and nationalists, the declaration, while acknowledging the 1915 genocide of Armenians by Turkey, did not pledge to recover lands ceded to Turkey. In December tensions between the government and the Communists intensified after a draft resolution banning activities of political parties in state organs and virtually all public institutions. With the return of Paruir Harikiyan, the Union of National Self-Determination and the splinter Republican Party of Armenia, launched confrontational tactics against the Communists, including occupying buildings.

On 2 February 1991, the Armenian Supreme Soviet adopted a law barring the activities of any party headquartered outside Armenia. The measure applied not only to the CPSU, but to traditional nationalist parties functioning abroad. The Supreme Soviet also reiterated that Armenia would boycott the 17 March referendum on preserving the Soviet Union. It voted to hold a republican referendum on secession from the USSR on 21 September in full compliance with a USSR law on the mechanics of secession. In April, parliament declared all Communist Party assets to be state property and authorized the government to sell the property.

Ter-Petrossyan's determination to improve economic and political ties with Turkey led to charges by the Communists and nationalists that the ANM had betrayed the Armenian cause. The criticism intensified after the Turkish ambassador to the USSR visited Armenia in April.

In the spring, violence broke out along the border with Azerbaijan, and continued through the year. In early May, Soviet army troops and Azerbaijani forces killed 35 people during an attack on the Armenian village of Getashen in Azerbaijan. Armenia announced on 9 May that Soviet forces had entered 10 villages since the beginning of the month, and blamed the violence on Moscow's attempts to undermine Armenia's non-Communist government and the republic's sovereignty.

In early July, USSR President Gorbachev decided to lift the state of emergency in two Azerbaijani areas, and almost immediately Azerbaijani forces attacked three Armenian villages in Azerbaijan. Border clashes continued through the month. The same month, a poll indicated that 80 percent of Armenians supported the republic's secession from the USSR, reflecting a loss of trust in Russia as Christian Armenia's protector against its Turkic, Muslim neighbors. Also in July, Prime Minister Vazgen Manukyan, a former Ter-Petrossyan ally, announced he was leaving the ANM and founding his own political party, the National Democratic Union.

On 15 August, the state of emergency imposed in Armenia in 1990 after the killing of a parliament member by paramilitaries was lifted by the Supreme Soviet.

The coup attempt against President Gorbachev gave further impetus to the secessionist movement, and led the Communist party to cease its activities in September. On 21 September, 94.39 percent of the electorate participated in the independence referendum; 99.31 percent voted in favor of secession. Parliament passed a formal declaration two days later.

On 16 October, Levon Ter-Petrossyan was elected President of Armenia, getting over 80 percent of the vote. Nationalist leader Pariur Harikiyan was second, as Sos Sarkisyan of the historic Armenian Revolutionary Party (Dashnak) was third. Ten days later, parliamentary delegations from Armenia and Azerbaijan met in Armenia for the first round of talks on Nagorno-Karabakh. The talks had been brokered by Russian President Boris Yeltsin in September. However, the talks collapsed in November when Azerbaijan refused to restore gas supplies to Armenia. On 10 December, residents of Nagorno-Karabakh overwhelmingly supported a referendum on independence.

With the collapse of the Soviet Union in December, Armenia ultimately agreed to join the Commonwealth of Independent States (CIS) created by Russia, Ukraine and Belarus.

In other issues, the Armenian economy continued to suffer from sporadic interruption of transportation links through Georgia and Azerbaijan. The government remained intent on privatizing the state sector under reform provisions passed in 1990. By the end of April, 60 percent of all land had been distributed to private owners, breaking up most of the collective farms in Armenia. Retail stores and businesses were auctioned off. The large state enterprises were scheduled to be privatized in 1992-93.

Azerbaijan

Population: 7,020,000
Ethnic Groups: Azeris, other Turkic, Armenian

Political Rights: 5
Civil Liberties: 5
Status: Partly Free

In 1991, Azerbaijan was plagued by political and ethnic turmoil. Bloody clashes flared up along the Armenian border, raids by Soviet and Azerbaijani forces into Armenia killed numerous civilians, and the conflict over the predominantly Armenian enclave of Nagorno-Karabakh continued for the third year. Independent opposition groups mounted protests against President Ayaz Mutalibov and a Communist-dominated Supreme Soviet (parliament) elected in 1990 in a vote marred by irregularities.

In January, hundreds of thousands marched through the capital, Baku, on the first anniversary of the Soviet military action that killed 150 Azerbaijanis. The Soviet army had intervened following a week of pogroms against Armenians. Many Azerbaijani's suspected Moscow used ethnic tensions as a pretense to squelch the growing power of the unofficial Popular Front.

On 5 February, the 350-member Supreme Soviet convened, with President Mutalibov urging deputies to work toward democratic reforms. Fifty non-Communist deputies walked out to protest police action against anti-government demonstrators outside the building. They demanded lifting the state of emergency in Baku, unedited television coverage of Supreme Soviet meetings, and the release of detainees. Workers backed the demands with republic-wide strikes which ended after the opposition and the Communists issued a joint statement calling for concrete proposals to the Supreme Soviet to ensure the security of Nagorno-Karabakh and the Armenian border. An opposition Azerbaijani Popular Front member was named deputy chairman of the Council of Ministers.

Later in the month, the opposition Democratic Bloc of Azerbaijan urged a boycott of the 17 March referendum on preserving the Soviet Union. Their statement was supported by several political and social groups. Nevertheless, 75 percent of eligible voters turned out, with 93 percent voting to maintaining the union.

On 19 April, President Mutalibov lifted the curfew in effect in Baku since January 1990. The state of emergency remained in force.

Ethnic clashes broke out along the Armenian-Azerbaijani border in spring, and continued through the year. On 1 May, Soviet troops and Azerbaijani police killed 35 during an attack on the Armenian village of Getashen in Azerbaijan. The next day, 50 more were killed and the village razed by Soviet Interior Ministry (MVD) troops. Armenia also reported attacks on villages within its borders. On 8 May, President Mutalibov ruled out talks with Armenia, saying there could be no compromise on territorial claims and that clashes were caused by Armenian terrorists.

In early July, Soviet President Gorbachev lifted the state of emergency in two Azerbaijani areas. Within days, Azerbaijani special forces OMON troops attacked three Armenian villages in Azerbaijan. More border fighting was reported at the end of the month.

The coup against President Gorbachev effected the political situation in Azerbaijan. After the junta seized power on 18-19 August, President Mutalibov, in Iran on a state visit, said he welcomed the coup as "the natural consequence of the policies that have brought chaos into the Soviet Union..." Returning to Baku, he denied supporting the plotters. The opposition launched demonstrations demanding Mutalibov's resignation, the postponement of 8 September presidential elections, and a declaration the republic's independence. At a 29 August Supreme Soviet session, Mutalibov resigned as Communist Party first secretary. The next day, the Azerbaijani parliament voted to "restore" the republic's independent status of 1918-20.

President Mutalibov had cast himself as a "pragmatic" Communist in 1990, blaming the nationalist Popular Front for the crackdown in Baku. In 1991 he modified his hard-line rhetoric, publicly embracing reconciliation, democracy, and free-market reforms as essential to stability. Polls indicated his approval rating rose from 20 to 76 percent over the year, although the absence of a serious alternative was a factor. Mutalibov ran virtually unopposed in the 8 September elections. The opposition had only one month to collect the requisite 20,000 signatures to get on the ballot because the election law was not published until June. The only alternative candidate, Zardusht Ali-Zade of the Azerbaijani Social Democratic Group, declared his candidacy in mid-July. According to reports, President Mutalibov was so anxious to be seen as promoting democratic elections that when Ali-Zade had trouble getting 20,000 signatures, provincial Communist Party bosses were ordered to make up the deficit.

Voter participation was reportedly over 80 percent, and Mutalibov was overwhelmingly elected. Less than a week later, the Azerbaijani Communist Party voted to disband itself. On 30 September, the Popular Front staged a rally in Baku calling for a dissolution of the Supreme Soviet, democratic elections, and "a mobilization of forces in order to ensure the security of the Azerbaijani population in Nagorno-Karabakh." President Mutalibov agreed on 2 October to begin talks with opposition leaders on dissolving parliament, holding new elections, and restructuring state bodies.

On 30 October, the Azerbaijani Supreme Soviet created the National Council, a permanent 50 seat legislative body, the National Council. Half the seats would be chosen by the president, half by the opposition.

On 26 October, parliamentary delegations from Azerbaijan and Armenia met in Armenia for the first round of formal talks on Nagorno-Karabakh. The talks were brokered by Russian President Boris Yeltsin in September. An appeal urged both sides to refrain from violence. A second round was scheduled for 15 November. Meanwhile, on 1 November, Armenian paramilitary forces reportedly launched a campaign to drive Azerbaijanis out of Nagorno-Karabakh. Thousands were reportedly evicted from their homes. Negotiations were suspended after talks to persuade Azerbaijan to restore gas supplies to Armenia broke down. At a 26 November special session, the Supreme Soviet voted to abolish the autonomous status of the Nagorno-Karabakh Autonomous Oblast. The same day, leaders of both republics flew to Moscow for talks to prevent escalation of the crisis and deputies from Nagorno-Karabakh resolved to hold an independence referendum in December.

On 10 December, the independence referendum in Nagorno-Karabakh was approved by 99 percent of voters. The Azerbaijani population boycotted the vote. On 12 December, Azerbaijan's parliament approved joining the Commonwealth of Independent States (CIS) established by Russia, Ukraine and Belarus after the collapse of the Soviet Union.

Belarus (Byelorussia)

Population: 10,149,000
Ethnic Groups: Byelorussians, Russian, Ukrainian

Political Rights: 4
Civil Liberties: 4
Status: Partly Free

In 1991, Belarus, a Slavic republic bordering Russia and Ukraine continued to shed its long-time pro-Soviet quiescence. Independent political groups, emboldened by the republic's 1990 sovereignty declaration, continued to assert national identity and challenge the ruling Communist party. When the Soviet Union collapsed at year's end, Belarus joined its Slavic neighbors as a founding member of the Commonwealth of Independent States (CIS).

More than glasnost and perestroika, it was Moscow's indifference to the 1986 Chernobyl nuclear disaster that galvanized Byelorussians, including reform-minded Communists, into seriously considering alternatives to central rule. About 20 percent of the population, or 2 million people, live on land contaminated by the radioactive fallout. By 1990 independent groups like the democratic Byelorussian Popular Front became an energetic minority in the Supreme Soviet (parliament) following the republic's first multi-candidate elections in the spring. Though the majority of the 345 seats went to mainstream Communists, the Popular Front, including the Social Democratic Party, Christian Democrats, and others, gained 37 seats. Along with the loose Democratic Club of liberal Communists numbering 80 to 100 deputies, the democratic movement was able to wield considerable influence on the government. In 1990 Byelorussian became the official language, several new parties were formed, and state sovereignty was declared. The Communist party under first secretary Anatoly

Malafeyeu was losing members and initiative. By year's end, it had drafted no new laws and introduced no new legislation.

Nevertheless, at the start of 1991, the Byelorussian Communist Party remained firmly in power. Prime Minister Vyacheslav Kebich and his government strongly supported a continued union with the USSR. Prior to the 17 March referendum on preserving the Soviet Union, authorities effectively silenced opponents of the union, denying them television and radio air time and using the media outlets to influence the public to vote "yes." On voting day, 83 percent of the electorate turned out, and an overwhelming 83 percent approved the proposition, the highest proportion in any republic outside Central Asia.

But in on 3 April, after massive price increases were introduced, tens of thousands of Byelorussian workers went on strike in Minsk—the capital—and other cities. Marches were organized by the newly formed independent Byelorussian Confederation of Labor, which held its inaugural congress on 31 March. On 4 April, tens of thousands of workers, students, doctors and even some government workers marched in central Minsk. The strikers demanded the resignation of the Communist government, new elections, the removal of Communist party committees from the workplace, the legalization of private property, and other political demands. They also demanded compensation for price hikes and a repeal of the USSR sales tax. An all-Byelorussian Strike Committee was organized. Sporadic strikes continued through the month. On 23 April, an estimated 200,000 workers went on strike throughout the republic.

Labor unrest surprised the Communist government and even some opposition leaders. The strikes further weakened the party's influence. The Supreme Soviet rejected a draft law on states of emergency and a proposal that the first president of the republic be elected by parliament rather than popular vote. In July, on the eve of the G-7 summit in London, authorities bowed to international pressure and released journalist Valery Syadou, held for 70 days in pretrial detention for his part in an anti-Communist rally in Minsk. In early August, labor activist Mikhail Razumau, arrested for organizing a blockade in Orsha, won a victory when the judge was disqualified on the grounds that, as a party member, he was subject to government interference.

On 19 August, after hardline Communists launched a coup against Soviet President Mikhail Gorbachev, Byelorussia's parliamentary opposition strongly condemned the coup. Two days later, on the last day of the coup, the Presidium belatedly published a cautious, noncommittal reaction. The Central Committee of the Byelorussian Communist Party strongly backed the putsch, issuing a 21 August statement that used phrases identical to ones issued by the junta.

An extraordinary session of the Byelorussian Supreme Soviet convened on 24 August. That evening, President Gorbachev announced his resignation as general secretary of the Communist Party of the Soviet Union (CPSU) and suspended all party activities. When the Byelorussian parliament reconvened the following day, Supreme Soviet Chairman Mikalai Dzemyantsei resigned and party First Secretary Malafeyeu called for Byelorussia to declare its independence and for the Byelorussian Party to sever CPSU ties. The opposition demanded a ban on party activities in law-enforcement agencies, the handing over of party property, placing KGB and Interior Ministry units under republican control, and a suspension of party activities pending an investigation into its actions during the coup. Communist deputies agreed. Prime Minister Kebich recommended a vote for national independence, which was supported by the Popular Front. The 256 deputies present voted unanimously to proclaim the independence of Byelorussia.

In September, parliament voted to change the name of the republic to Belarus and restore the traditional red-on-white flag. Physicist Stanislau Shushkevich, moderate first deputy chairman of the Supreme Soviet, was named Supreme Soviet chairman. On 2 October, parliament defeated a proposal to lift the temporary ban on the Communist party, but also rejected opposition attempts to dissolve the party and seize its property. In mid-November, Popular Front deputies demanded the resignation of the government, charging Prime Minister Kebich was incapable of creating a market economy.

On 8 December, Russian Leader Boris Yeltsin joined leaders from Belarus and Ukraine in Minsk, and announced the three Slavic republics were forming the nucleus for a new Commonwealth of Independent States (CIS). Later in the month, at a meeting in Alma-Ata representatives of eight other republics agreed to join the body.

Georgia

Population: 5,396,000
Ethnic Groups: Georgians (70 percent); Russians, Armenians, Azeris, Ossetians, others (30 percent)

Political Rights: 6
Civil Liberties: 5
Status: Not Free

Georgia's brief experience with democracy, launched in October 1990 when non-Communists won multi-party Supreme Soviet elections, degenerated in 1991 into escalating ethnic violence, increased repression by President Zviad Gamsakhudria, and ended with bloody clashes in the capital of Tbilisi between opposition militias and troops loyal to the president.

In October 1990 the separatist Round Table/Free Georgia coalition led by Gamsakhudria, a former human rights activist and political prisoner, won 60 percent of the vote and 155 of 250 parliamentary seats, short of the two-thirds majority needed to effect constitutional changes. Thirteen parties or coalitions participated in the election. In November the constituent parliamentary session elected Gamsakhudria chairman and proclaimed the Republic of Georgia, heir to the short-lived republic overthrown by the Bolshevik Army in 1921.

The popular Gamsakhudria had pledged his coalition to restore Georgia's state sovereignty by democratic means and reform the economy. But other parts of Gamsakhudria 's program reflected a Georgian chauvinism, as he became increasingly authoritarian.

By mid-December, violence broke out in South Ossetia, an autonomous region within Georgia and home to 60,000 Indo-European people who settled there in the sixth century. In September South Ossetia had proclaimed itself a union republic. Unrest was triggered by a unanimous vote in the Georgian parliament on 11 December to abolish South Ossetia as a territorial unit on the grounds that the Ossetian campaign for unification with the North Ossetian ASSR in Russia constituted a threat to Georgia's independence. Parliament then declared a state of emergency in response to the shooting of three Georgian policemen in the South Ossetian capital, Tskhinvali.

In early January 1991, with Georgian Interior Ministry (MVD) forces and KGB in South Ossetia to enforce the state of emergency, a decree by Soviet President Gorbachev declared South Ossetia's proclamation and Georgia's abolition of the region's autonomous status unconstitutional. On 9 January Georgia's parliament rejected the order. At the end of the month, Georgian MVD officials arrested Torez Kulumbegov, chairmen of the South Ossetian Oblast Soviet. The same day, the Georgian Supreme Soviet announced Georgia would boycott the 17 March Union-wide referendum on preserving the USSR, and hold an independence referendum on 31 March.

At the end of January, as violence intensified, Georgia's parliament established a 20,000-strong National Guard. In early February, Georgia cut off electricity to Tskhinvali. As fighting continued, Gamsakhudria blamed the Kremlin for fomenting rebellion to undermine Georgian sovereignty and insisted South Ossetia's autonomous status would not be restored.

Another problem was the proliferation of weapons and armed militias, including the ultra-nationalist, 2,000-man *Mkhedrioni* (The Knights of Georgia), formed in 1989 and led by Jaba Ioseliani. On 19 February Soviet forces raided a *Mkhedrioni* training camp outside Tbilisi. Ioseliani, who thought Gamsakhudria's government insufficiently militant, accused Gamsakhudria of planning the incident and pledged to join with other political parties to form "an anti-Facist union." Gamsakhudria had Ioseliani arrested for illegal firearms possession. Sporadic clashes and heavy fighting in South Ossetia continued through the year.

Gamsakhudria's authoritarian streak had emerged. At a 2 February news conference, he threatened to expel Western and Soviet journalists for "lack of objectivity." In December 1990 Georgian radio and television had barred access to government opponents, including the unofficial National Congress, which opposed the Round Table coalition and had boycotted the 1990 vote. In January Gamsakhudria oversaw the reorganization of local government structures, establishing a system of prefectures whose hand-picked leaders would report to him. Before the independence referendum, a National Congress figure said Gamsakhudria was becoming autocratic: "He's been in power only five months and he's effectively eliminated all opposition."

On 17 March Georgia boycotted Gorbachev's union referendum, though voting did take place in areas of South Ossetia and in the autonomous, Communist-governed Abkhaz ASSR. On 1 April the electoral commission announced that 90.5 percent of eligible voters participated in the 31 March independence referendum, and 98.93 percent voted to restore Georgia's independence based on the 1918-21 republic. One explanation for the overwhelming "yes" vote was Gamsakhudria's pre-vote threat to withhold Georgian citizenship—a prerequisite for land ownership—from the entire population of regions where the majority voted against independence.

The same day, the Soviet parliament recommended that President Gorbachev declare a state of emergency and send troops to South Ossetia. Federal troops carrying some 700 tons of food were deployed to Tskhinvali to break the three-month blockade by 15,000 armed Georgians. In response, Gamsakhudria on 8 April threatened a general strike unless Soviet troops were removed; two days later railway workers shut down traffic between Black Sea oil ports and the Russian republic. Some 10,000 auto workers also walked off the job.

On 9 April an emergency parliamentary session unanimously approved Gamsakhudria's decree proclaiming the republic's independence. Typical of Gamsakhudria's political style, the text of the declaration had not been debated, amended, or voted on, but was approved simply by acclamation. On 14 April, after amending the Georgian constitution to create the post, the Supreme Soviet unanimously elected Gamsakhudria president of the republic for a five-year term. Direct presidential elections were slated for 26 May, the anniversary of the 1918 declaration of Georgian independence.

In mid-April unrest erupted in Batumi, the capital of the autonomous Adzhar ASSR within Georgia. Demonstrators protested religious discrimination against the largely Muslim population, the presence of local prefects sent from Tbilisi, and President Gamsakhudria's desire to abolish local autonomy. The Georgian National Guard opened fire on demonstrators marching to the local Supreme Soviet building. Violence in South Ossetia also continued in May. On 15 May, the Georgian Supreme Soviet declared a state of emergency in Tskhinvali that included a nightly curfew.

On 26 May, Gamsakhudria was elected president by a majority of 86.5 percent in the first contested popular election of a republican leader in the USSR. Five other candidates charged the campaign was marked by intimidation and slander. Gamsakhudria's main rival, Valerian Advadze, chairman of the Union for National Accord and Rebirth, came in second, with 7.6 percent of the vote. Of nine original candidates, three withdrew after failing to gather the requisite 10,000 signatures. One of them, Kartlos Gharibashvili, had been assaulted. Advadze's office was raided by Internal Ministry officials and two supporters were beaten. The remaining candidates were barred from publishing election platforms in the republican press. Though all the candidates were pro-independence, they were attacked as "enemies of Georgia" by the press.

Anti-government feelings increased in summer, as opposition politicians challenged Gamsakhudria's high-handed rule and some even questioned his sanity. Protests became more vocal after the president's failure to condemn the 19 August hardline putsch against President Gorbachev. The Georgian Popular Front had immediately attacked the hardline junta, pledging its support of "the democratic forces of the Soviet Union."

On 2 September, the Popular Front and the National Democratic Party called for a demonstration in Tbilisi to demand Gamsakhudria's resignation, new parliamentary elections, and the release of *Mkhedrioni* leaders. Demonstrations were held daily. By 12 September up to 28 political groups staged anti-government sit-ins in Tbilisi. Students, members of the formerly pro-Gamsakhudria moderate intelligentsia, National Guard factions, and Gamsakhudria's ex-Prime Minister, Tengiz Sigua, sided with the opposition.

By mid-September there were defections from the Round Table Coalition; the chairman of the parliamentary Foreign Affairs Commission asserted that Gamsakhudria's government was "definitely an authoritarian regime." Later in the month, a rebel faction of the National Guard in Tbilisi was deployed to defend the local television station occupied by opposition supporters. A subsequent clash with pro-Gamsakhudria forces left several dead.

Gamsakhudria dismissed opponents as pro-Moscow puppets. Gamsakhudria supporters were bused into the capital for counter-demonstrations. Gamsakhudria tightened censorship, blacked out Soviet and Russian television, arrested key opposition figures, including National Democratic leader Gia Chanturia and filmmaker Georgi Hainsrava, and imposed martial law in Tbilisi.

Protests intensified in the following months. In December, as the Soviet Union

collapsed, Russia, Ukraine and Belarus created the Commonwealth of Independent
States (CIS) that was subsequently joined by all the remaining republics except
Georgia, which by then was embroiled in an armed uprising against the government.
On 22 December, dozens were killed or injured in skirmishes between Gamsakhudria
loyalists and opposition troops at the presidential headquarters. Rebel units were
reportedly led by former Prime Minister Tengiz Sigua. As fierce fighting raged for a
second day, Gamsakhudria told the BBC he was willing to share power with the
opposition and was not opposed to joining the CIS. On 27 December, rebels attacked
Georgian KGB headquarters and freed at least eight political prisoners, among them
Gia Chanturia, who ruled out negotiations with the president.

As the year ended, it seemed only a matter of days before rebel forces would
win. President Gamsakhudria was reportedly in a bunker under the parliament building
with less than 1,000 troops. The fighting had left scores dead and hundreds wounded.

Kazakhstan

Population: 16,463,000
Ethnic Groups: Russian (40
percent), Kazakh (36 percent),
Ukrainian (6 percent), others
(17 percent)

Political Rights: 5
Civil Liberties: 4
Status: Partly Free

Economic reform, simmering inter-ethnic tensions, direct presidential elections and the
dissolution of the Soviet Union were among major issues in 1991 facing Nursultan
Nazarbaev, president of this vast republic stretching from the Caspian Sea east to the
Chinese border.

By the end of 1990, unsolved economic and environmental problems and friction
between Kazakhs and Russians, the two largest ethnic groups, put pressure on the
government to implement changes. In October 1990 President Nazarbaev, to defuse
potential for violence, asked political groups and non-Communist organizations to curb
demonstrations, a request almost immediately ignored by two Kazakh nationalist
parties, Alash and Jeltoqsan. Toward the end of 1990, chronic housing shortages led
squatters to seize vacant land in the capital, Alma-Ata, compelling the government to
pass anti-squatter laws in November. Nevada-Semipalatinsk, a popular environmental
group, continued demonstrations against industrial pollution and for the closure of a
nuclear weapons test site. In September inter-ethnic tensions heightened after the
publication of exiled Soviet writer Aleksander Solzhenitsyn's view that northern
regions of Kazakhstan be attached to Russia.

In 1991 the government launched an economic restructuring program in the
republic, which has substantial mineral wealth and a well-developed industrial base. In
March President Nazarbaev met with heads of enterprises subordinate to all-Union
ministries to discuss ways to integrate these enterprises into a market economy. The
government announced progress in privatization of agricultural land. A one-day
warning strike in March by coal miners in the Karaganda region allowed Nazarbaev
to initiate transferring the jurisdiction of metallurgy and coal industries from all-Union
to republican agencies. In June the Supreme Soviet (legislature) approved a program

for privatizing state property which included provisions for foreign ownership. In October the government announced plans to give the republic its own currency. The new currency would function alongside the ruble and be convertible in the USSR and abroad. Its value was to backed by the republic's gold reserves.

A key political issue was the 17 March referendum on Soviet President Mikhail Gorbachev's All-Union Treaty. Given the size of the non-Kazakh population, President Nazarbaev had been careful the year before not to issue a provocative declaration of national sovereignty. The resolution adopted on 25 October 1990 asserted republican control over natural resources and technological potential, but carefully stressed the equality of all nationalities. Kazakh nationalists criticized the declaration. In the March treaty vote, 94.1 percent of voters chose to "preserve the USSR as a union of equal sovereign states." But by late July, Nazarbaev criticized central authorities for interfering with negotiations on the union treaty and it became clear the treaty was unworkable.

The August coup against President Gorbachev led Nazarbaev to quit the Politburo and the Central Committee of the Communist Party of the Soviet Union (CPSU) and call for the Communist party in Kazakhstan to become an independent organization. The president said he was outraged that an attempt was made during the coup to get him, as a Politburo member, to sign a CPSU Central Committee declaration supporting the junta. He also decreed the immediate cessation of organized activity by political parties and mass movements in the republic's prosecutor's office, security and law-enforcement agencies, courts, and the custom's service. The edict required law-enforcement officials to follow only the laws of Kazakhstan.

In September the Popular Congress of Kazakhstan was founded in Alma-Ata to unite independent groups. Among those represented were Nevada-Semipalatinsk, the Kazakh Azat Party (the largest non-Communist party), the Russian Edinstvo group, and the Kazakh Language Society. Nevada-Semipalatinsk Chairman Olzhas Suleimenov and poet-political activist Mukhtar Shahanov were elected co-chairmen of the new party, which had the approval of President Nazarbaev.

On 1 December Nazarbaev became the first directly elected president in the republic's history, reportedly garnering 99 percent of the vote. He said the vote was a mandate to pursue "resolute measures" for economic reform. He called for national unity, warning nationalist parties to work within legal structures. Later in the month, with the demise of the Soviet Union, the three Slavic republics—Russia, Ukraine and Belarus—proposed a Commonwealth of Independent States (CIS). On 12 December, leaders of five Central Asian republics met in Ashkabad to discuss the commonwealth. Most favored a genuine commonwealth of independent states as the most democratic way to organize a union. Their statement indicated a willingness to join the Commonwealth, but insisted that Central Asian states and the founding nations have equal rights.

As one of four republics with nuclear weapons, Kazakhstan was brought into negotiations with the three founding states, and at a 21 December meeting in Alma-Ata, eleven former Soviet republics formally constituted the CIS. Leaders of Russia, Belarus, Ukraine and Kazakhstan also signed a nuclear weapons accord.

The year also saw a revival of Islam in Kazakhstan. By August there were over 230 Muslim religious communities in the republic, 20 percent more than five years before. Translations of the Koran into Kazakh were made, mullahs became more active in public life, an Islamic Institute was functioning in Alma-Ata and an independent newspaper, *Islam shapagaty*, was established.

Kyrgyzstan (Kirgizia)

Population: 4,258,000
Ethnic Groups: Kirgiz (52.3 percent) Russian (21.5 percent) Uzbek (12.9 percent) others

Political Rights: 5
Civil Liberties: 4
Status: Partly Free

In 1991 this republic bordering China and Uzbekistan in Central Asia, continued to take cautious steps toward greater democratization begun the year before and known as the "silk revolution." Like other constituent republics in the disintegrating USSR, it declared full independence shortly after the abortive hardline coup attempt against Soviet President Mikhail Gorbachev in August. In October, President Askar Akaev became the first popularly elected president of Kirgizia.

The slow process toward political reform began in 1990. In February after orthodox Communist Party First Secretary Absamat Masaliev warned that democracy could only be achieved through Party discipline, the Party swept republican and local elections. Only two alternative candidates ran in the elections, and only one, representing the emerging Kirgiz Democratic Movement, was elected. Masaliev was subsequently elected chairman of the new Supreme Soviet. But in October, growing dissatisfaction with Masaliev coupled with socio-economic and political problems, as well as Kirgiz-Uzbek violence in the Osh region, led the Supreme Soviet to create the post of president of the republic and to name Askar Akaev, a liberal physicist and president of the Kirgiz Academy of Sciences, to the post. By December 1990 Masaliev had resigned as chairman of the Supreme Soviet, which the same month chose not to issue a formal declaration of sovereignty, opting instead to affirm that Kirgizia was an independent entity. Several informal associations emerged in 1990, the most important of which was the Kirgiz Democratic Movement, an umbrella group consisting of several opposition organizations. In late September, 120 democratic Supreme Soviet deputies organized the Deputies' Group for Democratic Renewal to press for new laws to accelerate economic restructuring and democratic change.

In January 1991 the Supreme Soviet elected a Cabinet of Ministers that replaced the Council of Ministers and reported directly to President Akaev, who proposed the change. On 5 February, the Supreme Soviet decided the republic's capital city, Frunze, should revert to its original name, Bishkek. During the first week of February, over 600 delegates attended the first congress of the Kirgiz Democratic Movement. The group's co-chairman, Kazat Akhmatov, said that Kirgizia should join with Russia, Ukraine, Byelorussia and Kazakhstan in discussing cooperation among the republics and avoid the dictates of the central government in Moscow.

On 17 March a reported 94 percent of the electorate voted "yes" to the referendum on Mikhail Gorbachev's All-Union Treaty to preserve the USSR. But on 22 April, the Kirgiz Supreme Soviet decided not to sign the draft Union Treaty. The next day, President Akaev criticized virtually all points of Gorbachev's proposal.

The president told the Supreme Soviet that an "anti-crisis program" was needed to avoid food shortages and social unrest. He advocated land reforms allowing peasants to make more efficient use of the land, and the right to sell 20 percent of their produce at free-market prices.

In June Kirgizia established its first free-economic zone in Naryn Oblast, a mineral-rich region on the Chinese border. The following month, the government announced the centerpiece of economic restructuring would be large-scale privatization of state holdings. The program also included laws to encourage foreign investment.

In August the Communist party leadership, which in April had replaced Party Secretary Masaliev with Dzhumgalbek Amanbaev, an Akaev associate, declared invalid a decision by the Party organization of the republic's Ministry of Internal Affairs to separate government and Party and end Party activities in the ministry. But the coup attempt against Soviet President Gorbachev broke the power of the local Communists. On 19 August, the day of the coup, the local military chief threatened to send tanks into the streets, and the local KGB chief arrived to arrest president Akaev. Instead, Akaev had him arrested, sent loyal troops to surround Communist headquarters, and began broadcasting Russian President Boris Yeltsin's appeal for resistance. On 20 August the Kirgiz Democratic Movement telegrammed Yeltsin condemning the unconstitutional removal of Gorbachev. The next day, President Akaev attacked the republic's Communists, noting that all progressive forces in Kirgizia, but not the Communist Party leadership, condemned the "military-Party putsch" against Gorbachev. The president also issued a decree banning organizations of political parties from all government structures. On 31 August the republic's Supreme Soviet declared Kirgizia's independence from the USSR.

President Akaev continued to gain respect from regional democrats. In October, the leader of the largest opposition party in neighboring Kazakhstan called Kirgizia "the real center of democracy in Central Asia," and it was reported that after the aborted coup Gorbachev had offered Akaev the post of Soviet vice-president. On 12 October, President Akaev ran unopposed and was elected president of Kirgizia. After the vote, he said he was distressed that no one was willing to run against him. A spokesman of the Kirgiz Democratic Movement, however, complained the opposition did not have enough time to gather 25,000 signatures needed to register.

In mid-December, Kirgizia agreed to join the new Commonwealth of Independent States which was hastily established by Russia, Ukraine and Belarus after the Soviet Union collapsed. Among the problems facing Kirgizia, one of the poorest of the former republics, is an end to Soviet budget subsidies.

Moldova (Moldavia)

Population: 4,332,000
Ethnic Groups: Romanian (64 percent), Russian, Ukrainians

Political Rights: 5
Civil Liberties: 4
Status: Partly Free

In 1991 this ethnically divided republic bordering Romania and Ukraine continued political democratization and the drive toward independence even as 150,000 non-Moldavian Gagauz (a Turkic Christian minority) and Russians and Ukrainians on the east bank of the Dniester River proclaimed independent republics. Other developments included a split in the Moldavian Communist Party and a presidential election won by incumbent Mircea Snegur.

The republic of Moldavia was established in 1940 when Joseph Stalin annexed the then-Romanian province of Bessarabia. In 1918 the Romanian majority of the former Tsarist province had voted for union with Romania. When Stalin seized the region, northern and southern Bessarabia were given to Ukraine, while a sliver of territory east of the Dniester River was tacked on to the old province. Tens of thousands Romanian-speaking Bessarabians were deported, and Russians and Ukrainians brought in. Bessarabians were told they were ethnic Moldavians not Romanians who spoke Moldavian, a non-existent language.

With the advent of glasnost, Moldavia began to assert its autonomy. By 1990 political power had passed from the Moldavian Communist Party to democratic forces representing the native majority. The transfer of power was accompanied by inter-ethnic conflict, as Russians and Ukrainians resented Moldavian separatism. The independent Moldavian Popular Front was radicalized, advocating the dismantling of the Soviet empire. Other political groups emerged, among them the Social Democratic Party, the Union of Peasants, the National Christian Party, the Ecological Movement of Moldavia and the Organization of Democratic Youth. All but the Social Democrats were overwhelmingly Moldavian. Aligned against them were two main Russian movements: the Inter-Movement Edinstvo, dominated by Communists, and the United Work Collectives.

In February-March 1990 Supreme Soviet (parliament) elections, the Popular Front won 40 percent of the 218 seats and nearly 30 percent went to groups sharing the Front's goals. Paradoxically, 80 percent of deputies remained Communist Party members. In April, parliament, rejecting a Communist candidate, named Popular Front ally Mircea Snegur as chairman (later changed to president). In May the Supreme Soviet brought down the government of Communist Petru Pascaru in a non-confidence vote. It installed a government dominated by reformers led by Prime Minister Mircea Druc, which enacted far-reaching political reforms: the constitutionally guaranteed leading role of the Communist Party was abolished; political movements were barred from organizing in state and public institutions; and the Communist party was stripped of its media outlets. The newly independent media began criticizing the Party. The Russian-language press remained loyal to the Communists. In June, parliament declared sovereignty, giving republican laws precedence over all-Union law.

In response, Gagauz and Slavic leaders proclaimed their own republics: the Gagauz SSR on 19 August, the Dniester SSR on 2 September. Both subsequently elected parliaments and asked for recognition from Moscow. Paramilitary organizations were formed, and inter-ethnic clashed erupted in November. Though not recognizing the breakaway republics, Moscow sent troops to protect the new governments.

In January 1991 the Moldavian Popular Front called for a boycott of the 17 March all-Union referendum on preserving the Soviet Union. Subsequently, the Moldavian Supreme Soviet decided to boycott the referendum, noting that it constituted direct interference by Moscow in Moldavia's internal affairs.

At the end of February, President Snegur announced he was resigning, accusing the Communist Party of launching a campaign to discredit him. He also cited his inability to work with Prime Minister Druc. He said he would stay on if parliament agreed to elect the president by popular vote. He formally quit the Communist Party. Parliament refused to accept his resignation and formed a commission to reform executive power.

In March Moldavian Communists belonging to the Democratic Platform faction split from the main party. Within days, a breakaway Independent Communist Party was constituted in the capital, Kishniev. Moldavia successfully mobilized popular support for the referendum boycott, and on 17 March turnout of ethnic Moldavians was only 5 percent. Non-Moldavians overwhelmingly approved the preservation of the union.

On 22 May, Prime Minister Druc was ousted by a non-confidence vote. Parliament replaced him with President Snegur's nominee, Valeriu Muravschi, supported by the Popular Front and opposed by Russian Communist deputies.

When hardliners staged an August coup against Soviet President Gorbachev, Moldavia immediately opposed the junta, supporting Russian President Boris Yeltsin and rejecting demands by Soviet generals to declare a state of emergency. Republican leadership mobilized over 100,000 citizens to defend public buildings in Kishniev. Huge crowds prevented troops from entering the capital. Pro-Soviet Gagauz SSR and the Dniester SSR leaders had sided with the junta. Following the coup's collapse, Moldavia suspended the Communist press, banned the Communist Party, and confiscated party assets. On 27 August, parliament proclaimed Moldavia's independence from the USSR. Follow-up legislation committed Moldavia to United Nations and Conference on Security and Cooperation in Europe (CSCE) human rights pacts. Negotiations began on Soviet troop withdrawals.

In September, the Gagauz republic declared it was seceding from Moldavia. Opening a new session of parliament, President Snegur said Moldavian independence was irreversible.

On 24 October, President Snegur launched his election campaign by stressing "there would be no question (of Moldavia) merging with another state," countering speculation that Moldavia might seek to rejoin Romania. In November, Popular Front and Romania officials met in Bucharest, with the opposition group asking Romania to grant citizenship rights for residents in Bessarabia and Bukovina. President Snegur told an electoral rally that the request was unlawful and incompatible with Moldavia's independence. Romania's president, Ion Iliescu, said he had turned down the request.

In December, the Dniester SSR and the Gagauz SSR held presidential elections and referenda on joining the Commonwealth of Independent States (CIS) proposed by Russia, Ukraine and Belarus after the collapse of the Soviet Union. On 10 December, President Snegur, running unopposed, won 93 percent of the vote, as 83 percent of voters turned out. Three days later, a gun battle broke out between police and separatists in the Dniester SSR. As the year ended, Moldavia and 11 other former republics joined the CIS.

Russia

Population: 147,386,000

Ethnic Groups: Russian, over 100 ethnic groups

Political Rights: 3

Civil Liberties: 3

Status: Partly Free

In 1991 Russia, the vast, rich land sweeping from the edge of Europe to the Pacific and the political center of two mighty empires, faced the challenge of building free-market and democratic institutions rooted in the very concepts it had rejected in its turbulent history. The burden to lead the transition fell on Boris Yeltsin, the popularly elected president whose courageous leadership during the August hardline coup attempt helped seal the collapse of the Soviet Union.

In December 1991, President Yeltsin joined leaders of Ukraine and Belarus, the two other Slavic republics, to forge a new Commonwealth of Independent States (CIS), subsequently joined by eight former republics (Georgia did not join and Moscow recognized the independence of the three Baltic republics). By year's end, with Russia and Ukraine at loggerheads over control of the Soviet fleet and other republics wary of Russian hegemony, it remained unclear whether Yeltsin envisioned the CIS as a true commonwealth of equals, a transitional body or, as Russia's Deputy Prime Minister Gennady Burbulsi suggested, a supra-state structure to replace the USSR with Russia at the center.

In 1991 the dynamic of Russian politics was the struggle between President Yeltsin and Soviet President Mikhail Gorbachev over restructuring the Soviet state. Yeltsin favored decentralization, a transfer of power to the republics, the elimination of Communist Party of the Soviet Union (CPSU) cells from all-Union and Russian institutions, and a new confederated union in which the Russian, not the Soviet, president would play the leading role. Yeltsin's pressure on the Soviet center, which included winning the support of the republican KGB and military forces on Russian territory, was economic as well as political. He sought to wrest the republic's economic wealth from Soviet control. Though having only 51 percent of the Soviet population, Russia accounted for 64 percent of Soviet industrial output, 55 percent of union budget revenues and 80 percent of export revenues. Yeltsin intensified efforts to keep Russia's wealth at home rather than subsidize a crumbling center and the poorer republics.

Other key events in 1991 included attempts by orthodox Communist republican legislators to strip Yeltsin's power, direct presidential elections, restiveness in several of Russia's 16 autonomous republics and 30 autonomous areas, and the impact of radical economic reforms.

Russia accelerated democratization in 1990, when voters elected 1,068 deputies to the new republican Congress of People's Deputies whose primary task was to elect the 152-member Supreme Soviet, the republic's standing legislature. Key blocks coalesced around old-line Communists and a loose alliance of democratic reformers. In May, Yeltsin, who was elected to the Congress with 90 percent support, won the chairmanship of parliament on the third round of balloting by only four votes. In June the republic declared sovereignty, though not full independence. At the 28th CPSU Congress in July, Yeltsin quit the party to protest the accumulation of power by Gorbachev, who had been elected president by the Congress of People's Deputies. With Russia's Communist party earlier electing Leninist Ivan Polozkov as leader, Yeltsin realized that the party would be a major impediment to economic reform and Russian sovereignty.

To circumvent the party, Yeltsin aimed to gain control of the Soviet armed forces and the KGB. He demanded that Russia be given veto rights over Soviet use of nuclear weapons, the right to control KGB communications on its territory and the right to nominate the USSR defense minister.

In January 1991, after Soviet forces cracked down in Lithuania, Yeltsin appealed to the Soviet military and the KGB not to support Gorbachev in his attempts to hold the disintegrating empire together. He visited the Baltics to show his support, and in a February live television interview publicly demanded the elimination of the Soviet presidency and transference of supreme power to the USSR Council of the Federation (the top consultative body of republican leaders). He maintained that a better concept of union could emerge from the alliance of leaders of the five largest republics: Russia, Ukraine, Belarus, Kazakhstan and Uzbekistan.

In response, a group of parliamentary leaders on 21 February proposed an extraordinary Russian Congress of Peoples Deputies in an effort to oust Yeltsin as chairman and derail his plans to hold direct presidential elections. During the weeklong session in late March and early April, Yeltsin skillfully managed to split the Communists, defeat the hardliners and win expanded powers to rule by decree. Reform Communists formed a Communists for Democracy group and backed Yeltsin. Tensions between Yeltsin and Gorbachev heightened on 28 March when the Soviet president ordered troops to block a rally of 100,000 pro-Yeltsin marchers in Moscow.

Even though Russians voted overwhelmingly for Gorbachev's 17 March referendum to preserve the Soviet Union, 69.85 percent also said "yes" to "the introduction of the post of President of the RSFSR, elected by a vote of all the people." Elections were set for 12 June.

During the so-called Nine-Plus-One talks between Gorbachev and leaders of nine of 15 republics in Novo-Ogarevo in April, Yeltsin and the other republican leaders convinced Gorbachev to recognize republican sovereignty. The 23 April Novo-Ogarevo agreement allowed Yeltsin to further strengthen Russia's state and government institutions and establish an independent banking system. Financial control was Yeltsin's most potent weapon against the center. During the first half of 1991, Russia weakened the USSR budget by withholding tax contribution.

Five candidates challenged Yeltsin for the presidency: former Soviet Prime Minister Nikolai Ryzhkov, who campaigned against hasty reforms; former Interior Minister Vadim Bakutin, a liberal Communist; Albert Makashov, a hard-line army general; Vladimir Zhirinovsky, the anti-Semitic founder of the small Liberal Democratic Party, who pledged to abolish national republics and restore Russian dominance; and Aman Tuleyev, a Siberian Kazakh who gained notoriety in the 1990 coal-miners' strike.

On 12 June, Yeltsin won the presidency with 60 percent of the vote. He again demanded a rapid transition to a market economy, the sale of state enterprises, the right to own and farm private land, and the ouster of Communist organizations from all enterprises and bureaucracies.

Yeltsin's election further shifted legitimacy from Gorbachev to the republic level, forcing the Soviet president to share power with the Russian leader. In late June, Yeltsin continued to express doubts about the union treaty, objecting to a tax system that placed an unfair burden on Russia.

On 20 July, a presidential decree banned Communist Party organizations from government offices and workplaces in Russia. Yeltsin also called for legislation to bar Party cells in the KGB, military and police. The decree required government officials to follow state law and ignore Party orders. At the end of the month, Yeltsin signed an unprecedented treaty with Lithuania, securing rights for Russians living in the breakaway republic and recognizing Lithuanian independence.

In early August, President Gorbachev announced that Yeltsin had agreed to sign a new union treaty and, despite Ukraine's late-June decision to postpone discussion of the treaty until September, Russia, Kazakhstan and Uzbekistan would sign the treaty on 20 August. Despite objections from deputies who warned that Russia's parliament might reject the pact, Yeltsin saw the treaty as a way to gain control of union enterprises.

President Gorbachev's concessions to Yeltsin and the growing superfluousness of the CPSU were clearly a factor in the ill-fated coup a day before the scheduled signing of the union treaty. Yeltsin's heroic stand against the junta undermined Gorbachev's remaining authority and enhanced his own political power. His cultivation of the army and KGB earlier in the year paid off, as most of the army and KGB ignored commands by the plotters and expressed loyalty to Yeltsin. With the CPSU completely discredited, Yeltsin undertook to transfer power from the center to the republics in the Council of Federation, a move he advocated in February.

After the coup collapsed, Yeltsin suspended five papers, including *Pravda* , and proclaimed himself commander-in-chief of Soviet forces on Russian territory. He also asserted control over ministries, the central media, banks and communication networks. He alarmed Russia's neighbors, especially Ukraine and Kazakhstan, when aides announced Russia would demand a review of its borders if its neighbors broke away from the union. Subsequent Russian-Ukrainian negotiations confirmed the articles of a 1990 treaty regarding territorial integrity and minority rights.

In early September, Yeltsin joined President Gorbachev in urging the adoption of a new, republican-based interim governing structure for the Soviet Union. He reassured republics concerned about Russian dominance: "The Russian state, having chosen democracy and freedom, will never be an empire, nor an elder brother, or a younger brother. It will be an equal among equals." He also called for the elimination of nuclear weapons in Russia.

On 28 October Yeltsin announced a new radical reform program to convert Russia to a market economy. He revamped the republic's government, replacing old-line bureaucrats with followers who believed Russia should declare itself the legal successor to the USSR, take control of all-Union structures on its territory, nationalize the armed forces, and dictate trade terms between republics. The reforms included price rises by 1 January 1992, state budget cuts and efforts to break state monopolies. Addressing the Russian parliament, Yeltsin said Russians should brace themselves for hardship. Yeltsin proposed assuming the vacant post of Russian prime minister, combining chief executive and administrative functions and taking full responsibility for reforms and their consequences. On 1 November, the Russian parliament approved Yeltsin's emergency blueprint to free consumer prices.

In mid-November, with a burst of new decrees, President Yeltsin moved to assert Russia's dominance over the foundering Soviet economy, proclaiming control over Russia's dwindling reserves of oil, gold and other precious metals and opening its doors to foreign trade. The measures lifted most controls over imports, exports and foreign-currency transactions on Russian territory and would allow the value of the ruble to float according to market rates starting in 1992. The steps undercut a union economic agreement signed earlier, which recognized individual republic's sovereignty over their economic output, but provided for a single currency administered by a Soviet central bank.

On 20 November, Russia, which had already stopped most of its payments to the Kremlin budget, rejected President Gorbachev's request for an emergency three-month appropriation, which would have widened the total Soviet deficit to 300 billion rubles. Russian officials maintained that the republic's moves were not a new "Russian imperialism," but a recognition that neither Russia nor any other republic could afford to waste any more time in starting long-overdue reforms. Yegor T. Gaidar, deputy prime minister for economic policy, told G-7 representatives that Russia was prepared to assume the entire Soviet debt if necessary. Later in the month, the Russian parliament voted to take control of the Soviet State Bank and the Bank for Foreign Economic Affairs, placing them under the control of the Russian central bank.

In early December, President Yeltsin guaranteed state employees' December salaries after the chairman of the Soviet Gosbank said there was not enough money in government coffers to meet Soviet budget requirements. Russia also took control of the Soviet Ministry of Finance, arguing the takeover was necessary to protect it from the introduction of separate currencies by other republics. On 3 December, Russia approved a program to revive the private peasant farm, but parliament stopped short of allowing the private sale of farmland.

On 8 December President Yeltsin oversaw the formation of a Commonwealth of Independent States (CIS). One week later, Russia asked the United States to recognize its independence and that of Belarus and Ukraine. On 19 December President Yeltsin took control of the Foreign Ministry, the KGB, the parliament and President Gorbachev's office. The timing of the takeover suggested the Russian government was eager to claim as much of the old union as possible before a scheduled meeting of republican leaders on 21 December in Alma-Ata to formalize the CIS. The presidium of the Russian parliament took over all the building and other property of the union parliament. On 20 December President Yeltsin told NATO Russia hoped to join the alliance in the future. With no legitimate base of authority, Soviet President Gorbachev resigned on 25 December.

On 27 December, in an indication of his growing authority, President Yeltsin removed Vice President Aleksandr Rutskoi—a staunch ally in their election campaign who had since become a voice of opposition—from the chairmanship of five special Russian executive committees. The following day, he signed an executive order to begin agricultural land reform. In a somber New Year's Eve address, President Yeltsin acknowledged Russia would be severely tested in early 1992 as measures were implemented to free the economy.

In other issues, several areas in Russia demanded greater autonomy. Leaders in the Chechen-Ingush ASSR (autonomous republic), a Muslim enclave of some 1 million bordering Georgia and Azerbaijan, pressed for independence. In October armed militias seized the KGB building in Groznyi, the capital, despite ongoing negotiations with Russian officials. On 27 October former Soviet Air Force General Dzhakhar Dudaev, chairman of the Executive Committee of the Congress of the Chechen People, was elected president in elections Russian authorities had earlier declared illegal. On 9 November, thousands of nationalists seized airports, barricaded roads and prevented 600 Soviet troops from enforcing emergency rule declared by President Yeltsin. On 11 November Russia's parliament refused to endorse Yeltsin's emergency rule, and instead authorized him to pursue negotiations. The region was potentially volatile given Ingushi claims on territory in mostly Christian North Ossetia, another autonomous region within Russia.

Unrest also hit Tatarstan, an autonomous region with a mixed population of 4 million Tatars and ethnic Russians. Tatarstan had long insisted that it be directly involved in union treaty negotiations, putting it on a collision course with President Yeltsin, who refused to compromise Russia's territorial integrity. On 24 October, the Supreme Soviet of Tatarstan adopted a state independence resolution calling for a referendum on the republic's status.

Tajikistan

Population: 5,090,000

Ethnic Groups: Tajiks (58 percent), Uzbeks (23 percent), Russians and Ukrainians (11 percent), Jews, Germans, Armenians, Gypsy, others (7 percent)

Political Rights: 5
Civil Liberties: 5
Status: Partly Free

A simmering dispute between hardline Communists rulers, democratic reformers and Islamic activists in this poor, remote Central Asian republic bordering Afghanistan and China intensified after the abortive coup against Soviet President Mikhail Gorbachev in August. The conflict included the reimposition of a state of emergency first imposed in February 1990 when federal and republican forces killed 22 people during a week of violence in the capital, Dushanbe. By year's end, several Communist governments had collapsed, but though the opposition grew in strength, a former Communist, Rakhman Nabiev, was elected president on 24 November amid charges of vote-rigging and other irregularities.

The momentum for political change began to accelerate in 1990. On 12 February persistent rumors that Armenian (Christian) refugees had been given apartments despite long waiting lists sparked demonstrations organized by the informal political group, Rastokhez, which had been demanding more rapid democratization in the republic. After Tadjik Communist Party First Secretary and Chairman of the Supreme Soviet Kakhar Makhkamov failed to address long-neglected social and economic problems, the crowd in Central Committee grew restless. Ministry of Interior (MVD) forces, KGB border guards and a USSR Ministry of Defense detachment guarding the Central Committee building opened fire, killing nine people. The government declared a state of emergency and a curfew in Dushanbe. The killings touched off days of rioting, looting and shootings that left 22 dead and 700 injured. Makhkamov resigned in 13 February, only to be reinstated later in the day at an emergency party plenum session.

With order restored, Makhkamov, who had tolerated some political and social pluralism, cracked down, blaming Rastokhez, the Democratic Party of Tadjikistan, and the Tadjikistan branch of the Islamic Renaissance Party for the disturbances. In the subsequent six months, 36,000 people, mainly professionals and skilled workers, left Tadjikistan, adversely affecting an economy already among the poorest in the USSR. A declaration of republican sovereignty on 24 August did little to slow the exodus.

On 1 January 1991, the curfew in Dushanbe was lifted, but the state of emergency in the city remained in force. In February, the republic's Supreme Soviet voted in favor of participating in the 17 March referendum on Gorbachev's All-Union Treaty for preserving the Soviet Union. The Democratic Party, however, announced it would boycott the poll. On election day, officials announced that 96.2 percent voted to maintain the union.

In July the Democratic Party, claiming 15,000 members, formally registered as a public organization. According to opposition leaders, authorities decided to tolerate the new party because it posed less of a threat than the banned Islamic Renaissance Party. President Makhkamov continued tightening his grip on power. On 15 July, the Tadjik Supreme Soviet passed a law calling for up to six years' imprisonment for defaming the president by disseminating "slanderous materials."

A turning point was the attempted coup against Gorbachev on 19 August. The day of the coup, President Makhkamov said he supported the hardline junta. When it was apparent the coup had failed, Makhkamov said the coup was a tragedy that could have caused a civil war. Within days, a Democratic Party rally called on the republic's leadership to resign.

With Communists badly discredited, Makhkamov resigned. He was replaced by Kadriddin Aslonov, a long-time Communist apparatchik. On 9 September the Supreme Soviet declared Tadjikistan's independence from the USSR. Ten days later, acting President Aslonov announced his resignation from the Communist party, explaining it would be improper for him to belong to any political organization. He subsequently suspended the Communist party and nationalized its property in a controversial decree.

On 23 September, with growing social unrest, the Supreme Soviet declared a state of emergency, replaced Aslonov with Rakhman Nabiev, a Communist traditionalist, and scheduled presidential elections for 27 October. Government officials and opposition representatives began a series of meetings on 28 September, with the opposition demanding the state of emergency be rescinded. On 30 September, as crowds of protestors swelled to 10,000, the government agreed.

On 2 October the Supreme Soviet suspended the activities of the republican Communist party. Demonstrators in front of the Supreme Soviet building continued to demand that the legislature dissolve itself. Leningrad Mayor Anatoly Sobchak, an envoy from Gorbachev, met with government and opposition leaders to resolve the impasse.

President Nabiev, bowing to opposition demands, resigned on 5 October. Elections were deferred to 24 November under an agreement that also called for a referendum on whether to dissolve the Supreme Soviet, reimposed the ban on the Communist Party, and recommended that representatives from Rastokhez, the Democratic Party and the Islamic Renaissance Party be added to election commissions and given equal access to television and radio.

On 21 October a Soviet constitutional committee ruled that the state of emergency in September had been illegal. The following day, the Tadjik Supreme Soviet lifted a ban on religious parties codified in the republic's law on freedom of conscience. This removed the main obstacle to the registration of the Islamic Renaissance Party, which held a congress on 27 October.

On 24 November, Rakhman Nabiev was elected president of Tadjikistan, gaining 58 percent of the vote in beating seven opponents. His main rival, Cinema Workers' Union Chairman Davlat Khudonazarov, backed by the Democratic and Islamic parties, got 25 percent. The opposition accused the republican leadership of falsifying results and claimed to have video proof of irregularities.

In early December, representatives of opposition groups met to organize a congress of a new umbrella organization, the Movement for Democratic Reforms. Later in the month, after the Soviet Union dissolved, President Nabiev said Tadjikistan would join the new Commonwealth of Independent States (CIS) founded by Russia, Ukraine and Belarus.

Turkmenistan

Population: 3,512,000

Ethnic Groups: Turkic, others

Political Rights: 6

Civil Liberties: 5

Status: Partly Free

In 1991 this republic bordering Iran and Afghanistan officially announced its independence from a rapidly disintegrating Soviet Union following a republic-wide referendum on 26 October. Unlike other former republics in Central Asia, Turkmenistan made only nominal progress toward genuine democratization.

Turkmenistan is led by Saparmurad Niyazov, who ran unopposed in January 1990 for the chairmanship of a new, largely conservative Supreme Soviet (parliament) and was also re-elected first secretary of the Communist party. Nearly 90 percent of those elected to the parliament were Party members. At the end of October—after the Supreme Soviet amended the republic's constitution in order to introduce an executive presidency—Niyazov, unanimously nominated by the Supreme Soviet, again became the sole candidate in the presidential elections. Despite its conservatism, the Turkmen Supreme Soviet adopted a declaration of sovereignty in mid-August 1990, asserting the republic's right to determine its own political and social system and to secede from the USSR.

The main opposition group, known as Agzybirlik, was formed in September 1989 by intellectuals meeting in the capital, Ashkhabad, to set up a popular front whose draft program dealt with the status of the Turkmen language, indigenous arts in the republic, the environment and the shortage of consumer goods. Officially registered in October 1989 and banned in January 1990, the group defied authorities the following month and held a congress. The meeting was attacked in the Party newspaper, which alleged Agzybirlik was promoting divisiveness. In June three of the groups officials were ordered to appear in court on charges of organizing an illegal public meeting.

In February 1991 the Turkmen Supreme Court overturned the conviction of writer and Agzybirlik activist Shiraly Nurmyradov, who was convicted on trumped-up charges in December 1990 because he had ridiculed President Niyazov in his books. Also in February, Turkmenistan's first independent newspaper, *Turkmen ili*, began publication. The weekly, which appeared in Russian, had a print run of only 999 copies because a publication of under 1,000 does not need to register with authorities.

In March, TASS reported that the Turkmenistan Supreme Soviet had approved the draft of Soviet President Mikhail Gorbachev's Union treaty. On 17 March, 97.9 percent of the people reportedly approved the referendum on the All-Union Treaty.

When Kremlin hardliners launched their coup against President Gorbachev on 19 August, President Niyazov refused to condemn the plotters until it was clear the putsch had failed. Agzybirlik had immediately condemned the overthrow of Gorbachev. Two days later, when it was evident the attempt would fail, President Niyazov issued a decree declaring that the decisions of the "putschists" were not valid in Turkmenistan. Government spokesman tried to blame the delay on lack of available information, but on 20 August—one day after the coup—the party daily had published the junta's appeal. Agzybirlik criticized Niyazov's failure to speak out against the plotters.

On 30 September, with Gorbachev's power seriously undermined and the Soviet Union rapidly unravelling, the Turkmenistan Supreme Soviet voted to hold a referendum on independence. It had been one of only three republics not to have declared independence; the others were Russia and Kazakhstan. On 26 October, 94 percent of Turkmenistan voters opted for independence. Accordingly, the Supreme Soviet proclaimed 27 October as Independence Day. The referendum on which voters cast their votes declared Turkmenistan to be a democratic state based on the rule of law, but Agzybirlik doubted the leadership's commitment to genuine pluralism and democracy.

On 19 December, Turkmenistan said it was prepared to join the newly formed Commonwealth of Independent States (CIS) set up earlier by the three Slavic former republics—Russia, Ukraine and Belarus. Three days earlier, the 25th Congress of the Turkmenian Communist Party decided to disband, and established the Democratic Party as a successor. As expected, President Niyazov was elected chairman of the "new" organization, which named a 108-member political council. The transformed party pledged itself to a strong presidential system, market reforms, and the sale of state property.

The Turkmenistan economy is based on cotton, gas and silk, most of which was previously exported to other Soviet republics. High unemployment, poverty and a declining living standard, which had led to violent unrest in 1989, continued to plague the economy in 1991.

Uzbekistan

Population: 19,808,000
Ethnic Groups: Uzbeks, Russians, Ukrainians, Meshketian Turks, others

Political Rights: 6
Civil Liberties: 5
Status: Partly Free

In 1991 major issues confronting President Islam Karimov of this Central Asian republic on the Afghan border were a sagging economy, the catastrophic ecological impact of the receding Aral Sea, and ethnic tensions. Amid complaints by the democratic and Islamic opposition regarding the pace and scope of political and economic reform, President Karimov also faced the challenge of charting Uzbekistan's future after the collapse of the Soviet Union.

The republic's Supreme Soviet (legislature), elected in early 1990, was dominated by old-line Communists. Karimov, who was elected party first secretary in 1989, reorganized the government, replaced the Council of Ministers with an advisory cabinet, and named himself president. His chief concerns were: to avoid the kind of inter-ethnic violence that erupted in 1989-90 between Uzbeks and Meshketian Turks in the Fergana Valley; reverse the brain-drain of mostly Russian professionals who began to leave in droves after the republic's sovereignty declaration; and recharge a slumping economy. Despite a bumper cotton crop and one of the world's largest natural gas deposits, Uzbekistan remained poor, and a skyrocketing population growth put pressure on the government to find solutions. To many, the Aral Sea disaster epitomized the inability of bloated, inefficient central and republican bureaucracies to solve major problems. An ill-conceived project diverting water from two rivers that fed the huge inland sea led to a 65 percent decrease in the sea's volume, resulting in oversalianated dust from emerging banks that destroyed soil already poisoned by pesticides. Fishing was ruined, and infant mortality and illness rose in ajoining regions.

Early in 1991, the government took some measures toward economic reform. In

January the legislature prepared a draft law on private enterprise, which allowed foreign investment. In February President Karimov decreed that more than 100,000 hectares of irrigated land be distributed to peasants to enlarge private plots. In mid-December, denationalization and privatization plans were formalized and would be submitted to the legislature in 1992-93.

In political affairs, President Karimov told the Supreme Soviet in February that Uzbekistan would not sign Soviet President Mikhail Gorbachev's Union Treaty. The independent Uzbek Popular Front (Birlik) and the Erk Democratic Party called for a boycott of the 17 March all-Union treaty referendum. The Supreme Soviet approved an additional ballot question: "Do you agree that Uzbekistan should remain part of the restructured Union as a sovereign republic." A February law on public association banned religious political parties, a response to the 26 January formation of a branch of the Islamic Renaissance Party. Police invaded the founding congress in the capital, Tashkent, detained participants, and fined them for holding an unauthorized assembly.

As the date for the treaty referendum approached, Uzbek officials complained the draft was an attempt to maintain a "unitary state" and inconsistent with Uzbekistan's sovereign status. On 17 March, a reported 93.7 percent of voters approved the referendum, and 94 percent voted "yes" on the additional question.

In April, the government closed Birlik headquarters for what the group's leaders said were political reasons. On 7 July, leaders of Birlik and the Erk Democratic Party announced they would work together, but that Erk would continue to function as a political party. Later that month, Birlik spokesmen told the press they believed Uzbekistan should remain in a union because independence would mean the current corrupt Communist regime would retain control.

With the disintegration of the Soviet Union accelerated by the attempted coup against President Gorbachev, Uzbekistan's Supreme Soviet voted on 31 August to declare the republic's independence from the USSR.

In mid-September, President Karimov told Western journalists Uzbekistan would follow the "Chinese model" of economic reform because the republic was not ready for full democracy or a market economy. He said privatization would take place primarily in the service sector, presumably leaving state-enterprises in tact. He said a ban on political rallies was justified to preclude violence, adding that only candidates nominated by registered political parties would be eligible to run. Only Karimov's large People's Democratic Party (the Communist Party changed its name after the coup) and the tiny Erk Party were registered. He doubted the Birlik Popular Front would ever qualify to register, and said the Islamic Renaissance Party remained prohibited. He later retracted the China-model statement.

On 28 October, Birlik proclaimed itself a political party headed by co-chairman Adburrakhim Pulatov. Officials told Birlik to present a membership list by 1 November, but the party said it was an unreasonable timetable. In November, a group of Uzbek deputies asked a parliamentary committee to schedule direct elections for the presidency, noting that Uzbekistan was the last of the Central Asian republics to hold popular elections. The vote was subsequently set for 29 December, and a referendum on independence was slated for the same day. At the end of the month, President Karimov rejected the latest union treaty draft.

As expected, President Karimov was nominated by the People's Democratic Party. Poet Mohammed Saleh was nominated by the Erk Party. Saleh, the party leader, represented a part of the Uzbek intelligentsia which saw national rebirth as a corner-stone for change: the revival of Islam, the Uzbek language and Uzbek culture. On 20 November Birlik nominated Chairman Pulatov, but needed to gather 60,000 signatures because it was not registered.

On 12 December, President Karimov and other Central Asian leaders met in Ashkabad to discuss the new Commonwealth of Independent States (CIS) organized by Russia, Ukraine and Belarus. On 21 December, Uzbekistan was among eleven former-Soviet republics that agreed to join the CIS at a meeting in Alma-Ata.

Predictably, Karimov was overwhelmingly elected president as the year drew to a close.

United Arab Emirates

Polity: Federation of traditional monarchies
Economy: Capitalist statist
Population: 2,400,000
PPP: $19,440
Life Expectancy: 70.5
Ethnic Groups: Native Arabs, Arab and other immigrant groups

Political Rights: 6
Civil Liberties: 5
Status: Not Free

Overview:

An independent state since 1971, the United Arab Emirates (UAE) is a federation of seven sheikdoms, each of which retains control over mineral rights, taxation and security. Each constituent state is a monarchy, dominated by a ruling family with powerful economic interests. The current head of state is Sheik Zayed bin Sultan al-Nahiyan. Sheik Zayed is also the principal shareholder in the scandal-ridden Bank of Credit and Commerce International (BCCI).

Together, the rulers of the seven sheikdoms constitute the Supreme Assembly seated in Abu Dhabi. The Council elects a president and vice-president for the federation. The president, in turn, appoints a prime minister and a cabinet. The seven rulers also appoint members to a forty-member Federal National Council that gives advice on legislation. No political parties are permitted, although some groups operate clandestinely. There are no elections. Three quarters of the population are non-citizens who play little or no political role. Most indigenous citizens are Sunni Muslims.

During the 1991 Gulf War, the oil-rich UAE welcomed troops from Arab nations and other countries to help in its national defense. The announcement came after a visit by U.S. Secretary of Defense Dick Cheney. Breaking with tradition, the UAE government allowed women into the armed forces. Although other Arab states also invited women to become part of the civil defense and first-aid squads, only the UAE decided to make the women an integral part of its armed forces.

Political Rights and Civil Liberties:

Citizens cannot change their government democratically. There are no political parties. Emirate rulers are generally accessible to citizens with particular problems or needs. The judicial system, divided into lay and clerical (*shari'a*) courts, is considered fair and independent. Trials, for the most part, are public. Although constitutionally guaranteed, there are limits on freedom of expression. The media practice self-censorship, with most private newspapers receiving subsidies from the government. The government monitors and screens all imported media. All television and radio are government owned and conform to government guidelines. Muslims are free to worship but not to proselytize. Private associations are free to organize, but public assembly requires government permission. Freedom of travel is respected. By law, unions and the right to strike are prohibited.

United Kingdom

Polity: Parliamentary democracy
Economy: Mixed capitalist
Population: 55,922,000
PPP: $13,060
Life Expectancy: 75.7
Ethnic Groups: English, Scottish, Welsh, Irish, and various Asian, African, and Caribbean immigrant groups

Political Rights: 1
Civil Liberties: 2
Status: Free

Overview:

The most important developments in 1991 included the government's proposed repeal of the so-called poll tax, British bargaining with the European Community, U.K. participation in the Persian Gulf War, military reform, preparations for the 1992 general election and rising economic and social problems.

The United Kingdom of Great Britain and Northern Ireland combines two formerly separate kingdoms (England and Scotland), an ancient principality (Wales) and six counties of the Irish province of Ulster. (A separate essay on Northern Ireland appears in the section on related territories.) Parliament has two houses: an elected House of Commons with 650 members chosen by plurality vote from single-member districts, and a House of Lords with over 1,000 hereditary and appointed members. The Lords have little power except for a suspensive veto, under which they can delay a piece of legislation for six months. If the House of Commons backs the legislation again, it becomes law. A section of the House of Lords serves as a supreme court. Parliament has a maximum term of five years. Queen Elizabeth II is the largely ceremonial head of state who nominates for prime minister the party leader who has the highest support in the House of Commons.

The Conservative Party has been in power since 1979. Facing declining popularity for the party in 1990, the Conservative parliamentary caucus unseated Prime Minister Margaret Thatcher, whom they replaced with John Major, a more moderate leader.

Labour, the main opposition party, led by Neil Kinnock, has moderated its socialist policies since losing its third consecutive general election in 1987. That year the Conservatives won 376 Commons seats to 229 for Labour and 22 for the centrist Alliance of Liberals and Social Democrats. Regional and nationalist parties from Scotland, Wales and Northern Ireland won the remaining seats. Most Liberals and Social Democrats merged into the Liberal Democratic Party in 1988. Its leader is Paddy Ashdown. A rump Social Democratic Party, led by Dr. David Owen, persisted after the Liberal Democratic merger, but Owen announced in 1990 that the party would cease contesting elections.

During Major's first year in office, he attempted to drop Thatcherite policies that endangered his party in the next general election, especially the unpopular local community charge, or poll tax, that had precipitated Thatcher's departure. The government announced in 1991 that local property taxes, adjusted for the number of household residents, would replace the hated poll tax.

Internationally, Major continued Britain's involvement in the anti-Iraq coalition which Thatcher had started. With the end of the cold war, Britain announced cutbacks in its military, including amalgamations of regiments and overall troop reductions. These measures angered many Conservatives, especially veterans.

Under pressure from Thatcher and other Conservatives hostile to a federal Europe, Major negotiated with the European Community to allow the U.K. to opt out of a single European currency. He also refused to join the other eleven EC members in a treaty which would harmonize social policies among member countries, because British Conservatives fear that the treaty would force the country to adopt more generous welfare and trade union policies.

Following Conservative losses in local elections, Major declined to call an early general election, and put off the vote until 1992. Major prepared for the campaign by issuing the "Big Idea" or the Citizen's Charter, a plan for greater government accountability for its services and more privatization. In 1991 the Labour Party expelled two MPs for their membership in the Trotskyist Militant Tendency. Labour hoped to make gains out of rising unemployment in the forthcoming general election. As the year closed, the Provisional Irish Republican Army carried out a terror campaign in England, bombing shopping areas during the Christmas season.

Political Rights and Civil Liberties:

Political rights and civil liberties are generally well-established by custom and precedence in Britain's largely unwritten constitution. The people have the right to change their government democratically. The electorate is registered to vote by a government survey. Irish citizens resident in Britain have the right to vote in British elections. Residents of Wales, Scotland and Northern Ireland do not have their own regional legislatures, but they elect members to the House of Commons.

The press is generally free, lively and competitive, but tough libel laws may have a chilling effect on some kinds of publishing and entertainment. For example, in 1991 MP Teresa Gorman won a libel suit over a mock press release from Anthony Mudd, a Conservative accountant. The Official Secrets Act provides the government with a tool to attempt halting publication of intelligence activities and other official matters. The media can challenge this restraint through appeals in the courts and publication overseas.

The British Broadcasting Corporation (BBC) is run as an autonomous public corporation. On occasion, it responds to government pressure not to broadcast certain controversial items such as those on terrorism. However, the BBC offers pluralistic points of view, and televises political programs of both government and opposition parties. There are also broadcast and satellite channels for private television corporations.

Since 1989 the courts have had to overturn several convictions in cases of alleged terrorism. For example, in 1991 an appeals court threw out the Maguire family's 1976 bombing conviction, citing the prosecution's use of invalid scientific evidence. In other overturned cases, the police had used forced confessions.

With a few exceptions involving Northern Ireland, there is freedom of movement. In November 1991 the government announced tighter rules for political asylum applications. This policy responded to public concerns about increasing immigration. Amnesty International called for repeal of the 1987 Immigration (Carriers' Liability) Act, under which the government fines airlines and shippers 2,000 pounds for each passenger they carry who has no valid passport or visa. Potential asylees often must flee without such travel documents.

Britain has free religious expression, but the Church of England and the Church of Scotland are established. The Queen is head of the Church of England. There is some possibility for political interference in religion, because the Queen appoints Anglican bishops from a church commission's short list on the advice of the prime minister.

Trade unions and business groups are powerful and active on political issues, but the unions declined in size and influence in the Thatcher era. In 1991 the government proposed several new restrictions on labor. If adopted, these rules would mandate such measures as: a seven-day cooling-off period before strikes; advance notice stating the precise kind of industrial action a union would take; and frequent, individual reauthorization of union dues withholding from wages.

United States of America

Polity: Federal presidential-legislative democracy
Economy: Capitalist
Population: 252,800,000
PPP: $19,850
Life Expectancy: 75.9
Ethnic Groups: Various white, black, Hispanic, Asian, native American (Indian) and others

Political Rights: 1
Civil Liberties: 1
Status: Free

Overview:

Significant developments in American domestic and foreign affairs in 1991 included the Persian Gulf War, the economic recession, the battle over Supreme Court nominee Clarence Thomas, signs of voter anger in the 1991 elections and the start of the 1992 presidential campaign.

Founded in 1776 during a revolution against British colonial rule, the U.S.A. began the modern movement for freedom and self-government in the world. The current system of government began functioning in 1789, following the ratification of the Constitution. Because the founders of the U.S. distrusted concentrations of centralized government power, they set up a system in which the federal government has three competing centers of power (executive, legislative and judicial branches), and left many powers with the state governments and the citizenry.

The U.S. Congress has two houses. There are 435 voting members of the House of Representatives and nonvoting delegates from Washington, D.C. and U.S. territories. Each state is guaranteed at least one representative. The rest are apportioned on the basis of population. The 100-seat Senate has two members from each state regardless of population.

The federal courts interpret the laws. The Supreme Court is the ultimate arbiter of the constitutionality of government actions. On occasion, the federal courts have ruled against the decisions of both other branches of the federal government.

President George Bush, a Republican, won the election in 1988 with 426 of the 538 electoral votes and 54 percent of the popular vote and took office in January 1989. The Republican Party, the more conservative of the two major parties, has won seven out of the last ten presidential elections. The Democratic Party, which is more liberal, has controlled both Houses of Congress for most years since the 1930s. In the 1990 Congressional elections, Democrats made modest gains: one seat in the Senate and eight in the House.

The Persian Gulf War dominated the news in early 1991. Led by the U.S., an international military coalition attacked Iraq and Iraqi-occupied Kuwait in January. The coalition drove Iraqi forces out of Kuwait and slashed Iraq's military capabilities. Internationally, the war showed that with the demise of the Soviet Union, the U.S. was the world's only superpower. Domestically, the war temporarily lifted both American spirits and President Bush's poll ratings dramatically. The conflict also gave Congress the opportunity to make a *de facto* declaration of war when it voted to authorize the use of force against Iraq. In light of America's decisive leadership in the Gulf War victory, President Bush seemed to be in a formidable position for re-election in 1992. One by one, numerous leading potential Democratic challengers announced they would not be presidential candidates.

The political afterglow of the war faded by late summer 1991 as Americans became increasingly concerned with unemployment, which rose officially to 7.1 percent by December. Public opinion polls reflected the perception that President Bush cared too much about overseas trips and foreign policy and too little about American jobs and living standards. The Bush Administration devoted a great deal of time to events in the now defunct Soviet Union and to thinking about the direction of post-cold war defense and foreign policy. However, substantial political currents, both Left and Right, concluded that the collapse of Communism meant that Americans should turn inward, and devote their energies to domestic problems.

The most publicized domestic political episode in 1991 was the battle over Bush's nomination of Clarence Thomas to the Supreme Court. Thomas, a black conservative, faced intense questions about his views on abortion. However, Thomas deflected questioners from the Senate Judiciary Committee with the claim that he had never discussed *Roe v. Wade*, the 1973 Supreme Court case which had legalized abortion. After Thomas' hearings, former aide Anita Hill accused him of sexual harassment. The Senate extended the hearings for several days of contradictory testimony from Hill, Thomas and several supporting witnesses. The Senate narrowly confirmed Thomas. Pressured by their large black constituencies which favored Thomas, Southern Democrats provided the conservative judge with his margin of victory.

In late 1991 Americans expressed their dissatisfaction with the political status quo through public opinion polls and state elections. By year's end, President Bush's support in opinion surveys dropped from over 80 percent during the Gulf War to under 50 percent. The 1991 off-year elections sent politicians angry messages in several states. In Louisiana, former Ku Klux Klan and Nazi leader David Duke, a Republican, won a place in the gubernatorial run-off election against former Governor Edwin Edwards, a flamboyant Democrat with a reputation for corruption. Embarrassed national Republican leaders, including President Bush, disowned Duke and backed Edwards. Although Duke lost, he won a majority of Louisiana's white vote, and announced an anti-Bush presidential campaign for 1992. Running on an anti-tax theme, Republicans trounced the Democrats in New Jersey's legislative election. Democrats attached national significance to Democrat Harris Wofford's victory over Bush's former Attorney General, Dick Thornburgh in Pennsylvania's U.S. Senate by-election. Wofford campaigned against federal economic and health policies. The Bush Administration was so shocked by Wofford's victory that it postponed a presidential trip to Japan, and began admitting that the economy was still in recession. The Pennsylvania result showed Bush's vulnerability on economic issues, and it encouraged the comparatively unknown field of Democratic presidential hopefuls. In late 1991 conservative Republican journalist Patrick Buchanan announced that he, too, would oppose Bush in the 1992 Republican primaries.

Throughout most of 1991, Bush opposed a civil rights bill which proposed shifting the burden of proof from employees to employers in job discrimination suits. He insisted repeatedly that the legislation would lead to racial quotas in hiring practices. After months of negotiation with Congress, President Bush reversed himself, signed the legislation and cut off his aides' attempt to issue an executive order against affirmative action.

Political Rights and Civil Liberties:

Americans have the right to change their government democratically. The electoral system allows Americans to change presidents every four years, the House of Representatives every two years and one-third of the Senate every two years. However, scarcely 50 percent of the voting age population takes part in presidential elections. The figure is even lower for midterm Congressional elections and some local contests. For example, only an estimated 36 percent of the voting age population turned out for the 1990 general elections. The party system is competitive, but 96 percent of Congress members seeking re-election won in 1990. Members spend an increasing amount of time raising funds from wealthy individuals and special interest groups in order to ward off potential opponents. This undermines the quality of representation and gives incumbents an unfair advantage in elections.

In presidential election years, an ideologically unrepresentative minority chooses Democratic and Republican presidential nominees through a chaotic, complicated and debilitating series of primary elections and local party meetings called caucuses. The first caucus and primary states, Iowa and New Hampshire, play a disproportionately powerful role in reducing the field of presidential contenders. Voters in the states that hold later primaries and caucuses often have little influence in deciding the outcome of the nomination process, even if their populations are larger or more representative of the nation as a whole.

Since the 1960s, the major parties have lost most of their traditional organizing functions to the news media and political advertising consultants. The latter specialize in negative campaigning, which they design to reduce voter turnout among the opposing campaign's potential supporters.

Several minor parties function, but the electoral system encourages pre-election coalitions within two parties rather than post-election coalitions among several parties, as it happens in many European countries. Several states, like New York, have daunting petitioning hurdles that make it difficult for small parties or major party insurgents to receive a place on the ballot. Many states allow the voters the rights of initiative and referendum. These devices allow citizens to collect petitions to place a public issue on the ballot and to decide the question directly, sometimes overturning the decisions of their elected representatives. California is especially noted for a high number of referenda each year.

The American media are generally free and competitive. However, there are some worrisome trends towards monopolization. As literacy rates fall, most Americans get their news from television. Broadcast news is highly superficial and is becoming increasingly difficult to distinguish from entertainment. During the Gulf War, the military controlled the flow of information from the front and limited reporters' access to American troops. Military police arrested a few reporters for trying to break through the restrictions. In Wilkes-Barre, Pennsylvania, authorities arrested four journalists for taping and publishing a telephone conversation with a murder suspect without his permission.

Public and private discussion are very open in America. However, a trend in universities to ban allegedly racist and sexist language is subject to broad interpretation and may have a chilling effect on academic freedom. There has been also a growing recognition that a tendency towards left-wing conformism among faculties resulted in a pressure on independent thinkers to mouth "politically correct" (p.c.) views. Certain large corporations may have a chilling effect on free speech when they hit their activist opponents with lawsuits, which are known as SLAPP suits (special litigation against public participation).

Since the early 1980s the Supreme Court has made increasingly conservative rulings, reversing the pattern of more liberal decisions in the 1960s and 1970s. Conservatives hope that Clarence Thomas' addition to the Court will intensify this recent trend.

Court systems at all levels of government suffer from a severe backlog of cases, delaying the course of justice in countless criminal and civil cases. The high crime rate and growing public demand to punish criminals have led to severe overcrowding in American prisons.

The nation was shocked in 1991 when several Los Angeles police officers repeatedly beat and kicked Rodney King, a black suspect. An amateur videotape of the incident played repeatedly on television and gave credence to complaints from racial minorities about police brutality against them.

The federal government's anti-drug measures have included seizing boats with trace elements of illegal drugs and random drug-testing of transport workers and civil servants. Public opinion supports additional measures to combat drugs, some of which would endanger the constitutional protection from unreasonable search and seizure.

The U.S. has freedom of association and thousands of clubs and associations of all kinds. Farm organizations and trade unions are free, but the labor movement is declining as its traditionally strong manufacturing base shrinks. U.S. trade unions have fewer legal protections than their counterparts in Western Europe. Due to management's increasing use of replacement workers during strikes, the strike has become a less effective weapon for discontented workers. In recent years, the federal government has used anti-racketeering laws to place some local and national unions under federal trusteeship, in order to remove corrupt officers and to attempt ending patterns of criminal activity. For example, in 1991 a trustee supervised the convention of the Teamsters' union and oversaw the union's first free rank-and-file presidential election. The labor movement opposes trusteeship as interference with freedom of association, but the new teamsters' president said that his union's old, corrupt leaders had nobody but themselves to blame for the federal intervention.

The country has a regulated, largely free market economy, with a growing number of service jobs and declining manufacturing employment. The entrepreneurial spirit remains strong. Most job growth takes place in small enterprises in the private sector.

The U.S. has many free religious institutions. Due to the constitutional separation of church and state, the Supreme Court has issued rulings limiting religious holiday displays on public property and prohibiting organized prayer in the public schools.

Most poor people in the U.S. are white, but there is a large, disproportionately black underclass that exists outside the economic mainstream. Characterized by seemingly permanent unemployment, the underclass lives to a great extent on welfare payments. Heavy drug use, high crime rates, female-headed households and large numbers of poorly fed, badly educated, illegitimate children characterize underclass neighborhoods. One report in 1990 suggested that men in Bangladesh have a better chance of living past age 40 than men in Harlem in New York City. The quality of life in America's older cities is in decline.

Despite the 1954 Supreme Court ruling against school segregation, some American school districts are experimenting with deliberately all-black or all-black male schools with special black curricular emphases. These are desperate attempts to motivate black youngsters who have poor skills and low self-esteem. There is also a black middle class that has made significant gains in housing, education and employment since the civil rights legislation of the 1960s.

American women have made significant gains in social and economic opportunities in recent decades, but still lag behind men in income. Affirmative action programs have increased the number of women in business and the professions, but they remain concentrated in low-paying occupations.

Under the terms of the 1986 immigration reform legislation, employers who hire illegal aliens face penalties. Studies in 1990 showed that employers took the possibility of sanctions so seriously that they discriminated against legal immigrants, especially Hispanics. In 1991, the U.S. turned back many Haitian asylum-seekers, and then switched to a policy of holding refugees at the American base at Guantanamo, Cuba. In 1991 the U.S. began the Morrison Visa Program, under which people from countries hurt by the 1965 immigration quotas can enter the country in greater numbers.

Environmentally, many parts of the U.S. have serious problems. Unacceptably high levels of air, water and ground pollution threaten inhabitants with higher disease rates and may lead to personal restrictions including limits on the use of automobiles and water supplies.

The U.S. government seems largely indifferent to the plight of the American Indians. Many descendants of the first Americans live in poverty on reservations. Several tribes have cases in court against the federal government, charging violation of treaty provisions relating to control over land and resources.

Uruguay

Polity: Presidential-legislative democracy
Economy: Capitalist-statist
Population: 3,100,000
PPP: $5,790
Life Expectancy: 72.2
Ethnic Groups: White, mostly Spanish and Italian, (89 percent), Meztizo (10 percent), Black and Mulatto (1 percent)

Political Rights: 1
Civil Liberties: 2
Status: Free

Overview:

The power-sharing agreement between President Luis Alberto Lacalle's National Party and the Colorado party, the country's other traditional political group, ran aground in 1991 over Lacalle's proposals for overhauling the statist economy. There was also grumbling in the military over the possibility of the left-wing Broad Front coalition winning the next national election in 1994.

After achieving independence from Spain in 1825, the Eastern Republic of Uruguay was established in 1830. The Colorado Party dominated the relatively democratic political system with few interruptions until it was finally ousted in the 1958 elections. It returned to power in 1966, the same year voters approved a constitutional amendment returning the political system to a one-man presidency. A sustained economic crisis, student and worker unrest, and the mounting activities of the Tupamaro urban guerrilla movement eventually led to a military takeover of the government in 1973.

The government was returned to civilian hands in 1985 following three years of protracted negotiations between the right-wing military regime and civilian politicians joined in the so-called Multipartidaria. Jose Sanguinetti of the Colorado party won the presidential election in November 1984 and took office, along with a newly elected congress, in March 1985.

The current political system is based on the 1967 democratic constitution. Both the president and a bicameral Congress consisting of a 99-member Chamber of Deputies and a 31-member Senate are elected for five years terms through a complicated system of electoral lists that allows parties to run multiple candidates. The leading presidential candidate of the party receiving the most votes overall is the winner; in essence, party primaries are conducted simultaneously with the general election. Congressional seats are allocated on the basis of each party's share of the total vote. Municipal and regional governments are also elected.

A major issue since the return to democratic rule has been civil-military relations. In the negotiated transition, the military backed down from demands for a permanent say in national security matters; its defense actions and the declaration of a state of siege are now subject to congressional approval. However, the nation divided in 1986 when the Sanguinetti government pushed through Congress an amnesty for officers accused of human rights violations during military rule. The constitution permits a referendum on laws passed by the legislature, provided that 25 percent of the electorate sign a petition requesting it. A sustained effort by predominantly leftist opponents of the amnesty led to the collection of enough signatures, and a plebiscite was held on 16 April 1989. Uruguayans voted, 57 percent to 43, to confirm the amnesty law.

After the plebiscite, the campaign for the 26 November 1989 general and municipal elections began. There were eleven candidates from seven parties and coalitions seeking to succeed President Sanguinetti. The ruling right-of-center Colorado party had three candidates. The centrist National (Blanco) party, the other traditional party, also had three. The predominantly Marxist Broad Front coalition had one.

The leading Blanco candidate was Luis Alberto Lacalle and the leading Colorado candidate was Jorge Batlle. The Broad Front candidate was Liber Seregni. Lacalle was elected president as the National Party obtained 37.4 percent of the vote, against 28.8 percent for the Colorados. Although the Broad Front only obtained 8 percent of the national vote, in municipal voting it captured Montevideo, the nation's capital and home to nearly half the country's population. In congressional races, the Blancos won 51 of 129 seats, with the Colorados taking 39, the Broad Front 29, and the remaining 10 going to smaller, predominantly social democratic parties.

To overcome the lack of a parliamentary majority, Lacalle secured a co-governing agreement with the Colorados by offering them three cabinet positions. After taking office in 1990, he began to push legislation on privatizing inefficient state enterprises and attracting foreign investment. Since then, however, his program has encountered strong opposition from Uruguay's powerful labor unions and the Broad Front administration in Montevideo under Mayor Tabare Vasquez.

In 1991 two Colorado factions withdrew from the government, leaving Lacalle with a tenuous legislative majority. By mid-year, opinion polls showed that the popularity of both traditional parties was dropping, suggesting that the Broad Front and the popular Tabare would make a strong run at the presidency in 1994. The prospect prompted a harsh statement by retired, hardline military officers that a Broad Front presidency would be "calamitous." When army chief General Guillermo de Nava backed the statement, President Lacalle moved quickly to establish a dialogue between the military and the political parties to ease the tension. But the army high command, while agreeing to talk with the Blancos and Colorados, was divided over whether to talk with the Broad Front.

Political Rights and Civil Liberties:

Citizens are able to change their government through free and fair elections. Constitutional guarantees regarding free expression, freedom of religion and the right to organize political parties, labor unions and civic organizations are respected. Elections and referendums are overseen by an independent electoral commission.

With the return to civilian rule in 1985, legal status was restored to all outlawed political organizations including the Communist party (PCU), as well as the country's trade union confederations. The Tupamaros renounced violence and registered as a political party, the National Liberation Movement, which formed a coalition with the Trotskyist Socialist Workers Party (PST) and other radical organizations. After the 1985 inauguration, the Sanguinetti government released all political prisoners, including former Tupamaro guerrillas, and permitted the return of an estimated 20,000 exiles.

Political expression is occasionally restricted by violence associated with hotly contested political campaigns and government-labor disputes. Labor is well organized, politically powerful, and frequently uses its right to strike. Since 1985, there have been nearly two dozen general strikes and numerous smaller stoppages over wages, government austerity policies, and the reinstatement of social welfare programs eliminated by the former military government.

The judiciary is independent and headed by a Supreme Court. The system includes courts of appeal, regional courts and justices of the peace.

A long tradition of press freedom was restored with the return of civilian government. The press is privately owned, and broadcasting is both commercial and public. There is no censorship. There are six daily newspapers, many associated with political parties, and a number of weeklies, including the influential *Busqueda*. Television has become an increasingly important part of the political landscape; the 1989 campaign featured a series of presidential debates and news coverage was extensive on the four channels that service the capital.

Vanuatu

Polity: Parliamentary democracy
Economy: Capitalist-statist
Population: 200,000
PPP: na
Life Expectancy: 69.5
Ethnic Groups: Indigenous Melanesian (90 percent), French, English, Vietnamese, Chinese, and other Pacific Islanders

Political Rights: 2
Civil Liberties: 3
Status: Free

Overview:

Vanuatu's major news story of 1991 was the ouster of the country's only prime minister since independence, Walter Lini. An archipelago of 80 islands north of New Caledonia, Vanuatu (formerly New Hebrides) gained independence in 1980 after 70 years of British-French rule.

The main opposition party, the Melanesian Progressive party (MPP) has become increasingly frustrated with their attempts to take power. The MPP is led by Lini's former ally, Barak Sope. In 1989 Sope's uncle, then-president George Sokomanu, the titular head of state, attempted to dissolve parliament and install Sope as prime minister. The two men were subsequently sentenced to five years' imprisonment on sedition and mutiny charges, but the country's Appeals Court overturned the convictions. Since then, the MPP has formed an opposition coalition with the more conservative Union of Moderate Parties (UMP).

Walter Lini faced increased dissatisfaction from his party in 1991, largely due to his failing health. In May 1991 Lini suffered a minor heart attack. Between October 1990 and August 1991, Lini fired or demoted 13 ministers and 40 civil servants, and demanded loyalty pledges from those that remained. Many of those fired were replaced by family and friends of the prime minister.

On 7 August the party moved to dump Lini during a party meeting. At first Lini tried to block the congress by declaring it illegal. When that didn't work and the order for his resignation was voted, Lini refused to step down as prime minister. However, on 6 September he decided to cede his spot as head of government to lead a new political group of Lini loyalists, the National United Party. In the election on 2 December the French-speaking UMP won 19 of the 46 parliamentary seats. To form a government, the UMP entered into a coalition with Lini's new party.

Political Rights and Civil Liberties: The people of Vanuatu can change their government democratically. Vanuatu has been dominated by Walter Lini's Party of Our Land since independence. The president, elected for a five-year term, has a largely ceremonial role. The prime minister and his cabinet, who must hold legislative seats, are elected by the Parliament. The unicameral Parliament is elected for four year terms. Parallel to the government is the National Council of Chiefs, whose members are elected from councils on the district level. The National Council can make recommendations to the government on matters of traditional culture and language. There are also various regional council. The judicial system is headed by a four-member Supreme Court. The chief justice is appointed by the president on the advice of both the prime minister and the leader of the opposition. The speaker of Parliament, the National Council of Chiefs and the presidents of the Regional Councils each appoint one of the other three judges.

At the time of independence, Vanuatu had five weekly newspapers and several monthly and quarterly publications. Now only one weekly newspaper, the state run *Vanuatu Weekly,* remains. There is also a new "independent" magazine; however, its editor-in-chief is Mrs. Hilda Lini, Walter Lini's wife. The radio is also government controlled and there are not television stations. Opposition views are tolerated, but the government has occasionally restricted the opposition's access to the media.

In July 1990 Father Lini called for a review committee to make adjustments to the ten-year-old constitution. The committee consists of 35 members, 24 of whom are VP members. One area of adjustment includes possible restrictions on religious cults. Father Lini, an Anglican priest, would like "traditional" sects (such as Catholicism, Protestantism, etc.) to be recognized officially in the constitution. This implies that those groups not recognized could be declared illegal.

Permits must be obtained from the government to hold demonstrations, but permission is usually granted. The judiciary is independent and proceedings are considered fair.

Workers are permitted to organize freely and to strike.

Venezuela

Polity: Presidential-legislative democracy
Economy: Capitalist-statist
Population: 20,100,000
PPP: $5,650
Life Expectancy: 70.0
Ethnic Groups: Mestizo (69 percent), White (Spanish, Portuguese, Italian, 20 percent), Black (9 percent), Indian (2 percent)

Political Rights: 1
Civil Liberties: 3
Status: Free

Overview: Midway through the five-year term of President Carlos Andres Perez, government optimism about its economic liberalization program was undercut by a series of official corruption scandals, national labor strikes, and the penetration of the nation's institutions by the region's expanding drug trade. Opinion polls showed increasing disillusionment with the country's traditional political parties, further evidence of strain on one of Latin America's oldest democracies.

The Republic of Venezuela was established in 1830, nine years after achieving independence from Spain. A history of political instability and long periods of military dictatorships culminated with the overthrow of the General Marcos Perez Jimenez regime by a popular democratic movement in 1958. The election of President Romulo Betancourt and the promulgation of a new constitution in 1961 established a system of democratic governance which has been in place ever since.

The 1961 constitution established a federal system consisting of 20 states and a federal district (Caracas); in 1991 the eastern federal territory of Delta Amacuro became the twenty-first state. The president and a bicameral Congress consisting of a Senate and a Chamber of Deputies are directly elected for five years. The Senate has at least two members from each of the states and from the federal district. All former presidents are life members of the Senate and additional seats are awarded to minority parties. There are currently 201 seats in the Chamber, also including seats awarded to small parties. State legislatures and municipal councils are elected.

Since 1958, the Venezuelan democracy has been dominated by two political parties, the social democratic Democratic Action (AD) party and the Christian democratic Christian Social Party (COPEI). The AD has won the last two national elections, including those in December 1988 when former President Carlos Andres Perez (1974-79) defeated COPEI's Eduardo Fernandez. COPEI has held the presidency twice since 1958, most recently under President Luis Herrera Campins (1979-84).

Less than a month after Perez's 2 February 1989 inauguration, the capital city of Caracas was torn by three days of violent street protests, remembered as the *caracazo*. The explosion of discontent was in response to deteriorating living standards and the government's austerity program intended to stabilize the debt-strapped economy. Under national emergency provisions of the constitution, the government declared martial law which lasted for ten days. The riots left over 300 people dead, according to official sources. A replay was feared during a series of labor strikes and student protests in the fall of 1991, but rioting on that occasion was quelled without police resorting to inordinate firepower.

The decline in popular support for the Perez government was further evident in the 3 December 1989 gubernatorial and municipal elections. AD lost in over half the country's 20 states and in over half the 269 municipal districts. Three governorships went to left-wing parties that ran anti-corruption campaigns.

Most surprising, however, was the overwhelming voter abstention—nearly 70 percent, despite the first-ever opportunity to directly elect governors and mayors—a trend which continued in 1990 and 1991 during intra-party elections. Also, there was little popular interest as the parties geared up for the next round of state and local elections scheduled for 1992. Voter abstention seemed to reflect the growing disenchantment not only with the ruling AD but with all established parties. The next presidential election will take place in December 1993.

In 1991, after a series of drug-related scandals involving high government officials and officers of the military, and as evidence emerged that the country had become not only a transshipment point but also a base of trafficking operations, the media began to speak of the "Colombianization of Venezuela." In June, President Perez for the first time acknowledged the problem and announced the formation of a national commission to coordinate the fight against the drug trade and strengthen anti-drug laws. However, opinion polls revealed that a majority of citizens had little confidence in the initiative or in the government's ability to weed out corruption in the nation's institutions.

Political Rights and Civil Liberties:

Citizens are able to change their government democratically. Constitutional guarantees regarding free expression, freedom of religion and the right to organize political parties, civic organizations and labor unions are generally respected. Political parties occupy the spectrum from right to left and labor unions are strong and well organized. A new labor law that went into effect in 1991 reduced the work week to 44 from 48 hours, and made it illegal for employers to dismiss workers without compensation.

Venezuelan laws also meet international human rights standards. However, the rule of law is often slow to be implemented and human rights abuses, while not systematic, have been on the rise in recent years as the police have cracked down on a growing crime wave, and as security forces have responded to the numerous popular demonstrations against the government's economic policies.

There are a number of independent human rights organizations. Since the February 1989 riots, these groups have fielded numerous complaints of abuses by police and security forces, including allegations of torture and arbitrary shootings. According to rights activists, the actual death toll exceeds official government figures. An investigation by a government commission led to the release of all detainees, but there has been no adequate response on the charges of abuse. There are no political prisoners, but there are continuing reports of deaths at the hands of security forces.

The judiciary is headed by a Supreme Court whose members are elected by the Congress. Although nominally independent, the judicial system is overly politicized. It is also slow and generally ineffective; less than a third of a prison population that totals about 30,000 has been convicted of a crime. Moreover, military courts investigating abuses by members of the armed forces are slow to cooperate with the civil court system, if they do at all. Military court decisions cannot be appealed in civilian courts. The judiciary also has been undermined by drug-related corruption, with growing evidence of bribery and intimidation of judges.

The press is privately owned. There are nearly a dozen independent daily newspapers. Radio and television are mostly private, supervised by an association of broadcasters under the government communications ministry. Censorship of the press and broadcasting media, however, occurs during states of emergency. In recent years a number of journalists investigating corruption charges and rights abuses have been arrested or anonymously threatened, and the media in general has encountered intimidation from official and unofficial sectors. Members of the media have accused the government of systematic spying on investigative journalists covering official corruption.

Vietnam

Polity: Communist one-party
Economy: Statist
Population: 67,600,000
PPP: na
Life Expectancy: 62.7
Ethnic Groups: Predominantly Vietnamese, with Chinese Khmer and other minorities

Political Rights: 7
Civil Liberties: 7
Status: Not Free

Overview:

In 1991 Vietnam's ruling Communist Party (VCP) continued its attempts to liberalize the economy without opening up the political system. The VCP has invited foreign investment, dismantled agricultural collectives and allowed small private enterprises, while prohibiting criticism of its commitment to socialism. The VCP's plans have been slowed by a loss of aid from the Soviet Union and a continuing U.S. economic embargo.

Vietnam's three historic regions of Tonkin, Annam and Cochin-China came under French control between 1862-1884. The French returned following a Japanese occupation during World War II and were attacked by a resistance movement led by Ho Chi Minh. In 1954, the French granted independence and the country was divided between a French-installed government in South Vietnam and a communist govern-ment in North Vietnam. Military forces and insurgent groups from the North battled troops from the U.S.-backed South until a 1972 cease fire. Reconciliation talks broke down and the North launched an offensive in late 1974, overtaking the South in 1975 and reuniting the country as the Socialist Republic of Vietnam in 1976. China and Vietnam fought a brief border war in 1979 after Vietnam's late 1978 invasion of Cambodia that drove out the Khmer Rouge.

With the nation struggling with mounting poverty, the seminal VCP Sixth Party Congress in 1986 introduced a program of economic renovation (*doi moi*), which has decentralized economic decision-making, encouraged small-scale private enterprise and largely dismantled the country's system of collective agriculture. Farmers can now obtain land on long-term leases from the government and sell products at market prices. The changes transformed the country into a rice exporter, but other areas of the economy have shown far less improvement. Malnutrition is a major problem and the country remains one of the poorest in the world, with an annual per capita income of less than $200.

The former East bloc countries have ended nearly all trade agreements and economic aid to Vietnam, which had totaled over $1 billion dollars annually. This has forced Vietnam to purchase goods at world market prices with hard currency and caused shortages in food, steel and other necessities. Nearly three-quarters of the population is in agriculture, but the country cannot afford enough fertilizer to raise crop yields. Inflation has been reduced but still runs at upwards of 75 percent per year. Unemployment has risen with the return of 200,000 guest workers from Eastern Europe and a major army demobilization of over 400,000 soldiers. Commenting on the woeful performance of the public sector, a government official told the *Financial Times* ,"State-owned enterprises produce 26 percent of GDP, using 75 percent of fixed capital and 86 percent of credit volume." Industries use outdated equipment and produce inferior goods. Civil servants often go for months without getting paid and many public sector workers are forced to engage in black-market trade to supplement their incomes.

The opening of VCP's Seventh Party Congress, originally scheduled for early 1991, was delayed for several months as economic policy questions were debated at a series of party plenums and local caucuses. Many cadres criticized the party's bureaucracy and the inefficiency of state enterprises. Disputes arose over the pace of economic reform as hard liners feared that rapid decentralization would lead to an eventual downfall of the government. Several younger party members demanded political liberalization. Following a party plenum in May, the VCP deleted a statement in the proposed Congress platform referring to socialism's eventual triumph over capitalism, but refused to allow criticism of the country's commitment to socialism itself. After articles questioning the validity of Marxism-Leninism appeared in the March issue of the party's ideological magazine, *Communist Review,* the April edition published a retraction entitled "Some Things Need to be Discussed Again." Editors were warned about publishing similar articles in the future.

Paranoia surrounded the Congress. Fear of anti-government activity in the south had led to the recent creation of a special security unit composed mainly of recruits from the Nghe An province, the birthplace of Ho Chi Minh. An estimated 50,000 VCP members have been purged since the 1986 Congress. In April, the party dismissed war hero and newspaper editor Colonel Bui Tin after he criticized the government in the Paris media while on an official assignment. Immediately prior to the opening of the Congress, several foreign journalists were expelled from the country.

Opening the Congress on 24 June, aging VCP general secretary Nguyen Van Linh, the chief proponent of *doi moi*, acknowledged "a crisis in theory and in practice" in socialism, but blamed "imperialist forces" for the events in Eastern Europe. While rejecting calls by "pseudo-democrats" and "demagogues" for a multi-party political system in Vietnam which would unleash "forces of reaction," Linh encouraged the development of a state-regulated market economy. He then resigned as part of an expected politburo shakeup, and was replaced as party leader by Prime Minister Do Muoi, who candidly referred to Vietnam as "a poor and backward country." Several others were dismissed from the politburo, including hard line Foreign Minister Nguyen Co Thach, who had failed to persuade the United States to normalize relations and had opposed improving relations with China.

A resulting thirteen member politburo, with eight new members, demonstrated Linh's success in bringing in younger, educated reformers who could apply modern economic principles while retaining the party's hold on power. Only two of the former members had received the equivalent of a high school education. Completing the transition, in August veteran revolutionary fighter and economic reformer Vo Van Kiet succeeded Do Muoi as prime minister.

The new leadership's biggest challenge in rebuilding the economy is to end the United States trade embargo, imposed in 1975 after the fall of South Vietnam and continued with the country's invasion of Cambodia. In April the U.S. State Department outlined a "road map" for a normalization of ties between the two countries, largely linked to the Cambodian peace process, which would result in a full restoration of relations after free elections are held in Cambodia. Vietnam claims its 1989 troop withdrawal from Cambodia met what had been the standing United States' condition at the time for improved relations, and that the October 1991 Cambodian peace agreement ended its control of the regime it installed there in 1979. In addition to the embargo, the U.S. has continuously blocked international lending organizations from providing aid. On 16 October the U.S. vetoed an attempt by the World Bank and International Monetary Fund to grant funds to allow the country to pay past debts, estimated at roughly $150 million.

The United States is also demanding a full accounting of the 2,273 American soldiers listed as "Missing in Action" (MIA) in Indochina. In July the U.S. established an office in Hanoi to use as a base in searching for MIAs, and on 18 November the U.S. State Department announced it would begin direct discussions with Vietnam on normalizing relations.

Vietnam is also seeking closer relations with China. In recent years, the two countries supported opposite sides in Cambodia and both claim possession of the Spratly Islands in the South China Sea. In November the countries announced relations were normalized, agreed to consider joint oil exploration in the Spratly Islands and signed trade agreements during a four-day meeting in Beijing. Small-scale trade has flourished along their 600-mile common border.

Political Rights and Civil Liberties:

Vietnamese citizens cannot change their government democratically. The ruling Vietnamese Communist Party (VCP) is the only legal political party and its politburo directly influences the policies of the state's Council of Ministers. An umbrella Vietnam Fatherland Front includes the VCP as well as youth, trade and peasant groups. Since 1975 some 100,000 political prisoners have been sent to "re-education camps." Late in 1991 the government began the release of some 100 prisoners it claimed were the last of those held from the former South Vietnam army and government. However, this amnesty does not extend to some 2,000 remaining political prisoners held for activities after 1975. The government said it would allow the International Red Cross to visit the last camp, in Thuan Hai province, early in 1992. The judicial system lacks civil law codes and is closely monitored by the government. New regulations provide a greater role for the defense counsel, although in practice few defendants receive adequate assistance and the appeals process provides a negligible safeguard. Those accused of common crimes are often beaten to extract confessions. Although judges are nominally elected, all candidates must be nominated by the party.

Freedom of speech and expression are provided for in the constitution, but in practice are severely limited by the government. Private media are not permitted and government broadcasts and publications are limited to party views. While the policy of *doi moi* has allowed for some critique of government problems and social issues, advocacy of a multi-party system or a non-socialist economy remain illegal. Several dissidents were arrested in early September 1991 following the distribution of leaflets calling for the overthrow of the regime, but a protest in front of the National Assembly in December calling for curbs on official corruption was permitted. In late November the government sentenced Nguyen Dan Que, who had attempted to form a human rights group, to 20 years in prison and five years of house arrest on charges of subversion. Prominent author Duong Thu Huong was held for several months in 1991 on the charge of "siphoning abroad documents detrimental to state security." Her anti-regime book, *Blind Paradises*, has been banned. Freedom of assembly is limited by regulations requiring a permit for group meetings, and some areas reportedly require permission for gatherings of more than three people.

One key test of the regime's commitment to human rights may come with the return of refugees who have fled since 1975. Some 100,000 remain in camps throughout Southeast Asia. The government agreed on 2 October to accept the forced return of refugees in Hong Kong and promised they would not be discriminated against.

In February two church leaders in Ho Chi Minh City were arrested on charges of using religion to foment political unrest. A resurgence of religious practice prompted a government decree in May which stipulated that religious activities must not violate "the Constitution and the law." It requires government approval of religious activities. The government has relaxed some restrictions on internal travel and in recent years has allowed more citizens to travel abroad, but citizens are still often required to obtain permits to cross provincial lines. The government controls all worker's unions, and strikes are not permitted.

Western Samoa

Polity: Elected parliament and family heads
Economy: Capitalist
Population: 200,000
PPP: $1,870
Life Expectancy: 66.5
Ethnic Groups: Samoan (88 percent), mixed race (10 percent), Europeans, other Pacific Islanders

Political Rights: 2
Civil Liberties: 2
Status: Free

Overview:

A devastating cyclone ripped across Western Samoa in December 1991, leaving thousands homeless, killing 12 and destroying food crops. Winds of up to 150 miles per hour damaged 95 percent of the houses on the island of Savaii and damaged 60 percent of the communal fishing boats. Damages were estimated at $278 million, and relief experts predict a shortage of fresh food through much of 1992. The storm came as the country continued to recover from a previous cyclone, which hit in February 1990.

Located 1600 miles northeast of New Zealand, the western Samoan islands became a German protectorate in 1899. New Zealand claimed the islands during World War I and administered them until 1962, when the country gained its independence. Malietoa Tanumafili II is the head of state for life, although future heads of state, who must approve all legislation passed by the parliament, will be elected by the parliament for five year terms. Citizens of Western Samoa enjoyed universal suffrage for the first time in 1991, but most of the seats in the 47-member parliament remained restricted to *matai*, the traditional tribal chiefs. In a special referendum in October 1990, 53 percent favored universal suffrage for all citizens over 21. Previously, only *matai*, who represent villages of extended families, could vote. Two seats in the parliament are still reserved for citizens of non-Samoan descent. Many *matai* had opposed universal suffrage and one member of parliament claimed the old system had been "perhaps the best form of democracy in the world" and decried "dictatorial rule pretending to be universal suffrage."

Prior to the 1991 election, the government passed legislation aimed at various interest groups that would be voting for the first time. It introduced a pension for those over 65, created an annual national holiday for women, promised money for women's committees in villages, and set up an ombudsman's office to hear complaints against government agencies.

The 5 April election had a turnout of roughly 90 percent. Ceremonial exchanges of gifts were banned prior to the election because of the difficulty in distinguishing between bribery and traditional gift-giving. Prime Minister Tofilau Eti Alesani's Human Rights Protection Party won twenty-six seats as well as the support of two independents. Opposition leader Tuiatua Tupua Tamasese of the Samoan National Development Party lost his seat in the election, but forced a by-election after a judge found evidence of bribery in his district. Tapua won the by-election, but the Supreme Court declared the seat vacant on 20 November pending additional review due of further election irregularities. The Court said Tapua bribed voters when he handed out 12 pounds of corned beef after an election speech. In all, post-election petitions were filed against eleven members of parliament for charges ranging from illegal distribution of food and drinks to votes cast under the names of people who were deceased or out of the country.

Political Rights and Civil Liberties:

Western Samoans can change their government democratically. Although there are two political parties, politics are generally based on individual loyalties.

Citizens have the right to a trial with procedural safeguards modeled on the British system, although in practice many disputes are adjudicated by village parliaments (*fonos*), whose decisions are legally recognized and subject to appeal to the Lands and Titles Courts. Punishments meted out by village fonos can include banishment from a village and destruction of property. Freedom of press, speech and association are are enumerated in the constitution and protected in practice. There is full freedom of religion in this near-completely Christian society. Citizens are free to travel abroad and internally, although village fono decisions have the effect of banning people from certain areas. Workers are free to bargain collectively, although no unions have formed in the private sector.

Yemen

Polity: Transitional military-civilian ruling council and parliament
Economy: Capitalist-statist
Population: 10,100,000
PPP: na
Life Expectancy: 51.5
Ethnic Groups: Arab majority, African and Asian minorities

Political Rights: 6
Civil Liberties: 5
Status: Partly Free

Overview:

In 1991 Yemen's reunification process and preparations for multi-party elections were hampered by an economy weakened by the Persian Gulf War. Having sided with Iraq, the country faced a cutoff of foreign aid and an expulsion of its expatriate workers in other Gulf states. The crisis highlighted tensions among Marxists, fundamentalists and tribal leaders and culminated in a series of assassination attempts against government figures and protests over a new constitution.

Located at the southern end of the Arabian peninsula, the Republic of Yemen was formed on 22 May 1990 with the merger of the conservative Yemen Arab Republic (YAR) and the Marxist People's Democratic Republic of Yemen (PDRY). The two countries had fought border skirmishes in 1971-1972 and a one-month war in 1979. Efforts to unify the countries, which had begun in the early 1970s, continued after the war and increased in the late 1980s, reportedly with prodding from the Soviet Union.

A constitution ratified by an announced 98.3 percent in a popular referendum on 15-16 May 1991 provides for a transitional Presidential Council composed of a president, a vice-president and three other officials, who will serve until elections are held in November 1992. Until elections, a 301-seat House of Representatives led by prime minister Haydar Abu Bakr al-Attas, a former DPRY president, will be carrying out legislative duties. The House is composed of MPs who had served in the parliaments of the two former countries and 31 new members. The government is dominated by the YAR's National Congress Party and the DPRY's Yemeni Socialist Party, but opposition parties from the far right to the radical left have emerged. Under arrangements made prior to reunification, Lieutenant-General Ali Abdallah Salih of the YAR serves as President and Ali Salim al-Biedh of the DPRY is Vice President.

The government's support of Iraq in the Persian Gulf War proved to be extremely costly. Over 1 million Yemenis working in Saudi Arabia and elsewhere, who had provided upwards of $1.2 billion in remittances per year, were expelled and several Western aid donors sharply curtailed assistance. During the war, pro-Iraqi demonstrations were held in cities and bombs exploded at four Western embassies. Sensing its international isolation, the government attempted to modify its original position by stressing that its support was for the Iraqi people rather than for Saddam Hussein. Official statements continued to condemn the American-led coalition. The loss of income has limited the government's ability to make payments on a foreign debt in excess of $7 billion and a 1991-92 budget deficit of $1.12 billion. Saudi Arabia's decision after the war to begin allowing some of the workers to return helped prevent a complete economic implosion.

Economic problems have increased tribal, religious and political rivalries. Citing an August assassination attempt on Ahmad al-Asbahi, an MP, and suggesting that two politicians who died in separate auto accidents were actually murdered, opposition groups claimed that popular unrest against the regime was growing due to economic problems and repression. In another apparent assassination attempt on 11 September, unidentified gunmen wounded Omar al Jawi, the head of the leftist opposition Unionist Rally Party and a critic of fundamentalist groups.

Fundamentalist Muslims, led by Sheik Hussein Abdullah al-Ahmar, the head of the confederation of Hashed tribes in the North, have demanded an Islamic state and have adopted an Islamic platform for the 1992 elections. In May more than 20,000 activists from the Yemeni Rally Party for Reform and other fundamentalist groups demonstrated against the proposed constitution, calling it secular and socialist.

The government's influence outside the cities is marginal. Territory is divided along traditional boundaries by Bedouin tribes and tribal leaders have the power to levy taxes and resolve disputes. The government engendered hostility in 1990 by forming a commission to redraw the boundaries of the local governorates, posing a territorial challenge to tribal leaders. In addition, a dispute reportedly occurred among the ruling parties in 1991 over President Salih's alleged payments to "persons unknown" for military expenses. The ex-PDRY leaders fear that purchased weapons could be used in a plot to force it out of the governing coalition.

In an effort to promote self-sufficiency in a country which imports roughly two-thirds of its food needs, the government announced a plan in early 1991 to give portions of land to returning expatriate workers for food production. The government is depending on the development of Aden as a free trade zone and newly discovered oil reserves to boost the economy. Eighteen foreign companies have been prospecting for oil and experts believe the country may be able to export up to 700,000 barrels a day by the mid-1990s.

Political Rights and Civil Liberties: Citizens of Yemen cannot democratically change their government. The ruling coalition says it will hold multi-party elections via secret ballot in November 1992 and there are 38 registered political parties representing a diversity of viewpoints. Political parties had been banned in the YAR and the Yemeni Socialist Party had been the only legal party in the PDRY. As the country is still in transition towards a unified legal system, many laws of the former countries still apply in their respective territory. Security forces reportedly search homes without authorization, monitor communications and carry out human rights violations against detainees. The new constitution calls for an independent judiciary, but few measures have been taken towards the establishment of a court system or legal code. Despite pressures from fundamentalist groups, the government says Islamic law will be only one element of the new legal system and not its entire basis.

While the new constitution provides for freedom of speech, press and association, Yemenis are generally cautious in criticizing the authorities. The government runs all electronic media and owns several large newspapers; foreign papers are generally available. Independent papers representing a wide range of opinions have been founded. All organizations must be registered with the government. Islam is the state religion, but the country's tiny, rural Jewish population is permitted to practice. Citizens with one non-Yemeni parent and descendents of former slaves are occasionally discriminated against. Citizens can travel relatively freely internally and abroad. While women are increasingly gaining access to middle-level jobs, domestic violence and clitorectomy reportedly occur frequently. Labor laws are in a flux, and strikes and union activity are sharply restricted.

Yugoslavia

Polity: Dominant party (military-influenced)
Economy: Mixed statist
Population: 17,300,000
PPP: $4,860
Life Expectancy: 72.6
Ethnic Groups: Serbian (36 percent), Croatian (20 percent), Bosnian (9 percent), Slovene (8 percent), Macedonian (6 percent)

Political Rights: 6
Civil Liberties: 5
Status: Not Free

Overview: In 1991 the federal system of government that kept this ethnically and religiously diverse confederation together finally collapsed. The resulting civil war launched by Serbia and the Serb-dominated national army against neighboring Croatia saw some of the worst fighting in Europe since World War II.

On the surface, the war seemed to be precipitated by declarations of independence by Slovenia and Croatia on 25 June, but in reality the conflict was an outgrowth of age-old Serbian-Croatian animosities exacerbated by Serbia's anti-reformist Communist President Slobodan Milosevic's repeated calls for a resurgence of a Greater Serbia. By year's end, the war had claimed over 6,000 lives and left at least 600,000 homeless. Serbian militias and army forces laid siege to the historic Croatian city of Dubrovnik and indiscriminate shelling destroyed medieval architectural and cultural treasures. The city of Vukovar also fell after heavy fighting.

As numerous cease-fires engineered by the European Community and the U.N. failed to hold, there was real danger the war could spread to Bosnia-Herzegovina, where ethnic Muslims made up 40 percent of the population, Serbs 33 percent, and Croats 18 percent. Another flashpoint was Macedonia. Nationalist Serbs never accepted Macedonians as a separate ethnic group and refer to the republic as "Southern Serbia." Greece, Bulgaria and Turkey have all claimed parts Macedonia in the past. In addition, Serbia's virtual annexation of formerly autonomous Kosovo, 90 percent Albanian, and Vojvodina, home to over 400,000 Hungarians, has increased tensions in those regions.

In 1991 the country that was forged in 1918 from the remnants of the Hapsburg and Ottoman empires and held together after World War II by former anti-Nazi partisan and Communist leader Marshal Josip Broz (Tito), ceased to exist. From its creation, Yugoslavia was divided by cultural and economic differences that separated the Roman Catholic, pro-European north (Slovenia and Croatia) from the poorer Eastern Orthodox and Muslim south. Under Tito, Yugoslavia became a one-party state with political power concentrated in the League of Communists of Yugoslavia (LCY). Federal republics were accorded national status and substantial self-government. Each of the six republics had its own party and government apparatus, with an indirectly elected assembly, an executive and a judiciary. State power was vested in a bicameral Federal Assembly, elected through a complex process to make it as representative as possible. After Tito's death in 1980, the duties of head of state were vested in a collective presidency, the Federal Executive Council, the presidency of which was to rotate annually between the republics. Ante Markovic was elected president of the Council and prime minister in March 1989.

1991 opened amid deep divisions and heightened ethnic tensions. The LCY had all but disappeared as a national party, separatist presidents were democratically elected in Slovenia (Milan Kucan) and Croatia (General Franjo Tudjman), Macedonia and Bosnia-Herzegovina elected non-Communist governments, Montenegro elected a moderate Communist leader, and in Serbia, Milosevic's Socialist Party (formerly Communist) triumphed.

In January a financial scandal with political ramifications threatened to topple the federal monetary system, undercutting Prime Minister Markovic's ambitious economic reform program. Federal officials disclosed that Serbia's parliament illegally and secretly approved a law a month earlier requiring Serbian-controlled national banks to issue $1.8 million worth of new money without any backing or federal approval. Under the country's decentralized banking system, republican banks, which issue currency, were technically required to follow the tight credit policy approved by the federal government as part of the prime minister's reform package. In effect, the move was the first salvo in Milosevic's war against the central government and angered leaders of other republics.

Tensions heightened when Croatia, which had been advocating a looser confederation, refused to disarm its paramilitary police, claiming the order by the federal presidency was a challenge from Serbia and the Serb-controlled army. In February the fourth round of talks between republic leaders failed to reach agreement on the future of the country. The failure resulted from irreconcilable differences on how loosely or tightly Yugoslavia's ethnic-based components should be knit, as well as differences on the political role of the Yugoslav People's Army (YPA). Croatia and Slovenia demanded a looser union, while Serbia insisted on a strong central government. At the end of the month, Slovenia approved legislation allowing it to take over functions like banking and defense from the central government in Belgrade.

The growth of Serbian nationalism, fueled by Milosevic's fiery oratory, further spurred Croatia's Serbian minority, 12 percent of the republic's 4.5 million people concentrated mainly in east Croatia, to expand armed militias and demand autonomy.

The political crisis intensified in March. Demonstrations in Belgrade calling for the ouster of Communist leaders and President Milosevic left two dead and 120 wounded by police. On 15 March the eight-member federal presidency rejected Serbian calls for a state of emergency to put down the protests. Borisav Jovic, Serbia's representative to the collective presidency resigned, precipitating a constitutional crisis. He was subsequently pressured to stay by the Communist majority in the Serbian parliament. On 16 March members from Montenegro and Vojvodina, the formerly autonomous region seized by Serbia, quit the presidency. The next day, Milosevic declared the Krajina region of Croatia a "Serbian autonomous region." On 17 March the Serbian-administered, predominantly Albanian enclave of Kosovo lost its representative to the federal presidency when he was removed by Serbia. With half its members removed, the presidency lost its quorum. The constitutional crisis was averted with the return of Jovic and the rescinding of the other resignations.

In 15 May the Serbian leadership again plunged the country into a constitutional crisis by blocking the installation of Croat Stipe Mesic as federal president, which was to be automatically rotated. Instead, the Serbian representative voted against Stipe, as did the Serb-appointed representatives of Kosovo an Vojvodina. Montenegro abstained, leaving Mesic, who was backed by Slovenia, Croatia and Bosnia-Herzegovina, one vote short of a majority. Two days later, republic representatives failed to fill the post. On 31 May, Croatia announced it was forming its own army and President Tudjman indicated that the republic could not stay in Yugoslavia. Croatia, Slovenia and Macedonia boycotted a meeting of the collective presidency, and derailed an effort to end a crisis that left the country without a head of state for two weeks.

The situation worsened on 25 June, when Croatia and Slovenia declared their independence. Within days, tanks from the YPA were sent to Slovenia. Prime Minister Markovic's pleas for unity were ignored, and Serbia's obstructionism in filling the collective presidency, which controls the military, suggested the army was acting on its own or under Serbian authority. Slovenia, a tiny, ethnically homogeneous and prosperous republic bordering Austria, had prepared for YPA intervention, and its well-armed defense forces managed to secure its borders and rout army forces. On 18 July the federal presidency decided to order the withdrawal of YPA units from Slovenia. The four Serbian-controlled members supported the army's retreat, immediately raising fears in Croatia that the units would intervene to block the republic's secession.

Those fears were justified, as YPA units joined Serbian irregulars in raids against Croatian police and militia. By 22 July fighting had erupted across Serbian-populated counties in Croatia. In early August, the European Community (EC) had sent a delegation to Yugoslavia, but all attempts by the Europeans and the federal presidency to broker a permanent cease-fire proved fruitless. Fierce fighting raged through August. The EC convened a peace conference in the The Hague on 7 September, which was dominated by name-calling by Serbian and Croatian representatives.

On 9 September, Macedonia declared its independence after 75 percent of eligible voters approved a referendum on state sovereignty. Bulgaria announced it was prepared to recognize Macedonia. Throughout the month, Croatia's outgunned defense forces were losing ground to Serbian militias and YPA units.

In another key development, Kosovo held an underground referendum and a clandestine legislative vote in favor of independence in spite of Serbia's declaration that the voting was illegal.

On 23 October, as fighting raged around the Croatian cities of Dubrovnik and Vukovar, top Serbian government, military and civilian leaders met in Belgrade to support a plan to create a rump Yugoslav state. The plan, which was proposed at a meeting of the pro-Serb members of Yugoslavia's collective presidency, countered a proposal for a six-republic Yugoslav confederation presented by the EC at The Hague. Serb leaders called for a nationwide referendum in which the people at large, and not republics, would decide whether they wanted to remain in Yugoslavia. The referendum would have likely produced a Serb-dominated state that included Serbia and Montenegro; large parts of Bosnia-Herzegovina, a patchwork of Muslim Slavs, Serbs and Croats; and areas of Croatia under the control of the YPA and Serbian militia. Two days later, Milosevic rejected the latest EC proposal for a loose confederation.

Frustrated by Serbian intransigence, the EC in November voted to impose sanctions against Yugoslavia, a decision that was joined by the United States. On 13 November, Britain, France and Belgium urged the United Nations Security Council to dispatch a peacekeeping force to Yugoslavia.

By the end of the month, Serbia's Communist regime took steps to takeover the Yugoslav government, aiming to transform federal institutions paralyzed by the civil war into a central administration for a Serb-dominated rump state. But the EC and the United States made it clear that it would regard the ouster of Prime Minister Markovic as illegal. The threat of punitive steps and a strident warning by U.N. special envoy Cyrus Vance apparently delayed Milosevic's replacement of Markovic.

By December, after several more ceasefires had collapsed, Vance announced that renewed fighting was hindering the dispatch of a peacekeeping force. On 5 December, Mesic, a Croat, resigned as the head of the collective presidency amid escalating fighting. Croatia voted to grant the Serb minority a degree of self-rule.

On 14 December, Germany announced that it would recognize Slovenia and Croatia as independent states, and three days later, the EC followed suit, declaring that formal recognition would become effective from 15 January 1992. As the year drew to a close with no apparent respite in the fighting, Bosnia-Herzegovina, home to 1.4 million Serbs, asked the EC to recognize its independence amid rising fears that the republic would be swallowed up by a rump Serb-dominated state or face outright invasion by Serbia.

Political Rights and Civil Liberties: The collapse of the federal government, the secession of three republics, and a bloody civil war undermined the political rights of what was Yugoslavia. In the absence of federal elections and the impotence of central authorities, Yugoslavs do not have the means to democratically change their government. Independent political parties function in all the republics, though the Serbian opposition has been cowed by pro-Milosevic forces. Each republic has its own judiciary and criminal code. Ordinary criminal and civil cases are usually open and fair.

Political violence was rampant in 1991. In the Serbian-controlled region of Kosovo, repression against the Albanian majority is systemic. Scores were killed and injured by police in Belgrade during protests against the hardline Serbian government. YPA forces and Serbian militias committed widescale atrocities in Croatia during the war; whole villages were destroyed and Croatian civilians were massacred. Croatian forces also committed atrocities against Serbs. Even before all out war, Serbian paramilitary groups conducted raids in Croatia, murdering and mutilating policemen. In September, Serbian police blocked voters in Kosovo from voting on an independence referendum.

Press freedom has been compromised, particularly in Serbia. Newspapers and government controlled media parrot the government line. The paper *Politika*, which had an international reputation as one of the most credible papers in the Communist world, has become a mouthpiece for Milosevic and the nationalists. In February, it printed a bizarre story charging that the Vatican was working to break up Yugoslavia by negotiating an $4 billion loan to the government of (Catholic) Croatia.

Religious freedom is guaranteed by law, but regulations and restrictions exist, particularly in activities deemed political or nationalist. Workers can join trade unions, and independent unions have been organized.

Zaire

Polity: Transitional
Economy: Capitalist statist
Population: 37,800,000
PPP: $430
Life Expectancy: 53.0
Ethnic Groups: Over 100, including the Azande, Babwe, Bang, Bangala, Kongo, Luba, Lulua, Mai-Ndombe, Mon, Mongo, and Pygmy

Political Rights: 6
Civil Liberties: 5
Status: Not Free

Overview: Despite his proclaimed commitment in 1990 to greater pluralism, in 1991 President Mobutu Sese Seko continued to evade all challenges posed to his 26 year monopoly on power in Zaire. Amidst international pressure for Mobutu's resignation, economic collapse sent looting crowds of soldiers and civilians to the street in cities throughout the country.

Known as the Belgian Congo until it gained independence in 1960, Zaire has been ruled since 1965 by Mobutu as a one-party state dominated by the Popular Movement of the Revolution (MPR). The internecine blood-letting and attempted secessions that followed independence took the lives of 100,000 people and only ended with Major General Mobutu's consolidation of power. The trade-off for a quarter-century of political stability under Mobutu (with occasional help from foreign troops) has been an impoverishing level of official corruption and the repression of political opposition. In the early '80s, the opposition group Union for Democracy and Social Progress (UDSP) was formed to push for multi-party rule, but its leaders were either arrested or forced into exile.

Only MPR-approved candidates may compete in elections to the unicameral National Legislative Council. The Council is subservient to the MPR's 38 member Political Bureau, whose members are all appointed by the president. In 1984, President Mobutu, running unopposed, was re-elected to his third seven-year term.

In 1990, facing growing popular pressures for political reform, Mobutu announced a series of changes ostensibly meant to introduce a multi-party system in this vast, central African country. He stated that all opposition parties would be permitted access to the state media and added that a new constitution would be submitted to a referendum in 1991. Nonetheless, opposition rallies and other meetings continued to be broken up by the police; a political meeting called in November 1990 by the revived UDSP in Kinshasa led to a violent response by the army in which dozens were wounded and hundreds arrested.

In 1991 it became clearer that the legalization of opposition political parties had little to do with limiting the President's hold on power. As Mobutu expressed it, he wished to remain head of state in the role of a mediating arbitrator above all parties. In early January, leaders of several opposition parties called for a strike to oust the President from power, but within days proposed instead the formation of a govern-ment of national unity. The President accepted the proposal, but the initiative failed when Mobutu refused to cede significant authority to a prime minister and cabinet.

Growing unrest with the regime led to clashes between security forces and demonstrators. In mid-April security forces killed over 40 protestors in the central mining town of Mbuji-Mayi. On 14 May two students were killed at a demonstration in the capital, Kinshasha. The president abandoned the role he had sought as a national moderator when he re-assumed the leadership of the ruling MPR on 21 April, only a year after having resigned as chairman. In July some 200 opposition groups joined together in a Sacred Union of Forces for Change. In an effort to relieve the tensions, a national conference was convened in the capital on 31 July, but was suspended two weeks later when opposition groups called a boycott to protest what it claimed was the government's stacking of the conference with Mobutu supporters. Hoping to placate the opposition, Mobutu offered to appoint as prime minister Tshisekedi wa Mulumba of the UDPS and the Sacred Union, a former interior minister who had joined the opposition nine years ago. Sensing Mobutu's weakness, Tshisekedi refused the offer.

In late September, paratroopers based in Kinshasa mutinied on grounds that they had not been paid for months. Looting shops and homes, they were soon joined by civilians. Entire commercial districts were stripped bare; many items were transported to military barracks and sold. Mines, factories, and utilities were vandalized in the wake of the flight of an estimated 15-20,000 foreign technicians to adjoining coun-tries. Hundreds were reported to have died and thousands injured. As rioting spread to cities in the west and far south of the country, France and Belgium sent in troops to protect and evacuate their nationals and other expatriates on 24 September. The regime reimposed order with a curfew. The West warned Mobutu they would not come to his assistance should the breakdown in military discipline turn into revolt against him. On 28 September, Tshisekedi accepted Mobutu's offer to share power and accepted the post of prime minister.

At a swearing-in ceremony, Tshisekedi altered his oath of office so as not to swear allegiance to the president or the constitution. The new prime minister indicated that he considered Mobutu nothing more than a figurehead awaiting banishment or arrest. Tshisekedi asserted that he was now in charge of the armed forces and cabinet ministries of foreign affairs, the treasury, and the interior.

Mobutu accused the opposition of trying to seize total control through a "civilian coup d'etat" and, in a show of strength, dismissed Tshisekedi in early October 1991. The President, demanding the opposition put forward another candidate, emphasized that he would retain control of key ministries and general oversight in any future government. The leaders of two opposition parties successively accepted the vacated position of prime minister, but other elements of the Sacred Union rejected the appointments and demanded the reinstatement of Tshisekedi. Opposition leaders formed a "parallel government" on 1 November, calling for a campaign of civil disobedience and strikes to force Mobutu out. On 25 November, Nguza Karl-i-Bond of the Union of Federalists and Independent Republicans, an expelled member of the Sacred Union, became the sixth and last prime minister appointed in 1991. In early December, Mobutu refused to step down as his presidential term ended.

Apart from intense pressure at home the president has had to deal with growing disillusionment with his regime by international banking institutions and by Western governments, which for decades gave the country substantial financial and military support as a bulwark against communism in the region. The American, Belgian, and French governments have cut off financial aid. The International Monetary Fund and the World Bank, disturbed by widescale graft and paltry spending on education, public health, and infrastructure, withheld further loans. International donors agreed in December 1991, however, to take over management of the central bank. The regime continued to blame the country's economic woes on a fall in the world price of copper and cobalt, both significant exports. Hyperinflation of 3,000 percent squeezed the resources of the average Zairian; only 25 percent of the population was employed in 1991. Mobutu himself is reputed to have amassed a fortune of somewhere between $3 and $6 billion by skimming off the assets of parastatals and the central bank.

Political Rights and Civil Liberties:

Citizens of Zaire cannot change their government democratically. Although opposition parties were legalized in 1990, President Mobutu wields absolute power. The judiciary is firmly controlled by the executive. Arbitrary arrest and detention are commonplace and corruption and abuse are rife in the security and police forces. Opposition leaders, human rights workers, and political activists continued to be arrested and detained in 1991, although President Mobutu granted amnesty to political exiles in February 1991.

In 1990 a number of independent newspapers critical of the regime began publication. State-run papers provide only pro-regime views. Journalists can and have been detained on grounds of having "insulted the head of state" when criticizing Mobutu's rule or having purportedly "diffused false information" when speculating about his political future. The offices of prominent independent periodicals were ransacked and bombed by parties unknown in 1991. Despite promises of opposition access to the broadcast media, all of which are owned and controlled by the regime, dissent is almost nonexistent on the airwaves.

The rights of assembly and expression are not recognized by the regime; authorization for opposition meetings and rallies are routinely refused by government officials, and nonviolent gatherings without permit are subject to brutal dispersal. Nonpolitical associations must register with the government. Churches need government permission to operate. Travel is often restricted and citizens must carry identification cards. The umbrella National Union of Zairian Workers (UNTZA) is controlled by the MPR; membership is compulsory for state employees.

Zambia

Polity: Presidential parliamentary democracy
Economy: Mixed statist
Population: 8,400,000
PPP: $870
Life Expectancy: 54.4
Ethnic Groups: One of the most ethnically diverse countries in Africa, with major groups including the Aushi, Bemba, Bisa, Ila, Kaonde, Lala, Lamba, Lambya, Lozi, Luapula, Lukolwe, Lungu, Mashasha, Mashi, Mpenzeni, Nkoya, Nsenga, Senga, Subia, Tabwa, Tonga, Totela, Unga

Political Rights: 2
Civil Liberties: 3
Status: Free

Overview:

The Republic of Zambia, formerly Northern Rhodesia, returned to multi-party democracy on 31 October 1991 after eighteen years of one-party rule by Kenneth Kaunda's United National Independence Party (UNIP). Zambia Congress of Trade Unions (ZCTU) Chairman Frederick Chiluba, running under the banner of the recently formed, multi-ethnic Movement for Multiparty Democracy (MMD), was elected president with an estimated 80 percent of the vote in what was described as a generally free and fair election. The MMD also gained some 125 of the 150 seats in parliament. Kaunda conceded defeat gracefully, even though he had warned before the balloting that a civil war was possible if the UNIP lost.

The 1972 constitution, promulgated eight years after independence from Britain, institutionalized "one-party participatory democracy" and banned all parties except UNIP. Running as the sole candidate, President Kaunda was re-elected in October 1988 to a sixth five-year term. Until the 1991 elections, all candidates for the unicameral National Assembly had to be UNIP members.

Kaunda and the UNIP vigorously resisted the Zambian movement in support of multi-partyism. In December 1989, ZCTU Chairman Chiluba, a temporary political detainee eight years before, called for multi-partyism in light of the fall of one-party regimes throughout Eastern Europe. In response, the UNIP-owned *Times of Zambia* indicated that the Zambian one-party system had been popularly endorsed in a "referendum to end all referenda" in the early 1970s, and asserted that trade union officials were taking a "reactionary stand" contrary to workers' interests.

Nevertheless, after considerable public pressure, President Kaunda announced in May 1990 that a national referendum would be held on the introduction of multi-party democracy. He abandoned this idea in September 1990 in favor of multi-party parliamentary and presidential elections in 1991. Kaunda's administration prevaricated for three months before creating and signing the necessary amendments. In the meantime, partisans of the MMD, a coalition of opposition groups formed in July 1990, were denied the right to organize politically. Unable to obtain police permits to hold a party convention and public rallies, they were arrested and charged with unlawful assembly and membership in an illegal political organization whenever they gathered. By December 1990, however, Kaunda signed amendments to the constitution which legalized the formation of opposition political parties.

During the MMD convention in February 1991, Party Chairman Arthur Wina lost to Frederick Chiluba in balloting for the party's presidential nomination. The UNIP pulled out all the stops prior to the elections in an effort to retain power. Officials were reported to be lavishly spending public funds during the campaign as well as intimidating voters. MMD activists were beaten, fired, arrested, and had property damaged by suspected UNIP vigilantes. The president refused to lift the state of emergency that had been in force since 1965, and refused to permit any additional registration of voters after the MMD itself was legally registered. There were also attempts at muzzling independent voices in the media. The UNIP expelled from Parliament legislators who had left the party to join the MMD, but the country's High Court ruled in July that the defectors must be reinstated. Kaunda delayed fixing a specific day for elections until less than two months before the 31 October date that was announced.

In the midst of the campaign, Kaunda broke an earlier commitment to international lenders when he vowed not to raise the subsidized price of maize before the election. The UNIP clearly feared alienating any potential supporters who depended on maize as a staple. Zambia defaulted on a loan repayment to the World Bank, and international creditors suspended further aid. Some members of the UNIP called for Kaunda to step down as chairman of the party, but a brief challenge to his role as party standard-bearer in the up-coming election was abandoned at the UNIP's convention in August 1991.

Within days of his victory, President Chiluba moved to alter the status quo. Executives of many state enterprises were fired or suspended and government-financed vehicles and homes were seized from UNIP officials who had attempted to permanently appropriate them for personal use.

Political Rights and Civil Liberties: Zambians can now democratically change their government. The first multi-party elections since independence were held in October 1991. Even under the one-party system, parliamentary sessions were marked by free and open debate. The court system is now increasingly independent of executive interference. A major turning point came in December 1990, before opposition parties were legalized, when a High Court ruled that the government had violated constitutional assurances of the right to peacefully assemble when it denied the MMD permits to assemble.

Free expression generally increased during the multi-party election campaign, including substantial criticism of President Kaunda and the UNIP. Kaunda attempted to pressure journalists of the official media into exclusively presenting the UNIP's perspective on events and fired those who did not. However, the Press Association of Zambia managed to obtain an injunction from the High Court to suspend official media heads for biased pro-UNIP coverage before the election. The state owns two national dailies as well as radio and television service, all of which had previously parroted the UNIP line. The independent press—including the Church-funded *National Mirror,* the new *Weekly Post,* and a variety of broadsheets—frequently publishes diverse views and criticized actions by the MMD even before its electoral victory.

Police permits for demonstrations and rallies are needed and are usually granted, although authorities of the UNIP regime were reluctant to cooperate with the opposition during the campaign. There have long been many autonomous cultural, professional, and civic associations. Freedom of religion is respected. Zambia has a strong industrial trade union tradition. All large unions belong to the independent and democratic ZCTU, the only legal confederation.

Zimbabwe

Polity: Dominant party
Economy: Capitalist-statist
Population: 10,000,000
PPP: $1,370
Life Expectancy: 59.6
Ethnic Groups: Shona, Ndebele, white, and others

Political Rights: 5
Civil Liberties: 4
Status: Partly Free

Overview:

The year 1991 saw controversy over the attempt by the government, controlled by the ruling Zimbabwe African National Union-Patriotic Front (ZANU-PF), to limit the judiciary's power to review the public seizure of white-owned land. The government plans to redistribute the land to poor black families.

The Republic of Zimbabwe, formerly white-ruled Rhodesia, was established on 18 April 1980 after years of guerrilla activity and diplomatic negotiations forced Prime Minister Ian Smith to accept black majority rule. One of the most important measures agreed to by all the parties to the negotiations was a Declaration of Rights to be made part of a new constitution. It specified certain fundamental rights that could not be modified by less than the full Parliament until ten years after independence. Following parliamentary elections in February 1980, Robert Mugabe, leader of the original ZANU, one of two main guerrilla groups making up the rebel Patriotic Front struggling for majority rule, was asked to form a government.

After independence, fighting broke out between ZANU armed forces and those of Zimbabwe African People's Union (ZAPU), the other main group in the Patriotic Front. The conflict was largely rooted in traditional ethnic rivalry between the northern Shona group represented in ZANU and the southern Ndebele that made up ZAPU, led by Joshua Nkomo. Violence between the two movements subsided in 1981 and their guerrilla forces were merged to form a national army. Nkomo became a member of the cabinet but was dismissed in February 1982 following continuing differences between the groups. Talks beginning in 1985 resulted in a December 1987 agreement which saw the merger of ZANU and ZAPU into the ZANU-PF. With the approval of the ZANU-PF dominated Assembly, Mugabe became president of the country that same month and Nkomo became one of two vice-presidents.

Parliament consists of the 150-member unicameral House of Assembly, with 30 seats reserved for chiefs and nominated members. Although the White Roll (guaranteed white seats), a product of pre-independence negotiations, has now been abolished, some whites have been appointed to non-elective seats by President Mugabe. Following the 1990 election, three parties were represented in the legislature: the ZANU-PF with 147 seats, the opposition Zimbabwean Unity Movement (ZUM) with two seats, and the remains of a pre-Mugabe ZANU with one seat. In 1991 a Democratic Party was formed, which plans to contest the next election in 1995. President Mugabe was re-elected in 1990 in an election characterized by an aggressively negative tone and acts of physical intimidation by both ZANU-PF and ZUM partisans. ZANU-PF won over 75 percent of the vote.

In its election manifesto of 1990, ZANU-PF said it intended to introduce a land acquisition bill in Parliament that would allow for massive redistribution of land and the resettlement of peasant farmers. The manifesto also vowed to continue efforts to bring schools, health facilities, and other social services to rural areas within the country, and to preserve Zimbabwe's foreign policy of non-alignment. The party constitution adopted in 1989 referred to the goal of establishing a "socialist" society, under a guiding ideology of Marxism-Leninism.

As the requisite ten years had passed since independence, the ZANU-PF majority in the House of Assembly was free to amend the Declaration of Rights in order to address the problem of peasant landlessness. The Declaration was amended in December 1990 to ensure that neither the sum offered in compensation for the land taken for redistribution nor the confiscation itself could be judicially appealed. As President Mugabe put it, "nothing must stand in our way to the acquisition of any land we identify and designate for resettlement." His justice minister asserted that the issue of fair compensation for confiscated land was based on what the state "could afford to pay." The nation's Chief Justice, however, denounced the constitutional amendment, warning that the High Court would invalidate limits on the right of appeal. The President responded in January 1991 by inviting judges who disagreed with the government's program to step down from the bench.

During 1991 ZANU-PF backed off from its earlier commitment to Marxism-Leninism and the one-party state. In January President Mugabe publicly renounced his long-held goal of constitutionally abolishing all political parties but ZANU-PF. This was reassuring to Zimbabweans who feared that the 1990 election was to be the last multi-party competition for votes. At the same time, Mugabe has called the Wests' attempts to tie further economic assistance in Africa to democratization as "blackmail." Despite keeping its formal multi-party system, the Zimbabwean government still shows clear favoritism toward the ruling ZANU-PF. A Ministry of Political Affairs was created in 1991 to funnel public money to that party in support of its organizing activities; no other party appears to qualify for these funds. In June, Mugabe claimed that the regime's belief in a mixed economy meant that it was a social democracy and no longer wished to be considered Marxist-Leninist.

The 6 million hectares of farmland which the government announced in March 1991 it plans to nationalize belong to the nation's 4,500 white farmers. The lands have a reported aggregate value of almost six times the amount the government is prepared to pay for them. The land is intended to be distributed among 110,000 peasants.

Political Rights and Civil Liberties: Although Zimbabwe is a *de facto* one-party state, citizens freely elect parliamentary representatives and local officials, and a few minor parties are in existence. The judiciary is independent, and the president cannot dismiss judges. In 1991, however, the government moved to amend the constitution in order to sharply limit the scope of judicial review over various legislative actions which allow for capital punishment, tighten government control over universities and restrict private property rights. With the expiration of the ten-year old British-brokered Lancaster House constitution in April 1991, the House of Assembly is empowered to overturn by a two-thirds majority any clause in the bill of rights. There are reportedly no political prisoners, though there are allegations that some individuals have been convicted as South African spies after confessions were extracted by torture.

The major print media, television, and radio are government owned. All reflect a ZANU point of view in their coverage and presentation of the news. Small, private print media, such as the *Financial Gazette,* are freer to offer critical assessments of the government since the state of emergency was lifted.

Political and non-political organizations are permitted, although the former face some restrictions. Political meetings and rallies require police permits, which may be denied on "security" grounds under a state of emergency. In June of 1991, police broke up a legally-convened meeting of ZUM and detained some attendees for two days before releasing them. Business, professional, and social organizations are free from government interference. Freedom of religion is respected, and there are no restrictions on travel. Unions belong to the Zimbabwe Congress of Trade Unions (ZCTU), but there are increasing restrictions on the right to strike in services and industries deemed "essential." Private human rights groups are permitted to operate in the country.

Australia
Christmas Island (Kiritimati)

Polity: Appointed administrator
Economy: Capitalist-statist
Population: 1,500
Ethnic Groups: Chinese and Malay

Political Rights: 3
Civil Liberties: 2
Status: Free

Overview:

Located in the Indian Ocean, Christmas Island is the home of a disappearing phosphate industry, which is owned by the Australian government's Australian Phosphate Corporation. Under Australian administration since 1958, Christmas Island has a government run by an administrator who is appointed by the Governor General, Queen Elizabeth's representative in Australia. Australia classifies the island as an external territory, but residents have the right to opt for Australian citizenship or residency status. Due to the near exhaustion of phosphate, the chief source of employment, many islanders have moved to Western Australia, Singapore, and Malaysia. The Australian government proposed laying off 150 phosphate miners in 1986. This caused labor and ethnic strife. The government decided to reduce the mine labor force gradually during 1986-89.

To reinvigorate the economy, Australia approved construction of a gambling resort complex. Pacific Consultants International of Japan suggested in 1989 that the island needed a new resort hotel, recreational and marine facilities, harbor facilities, and a better airport. A Melbourne-based consulting firm began studying the airport and tourism issues in 1990.

Two weeks after the 1987 election, the Australian government dismissed Christmas Island's democratically elected nine-member assembly, citing fiscal mismanagement. However, the islanders retain the right to vote in Australian national elections as part of the mainland's Northern Territory.

Cocos (Keeling) Islands

Polity: Appointed administrator and elected council
Economy: Capitalist-statist
Population: 616
Ethnic Groups: Malay

Political Rights: 1
Civil Liberties: 2
Status: Free

Overview:

Located in the Indian Ocean and discovered by Captain William Keeling in 1609, the Cocos Islands were a personal fiefdom of the Clunies-Ross family until 1978. An Australian-appointed administrator is the chief executive. An elected local council began functioning in 1978. In a 1984 referendum, the inhabitants voted to integrate with Australia. They are now part of Australia's Northern Territory, which elects members of the Australian Parliament. The population is mostly Malay.

Norfolk Island

Polity: Appointed administrator and elected assembly
Economy: Capitalist
Population: 2,490
Ethnic Groups: *Bounty* families, Australians, New Zealanders

Political Rights: 2
Civil Liberties: 1
Status: Free

Overview:

Located in the South Pacific, Norfolk Island is the home to many descendants of *Bounty* mutineers. An Australian-appointed administrator is the chief executive, but there has been a freely elected, nine-member assembly since Australia's passage of the Norfolk Island Act in 1979. This legislation provided for substantial self-government. The assembly executive committee acts like a cabinet on the island.

Chile
Rapanui (Easter Island)

Polity: Appointed governor and elected local government
Economy: Capitalist-statist
Population: 2,000
Ethnic Groups: Spanish-speaking Polynesian natives, 70 percent, and Chilean settlers, 30 percent

Political Rights: 3
Civil Liberties: 2
Status: Free

Overview:

The leading news story of 1991 was the visit of Chilean President Patricio Aylwin. He asserted the need to update local laws to protect the native culture and announced that the island would join the Chilean mainland in holding democratic municipal elections in June 1992. Located in the Pacific Ocean, 2,360 miles from Chile, Rapanui (Easter Island) is the home of an ancient Polynesian culture. Under Chilean ownership since 1888, the island is isolated from the world with the exception of twice-weekly airline flights and twice-yearly cargo ships. There are no newspapers, but there is a local radio station. Tourism is the main source of income. Visitors come to see the island's hundreds of giant, long-faced statues. Islanders hope to save these crumbling attractions with foreign funding.

Formerly run by the Chilean navy, the island became a Chilean municipality with voting rights in 1966. The territory has had fairly open discussion and its own local government. Every family has the right to a house and five hectares of land. The government subsidizes energy and utility costs. Island students are eligible for government university scholarships in Chile.

The natives' Council of Elders favors more autonomy for the island. Chilean authorities (the forestry commission and the farm administrator) control 80 percent of the land, but the elders would prefer communal ownership and native control.

China
Tibet

Polity: Communist one-party
Economy: Statist
Population: 3,000,000
Ethnic Groups: Tibetans, Han Chinese

Political Rights: 7
Civil Liberties: 7
Status: Not Free

(*3 million Tibetans live under Chinese control, including 1.9 million in the Tibetan Autonomous Region)

Overview:

1991 marked the 40th anniversary of China's often brutal occupation of this former Buddhist suzerainty in the Himalayas. The four decades of Chinese rule have brought deadly famines, the destruction of some 6,000 monasteries and temples, often bloody suppression of dissent, the pillaging of sacred religious objects and cultural genocide reinforced by the influx of ethnic Chinese who made native Tibetans a minority in several regions.

Chinese troops invaded Tibet in 1950. A year later, on 23 May, a 17-point agreement was forced upon a Tibetan delegation, after Chinese troops had already wiped out most of the inexperienced Tibetan army and occupied eastern Tibet. The spiritual leader of Tibet, the 14th Dalai Lama, Tenzin Gyatso, acquiesced to the agreement, fearing a slaughter in the capital of Lhasa if he refused. The 17 points delineated a framework for the future status of Tibet. Peking agreed to not change the existing political system, alter the status of the Dalai or the Panchen Lamas or compel communist-style reforms. It also guaranteed freedom of religion. Less than eight years later, Tibetans rebelled, as radical "reforms" under Mao Zedong's Great Leap Forward violated virtually every point of the agreement.

The Chinese put down the 1959 revolt with unbridled ferocity. As reported by the International Commission of Jurists, monks and civilians were crucified, disemboweled, and many had their tongues torn out to prevent them shouting "Long Live the Dalai Lama" before they were executed. The Dalai Lama and thousands of followers fled to neighboring India just ahead of pursuing Chinese forces. An estimated 1.2 million Tibetans died in the 1959 uprising and its aftermath. The wholesale destruction of monasteries was launched. Western experts recently estimated that the sale on world markets of looted religious art and precious metals and minerals brought the Chinese (over a 30-year period) $80 billion.

In 1991 a lavish program of festivities and propaganda for what China called the 40th anniversary of the "Peaceful Liberation of Tibet" were planned for Lhasa for 23 May. Security precautions were massive. Analysts estimated that the combined strength of the People's Liberation Army, Public Security Bureau, and People's Armed Police personnel in Tibet by the end of March was roughly equivalent to the entire population of the region. In March a Great Prayer Festival was banned to prevent protests commemorating the 1959 uprising. Officials bulldozed a path near the central Jokhang Temple on 2 March; five monks were subsequently arrested for demonstrating. Authorities feared a repeat of huge demonstrations like those in Lhasa in 1988 that led to massive repressions and martial law.

To countervail Chinese propaganda, the 14th Dalai Lama in 1991 embarked on a world tour to publicize Tibet's plight. In April he met with President George Bush, who met with Tibet's spiritual leader despite strong objections by China. In 1988 the Dalai Lama softened his demand for Tibet's complete independence, proposing that

China retain control of Tibet's foreign and defense policies in exchange for self-governance and limited autonomy.

In December, more than 350 Tibetans were arrested in New Delhi while protesting the visit to India by Chinese Prime Minister Li Peng.

Political Rights and Civil Liberties: Tibetans cannot democratically change their government. Although martial law was rescinded in April 1990, the Chinese occupation administration maintains the right to deny persons suspected of anti-government activities the fundamental rights of due process. Suspects can be arrested without warrants and detained indefinitely without charge. In the last two years, hundreds of monks have been detained for political activities. Five monks were known to have been arrested on 17 March while trying to unfurl a nationalist banner. Witnesses alleged that the monks were beaten by members of the Public Safety Bureau. Torture is routinely used in Tibetan prisons. Buddhists nuns are treated worse than other prisoners. Other sanctions include job loss, docking pay for time spent in prison and billing for food eaten in jail.

The occupation administration strictly prohibits any assembly or speech opposing Chinese rule. There are restrictions on movement so authorities can better track nationalists. Emigration is illegal, and Tibetans caught trying to flee the country are imprisoned and often tortured.

Because Tibetan Buddhism and national identity are so closely bonded, religious activity is strictly regulated. The state trains monks, decides their numbers and approves their prayer books. Certain traditional rites and rituals are banned.

In addition to encouraging the immigration of ethnic Chinese to Tibet, authorities also use forced birth control and sterilization to keep down the number of Tibetans. Some 10,000 Tibetan children have been sent to mainland China to study in what Tibetans see as a clear attempt by China to undermine Tibetan culture and traditions in future generations.

Denmark
Faeroe Islands

Polity: Parliamentary democracy
Economy: Mixed capitalist
Population: 47,840
Ethnic Groups: Faeroese

Political Rights: 1
Civil Liberties: 1
Status: Free

Overview: Since 1948 the Faeroe Islands have had substantial autonomy within the Kingdom of Denmark. The Danish government maintains authority over foreign affairs, defence, finance and justice. A high commissioner (ombudsman) represents Denmark. The Faeroese government has responsibility for communications, culture, and industry. The islands send two representatives to the Danish parliament, but pay no Danish taxes. The territory has the right to opt out of Denmark's European Community membership. There are 50 local authorities. Presently, six political parties with diverse ideological perspectives compete in elections. The parliament, the *Løgting*, is composed of 27 members chosen by proportional representation in seven districts, plus up to five supplementary members.

Elections in late 1990 weakened the conservative People's Party, causing the collapse of its coalition government. After two months of negotiations, the Social Democratic Party and the People's Party formed a new coalition in January 1991. Atli Dam, the Social Democratic leader, became premier for the sixth time. His People's Party predecessor, Jogvan Sundstein, remained in the cabinet as the minister of finance.

The Faeroese have a full range of political rights and civil liberties. Eight newspapers publish freely. There are public radio and television stations. Although the established Lutheran Church represents almost 90 percent of the population, worship is free, and there are several independent churches.

Greenland	**Polity:** Parliamentary democracy	**Political Rights:** 1
	Economy: Mixed-capitalist	**Civil Liberties:** 1
	Population: 55,558	**Status:** Free
	Ethnic Groups: Inuit (Eskimo), native whites, Danish	

Overview:

The major developments in Greenland in 1991 were parliamentary elections and a change of leadership within the ruling political party. The first elections to the territory's parliament (*Landsting*) since 1987 took place on 5 March 1991. The legislature consists of 23 members chosen by proportional representation and up to an additional four members for parties failing to win seats in districts. Jonathan Motzfeldt was premier of Greenland (1979-91) and head of the socialist Forward (*Siumut*) Party. Although his party remained dominant after the 1991 elections, he was replaced by Lars Emil Johansen after allegations of financial mismanagement. The Forward party won eleven seats in the election and formed a coalition with the Marxist-Leninist Eskimo Brotherhood (*Inuit Ataqatigiit)* Party, which won five seats. The new government is expected to seek increased independence from Denmark and adopt a new tax system favoring lower income groups. The opposition parties in the legislature are: the conservative Feeling of Community or Solidarity (*Attasut*) Party with eight seats; the new Center Party with two seats; and the pro-business Polar (*Issittrup*) Party with one seat.

Located in the North Atlantic, Greenland has had substantial autonomy from Denmark since 1979. Denmark still controls Greenland's foreign and defence policy, but the local authorities handle most other matters. Greenland sends two representatives to the Danish parliament in Copenhagen. Although Denmark has European Community membership, in 1985 Greenland used its right to opt out of the EC.

Political Rights and Civil Liberties:

Political rights and civil liberties are generally respected. There is full freedom of expression and association. However, published reports suggest evidence of discrimination against Inuits in a contraception program. Doctors administer a disproportionately high number of contraceptive injections to Inuits, and fail to explain side-effects and other implications of the shots. In Denmark, doctors give these same shots only to those who cannot take care of themselves.

Ethiopia
Eritrea

Polity: One-party
Economy: Mixed
Population: 3,200,000
Ethnic Groups: Afar, Arab, Beja,
Bilin, Jabarti, Kunama, Saho, Tigrawi

Political Rights: 6
Civil Liberties: 6
Status: Not Free

Overview:

In 1991 Eritrea took steps toward becoming the first territory in post-colonial Africa to gain internationally recognized independence after detaching itself from another African country.

Eritrea, which extends from Djibouti to Sudan along the Red Sea in northeastern Africa, bases its claim for independence on the assertion that it is a territory related to, but distinctive from, Ethiopia. Much of Eritrea has been culturally, and at times politically, tied to the Christian Ethiopian highlands to its south since the Kingdom of Axum arose in the first century A.D. Eritrea was colonized by Italy in 1890. In 1936 Italian troops based in Eritrea overran the forces of Emperor Haile Selassie and conquered Ethiopia, and until 1941 Eritrea and Ethiopia were administered as a single Italian colony. After the resident forces of Mussolini's Army were routed during World War II, Eritrea was administered by Britain as a U.N. trusteeship until it was federated with Ethiopia in 1952.

Despite Eritrea's constitutionally guaranteed autonomy, its trade unions and pro-independence political parties were banned and Ethiopia's Amharic was illegally imposed as the language of administration. In 1962 it lost its formal autonomous status when Haile Selassie's government exerted heavy pressure on the Eritrean legislative assembly to approve the assimilation of Eritrea into a unitary Ethiopia, making it a regular province.

The Eritrean Liberation Front (ELF) began its armed drive for secession from Ethiopia in late 1961. It drew its support from Muslims in Eritrea's western lowlands who opposed incorporation into Christian-dominated Ethiopia. The ELF was gradually supplanted during the 1970s by another group, the radical Eritrean People's Liberation Front (EPLF). The EPLF, whose Marxist-Leninist leadership came from western Eritrea's Christian highlands, accused the ELF of solely representing the interests of a conservative Muslim elite. It drew its financial support from radical Arab and communist European states.

In 1974 Emperor Selassie was overthrown by an Ethiopian military clique, the Marxist-Leninist Dergue, which was opposed to an independent Eritrea. Military control of Eritrean territory see-sawed between the EPLF and the Dergue during the next 17 years. The EPLF gradually extended its authority over most of Eritrea, except for the capital of Asmara, the Red Sea port of Asab, and certain adjacent areas. During on-again, off-again peace negotiations, the Ethiopian government repeatedly stated that it might accept some form of arrangement for Eritrea short of independence, while the EPLF demanded a referendum within Eritrea that would have independence as an one of its options.

In February 1991 formal peace talks between the Dergue and the EPLF briefly recommenced in Washington but soon reached an impasse. The American-mediated negotiations did not resume for three months; in the interim the military position of the Dergue seriously deteriorated. In the face of a coordinated offensive waged by the

EPLF in Eritrea and the rebel Ethiopian People's Revolutionary Democratic Front (EPRDF) in Ethiopia itself, Ethiopian troops had fallen back on all fronts. Months of shelling by EPLF forces surrounding Asmara preceded block-to-block combat in the city after the insurgents penetrated Ethiopian army defenses. Ethiopian troops finally capitulated in May, with the EPLF also seizing the port of Asab, and the EPRDF emerging victorious in Ethiopia.

The EPRDF, now running Ethiopia, has stated that it does not intend to block the U.N.-sponsored referendum in Eritrea on independence in 1992 or 1993. A July 1991 conference of most the Ethiopian political movements formally supported this position. The EPRDF hopes to convince the Eritreans before the referendum that continued political association with Ethiopia would be to Eritrea's advantage. When Eritreans opt for independence, as it is virtually certain that they will, even the strength of "Greater Ethiopia" nationalism among the long-dominant Amhara ethnic group in Ethiopia will not be enough to seriously threaten Eritrea and its well armed EPLF. An independent Eritrea would mean a land-locked Ethiopia, although the EPRDF and the EPLF have agreed that the port of Asab would be a free port for Ethiopia.

The EPLF's political and economic program was explicitly Marxist-Leninist and anti-pluralist until the 1980s, when its party manifesto began to claim that the movement had become social democratic. After its victory in 1991, it publicly underscored its commitment to a multi-party democracy after the referendum is held. However, the EPLF's subsequent comments about the lack of legitimacy of Eritrean political groups other than itself puts such promises into question. Elections for a national assembly are to be held before the internationally supervised referendum. Isaias Afwerki, secretary-general of the Party, heads an provisional administration which has decided not to formally participate in the political reorganization of Ethiopia. The EPLF also now claims to support a mixed economy for Eritrea and was reportedly quick to "privatize" much of the state sector when it extended its control over areas formerly in the hands of the Dergue. Tens of thousands of Ethiopian soldiers fled Eritrea to Djibouti, Sudan, and Ethiopia following the EPLF's victory. Many died within days, lacking water and food in this arid region. Thousands more, along with over 100,000 civilian Ethiopian residents in Eritrea, were summarily deported by the EPLF to the border with Ethiopia. The new Eritrean regime disclaimed responsibility for the well-being of the deportees, asserting that Ethiopian authorities ought to have provided for them.

Political Rights and Civil Liberties: Although the Eritrean people have achieved *de facto* independence, they have not yet been given the opportunity to change their leaders democratically. The question is whether *de jure* independence will mean the installation of an EPLF one-party regime. EPLF's Aferwerki has stated that there is no justification for political groups other than the EPLF in a liberated Eritrea. Other groups include the long-dormant ELF, the Sudan-sponsored Eritrea Islamic Front, and the EPRDF-linked, anti-independence Eritrean People's Democratic Organization. The EPLF maintains a security force which reportedly stifles non-violent political opposition to EPLF rule.

Although the EPLF released Ethiopian-held political prisoners after its victory, some 500 Ethiopian officers are detained for war crimes trials which the new government promises will be fair and open. Until Ethiopian forces were decisively defeated in May 1991, agents of the Dergue and the EPLF engaged in a campaign of assassination and counter-terror within Eritrea. Ethiopian troops continued forced conscriptions, extrajudicial executions, beatings, and rapes until their defeat. They also forcibly requisitioned food from civilians in the famine-struck region. In and around Asmara, the Dergue's security forces detained hundreds of people on suspicion of having assisted the EPLF. Meanwhile, the EPLF assassinated Eritreans who it judged to be collaborators with the Ethiopian government.

In an attempt to cut off supplies to the Ethiopian military garrison in Asmara, the EPLF prevented an airlift of humanitarian relief to the city's civilian population by shelling in-coming flights. Foreign relief agencies have accused the EPLF of impeding the overland transport of famine assistance needed for civilians in both Eritrea and Ethiopia, a charge the EPLF denied. As no constitution has been adopted yet in Eritrea and the EPLF rejects the interim political charter adopted by Ethiopia in mid-1991; there are no human rights guarantees yet in effect dealing with expression, association and assembly.

France
French Guiana

Polity: Appointed prefect and elected assembly and council
Economy: Capitalist-statist
Population: 114,900
Ethnic Groups: Complex, black (66 percent), Caucasian (French) (12 percent), East Indian, Chinese and Amerindian (12 percent), and other (10 percent)

Political Rights: 2
Civil Liberties: 2
Status: Free

Overview:

As one of four French Overseas Departments, French Guiana is ruled according to French law and the administrative establishment is headed by a commissioner of the Republic who is appointed by the French Ministry of the Interior. Representatives to the French parliament are elected. A nineteen-member General Council is elected for six years; councilors represent individual districts. Since 1982 the Council has been given increased powers, particularly in financial matters.

When French Guiana was given regional status in 1974, a Regional Assembly was set up, distinct from the General Council, with limited control over the economy. This control was expanded under the Mitterrand reforms of 1982-83. The first direct elections to the Regional Assembly, on the basis of proportional representation, were held in February 1983. Mayors and municipal councils are also directly elected. The two main political parties are the right-wing Rally for the Republic (RPR), and the Guianese Socialist Party (PSG), which currently advocates autonomous rule as the first step toward full independence. The smaller Guianan Unity (UG) advocates immediate independence. At the most recent General Council elections in fall 1988, the PSG retained control by taking twelve seats against seven for the RPR and other right-wing parties.

In recent years there has been growing concern about the condition of the estimated 10,000 Bush Negro and Amerindian refugees who have fled into western French Guiana because of guerrilla conflict in neighboring Suriname. Local and international human rights groups charge the refugees are denied basic rights in camps controlled by the French army. The French government denies the allegations, saying it spends $10 million annually to care for the refugees, and that they are free to travel anywhere in the department.

Pluralistic points of view are presented in the media including two major newspapers and several radio and television stations.

French Polynesia

Polity: Elected Assembly
Economy: Capitalist-statist
Population: 188,814
Ethnic Groups: Polynesian (83 percent), French and other European (11 percent), and Chinese and other Asian (6 percent)

Political Rights: 2
Civil Liberties: 2
Status: Free

Overview:

In 1991 French Polynesia was rocked by a devastating cyclone and violent confrontations between police and anti-tax protestors.

French Polynesia consists of 120 South Pacific Islands, the most populous of which is Tahiti. A High Commissioner represents the French government. France controls defense, the courts, the police, some education, immigration, and international airline traffic, but the territory has significant autonomy. The Polynesian Territorial Assembly consists of 41 members elected for a maximum term of five years. The Assembly elects the President, who selects the ministers with the Assembly's approval. In the general election of 17 March 1991, Gaston Flosse's People's Rally Party, the Polynesian section of the French Gaullist Rally for the Republic, won 18 of the 41 seats. An alliance between supporters of outgoing President Alexandre Leontieff and Assembly President Jean Juventin captured only fourteen seats. A grouping around French Assembly Deputy Emile Vernaudon won five seats. Led by Oscar Temaru, the Polynesian Liberation Front won four seats, while more moderate nationalists under Jacques Drollet lost their three seats. Flosse and Vernaudon formed a governing coalition. Subsequently, their coalition picked up two more seats.

To deal with the budget deficit, Flosse instituted an audit of territorial finances, significant budget cuts, and higher consumption taxes. Despite suggestions from French President Mitterrand, the territory has no income tax. In Paris, a Gaullist Deputy charged that the French government had offered to cancel Tahiti's debts if Leontieff had returned to power. Flosse and Vernaudon hinted that without a deal on the debt with France, the pro-independence forces would make gains.

In June 1991 the island of Moorea voted in an advisory referendum against a proposed Japanese resort. Flosse had expected an easy victory on this question. Although the government could have ignored the referendum results, it chose to cancel the project.

On 10 July striking workers blocked roads and manned barricades in an anti-tax protest. The crowd overturned cars and surged through the streets. Police broke up the crowd and the barricades. Several policemen and civilians were injured. The next day the French High Commissioner and religious leaders negotiated a deal between the territorial government and the labor unions. Flosse agreed to roll back the taxes, and

France agreed to make up the difference in revenue with subsidies. France and the territory each provide about half the expenses of running the Polynesian government. After the violent episode ended, *Pacific Islands Monthly* reported that Hiro Tefaarere, one of the union leaders involved in the illegal blockade, is a former police official still on the payroll of the French Interior Ministry.

In December, Cyclone Wasa hit the islands, causing flooding, property damage, and at least two deaths.

Political Rights and Civil Liberties: Polynesians elect a member of the French Senate and two National Assembly deputies. Peaceful advocates of independence have freedom of expression and association. There are three daily newspapers and a public broadcasting service. The Chinese minority prospers in business, and enjoys much greater acceptance than the Chinese communities on other Pacific islands. The nuclear industry is a major employer, but the natives resent French indifference to their environmental concerns.

French Southern and Antarctic Territories

Polity: Appointed administrator and consultative council
Economy: Capitalist-statist
Population: 180
Ethnic Groups: French

Political Rights: 3
Civil Liberties: 1
Status: Free

Overview: The French Southern and Antartic Territories consist of the Indian Ocean islands of St. Paul, Amsterdam, the Kerguelen and Crozet archipelagos, and the French-claimed sector of Antarctica. Due to the small population and scattered locations of these territories, the French administrator is based in Paris, where the consultative council meets twice annually. The administrator also appoints heads of the territories' four districts. Kerguelen's 100 inhabitants comprise the largest population of the territories. The chief activities are scientific research and fishing. Since 1977 Port-aux-Francais (Kerguelen) has served as a registry point for supply ships and bulk cargo ships. This registry allows French shippers to use non-French seafarers to sail under the French flag.

Guadeloupe

Polity: Appointed commissioner and elected assembly andcouncil
Economy: Capitalist-statist
Population: 386,000
Ethnic Groups: Predominantly black with white French minority

Political Rights: 2
Civil Liberties: 2
Status: Free

Overview: As one of four French Overseas Departments, the Department of Guadeloupe is ruled according to French law and the administrative establishment is headed by a commissioner appointed by the French Ministry of the Interior. In the wake of Hurricane Hugo, which ravaged Guadeloupe in 1989, the interior ministry appointed a new commissioner, Jean-Pierre Truce. Representatives to the French parliament are elected.

A 36-member General Council is directly elected to a five-year term, with each member elected to represent individual districts. Since 1982, the Council has been given increased powers, particularly in financial matters.

When Guadeloupe was given regional status in 1974, and a Regional Assembly was set up, parallel to the General Council, with limited control over the economy. This control was expanded under the Mitterand reforms of 1983-83. The first direct elections to the Regional Assembly, on the basis of proportional representation, were held in February 1983. Mayors and municipal councils are also directly elected.

The two main political parties are the Socialist Party (PS) and the right-wing Rally for the Republic (RPR). In the 1988 General Council elections, the PS increased its majority by one seat, defeating opponents 26-16. The Communist Party of Guadeloupe (PCG), which normally secures a quarter of the vote, is pro-independence but non-violent. Since the late 1960s, there have been a number of militant pro-independence groups. Those that resorted to armed tactics were outlawed. Since 1985, however, violent activity has nearly died out. The semi-clandestine Popular Union for the Liberation of Guadeloupe (UPLG), as well as other remaining radical groups, have boycotted recent elections. Labor unions are legal and there are two main labor federations.

There is one daily newspaper and a handful of radio and television transmitters. International news agencies maintain local offices.

Martinique

Polity: Appointed commissioner and elected assembly and council
Economy: Capitalist-statist
Population: 359,800
Ethnic Groups: Predominantly black with French minority

Political Rights: 2
Civil Liberties: 1
Status: Free

Overview:

As one of four French Overseas Departments, the department of Martinique is ruled according to French law, and the administrative establishment is headed by a commissioner appointed by the French Ministry of the Interior. Representatives to the French parliament are elected.

A 44-member General Council is directly elected to a five-year term, with each member elected to represent individual districts. Since 1982, the Council has been given increased powers, particularly in financial matters.

When Martinique was given regional status in 1974 and a Regional Assembly was set up, parallel to the General Council, with limited control over the economy. This control was expanded under the 1982-83 Mitterand reforms. The first direct elections to the Regional Assembly on the basis of proportional representation were held in February 1983. Mayors and municipal councils are also directly elected.

The main political parties are the right-wing Rally for the Republic (RPR), the

Martinique Progressive Party (PPM), the Socialist Federation of Martinique (FSM), and the Martinique Communist Party (PCM). In recent years, the last three have formed an electoral alliance, the Left Union (UG). Both the PCM and PPM advocate autonomy for the island as the first step toward independence. The UG obtained a one-seat margin in the 1988 General Council elections. A number of militant separatist groups resorted to violence in the mid-1980s and were banned. Separatist violence has nearly disappeared in recent years. Labor unions are legal and permitted to strike. There are two main labor confederations.

The media are varied and reflect pluralistic points of view. There are several radio and television stations. There are one daily and several weekly newspapers.

Mayotte (Mahore)

Polity: Appointed commissioner and elected council
Economy: Capitalist
Population: 79,300
Ethnic Groups: A mixture of Mahorais, French, Comoran, and Malagasy speakers of African and European descent

Political Rights: 2
Civil Liberties: 2
Status: Free

Overview:

Part of the Comoro archipelago, Mayotte is located in the Indian Ocean east of Mozambique and northwest of Madagascar. In two referenda, the largely Catholic population has rejected joining the adjacent Federal Islamic Republic of the Comoros. Nonetheless, the Comoran government has continued to claim Mayotte, regarding the referenda supporting continued association with France as null and void. In March 1991 the French prime minister stated that France would not turn Mayotte over to the Comoros against Mahorais wishes.

The French government appoints a commissioner, and the residents elect a seventeen-member council. The economy is based largely on primary products and tourism. The political parties are the Mahoran Popular Movement, which wants the island made a French department; the Party for the Mahoran Democratic Rally, which supports merger with the Comoros; and the Gaullist Mahoran Rally for the Republic. The island sends one member to the French Senate and elects one to the National Assembly. The government-owned radio station broadcasts in French and Mahorais.

Monaco

Polity: Prince and elected council
Economy: Capitalist-statist
Population: 28,500
Ethnic Groups: French, Monegasque, Italian, and others

Political Rights: 3
Civil Liberties: 1
Status: Free

Overview:

The Principality of Monaco is located on the French Mediterranean coast. Prince Rainier is the hereditary chief of state, but the French government nominates the Minister of State (the prime minister) and has the right to veto the heir to the throne. Monaco has a customs union with France, which controls the principality's foreign relations. However, Monaco belongs to several U.N. agencies and intergovernmental organizations. The voters elect an eighteen-member National Council for a five-year term. In the 1988 election, the National and Democratic Union won all eighteen seats. The Monaco Socialist Party has contested elections unsuccessfully. Other parties include the Communist Democratic Union Movement and the liberal Monaco Action. There is also an elected fifteen-member municipal council, headed by a mayor and assistants appointed by the council.

Newspapers in nearby Nice print Monaco editions, which they distribute freely in the principality. Radio and television are government-operated. Trans World Radio broadcasts religious programs. The French government has a controlling interest in Radio Monte Carlo. A tax haven, Monaco is the home of gambling casinos and light industry. Roman Catholicism is the state religion, but the constitution guarantees religious freedom.

New Caledonia

Polity: Appointed commissioner and elected congress and assemblies
Economy: Capitalist-statist
Population: 164,173
Ethnic Groups: Kanaky, Wallisian-Futunians, Javanese, French, Tahitians, West Indians, Vietnamese, other Asian Pacific groups

Political Rights: 2
Civil Liberties: 2
Status: Free

Overview:

In 1991 New Caledonia's leading political groups began positioning themselves for the planned 1998 referendum on independence. Because the indigenous Melanesian Kanaky only make up 43 percent of the population of this French colony in the South Pacific, the Kanak Socialist National Liberation Front (FLNKS) needs the electoral support of other ethnic groups to form a majority in favor of independence. FLNKS' position is that on-going decolonization and sentiment in favor of national self-determination throughout the world obligates France to grant independence, even if the settler population forms a majority in opposition.

In June 1991 FLNKS re-elected Paul Tyaou Neaoutyine as its president. Neaoutyine became leader in March 1990, replacing Jean-Marie Tjibaou, who was killed by a Kanak radical in 1989. Tjibaou had made a compromise agreement—the Matignon Accords—with the French government, which postponed the question of independence until 1998. The Matignon Accords also granted increase autonomy to the island and called for a fairer distribution of the wealth, much of it derived from the island's nickel mines. The FLNKS and the pro-colonial Rally for Caledonia in the Republic (RPCR) back the agreement.

Under the Kanak-French arrangement, there are three regional assemblies, which also form a combined Congress. The Kanaky dominate the North and Islands assemblies, and the RPCR controls the South assembly. The RPCR holds 27 of 54 seats in the combined congress; FLNKS holds nineteen seats. Paris appoints a high commissioner to represent French interests. New Caledonia elects two National Assembly deputies and sends one senator to the French Parliament.

One of the deputies is Jacques LaFleur, recently re-elected leader of the RPCR.

In early 1991 he suggested that all parties in New Caledonia attempt to reach a "consensual" solution before the referendum that would allow greater autonomy for the colony without leading to independence. FLNKS rejected the proposal just as it had rejected the suggestion that the island should be partitioned and only the Kanaky-majority areas given independence. In demanding full independence and territorial unity, FLNK's position is bolstered by United Nations Resolution 1514, which declared New Caledonia in 1986 a non-self-governing territory.

Reunion

Polity: Appointed commissioner and elected assembly and council
Economy: Capitalist-statist
Population: 596,000
Ethnic Groups: Creole (Afro-European), French, Malagache, Malay, South Asian, and Vietnamese

Political Rights: 2
Civil Liberties: 2
Status: Free

Overview:

Located in the Indian Ocean east of Madagascar, Reunion has been in French hands since the seventeenth century. The population is multi-racial and largely Catholic. Sugar cane is the most important crop. A French commissioner carries out executive functions. There is a competitive, multi-party system, which ranges from pro-French conservatives to pro-independence Communists. Reunion has a bicameral legislature, consisting of an elected 36-member General Council and an elected 45-member Regional Assembly. The territory elects three National Assembly deputies and one Senator to the French Parliament. There are three daily newspapers and a government radio and television system.

The working class quarter of Saint-Denis, the capital, was rocked in February 1991 by three days of rioting; more than 60 people were injured and 11 were killed. The disorders were precipitated by the government's seizure of the transmitters of a pirate television station that was popular among the poor creole-speaking portion of the population. The station had been on the air without a license for five years, ignoring orders to suspend broadcasting. Government troops soon questions quashed the disturbance. Protests returned in March during visits by French dignitaries.

St. Pierre and Miquelon

Polity: Appointed commissioner and elected council
Economy: Capitalist
Population: 6,392
Ethnic Groups: French

Political Rights: 2
Civil Liberties: 2
Status: Free

Overview:

Located south of Newfoundland in the North Atlantic, the islands of St. Pierre and Miquelon are the only remaining French possessions in North America. Fishing is the mainstay of the economy. A quota agreement governing French and Canadian fishing in the area expired at the end of 1991. The French government appoints a commissioner, and local residents elect a fourteen-member general council and municipal councils. The islanders also choose a National Assembly deputy and a senator to the French Parliament. The Socialist Party and the center-right Union for French Democracy, are the active political parties. There is freedom of association. Unionized workers belong to *Force Ouvriere* (Workers' Force). The only newspaper is a bulletin of government announcements. There is a medium-wave radio transmitter and a government radio and television station.

Wallis and Futuna Islands

Polity: Appointed administrator and elected council
Economy: Capitalist-statist
Population: 12,408
Ethnic Groups: Polynesian

Political Rights: 3
Civil Liberties: 2
Status: Free

Overview:

Located in the South Pacific, Wallis and Futuna Islands have almost completely Polynesian populations. The islands voted to become a French territory in 1959. There is a French-appointed administrator and a locally elected 20-member council. Three traditional chiefs are council members. In 1989, local leaders attacked the administrator for governing without their participation. Local affiliates of the French center-right parties predominate. The territory elects a National Assembly deputy and a senator to the French Parliament. In 1991 there were talks on the islands' future between the French and the local leadership. The only radio station broadcasts in both French and Wallisian.

France-Spain Condominium
Andorra

Polity: Co-Princes and parliament
Economy: Capitalist
Population: 56,000
Ethnic Groups: Andorran (Catalan), Spanish, Portuguese, French, other European

Political Rights: 2
Civil Liberties: 1
Status: Free

Overview:

Continuing to feel pressure from its French and Spanish neighbors to liberalize and modernize its economy, Andorra joined the European Community customs union in 1991.

Located in the Pyrenees Mountains between France and Spain, Andorra has been a joint territory of the French government and the Bishop of Urgel, Spain since 1278. Before 1981, there was no clear power structure to rule the country. As Co-Princes, the French President and the Spanish Bishop had representatives there, but Andorra had no locally chosen head of government. The Co-Princes' representatives (vicars) still play a role, especially in the court system. Since 1981, there has been a head of government (cap del govern). The 28 members of the elected General Council serve four-year terms and choose one of their number as head. In 1982 Andorran voters approved a system of proportional representation in a referendum, but the French and

Spanish sides have not enacted this reform, due to 48 percent voter abstention. There are some limitations on voting rights for young, first-generation Andorrans. Otherwise, there is universal suffrage at age 18 and over. Andorra took a major step towards political reform on 18 June 1990 when its General Council decided unanimously to draft the territory's first constitution.

Andorrans represent only a minority of the population and the number of Spanish and Portuguese immigrants is growing faster than the native population. The government has proposed easing citizenship requirements. Technically, there are no political parties, but there are factions and associations which have effective party functions. The French and Spanish governments pressed Andorra to legalize trade unions in 1991. The French have generally handled Andorra's foreign relations. There are two private weekly newspapers, a local public radio, and television service. French and Spanish media are easily available.

India
Kashmir

Polity: Indian-administered
Economy: Capitalist-statist
Population: 6,000,000
Ethnic Groups: Kashmiris (Muslim majority, Hindu minority)

Political Rights: 6
Civil Liberties: 6
Status: Not Free

Overview:

In 1991 over 1,600 soldiers, civilians and separatist militants died in the Indian-administered portion of Kashmir in the latest round of unrest that began in January 1990. Kashmir is the only Muslim-majority state in predominantly Hindu India, and the Muslim population leads the separatist cause. Over 200,000 Indian troops line the tense border with Pakistan, which India blames for arming and training separatist militants within its borders and for sending them into Kashmir.

Until 1947 all of Kashmir belonged to the British-ruled Indian territories. Headed by a Hindu ruler, the Maharajah of Kashmir, the area had a Muslim majority that did not wish to join India after the British decided to partition their holdings into Muslim Pakistan and Hindu-dominated India. Caught in the subsequent fighting between between India and Pakistan, the Maharajah decided his domain should join India. The Indian government announced that it would hold a referendum to settle the territory's fate, but the plebiscite has never taken place. India also included a provision in its constitution, Article 370, which limited the Indian parliament's power to make laws for Kashmir. Following the first Indo-Pakistani war, the United Nations divided Kashmir into Indian- and Pakistani-administered areas in 1949. In 1957 India made its portion of Kashmir an official part of its territory as the state of Jammu and Kashmir. Following Chinese-Indian clashes in 1962, India ceded a portion of Kashmir to China. India and Pakistan warred over Kashmir again in 1965 and in 1971-72. The two countries agreed in principle in the 1972 Simla agreement that they would respect the truce line in Kashmir as a *de facto* border between their areas of control.

The Kashmiris in the Indian-held areas have become increasingly anti-Indian since the late 1980s. Their grievances include their political status, unemployment, and underdevelopment. India's central government appointed a new Kashmiri government in January 1990 and the elected government of Chief Minister Farooq Abdullah resigned.

Abdullah had headed the National Conference coalition which included the Indian Congress Party. Most Kashmiris believed that the most recent elections, held in 1987, had been rigged. The Indian government replaced Abdullah with Governor Jagmohan, who had held the post before. There was some hope for a new election for the state when the Indian government dissolved Kashmir's legislature in February 1990, although a new date was never set. In May 1990 three young men assassinated the senior Muslim religious leader Maulvi Mohammed Farooq. Indian troops opened fire on mourners, killing up to 100 and wounding 200. Following the violence after Farooq's death, India imposed direct central government rule in over Kashmir in July 1990.

In 1991 separatist militants kidnapped foreigners for the first time in order to publicize their claims. On 31 March two Swedish engineers working on a hydroelectric project were seized by the obscure Muslim Crusade force, which demanded that India allow international human rights groups and the United Nations Human Rights Commission to conduct investigations in Kashmir. On 27 June, militants kidnapped seven Israeli tourists and one Dutch tourist. One of the Israelis died in a struggle and the rest escaped. Militants also kidnapped an Indian oil executive in June and several government officials throughout the year.

Indian security forces continued to launch raids into villages in search of separatist militants. On the night of 24 February, 160 Indian soldiers surrounded the village of Kunan-Poshpora near Kupwara. Although the army claims the search proceeded as planned, 53 women claimed they had been raped by the Indian troops. On 4 October troops shot at least 13 people during a sweep of several villages. Kashmiri human rights groups also claim that on 10 June Indian paramilitary forces fired indiscriminately from vehicles into crowds of civilians in Kashmir's capital, Srinagar, resulting in over 20 deaths and dozens of injuries. This was viewed as a retaliatory action for an earlier ambush of Indian forces by separatist militants. Several strikes occurred throughout the year in the Srinager, the capital, to protest the actions of the Indian troops.

Pakistani forces launched their second major attack since the fall of 1990 into Indian-controlled Pakistan in March. Indian troops quickly repulsed the intrusion. A smaller border clash occurred in late August 1991. Throughout the year, Indian troops confronted and killed militants entering Kashmir from Pakistan. The Indian government frequently publicly displays Pakistani arms claimed to have been taken from the infiltrators as proof of Pakistan's aid to the guerrillas.

Political Rights and Civil Liberties:

Kashmiris cannot change their government democratically. Kashmir has been under direct presidential rule from New Delhi since January 1990 and Kashmiris did not vote in May-June 1991 Indian elections. Elections were last held in Kashmir in 1987, and were widely alleged to have been rigged by the victorious National Conference/Congress Party. There is no sign that New Delhi is planning to reinstitute democratic government in Kashmir. Political parties are allowed, but the Indian government outlawed several militant organizations in 1990.

Kashmiris are deprived of basic rights both by Indian security forces and rebel militants. Over 3,400 people have been killed since the beginning of the current unrest in January 1990, a majority of them by militants. The Indian authorities have detained thousands without trial since January 1990. The autonomy of Kashmir in domestic matters, although protected by the terms of Kashmir's accession to India in 1947, is not respected by New Delhi.

The media are restricted both by the Indian government and the militants, the latter doing so mainly through threats of violence. Indian security forces frequently break up peaceful anti-Indian demonstrations. Although Kashmiri courts are putatively sovereign and their decisions not subject to appeal in Indian courts, the Army Act gives army forces the often-exercised option of assuming jurisdiction and trying any case in a court martial.

The rebel insurgency and the government's continuing military response affect nearly all Kashmiris. Army patrols and curfews often restrict freedom of movement. Militants and suspected militants are subject to torture and extrajudicial execution by security forces, who also have been accused on several occasions of mass rape and burning whole villages to the ground.

Indonesia
East Timor

Polity: Dominant party (military-dominated)
Economy: Capitalist-statist
Population: 750,000
Ethnic Groups: Timorese, Javanese, others

Political Rights: 7
Civil Liberties: 7
Status: Not Free

Overview:

On 12 November Indonesian troops opened fire on pro-independence demonstrators in Dili, the capital of this former Portuguese colony. The government initially reported that 19 were killed and some 90 wounded in the shootings, which took place after a funeral. Eyewitnesses and human rights activists put the death toll at 200.

The incident sparked international protests, including condemnation from the Vatican, which cited continued repression of the overwhelmingly Catholic East Timorese. Seventy East Timorese students protesting the deaths were arrested in Jakarta on 22 November. In late December, the Indonesian government reported that 50 had been killed and that Indonesian troops had overreacted. On 28 December, Indonesian President Suharto relieved two generals of their posts after holding them responsible for the deaths.

Portugal and Indonesia continued their long-standing dispute over the status of East Timor in 1991. Portugal, which ruled this half of the island of Timor for 400 years, called for Timorese self-determination in 1974. The Timorese People's Association (Apodeti) advocated an autonomous status within Indonesia, while the Democratic Union of Timor (UDT) campaigned for independence. In August 1975 the UDT and the leftist Revolutionary Front for an Independent East Timor (Fretilin) launched separate revolts. Fretilin declared an independent republic in late November 1975. Indonesia invaded nine days later and annexed East Timor in July 1976.

The United Nations still recognizes Portugal as the "administering power" in East Timor. Portugal has called for the right of self-determination for the region; Indonesia has rejected any such demand by what it considers to be a former colonial power. A Portuguese parliamentary visit to the disputed territory, delayed since 1988, stalled again at the start of 1991, as both nations exchanged verbal attacks. After the November violence, Portugal called for a trade embargo against Indonesia.

Estimates of those who died during 1975-1979 as Indonesia strove to crush Fretilin resistance vary from 100,000 to 200,000. Many of the casualties starved to death during a famine, allegedly exacerbated by Indonesia deliberately destroying croplands. Periodic skirmishes and military abuses have continued ever since.

Political Rights and Civil Liberties: The November shootings seriously damaged Indonesia's campaign to counter persistent charges of human rights abuses in East Timor and its claim that the military had adopted a "smiling policy" toward East Timorese. Allegations of serious human rights abuses continued, including reports of unfair trials, torture and disappearances before the November violence. Indonesia attacked the European Community for its statement on the incident, and blamed Portugal for the EC's harsh attitude. In 1989 Indonesia declared East Timor to be an open province, lifting many travel restrictions, allowing foreign investment, and demilitarizing the local government. Although some travel restrictions remain, Indonesia permitted visits by the International Committee of the Red Cross.

The government allows East Timorese to practice Catholicism, the dominant religion. Freedom of assembly is restricted. Ethnic tension between East Timorese and migrants from the more populated regions of Indonesia continued in 1991.

Irian Jaya

Polity: Dominant Party (military dominated)
Economy: Capitalist-statist
Population: 1,200,000
Ethnic Groups: Mainly Papuan

Political Rights: 7
Civil Liberties: 6
Status: Free

Overview: Indonesia's controversial Transmigration Program—designed to move people from overpopulated islands, such as Java, to less crowded areas—came under increasing criticism from ethnic Irianese in 1991. After an intensive start in the 1980s, the program has slowed to a virtual halt, due to problems between immigrants and Irianese. A large influx of immigrants not associated with the government program has exacerbated the problem. Non-governmental activists grew increasingly adamant throughout 1991 that quotas be established to protect market share, jobs, and equity ownership for indigenous Irianese.

When the Dutch government recognized Indonesia's independence in 1949, it retained control over the Netherlands New Guinea which occupied the western half of the island of New Guinea. The Dutch later surrendered control over the territory to the United Nations on the understanding that Indonesia would administer Irian Jaya from 1963 until a referendum could be held on its future status, by 1969. The mainly Papuan population seemed to favor independence, but the Indonesian government, rather than hold an open referendum, convened 8 regional assemblies during the summer of 1969. All eight voted for incorporation into Indonesia. The Free Papua Organization (OPM), whose major objective was the establishment of a separate "West Papua," emerged in the mid-1960s and have fought for secession from Indonesia ever since. In 1984 the Indonesian army launched an offensive against the OPM. In the two years which followed, over 11,000 Irianese sought refuge in neighboring Papua New Guinea. Another offensive in 1989 has left the OPM with dwindling overt support; its active members reported to number no more than 200. Yet, the Indonesian military has used the OPM as its excuse for the maintenance of an estimated 4,000 troops in Irian Jaya.

Despite abundant mineral resources, Irian Jaya is economically backward and suffers from a poor quality of life. Infant mortality in Irian Jaya is 85 percent higher than the national average and life expectancy is just 48 years.

Political Rights and Civil Liberties: Reports of mistreatment at the hands of both the Indonesian military and the OPM continued to emerge from Irian Jaya. Amnesty International was highly critical of the military's brutality against suspected secessionists and political prisoners. An Amnesty report released in April, 1991 stated that 80 Irianese in prison at that time were "prisoners of conscience—persons held for their non-violent political or other activities or beliefs." All were tried under Indonesia's anti-subversion laws. The report alleges that many of the prisoners were beaten or tortured under detention and that those accused of subversion are automatically presumed guilty by Indonesian courts.

The government continues to restrict both access to and movement within Irian Jaya for both Indonesians and foreigners. The government nevertheless allowed the International Committee of the Red Cross to open an office in Irian Jaya during 1989 to assist with returning refugees and to monitor prison conditions. Although Irian Jaya enjoys relative freedom of religion, there have been accusations that the government has been indirectly forcing Islam on the mostly Christian population through the transmigration of so many Muslim citizens to the region.

Israel
Occupied Territories

Polity: Military-administered (West Bank and Gaza)
Economy: Capitalist
Population: 1,538,000
Ethnic Groups: Palestinian Arab, Jewish

Political Rights: 6
Civil Liberties: 6
Status: Not Free

Overview: Major developments in the territories in 1991 included the strict Israeli curfew during the Gulf War, new Israeli settlements, and Palestinian participation in Arab-Israeli peace talks.

The West Bank and Gaza were part of the Arab state envisioned in the United Nations 1947 partition plan for the lands of the British-occupied Palestine Mandate. After Israel's victory over the Arabs in its 1948-49 war of independence, Egypt occupied the Gaza Strip, and Jordan took over the West Bank and East Jerusalem. Israel captured East Jerusalem, the West Bank and Gaza in the 1967 war. It also gained the strategically important Golan Heights from Syria. Israel annexed East Jerusalem in 1967 and the Golan Heights in 1981.

The Israeli Defense Ministry runs the West Bank and Gaza. The Israelis sponsored the most recent local elections there in 1976. Only a few of the elected officials remain. After the Palestinian uprising (intifada) began in 1987, King Hussein of Jordan cut legal and administrative ties to the West Bank; as a result, West Bank Palestinians have no representation in Jordan's parliament. During the intifada, more than 876 Palestinians and 75 Israelis have been killed.

Before the start of the Gulf War in January 1991, the Palestine Liberation Organization (PLO) had expressed clear support for Iraqi President Saddam Hussein. The Iraqi leader gained the sympathy of the Palestinians for his harsh attacks on Israel and the West. During the war, Israel imposed a curfew on the West Bank and Gaza. This policy cut the residents off from work, food, and medical care. Despite an Israeli court order requiring the authorities to distribute an adequate number of gas masks to the Palestinians, the government provided only a small number. This left the Palestinians defenseless in the event of an Iraqi poison gas attack.

Before the Gulf War, about 120,000 Arabs from the territories worked in Israel, especially in agriculture and construction. A strict work permit system in 1991 practically eliminated Palestinian casual labor in Israel and drove up unemployment in the territories. Israel is a signatory to the Fourth Geneva Convention on the rights of civilians in military-occupied areas, but says that the agreement does not apply to the West Bank and Gaza since Jordan and Egypt had no legal claim to those areas when they ruled them before the 1967 war.

Since the Palestinians had backed Saddam Hussein, they appeared to be in a weak position after the allied victory in the Gulf War. However, America's Arab allies expected the U.S. to use that victory to press Israel to negotiate with its neighbors. The Israelis strengthened their hold on the territories with more Jewish settlements in 1991. Israeli Housing Minister Ariel Sharon announced plans for 13,000 more Jewish housing units. The arrival of thousands of Jews from the former Soviet Union, combined with the Palestinian fear that the newcomers would settle in the occupied areas, increased the Palestinians' willingness to negotiate with Israel. Israel was unwilling to deal directly with the PLO. The Americans and Israelis worked out an arrangement under which the PLO gave effective approval to a Palestinian delegation which the Israelis accepted as part of a joint Jordanian-Palestinian negotiating team.

The Arab-Israeli peace talks opened in Madrid in November 1991 under the joint American-Soviet sponsorship. The discussions moved later to Washington. For the West Bank and Gaza, the Israelis and Palestinians began attempting to make an interim deal for Palestinian autonomy before negotiating a more permanent settlement. Syria joined the opening round of talks reluctantly, but its case may be more problematic. Both the Likud bloc and the Israeli Labor Party support Israeli settlements in the Golan Heights and appear unwilling to cede the area to Syria for security reasons.

Political Rights and Civil Liberties:

Palestinians in the West Bank and Gaza have no right to change their government democratically. Israel allows them no political parties. Both Arab and Israeli residents of annexed areas have the right to vote in Israeli elections, but few Arabs do so. In the West Bank and Gaza, only Jewish settlers have Israeli voting rights.

Israel places strict limits on press freedom, free speech, and cultural expression. The occupying forces allow only limited criticism. The Israelis censor and ban local Arab and foreign publications, declare certain towns closed to journalists, and detain uncooperative journalists. In January 1991 the Israelis arrested Taher Shiteh, a Gaza journalist, because he was working on a story about Hamas, the Islamic fundamentalist movement. He used an illegal fax machine to send information. The Israelis released him in March after an international campaign on his behalf. Also in January the authorities arrested Professor Sari Nusseibeh of the closed Bir Zeit University. They claimed he was aiding Iraqi "espionage," but Amnesty International declared him to be a prisoner of conscience, held for his nationalistic views. Israel released him in April. The administration allowed the reopening of An-Najah University in August after it had been closed for 44 months.

The Israelis respect freedom of religion for Arab Moslems and Christians, and for Jewish settlers. However, there is tight security around mosques, which are occasional gathering places for stone-throwers. Islamic fundamentalism has become very popular in the territories, especially Gaza. In October 1991 the Israelis sentenced fundamentalist movement leader Sheik Ahmed Yassin, a quadriplegic, to concurrent life and fifteen-year terms for manslaughter, incitement, and leading an illegal organization.

Israeli security forces carry out numerous violations of human rights in the territories. In March 1991 the Israeli police minister urged the forces to shoot to kill Arab assailants who attacked or threatened to attack Israeli civilians. Soldiers killed a youth in riots during a general strike. The Israeli public was shocked in June by a televised documentary which showed Israeli undercover teams dressed as Arabs. The teams attacked and arrested people on the streets. The army allowed the broadcast, in order to intimidate Palestinians.

Reports persisted about unacceptable prison conditions in 1991. Palestinian prisoners went on a hunger strike in several facilities in June to protest maltreatment. The Israeli police ministry comptroller commented that prison authorities allow prisoners too much autonomy. Palestinian human rights groups complained that they had difficulty in locating some detainees, but the situation had improved somewhat over that of earlier years. There were allegations that interrogators used electric shocks on prisoners.

Israel permits trade union activity in the territories, but it tries to discourage it. Nonetheless, several trade unions and competing labor federations function. Many Palestinians must work in Israel, but Jews from the former Soviet Union replaced Arabs at many Israeli job sites in 1991. Fundamentalists called a general strike in the territories which shut down the territories' commerce in March. After years of discouraging business in the territories, Israel announced easier licensing practices and tax breaks to take effect in January 1992. Israel allowed competitive elections for the Chamber of Commerce board in Hebron. It was a trial run for possible municipal elections.

There are several restrictions on freedom of movement. Israel has deported more than 67 Palestinians from the West Bank and Gaza since 1987. In March 1991 Israel announced that it would deport Palestinians who incited attacks against Jews. Although Palestinians are free to emigrate, various restrictions have complicated their travel abroad. They must endure long waits for travel permits. The Israelis often deny them after people have waited for hours. Authorities have carried out some illegal confiscations of identity cards. Israel has refused some family reunifications and has prevented the return of thousands of Palestinians from Kuwait. A group of 200

Ethiopian Jews on the West Bank wants to leave the area, but the government will not provide them with relocation assistance. In December Israel announced a new rule that requires people to stay 165 yards clear of roadsides from sunset to sunrise.

Israel punishes Palestinians by bulldozing or blowing up their homes. Since 1987 the security forces have destroyed over 300 homes and sealed over 200 others. In a bizarre case in 1991, the Israelis punished Munzer Abdallah by blowing up his home *after* his death. The Israelis claim this punishment is legal under the emergency laws of the British Palestine Mandate.

Italy
San Marino

Polity: Parliamentary democracy
Economy: Capitalist
Population: 23,900
Ethnic Groups: Italian

Political Rights: 1
Civil Liberties: 1
Status: Free

Overview:

According to tradition, a Christian stonecutter named Marinus founded San Marino in 301 A.D. Surrounded entirely by Italian territory, San Marino is the world's oldest republic. The country signed the first of several friendship treaties with Italy in 1862. Italy handles many of San Marino's foreign and security affairs. In 1979, they upgraded their relations to the ambassadorial level. The tiny republic has a lively multi-party system, similar to Italy's. In recent years, Socialists, Communists, Christian Democrats, and Social Democrats have participated in coalition governments. Cabinets have changed frequently, due to a lack of consensus on policy. In the May 1988 election, the Christian Democrats and Communists won enough seats to continue their coalition government. Since 1600, San Marino's Grand and General Council has served as the legislature. Its sixty members serve for a maximum term of five years. The Council chooses the State Congress, which functions as a cabinet. Chosen by the Council for six-month terms, two Captains Regent supervise the State Congress. One Captain Regent represents the city of San Marino, and the other stands for the surrounding area. The media are free, and Italian newspapers and broadcasts are freely available.

Morocco
Western Sahara

Polity: Appointed governors
Economy: Capitalist
Population: 200,000
Ethnic Groups: Arab, Sahrawi

Political Rights: 6
Civil Liberties: 5
Status: Partly Free

Overview:

In 1991 the U.N. attempted to solve the Western Sahara dispute through a peace-plan featuring a referendum allowing the territories' inhabitants, the Sahrawi people, to choose freely whether they want independence or integration with Morocco. By year's end, however, hopes for a solution faded as Morocco obstructed U.N. activities and launched a "Second Green March," by which tens of thousands of Moroccans entered the disputed territory with the intention of voting in favor of Morocco in the referendum.

The conflict over Western Sahara began in 1975, when, as Spain prepared to withdraw from its last colony, Morroccan King Hassan II sent 300,000 civilians into Western Sahara, in the first "Green March," to claim it as Moroccan territory, despite calls by the United Nations and the World Court for the self-determination of the area's inhabitants. Morocco then sent troops to occupy the land and bombarded the area with napalm, sending hordes of refugees, which today amount to 160,000, into southern Algeria. In 1991 only 10 percent of Western Sahara remained outside of Moroccan control.

The Algerian-based Polisario (the Front for the Liberation of Western Sahara and Rio Oro) guerillas, whose motto is "Our entire fatherland or death," have repeatedly attacking the thousand kilometer-long sand wall built by the Moroccans across the West Sahara. Major Western powers have not recognized Moroccan title to the territory, and over seventy nations, mostly African, have recognized the Polisario's government in exile in Algeria, the Saharan Democratic Arab Republic (SADR). In 1991 United Nations Secretary General Javier Perez de Cuellar affirmed a commitment to bring to fruition his six-year effort to make peace between Morocco and the Polisario. In April the U.N. Security Council unanimously authorized the establishment of UN Mission for the Referendum in Western Sahara (MINURSO), which would plan and implement a vote allowing the Sahrawi people to choose between independence or official annexation by Morocco.

On 17 May the U.N. General Assembly approved Resolution 690, which proposed a budget of $200 million for the referendum program, limited the number of Moroccan forces to 65,000 (from the estimated 190,000), set a cease-fire date of 6 September, and stipulated the completion of the referendum by the end of January 1992. An Identification Commission set up to determine who would be included in the referendum decided that all the people who were in the last census in Western Sahara in 1974 were eligible to vote and that all the Sahrawi refugees in camps in southern Algeria would be repatriated within six weeks of the ceasefire date. Thirty-six countries, including the five permanent members of the Security Council, were to participate in a 3,000-strong team to supervise the cease-fire and the referendum.

Despite their acceptance of the U.N. plan and the ceasefire date, Morocco and the Polisario Front resumed their hostile exchange, which had lulled for almost two years. In early August, the Moroccan Air Force bombed the villages of Tifariti and Meharise, areas on the Mauritanian border which lie outside the Moroccan defensive line. Later that month, King Hassan requested that the referendum be delayed by four months and refused to allow U.N. Secretary General's special envoy Johannes Manz to travel to Western Sahara.

From August 22-29, an estimated seven regiments of Morocco's Royal Armed Forces conducted "clearing" operations in the small area under Polisario control. Though no fighting took place after 6 September, security problems persisted, no prisoners were exchanged, and Morocco's estimated 130,000 troops were not reduced to 65,000.

Disagreement continued over the status of thousands of Moroccan immigrants who make up a considerable proportion of Western Saharan residents. The Moroccans moved to Western Sahara for the high salaries and cheap prices, all subsidized by the Moroccan government to encourage immigration to the region. Sympathetic to Moroccan claims to Western Sahara, these Moroccans could be deciding factor in the referendum. On 23 September Morocco launched a "Second Green March," sending an estimated 35,000 more Moroccans into El-Ayoun, the capital of Western Sahara, and other towns; an estimated 200,000 more were due to arrive before the referendum. Morocco claims these people are native Sahrawis who sought refuge from European colonization. In November the U.N. conceded to Moroccan demands that the census be widened to include those not included in the 1974 consensus. Morocco had earlier submitted a list of 120,000 Sahrawis to be added to the 160,000 living in Algeria.

Morocco continued to block movement of Minurso equipment and U.N. troops into Western Sahara, insisting that full U.N. deployment could not take place until the voting consensus was agreed upon. The blockade on U.N. material, the census disagreement, and security problems resulting from August's combat put the referendum six-months behind schedule. The repatriation of the refugees, due to start in October, was delayed until May 1992.

Political Rights and Civil Liberties:

The portion of the population that Morocco administers has generally the same civil liberties as those in Morocco proper (*see Morocco*). Moroccan authorities monitor Saharans for their political beliefs and possible Polisario support. The territory has ten parliamentary seats in the Moroccan parliament. Those elected are native Saharans. King Hassan appoints natives to govern the four provinces of the region. Politically suspect Saharans are subject to abuse.

Netherlands
Aruba

Polity: Appointed governor and parliamentary democracy
Economy: Mixed capitalist
Population: 67,3000
Ethnic Groups: Black majority with Carib Indian and European minorities

Political Rights: 1
Civil Liberties: 1
Status: Free

Overview:

Aruba was part of the Netherland Antilles from 1954 until 1986 when it achieved formal parity with the Netherlands and Netherlands Antilles under the Dutch crown. Under the assumption of domestic autonomy, Aruba agreed to retain economic and political links to the Netherland Antilles until 1996.

The Netherlands is represented in Aruba by an appointed governor, but the island is largely self-governing. Domestic affairs are the responsibility of the prime minister appointed by the freely elected unicameral Staten (legislature). Full freedom of party organization and expression is respected. The Council of Ministers at the Hague remains responsible for foreign affairs and defense.

The 21-member Staten is directly elected for four-year terms. The People's Electoral Movement (MEP) won the 7 January 1989 election, taking ten seats against the incumbent, center-right Aruba People's Party (AVP), won eight seats. Three smaller parties obtained one seat each. Following the election, a three-party government was formed, headed by the MEP's Nelson Oduber.

The MEP has traditionally been the major force for independence. In 1989, however, Prime Minister Oduber appeared to be shifting in favor of commonwealth status to ensure a full defense commitment from the Netherlands against the threat of the Colombian cocaine cartels, and to guarantee certain forms of financial assistance. During discussions in July 1990, Oduber and the Dutch government agreed that a new constitutional relationship, to be negotiated in the future, would not involve transition to full independence in 1996.

The press, radio and television are private, free and varied. Three daily newspapers are published, one in Dutch, one in English, and one in the local Papiamento. There are five privately run radio stations and one commercial television station.

Netherlands Antilles

Polity: Appointed governor and parliamentary democracy
Economy: Mixed capitalist
Population: 207,000
Ethnic Groups: Black majority with Carib Indian and European minorities

Political Rights: 1
Civil Liberties: 1
Status: Free

Overview:

In 1954 the Netherlands Antilles was granted constitutional equality with the Netherlands and Suriname (which became independent in 1975). In 1986, Aruba split off and was given formal parity with the Netherlands and the Netherlands Antilles. The Netherlands Antilles currently consists of two groups of two and three islands each, the southern (Leeward) islands of Curacao and Bonaire and the northern (Windward) islands of St. Maarten, St. Eustatius, and Saba.

Although the Netherlands is represented by an appointed governor, the Netherlands Antilles is largely self-governing. Domestic affairs are the responsibility of the prime minister appointed by the unicameral Staten (legislature) of twenty-two deputies (fourteen from Curacao, three each from Bonaire and St. Maarten, and one each from St. Eustatius and Saba) elected for four years. Full freedom of party organization and expression is respected. Foreign affairs and defense remain the responsibility of the Council of Ministers at the Hague.

Coalition governments have been highly unstable given the geographical range of the islands and island-based political differences, particularly over the issue of island independence. There have been seven governments since 1977 as eight different political parties have entered in and out of a variety of coalitions. The two main parties are the center-right National People's Party (NPP), which formed the government in 1988 under Maria Liberia-Peters, and the social democratic New Antilles Movement (MAN) headed by former prime minister Dom Martina.

The Liberia-Peters government retained office in new elections held on 16 May 1990. The PNP increased its representation to seven seats, and its coalition partner, the Workers Liberation Front (FOL), won three seats. With 10 out of 14 seats on Curacao, the PNP also had the support of the Democratic Party (St. Eustatius) and the Windward Islands Patriotic Movement (Saba), both of which retained their seats, and the Bonaire Patriotic Union, which took all three seats on Bonaire. Claude Wathey, the leader of the Democratic Party (St. Maarten) and powerbroker of most federation governments over the last three decades, lost his seat.

Local government on each of the islands is constituted by freely elected Island Councils.

Since 1990, the Netherlands has shifted on its long-held policy of encouraging full independence. In May 1990, the Dutch government announced plans for drawing up a new constitution governing relations between the Netherlands, the Netherlands Antilles, and Aruba. The Liberia-Peters government responded by announcing that it hoped to hold by 1992 a round-table conference in which all three parties would discuss the basis for future relations. In the Netherland Antilles, there continued to be great differences of opinion, between political parties and islands alike, over the issue.

The press, radio and television are private, free and varied. The islands are serviced by six daily newspapers, two in Dutch and four in the local Papiamento. Privately owned radio stations operate on all islands except St. Eustatius. There is a television station on Curacao.

New Zealand
Cook Islands

Polity: Parliamentary democracy
Economy: Capitalist-statist
Population: 18,092
Ethnic Groups: Polynesian majority, European and mixed race minorities

Political Rights: 2
Civil Liberties: 2
Status: Free

Overview:

The major developments in 1991 were a government party by-election victory, an abrupt change in telecommunications, and a corporate windfall from Hong Kong.

Located in the South Pacific, the Cook Islands are in free association with New Zealand and have the right to independence at any time. Aside from defense and foreign affairs, they are largely self-governing. The inhabitants have New Zealand citizenship rights. The governor-general of New Zealand appoints a Queen's representative who appoints the prime minister. The 24 seat parliament has a maximum term of five years. There is also an advisory council of chiefs. Prime Minister Geoffrey Henry of the Cook Islands Party has been in power since the 1989 election. The previous coalition government had banned politics from the media in 1988, but lifted the ban for the 1989 campaign.

Ben Toma won the Manihiki constituency for the Cook Islands Party in the March 1991 by-election. He had switched from the opposition Democrat Taokoti in 1990. The opposition responded to his switch by filing a suit to remove him from office, on the grounds that he spent most of his time in Australia. A court removed him from office and triggered a by-election. Toma won easily and gave the government the two-thirds of parliament needed for amending the constitution.

In June 1991 the government terminated the British Cable and Wireless Company's telecommunications franchise abruptly, four years before the end of its contract. The government took control of telecommunications, in order to fulfill its campaign promise to develop inter-island communications. Prime Minister Henry refused to divert New Zealand aid funds to pay for the contractual buy-out.

Hong Kong's Securities and Futures Commission assisted the Cook Islands' economy in 1991 by deciding to allow Hong Kong companies to use the islands as an offshore locus of incorporation. Many companies may switch their registration in advance of Hong Kong's accession to China in 1997.

The Cook Islands have one newspaper, two radio stations, and one television station.

Niue

Polity: Parliamentary democracy   **Political Rights:** 2
Economy: Capitalist-statist   **Civil Liberties:** 2
Population: 2,112   **Status:** Free
Ethnic Groups: Polynesian, other Pacific Islanders, Europeans

Overview:

Niue's top news story in 1991 was a $500,000 cut in aid from New Zealand. The territory explored ways to justify its existence and revive its economy.

Located northeast of New Zealand in the South Pacific, the island is in free association with New Zealand, which gives Niueans full citizenship rights. The small population is more than 90 percent Polynesian. The island has a very poor economy, and endures such natural disasters as long droughts and cyclones. Subsidies from New Zealand sustain the relatively large local government and the declining population. In the labor force, 600 (a majority of paid employees) work in the public sector. However, a cut in aid in 1991 threatened 150 local jobs. In a last-ditch effort to save the island, the larger country is pouring in funds to develop local business. This may be cut off altogether, due to poor economic performance. Niue is attempting to promote such natural resources as rock pools and volcanic caves. The island hopes to build links to Fiji as an alternative market to New Zealand. In a potentially more promising development, the Sydney-based Roycol exploration company hoped to find uranium on the island. However, the Australian Stock Exchange suspended the trading in the company's shares. If all economic plans fail, some or all of the remaining Niueans could move or be moved fairly cheaply to New Zealand. About 10,000 Niueans live there already.

The island's politics are characterized by shifting alliances of personalities and family squabbles. The twenty-member Assembly is elected every three years. Fourteen win election from village constituencies. Six stand for office at-large. Sir Robert Rex has been the political leader since the 1950s. Many islanders grew tired of his longevity, and elected six new members of the Assembly in the spring 1990 election. Many candidates on both sides were members or inlaws of the Rex family. The only formal party, People's Action, and its sympathizers won the most votes in the election. On election night People's Action leader Young Vivian thought he would have a 12-8 majority in the Assembly. However, splits developed on the People's Action side, and Sir Robert took advantage of them. He managed to switch enough Assembly members to give himself a 12-8 majority. Both Young Vivian and the voters were stunned.

After a few months in office Rex dumped two of his ministers, charging that they "stabbed me in the back." The pair had sought to replace Sir Robert. Then the leader named two new ministers including his electoral opponent, Young Vivian.

There is only one newspaper. Most islanders belong to the Christian Council of World Missions, but other groups have freedom of worship.

Tokelau

Polity: Administrator, elected leaders and elders
Economy: Capitalist-statist
Population: 1,700
Ethnic Groups: Polynesian

Political Rights: 2
Civil Liberties: 2
Status: Free

Overview:

In 1991 the United Nations Decolonization Subcommittee on Small Territories examined the question of independence for Tokelau, but its status is unchanged. Tokelau is a collection of Polynesian islands in the south Pacific. New Zealand appoints the territorial administrator. Each village elects a Faipule, who represents the community and presides over the council of elders, and a Pulenuku, who is responsible for village administration. Elections take place every three years. The next one is due in January 1993. Land may not pass to non-indigenous people. Some land belongs to families, while some is common property. There are no newspapers or broadcast media. There is freedom of worship. Islanders belong to various Christian groups. New Zealand subsidizes the local economy.

Portugal
Azores

Polity: Elected assembly
Economy: Capitalist-statist
Population: 260,000
Ethnic Groups: Portuguese

Political Rights: 1
Civil Liberties: 1
Status: Free

Overview:

The Azores are three groups of islands located 800 miles west of Portugal in the Atlantic Ocean. After the 1974 revolution in Portugal, separatist sentiment increased. Subsequently, the Lisbon government surrendered administration of the island to local political leaders. A multi-party, 43-seat Assembly was established in 1976, and a regional government formed under the leadership of the Popular Democratic Front, currently called the Social Democratic Party (PSD). The Social Democrats have remained the dominant party. Statutes passed by the regional assembly of the Azores remain subject to the Portugese Assembly's approval. The islands have elected representatives in the Portuguese parliament. Azoreans have the same civil liberties as Portugese mainlanders.

Macao

Polity: Appointed governor and partially elected legislature
Economy: Capitalist-statist
Population: 500,000
Ethnic Groups: Chinese, Mecanese, Portuguese

Political Rights: 3
Civil Liberties: 3
Status: Partly Free

Overview:

In March 1991 Portuguese President Mario Soares appointed General Vasco Rocha Vieira as governor of this Portuegese territory. General Vieira replaced the interim governor, Francisco Murteira Nabo, who had been appointed in September 1990 following the resignation of Carlos Melancia for allegedly accepting bribes from a German contractor. Melancia's resignation—the third in five years—raised doubts about Portugal's ability to ensure a smooth transition to Chinese rule on 20 December 1999.

Founded in 1557 as the first Western trading post on the Chinese coast, Macao—which consists of two islands, a peninsula, a bridge and causeway—will revert to Chinese control on the basis of a 1987 Sino-Portuguese agreement modelled on a similar pact between Beijing and Great Britain on the transfer of Hong Kong, in 1997. The treaty guaranteed Macao's semi-democratic, capitalist system for 50 years.

An urgent problem facing the new governor was putting a stop to a wave of murders and armed robberies that wracked the island from the beginning of the year. Some on the island attributed the violent crime to competition among the enclave's casino bosses, while other blamed illegal immigrants from China. In other developments, on 12 December the government approved a decree making Chinese an official language, giving it equal status with Portuguese.

Political Rights and Civil Liberties:

The Portuguese constitution guarantees the civil liberties of Macao's residents. Approximately 100,000 residents hold Portuguese passports and it appears Portugal will allow immigration for those who want to leave. Portugal also grants the same rights to the descendants of those who stay past 1999, though China views passports only as travel documents and has refused to allow consular protection. A 1991 draft of the future Basic Law, unlike similar legislation in Hong Kong, places no restrictions on foreign passport holders taking important posts in the Macao administration after 1999. The only exception is the future chief executive, who is not allowed to acquire the right of abode in a foreign country while holding office. One quarter of Macao's Chinese residents qualify for full Portuguese passports, a point the Portuguese would not yield, despite Beijing's objections. Another key concession is the absence of provisions for China's People's Liberation Army to be stationed in Macao after 1999, as it will be in Hong Kong after 1997. And Macao's Basic Law is stronger than Hong Kong in limiting immigration from the mainland after 1999.

Macao's Legislative Assembly has 18 members who serve three-year terms. Five are appointed by the governor, six directly elected, and six indirectly elected by business associations. The Assembly can be dissolved by the president of Portugal on the recommendation of the governor. Public representatives also serve on the Constitutional Council which advises the governor.

In January 1991 the governor took over control of all internal security units after 1990 amendments to the Organic Law disbanded the Security Force Command in a major shake-up of security affairs on the enclave. The governor has overall control of all internal security affairs, including public order, crime prevention and border control.

Madeira	**Polity:** Elected assembly	**Political Rights:** 1
	Economy: Capitalist-statist	**Civil Liberties:** 1
	Population: 277,000	**Status:** Free
	Ethnic Groups: Portuguese	

Overview:

The Madeira Islands are located in the Atlantic 500 miles southwest of Portugal. On 29 August 1975 the Madeira Archipelago Liberation Front (FLAMA) announced a provisional government. The Social Democratic Center Party has controlled the regional Assembly since this legislature's establishment in October 1976. Statutes passed by the Assembly are subject to approval by the legislative Assembly in Portugal. Madeira has representatives in the Portugese parliament. Civil liberties are the same as on the mainland.

South Africa	**Polity:** Dominant party	**Political Rights:** 6
Bophutatswana	**Economy:** Capitalist-statist	**Civil Liberties:** 5
	Population: 2,334,000	**Status:** Not Free
	Ethnic Groups: Tswana majority,	
	Pedis, Shangaans, Xhosas, South Sothos, and Swazis	

Overview:

In 1991, the significant political developments Bophutatswana were an outbreak of violence in a former South African village incorporated into the territory two years ago, and the release of political prisoners arrested after a failed coup attempt in 1988.

Located in north-central South Africa, Bophutatswana consists of seven arid and noncontiguous territories. South Africa granted the territory nominal independence in 1977, but no other country has recognized this status. Kgosi (Chief) Lucas Lawrence Manyane Mangope has been president since 1977, and was re-elected for a third seven-year term in 1991. He holds most executive power, and under a 1984 constitutional amendment has the right to run any government ministries. Mangope's dominant Bophuthatswana Democratic Party (BDP) held 102 of 108 seats in the National Assembly after the 1987 elections, with the remainder held by the opposition Progressive People's Party (PPP). In February 1988 the army attempted to force Mangope from power and install PPP leader Rocky Ismael Malabane-Metsing, but South African troops put down the rebellion within 15 hours. The government then banned the PPP, an ally of South Africa's African National Congress. The BDP currently holds all the seats in parliament. The ANC's support among the territorie's residents continues to grow and threatens Mangope's hold on power.

In January 1991 street fighting occurred in the village of Braklaagte, given by South Africa to Bophuthatswana two years before, between residents unwilling to lose their South African citizenship and vigilantes sent by the Mangope regime. Several deaths and injuries were reported, and approximately half the town's population of 5,000 fled to the South African town of Zeerust, twelve miles away. In March, Mangope ended a year-long state of emergency imposed to stifle ANC protests, but continued to detain its supporters and ban all demonstrations under substitute legislation. Despite going on hunger strikes in 1991 to force their early release, most political detainees linked to the 1988 coup remained imprisoned until December, when all except coup leader Timothy Phiri were released. The ANC had considered them South African prisoners of conscience and demanded that South African President de Klerk put pressure on Mangope to release them.

Bophutatswana has some economic strength, derived from platinum and vanadium mines, and the Sun City resort complex. However it depends on the South African government for 80 percent of its budget.

As of late 1991, despite Mangope's insistence that Bophutatswana will remain independent regardless of political changes in South Africa, re-incorporation still appeared likely. Supporters of the ANC consider Mangope's regime illegitimate and demand an immediate end to the territory's independent status.

Ciskei

Polity: Military
Economy: Capitalist-statist
Population: 1,143,000
Ethnic Groups: Xhosa-speaking south Nguni tribes

Political Rights: 6
Civil Liberties: 5
Status: Not Free

Overview:

In 1991 Brigadier Oupa Gqozo, who overthrew the civilian one-party regime of President Lennox Sebe in March 1990, found his attempts to extend government control throughout Ciskei resisted by groups affiliated with the African National Congress (ANC).

Located in southcentral South Africa, Ciskei is composed of two noncontiguous territories and is considered the poorest of the country's nominally independent black ethnic homelands. Ciskei's "independence" was granted in 1980 by South Africa, which still provides three-fourths of it's budget in the form of direct aid. An eight-member Council of State has ruled Ciskei since the coup, but in February 1991 the homeland gave up some of its sovereignty when it yielded four of its ministries to South Africa. Gqozo characterized the move as "the first step on the road to incorporation into a new, non-racial South Africa." Ciskei attended the December 1991 preliminary round of the all-party Conference for a Democratic South Africa.

Two men, one the brother of ex-President Sebe, were killed after a confrontation with Ciskei police at a roadblock in January 1991. The government claimed it had foiled a coup attempt, and asserted that Chris Hani, then leader of the ANC's military wing, was implicated. Less than three weeks later, another alleged coup was stymied with the help of the South African Defense Forces. Civil servants organized by the ANC-affiliated trade union federation went on strike for salary parity with South African civil servants, and also demanded Gqozo's resignation. Three thousand were fired after the strike continued into late April.

In October Ciskei declared a state of emergency as confrontations increased between the ANC and the security police. The ANC accused Gqozo of trying to "impose" himself on Ciskei and called upon South Africa to replace Gqozo with an interim administrator, a suggestion that Pretoria rejected. Gqozo restricted ANC organizing efforts and detained several ANC activists. After high-level talks with the

ANC the state of emergency was lifted three months later. In November 1991 local community residents associations were banned by the regime in order to stop further resistance to government-appointed headmen assuming control over local administration.

Transkei

Polity: Military
Economy: Capitalist
Population: 3,051,000
Ethnic Groups: Xhosa

Political Rights: 6
Civil Liberties: 5
Status: Not Free

Overview:

In 1991 Transkei's military government projected a militantly pro-ANC stance. Ruled by Major General Harrington Bantubonke Holomisa at the head of a five-man Military Council, the territory provides a secure base for Chris Hani, the ANC's former military chief of staff and new general secretary of the South African Communist Party. The Transkei government denied reports that it has allowed the ANC to store arms and ammunition on its territory. However, the regime did state in December 1991 that it would support the ANC's military wing if negotiations with the de Klerk government fail.

Located in southeastern South Africa, Transkei is a nominally independent black homeland consisting of three noncontiguous territories. It has been self-governing since 1976, but its independence has only been recognized by the South African government. The Transkei army seized power from a civilian government in 1987, and successfully defeated a coup attempt in late 1990. The government states that it is willing to be re-incorporated into South Africa after transition to majority rule; representatives of Transkei attended the first meeting of the Conference for a Democratic South Africa in December 1991.

Venda

Polity: Military
Economy: Capitalist-statist
Population: 650,000
Ethnic Groups: Venda majority, Sangaan and Pedi minorities

Political Rights: 7
Civil Liberties: 5
Status: Not Free

Overview:

In 1991 the military government of Venda indicated its willingness to be re-incorporated into a united, post-apartheid South Africa. Brigadier Gabriel Ramushwana, chairman of the ruling Council of National Unity, said that his regime would create a broad-based forum in the homeland to set the terms for any such re-incorporation. Although no general elections will be held prior to the end of Venda's separate political status, political parties such as the African National Congress were free to organize in 1991. In November 1991, Venda accepted an invitation to attend South Africa's all-party Conference for a Democratic South Africa, which is to create the basis for a new non-racial and democratic government in Pretoria.

Situated in northeastern South Africa along the Limpopo River, Venda was granted nominal independence in 1979. The homeland was created in accordance with the South African plan for setting up separate political entities for various black ethnic groups in their historic territories, with the object of depriving the black majority in South Africa proper of their citizenship rights. Under its original form of government, the territory of Venda had a legislative assembly with a combination of elected and appointed members. By the time Ramushwana overthrew the civilian government of President Frank Ravele in April 1990, it had devolved into a closely-controlled one-party state.

Spain
Canary Islands

Polity: Regional legislature
Economy: Capitalist
Population: 1,535,000
Ethnic Groups: Mostly Hispanic

Political Rights: 1
Civil Liberties: 1
Status: Free

Overview:

The mysterious death of British publisher Robert Maxwell off the Canary Islands was a major international story in 1991.
A judge on Tenerife Island ruled that there was no evidence to charge anyone with Maxwell's death, which took place on 5 November 1991.

The Canary Islands, located off the northwest coast of Africa, are administered as two provinces by Spain. Although the people are largely Hispanic, they are of diverse origins and maintain pre-Spanish customs. There have been periodic separatist movements, but the development of internal self-determination has helped to diffuse such sentiments. In terms of civil liberties, the population enjoys the same rights and guarantees as citizens of Spain.

Ceuta

Polity: Municipal administration
Economy: Capitalist-statist
Population: 80,000
Ethnic Groups: Moroccan, Spanish

Political Rights: 2
Civil Liberties: 1
Status: Free

Melilla

Polity: Municipal administration
Economy: Capitalist-statist
Population: 65,000
Ethnic Groups: Moroccan, Spanish

Political Rights: 2
Civil Liberties: 1
Status: Free

Overview:

Ceuta and Melilla, located on the coast of Morocco, are governed as municipalities of Cadiz and Malaga, respectively. Both areas have Muslim populations with Moroccan roots who have lived there for generations. In 1986 the government created a commission to examine how to integrate the Muslims into Spanish society. After demonstrations in 1986, the Spanish government made a move to give most Muslims citizenship over time. There is now an Islamic party in Melilla.

Switzerland
Liechtenstein

Polity: Prince and parliamentary democracy
Economy: Capitalist-statist
Population: 29,000
Ethnic Groups: Alemannic German, Italian, other European

Political Rights: 1
Civil Liberties: 1
Status: Free

Overview:

The Principality of Liechtenstein was created in the eighteenth century. Most Liechtensteiners are descended from the Germanic Alemanni tribe. The head of state is Prince Hans Adam, whose Austrian ancestors purchased this country's land. The prince appoints a prime minister from the majority party or coalition in the fifteen-member Landtag, whose members serve for four-year terms. Called "hallowed and sacrosanct" by the constitution, the monarch has the right to veto legislation. Hans Adam's father vetoed only one bill, a proposed hunting law. Parties with at least eight percent of the vote receive proportional representation in the Landtag. The leading parties are the moderately liberal Fatherland's Union, the conservative Progressive Citizens' Party, the Christian Social Party, and the liberal, Green-oriented Free Voters' List. The major issue in the March 1989 elections was whether or not to build a museum. Major local concerns include overdevelopment and the large number of outsiders in the labor force. Liechtenstein uses Swiss currency, and has a customs union with its larger neighbor. The Swiss handle Liechtenstein's defense and foreign affairs, but the principality joined the United Nations in 1990.

Political Rights and Civil Liberties:

Liechtensteiners can change their government democratically. Control has shifted back and forth between parties. Voters may decide issues directly through referenda. Despite the dependence on Switzerland, Liechtenstein retains its own traditions and power over local concerns. Women have had voting rights nationally since 1984. The leading parties publish newspapers five times each week. Residents receive radio and television freely from other countries. Liechtenstein has no broadcast media. The country is too small to have numerous organizations, but association is free. The highly prosperous economy is a combination of private and state enterprises. Per capita GDP is over $26,000.

United
Kingdom
Anguilla

Polity: Appointed governor and elected assembly
Economy: Mixed capitalist
Population: 6,815
Ethnic Groups: Relatively homogeneous, black majority

Political Rights: 1
Civil Liberties: 1
Status: Free

Overview:

Following the establishment of the Associated State of St. Kitts-Nevis-Anguilla, Anguillans rejected governmental authority from St. Kitts and in 1969 a British commissioner was appointed. A separate constitution was provided in 1976 giving the commissioner (now governor) authority over foreign affairs, defense, civil service and internal security. In January 1990 the governor (currently Brian Canty) also assumed responsibility for international financial affairs. All other governmental responsibilities are carried out by a freely elected seven-member House of Assembly. The first House elections were held in 1976. In December 1980, the dependent status of the territory was formally confirmed.

In the 27 February 1989 elections, the incumbent Anguilla National Alliance (ANA) headed by Chief Minister Emile Gumbs retained control of the House over the opposition Anguilla United Party (AUP).

Anguillans enjoy all civil rights common to the homeland. The press is government owned and operated. Radio is both government owned and private. There is no television.

Bermuda

Polity: Appointed governor and parliamentary democracy
Economy: Mixed capitalist
Population: 59,066
Ethnic Groups: Black (approximately 60 percent), large British minority

Political Rights: 1
Civil Liberties: 1
Status: Free

Overview:

Under a constitution approved in 1967, Bermuda was granted the right of internal self-government in 1968. A British-appointed governor exercises responsibility for external affairs, defense, internal security and police. A premier is appointed by the governor but is responsible to a freely elected 40-member House of Assembly for all internal matters.

In the 9 February 1989 general election the incumbent center-right, multiracial United Bermuda Party (UBP) of Premier John Swan retained control of the House over the left-wing, predominantly black Progressive Labour Party (PLP). The UBP obtained 23 seats, the PLP fifteen, and the National Liberal Party (NLP) and an independent environmentalist, one each. Poverty, race and immigration were the main issues; the question of independence has diminished in importance as most of the electorate has demonstrated its support for the status quo.

A non-binding referendum on the future of capital punishment, held on 28 August 1990, produced a 78.4 percent vote for its retention, on a turnout of less than a third of the 33,330 registered voters. The turnout at general elections is usually around 70 percent. The decision to hold the referendum was taken by the House of Assembly in 1989, after a tied vote on a motion to abolish the death penalty. The last executions were in December 1977. Capital punishment is limited to cases of premeditated murder.

Bermudians enjoy all civil rights common to the homeland. There are several newspapers, all privately owned. There are over half a dozen radio stations and two television stations. Labor unions, the largest being the 6,000-member Bermuda Industrial Union, are well organized. The right to strike is recognized by law and in practice.

British Virgin Islands

Polity: Appointed governor and elected council
Economy: Mixed statist
Population: 14,000
Ethnic Groups: Relatively homogeneous with black majority

Political Rights: 2
Civil Liberties: 1
Status: Free

Overview:

The 1977 constitution granted the government of the British Virgin Islands greater responsibility over internal affairs. A British-appointed governor retains responsibility for external affairs, civil service, defense and internal security. On other matters the governor acts on the advice of the Executive Council whose members are the governor, the chief minister, four members of the legislature and the attorney general. The chief minister, representing the majority party in the elected nine-member Legislative Council, is appointed by the governor.

The 1986 Legislative Council elections were won by the Virgin Islands Party (VIP) headed by the chief minister H. Lavity Stoutt. In October 1990 the legislature was dissolved and campaigning began for new elections. A total of 36 candidates were announced by the ruling VIP, the People's Progressive Democratic Party, and the British Virgin Islands United Party, as well as independents. On 12 November 1990, Stoutt was re-elected to a second term as the VIP won six of nine legislative seats.

Residents enjoy all civil liberties common to the homeland. There is one weekly newspaper, one radio station and one television station.

Cayman Islands

Polity: Appointed governor and mostly elected assembly
Economy: Capitalist
Population: 25,800
Ethnic Groups: Mixed (40 percent), Caucasian (20 percent), black (20 percent), various ethnic groups (20 percent)

Political Rights: 2
Civil Liberties: 1
Status: Free

Overview:

Previously governed from Jamaica, the Cayman Islands were placed under a British administration in 1962. A British-appointed governor is assisted by an Executive Council and a Legislative Assembly, over which he presides. The Council consists of seven members, four of whom are elected. The Assembly consists of three members appointed by the governor and twelve elected members, with a new Assembly elected every four years.

In September 1990 the United Kingdom agreed to a request by the Legislative Assembly for a review of the 1972 constitution. A review was conducted in 1991 by a team appointed by the Foreign and Commonwealth Office and a report released in June. The main recommendations were for establishing the post of chief minister to head the Legislative Assembly; increasing the number of elected Assembly members from twelve to fifteen; increasing the number of elected members on the Executive Council from four to five; and including a bill of rights in the constitution. By the end of 1991, debate over the recommendations continued. The enactment of any of the changes would require a majority vote in the Assembly and approval by the Foreign and Commonwealth office in London.

In August the Progressive Democratic Party, the first political party to be formed since the collapse of party politics in the 1960s, was launched by Assembly member McKeeva Bush.

Residents enjoy all civil liberties common to the homeland. There is one daily newspaper and at least one weekly publication. There is at least one radio and one television station.

Channel Islands

Polity: Appointed executives and legislatures (varies by island)
Economy: Capitalist
Population: 139,000
Ethnic Groups: British, Norman French

Political Rights: 2
Civil Liberties: 1
Status: Free

Overview:

The Channel Islands are located in the English Channel. The territories included are the islands of Jersey and Guernsey and their dependencies. Surviving fragments of the medieval Duchy of Normandy, the islands are Crown fiefdoms. They are connected to Britain through the person of the monarch. The Queen appoints her representatives, who are called lieutenant governors and commanders-in-chief. British laws do not apply unless the parliamentary legislation specifies that they do or unless the British Privy Council extends coverage of the laws to the islands. Under an ancient practice called doleance, islanders can make certain legal appeals directly to the Privy Council. In Jersey and Guernsey the appointed bailiffs preside over the royal courts and legislatures. Jersey's legislature, the States, is elected directly by universal suffrage. Guernsey's legislature, the States of Deliberation, has a mixture of directly and indirectly elected members. Two of Guernsey's dependencies, Alderney and Sark, have local legislatures, the States of Alderney and the Chief Pleas of Sark. Sark also has a hereditary head. There are two representatives of Alderney in the States of Guernsey. Residents speak either English, French, or Norman French. Farming and tourism are major industries. There was a controversy in late 1990 when the association controlling the main public hall in Guernsey refused to stage a play showing how the island's leaders helped send three Jewish women to their deaths during World War II.

Falkland Islands

Polity: Appointed governor and partly elected legislative council
Economy: Capitalist-statist
Population: 2,121
Ethnic Groups: British

Political Rights: 2
Civil Liberties: 1
Status: Free

Overview:

British and Argentine announcements about oil exploration, and a bilateral fishing agreement were the major developments in 1991.

Britain opened the waters around the islands for oil exploration, and Argentina issued a decree claiming its continental shelf, including the Falklands, for commercial development. The issue of these conflicting sovereignty claims remains unsettled, but future negotiations are possible. Early in 1991, the two countries reached a fishing agreement to control squid fishing in the surrounding waters and to designate boundaries for each country's fishing rights. Since February 1990, the United Kingdom and Argentina have had diplomatic relations and have attempted to relax tensions around the Falkland Islands.

Englishmen landed on these islands for the first time in 1610. Spain and Britain clashed over ownership of the Falklands in the eighteenth century. Argentina claimed the territory in 1820, but Britain rejected that. Britain and Argentina negotiated over the Falklands' status in the 1960s and 1970s, but never reached agreement. In 1982, Argentina's military government decided to invade and seize control of the islands. Britain defeated Argentina after several weeks of fighting.

Britain appoints a governor to represent the Queen. A chief executive assists in administering the islands. The Legislative Council consists of six members elected by the people, the chief executive, and the financial secretary. The latter two officials, nominees of the governor, and two nominees of the Legislative council form an Executive Council. There are two newspapers, one of them government-published. The public Falkland Islands Broadcasting Service operates two radio stations. Sheep and marine life provide the bases of the local economy.

Gibraltar

Polity: Appointed governor and mostly elected assembly
Economy: Capitalist-statist
Population: 31,000
Ethnic Groups: Italian, English, Maltese, Portuguese, and Spanish

Political Rights: 1
Civil Liberties: 1
Status: Free

Overview:

Located at the southern tip of the Iberian peninsula, Gibraltar came under British control in 1704 after the War of the Spanish Succession. Due to its strategic location between the Atlantic and the Mediterranean, Gibraltar has served as a key British naval base. Spain still claims sovereignty over the territory, but Britain and Spain have reached agreements to ease their earlier tensions over the area. In 1990, the two countries announced closer cooperation in civil aviation and agreed to extend a 1985 extradition treaty and a 1989 anti-drug agreement. However, Spain refused to sign a European Community border treaty by 1 January 1992. Madrid argued the treaty would have implicitly recognized Gibraltar's status as a British possession.

The colony gained a measure of self-government in 1964. In 1967 the majority of Gibraltarians voted for continued British rule. A new constitution in 1969 established the assembly. Anglo-Spanish relations worsened in 1969 when Britain refused to accept a U.N. deadline for decolonization. Spain cut off land links with Gibraltar, in order to press its claim against the British. The two governments began negotiating in 1982, but postponed talks as a result of the Falklands War. They normalized relations and Spain lifted the land link embargo in 1984.

Britain appoints a territorial governor. A Council of Ministers advises him. The Council consists of four ex officio members and five elected members of the legislature, the House of Assembly. The Assembly has fifteen directly elected members, two ex officio members, and an appointed speaker. The House has been responsible for most domestic affairs since 1969. Britain is responsible for defense and foreign affairs. In the legislative election of 1988, the Socialist Labour Party, led by Joe Bossano, won eight seats. The Gibraltar Labour Party/Association for the Advancement of Civil Rights (AACR), led by Adolfo Canepa, won seven seats. A former AACR member, Peter Montegritto, has formed a separate Gibraltar Social Democratic Party (GSD) since the national election. The GSD calls for representation by Gibraltar in negotiations on the future of the colony by Spain and Britain. On 16 May 1991, the GSD won a by-election for a seat in the House of Assembly, defeating an AACR candidate. Bossano sees complete independence as the ideal solution for Gibraltar. He fears that British troop reductions in Gibraltar may lead to Spanish sovereignty. Association is free. There are seven newspapers and a public broadcasting corporation.

Hong Kong

Polity: Colonial appointed governor and partly elected legislature
Economy: Capitalist
Population: 5,900,000
Ethnic Groups: Chinese (98 percent)

Political Rights: 4
Civil Liberties: 3
Status: Partly Free

Overview:

In 1991 major issues in this British crown colony on the South China Sea included ongoing friction between Britain and China, which is to take control of Hong Kong in 1997, over the right to build a new airport; the first direct elections to the Legislative Council (Legco); and the forced repatriation of thousands of Vietnamese boat people.

The airport controversy marked a political struggle between the British administration under Governor Sir David Wilson and Beijing over which side had ultimate decision-making power in the interim before 1997. The 1984 joint declaration on the transfer of power called for democracy and autonomy before the transfer, and China guaranteed that after 1997 "Hong Kong people would rule Hong Kong" through an elected legislature and enjoy autonomy except in defense and foreign affairs.

In January 1991 China and Britain remained at loggerheads over plans to build the airport and transportation infrastructure at a cost of $16.3 billion. China complained they had not been consulted in the planning, and that the project was an attempt by Britain to empty colony coffers before the takeover. Beijing wanted assurances it would inherit a substantial portion of the prosperous colony's estimated $75-billion in fiscal reserves.

In April, British Foreign Secretary Douglas Hurd consulted with Chinese Prime Minister Li Peng in Beijing, but they could not reach an agreement. In July, Britain and China announced a breakthrough in the 18-month dispute. The colony could build the airport, but on condition that China gain even more influence over Hong Kong's affairs. Britain agreed that China would be formally consulted on all major decisions about the project.

Another major development was the 15 September elections to the 60-member Legco, the colony's law-making body. The Executive Council (Exco), the colony's highest policy-making body, is presided over by the governor, who appoints the 15 members, of whom 10 are from the public sector. An election preview was offered in March elections to 19 district boards that deal with strictly local issues and have little power. The vote included three factions: the pro-business Liberal Democratic Federation (LDF); Beijing-controlled trade unions, education and residents groups; and the pro-democracy United Democrats of Hong Kong (UDHK) under Legco member and prominent attorney Martin Lee, whose group was distrusted by Beijing, which indicated its members have "no place" in Hong Kong's political future.

Only 18 of 60 Legco seats were openly contested. Twenty-one seats were to be indirectly elected by business and professional groups like industry, financial services and accountancy. The remaining seats are filled by three government officials, a vice president and 17 councillors appointed by the governor. The UDHK won 12 of 18 seats contested and called for an appointment to Exco. However, when the governor appointed Exco members on 24 October, no UDHK members were included, presumably to placate the Chinese.

A controversial issue in 1991 was Hong Kong's forced expulsion of most of the 64,000 Vietnamese boat people, a plan criticized by human rights advocates and governments, including the U.S. Hong Kong officials maintained that the Vietnamese were economic migrants not fleeing political repression. Vietnam consistently maintained it would not accept people returned against their will.

On 29 October Vietnam and Britain signed an agreement opening the way for the non-voluntary return of refugees. The following day, refugees at Hong Kong's biggest camp appealed to the United States to stop the repatriation. Violence broke out at several camps. Repatriations began in earnest in November, as authorities dragged 59 men, women and children, many struggling fiercely, onto a chartered plane. Some 28 Vietnamese were forced back on 10 December—International Human Rights Day.

Political Rights and Civil Liberties:

Hong Kong residents cannot change their government democratically. While some seats in the 1991 Legco elections were contested and pro-democracy advocates did well in March council elections, calls for greater democratization before the Chinese takeover have been resisted. Residents had no say in the 1984 British decision to return the colony to China.

In June 1991 Legco approved a Bill of Rights watered down by the government to avoid a public clash with China. Human rights lawyers feared the bill will be scrapped by the Chinese after 1997 because it strengthened the legal basis of civil liberties such as freedom of speech and privacy contained in international covenants on civil and political rights, which China does not recognize. Another human rights issue was the forced detention and subsequent repatriation of Vietnamese boat people.

The draft Basic Law, Hong Kong's post-1997 constitution, contains articles that could restrict freedom of expression. Censorship and self-censorship rose in 1991, as British and Hong Kong officials sought to avoid offending China. The government refused to allow foreign students into Hong Kong for a conference on the Chinese democracy movement. Five UDHK activists were tried under an obscure law prohibiting the public use of a megaphone (their convictions were overturned).

The Chinese Communist Party dominates the Federation of Trade Unions, but independent unions exist. The effective right to collective bargaining, however, does not exist.

Isle of Man

Polity: Appointed executive and elected legislature
Economy: Capitalist
Population: 64,282
Ethnic Groups: Mostly Manx (of mixed Celtic and Scandinavian descent)

Political Rights: 2
Civil Liberties: 1
Status: Free

Overview:

The Isle of Man is located west of Britain in the Irish Sea. Like the Channel Islands, it is a crown fiefdom, tied to Britain through the monarch. The queen appoints an executive, the lieutenant governor. The Court of Tynwald is the bicameral legislature. Claiming to be the world's oldest functioning legislature, it consists of a twelve-member Legislative Council, of which the lieutenant governor is a member, and an elected twenty-four-member House of Keys. For most matters, the two houses sit in joint session. Two members of the Legislative Council and five members of the House form an executive council. The Isle has its own laws. Acts of the British Parliament apply to Man only if they state so specifically.

The major issue in 1991 was the government's announced reduction in the tax rate on the fees earned by fund management companies from twenty to five percent effective April 1992. The island is attempting to become Europe's leading offshore funds center. In 1990 the government proposed legalizing homosexual acts. Britain's acceptance of the European Human Rights Convention on behalf of its territories had put the island in breach of continental rights standards on this issue. The island is the only European territory of the U.K. where people do not have the right of individual petition to the convention. Some supporters of Manx autonomy opposed the homosexual reform measure, because they feared it would jeopardize the territory's special legal status. The Isle of Man owes its success as a tax haven to its freedom from British tax laws. Manx economic interests feared that the homosexual reform would set a precedent that would undermine the island's ability to write its own tax laws, but the change in the fund management tax in 1991 suggested otherwise.

Montserrat

Polity: Appointed governor and partly elected council
Economy: Capitalist
Population: 12,700
Ethnic Groups: Mostly black with European minority

Political Rights: 2
Civil Liberties: 1
Status: Free

Overview:

A British-appointed governor presides over an appointed Executive Council. Local legislative matters are the responsibility of an eleven-member Legislative Council. Of the eleven members, who serve five-year terms, seven are directly elected, two are official members, and two are nominated. The chief minister is the leader of the majority party in the Council.

In the 25 August 1987 Council elections, the People's Liberation Movement

(PLM) headed by incumbent chief minister John Osborne retained its four-seat majority.

David Brandt, a founder of the National Development Party (NDP), which held two seats in the Council, resigned in early September 1989 after accusations of involvement in the 1989 offshore banking scandal. The scandal also caused friction between chief minister Osborne and governor Christopher Turner. Osborne accused Turner of overstepping legal bounds by ordering police to raid one of the banks involved.

In December 1989 negotiations in London between Osborne and the British government led to an agreement on a new constitution. The new constitution, which was instituted on 13 February 1990, consolidates the provisions of the Montserrat Letters Patent of 1959 and other legislation, and adds a statement on the fundamental rights and freedoms of the individual. On disputed matters, Osborne agreed that the chief minister would relinquish to the governor responsibility for international financial affairs, as proposed by the British government in the wake of the banking scandal. In exchange, the British government agreed to add a provision recognizing Montserrat's right to self-determination, and to eliminate the governor's power to overrule the Legislative Council on certain types of legislation.

In April 1990, Turner ended his three-year term as governor and was replaced by David George Pendleton Taylor.

In elections held on 10 October 1991, Osborne and the PLM were swept out of office after thirteen years by the newly formed National Progressive Party (NPP) which won four of seven legislative seats. The PLM won one seat, the NDP one seat, and the last seat was taken by an independent. NPP leader Ryeben Meade, a 37-year-old former civil servant, was named chief minister.

Residents enjoy all civil liberties common to the homeland. There are at least two newspapers, including the opposition Montserrat Reporter, several radio stations and one television station. Labor unions are well organized and the right to strike is recognized by law and in practice.

Northern Ireland

Polity: British administration and elected local councils (military-occupied)
Economy: Mixed capitalist
Population: 1,670,000
Ethnic Groups: Protestants, Catholics

Political Rights: 3
Civil Liberties: 3
Status: Partly Free

Overview:

Major developments in 1991 included failed peace talks and rising levels of violence.

Northern Ireland consists of six of the nine counties of the Irish province of Ulster. At the insistence of the locally dominant Protestants, these counties remained within the United Kingdom after the other 26 largely Catholic Irish counties gained home rule in 1921. Protestants comprise over 60% of the general population, but Catholics form a majority of the youth under age fifteen. Generally, Protestants favor continued political union with Britain and thus have the political labels "Loyalist" and "Unionist," while the "Nationalist" or "Republican" Catholic population favors unification with the Republic of Ireland. Britain's Government of Ireland Act (1920), which partitioned Ireland, set up a Northern Irish parliament which functioned until the British imposed direct rule from London in 1972. There was a Northern Ireland Assembly under a Catholic-Protestant power-sharing agreement in 1973-74, but Protestant resistance ended this legislative experiment. The two communities came to no consensus at a constitutional convention in 1975-76 and the convention dissolved. Similarly, voters chose a consultative Northern Ireland Assembly in 1982, but the Nationalists boycotted the body and the British dissolved it in 1986.

Until the late 1960s, electoral regulations favored the economically dominant Protestants by according business property owners voting rights for both their residential and commercial addresses. A non-violent Catholic civil rights movement in the 1960s met with limited success and a violent response from the Protestants. Attempting to impose order in 1969, the British government sent in the army, which originally appealed to some Catholics as a preferable security force to the Protestant-controlled local police. However, Catholics soon viewed the troops as an army of occupation. The violently confrontational situation of the late 1960s and 1970s led to polarizations in both the Unionist and Nationalist communities. There are now several Unionist and Nationalist parties. The most important of these are: the conservative Official Unionist Party, led by James Molyneaux; the hardline Democratic Unionist Party, led by Rev. Ian Paisley; the moderate, pro-Nationalist Social Democratic and Labour Party, led by John Hume; the militant, pro-Nationalist Sinn Fein, led by Gerry Adams; and John Alderdice's moderate Alliance Party, which attempts to combine Protestants and Catholics. Sinn Fein is the political wing of the Irish Republican movement, whose military wing is the Provisional Irish Republican Army (IRA).

In 1990-91 Britain's Secretary of State for Northern Ireland, Peter Brooke, organized preliminary negotiations on Northern Ireland's political future. He planned rounds of talks involving Northern Ireland's political parties (except Sinn Fein) and the British and Irish governments. Sinn Fein's refusal to renounce violence kept it out of the discussions. Brooke hoped to get all sides to agree on a new power-sharing formula. However, the talks bogged down in procedural wrangling early in the year and broke down altogether in July. The Nationalists charged the Unionists with being more interested in scuttling the Anglo-Irish Accord than in agreeing to share power.

Political Rights and Civil Liberties:

The people of Northern Ireland have the right to elect members of the British House of Commons and local government bodies. However, the regional parliament remains suspended. Nationalists argue that they lack the right of self-determination, because Britain has effectively granted the Unionists a veto over the six counties' entrance into a united Ireland. Unionists, on the other hand, insist that the Irish Republic should have no role in governing them; they resent Dublin's consultative role in Northern Ireland under the terms of the 1985 Anglo-Irish Accord. Elections appear to be conducted fairly and allow Sinn Fein to win both parliamentary and local council seats. The situation regarding political rights may change if peace talks succeed at working out a regional power-sharing agreement between Protestants and Catholics.

British law bans broadcast appearances by members or supporters of terrorist organizations. Although there is generally freedom of association, the government has banned the IRA, the Irish National Liberation Army (INLA), the Irish People's Liberation Organization (IPLO), the Ulster Volunteer Force (UVF), the Ulster Freedom Fighters (UFF), and the Red Hand Commandos. The Ulster Defense Association (UDA), a front for the UFF, remains legal, as does Sinn Fein. In 1991 some Nationalists called for the banning of the Loyalist UDA. Reports persist that elements of the security forces share information with Loyalist paramilitaries. Under Britain's military reforms announced in 1991, the Ulster Defense Regiment (UDR) will merge with the Royal Irish Rangers. Unlike the UDR, the Rangers have had a substantial Catholic enlistment.

The traditional British right to trial by jury does not exist for suspected terrorists in Northern Ireland. A judge tries such cases, and there is an extremely high conviction rate. Under the Prevention of Terrorism Act, the security forces may arrest suspects without warrants. The authorities may also prevent suspected terrorists from entering Britain from Northern Ireland and may keep non-natives out of Northern Ireland.

1991 was Northern Ireland's deadliest year since 1982. At least 94 people died in political and sectarian violence. The death toll since the start of "the troubles" in 1969 exceeds 2,900. Violence escalated in the second half of the year after the failed talks. Loyalist death squads increased their activities, causing nearly half the year's terrorist fatalities. In previous years, Republican terrorists had caused a much higher proportion of fatalities. Republican or Nationalist terrorists tend to attack policemen, soldiers, alleged Protestant paramilitaries, and alleged Catholic informers and collaborators. Loyalist or Unionist terrorists usually target alleged IRA members and sympathizers. Both sides often kill innocent, unintended victims. For example, the IRA received international criticism for its bombing of a Belfast hospital's military wing in November 1991. The attack killed two soldiers and wounded several children.

Traditionally, the six counties have had gross inequality of opportunity. The Protestants have discriminated against Catholics throughout the economy. The British Parliament passed the Fair Employment Act of 1989, which set up a commission to monitor employer compliance with anti-discrimination policies. Numerous labor and human rights groups and Irish ethnic organizations around the world have campaigned for the MacBride Principles, a set of standards designed to direct investment only to Northern Irish firms which adopt affirmative action hiring practices. Unemployment is high in general and highest in Catholic ghettoes.

Pitcairn Islands

Polity: Appointed governor and council
Economy: Capitalist-statist
Population: 59
Ethnic Groups: *Bounty* families (Mixed Anglo-Tahitian)

Political Rights: 2
Civil Liberties: 1
Status: Free

Overview:

Located in the South Pacific, the territory consists of Pitcairn and three uninhabited islands. The inhabitants are descended from the *Bounty* mutineers and Tahitian women. In 1990 the island observed the bicentennial of the community's founding. In 1790 mutiny leader Fletcher Christian and his fellow muntineers settled there with a dozen Tahitian women.

The island's major news story in 1990 was the withdrawal of Japan Tuna's trawlers from the colony's waters after a three-year trial. The island had hoped to profit from selling fishing licenses, but the Japanese found the local catch insufficient to justify continuing fishing there. Aside from fishing, the local economy is based on plant life, postage stamp sales, and crafts. Islanders make money by carving orna-ments to sell to passing ships. In 1989, the island's gross income was 958,733 Pitcairn dollars, but the outgo was 923,355 Pitcairn dollars, leaving a surplus of 35,378 Pitcairn dollars.

The appointed governor is the British High Commissioner in New Zealand. Ten residents serve on the Pitcairn Island Council. They include the elected magistrate, Brian Young, and three other elected members; the island secretary; one member appointed by the governor; two members appointed by the elected members; one non-voting member appointed by the governor; and one non-voting member named by the council. The council controls immigration by issuing licenses to land only in rare circumstances. Magistrate Young and his wife visted London in July 1990, and met with Queen Elizabeth at a Buckingham Palace garden party. "We pay no taxes but we all do some form of public works," Young said. Among other tasks, the island's twelve able-bodied men maintain 17.5 miles of mud roads. Local law forbids public displays of affection. The islanders are Seventh-Day Adventists, and observe a strict Sabbath on Saturdays.

St. Helena and Dependencies

Polity: Appointed governor and elected council
Economy: Capitalist statist
Population: 4
Ethnic Groups: British, Asian Africa

Political Rights: 2
Civil Liberties: 1
Status: Free

Overview:

St. Helena, Ascension Island, and the Tristan da Cunha island group are scattered across the South Atlantic between Africa and South America. The British governor administers the islands with an executive council of two *ex officio* members and the chairmen of the council committees. Residents elect a twelve-member Legislative Council for a four-year term. The Legislative council started in 1967. Political parties are legal, and took part in earlier elections, but have become inactive. Tristan da Cunha and Ascension have appointed administrators who are responsible to the governor of St. Helena. Advisory councils assist them. The Ascension advisory council includes representatives of the BBC, South Atlantic Cable Company, Cable Wireless Ltd., the U.S. National Aeronautics and Space Administration, and the U.S. Air Force, all of which have facilities there. Ascension has no native population. In 1981 the governor appointed a constitutional commission to determine desired constitutional changes, but the commission found too little interest among the population to draw any conclu-sions. The island economies are dominated by British and American bases. There are also local fishing, timber, craft, and agricultural industries. The colony has a government-run broadcasting service and a weekly newspaper. The trade union is the St. Helena General Workers Union.

Turks and Caicos	**Polity:** Appointed governor and elected council **Economy:** Capitalist **Population:** 11,700 **Ethnic Groups:** Relatively homogeneous with black majority	**Political Rights:** 2 **Civil Liberties:** 1 **Status:** Free

Overview: **P**reviously governed from Jamaica, the islands were placed under a British administration in 1962. A constitution adopted in 1976 provides for a governor, an eight-member Executive Council, and a Legislative Council of thirteen elected, four ex-officio, and three nominated members. The chief minister is the leader of the majority party in the Legislative Council.

In 1985, chief minister Norman Saunders of the conservative Progressive National Party (PNP) was arrested in Miami on drug trafficking charges and forced to resign. He was replaced by his deputy Nathaniel Francis, who was forced to resign in 1986 on corruption and patronage charges. The British government then imposed direct rule under the governor and established a commission for making constitutional reforms designed to inhibit corruption.

In the 3 March 1988 elections that marked the return to constitutional rule, the People's Democratic Movement (PDM), formerly in opposition, took nine of eleven seats and Oswald Skippings became chief minister. In the 3 April 1991 elections, the PNP returned to power by winning eight legislative seats to the PDM's five and PNP leader Washington Missick became chief minister.

Residents enjoy all the civil liberties common to the homeland. There are at least one weekly newspaper and several radio stations.

United States of America **American Samoa**	**Polity:** Elected governor and legislature **Economy:** Capitalist **Population:** 41,000 **Ethnic Groups:** Samoan (Polynesian)	**Political Rights:** 1 **Civil Liberties:** 1 **Status:** Free

Overview: **A**merican Samoa is located in the South Pacific. The U.S. had ruled the territory through an appointed governor for most of this century, but Samoans have elected their own governor since 1977. The current Governor is Peter Tali Coleman. The bicameral legislature is called the Fono. It consists of a twenty-member House of Representatives and an eighteen-member Senate. The House is elected by popular vote for two-year terms. The *matai,* the chiefs of extended Samoan families, elect senators from among themselves for four-year terms. Governor Coleman suggested a major constitutional overhaul in 1991, but it is not clear what form this change would take. There are local affiliates of the U.S. Democratic and Republican parties. The territory sends Eni F.H. Faleomaveaga, a non-voting delegate, to the U.S. House of Representatives. Tourism, fishing, and agriculture are major industries. There are free and competing newspapers. There is a private radio station and a government-owned television station.

In 1991, there was a major development over the application of American wage structures to Samoans. There is a special provision for American Samoa in the mainland's federal wage laws. A subminimum wage prevails, subject to periodic review by a six-member, joint Samoan-American commission. Both public and private sector leaders opposed higher minimum wages. Governor Coleman, whose administration is running a deficit, opposed a wage increase on the grounds that higher pay for government workers would have meant a higher deficit, higher taxes, or layoffs. Congressman Faleomaveaga also opposed higher wages out of the fear that the important tuna industry would have left for a lower-wage country. Most tuna workers are Western Samoan citizens who lack an electoral voice in the territory, so there was little or no political pressure from those workers to raise their pay. The six-member pay panel split evenly, so the minimum wages stayed the same in 1991.

The territory receives $80 million is U.S. grants. There was a dispute in 1991 over the government's switching recreational aid funds to other budgetary purposes. About 500 Samoans served in American forces in the Persian Gulf War.

The United Nations Decolonization Subcommittee on Small Territories held hearings on American Samoa in 1991, but the territory's status remains unchanged.

Guam

Polity: Elected governor and legislature
Economy: Capitalist-statist
Population: 134,000
Ethnic Groups: Guamanian or Chamorro (Micronesian) majority, U.S. mainlanders, Filipinos

Political Rights: 1
Civil Liberties: 1
Status: Free

Overview:

The leading issues on Guam in 1991 were anti-abortion legislation and the territory's political status.

In 1991 a federal district court judge declared Guam's abortion law unconstitutional. The legislation would have prohibited abortion, even in cases involving rape, incest, and fetal abnormality. The only exceptions to the abortion ban would have been situations involving medically certified threats to the mother's life or health.

An unincorporated territory of the U.S., Guam lobbied Washington in 1990-91 for commonwealth status. In 1982 the voters chose commonwealth status, but the U.S. has not passed the required enabling legislation. Guam's Commission on Self-Determination and a federal task force met in 1991 to discuss constitutional issues. The Guamanians want to end the U.S. Congress's theoretical right to abolish the island's constitution. They also want direct access to the federal Supreme Court in any plan for commonwealth. Negotiations went on for months, and opinion polls showed the Guamanian public was worn out by the process. There may be commonwealth enabling legislation in Congress in 1992.

Located west of Hawaii, Guam became American territory as a result of the Spanish-American War in 1898. Guam has a twenty-one member, unicameral legislature elected for two-year terms. Since 1970 the territory has had an elected governor who serves a four-year term. Former two-term, Democratic Governor Ricardo Bordallo, who was found guilty of corruption, killed himself in January 1990. Shortly before his scheduled trip to prison in California, Bordallo chained himself to a statue of an island chief, covered himself with the territorial flag, and shot himself. Despite Bodallo's departure from office in 1987 and his death in 1990, the White House sent him a perfunctory thank-you note in 1991. This letter caused islanders to complain about Washington's ignorance of their situation.

Guam has a nonvoting representative to the U.S. Congress. American bases and U.S. subsidies contribute significantly to the local economy. Tourism declined significantly during the Persian Gulf War. There are free and competitive print and broadcast media.

Northern Marianas

Polity: Elected governor and legislature
Economy: Capitalist
Population: 22,300
Ethnic Groups: Highly diversified populations of Pacific Islanders, Asians, Europeans, and Americans

Political Rights: 1
Civil Liberties: 1
Status: Free

Overview:

Major news stories in 1991 included a debate over representation in Washington, disputes over economic development, and a wage scandal.

Situated west of Hawaii in the Pacific, the Northern Marianas formed part of the former U.S. Trust Territory of the Pacific. The U.N. recognized the end of the trusteeship in 1990. The islands have Commonwealth status, and the residents have U.S. citizenship. The U.S. has responsibility for the islands' defense. The territory has no representation in the U.S. Congress, but in 1991 the Commonwealth's representative in Washington suggested that he should be elected as a non-voting member of Congress. His predecessor favored keeping the appointed status. The directly elected governor serves for four years. The Senate has a four-year term, while the House of Representatives has a two-year term.The Commonwealth government has responsibility for immigration. There is a very high number of Asian workers, possibly a majority of the labor force. Reportedly, many are illegal aliens. In October 1991, the U.S. Department of Labor sued a family on the island of Saipan for underpaying 1,350 Chinese workers. Handicrafts, fishing, tourism, and agriculture are significant industries. Legislators passed a bill making developers pay impact fees to underwrite the cost of the new infrastructure which development requires. However, Governor Lorenzo Deleon Guererro vetoed it. On the island of Tinian, the gambling enforcement division recommended excluding a Japanese firm with alleged ties to organized crime. The company decided to appeal the ruling. There are three competing newspapers, three radio stations, and several cable television channels.

Palau (Belau)

Polity: Elected president and legislature
Economy: Capitalist
Population: 14,390
Ethnic Groups: Palauan (a mixture of Micronesian, Malayan and Melanesian) and mixed Palauan-European-Asian

Political Rights: 1
Civil Liberties: 2
Status: Free

Overview:

Palau (Belau) became part of the U.N. supervised Trust Territory of the Pacific after World War II, and is the only remaining trust territory. The territory took the name of Republic of Palau in 1978. It has tried on many occasions to pass a referendum on a compact of free association with the U.S., but they have all failed to pass with the constitutionally required 75 percent. In the most recent referendum held in February 1990, only 60.5 percent approved a proposed deal with the U.S. Many residents objected to U.S. nuclear storage rights on the island, and expressed fears that the Pentagon would control too much land under the proposed arrangement. The U.S. part of the plan included proposed independence and economic aid. Some voices in Palau have pointed out that independence will not substantially change the political situation on the island chain, while depriving the archipelago of $16 million in annual aid; the standards of living in the Federated States of Micronesia, the Marianas, and the Marshalls have been falling since the trusteeship status of these islands was terminated in December 1990. In 1990 the U.S. Department of the Interior Order No. 3142 outlined an increase in American interference in island affairs, necessitated by reports of corruption and fiscal mismanagement. In 1991 Ibedul (Paramount Chief) Yukata Gibbons of the Council of Chiefs (traditional government, but merely an advisory body under the new constitution) filed a suit against Manuel Lujan, U.S. Secretary of the Interior. Gibbons vaguely outlined objectives include: termination of trusteeship on terms acceptable to Palau, U.S. funds to bring Palau's infrastructure to the level it enjoyed at the height of Japanese activity there, and repeal of Order 3142. He cited the fact that under Japanese occupation Palau had 95 miles of paved road, compared to 9 miles in 1991. Although the chiefs and the governors of Palau's 16 regions backed the suit, neither President Ngiratkel Etpison or the legislature (OEK) supported the suit.

During the unsuccessful attempts to settle its constitutional arrangements, two of Palau's presidents have died, and the territory has experienced some political violence. President Remelii was assassinated in 1985, and President Salii killed himself in 1988, apparently over a bribery scandal involving a power company. A U.S. High Commissioner is technically still in charge of administration, but the directly elected president exercises effective power.

Palau is very clannish and traditional. Historically, the main chief was selected by the highest ranking woman, the *Bilung*, and behind the scenes women held real power on the islands, although their influence has dwindled since the implementation of the

Constitution. Social rank depends on the family's standing in the home village. Non-Palauan citizens and firms may not own land, but leases are available. Tourism, fishing, and agriculture are the major industries. The only newspaper is government-owned.

Puerto Rico

Polity: Elected governor and legislature
Economy: Capitalist
Population: 3,289,000
Ethnic Groups: Relatively homogeneous, Hispanic

Political Rights: 1
Civil Liberties: 1
Status: Free

Overview:

Following approval by plebiscite, Puerto Rico acquired the status of a commonwealth in free association with the U.S. in 1952. Under its terms, Puerto Rico exercises approximately the same control over its internal affairs as do the fifty U.S. states. Residents, though U.S. citizens, do not vote in presidential election and are represented in the U.S. Congress only by a delegate to the House of Representatives who can vote in committee but not on the floor.

The Commonwealth constitution, modeled on that of the The Commonwealth constitution, modeled on that of the U.S., provides for a governor and a bicameral Legislature, consisting of a 27-member Senate and a 50-member House of Representatives, directly elected for four-year terms. An appointed Supreme Court heads an independent judiciary; the legal system is based on U.S. law.

The fundamental issue of the island's politics remains Puerto Rico's relationship with the U.S. In a 1967 plebiscite, 60.4 percent opted for continued commonwealth status, 39 percent for statehood, and 0.6 percent for independence. The Popular Democratic party (PDP) led by Rafael Hernandez Colon, the current governor, supports continued commonwealth status. The New Progressive party (PNP) led by Pedro Rosello is pro-statehood. The social democratic Puerto Rican Independence party (PIP) led by Ruben Berrios is pro-independence, as is the Marxist Puerto Rican Socialist Party (PSP). The armed activities of two far-left separatist groups, the Armed Forces for National Liberation (FALN) and the Boricua Popular Army (also known as the Macheteros), have diminished substantially in recent years.

At the request of the PDP, the PNP, and the PIP, both the U.S. Senate and House of Representatives in 1989 began working on bills for a new status vote tentatively scheduled for 1991, a year before the scheduled 1992 general elections. By mid-1990, the Senate had chosen a one-step process, drafting a detailed plan that would become self-executing after the voters speak. The House, however, decided for a two-step process that would give Congress a second chance to review the issue and spell out details of whatever option, broadly defined, the voters select.

In early 1991, however, the U.S. Congress failed to resolve the substantial differences between the House and Senate bills, with many legislators balking because of the projected difficulty in absorbing Puerto Rico as the 51st state in the event Puerto Rican voters chose the statehood option.

In September, Governor Hernandez, backed by the PIP, authorized a referendum designed to pressure the U.S. Congress to re-address the status issue and strengthen the commonwealth option as well. A key clause in the proposal would have blocked any future yes or no vote on statehood. But Hernandez was rebuked on 8 December 1991 when Puerto Rican voters rejected, by 53 to 45 percent, the complex measure designed to strengthen the island's political sovereignty. During the campaign, commonwealth proponents tried to exploit anger at the U.S. Congress's failure to deliver on promises to hold a status plebiscite in 1991. However, statehood supporters won the day with an exaggerated argument that approval could have meant the loss of U.S. citizenship and welfare benefits.

In recent years, polls consistently have shown voters almost evenly divided between staying a commonwealth and becoming a state, with less than ten percent favoring independence. But the December referendum suggested a tilt toward statehood and seemed to auger trouble for the PDP in the 1992 gubernatorial election.

As U.S. citizens, Puerto Ricans enjoy all civil liberties granted in the U.S. The press and broadcast media are well developed, highly varied, uncensored and critical.

United States Virgin Islands

Polity: Elected governor and senate
Economy: Capitalist
Population: 3,289,000
Ethnic Groups: Approximately two-thirds black with one-quarter of Puerto Rican descent

Political Rights: 1
Civil Liberties: 1
Status: Free

Overview:

The U.S. Virgin Islands, consisting of St. Croix, St. Thomas, St. John and four dozen smaller islands, are governed as an unincorporated territory of the U.S. The inhabitants were made U.S. citizens in 1927 and granted a considerable measure of self-government in 1954. Since 1970, executive authority has resided in a governor and lieutenant governor directly elected for a four-year term. There is also a unicameral fifteen-member Senate elected for two years; each of the three main islands are proportionately represented. Since 1973 the territory has sent one non-voting delegate to the U.S. House of Representatives.

In September 1989, the islands were ravaged by Hurricane Hugo, with St. Croix the hardest hit. After looting broke out, President Bush ordered U.S. troops and federal marshals onto St. Croix for twenty days to keep order. Governor Alexander Farrelly of the Democratic Party was criticized in some quarters for his handling of the crisis. Nonetheless, in November 1990, he scored a landslide victory over his main challenger, former governor Juan Luis, to secure a second term. The other main political party is the Independent Citizens' Movement.

As U.S. citizens, island residents enjoy all civil liberties granted in the U.S. There are at least two newspapers and several radio and television stations.

Tables and Ratings

Table of Independent Countries
Comparative Measures of Freedom

Country	PR	CL	Freedom Rating	Country	PR	CL	Freedom Rating	Country	PR	CL	Freedom Rating
Afghanistan	7	7	Not Free	Cuba	7	7	Not Free	Japan	1	2▼	Free
↑Albania	4▲	4▲	Partly Free	Cyprus (G)	1	1	Free	↑Jordan	4▲	4▲	Partly Free
Algeria	4	4	Partly Free	Cyprus (T)	2	2	Free	○Kazakhstan	5	4	Partly Free
↑Angola	6▲	4▲	Partly Free	Czechoslovakia	2	2	Free	Kenya	6	6	Not Free
Antigua and Barbuda	3	3▼	Partly Free	Denmark	1	1	Free	○Kyrgyzstan (Kirgizia)	5	4	Partly Free
↓Argentina	1	3	Free	Djibouti	6	5	Not Free	Kiribati	1	2	Free
○Armenia	5	5	Partly Free	Dominica	2	1	Free	Korea, North	7	7	Not Free
Australia	1	1	Free	↓Dominican Republic	2	3	Free	Korea, South	2	3	Free
Austria	1	1	Free	Ecuador	2	3▼	Free	Kuwait	6▲	5▲	Not Free
○Azerbaijan	5	5	Partly Free	↓Egypt	5	5▼	Partly Free	Laos	6	7	Not Free
Bahamas	2	3	Free	El Salvador	3	4	Partly Free	○Latvia	2	3	Free
Bahrain	6	5	Partly Free	Equatorial Guinea	7	7	Not Free	↑Lebanon	6	4▲	Partly Free
Bangladesh	2▲	3▲	Free	○Estonia	2	3	Free	↑Lesotho	6	4▲	Partly Free
Barbados	1	1	Free	Ethiopia	6▲	5▲	Partly Free	Liberia	7	6▲	Not Free
○Belarus (Byelorrussia)	4	4	Partly Free	Fiji	6	4	Partly Free	Libya	7	7	Not Free
Belgium	1	1	Free	Finland	1	1	Free	○Lithuania	2	3	Free
Belize	1	1▲	Free	↓France	1	2	Free	Luxembourg	1	1	Free
Benin	2▲	3▲	Free	Gabon	4	3▲	Partly Free	Madagascar	4	4	Partly Free
Bhutan	6	5	Partly Free	The Gambia	2	2	Free	Malawi	7	6	Not Free
Bolivia	2	3	Free	○Georgia	6	5	Not Free	Malaysia	5	4	Partly Free
Botswana	1	2	Free	↓Germany	1	2	Free	Maldives	6	5	Not Free
↓Brazil	2	3	Free	Ghana	6	6▼	Not Free	↑Mali	6	4▲	Partly Free
Brunei	6	5	Not Free	Greece	1	2	Free	Malta	1	1	Free
↑Bulgaria	2▲	3▲	Free	Grenada	1▲	2	Free	○Marshall Islands	1	1	Free
Burkina Faso	6	5	Not Free	Guatemala	3	5▼	Partly Free	Mauritania	7	6	Not Free
Burma (Myanmar)	7	7	Not Free	Guinea	6	5	Not Free	Mauritius	1▲	2	Free
Burundi	7	6	Not Free	↑Guinea-Bissau	6	5	Partly Free	Mexico	4	4	Partly Free
↑Cambodia	6▲	6▲	Not Free	Guyana	5	4	Partly Free	○Micronesia	1	1	Free
Cameroon	6	6	Not Free	Haiti	7▼	7▼	Not Free	○Moldova (Moldavia)	5	4	Partly Free
Canada	1	1	Free	Honduras	2	3	Free	Mongolia	2▲	3▲	Free
Cape Verde	2▲	3▲	Free	Hungary	2	2	Free	Morocco	5▼	5▼	Partly Free
Central African Republic	6	5	Partly Free	Iceland	1	1	Free	Mozambique	6	4▲	Partly Free
Chad	6▲	6	Not Free	India	3▼	4▼	Partly Free	Namibia	2	3	Free
Chile	2	2	Free	Indonesia	6	5	Partly Free	Nauru	1	2	Free
China (P.R.C.)	7	7	Not Free	Iran	6	5	Not Free	Nepal	2▲	3▲	Free
Colombia	2▲	4	Partly Free	Iraq	7	7	Not Free	Netherlands	1	1	Free
↑Comoros	4▲	3▲	Partly Free	Ireland	1	1	Free	New Zealand	1	1	Free
Congo	6	4▲	Partly Free	Israel	2	2	Free	↓Nicaragua	3	3	Partly Free
Costa Rica	1	1	Free	Italy	1	1	Free	↑Niger	6	5	Partly Free
Croatia	3	4	Partly Free	Ivory Coast	6	4	Partly Free	Nigeria	5	4▲	Partly Free
				Jamaica	2	2	Free	Norway	1	1	Free
								Oman	6	6	Not Free

Table of Independent Countries
Comparative Measures of Freedom

Country	PR	CL	Freedom Rating	Country	PR	CL	Freedom Rating	Country	PR	CL	Freedom Rating
Pakistan	4	5▾	Partly Free	Sierra Leone	6	5	Partly Free	↓Tunisia	5	5▾	Partly Free
Panama	4	2	Partly Free	Singapore	4	4	Partly Free	Turkey	2	4	Partly Free
Papua New Guinea	2	3	Free	Slovenia	2	3	Free	○Turkmenia (Turkmenistan)	6	5	Partly Free
Paraguay	3▲	3	Partly Free	Solomon Islands	1	1	Free	Tuvalu	1	1	Free
Peru	3	5▾	Partly Free	Somalia	7	7	Not Free	Uganda	6	6▾	Not Free
Philippines	3	3	Partly Free	South Africa	5	4	Partly Free	○Ukraine	3	3	Partly Free
Poland	2	2	Free	Spain	1	1	Free	United Arab Emirates	6	5	Not Free
Portugal	1	1▲	Free	Sri Lanka	4	5	Partly Free	United Kingdom	1	2	Free
Qatar	7	5	Not Free	Sudan	7	7	Not Free	United States	1	1	Free
Romania	5▲	5	Partly Free	*Suriname	4	4▾	Partly Free	Uruguay	1	2	Free
○Russia	3	3	Partly Free	Swaziland	6	5	Partly Free	○Uzbekistan	6	5	Partly Free
Rwanda	6	6	Not Free	Sweden	1	1	Free	↑Vanuatu	2	3	Free
St. Christopher and Nevis	1	1	Free	Switzerland	1	1	Free	↓Venezuela	1	3	Free
St. Lucia	1	2	Free	Syria	7	7	Not Free	Vietnam	7	7	Not Free
St. Vincent and the Grenadines	1	2	Free	○Tajikstan	5	5	Partly Free	Western Samoa	2	2	Free
Sao Tome and Principe	2▲	3▲	Free	↑Taiwan (Rep. of China)	3	3	Partly Free	Yemen	6	5	Partly Free
Saudi Arabia	7	6	Not Free	↑Tanzania	6	5	Not Free	Yugoslavia	6▾	5▾	Not Free
Senegal	4	3	Partly Free	Thailand	6▾	4▾	Partly Free	Zaire	6	5▲	Not Free
Seychelles	6	6	Not Free	Togo	6	5▲	Not Free	Zambia	2▲	3▲	Free
				Tonga	3	3	Partly Free	Zimbabwe	5▲	4	Partly Free
				Trinidad and Tobago	1	1	Free				

↑↓ Arrows up or down indicate a general trend in freedom. PR and CL stand for Political Rights and Civil Liberties. 1 represents the most free and 7 the least free category.

▲▾ Triangles up or down indicate a change in Political Rights or Civil Liberties since the last survey. The Freedom Rating is an overall judgment based on *Survey* results. See the "Methodological Essay" for more details. The table does not indicate changes made for purely methodological reasons since last year.

○ New as a country in this *Survey*.

* Moved from 4,3 to 6,4 to 4,4 within the year.

Table of Related Territories
Comparative Measures of Freedom

Country & Territory	PR	CL	Freedom Rating
Australia			
Christmas Island	3	2	Free
Cocos (Keeling) Islands	1	2	Free
Norfolk Island	2	1	Free
Chile			
Rapanui (Easter Island)	3	2	Free
China			
Tibet	7	7	Not Free
Denmark			
Faeroe Islands	1	1	Free
Greenland	1	1	Free
Ethiopia			
* Eritrea	6	6	Not Free
France			
French Guiana	2	2	Free
French Polynesia	2	2	Free
French Southern and Antarctic Territories	3	1	Free
Guadeloupe	2	2	Free
Martinique	2	1	Free
Mayotte (Mahore)	2	2	Free
Monaco	3	1	Free
New Caledonia	2	2	Free
Reunion	2	2	Free
St. Pierre and Miquelon	2	2	Free
Wallis and Futuna Islands	3	2	Free
France-Spain Condominium			
Andorra	2	1	Free

Country & Territory	PR	CL	Freedom Rating
India			
Kashmir	6	6▼	Not Free
Indonesia			
East Timor	7	7▼	Not Free
Irian Jaya	7	6	Not Free
Israel			
Occupied Territories	6	6	Not Free
Italy			
San Marino	1	1	Free
Morocco			
Western Sahara	6▼	5▼	Partly Free
Netherlands			
Aruba	1	1	Free
Netherlands Antilles	1	1	Free
New Zealand			
Cook Islands	2	2	Free
Niue	2	2	Free
Tokelau	2	2	Free
Portugal			
Azores	1	1▲	Free
Macao	3	3	Partly Free
Madeira	1	1▲	Free
South Africa			
Bophutatswana	6	5	Not Free
Ciskei	6	5	Not Free
Transkei	6	5	Not Free
Venda	7	5	Not Free
Spain			
Canary Islands	1	1	Free
Ceuta	2	1	Free

Country & Territory	PR	CL	Freedom Rating
Melilla	2	1	Free
Switzerland			
Liechtenstein	1	1	Free
United Kingdom			
Anguilla	1	1	Free
Bermuda	1	1	Free
British Virgin Islands	2	1	Free
Cayman Islands	2	1	Free
Channel Islands	2	1	Free
Falkland Islands	2	1	Free
Gibraltar	1	1	Free
↑ Hong Kong	4	3	Partly Free
Isle of Man	2	1	Free
Montserrat	2	1	Free
* Northern Ireland	3	3	Partly Free
Pitcairn Islands	2	1	Free
St. Helena and Dependencies	2	1	Free
Turks and Caicos	2	1	Free
United States of America			
American Samoa	1	1	Free
Guam	1	1	Free
Northern Marianas	1	1	Free
Palau (Belau)	1	2	Free
Puerto Rico	1	1	Free
United States Virgin Islands	1	1	Free

* New in this Survey

Table of Social and Economic Comparisons

Country	PPP ($)	Per Capita GNP ($)	Life expectancy	Country	PPP ($)	Per Capita GNP ($)	Life expectancy
Afghanistan	710	200	42.5	Cambodia	na	130	49.7
Albania	na	1,200	72.2	Cameroon	1,670	1,010	53.7
Algeria	2,470	2,360	65.1	Canada	17,680	16,960	77.0
Angola	840	870	45.5	Cape Verde	1,410	680	67.0
Antigua and Barbuda	na	3,690	72.0	Central African Republic	780	380	49.5
Argentina	4,360	2,520	71.0	Chad	510	160	46.5
Armenia	na	na	na	Chile	4,720	1,510	71.8
Australia	14,530	12,340	76.5	China (PRC)	2,470	330	70.1
Austria	12,350	15,470	74.8	Colombia	3,810	1,180	68.8
Azerbaijan	na	na	na	Comoros	na	440	55.0
Bahamas	10,590	10,700	71.5	Congo	2,120	910	53.7
Bahrain	9,490	6,340	71.0	Costa Rica	4,320	1,690	74.9
Bangladesh	720	170	51.8	Croatia	na	na	na
Barbados	6,020	6,010	75.1	Cuba	na	2,000	75.4
Belarus	na	na	na	Cyprus	8,380	6,260	76.2
Belgium	13,010	14,490	75.2	Czechoslovakia	na	5,820	71.8
Belize	na	1,500	69.5	Denmark	13,610	18,450	75.8
Benin	1,050	390	47.0	Djibouti	na	480	48.0
Bhutan	na	180	48.9	Dominica	na	1,680	76.0
Bolivia	1,480	570	54.5	Dominican Republic	2,420	720	66.7
Botswana	2,510	1,010	59.8	Ecuador	2,810	1,120	66.0
Brazil	4,620	2,160	65.6	Egypt	1,930	660	60.3
Brunei	na	15,390	73.5	El Salvador	1,950	940	64.4
Bulgaria	na	4,150	72.6	Equatorial Guinea	na	410	47.0
Burkina Faso	650	210	48.2	Estonia	na	na	na
Burma (Myanmar)	660	200	61.3	Ethiopia	350	120	45.5
Burundi	550	240	48.5				

Notes: Freedom House obtained the figures for purchasing power parities (PPP), per capita GNP, and life expectancy from the U.N.'s *Human Development Report 1991* (Oxford University Press, 1991). PPP's are real GDP per capita figures which economists have adjusted to account for detailed price comparisons of individual items covering over 150 categories of expenditure. In a few cases the U.N. report does not list GNP figures. For these countries, the chart lists GNP or GDP data from the Rand McNally *World Map and Facts* (1990 edition). For countries marked with (GDP) Rand McNally lists no GNP figure. The U.N. life expectancy figures represent overall expectancy, not differentiated by sex. In some cases not covered by the U.N., the chart lists a combined average of male and female life expectancy obtained from Rand McNally. For Kiribati, Taiwan, Tonga and Tuvalu the chart lists these combined averages.

Table of Social and Economic Comparisons

Country	PPP ($)	Per Capita GNP ($)	Life expectancy	Country	PPP ($)	Per Capita GNP ($)	Life expectancy
Fiji	3,610	1,520	64.8	Lebanon	na	880	66.1
Finland	13,980	18,590	75.5	Lesotho	1,390	420	57.3
France	13,590	16,090	76.4	Liberia	890	450	54.2
Gabon	3,960	2,970	52.5	Libya	na	5,420	61.8
Gambia	650	200	44.0	Lithuania	na	na	na
Georgia	na	na	na	Luxembourg	14,290	22,400	74.9
Germany	14,620	16,570	75.2	Madagascar	670	190	54.5
Ghana	970	400	55.0	Malawi	620	170	48.1
Greece	6,440	4,800	76.1	Malaysia	5,070	1,940	70.1
Grenada	na	1,720	71.5	Maldives	na	410	62.5
Guatemala	2,430	900	63.4	Mali	500	230	45.0
Guinea	910	430	43.5	Malta	7,490	5,190	73.4
Guinea-Bissau	670	190	42.5	Marshall Islands	na	na	na
				Mauritania	960	480	47.0
Guyana	1,480	420	64.2	Mauritius	5,320	1,800	69.6
Haiti	970	380	55.7	Mexico	5,320	1,760	69.7
Honduras	1,490	860	64.9	Micronesia	na	na	na
Hungary	5,920	2,460	70.9	Moldova	na	na	na
Iceland	16,820	20,190	77.8	Mongolia	na	880	62.5
India	870	340	59.1	Morocco	2,380	830	62.0
Indonesia	1,820	440	61.5	Mozambique	1,070	100	47.5
Iran	3,560	1,800	66.2	Namibia	na	1,250	57.5
Iraq	3,510	3,020	65.0	Nauru	na	19,512	na
Ireland	7,020	7,750	74.6	Nepal	770	180	52.2
Israel	10,860	8,650	75.9	Netherlands	12,680	14,520	77.2
Italy	13,000	13,330	76.0	New Zealand	11,310	10,000	75.2
Ivory Coast (Cote D'Ivoire)	1,430	770	53.4	Nicaragua	2,660	830	64.8
				Niger	610	300	44.5
Jamaica	2,630	1,070	73.1	Nigeria	1,030	290	51.5
Japan	13,650	21,020	78.6	Norway	13,820	19,990	77.1
Jordan	2,570	1,500	66.9	Oman	9,290	5,000	65.9
Kazakhstan	na	na	na	Pakistan	1,790	350	57.7
Kenya	1,010	370	59.7	Panama	3,790	2,120	72.4
Kirgizia	na	na	na	Papua New Guinea	1,960	810	54.9
Kiribati	na	475 (GDP)	52(a)				
Korea				Paraguay	2,590	1,180	67.1
North	na	1,240	70.4	Peru	3,080	1,300	63.0
South	5,680	3,600	70.1	Philippines	2,170	630	64.2
Kuwait	9,310	13,400	73.4	Poland	4,190	1,860	71.8
Laos	na	180	49.7	Portugal	5,980	3,650	74.0
Latvia	na	na	na	Qatar	na	9,930	69.2

Table of Social and Economic Comparisons

Country	PPP ($)	Per Capita GNP ($)	Life expectancy	Country	PPP ($)	Per Capita GNP ($)	Life expectancy
Romania	na	2,560	70.8	Taiwan (China)	na	3,143 (GDP)	71.5
Russia	na	na	na	Tanzania	570	160	54.0
Rwanda	730	320	49.5	Thailand	3,280	1,000	66.1
St. Christopher-	na	2,630	67.5	Togo	700	370	54.0
Nevis (St.				Tonga	na	647	59.0
Kitts-Nevis)				Trinidad and	4,580	3,350	71.6
St. Lucia	na	1,540	70.5	Tobago			
St. Vincent and	na	1,200	70.0	Tunisia	3,170	1,230	66.7
the Grenadines				Turkey	3,900	1,280	65.1
Sao Tome and	na	490	65.5	Turkmenia	na	na	na
Principe				Tuvalu	na	513	58.5
Saudi Arabia	9,350	6,200	64.5	Uganda	410	280	52.0
Senegal	1,250	650	48.3	Ukraine	na	4,550	70.6
Seychelles	na	3,800	70.0	United Arab	19,440	15,770	70.5
Sierra Leone	1,030	300	42.0	Emirates			
Singapore	10,540	9,070	74.0	United	13,060	12,810	75.7
Slovenia	na	na	na	Kingdom			
Solomon	2,540	630	69.5	United States	19,850	19,840	75.9
Islands				Uruguay	5,790	2,470	72.2
Somalia	1,330	170	46.1	Uzbekistan	na	na	na
South Africa	5,480	2,290	61.7	Vanuatu	na	840	69.5
Spain	8,250	7,740	77.0	Venezuela	5,650	3,250	70.0
Sri Lanka	2,120	420	70.9	Vietnam	na	220	62.7
Sudan	970	480	50.8	Western Samoa	1,870	640	66.5
Suriname	3,830	2,460	69.5	Yemen	na	595	51.5
Swaziland	2,110	810	56.8	Yugoslavia	4,860	2,520	72.6
Sweden	14,940	19,300	77.4	Zaire	430	170	53.0
Switzerland	17,220	27,500	77.4	Zambia	870	290	54.4
Syria	4,460	1,680	66.1	Zimbabwe	1,370	650	59.6
Tajikstan	na	na	na				

Combined Average Ratings—
Independent Countries

FREE

1
Australia
Austria
Barbados
Belgium
Belize
Canada
Costa Rica
Cyprus (G)
Denmark
Finland
Iceland
Ireland
Italy
Luxembourg
Malta
Marshall Islands
Micronesia
Netherlands
New Zealand
Norway
Portugal
St. Christopher-Nevis
   (St. Kitts-Nevis)
Solomon Islands
Spain
Sweden
Switzerland
Trinidad and
   Tobago
Tuvalu
United States
   of America

1.5
Botswana
Dominica
France
Germany
Greece
Grenada
Japan
Kiribati
Mauritius
Nauru
St. Lucia
St. Vincent and
   the Grenadines
United Kingdom
Uruguay

2
Argentina
Chile

Cyprus (T)
Czechoslovakia
The Gambia
Hungary
Israel
Jamaica
Poland
Venezuela
Western Samoa

2.5
Bahamas
Bangladesh
Benin
Bolivia
Brazil
Bulgaria
Cape Verde
Dominican Republic
Ecuador
Estonia
Honduras
Korea, South
Latvia
Lithuania
Mongolia
Namibia
Nepal
Papua New Guinea
Sao Tome and Principe
Slovenia
Vanuatu
Zambia

PARTLY FREE

3
Antigua & Barbuda
Colombia
Nicaragua
Panama
Paraguay
Philippines
Russia
Taiwan (Rep. of China)
Tonga
Turkey
Ukraine

3.5
Comoros
Croatia
El Salvador
Gabon
India
Senegal

4
Albania
Algeria
Belarus (Byelorussia)
Guatemala
Jordan
Madagascar
Mexico
Peru
Singapore
Suriname

4.5
Guyana
Kazakhstan
Kyrgyzstan (Kirgizia)
Malaysia
Moldova (Moldavia)
Nigeria
Pakistan
South Africa
Sri Lanka
Zimbabwe

5
Angola
Azerbaijan
Armenia
Congo
Egypt
Fiji
Ivory Coast (Cote D'Ivoire)
Lebanon
Lesotho
Mali
Morocco
Mozambique
Romania
Tajikstan (Tajikistan)
Thailand
Tunisia

5.5
Bahrain
Bhutan
Central African Republic
Ethiopia
Guinea-Bissau
Indonesia
Niger
Sierra Leone
Swaziland
Turkmenia (Turkmenistan)
Uzbekistan
Yemen

NOT FREE

5.5
Brunei
Burkina Faso
Georgia
Guinea
Iran
Kuwait
Maldives
Tanzania
Togo
United Arab
   Emirates
Yugoslavia
Zaire

6
Cambodia
Cameroon
Chad
Djibouti
Ghana
Kenya
Oman
Qatar
Rwanda
Seychelles
Uganda

6.5
Burundi
Laos
Liberia
Malawi
Mauritania
Saudi Arabia

7
Afghanistan
Burma (Myanmar)
China
Cuba
Equatorial Guinea
Haiti
Iraq
Korea, North
Libya
Somalia
Sudan
Syria
Vietnam

Combined Average Ratings—Related Territories

FREE

1
American Samoa (U.S.)
Anguilla (U.K.)
Aruba (Netherlands)
Azores (Portugal)
Bermuda (U.K.)
Canary Islands (Spain)
Faeroe Islands (Denmark)
Gibraltar (U.K.)
Greenland (Denmark)
Guam (U.S.)
Liechtenstein (Switzerland)
Madeira (Portugal)
Netherlands Antilles (Netherlands)
Northern Marianas (U.S.)
Puerto Rico (U.S.)
San Marino (Italy)
U.S. Virgin Islands (U.S.)

1.5
Andorra (France-Spain)
British Virgin Islands (U.K.)
Cayman Islands (U.K.)
Ceuta (Spain)
Channel Islands (U.K.)
Cocos (Keeling) Islands (Australia)
Falkland Islands (U.K.)
Isle of Man (U.K.)
Martinique (France)
Melilla (Spain)

Montserrat (U.K.)
Norfolk Island (Australia)
Palau (Belau) (U.S.)
Pitcairn Islands (U.K.)
St. Helena and Dependencies (U.K.)
Turks and Caicos (U.K.)

2
Cook Islands (New Zealand)
French Guiana (France)
French Polynesia (France)
French Southern and Antarctic Territories (France)
Guadeloupe (France)
Mayotte (Mahore) (France)
Monaco (France)
New Caledonia (France)
Niue (New Zealand)
Reunion (France)
St. Pierre and Miquelon (France)
Tokelau (New Zealand)

2.5
Christmas Island (Australia)
Rapanui (Easter Island) (Chile)
Wallis and Futuna Islands (France)

PARTLY FREE

3
Northern Ireland (U.K.)
Macao (Portugal)

3.5
Hong Kong (U.K.)

5.5
Western Sahara (Morocco)

NOT FREE

5.5
Bophutatswana (South Africa)
Ciskei (South Africa)
Transkei (South Africa)

6
Eritrea (Ethiopia)
Kashmir (India)
Occupied Territories (Israel)
Venda (South Africa)

6.5
Irian Jaya (Indonesia)

7
East Timor (Indonesia)
Tibet (China)

National Elections and Referenda

Country	Date/Type	Results and Comments
Albania 31 March 1991	legislative (first round)	The Communists won 162 seats out of 250. The Democrats won 65 seats. The Greek Omonia organization won three seats and the pro-Communist Veterans' Committee won one seat. Run-offs were scheduled for 19 districts where no candidate won a majority. The opposition charged that the Communists used vote-rigging and intimidation in rural areas. Election officials assigned voters and their ballots corresponding numbers. Opposition candidates had only limited access to government media. The chairman of the electoral commission was a Communist candidate, but he lost. President Ramiz Alia and other Communists lost in urban districts.
7 April 1991	legislative (second round)	The Communists won 6 of 18 contested seats; the Democrats 10; and the Greek Omonia 2 seats.
14 April 1991	legislative (third round)	The Communists won the last unfilled seat, bringing their total to 169 of 250 seats.
Algeria 27 June 1991	legislative	The government postponed the elections until late 1991 following civil unrest in June 1991.
26 December 1991	rescheduled elections (first round)	The fundamentalist Islamic Salvation Front (FIS) led in the first round of voting for the Algerian parliament. 4,503 candidates from 49 parties and 1,209 independents contested 430 legislative seats. For the 199 seats where no party won outright, the two top finishers from round one were scheduled to contest the run-off in January 1992. The voting was generally peaceful, but there were some irregularities such as the failure of 900,000 of 13 million voter identification cards to reach the electorate. Turnout was 58 percent. Some traditional males may have prevented women in their families from voting. Of the 231 seats decided in round one, the FIS led in 188; the Front for Socialist Forces, 25; the governing National Liberation Front (FLN),15; and independents, 3. Losers filed complaints about alleged procedural errors and other irregularities in numerous districts.
Argentina various dates- August-October 1991	legislative	Legislative elections held in three stages from August to October. The ruling Peronists, officially the Justicialist Party (PJ), increased their total in the 254-seat Chamber of Deputies from 112 to 119 seats. The Radical Party (UCR) fell from 90 to 85 seats, and the Center Democratic Union (UCD) from 11 to 10 seats. The remaining 13 seats were split among three smaller parties.
Armenia 21 September 1991	referendum	Armenians voted by over 99 percent to make the republic an independent, democratic state outside the Soviet Union.
16 October 1991	presidential	President Levon Ter-Petrossyan won with more than 80 percent over a field of opposition candidates.
Azerbaijan 8 September 1991	presidential	President Ayaz Mutalibov won the election overwhelmingly. His supporters helped the only opposing candidate, Zardusht Ali-Zade, a Social Democrat, get enough petitions signed to get on the ballot.
Bangladesh 27 February 1991	general	2,774 candidates from over 90 parties contested 298 seats. The Bangladesh Nationalist Party of Khaleda Zia won 140 seats. An eight-party coalition dominated by the Awami League placed second with 84 seats. Former President H.M. Ershad's Jatiya Party and the Jamaat-e-Islami Party also made strong showings. Two constituencies held elections later. The elected representatives filled another thirty seats reserved for women. The Nationalist Party formed a government with Jamaat-e-Islami support.
15 September 1991	referendum	Voters ratified the reduction in presidential powers and the return to a figurehead president chosen by the parliament.

National Elections and Referenda

Country	Date/Type	Results and Comments
Barbados 22 January 1991	general	Prime Minister Erskine Sandiford's Democratic Labour Party won re-election with 18 of the 28 parliamentary seats. The Barbados Labour Party placed second. The National Democratic Party failed to win a seat.
Belgium 24 November 1991	general	The governing coalition of four Christian Democratic and Socialist parties lost ground to right-wing, anti-immigrant parties and to environmentalists. The coalition lost 14 seats. The anti-immigrant Vlaams Blok (Flemish Block) increased from 10 to 12 seats, and the extreme right National Front won its first parliamentary seat. The French-speaking, environmental Ecolo Party gained 7 seats, and Agalev, the Flemish environmental party, won 7 seats, a gain of one.
Benin 23 February 1991	legislative	The Union for the Triumph of Renewal, which supported interim Prime Minister Soglo, won 12 of 64 parliamentary seats in a multiparty field. No party was capable of winning a majority of seats. The National Party for Democracy and Development placed second with 9 seats. Our Common Cause came in third with 7 seats. Several other parties won the remaining seats.
10 March 1991	presidential (first round)	Interim Prime Minister Nicephore Soglo led President (General) Mathieu Kerekou 37 percent to 26 percent in a thirteen-candidate field. Albert Tevoedjre, former head of the ILO, placed third with 11 percent.
24 March 1991	presidential (second round)	Soglo defeated Kerekou with 67 percent of the vote.
Bulgaria 13 October 1991	general	Several parties contested the 240 parliamentary seats. The anti-Communist Union of Democratic Forces won 110 seats. The Socialist Party (formerly the Communists) took 106 seats. The remaining 24 seats went to the Movement of Rights and Freedoms, a Turkish ethnic party. The voting system allowed no seats to small, anti-Communist parties which won a combined total of 20 percent of the vote. The UDF announced the intention to form a minority government with the support of the Movement of Rights and Freedoms.
Burkina Faso 2 June 1991	referendum	Voters approved a draft constitution which provides for separate executive, legislative, and judicial branches of government. The document also calls for presidential elections every seven years. Of those voting, 93 percent voted "yes," and 7 percent voted "no." Only 1.6 million of the 3.4 million registered voters participated. Incompetent distribution of electoral materials and the planting season kept turnout down.
1 December 1991	presidential	President Blaise Compaore received 86.63 percent of the vote. His opponents had boycotted the contest, on the grounds that there was no transitional government set up to supervise the voting. Only 25 percent of the voters turned out. The opposition complained about bombing attacks on their homes and offices before the election. The National Electoral Organizing Committee reported attacks on 42 polling stations and arrests of 20 people for election day activities. Some major opposition leaders were killed or injured the week after the election.
Burundi 5 February	referendum	Voters approved a new National Unity Charter by a 9-1 margin.
Cape Verde 13 January 1991	parliamentary	In the country's first multi-party election, the Movement for Democracy won 56 of the 79 seats. The Movement defeated the former ruling party, the African Party for the Independence of Cape Verde (PAICV), which won the remaining seats.

National Elections and Referenda

Country	Date/Type	Results and Comments
17 February 1991	presidential	Antonio Mascarenhas defeated President Aristede Pereira with 72 percent of the vote. The Movement for Democracy backed Mascarenhas against the long-time PAICV leader.
Colombia 27 October 1991	legislative	The ruling Liberal Party took 56 of 102 seats in the senate and 86 of 161 seats in the chamber of representatives. Three factions of the divided Conservative Party won a total of 24 seats in the senate and 44 in the lower chamber. The left-wing Democratic Alliance M-19 took nine seats in the senate. For the first time, there were two Senate seats reserved for the Indians. Turnout was only 30 percent. There were terrorist bombings in several locations at the close of the campaign.
Croatia 19 May 1991	referendum	Croatians voted by a 9-1 margin to declare independence from Yugoslavia.
Cyprus (G) 19 May 1991	legislative	The right-wing Democratic Rally (DISI) received 35.8 percent of the vote, and 20 seats in the House of Representatives. The left-wing AKEL won 30.6 percent of the vote and 18 seats. The center-right Democratic Party (DIKO) received 19.5 percent of the vote and 11 seats. The socialist EDEK won 10.9 percent of the vote and 7 seats.
El Salvador 10 March 1991	legislative	The National Assembly, the nation's legislative body, was expanded from 60 to 84 seats in 1991. In the March elections, the ruling ARENA party won 39 seats, the Christian Democrats (PDC) 26 seats, the left-wing Democratic Convergence 8 seats, the right-wing National Reconciliation Party (PCN) nine seats, and the Communists National Democratic Union (UDN) one seat. The electoral council took nearly two weeks to announce the results. International observers criticized various irregularities, and opposition politicians suggested that the government manipulated the results to reduce their seats. However, the polling itself was generally orderly and competitive.
Equatorial Guinea 17 November	referendum (constitutional)	Voters ratified a constitution permitting multi-partyism by a reported 98.78 percent.
Estonia 3 March 1991	poll-pebiscite	Estonians voted for independence from the Soviet Union by a 3-1 margin.
Fiji 1991	general	The interim government cancelled the promised election, claiming the country needed more time to prepare. The new constitution will enshrine native Fijian dominance in politics.
Finland 17 March 1991	general	The Conservatives lost 13 seats, dropping to 40. The moderate Center Party gained 15 seats, rising to 55. The Social Democrats lost 8 seats, falling to 56. The Green Party gained 6 seats, for a total of 10. The Left-wing Alliance, a replacement for the Communists and left-wing Socialists, won 19 seats, a loss of 1. The Rural Party won 7 seats, declining by 2. The Swedish People's Party won 11 seats, a decline of 1. Other parties won the remaining seats. The Conservatives had led a multi-party coalition government.
Georgia 31 March 1991	referendum	Georgians voted by 99 percent to restore their independence.
26 May 1991	presidential	Zviad Gamsakhurdia won the first popular presidential election in Georgia with 87 percent. Several rivals split the rest of the vote. The runner-up, Valerian Advadze, won 6 percent. Critics charged the president with ordering too many curbs on the press. Georgian security forces arrested candidate Advadze's Russian bodyguards.

National Elections and Referenda

Country	Date/Type	Results and Comments
Guatemala 6 January 1991	presidential run-off	Jorge Serrano, a right-wing ally of the former dictator, General Rios Montt, defeated conservative publisher Jorge Carpio by a two-to-one margin in a vote marked by a 55 percent abstention rate.
Guyana 16 December 1991	general	National elections, having been rescheduled for 16 December 1991, were postponed yet again because of the government's failure to carry out a voter registration process acceptable to opposition parties and international observers.
Haiti 20 January 1991	legislative run-off	There was a very low turnout. No party won a clear majority. President Aristide's supporters, the National Front for Change and Democracy (NFCD), won 13 of 27 senate seats and 27 of 83 seats in the assembly.
Iceland 20 April	general	The conservative opposition Independence Party made gains, winning 26 of the 63 seats. It formed a coalition government with the Social Democrats who took 10 seats. The Progressive Party (13 seats) moved into opposition. The left-wing People's Alliance and Women's List hold the remaining 14 seats.
India 20, 23, 26 May (original schedule)	general	The government excluded the provinces of Punjab, Assam, and Jammu and Kashmir from taking part in the election, because there are violent separatist movements there. There was a high level of violence during the campaign and on the first election day. Former Prime Minister Rajiv Gandhi, the leader of the Congress Party, was assassinated. Election officials overturned results in many areas due to irregularities in many of the 204 constituencies voting in the first round. The government postponed the rest of the voting until June.
12, 15, and general 22 June 1991	(continuation of May voting)	115 constituencies voted on 12 June. At least 13 people died in electoral violence. There were several incidents of voting booth capturing and voter intimidation. Thugs stole ballot boxes and dumped them in the Ganges River. A polling official was caught stuffing ballot boxes.186 constituencies were scheduled to vote on 15 June.The campaign was the most violent in Indian history. Of the 511 constituencies contested, the Congress Party won 217 and its allies captured 20. The Hindu nationalist party, Bhaharatiya Janata, placed second with 121 seats. The Janata Dal-National Front coalition and the Left Front coalition controlled a combined 126 seats. Several splinter parties also won seats. Congress formed the government under P.V.N. Rao. The old government had scheduled voting in Punjab for 22 June, but violence caused a postponement. Since Sikh militants assassinated 22 candidates, many other contestants went into hiding out of fear for their lives.
Italy 9-10 June	referendum	Italians voted by a 19-1 margin to reform the system of parliamentary elections. Previously, voters had the option of listing four parliamentary candidates from a particular party in order of preference. With paper ballots, corrupt local officials abused this practice. Under the new system, voters will have the chance to list only one preferred candidate. There was a 62.5 percent turnout.
Kazakhstan 1 December 1991	presidential	Almost 99 percent of the voters backed Nursultan Nazarbayev in this "yes/no" presidential election. Kazakhs living in Moscow, Russia, cast ballots at a polling station there.
Kiribati 8 May 1991	parliamentary	Teatao Teannaki was elected president. The parliament nominates presidential candidates, who are subject to popular election, and who must retain the legislature's confidence.
Kyrgyzstan (Kirgizia) 12 October 1991	presidential	Askar Akayev was re-elected with 95 percent of the vote in this one-candidate election. The opposition coalition, the Democratic Movement, supported Akayev's

National Elections and Referenda

Country	Date/Type	Results and Comments
		candidacy reluctantly, and did not persuade him to dissolve the Communist-dominated parliament to face the voters in the 1991 election.
Latvia 3 March 1991	poll-plebiscite	Latvians voted for independence from the Soviet Union by a 3-1 margin.
Liberia 8 October 1991	general	Postponed until 1992.
Lithuania 9 February 1991	poll-plebiscite	90 percent of Lithuanians voted for independence from the Soviet Union. Despite Soviet intimidation, 84 percent of eligible voters turned out. Turnout was lower in Russian and Polish areas.
Mauritania 12 July 1991	referendum (constitutional)	Black and leftist opposition parties boycotted the vote. There was a poor turnout in Nouakchott. The electors who participated approved a document which endorses multipartyism and cites Islam as a basis for the system. The constitution designates the country "an Arab and African Islamic Republic."
Mauritius 15 September	general	The governing coalition of the Mauritian Socialist Movement and Mauritian Militant Movement won 57 of the 62 seats in parliament. With this mandate, the government announced plans to remove Queen Elizabeth as its head of state and to switch to a republican form of government.
Mexico 18 August 1991	legislative	All 500 deputies and 32 of the 64 senators faced the voters. Opposition parties and international observers charged the ruling PRI with systematic fraud: stolen ballot boxes, unannounced moving of polling places, intimidation of voters, and widespread registration foul-ups. At least 8 percent of citizens could not vote, because the government did not send them registration credentials. Reportedly, PRI supporters voted illegally in many areas. The conservative opposition party, PAN, said the government excluded its poll watchers from voting places in several districts. In the lower house election, the PRI won 61.41 percent of the vote and 320 seats. The PAN won 17.7 percent of the vote and 89 seats. The leftist PRD won 8.27 percent of the vote and 41 seats. The leftist PFCRN took 4.37 percent of the vote and 23 seats. The PARM, a PRI splinter, took 2.14 percent of the vote and 15 seats. The leftist PPS captured 1.8 percent of the vote and 12 seats. In the Senate election, the PRI took 31 seats to 1 for the PAN
Moldova (Moldavia) 10 December 1991	presidential	President Mireca Snegur won with 98 percent in this one-candidate election. Turnout was 83 percent
Nepal 12 May	legislative	Candidates from 47 parties took part in generally free legislative elections. Voters chose 205 members of the lower house of parliament. The centrist Congress Party and a Communist alliance emerged as the leading parties. The government ordered new polling at 37 locations because of vote fraud and violence. Election day violence injured at least 25 people. Campaign violence killed nine people. The Congress Party won 110 seats to 82 for the Communists. Others won 13 seats. Many Congress leaders from the interim government lost their seats. G.P. Koirala (Congress Party) became Prime Minister.
Paraguay 1 December 1991	constitutional convention election	In the election for the 198-member constituent assembly held 1 December 1991, the ruling Colorado Party won 123 seats, the Authentic Radical Liberal Party (PLRA) 57 seats, the Constitution for All movement 16 seats, the social democratic Febrerista Party one seat, and the Christian Democrats one seat.

National Elections and Referenda

Country	Date/Type	Results and Comments
Poland 27 October 1991	legislative	In the contest for the 560-seat Sejm, the lower house of parliament, no party won more than 13 percent of the vote. 7,600 candidates competed. The center-left Democratic Union placed first, followed by the Democratic Left Alliance (the former Communists), the People's (Peasants) Party, Catholic Action, the Center Alliance, the Nationalists, the Liberals, the Solidarity trade union, a small Catholic party, and the Friends of Beer Party, among others. Apathy, bad weather, and a complicated ballot may have caused the mere 40 percent turnout.
Portugal 13 January 1991	presidential	Backed by the governing Social Democrats and the opposition Socialists, former Socialist Prime Minister Mario Soares won reelection to the presidency with 70.43 percent. Finishing second, Basilio Horta (Social Democratic Center) took 14.07 percent. Carlos Carvalhas (Communist) carried 12.92 percent, and Carlos Marques (Popular Democratic Union) received 2.57 percent
6 October 1991	general	With 50.4 percent of the vote, the ruling Social Democrats won a 20-seat majority in the 230-member parliament. The Socialist Party placed second with 29.3 percent. The Communists came in third with 8.8 percent. Eleven other parties received a combined 11.5 percent.
Romania 8 December 1991	referendum	Two-thirds of the voters turned out and 77 percent voted "yes" in this referendum on a new constitution.
Russia 15 June 1991	presidential	In the first Russian popular presidential election, Boris Yeltsin won with 60 percent of the vote. Former Soviet Prime Minister Nikolai Ryzhkov finished second with 10 percent. Vladimir Zhirinovsky, the anti-Semitic leader of the Liberal Democrats, came in third with 6 percent. Other candidates received less than 4 percent each.
Sao Tome and Principe 20 January 1991	legislative	In the country's first free election, the opposition Democratic Convergence Party defeated the governing Movement for the Liberation of Sao Tome and Principe (MLSTP) by a nearly two to one margin. Voters gave the Convergence 33 seats, the MLSTP 21 seats, and the Democratic Coalition 1 seat.
3 March 1991	presidential	Backed by Democratic Convergence, former Prime Minister Miguel Trovoada won without opposition. His two opponents dropped out, charging him with embezzlement in government in 1976. About 20 percent cast spoiled ballots.
Sierra Leone May 1991	legislative	Widespread irregularities in voter registration preceded the vote in this one-party election.
23, 26, 28, and 30 August 1991	referendum	Voters decided by a 3-1 margin to end one-party rule.
Singapore 31 August 1991	general	The ruling People's Action Party won 61 percent of the vote and 77 of 81 parliamentary seats. This represented a slight decline in the PAP's standing from the previous election. The opposition contested only 40 constituencies.
Suriname 25 May 1991	general	In national elections held on 25 May 1991, the New Front for Democracy and Development won 30 of the 51 National Assembly seats, four short of the two-thirds majority required to elect a President. The military-aligned

National Elections and Referenda

Country	Date/Type	Results and Comments

National Democratic Party (NDP) won 12 seats and the Democratic Alternative (DA) coalition won nine seats. The election was relatively free, but there were numerous incidents of intimidation in rural areas.

With neither the NDP nor DA willing to back the New Front's presidential candidate, Ronald Venetiaan, the selection process, as per the constitution, was turned over to the 800-plus People's Councils that also had been elected in May, with the New Front having won a majority in more than 600 of them. On 6 September, 645 councils voted for Venetiaan who was inaugurated as President later in the month.

Sweden
15 September 1991 general

The long-governing Social Democrats lost control of parliament to a collection of non-socialist parties. Five centrist and conservative parties won a combined total of 195 of 349 seats. Four of the five formed a coalition under Carl Bildt, leader of the Moderate Party. The New Democracy Party, a new, sometimes whimsical, libertarian party, won 25 seats, but most traditional non-socialist parties rejected dealing with it.

Switzerland
3 March 1991 referendum

Voters decided by a three to one margin to lower the voting age from 20 to 18.

20 October 1991 general

Backing limits on immigration, the right-wing Auto Party made gains at the expense of the ruling, four-party, center-left, center-right coalition. The center-right Radical Democrats and the centrist Christian Democrats lost seats, but their coalition partners, the Social Democrats and the conservative Swiss People's Party, held their ground. The Greens made gains. The coalition retained control of three-fourths of the seats in the lower house and an overwhelming majority in the upper house.

Syria
2 December 1991 presidential

President Hafez Assad won re-election against no opposition. He received an alleged 99.9 percent of the vote in a "yes/no" election.

Taiwan (Republic of China)
21 December 1991 National Assembly

The ruling Nationalist Party (Kuomintang) won 71.2 percent of the vote and the overwhelming majority of seats in Taiwan's freest legislative election. The chief opposition, the Democratic Progressive Party, finished second with 23.9 percent. Also winning seats, the National Democratic Independent Alliance captured 2.3 percent. The Chinese Social Democrats finished fourth with 2.2 percent, but captured no seats. Combining seats from regional and national lists with places allocated for overseas Chinese, the Nationalists will have 254, the Democratic Progressives 66, and the NDIPA 3 members in the new Assembly. Election officials forbade the printing of the opposition's pro-Taiwan independence sentiments in the official election bulletins. The opposition complained that this prohibition was a restriction on free expression. Some local officials ignored the ban and distributed the illegal bulletins.

Tajikistan
24 November 1991 presidential

Rakhman Nabiyev, leader of the hard-line Communists, won the presidency with 58 percent of the vote. Reformer Davlat Khudonazarov finished second with 30 percent. Filing charges with the election commission, Khudonazarov alleged that Nabiyev won using numerous fraudulent and irregular techniques, such as voting

National Elections and Referenda

Country	Date/Type	Results and Comments
		without identification checks, pro-Nabiyev intimidation, barring of independent and opposition observers from several polling places, and preventing observation of the vote count. There were originally ten candidates. Reports vary, but at least two withdrew on election eve.
Trinidad and Tobago 16 December 1991	general	The People's National Movement (PNM) returned to office by winning 21 of 36 seats in Parliament and PNM leader Patrick Manning became Prime Minister. The left-of-center United National Congress (UNC) led by Basdeo Panday came second with 13 seats. The National Alliance for Reconstruction, led by outgoing prime minister A.N.R. Robinson, won only two seats.
Turkey 20 October 1991	general	The center-right True Path Party led the field with 27 percent in the parliamentary vote. The ruling conservative Motherland Party plunged in popularity, and garnered only 24 percent. The Social Democratic Populist Party came in third, and formed a coalition with True Path. The fundamentalist Islamic Welfare Party and allied right-wing nationalists gained support, and finished a strong fourth. In Turkish Kurdistan, 20 Kurdish nationalists won seats. The Democratic Left Party and other minor parties won the remainder. Some of the small groups backed the new coalition government.
Ukraine 1 December 1991	referendum	Ukrainians voted by a 9-1 margin for independence from the Soviet Union.
1 December 1991	presidential	In their first popular presidential election, Ukrainians elected the incumbent ex-Communist, Leonid Kravchuk, over several opponents, with 61.5 percent of the vote.
USSR 17 March 1991	referendum	Soviets voted on this question: "Do you consider it necessary to preserve the Union of Soviet Socialist Republics as a renewed federation of equal sovereign republics, in which human rights and the freedom of all nationalities will be fully guaranteed?" The referendum passed. Four republics accepted this wording as is: Byelorussia, Kirghizia, Tadzhikistan, and Turkmenistan. Six republics boycotted the referendum: Armenia, Georgia, Moldavia, Lithuania, Latvia, and Estonia. Some regions of Russia also boycotted. The subsequent break-up of the U.S.S.R. made this referendum irrelevant.
Uzbekistan 29 December 1991	referendum	98 percent voted to confirm Uzbek independence from the defunct Soviet Union.
29 December 1991	presidential	President Islam Karimov of the Popular Democratic (formerly Communist) Party was reelected with 86 percent over poet Mohammed Saleh, the Erk Democratic Party candidate. The Birlik (Popular Front) Party wanted to run its chairman, Pulatov, but the party was not registered, so he was disqualified. Earlier in the year, the government had banned the Islamic Renaissance Party.
Vanuatu 2 December 1991	general	The French-speaking Union of Moderate Parties won 19 of the 46 parliamentary seats. It formed a coalition with the National United Party of former Prime Minister Walter Lini. The Melanesian Progressive Party is the main opposition group.
Western Samoa 5 April 1991	general	In the first election with universal suffrage, only *matai* (family chiefs) were allowed to be candidates. However, voters chose among candidates from

National Elections and Referenda

Country	Date/Type	Results and Comments
		competing parties and tendencies. There was a 90 percent turnout. The governing Human Rights Protection Party won 26 of the 44 parliamentary seats. Pro-HRPP independents won 2 seats. Tofilau Eti Alesana remained prime minister. Opposition leader Tuiatua Tupua Tamasese of the Samoa National Development Party (SNDP) lost his seat. The SNDP declined to estimate its number of seats.
Yugoslavia Kosovo 25 September 1991	referendum (aborted)	The ethnic Albanians in this region attempted to hold a referendum on independence from Yugoslavia, but the military cut it off.
Zaire December 1991	presidential/legislative	This election did not take place. President Mobutu remained in office.
Zambia October 1991	general	In the presidential race, Chilunda (Movement for Multiparty Democracy) defeated Kenneth Kaunda (United National Independence Party) with 80 percent of the vote. The MMD also captured more than two-thirds of the legislative seats.

Sources

Publications, organizations

AFL-CIO *Bulletin*
Africa Confidential
Africa Fund
Africa News
Africa Report
Agence France Presse
Al Haq Report on Human Rights
American Institute for Free Labor Development
American-Jewish Committee
Amnesty International *Urgent Action Bulletins*
Amnesty International: *Report 1991*
Andean Newsletter
Anti-Censorship Action Group
Asian Bulletin
Asian Survey
Assembly of Turkish-American Association
Associated Press
Attacks on Justice
Australian Encyclopedia (1988 Edition)
Austrian Information
Beijing Review
Bougainville Information Service
British Information Service
Carib News
Caribbean Affairs
Caribbean Insight
Caribbean Review
The *Carter Center News*
Catholic Standard (Guyana)
CBS News Almanac 1978
Center for Security Policy Press Release
Center for Strategic and International Studies
Central America Report
Chickasha Daily Express
China Daily
The *Chinese Free Journal*
Chinese Information and Cultural Center
Christian Science Monitor
Civil Justice Memo
Civil Rights Update
Committee to Protect Journalists *Update*
Commonwealth Correspondence
Crusade for Democracy in Seychelles
Cyprus Newsletter
Dawn News Bulletin (All Burma Students Democratic Front)
Defense and Foreign Affairs Handbook 1989
Democracy Today
Deutschland Nachrichten
Droits de L'Homme
East European Reporter
Economic & Commercial Information

The *Economist*
EFE Spainish news agency
El Nuevo Herald (Miami)
Encyclopaedia Britannica 1991 Yearbook
The *European*
L'Express
Facts About Greenland
Far Eastern Economic Review
Foreign Broadcast Information Service:
    FBIS Africa
    FBIS China
    FBIS East Europe
    FBIS Latin America
    FBIS Near East & South Asia
    FBIS East Asia
    FBIS Soviet Union/Central Eurasia
    FBIS Sub-Saharan Africa
The *Financial Times*
Focus
Forum
Free Angola Information Service
Free China Journal
Free China Review
Free Labour World
Freedom First
Freedom to Write Bulletin
Frontline
The *Globe & Mail* (Toronto)
Greece Bulletin
The *Guardian*
Guatemala Watch (Guatemala City)
Gulf-Kuwait Newspaper
Hemisfile
Hemisphere
The *Herald Tribune*
Hong Kong Digest
Houston *Post*
Human Rights Watch:
    Africa Watch
    Americas Watch
    Asia Watch
    Helsinki Watch
    Middle East Watch
Immigration and Refugee Board
The *Independent*
Index on Censorship
India News
India Today
Indian Law Resource Center
The *Indochina Institute Report*
Inside China Mainland
Institute on Religion and Democracy
Inter-American Press Association
International Commission of Jurists

International Herald Tribune
International Organization for Migration
International Organization of Journalists
International Union of Food and Allied Workers
Internet on the Holocaust and Genocide
Iran Times (International)
Irish Echo
The Irish Emigrant Vote Campaign
Irish Voice
Issues + Views
Japan Access
The Jarkow Institute for Latin America of the
    Anti-Defamation League of B'nai B'rith
Jeune Afrique
Journal of Afghan Affairs
Journal of Commerce
Journal of Democracy
*Keesing's Revolutionary and Dissident
    Movements*
Keesing's Border and Territorial Disputes
Korea Update
Kwacha News
Latin American Perspectives
Latin American Regional Reports
Latin American Weekly Report
Lithuanian Information Center
Los Angeles *Times*
Mainstream
Middle East International
Middle East Monitor
Le Monde
National Catholic Register
National Council of Trade Unions
National Democratic Institute for International
    Affairs
National Spiritual Assembly for the Baha'is of
    the U.S.
New Observer
New Pittsburgh Courier
New Republic
New York
New York *Newsday*
New York *Times*
New Yorker
The *News + Courier*
News Digest
News From Austria
Newsletter (Nepal)
Newsweek
North-South Magazine
Norwegian Information Service
Le Nouvelle Observateur
Organization of American States
Pacific Islands Monthly
People's Mojahedin of Iran
Le Point
Political Handbook of the World: 1991
Political Handbook of the World: 1992

Portuguese Tourist Office of Publications
Proceso (Mexico City)
Problems of Communism
Radio Free Europe/Radio Liberty: RFE/RL
Report on Eastern Europe
    RFE/RL *Report on Soviet Union*
    RFE/RL *Soviet/East European Report*
Rand McNally *World Facts & Maps,*
    1990 edition
Red Cross/Red Crescent
Record
Religion-Economics Quarterly
Report on Science
Respekt (Czechoslovakia)
Response
Roundup
Royal Danish Ministry of Foreign Affairs
Select Committee on Hunger
The *Seychellois International*
South
South Africa Briefing Paper
South Africa Institute on Race Relations
South Africa Update
South East Asia Monitor
Sri Lanka News Bulletin
State Department *Country Reports on Human
    Rights Practices for 1990*
The *Statesman*
Strategic World
Sudan Democratic Gazette
The *Sunday Tribune*
Survey on Refugees
Swedish Information Service
Swiss Press Review
Swiss Review of World Affairs
Taiwan Communique
Tampa Florida Tribune
Third World Quarterly
The *Tico Times* (Costa Rica)
Time
Time & Money
The *Times Atlas of the World*
The *Times of the Americas*
Togo Information Service
U.S. News and World Report
Ukrainian Press Agency
Ukrainian Reporter
Ukrainian Weekly
Uncaptive Minds (Institute for Democracy in
    Eastern Europe)
UNDP *Human Development Report*
UNICEF
Universal Almanac 1991
Vanity Fair
Vietnam Insight
The Vietnamese Resistance
Voice of Democracy in China
Wall Street Journal

Washington *Post*
Washington *Times*
The *Week in Germany*
Week in South Africa
West Africa

World Almanac 1992
World Population Data Sheet 1991 (Population
    Reference Bureau)
World Press Review

Human Rights Organizations

Americas Watch
Amnesty International
Andean Commission of Jurists
Caribbean Institute for the Promotion of
    Human Rights
Caribbean Rights
Center for Democracy
Chilean Human Rights Commission
Committee of Churches for Emergency Help
    (Paraguay)
Cuban Commission for Human Rights and
    National Reconciliation
Cuban Committee for Human Rights
Group for Mutual Support (Guatemala)
Guyana Human Rights Association
Haitian Center for Human Rights
Helsinki Watch
Honduran Committee for the Defense of
    Human Rights
Human Rights Commission (El Salvador)
International League for Human Rights

Institute on Religion and Democracy
Inter-American Commission on Human Rights,
    Organization of American States
International League for Human Rights
Jamaica Council for Human Rights
Lawyers Committee for Human Rights
National Coalition for Haitian Refugees
National Coordinating Office for
    Human Rights (Peru)
Of Human Rights
Panamanian Committee for Human Rights
Permanent Commission on Human Rights
    (Nicaragua)
Permanent Committee for the Defense of
Human Rights (Colombia)
Puebla Institute
Runejel Junam Council of Ethnic
    Communities (Guatemala)
Tutela Legal (El Salvador)
Vicaria de la Solidaridad (Chile)

Delegations/visitors to Freedom House

Africa/Middle East
Algeria
Angola
Benin
Burkina Faso
Cameroon
Cote D'Ivoire
Egypt
Ethiopia
Iran
Israel
Mauritius
Mozambique
Niger
Nigeria
Rwanda
South Africa
Tanzania
Tunisia
Turkey
Zaire

Asia/Southeast Asia/Pacific
Australia
Bangladesh
Burma (Myanmar)
Cambodia
China (PRC)
Hong Kong
Indonesia
(South) Korea
Malaysia

Eastern Europe
Bulgaria
Czechoslovakia
Hungary
Poland
Romania
Yugoslavia

former USSR
Belarus (Byelorussia)

Estonia
Latvia
Lithuania
Russia
Ukraine

Western Europe
Netherlands

Western Hemisphere
Argentina
Brazil
Canada
Chile

Costa Rica
Cuba
Ecuador
El Salvador
Guatemala
Guyana
Haiti
Mexico
Nicaragua
Panama
Peru
Suriname
Venezuela

Delegations from Freedom House to:

Cuba
Czechoslovakia
El Salvador
Guatemala
Haiti
Hong Kong
Hungary
India

Indonesia
Japan
Mexico
Poland
Romania
South Africa
Suriname
USSR (former)